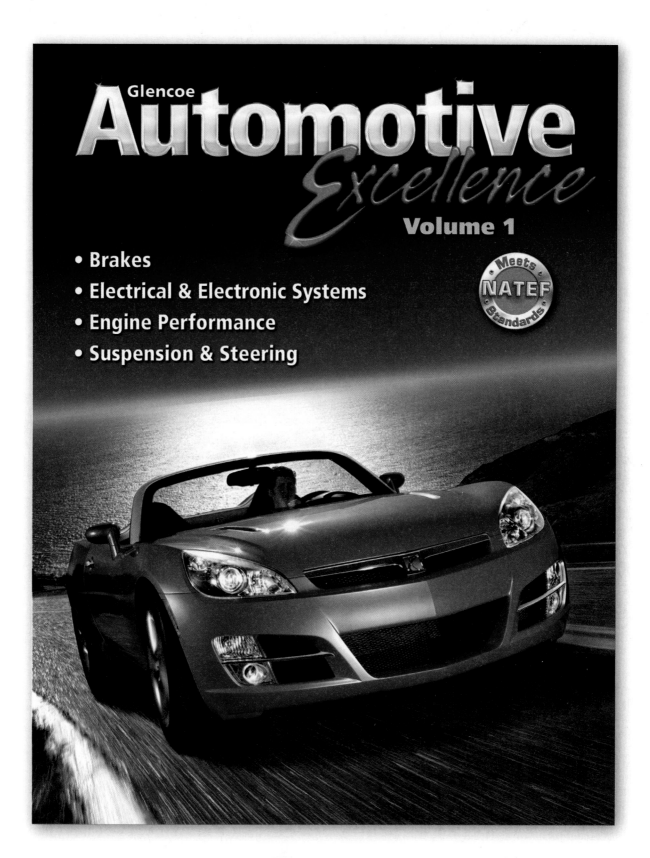

Glencoe
Automotive
Excellence
Volume 1

- Brakes
- Electrical & Electronic Systems
- Engine Performance
- Suspension & Steering

Meets NATEF Standards

McGraw Hill Glencoe

New York, New York   Columbus, Ohio   Chicago, Illinois   Peoria, Illinois   Woodland Hills, California

Brand Disclaimer

Publisher does not necessarily recommend or endorse any particular company or brand name product that may be discussed or pictured in *Automotive Excellence*. Brand name products are used because they are readily available, likely to be known to the reader, and their use may aid in the understanding of the text. Publisher recognizes that other brand name or generic products may be substituted and work as well or better than those featured in *Automotive Excellence*.

Safety Notice

The reader is expressly advised to consider and use all safety precautions described in *Automotive Excellence* or that might also be indicated by undertaking the activities described herein. In addition, common sense should be exercised to help avoid all potential hazards.

Publisher and Author assume no responsibility for the activities of the reader or for the subject matter experts who prepared *Automotive Excellence*. Publisher and Author make no representation or warranties of any kind, including but not limited to, the warranties of fitness for particular purpose or merchantability, nor for any implied warranties related thereto, or otherwise. Publisher and Author will not be liable for damages of any type, including any consequential, special or exemplary damages resulting, in whole or in part, from reader's use or reliance upon the information, instructions, warnings or other matter contained in *Automotive Excellence*.

Road Test Before performing a road test, be sure to obtain written permissions from appropriate authorities.

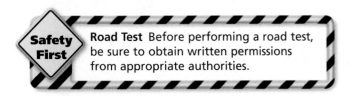

Send all inquiries to:
Glencoe/McGraw-Hill
3008 W. Willow Knolls Drive
Peoria, IL 61614

ISBN (13-digit) 978-0-07-874412-9
ISBN (10-digit) 0-07-874412-1

Printed in the United States of America
2 3 4 5 6 7 8 9 10 071 10 09 08 07 06

Contents in Brief

Automotive Technician's Handbook

Chapter 1 **The Automotive Industry** HB-32
Chapter 2 **Automotive Tools & Equipment** HB-50
Chapter 3 **Automotive Safety Practices** HB-88

Brakes

Chapter 1 **Brake System Operation** BR-108
Chapter 2 **Diagnosing & Repairing the Hydraulic System** BR-120
Chapter 3 **Diagnosing & Repairing Drum Brakes** BR-138
Chapter 4 **Diagnosing & Repairing Disc Brakes** BR-158
Chapter 5 **Diagnosing & Repairing Power Boosters** BR-180
Chapter 6 **Diagnosing & Repairing Parking Brakes** BR-192
Chapter 7 **Diagnosing & Repairing Antilock Brakes** BR-206

Electrical & Electronic Systems

Chapter 1 **Electrical System Operation** EL-228
Chapter 2 **Diagnosing & Servicing the Battery** EL-252
Chapter 3 **Diagnosing & Repairing the Starting System** EL-272
Chapter 4 **Diagnosing & Repairing the Charging System** EL-288
Chapter 5 **Diagnosing & Repairing Lighting Systems** EL-308
Chapter 6 **Diagnosing & Repairing Accessory and Safety Systems** ... EL-330

Engine Performance

Chapter 1 **Piston Engine Operation** EP-354
Chapter 2 **Diagnosing Engine Mechanical Problems** EP-370
Chapter 3 **Computerized Engine Controls** EP-388
Chapter 4 **Diagnosing & Repairing Ignition Systems** EP-416
Chapter 5 **Diagnosing & Repairing Air Induction Systems** EP-436
Chapter 6 **Diagnosing & Repairing Fuel Systems** EP-448
Chapter 7 **Using Computer Diagnostics** EP-470
Chapter 8 **Diagnosing & Repairing Emission Control Systems** ... EP-486

Suspension & Steering

Chapter 1 **Diagnosing & Repairing Tires and Wheels** SS-506
Chapter 2 **Diagnosing & Repairing Steering Systems** SS-530
Chapter 3 **Diagnosing & Repairing Suspension Systems** SS-550
Chapter 4 **Diagnosing, Adjusting, & Repairing Wheel Alignment** ... SS-576

Automotive Excellence Team

Excellence in Automotive Technology

Ron Chappell
Santa Fe Community College
Gainesville, Florida

Al Blethen
Shelton State Community College
Tuscaloosa, Alabama

Erick Dodge
OCM BOCES
Syracuse, New York

Terry Wicker
Franklin County High School
Carnesville, Georgia

Patrick Hart
New York Automotive and Diesel Institute
Jamaica, New York

John Campanella
New York Automotive and Diesel Institute
Jamaica, New York

Leo Van Delft
Tulsa Technology Center
Tulsa, Oklahoma

Robert Porter
Center for Technical Studies
    of Montgomery County
Plymouth Meeting, Pennsylvania

Ted Grekowicz
Michigan Technical Academy
Romulus, Michigan

Darrell L. Parks
NATEF Educational Consultant
Columbus, Ohio

Excellence in Math

Jason Feldner, Applied Math
Mid-East Career & Technology Centers
Buffalo Campus
Senecaville, Ohio

Janet Capps, Applied Math
Gordon Cooper Technology Center
Shawnee, Oklahoma

Excellence in Science

Charlotte Sanders, Applied Science
Francis Tuttle Vo-Tech Center
Oklahoma City, Oklahoma

Barbara Carstens, Applied Science
Butler Career & Technology Development Schools
Hamilton, Ohio

Excellence in Communication

Laura Marcy, Applied Communications
Licking County Career & Technology Center
Newark, Ohio

Patsy Kline, Applied Communications
Jones, Oklahoma

Your Road Map to Excellence!

Safety First The contents of this eye-catching feature stress safety practices that must be followed in the lab/service facility and on the job.

TECH TIP These timesaving bits of technical advice will help you perform diagnostic and repair procedures.

HYBRID TECHNOLOGY

These features introduce you to the emerging technologies that are being introduced in hybrid vehicles.

Excellence in Math

Each feature correlates a NATEF Mathematics Standard to automotive content. It provides you with information and then prompts you to *Apply It!* by working through a set of problems.

Excellence in Science

Each feature correlates a NATEF Science Standard to automotive content. Placed at "point of use," it provides you with critical information and then prompts you to *Apply It!* by performing a hands-on experiment.

Excellence in Communication

Each feature correlates a NATEF Communications Standard to automotive content. It provides you with background information or a situation and then prompts you to *Apply It!* by responding to a set of questions.

Special Features

Excellence in Math

Brakes
Converting Temperatures................... BR-116
Calculating Hydraulic Pressure............. BR-123
Measuring Out-of-Round Brake Drums........ BR-149
Measuring Brake Rotors.................... BR-177
Brake Pedal Ratios BR-183
Parking on a Hill BR-203
Interpreting ABS Graphs BR-210

Electrical & Electronic Systems
Using Ohm's Law EL-232
Applying Ohm's Law to Series Circuits EL-257
Calculating Resistance EL-282
Analyzing Sine Waves EL-294
Calculating Wattage.......................EL-310
Using Metric Prefixes EL-334

Engine Performance
Calculating Engine Displacement EP-361
Measuring Compression..................... EP-374
Determining Rate of Change EP-405
Calculating MAF Values EP-424
Calculating Airflow....................... EP-438
Calculating Miles Per Gallon EP-463
Testing a MAP Sensor..................... EP-482
Calculating Carbon Dioxide EP-499

Suspension & Steering
Determining Tire Diameter SS-526
Reading a Variable-Ratio Steering Graph SS-543
Calculating Spring Loads SS-572
Measuring Camber SS-588

Excellence in Science

Brakes
Friction Stops!.......................... BR-110
Using Hydraulics to Multiply Force BR-134
Inertia and Friction BR-144
Graphing Deceleration BR-174
Levers Multiply Force BR-188
Levers in Braking Systems BR-197
Converting Kinetic Energy BR-222

Electrical & Electronic Systems
Measuring Circuit Resistance EL-244
Investigating Electrolytes....................EL-262
Demonstrating Magnetism EL-277
Demonstrating Generator Action EL-290
Demonstrating an Electrical Ground EL-323
Using a Switching Transistor EL-346

Engine Performance
Hot Gases Are Really Cool EP-358
Analyzing Fluids EP-382
Finding Resistance EP-399
Converting Sensor Signals EP-409
How Does a Coil Work? EP-431
Measuring Pressure and Vacuum............. EP-442
Increasing Oxygen in Fuel EP-451
Identifying the Role of a Catalyst EP-472
Vapor Pressure and Temperature............. EP-493

Suspension & Steering
Measuring Torque........................ SS-519
Altering Force with Levers.................. SS-536
How Stress Affects Springs SS-557
Angles in Wheel Alignment................. SS-582

Excellence in Communication

Brakes
Taking Notes BR-118
"Reading" Your Customer BR-136
Reading Exploded Views BR-156
Reading Diagrams........................ BR-178
Recording Information BR-190
Remember—Safety First................... BR-204
Interpreting Technical Illustrations BR-224

Electrical & Electronic Systems
Using Electrical Symbols....................EL-250
Writing a Memo EL-270
Ask the Right Questions....................EL-286
Using Electrical Schematics EL-306
Recognizing Consequences EL-328
Researching Specialty Tools EL-350

Engine Performance
Explaining Things to Your Customer........... EP-368
Using the Scientific Method.................. EP-386
Decoding Words EP-414
Locating Information EP-434
Decoding Acronyms EP-446
Searching a Database..................... EP-468
Using Communication Strategies EP-484
Using J1930 Terminology EP-502

Suspension & Steering
Interpreting Information SS-528
Learning About New Systems SS-548
Using a Dictionary....................... SS-574
Reading Service Manuals SS-592

Contents

Automotive Technician's Handbook

CHAPTER 1 The Automotive Industry HB-32

Section 1 The Automotive Profession HB-33
  The Automotive Industry
  Automotive Systems
  Automotive Service Excellence (ASE) Certification
  The National Institute for Automotive Service Excellence
  ASE Certification Exams
  NATEF's Role
  Service Technicians Society
  Section 1 Knowledge Check

Section 2 Automotive Career Opportunities . . .HB-38
  Job Outlook
  Automotive Employers
  Dealerships
  Independent Service Facilities
  Large Retail Facilities
  Specialty Centers
  Fleet Facilities
  The Automotive Work Environment
  Becoming an ASE-Certified Automotive Technician
  A Well-Paid Profession
  Preparing for an Automotive Career
  Reading Skills
  Completing a Repair Order
  Writing Skills
  Science Skills
  Employability Skills
  Positive Attitude
  Responsibility
  Teamwork
  Respecting Others
  Honesty
  Commitment
  Willingness to Learn
  Initiative
  Personal Appearance
  A Diverse Workplace
  Communicating Clearly
  Telephone Skills
  Listening Skills
  Speaking Skills
  Nonverbal Communication
  Section 2 Knowledge Check

Chapter 1 Review

HYBRID TECHNOLOGY Alternative Energy Sources HB-48

Automotive Service Excellence Test Prep HB-49

8

Contents

CHAPTER 2 Automotive Tools & Equipment HB-50

Section 1 Hand Tools HB-51
Tool Safety
Using Tools Properly
Types of Tools
Storing and Maintaining Tools
Section 1 Knowledge Check

Section 2 General Workplace Equipment HB-64
Using General Workplace Equipment
Section 2 Knowledge Check

Section 3 Measuring Systems and Tools HB-74
Measuring Systems
The SI System
The USC System
Converting Measurements
Measurement Tools
Section 3 Knowledge Check

Section 4 Fasteners, Gaskets, and Sealants HB-79
Characteristics of Fasteners
Fastener Strength Groups
Screw Threads
Complete Thread Designation
Fastener Size
Fastener Pitch
Nuts and Lock Washers
Other Fasteners
Snap Rings
Thread Inserts
Setscrews
Self-Tapping Screws
Rivets
Removing a Broken Bolt
Restoring Threads
Repairing Internal Threads
Thread Dressings
Thread Lubrication
Thread-locking Compounds
Gaskets and Sealants
Preformed Gaskets
Formed-in-Place Gaskets
Welding
Section 4 Knowledge Check
Chapter 2 Review
HYBRID TECHNOLOGY Tools for Hybrids HB-86
Automotive Service Excellence Test Prep HB-87

CHAPTER **3 Automotive Safety Practices** HB-88

Section 1 General Workplace Safety HB-89
OSHA
Workplace Precautions
Hazardous Materials and Wastes
Fire Safety
Safety Notices
Evacuation Routes
Lockout/Tagout
Section 1 Knowledge Check

Section 2 Personal Safety Practices HB-94
Personal Protective Equipment
Eye Protection
Foot Protection
Hand and Arm Protection
Lung Protection
Head and Ear Protection
Ergonomics
Preventing Arm and Hand Injuries
Preventing Back Injuries
Emergency Response to Injuries
Avoiding Bloodborne Pathogens
Section 2 Knowledge Check

Section 3 Tool and Equipment Safety HB-98
Hand Tools
Electric Power Tools
Machine Guards
Pneumatic Tools
Drive Belts and Pulleys
Lifts, Jacks, and Safety Stands
Vehicle Lifts
Floor Jacks and Safety Stands
Hoists
Transmission Jacks
Electrical Safety
Welding Safety
Compressed Gases
Section 3 Knowledge Check

Chapter 3 Review

HYBRID TECHNOLOGY Safety Precautions HB-104

Automotive Service Excellence Test Prep HB-105

Contents

Brakes

CHAPTER 1 Brake System Operation BR-108

Section 1 **Brake Systems** BR-109
Types of Brakes
Service Brakes
Parking Brakes
Friction and Braking
Excellence **in Science** Friction Stops! BR-110
Static Friction
Kinetic Friction
Section 1 Knowledge Check

Section 2 **Service Brake System** BR-112
Service Brake Action
Dual Braking Systems
Section 2 Knowledge Check

Section 3 **Brake Fluid** BR-114
Brake Fluid Properties
Installing Brake Fluid
Brake Service Safety
Vehicle Support
Brake Dust and Chemical Safety
Excellence **in Math** Converting Temperatures BR-116
Section 3 Knowledge Check

Chapter 1 Review
Excellence **in Communication** Taking Notes BR-118
Automotive Service Excellence Test Prep BR-119

CHAPTER 2 Diagnosing & Repairing the Hydraulic System BR-120

Section 1 **Hydraulics** BR-121
Properties of Hydraulics
The Transfer of Motion
The Transfer of Force
Excellence **in Math** Calculating Hydraulic Pressure BR-123
Section 1 Knowledge Check

Section 2 **Brake Master Cylinder** BR-124
Types of Master Cylinders
Integral Master Cylinder
Composite Master Cylinder
Master Cylinder Operation
Master Cylinder Diagnosis
Brake Drag
Master Cylinder Bench Bleed
Brake Lines

Hydraulic Circuits
Front-Rear Split Systems
Diagonally Split Systems
Section 2 Knowledge Check

Section 3 Brake System Valves. BR-131
Types of Control Valves
Metering Valve
Pressure Differential Valve
Proportioning Valve
Excellence in Science Using Hydraulics to Multiply Force BR-134
Residual Pressure Check Valve
Combination Valve
Bleeding a Hydraulic Braking System
Manual Bleeding
Pressure Bleeding
Vacuum Bleeding
Section 3 Knowledge Check
Chapter 2 Review
Excellence in Communication "Reading" Your Customer BR-136
Automotive Service Excellence Test Prep BR-137

CHAPTER 3 Diagnosing & Repairing Drum Brakes BR-138

Section 1 Drum Brake Operation BR-139
Drum Brake Construction
Backing Plate
Brake Shoes
Brake Hardware
Wheel Cylinders
Types of Drum Brakes
Leading-Trailing Drum Brakes
Duo-Servo Drum Brakes
Drum-Brake Self-Adjusters
Excellence in Science Inertia and Friction BR-144
Section 1 Knowledge Check

Section 2 Diagnosing Drum Brakes BR-145
Dragging, Pulling, or Grabbing Brakes
One Brake Drags
Rear Brakes Drag
All Brakes Drag
Pulls to One Side When Braking
Brakes Grab
Brake Pedal Symptoms
Brake Pedal Free Play
Soft or Spongy Pedal
Poor Braking Requiring Excessive Pedal Force
Brakes Do Not Self-Adjust
Pedal Pulsation or Vibration
Excellence in Math Measuring Out-of-Round Brake Drums BR-149

Contents

Fluid Leaks, Noise, and Warning Lights
Loss of Brake Fluid
Noisy Brakes
Brake Warning Light Comes On While Braking
Section 2 Knowledge Check

Section 3 Servicing Drum Brakes BR-151
Drum Brake Self-Adjusters
Brake Drums
Removing the Brake Drum
Cleaning and Inspecting Brake Drums
Measuring Brake Drums
Machining Brake Drums
Brake Shoes
Inspecting Brake Shoes
Removing Brake Shoes
Wheel Cylinders
Removing a Wheel Cylinder
Installing a Wheel Cylinder
Inspecting, Installing,
    and Adjusting Brakes
Inspecting Hardware
Installing Brake Shoes
Adjusting Brake Shoes
Installing Brake Drums
Section 3 Knowledge Check

Chapter 3 Review
Excellence in Communication Reading Exploded Views. BR-156
Automotive Service Excellence Test Prep BR-157

CHAPTER **4 Diagnosing & Repairing Disc Brakes**. BR-158

Section 1 Disc Brake Construction and Operation. BR-159
Disc Brake Construction
Brake Pads
Rotors
Calipers
Disc Brake Operation
Fixed Caliper Disc Brakes
Floating Caliper Disc Brakes
Sliding Caliper Disc Brakes
Self-Adjusting Disc Brakes
Disc Brake Wear Indicators
Section 1 Knowledge Check

Section 2 Disc Brake Diagnosis BR-164
General Complaints
Pulling to One Side While Braking
Front Disc Brakes Grabbing
Failing to Release

Excessive Pedal Travel
Pedal Pulsations
Excessive Pedal Force, Grabbing, and Uneven Braking
No Braking with Pedal Fully Depressed
Fluid Leaking from Caliper
Low Fluid Level in Master Cylinder
Noise
Brake Warning Light On
Parking Brake Complaints
Section 2 Knowledge Check

Section 3 Disc Brake Service BR-169

Disc Brake Pad and Caliper Service
Inspecting Disc Brake Pads
Replacing Disc Brake Pads
Removing and Replacing Disc Brake Pads and Calipers (Floating or Sliding Calipers)
Repairing Disc Brake Calipers
Disc Brake Rotor Service
Measuring Disc Brake Rotors

Excellence **in Science** Graphing Deceleration BR-174

Removing Disc Brake Rotors
Inspecting and Replacing Wheel Studs
Machining Disc Brake Rotors
Installing Disc Brake Rotors

Excellence **in Math** Measuring Brake Rotors BR-177

Section 3 Knowledge Check

Chapter 4 Review

Excellence **in Communication** Reading Diagrams BR-178

Automotive Service Excellence Test Prep BR-179

CHAPTER 5 Diagnosing & Repairing Power Boosters BR-180

Section 1 Power Boosters BR-181

Types of Power Boosters
Vacuum Boosters
Vacuum Supply
Single-Diaphragm Vacuum Boosters

Excellence **in Math** Brake Pedal Ratios BR-183

Tandem (Dual) Diaphragm Vacuum Boosters
Hydraulic Boosters
Hydraulically Assisted Boosters
Electrohydraulically Assisted Boosters
Section 1 Knowledge Check

Section 2 Diagnosing Power Boosters BR-187

Diagnosing Vacuum Boosters
Testing Vacuum Booster Operation
Testing Vacuum Storage System Operation

Excellence **in Science** Levers Multiply Force BR-188

Contents

Diagnosing Hydraulically Assisted Boosters
Testing Hydraulically Assisted Booster Operation
Testing Hydraulic Pressure Storage System Operation
Section 2 Knowledge Check
Chapter 5 Review
Excellence in Communication Recording Information BR-190
Automotive Service Excellence Test Prep BR-191

CHAPTER **6 Diagnosing & Repairing Parking Brakes** BR-192

Section 1 Parking Brake Basics BR-193
Parking Brake Components
Braking Mechanisms
Actuating Mechanisms
Brake Warning Lights
Parking Brake Construction and Operation
Rear Drum Integral Parking Brakes
Rear Disc Integral Parking Brakes
Excellence in Science Levers in Braking Systems BR-197
Auxiliary Parking Brakes
Section 1 Knowledge Check

Section 2 Parking Brake Controls, Diagnosis, and Repair BR-199
Mechanical Components
Parking Brake Hand Levers
Parking Brake Pedals
Parking Brake Linkage
Parking Brake Equalizer
Parking Brake Complaints
Parking Brake Fails to Hold
Parking Brake Fails to Release
Parking Brake Repair
Adjusting Parking Brake Cables
Replacing Parking Brake Cables
Auxiliary Parking Brake Shoes
Excellence in Math Parking on a Hill BR-203
Section 2 Knowledge Check
Chapter 6 Review
Excellence in Communication Remember—Safety First BR-204
Automotive Service Excellence Test Prep BR-205

CHAPTER **7 Diagnosing & Repairing Antilock Brakes** BR-206

Section 1 Antilock Brake System Operation BR-207
Benefits of an Antilock Brake System
The Role of Sensors
Integral and Nonintegral Antilock Brake Systems
Excellence **in Math** Interpreting ABS Graphs BR-210
Understanding ABS Channels
One-Channel ABS
Three-Channel ABS
Four-Channel ABS
Section 1 Knowledge Check

Section 2 Antilock Brake Diagnosis and Repair BR-213
Antilock Brake System Control Module
Hydraulic Components
Pump, Accumulator, and Reservoir
Hydraulic Actuator
Sensors and Warning Lights
Speed Sensors
Deceleration Sensor
Lateral Acceleration Sensor
ABS Warning Light
Brake Warning Light
Four-Wheel-Drive Switch
Diagnosing and Repairing Antilock Brakes
Diagnosing Antilock Brakes
Testing and Diagnosing ABS Speed Sensors
Bleeding Antilock Brakes
HYBRID TECHNOLOGY Regenerative Braking BR-220
Section 2 Knowledge Check

Section 3 Controlling Torque BR-221
Traction Control
Excellence **in Science** Converting Kinetic Energy BR-222
Vehicle Stability Control
Section 3 Knowledge Check

Chapter 7 Review
Excellence in Communication Interpreting Technical Illustrations BR-224
Automotive Service Excellence Test Prep BR-225

Contents

Electrical & Electronic Systems

CHAPTER 1 Electrical System Operation EL-228

Section 1 The Nature of Electricity EL-229
Understanding the Atom
Conductors
Insulators
The Flow of Electricity
Voltage
Current
Resistance
Electrical Circuits
Series Circuits
Excellence in Math Using Ohm's Law EL-232
Parallel Circuits
Ohm's Law
Section 1 Knowledge Check

Section 2 Electrical Automotive Components EL-234
Storing and Generating Electricity
Generator
Battery
Conducting Electricity
Conductors
Terminals
Connectors
Controlling Electricity
Fuses, Fusible Links, and Circuit Breakers
Switches
Load Devices
Section 2 Knowledge Check

Section 3 Reading and Testing Electrical Circuits EL-239
Wiring Diagrams
Electrical Symbols
Electrical Test Equipment
Volt-Ohm-Meters
Test Lights
Logic Probes
Scan Tools
Oscilloscopes
Jumper Wire
Electrical Circuit Problems
Open Circuit
Excellence in Science Measuring Circuit Resistance EL-244
Short Circuit
Grounded Circuit

Excessive Circuit Resistance
Solder Repair of Wiring
Section 3 Knowledge Check

Section 4 Electronic Automotive Components EL-247

Uses of Semiconductors
Solid-State Components
Diodes
Zener Diodes
Light-Emitting Diodes
Transistors
Thermistors
Handling Solid-State Components
Section 4 Knowledge Check

Chapter 1 Review

Excellence in Communication Using Electrical Symbols EL-250

Automotive Service Excellence Test Prep EL-251

CHAPTER **2 Diagnosing & Servicing the Battery** EL-252

Section 1 Automotive Batteries EL-253

Purpose of the Battery
Battery Construction
Battery Operation
HYBRID TECHNOLOGY Hybrid Vehicle Auxiliary Battery EL-255
Battery Management Systems
Battery Performance
Battery Ratings
Cold-Cranking Amps (CCA)
Reserve Capacity
Excellence in Math Applying Ohm's Law to Series Circuits EL-257
Terminal Voltage
Section 1 Knowledge Check

Section 2 Battery Inspection and Testing EL-258

Battery Inspection
Battery Testing
Built-in Hydrometers
Open-Circuit Voltage (OCV) Test
Battery Load Test
State-of-Charge Testing
Excellence in Science Investigating Electrolytes EL-262
Key-Off Loads (Parasitic Drains) Testing
Section 2 Knowledge Check

Section 3 Battery Servicing EL-264

Battery Maintenance
Battery Cleaning
Battery Charging
Battery Replacement
Battery Removal
Battery Installation
Battery Damage

NOTICE

CONTENTS SENSITIVE
TO
STATIC ELECTRICITY

Contents

Jump Starting

HYBRID TECHNOLOGY High-Voltage in Hybrids EL-268

Using a Battery Jumper Box

Section 3 Knowledge Check

Chapter 2 Review

Excellence in Communication Writing a Memo EL-270

Automotive Service Excellence Test Prep EL-271

CHAPTER 3 Diagnosing & Repairing the Starting System EL-272

Section 1 The Starter EL-273

The Starter and the Starting System

Starter Construction

Field Coil Starter

Permanent Magnet Starter

Starter Operation

Solenoid Starter

Relay and Solenoid Starters

Excellence in Science Demonstrating Magnetism EL-277

Starter Drive Assembly

Section 1 Knowledge Check

Section 2 Diagnosing the Starting System EL-280

Starting System Tests

Cranking Voltage/Current Draw Test

Voltage Drop Test

Excellence in Math Calculating Resistance EL-282

Starter No-Load Bench Test

Testing Relays and Solenoids

Starter Service

Section 2 Knowledge Check

Chapter 3 Review

Excellence in Communication Ask the Right Questions EL-286

Automotive Service Excellence Test Prep EL-287

CHAPTER 4 Diagnosing & Repairing the Charging System EL-288

Section 1 Charging System Components and Operation EL-289

Charging System Components

Excellence in Science Demonstrating Generator Action EL-290

Generator Construction

Charging System Operation

Rectifying AC Voltage

Excellence in Math Analyzing Sine Waves EL-294

Temperature Compensation

Regulating the Generator

Instrument Panel Charge Indicators

Indicator Light

Voltmeter

HYBRID TECHNOLOGY Regenerative Braking System EL-297

Section 1 Knowledge Check

Section 2 Charging System Testing and Service EL-298

Preliminary Checks
Common System Problems
Checking Drive-Belt Tension
Charging System Tests
Charging Voltage Test
Charging Current Test
Voltage Regulator Test
Voltage Drop Test
Charging System Diagnosis
Undercharged Battery
Overcharged Battery
Charging System Noise
Removing the Generator
Generator Bench Testing
Installing the Generator
HYBRID TECHNOLOGY Recharging by Braking EL-305
Section 2 Knowledge Check

Chapter 4 Review
Excellence in Communication Using Electrical Schematics EL-306
Automotive Service Excellence Test Prep EL-307

CHAPTER 5 Diagnosing & Repairing Lighting Systems EL-308

Section 1 Lighting Systems EL-309

Light Sources
Incandescent Bulbs
Excellence in Math Calculating Wattage EL-310
Gas-Filled Bulbs
Light-Emitting Diodes
Basic Lighting Circuits
Headlight and Related Circuits
Parking/Tail/License/Side Marker Lights
Instrument Panel Lighting
Interior/Courtesy Lights
Electronic Lighting Controls
Automatic Lighting Control
Automatic Headlight Dimming
Lamp and Body Control Modules
Daytime Running Lights
Brake, Turn Signal, and Hazard Warning Lights
Brake Light Circuits
Turn Signal Circuits
Hazard Warning Circuits
Backup Light Circuit
Diagnosing Lighting Problems
Headlight Aiming
Section 1 Knowledge Check

Contents

Section 2 Instrument Panel Displays EL-320
Types of Displays
Electromagnetic Displays
Solid State Digital Displays
Light-Emitting Diodes
Liquid Crystal Displays
Instrument Panel Warning Lights
Excellence in Science Demonstrating an Electrical Ground EL-323
Diagnosing and Servicing Instrument Panel Displays
Gauges and Graphic Displays
Warning Lights
Section 2 Knowledge Check

Section 3 Brake Warning Lights, Switches, and Sensors EL-325
Activating Switches and Sensors
Brake Light Switches
Parking Brake Switch
Brake Fluid Level Sensors
HYBRID TECHNOLOGY Hybrid Warning Lights EL-326
Brake Wear Indicator Light
Section 3 Knowledge Check

Chapter 5 Review
Excellence in Communication Recognizing Consequences EL-328
Automotive Service Excellence Test Prep EL-329

CHAPTER 6 Diagnosing & Repairing Accessory and Safety Systems . . . EL-330

Section 1 Accessory Motors and Circuits EL-331
Permanent Magnet Motors
Accessory Motors
Nonreversing Motors
Reversing Motors
Accessory Circuits
Windshield Wiper Circuits
Windshield Washer Circuits
Heated Glass, Power Seats, and Mirrors
Excellence in Math Using Metric Prefixes EL-334
Diagnosing Motor Circuits
Checking the Ground Circuit
Checking Power Source
Electric Lock Diagnosis
Removing and Reinstalling a Door Panel
Section 1 Knowledge Check

Section 2 Cruise Control Systems EL-337
Types of Cruise Control Systems
Electronic/Vacuum Systems

Electronic Systems

Diagnosing and Repairing Cruise Control Systems

Failure to Engage

Failure to Maintain a Set Speed

Section 2 Knowledge Check

Section 3 Supplemental Restraint Systems EL-341

Air Bag Systems

Components of Air Bag Systems

Operation of Air Bag Systems

Excellence **in Science** Using a Switching Transistor EL-346

Seat Belts

Seat Belt Retractors and Pretensioners

Inspecting Seat Belts

Servicing Seat Belts

Section 3 Knowledge Check

Section 4 Horn Circuits EL-348

Horn Circuit Components

Diagnosing Horn Circuit Problems

Section 4 Knowledge Check

Chapter 6 Review

Excellence in Communication Researching Specialty Tools EL-350

Automotive Service Excellence Test Prep EL-351

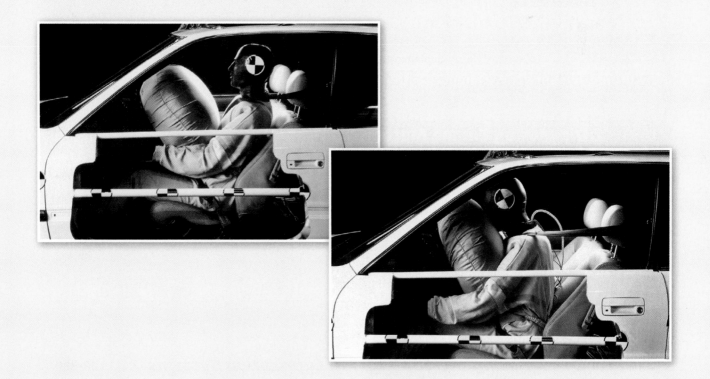

Contents

Engine Performance

CHAPTER 1 Piston Engine Operation **EP-354**

Section 1 Internal Combustion Engines EP-355
Types of Engines
Spark-Ignition Engine
Compression-Ignition Engine
Engine Construction
The Engine Block
The Cylinder Head
Excellence in Science Hot Gases Are Really Cool EP-358
Section 1 Knowledge Check

Section 2 Engine Operation EP-360
Conversion of Energy
Piston Action
Excellence in Math Calculating Engine Displacement EP-361
Valve Action
Power Flow
Basic Engine Systems
Air Induction System
Fuel System
HYBRID TECHNOLOGY Hybrid Systems EP-365
Ignition System
Lubricating System
Cooling System
Exhaust System
Section 2 Knowledge Check

Chapter 1 Review
Excellence in Communication Explaining Things to Your Customer EP-368
Automotive Service Excellence Test Prep EP-369

CHAPTER 2 Diagnosing Engine Mechanical Problems **EP-370**

Section 1 General Engine Diagnosis EP-371
Diagnostic Strategy
Diagnostic Tests
Cylinder Compression Tests
Cylinder Leakage Test
Excellence in Math Measuring Compression EP-374
Cylinder Power Balance Test
Engine Vacuum
Valve Train Noises
Engine Block Noises
Section 1 Knowledge Check

Section 2 Diagnosing the Cooling and Lubrication Systems EP-380
Cooling System Tests
Cooling System Pressure Test
Cooling System Temperature Test

Excellence **in Science** Analyzing Fluids EP-382

HYBRID TECHNOLOGY Coolant Heat Storage Tanks EP-383

Lubrication System Service
Checking Oil Level
Section 2 Knowledge Check

Chapter 2 Review

Excellence in Communication Using the Scientific Method EP-386

Automotive Service Excellence Test Prep EP-387

CHAPTER **3 Computerized Engine Controls** EP-388

Section 1 Sensors EP-389

Sensors and Electronic Signals
Reading the Data Stream
Speed and Position Sensors
Permanent Magnet Sensors
Hall-Effect Sensors
Optical Sensors
Variable Resistance Sensors
Thermistors
Potentiometers
Load Sensors
Manifold Absolute Pressure Sensors
Airflow Sensors
Oxygen Sensors
Zirconia Oxygen Sensors
Titania Oxygen Sensors
Checking Oxygen Sensors

Excellence **in Science** Finding Resistance EP-399

Knock Sensors
Switches
Power Side Switches
Ground Side Switches
Section 1 Knowledge Check

Section 2 Actuators EP-402

Types of Actuators
Solenoids
Relays
Stepper Motors
Other PCM-Controlled Outputs

Excellence **in Math** Determining Rate of Change EP-405

Testing an Actuator by Using a Scan Tool
Current Ramping
Section 2 Knowledge Check

Section 3 Computerized Controls EP-407

On-Board Diagnostic Systems
Powertrain Control Module
Diagnostic Trouble Codes

Excellence **in Science** Converting Sensor Signals EP-409

Displaying Diagnostic Trouble Codes

Contents

Using a Scanner
Snapshot Testing
Interpreting Diagnostic Trouble Codes
Replacing Sensors and Actuators
Verifying the Problem
Data Bus Problems
Mechanical Factors
Sensor and Actuator Failures
Precautions
Section 3 Knowledge Check

Chapter 3 Review
Excellence in Communication Decoding Words......................EP-414
Automotive Service Excellence Test Prep EP-415

CHAPTER 4 Diagnosing & Repairing Ignition Systems EP-416

Section 1 The Ignition System EP-417
Ignition System Components
The Ignition Switch
The Ignition Coil
The Distributor
The Powertrain Control Module
The Ignition Module
Excellence in Math Calculating MAF Values..EP-424
The Ignition Wires
The Spark Plugs
Section 1 Knowledge Check

Section 2 Spark Distribution Systems EP-429
Types of Spark Distribution Systems
Distributor Ignition Systems
Excellence in Science How Does a Coil Work?.................................EP-431
Distributorless Ignition Systems
Direct Ignition Systems
Section 2 Knowledge Check

Chapter 4 Review
Excellence in Communication Locating Information....................................EP-434
Automotive Service Excellence Test Prep EP-435

CHAPTER 5 Diagnosing & Repairing Air Induction Systems EP-436

Section 1 Air Induction Systems EP-437
Air Induction System Components
The Air Filter and Housing
Excellence in Math Calculating Airflow EP-438
The Throttle Body
Check Idle Speed
The Intake Manifold
Excellence in Science Measuring Pressure and Vacuum........ EP-442
Section 1 Knowledge Check

Section 2 Sensing Induction Airflow EP-443
Calculating Airflow
Airflow Sensors
Measuring Airflow Directly
Diagnosing Airflow Sensor Failures
Section 2 Knowledge Check

Chapter 5 Review
Excellence in Communication Decoding Acronyms............................ EP-446

Automotive Service Excellence Test Prep EP-447

CHAPTER 6 Diagnosing & Repairing Fuel Systems.................... EP-448

Section 1 Automotive Fuels............................... EP-449
Characteristics of Automotive Fuels
Gasoline
Excellence in Science Increasing Oxygen in Fuel EP-451
Gaseous Fuels
Air/Fuel Ratio
Section 1 Knowledge Check

Section 2 The Combustion Process.............................. EP-453
Factors Affecting Combustion
Atmospheric Air Pressure
Manifold Absolute Pressure
Humidity
Air Temperature
Abnormal Combustion
Composition of Exhaust Gases
Section 2 Knowledge Check

Section 3 The Fuel Management System EP-456
The Fuel Supply System
Fuel Tank
Fuel Pump
Fuel Filters
Fuel Pressure Regulator
Fuel Lines
Fuel Rails
Vapor Recovery System
Fuel Metering System
Electronic Fuel Injection
Powertrain Control Module
Excellence in Math Calculating Miles Per Gallon EP-463
The Fuel Injector
Fuel Management Sensors
Section 3 Knowledge Check

Chapter 6 Review
Excellence in Communication Searching a Database EP-468

Automotive Service Excellence Test Prep EP-469

Contents

CHAPTER 7 Using Computer Diagnostics **EP-470**

Section 1 OBD-II Systems EP-471
Purpose of OBD-II
Excellence in Science Identifying the Role of a Catalyst EP-472
OBD-II Hardware
OBD-II Terminology
Section 1 Knowledge Check

Section 2 OBD-II Diagnostics EP-475
OBD-II Monitors
OBD-II Diagnostic Trouble Codes
Setting OBD-II DTCs
Diagnostic Flowcharts
Using a Lab Scope
Comparing Sensor Readings
Interpreting Serial Data
Excellence in Math Testing a MAP Sensor EP-482
Retrieving OBD-II DTCs
Clearing OBD-II DTCs
Section 2 Knowledge Check

Chapter 7 Review
Excellence in Communication Using Communication Strategies EP-484
Automotive Service Excellence Test Prep EP-485

CHAPTER 8 Diagnosing & Repairing Emission Control Systems **EP-486**

Section 1 Automotive Emissions Controls EP-487
Emissions Control Subsystems
Positive Crankcase Ventilation System
Exhaust Gas Recirculation System
Air Injection System
Excellence in Science Vapor Pressure and Temperature EP-493
Catalytic Converter
Evaporative Control System
Section 1 Knowledge Check

Section 2 Emissions Testing EP-498
Emissions Testing Programs
Excellence in Math Calculating Carbon Dioxide EP-499
Exhaust Gas Analyzers
Section 2 Knowledge Check

Chapter 8 Review
Excellence in Communication Using J1930 Terminology EP-502
Automotive Service Excellence Test Prep EP-503

Suspension & Steering

CHAPTER 1 Diagnosing & Repairing Tires and Wheels SS-506

Section 1 Tires SS-507
Tire Construction
Bias-Ply, Bias-Belted, and Radial
Run-Flat Tires
Tire Dimensions
Aspect Ratio
Tire Tread
Tire Sidewall Markings
Checking Tire Pressure
Tire Inspection
Tire Rotation
Section 1 Knowledge Check

Section 2 Wheels SS-516
Wheel Construction
Wheel Dimensions
Wheel Fasteners
Wheel Inspection
Tire and Wheel Assembly
Removing a Tire and Wheel Assembly
Installing a Tire and Wheel Assembly
Excellence in Science Measuring Torque SS-519
Applying Torque
Section 2 Knowledge Check

Section 3 Tire Dismounting, Mounting, and Balancing SS-521
Dismounting
Mounting
Tire and Wheel Repair
Valve Stems
Mounting Procedure
Balancing
Static Balancing
Dynamic Balancing
Excellence in Math Determining Tire Diameter SS-526
On-the-Vehicle Balancing
Section 3 Knowledge Check
Chapter 1 Review
Excellence in Communication Interpreting Information SS-528
Automotive Service Excellence Test Prep SS-529

Contents

CHAPTER 2 Diagnosing & Repairing Steering Systems SS-530

Section 1 The Steering System SS-531

Steering System Components
Steering Wheel
Steering Column
Steering Gear Systems
Special Tools
Excellence in Science Altering Force with Levers SS-536
Steering Ratio
Section 1 Knowledge Check

Section 2 Power-Assisted Steering Systems SS-538

Power-Assisted Steering System Components
Power Steering Pump
Power Steering Fluid
Power Rack-and-Pinion Steering Gearbox
Excellence in Math Reading a Variable-Ratio Steering Graph SS-543
Power Steering Pressure Switch
Electronic Controls
HYBRID TECHNOLOGY Electric Motor-Assisted Power Steering SS-545
Steering-Wheel Air Bags
Steering Angle Sensor
Clock Spring
Section 2 Knowledge Check

Chapter 2 Review

Excellence in Communication Learning About New Systems SS-548
Automotive Service Excellence Test Prep SS-549

CHAPTER 3 Diagnosing & Repairing Suspension Systems **SS-550**

Section 1 The Suspension System **SS-551**
Suspension System Components
Springs
Shock Absorbers
Anti-Sway Bars
Control Arms
Excellence **in Science** How Stress Affects Springs SS-557
Ball Joints
Axles
Wheel Bearings
Active Suspension Systems
Section 1 Knowledge Check

Section 2 Front Suspension Systems **SS-563**
Preliminary Suspension Checks
Coil-Spring Front Suspension
Steering Knuckle Service
Servicing Coil-Spring Front Suspensions
Strut-Type Front Suspension
Inspecting Strut-Type Front Suspensions
Servicing Strut-Type Front Suspensions
Torsion Bar Front Suspension
Twin I-Beam Front Suspension
Section 2 Knowledge Check

Section 3 Rear Suspension Systems **SS-570**
Preliminary Suspension Checks
Leaf-Spring Rear Suspension
Servicing Leaf-Spring Rear Suspensions
Excellence **in Math** Calculating Spring Loads SS-572
Coil-Spring Rear Suspension
Servicing Coil-Spring Rear Suspensions
Strut-Type Rear Suspension
Servicing Strut-Type Rear Suspensions
Section 3 Knowledge Check
Chapter 3 Review
Excellence in Communication Using a Dictionary SS-574
Automotive Service Excellence Test Prep **SS-575**

Contents

CHAPTER 4 Diagnosing, Adjusting, & Repairing Wheel Alignment . . . SS-576

Section 1 Alignment and Driveability SS-577
Driveability
Wheel Alignment Angles
Camber Angle
Caster Angle
Toe
Steering Axis Inclination
Scrub Radius
Included Angle
Turning Radius
Setback
Excellence in Science Angles in Wheel Alignment SS-582
Thrust Angle
Section 1 Knowledge Check

Section 2 Wheel Alignment Procedures SS-584
Complaints
Pre-alignment Inspection
Alignment Equipment
Types of Wheel Alignment
Four-Wheel Alignment
Rear-Wheel Alignment
Excellence in Math Measuring Camber SS-588
Alignment Adjustments
Camber
Caster
Toe
General Procedure
Section 2 Knowledge Check

Chapter 4 Review
Excellence in Communication Reading Service Manuals SS-592
Automotive Service Excellence Test Prep SS-593

Glossary 594

Index 605

Credits 624

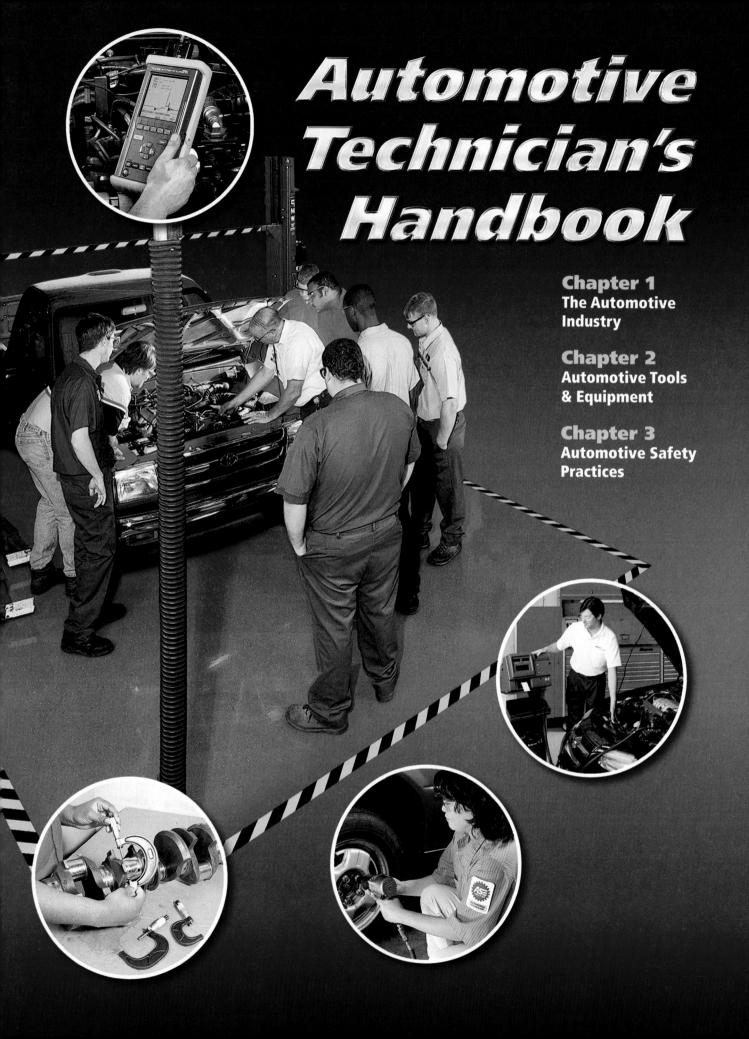

Automotive Technician's Handbook

Chapter 1
The Automotive Industry

Chapter 2
Automotive Tools & Equipment

Chapter 3
Automotive Safety Practices

Section 1
The Automotive
Profession

Section 2
Automotive Career
Opportunities

The Automotive Industry

Customer's Concern

You have always known that you wanted to work with your hands. No office cubicles, no telephone headsets. You want a job that offers new challenges every day. You want a technical career. You have always loved cars. Maybe you are interested in a career as an automotive technician.

Before you make your final career choice, you have several factors to consider. You need to decide if your love of cars also relates to the detailed diagnostic and repair work required of a technician. Job availability and security are very important. Financial stability is critical. Finally, you want to gain the education that will set you on a solid career path.

Technician's Challenge

After reading this chapter, you will have general answers to these questions:

1. What do automotive technicians do on the job? Consider making an appointment with a technician at a local service center to discuss this.

2. What are the employment opportunities for automotive technicians? Check employment classifieds in your local newspaper. You might also visit employment Web sites.

3. What is the average annual income for an automotive technician? Local service centers may share a range of wages related to your area's job market. If not, check Internet employment sites.

● Section 1
The Automotive Profession

Objectives:

- Identify the major systems of an automotive vehicle and briefly explain the purpose of each system.
- Identify the purposes and explain the importance of ASE, NATEF, and STS to the automotive service industry.
- Complete repair order to include customer information, vehicle identifying information, customer concern, related service history, cause, and correction.
- Locate and interpret vehicle and major component identification numbers (VIN, vehicle certification labels, and calibration decals).

Vocabulary:

- **automotive system**
- **Automotive Service Excellence (ASE)**
- **master technician**
- **National Automotive Technicians Education Foundation (NATEF)**
- **Service Technicians Society (STS)**

The Automotive Industry

Starting with the first patented gasoline-powered Benz Motorwagen in 1886, the automotive industry has seen continuous and exciting changes for over a century. See **Fig. 1-1**. The early gasoline-powered automobile generated 1.5 horsepower. It reached top speeds of 3–5 mph [5–8 kph]. Today's vehicles have 76–543 horsepower engines and cruise at 65–122 mph [106–196 kph], depending on the legal speed limit. For many people around the world, automobiles are the most important means of personal transportation.

In the United States, the automotive industry and its 350,000 related industries employ about 7 million workers. More than 30 percent of all passenger cars are in the United States. Ninety percent of Americans own at least one car, and 55 percent own two or more. Americans drive 2.7 trillion miles a year. Their vehicles consume 163 billion gallons of fuel per year. Annually, motorists in the United States spend $100 billion on vehicle insurance. They also use more than $300 billion of credit in the purchase and maintenance of vehicles. The automotive industry affects many areas of the economy.

Automotive Systems

Automobiles are highly complex vehicles with multiple computer-controlled systems. An automobile today has more computers in it than did the first spaceship. A new car may have as many as 50 computers operating everything from the engine to the sound system.

Automotive vehicles are available in a wide variety of models, sizes, and body styles. Vehicles range from compacts to full-size cars and from minivans to sport utility vehicles (SUVs). There are also sedans, convertibles, hatchbacks, station wagons, luxury models, and a wide variety of trucks.

Technology has improved automotive vehicles over the past century. Vehicles are designed according to a variety of factors, including the number of engine cylinders, the type of drive-train system, and vehicle application.

Mercedes-Benz of North America, Inc.

Fig. 1-1 An 1886 Daimler motor carriage, the forerunner of today's automobile. *What was the top speed of this vehicle?*

Fig. 1-2 The basic automotive systems.
What task does each system perform?

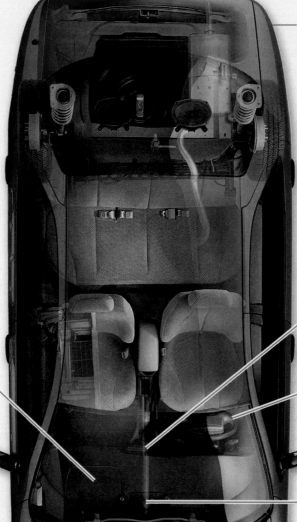

A **body and frame system** supports the vehicle and provides enclosures or compartments for the engine, passengers, luggage, and cargo.

An **accessory system** includes devices that increase comfort, safety, and security.

A **safety system** provides added passenger safety and includes devices such as air bags, antilock brakes, side-door panel steel rails, and shock-absorbing bumpers.

A **steering system** controls the direction of vehicle travel.

A **heating and air conditioning system** controls climate within the passenger compartment.

A **suspension system** absorbs the shocks of the tires and wheels from bumps and holes in the road.

A **power train system** includes the transmission, drive train, and axles that carry the power from the engine to the drive wheels.

A **braking system** slows and stops the vehicle.

An **electrical/electronic system** produces and directs electrical power needed to operate the vehicle's electrical and electronic components.

An **engine** or **power plant** (including the fuel, exhaust, cooling, and lubrication systems) produces dependable and efficient power to move the vehicle.

A **lighting system** includes headlights and taillights, directional signals, brake warning lights, interior convenience and courtesy lights, and instrument control-panel information and warning lights.

About 20,000 separate parts are assembled to make an automotive vehicle. These parts are grouped into several systems, known as automotive vehicle systems. An **automotive system** is a system made up of two or more parts that work together to perform a specific task. See **Fig. 1-2.**

As automotive vehicles become more complex, vehicle service, maintenance, and repair must keep up with changing technology. Many people who serviced and repaired their own vehicles have turned to highly skilled professional service technicians. Specialized equipment is used to troubleshoot and diagnose modern-day automotive vehicle problems to determine service and repair options. See **Fig. 1-3.**

Anyone whose vehicle has failed to start knows the importance of an automotive technician's job. A competent automotive technician can diagnose the cause of the problem quickly and accurately. The technician can then perform the necessary service or repair.

Jack Holtel

Fig. 1-3 An automotive service technician using a scan tool to check engine performance. *Why do people who serviced their own vehicles now rely on professional service technicians?*

Automotive Service Excellence (ASE) Certification

As the need for skilled technicians has grown, a number of automotive service-related organizations have been created. These organizations help ensure the quality of training received by today's automotive technicians. These organizations also support automotive service technicians as they grow in their careers.

The National Institute for Automotive Service Excellence

In 1972 the automotive service industry created the independent, nonprofit National Institute for Automotive Service Excellence. **Automotive Service Excellence (ASE)** is an organization of automotive professionals whose purpose is to improve the quality of vehicle service and repair. ASE does this through the testing and certification of service and repair professionals. See **Fig. 1-4.** ASE is governed by a member board of directors.

National Institute for Automotive Service Excellence

Fig. 1-4 The industry-recognized ASE Blue Seal of Excellence. *Why do consumers look for the ASE seal?*

ASE administers a series of certification exams. Individuals can become certified as automobile and light truck technicians, collision repair technicians, medium- and heavy-duty truck technicians, alternative fuel technicians, engine machinists, and parts specialists. There are a total of 43 areas in which one or more individual certification exams are given. See **Fig. 1-5.**

To achieve ASE certification, a technician must first pass at least one certification exam. Second, the technician must provide proof of two years of relevant work experience. A technician who is certified in all eight auto/light truck areas is a **master technician.** These areas are:

- Brakes.
- Electrical/Electronic Systems.
- Engine Performance.
- Suspension and Steering.
- Engine Repair.
- Heating and Air Conditioning.
- Automotive Transmission/Transaxle.
- Manual Drive Train and Axles.

Fig. 1-5 — ASE CERTIFICATION AREAS

Automobile/Light Truck

- Engine Repair
- Automatic Transmission/Transaxle
- Manual Drive Train and Axles
- Suspension and Steering
- Brakes
- Electrical/Electronic Systems
- Heating and Air Conditioning
- Engine Performance

Automobile Service Consultant

- Communications Skills
- Customer Relations Skills
- Vehicle Systems Knowledge
- Sales Skills
- Knowledge of Facility Operation

Medium/Heavy Truck

- Gasoline Engines
- Diesel Engines
- Drive Train
- Brakes
- Suspension and Steering
- Electrical/Electronic Systems
- Heating, Ventilation, and Air Conditioning (HVAC)
- Preventive Maintenance Inspection (PMI)

Truck Equipment Technician

- Truck Equipment Installation and Repair
- Electrical/Electronic Systems Installation and Repair
- Auxiliary Power Systems Installation and Repair

School Bus

- Body Systems and Special Equipment
- Diesel Engines
- Drive Train
- Brakes
- Suspension and Steering
- Electrical/Electronic Systems
- Air Conditioning Systems and Controls

Collision Repair

- Paint Refinishers
- Nonstructural Damage Repair
- Structural Damage Repair
- Vehicle Mechanical and Electrical Systems Repair
- Collision Damage Estimators

Engine Machinist

- Assembly Specialist
- Cylinder Block Specialist
- Cylinder Head Specialist

Alternative Fuels

- Light Vehicle Compressed Natural Gas

Parts Specialist

- Automobile Parts Specialist
- Medium/Heavy Truck Dealership Parts Specialist
- Medium/Heavy Truck Aftermarket Brake Parts Specialist
- Medium/Heavy Truck Aftermarket Suspension and Steering Parts Specialist
- General Motors Parts Consultant

Advanced Series

- General Powertrain Diagnosis
- Computerized Powertrain Controls Diagnosis (including OBD-II)
- Ignition Systems Diagnosis
- Fuel Systems and Air Induction Systems Diagnosis
- Emission Control Systems Diagnosis
- I/M Failure Diagnosis

- Automobile Advanced Engine Performance Specialist
- Truck Electronic Diesel Engine Diagnosis Specialist
- Diesel Engines

Undercar Specialist

UNDERCAR SPECIALIST

- Brake Systems
- Suspension and Steering Systems
- Exhaust Systems

ASE Certification Exams

ASE certification exams are offered twice a year at more than 750 locations in the United States. Many tests are computer based. These are offered at secure locations. See **Fig. 1-6**. The exams stress knowledge and job-related skills.

Nearly 420,000 professional technicians have been certified under this voluntary certification program. Many employers now make ASE certification a condition for employment. Many employers pay higher wages to ASE-certified technicians. To remain certified, a technician must pass a recertification test every five years.

ASE-certified technicians work in every area of the automotive service industry. ASE-certified technicians usually wear the blue-and-white ASE logo on their shirts.

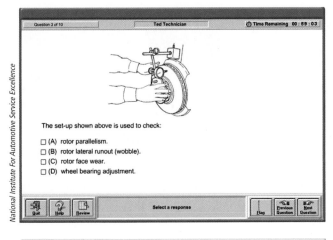

National Institute For Automotive Service Excellence

Fig. 1-6 A sample question from an ASE computer-based test (CBT).

NATEF's Role

In 1978 the **National Automotive Technicians Education Foundation** (**NATEF**) was created as an organization that certifies automotive training programs. See **Fig. 1-7**. NATEF was formed through the work of the Industry Planning Council (IPC) of the then American Vocational Association (AVA). The AVA is now known as the Association for Career and Technical Education (ACTE).

The IPC, working with ASE, developed a process for certifying automotive training programs. NATEF was formed to evaluate individual automotive training programs. It also recommends programs for ASE certification and certifies those programs.

National Institute for Automotive Service Excellence

Fig. 1-7 The National Automotive Technicians Education Foundation (NATEF) logo.

Service Technicians Society

Formed by the Society of Automotive Engineers (SAE), the **Service Technicians Society** (**STS**) is an association for automotive and transportation professionals. Students enrolled in automotive technician training programs are eligible to join STS.

SECTION 1 KNOWLEDGE CHECK

1. Explain how automotive engines have changed in the past 120 years.

2. Identify the major automotive systems and relate the major purpose of each system.

3. What is the mission of ASE?

4. How does one achieve ASE certification?

5. What is NATEF and what is its mission?

6. What does STS stand for?

ASE TEST PREP

7. The organization created to evaluate and certify individual automotive training programs is the:

   ⓐ National Institute for Automotive Service Excellence (ASE).

   ⓑ Service Technicians Society (STS).

   ⓒ National Automotive Technicians Education Foundation (NATEF).

   ⓓ Association for Career and Technical Education (ACTE).

Section 2
Automotive Career Opportunities

Objectives:
- Identify career opportunities in the automotive industry.
- Explain how to become an ASE-certified automotive technician.

Vocabulary:
- repair order
- diversity
- active listening

Job Outlook

According to the U.S. Department of Labor, 82,000 to 164,000 additional automotive technicians will be needed in the near future. Jobs will be plentiful for those who finish training programs in high school, career and technical school, or college. Most technicians who enter the field can expect steady work. Changes in economic conditions have little effect on the automotive service and repair business. See **Fig. 1-8.**

Jack Holtel

Fig. 1-8 A student learning from a master automotive technician. *Why is it important for students to visit automotive businesses?*

Automotive Employers

A variety of businesses employ trained automotive technicians to perform service and repairs. These include:
- Dealerships that sell and service specific brands of vehicles.
- Independent service facilities that service all types of automotive vehicles.
- Large retail facilities that are owned by mass merchandisers.
- Specialty centers that handle brakes, tune-ups, transmission repair, and wheel alignment.
- Fleet facilities operated by the government or private companies to service their own vehicles.

Dealerships

There are about 24,000 new-car dealers in the United States. There are also several hundred truck dealers. The dealer must prepare and service each new vehicle before delivery to the customer. Sometimes vehicle problems develop after the sale. The dealer must fix vehicles that are under warranty. Warranty work is paid for by the vehicle manufacturer. The warranty covers repairs only for a specified period of time or mileage amount after the date the vehicle was sold.

A manufacturer may recall a vehicle. This means the manufacturer asks the owner to return the vehicle to the dealer for inspection and possible repair. The manufacturer pays for any required parts or service. Recalls are frequently safety-related. Technicians should never allow the vehicle owner to ignore a recall.

New-car dealers also sell the used vehicles traded in when customers buy new vehicles. After inspecting and reconditioning the vehicle, the dealer sells the trade-in, often with a limited warranty. This warranty protects the buyer if a defect shows up shortly after the sale. Dealers also sell used vehicles "as is." In this case, the buyer does not receive any warranty.

The dealership has a service department to handle the automotive service work. This is a properly equipped service facility staffed with trained technicians who do warranty work and work for which the customer pays. Diagnostic equipment, special tools, and parts must be available. Some service departments are small, employing fewer than five technicians. Larger dealerships may employ 25 or more technicians.

Most dealerships have personal computers in the service department so they can be online with the vehicle manufacturer. See **Fig. 1-9**. This means the computers at the dealership are connected to the manufacturer's computer. A telephone line or satellite link connects the two. If a vehicle has a difficult problem, the technician can connect to the manufacturer's computer, which shows how to diagnose and repair the problem. The screen may also display the parts needed, along with their prices and availability.

William Taufic/The Stock Market

Fig. 1-9 Today's technicians must have a variety of skills including the ability to use computer diagnostic equipment.

Independent Service Facilities

There are more than 120,000 non-dealership automotive repair facilities in the United States. These are independent service facilities. Some are one-person specialty businesses. Others are general repair facilities that employ many automotive technicians. The larger facilities often operate like dealership service departments. See **Fig. 1-10**.

Terry Wild Studio

Fig. 1-10 A service department in an automotive dealership. *Why is a warranty important to the consumer?*

Large Retail Facilities

Service facilities owned by mass merchandisers operate much like independent service facilities. However, these centers usually specialize in engine tune-up, electrical/electronic systems, suspension and steering, lighting systems, and tire replacement and repair.

Specialty Centers

Specialty centers provide various "trade services" for the automotive service industry. These services usually include brake repair, wheel alignments, tune-ups, transmission repair, lube and oil changes, exhaust and muffler replacement, and radiator service. Many large and small dealership service departments now take their machine work to specialized automotive machinists. Such machinists refinish brake drums, rotors, and engine flywheels. The machinist may also repair cracks in cylinder blocks and heads, as well as bore and sleeve engine cylinders.

Fleet Facilities

A fleet is a group of five or more vehicles owned and maintained by a single company. Automotive dealers and independent service facilities maintain some fleet vehicles. However, there are more than 35,000 fleet facilities in the United States. Companies that do their own service and repair work operate these facilities. They include bus and trucking companies as well as taxicab and delivery fleets.

The technician in a fleet facility usually works for the company that owns the fleet. Often, the work is done on a preset schedule. This scheduled periodic service, or preventive maintenance, helps prevent unexpected vehicle breakdown and costly repairs.

The fleet driver checks some items daily before driving the vehicle. Then at scheduled intervals, the vehicle is brought into the facility. The technician checks the fluid levels, changing the fluids and filters if necessary. A visual inspection evaluates the condition of the belts, tires, and other parts. Meters and gauges show the condition of the battery and electrical system. A road test may be conducted to check vehicle performance. Any problems found during these checks are corrected. See **Fig. 1-11.**

Chris Sorensen/CORBIS

Fig. 1-11 Fleet facility technicians perform preventive maintenance to prevent unexpected breakdowns and repairs.

The Automotive Work Environment

Automotive technicians enjoy varied and interesting day-to-day encounters. Many consider diagnosing hard-to-find problems one of their most challenging and satisfying duties. While the use of hand tools is still an important part of the technicians' responsibilities, they also use electronic analyzers and computerized diagnostic equipment. This technology helps technicians find problems and make precision adjustments. Modern automotive service and repair facilities are clean and well ventilated. They are pleasant and safe places to work. See **Fig. 1-12.**

Technicians generally work a standard 40-hour week. Opportunities for overtime work are usually available. To better satisfy customer needs, some dealerships and independent repair facilities provide evening and weekend hours.

There are career opportunities in the automotive service industry other than that of a technician. The following are some of these careers.

Service Consultant The service consultant greets the customer and listens carefully as the customer describes the vehicle's problem. The service consultant writes the repair order in enough detail to assist the technician in diagnosing and repairing the problem.

Service Dispatcher The service dispatcher schedules each vehicle service and repair job. He or she also assigns the technician to perform the job. The service dispatcher tracks all repair jobs. This helps ensure that the jobs are completed correctly and that billings for the technicians' time are recorded.

Supervisor The supervisor is responsible for the overall supervision of the service department. The supervisor helps other technicians troubleshoot problems in all automotive areas. He or she provides a communication link between the service floor, the service manager, and the parts department. The supervisor is also responsible for communicating effectively with technicians and resolving any personnel disputes. The supervisor usually has been a successful automotive technician before being promoted.

Peoria Toyota Scion

Fig. 1-12 The design of this service facility, which is open and well-lighted, contributes to on-the-job efficiency. It also makes a good impression on customers.

Service Manager The service manager coordinates the service and repair activities of the service and parts departments. The service manager also responds to customer questions and complaints and ensures quality service.

Parts Manager The parts manager knows the components and systems of an automotive vehicle. He or she can quickly locate, price, and dispense the requested parts. See **Fig. 1-13**.

Automotive Salesperson The automotive salesperson works in the dealer's showroom or used-car department. He or she is responsible for selling vehicles to interested buyers. The salesperson must have good sales skills. He or she must also know about each vehicle's features, options, and price.

Additional formal education will present other career options in the automotive industry. These include engineers, designers, technical writers, and automotive technician trainers and instructors.

Pep Boys

Fig. 1-13 An automotive parts store. *What is the primary responsibility of a parts manager?*

Becoming an ASE-Certified Automotive Technician

There are three major requirements for getting started as a technician in the automotive service industry. The first requirement is to have a mechanical aptitude and an interest in automotive vehicles and how they work. Visit businesses that do automotive service and repair. Observe the automotive service and repair technicians' work environment. Discuss job requirements and career opportunities with working technicians.

The second requirement is to complete an automotive technician training program in high school, a vocational or technical institution, or a two- or four-year college. If available, the training program should be certified. Such certified programs have met rigid industry standards for training automotive technicians. These programs should display a NATEF/ASE logo. See **Fig. 1-14**.

To be ASE certified in a certain area, a technician must pass a written exam in that program area. He or she must also have at least two years of relevant work experience. Completion of an ASE-certified automotive technology training program may be substituted for one year of work experience toward ASE technician certification. This could lead to finding employment more quickly as well as a higher-paying job.

The third requirement is to gain work experience in a modern automotive service and repair facility. This could be at a dealership or an independent repair facility. Ideally, some of the work experience should occur while going to school. This experience could take place through cooperative education or part-time employment. Work experience adds relevance and provides an excellent opportunity to apply your technical and academic skills. These skills are critical to every automotive technician's success.

A Well-Paid Profession

Today's automotive technician is a respected, well-paid professional. Most technicians work on what the industry refers to as a flat rate. The industry has predetermined the amount of time it should take to perform a specific service or repair job. If it takes the technician an hour to complete a job listed in the flat rate manual as a two-hour job, he or she is paid for two hours of labor. However, if it takes the technician three hours to do that same job, the technician is paid only the two-hour flat rate.

Many experienced technicians employed by automotive dealers and independent repair facilities receive a guaranteed annual salary plus a commission. This commission is a percentage of the labor costs charged to customers. Under this method, weekly earnings depend on the work completed by the technician.

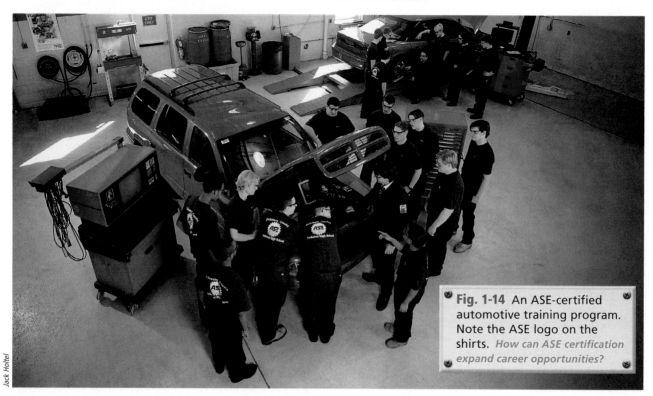

Jack Holtel

Fig. 1-14 An ASE-certified automotive training program. Note the ASE logo on the shirts. *How can ASE certification expand career opportunities?*

Preparing for an Automotive Career

For a successful automotive technician, learning never ends. Technological improvements continue with each new generation of cars and trucks. Automotive technology is becoming more complex with the addition of hybrid and fuel cell technology. State and federal regulations that affect the automotive industry are also increasing. For these reasons, you must continue to learn in order to become a successful automotive technician.

In addition to technical skills, automotive technicians need key academic skills to be successful. Reading, writing, math, and science skills are very important. They support and clarify the application of your technical knowledge.

Reading Skills

Whether you are reading repair orders, service manuals, or company memos, you need to understand what you read. Use these three reading comprehension strategies:

- **Preview** Before you actually read a document, preview the material by looking at the titles and headings. Doing so will give you an overall idea of what you are about to read.
- **Question** As you read, ask yourself questions to check your understanding. Finding answers to those questions will help you concentrate on what you are reading.
- **Visualize** Creating a mental picture of the material can help you understand what you are reading. For example, when you are reading a repair order, picture the steps in the repair process as you read. Doing so will help you recall the steps.

Sometimes you may need to reread a document to understand it. The following tips may help:

- Read to the end of a section to get a sense of the whole story.
- Reread what you do not understand.
- Look at the illustrations, diagrams, and charts. They can help explain the words.
- Use a dictionary to look up any words that you do not understand.

Writing Skills

Your ability to communicate in writing may include creating work orders or writing memos to coworkers. You can improve your writing by following these guidelines.

Identify Your Purpose Determine what you want your readers to learn. Use language that fulfills that purpose. Most written communication fulfills one of the following purposes:

- To inform or give instructions.
- To make a request, ask for information, seek a decision, or call for action.
- To persuade the reader to take action.

Consider Your Audience Tailor your writing to the needs of your readers. Knowing your purpose and your audience can help you determine what you will say and how you will say it. You can improve your writing if you follow these suggestions:

- Prepare a quick outline of the topics you need to write about.
- Get to your main point quickly. For example, if you need to alert your customer to a potential safety problem, make that point in the first sentence.
- Write clearly, simply, and directly.
- Follow basic rules of grammar and punctuation.
- Thoroughly proofread the document and correct any mistakes.
- Check the document for content accuracy. Make sure that all of the facts and figures are correct.
- Reread the document one last time.
- Ask someone else to read the document and suggest ideas for improvement.

Math Skills

The ability to calculate, or work with numbers, is an essential skill that every automotive technician must have. On the job, you will add, subtract, multiply, and divide. You will also calculate percentages and ratios, as well as measure and weigh items. Throughout this textbook you will learn to apply math skills within each automotive area.

Science Skills

It is equally important to understand how and why things work the way they do. The science principles that make automobiles work are fascinating. You will learn physics and chemistry as you read and apply the science skills taught within each automotive area of this textbook.

SAMPLE REPAIR ORDER

Vehicle Repair Order # _____

Date ____/____/____

Customer Name: _____   Vehicle Make/Type: _____   VIN: _____   Mileage: _____

Service History: _____

Customer Concern: _____

Cause of Concern: _____

Suggested Repairs/Maintenance: _____

Services Performed: _____

Parts		
Item	Description	Price
1.		
2.		
3.		
4.		
5.		
6.		

Labor	Time In:
Diagnosis Time:	Time Complete:
Repair Time:	Total Hours:

I hereby authorize the above repair work to be done using the necessary material, and hereby grant you and/or your employees permission to operate the vehicle herein described on streets, highways, or elsewhere for the purpose of testing and/or inspection. An express mechanic's lien is hereby acknowledged on above vehicle to secure the amount of repairs thereof.

X _____

Fig. 1-15 Correct completion of a repair order is the first step in solving the customer's concern.

Completing and Reading a Repair Order

A **repair order** is a document that organizes the information the service technician needs to know about the vehicle in order to service it properly. See **Fig. 1-15**. Repair orders are sometimes called work orders. State laws regulate repair orders, so they vary from state to state.

In completing a repair order, write legibly. Make sure all information is accurate. Double-check customer contact information.

Despite their differences, repair orders contain the same basic information. Important information includes the vehicle identification number, the service history, and the customer concern. The repair order should remain with the vehicle as the vehicle is being repaired.

Vehicle Identification Number (VIN) The vehicle identification number (VIN) is a string of coded data that is unique to the vehicle. The VIN indicates:
- When the vehicle was made.
- The country in which the vehicle was made.
- The vehicle make and type.
- The passenger safety system.
- The type of engine.
- The line, series, and body style.
- The assembly plant where the vehicle was produced.

The VIN is a rich source of information. It is also needed to properly use a scan tool to read diagnostic trouble codes.

Service History The service history is a history of all service operations performed on a vehicle. A detailed service history for a vehicle is regularly serviced. Information on service performed on the vehicle at other service centers is not available unless the customer makes it available. For this reason, it is usually a good idea to ask the customer about service performed outside of the present service center.

The service history alerts the technician to previous problems. For recurring problems, it helps identify ineffective solutions.

Customer Concern The customer concern is a reasonably detailed description of the problem that the customer is having with the vehicle. The customer is familiar with his or her vehicle. This often makes the customer the best source of information regarding the problem. This information can be used to perform the initial diagnosis. This will help identify both the problem and the solution.

Employability Skills

Finding and keeping a good job requires more than academic and technical skills. You must also work well with other people and show that you are a reliable employee. The following are personal characteristics that will help you become a successful automotive technician.

Positive Attitude

Whether to be positive or negative about your job is your choice. If you have a positive attitude, people are far more likely to respond positively to you.

Responsibility

Employers want employees to do their work promptly and properly and to take responsibility for their actions. What one person fails to do affects other people. If an employee does not show up for work or leaves early without permission, his or her coworkers may not be able to finish their tasks.

Teamwork

Throughout the automotive industry, automotive technicians work in teams. A team is a group of people working together to reach a common goal. The success of each team depends on cooperation and respect for each team member's contributions. Team members who work well together can achieve more than each of the members individually. Team efforts can lead to improvements in quality, safety, and customer service. Teamwork also results in better morale. Each team member makes a unique contribution to the whole.

Respecting Others

Without respect for one another, there can be little cooperation among coworkers. Respect is a two-way street, so the more you give, the more you are likely to receive.

Honesty

Employers expect their employees to be honest. Keep in mind that one dishonest act can destroy your reputation. Be sure to return the tools and equipment you use on the job. Never "borrow" company property for your personal use. Do not use a customer's vehicle for personal errands or keep it overnight.

Commitment

Automotive technicians who are committed to excellence strive to do their best at all times. They are committed to quality and strive to meet the highest standards. See **Fig. 1-16.**

Jack Holtel

Fig. 1-16 Commitment to excellence means commitment to quality and striving to meet the highest standards.

Willingness to Learn

Every company has its own ways of doing things. You need to learn the system. Be willing to learn any job, no matter how small. Take advantage of training opportunities to learn more.

Initiative

Taking initiative means doing what needs to be done without being told to do it. Employers value workers who look for opportunities to do and learn more than just the job for which they were hired.

Personal Appearance

Appearance can affect your success on the job. It is important to be clean and to dress appropriately. Likewise, if you don't feel your best, your job performance will suffer. Take good care of your health, eat nutritious foods, and exercise regularly.

A Diverse Workplace

In the automotive industry, you can expect to work with people of every race, gender, age, and ability level. This mix of different people is called **diversity.** The key challenge in a diverse workplace is learning to communicate. People with different backgrounds bring different skills and perspectives about how to solve problems and get work done.

Communicating Clearly

Strong communication skills help you establish and maintain effective relationships with customers as well as with coworkers and supervisors. Your ability to communicate will make or break your success in the automotive workplace. Make sure that you communicate with customers clearly, accurately, and promptly. You will also need to write clear repair orders, understand oral instructions, read to learn about new technologies, and communicate with customers on a daily basis.

What does it take to be a good communicator? Here are some general guidelines:

- Recognize that communication is an exchange between two or more people. See **Fig. 1-17.**
- Be respectful, courteous, and professional at all times.
- Listen carefully to your customer's concerns.
- Ask questions to understand your customer's needs.
- Notify your customer if problems occur that will affect delivery time.
- Follow up with your customers to make sure that your work is satisfactory.
- If there is a problem, explain actions that will be taken to address it.

The Communication Process

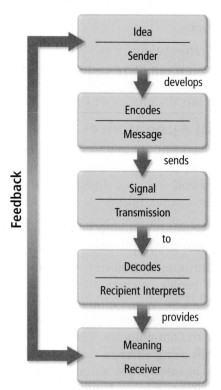

Fig. 1-17 Communication occurs when a message is sent and the meaning of that message is received.

Telephone Skills

Speak clearly and politely on the telephone. Your voice may be the listener's first and only impression of you and the company. Take accurate messages. Include the date and time of the call and the caller's name and phone number.

You may need to make notes during an incoming call. Be sure to have a pen and paper nearby. If you leave a voice message, keep it short and to the point. Repeat your phone number twice so that the person can return your call.

Listening Skills

You will be listening constantly on the job, so it is important to develop your listening skills. Listening is not the same as hearing. You can hear what someone says and still not understand the message. Listening means understanding what you hear and responding to it. The skill of paying attention and interacting with the speaker is known as **active listening.** Follow these guidelines to develop active listening skills:

- **Identify the purpose.** Think about the purpose of the message. Why are you listening?
- **Maintain eye contact.** Keep your eyes on the speaker. Doing so will help you focus on what the speaker is saying and concentrate on what you are hearing.
- **Ask questions.** If you don't understand, ask questions.
- **Take notes.** In some cases, you may need to take notes about details such as deadlines.
- **Restate the message.** Repeat the message in your own words to make sure that you understand it.

Speaking Skills

At times you will need to explain procedures to a coworker and/or a customer. You may even be asked to make a presentation to a group. You will need to speak clearly and concisely so that your listeners will understand. To develop effective speaking skills, follow these guidelines.

- **Consider your audience.** Keep in mind that listeners are not always familiar with the terms you use on the job. You will probably use more jargon when speaking to a coworker than you would with a customer.
- **Check for understanding.** Make sure that your listeners understand your message. Ask whether they have any questions.

- **Speak with confidence.** Remember that you have something important to say. Maintain eye contact by moving your eyes from person to person when speaking to a group.
- **Speak clearly.** Pronounce each word clearly and correctly. Do not cover your mouth while speaking.
- **Speak at a normal pace.** Do not speak so fast that no one can follow you or so slowly that people lose interest.
- **Control your volume.** Listeners cannot hear you if you speak too softly. Speaking too loudly will annoy listeners.

Nonverbal Communication

The use of behaviors other than speaking to convey meaning is known as nonverbal communication. Such behaviors may include gestures, facial expressions and other body language, laughter, and sighing. These movements and sounds often indicate thoughts and feelings that do not support what the person says.

Sending Nonverbal Signals Nonverbal signals can help or hinder communication. Be aware of your body language. Rolling your eyes or failing to look directly at the person with whom you are speaking can interfere with communication.

Interpreting Nonverbal Signals You can study a person's body language for clues to what he or she is thinking or feeling. You can then use that information to improve your communication. See Table 1-A.

Table 1-A	NONVERBAL SIGNALS
Body Language	**Messages**
Facial Expressions	Your facial expressions can convey your mood. Look calm and confident.
Gestures	Gestures can both complement and contradict your message. Use hand gestures to emphasize key points. Do not overuse gestures.
Posture	Good posture conveys confidence. Stand or sit upright as you face other people.
Personal Space	Be mindful of another person's personal space. Do not sit or stand too close.

SECTION 2 KNOWLEDGE CHECK

1. List five types of businesses that employ automotive service technicians.

2. Explain the difference between a dealership service department and an independent service facility.

3. Describe an automotive service technician's work environment in a modern automotive service and repair establishment.

4. List the three major requirements for getting started as a technician in the automotive service industry.

5. Why is an automotive service technician's learning never finished?

ASE TEST PREP

6. Technician A says that the vehicle repair order should stay with the vehicle during the service procedure. Technician B says that the vehicle repair order should remain at the service desk. Who is correct?
   - ⓐ Technician A.
   - ⓑ Technician B.
   - ⓒ Both Technician A and Technician B.
   - ⓓ Neither Technician A nor Technician B.

7. Technician A says that when listening to a customer it is important to ask questions about things you do not understand. Technician B says that when listening to a customer it is important to restate the customer's message in your own words in order to clarify the meaning. Who is correct?
   - ⓐ Technician A.
   - ⓑ Technician B.
   - ⓒ Both Technician A and Technician B.
   - ⓓ Neither Technician A nor Technician B.

CHAPTER 1 REVIEW

Key Points

Addresses NATEF program guidelines and career opportunities in the automotive industry.

- The automobile has evolved from a very simple to a very complex vehicle.
- Each major system has a specific purpose in the vehicle's operation.
- Three organizations that serve the automotive service industry are the National Institute for Automotive Service Excellence (ASE), the National Automotive Technicians Education Foundation (NATEF), and the Service Technicians Society (STS).
- The employment outlook for automotive technicians is very positive over the next several years.
- Many automotive technicians receive a guaranteed annual salary plus a commission.
- A correctly completed repair order includes all of the information needed to complete the repair, including the VIN.

Review Questions

1. How have automobiles changed over the past century? How have they remained the same?
2. Identify the major automotive systems and explain the purpose of each.
3. Distinguish between an automotive part, system, and task.
4. Identify the purposes of ASE, NATEF, and STS.
5. What are the advantages of being an ASE-certified master technician?
6. How does one get started on the pathway to a successful career as an automotive technician?
7. In obtaining ASE certification, what can be substituted for one year of work experience?
8. **Critical Thinking** Explain how strong skills in each of the following academic areas can help you in the automotive services field: science, math, and communication.

HYBRID TECHNOLOGY

Alternative Energy Sources

Imagine an automobile powered by an energy source other than gasoline. To reduce gasoline consumption, automobile manufacturers are exploring hybrid power sources and alternative fuels. Hybrid power sources include the use of fuel cells and high-voltage batteries with internal combustion engines. Alternative fuels include hydrogen, biodiesel, ethanol, and others.

Though not in common use, hydrogen fuel cells represent a potential alternative power source to gasoline.

Like a battery, a fuel cell is used to produce electricity. A single fuel cell consists of an electrolyte sandwiched between two porous electrodes. Flanking each electrode is a conductive plate with channels. The channels allow hydrogen and oxygen to reach the electrodes while the plate itself conducts current away from the electrodes.

Hydrogen gas is fed to one electrode where a catalyst impregnated in the electrode helps to separate electrons from the hydrogen. The electrons are conducted away from the electrode, creating current flow. The remaining hydrogen protons are transferred to the electrolyte. Oxygen is fed to the electrode opposite the hydrogen electrode. Hydrogen protons pass from the electrolyte to the oxygen electrode. There, with the help of a catalyst, the hydrogen protons combine with oxygen to produce water and give off heat in the process.

A single fuel cell produces very little electricity. However, when many fuel cells are combined in a fuel cell stack enough power can be produced to run a car.

Internal combustion engines powered by hydrogen have been produced. One such engine is bi-fuel, allowing it to run on either hydrogen or gasoline. Such an engine produces far less pollution than a gasoline engine. In a combustion engine, hydrogen generates only small amounts of nitrogen oxides (NO_x). The high cost of producing hydrogen prevents mass production of the engines.

AUTOMOTIVE SERVICE EXCELLENCE
TEST PREP

Answering the following practice questions will help you prepare for the ASE certification tests.

1. Which of the following statements about today's new automobiles is correct?

   a There are more computers in a car today than aboard the first spaceship.

   b A new car today may have as many as 50 computers onboard.

   c Both a and b.

   d Neither a nor b.

2. Which of the following is not considered an automotive system?

   a Power train.

   b Computer.

   c Electrical/electronic.

   d Engine/power plant.

3. The purpose of Automotive Service Excellence (ASE) is to:

   a improve the quality of vehicle service and repair.

   b test and certify automotive service and repair professionals.

   c Both a and b.

   d Neither a nor b.

4. To be ASE certified in a certain area, a technician must:

   a pass a written exam.

   b have at least two years relevant work experience.

   c complete an ASE-certified automotive training program.

   d Both a and b.

5. Which of the following statements about the automotive industry outlook is true?

   a Changes in economic conditions have little effect on the automotive service and repair business.

   b The demand for automotive technicians has never been lower.

   c Both a and b.

   d Neither a nor b.

6. The National Automotive Technicians Education Foundation (NATEF) does which of the following?

   a Provides a forum for technical information and exchange.

   b Tests automotive technicians on their knowledge and skills.

   c Evaluates automotive training programs and recommends programs for ASE certification.

   d Recommends automotive students to prospective employers.

7. Predelivery is the preparation and service of a new vehicle before delivery to a customer. This is performed in a(n):

   a independent service facility.

   b specialty service facility.

   c dealership.

   d fleet facility.

8. An automotive parts catalog comes in which of the following forms?

   a Paper.

   b Microfiche.

   c Online.

   d All of the above.

9. Which of the following is a "nontechnical" automotive career?

   a Service technician.

   b Brake specialist.

   c Automotive salesperson.

   d Engine machinist.

10. To get started in a career as an automotive service technician, you should:

   a have a mechanical aptitude and interest in vehicles and how they work.

   b complete an automotive training program.

   c gain work experience in a modern automotive service facility.

   d All of the above.

Section 1
Hand Tools

Section 2
General Workplace Equipment

Section 3
Measuring Systems and Tools

Section 4
Fasteners, Gaskets, and Sealants

Automotive Tools & Equipment

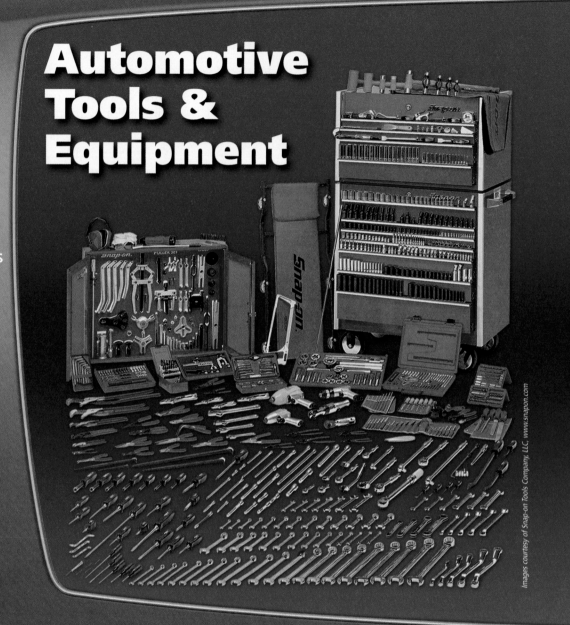

Images courtesy of Snap-on Tools Company, LLC. www.snapon.com

Customer's Concern

Socket wrenches, screwdrivers, wire cutters, Allen wrenches, hammers, and diagnostic scanners. These are just a few tools of the trade for an automotive technician. Because most service facilities require their technicians to supply and maintain their own tools, it is important to know what you will need. You are likely to develop your tool set gradually over a long period of time, but you will need some basics as you begin your career as a technician.

Like buying anything else, you want to look for value. Value is found in the best quality tools offered at the most economical prices. You will also want to consider the length of the warranty on the tools you purchase. A technician just starting his or her career should probably pass on a tool with a one-year warranty.

Technician's Challenge

When looking for tools, you need to find answers to these questions:

1. What tools should I buy for my starter set? What are the basic tools involved in automotive repair? What tools will I use most frequently?

2. How much can I afford to spend on my first tool investment? Will my employer loan me tools until I can afford my own?

3. Will I get the best value from a mobile tool service, a national department store chain, a national hardware store chain, or a locally owned hardware store?

● Section 1
Hand Tools

Objectives:
- ● Identify hand tools used in automotive technology.
- ● Demonstrate the correct use of automotive hand tools.

Vocabulary:
- ● **specialized tool**
- ● **hand tool**
- ● **pneumatic motor**

Automotive repair technicians must be familiar with a wide variety of tools. The correct tools must be used in the correct manner. As automobiles have become more complex, many of the required tools have become more specialized. A **specialized tool** is a tool designed for a certain use. A specialized tool may be a hand tool or a power tool. Specialized tools will be covered in the sections of this book in which they have application.

Tool Safety

Practice good safety habits when using tools. Chapter 3 of this handbook, "Automotive Safety Practices" provides specific recommendations for tool safety.

There are many possible safety hazards in an automotive repair facility. To avoid these hazards, technicians must always be aware of them. Keep informed of the safety issues involved with the use of tools by following the manufacturer's instructions. All of your questions about tool safety should be answered before you use the tool.

Paying attention to the task at hand and to the potential hazards are the bottom line in tool safety. In most situations there will be some warning of a hazard before it causes an accident.

Many workplace hazards are created by the careless use of hand tools. Some hazards are obvious and easy to avoid. For example, if you hammer a chisel against a metal part, it is likely that chips of metal could fly out and strike a hand or eye. Always wear eye protection.

Not all tool hazards are obvious. For example, using a pedestal grinder with a wheel out of balance can result in serious injury. A grinding wheel that has turned glassy from heat can break up. Pieces of the wheel can fly off. This can cause injury or death.

There is no "acceptable risk level" when using tools. There should be no dangerous situation in auto repair. Every operation and procedure is safe if performed properly. If a situation seems unsafe, something may be wrong. Correct the problem immediately.

Using Tools Properly

Most shops will require the technician to have a complete set of professional hand tools as a condition of employment. A starter set of hand tools can cost $1,000 to $2,000. A basic set of hand tools could easily cost more than $5,000. However, students enrolled in automotive training programs are often offered tools at a reduced price. See **Fig. 2-1.** Automotive technicians must upgrade their tools as needed. Because tools are costly, it makes sense to take care of them.

Images courtesy of Snap-on Tools Company, LLC, www.snapon.com

Fig. 2-1 Owning a complete set of tools is often a condition of employment. *Why are some tools packaged in pouches or anti-corrosion wrapping papers?*

Tool manufacturers usually include care and storage instructions with their tools. Some tools come with custom packages for storage. For example, measuring tools often come in pouches or in anti-corrosion wrapping papers. These protect the tools' delicate precision surfaces. Carefully read the manufacturer's instructions for tool use and care.

To take good care of tools, technicians must know the capabilities and limits of the tools. They must know when and how the tools should be used. A technician must also know how tools should not be used. For example, using a screwdriver in place of a chisel or punch may get the job done. But it may also damage the part on which it is being misused, and may also cause personal injury.

A good technician has respect for his or her tools. Such a technician uses the correct tool for the job. For example, pliers are grasping tools useful for holding nonprecision surfaces, such as a thick pipe. But pliers are not a good choice for holding bolt heads or the threaded surface of a bolt. Pliers can easily damage a threaded surface or the corners of a nut or bolt head. Using a hand socket on a powerful impact wrench, instead of using a special impact socket, defies common sense. Such misuse of tools also ignores manufacturer's instructions and can void the warranty.

It can be tempting to use the tool-in-hand rather than make the effort to find the right tool. It is important to know which tool is best for a job and to use that tool. See **Fig. 2-2.**

Fig. 2-2 Always use the right tool for the job.

Types of Tools

In some cases different types of tools can be used to do the same work. Different tools can provide different efficiencies in doing the same job.

Hand Tools A **hand tool** is a tool that does not use a motor and obtains its energy from the person using it. The most basic tools are hand tools such

as wrenches, screwdrivers, and pliers. Hand tools are used to tighten and loosen fasteners and move tightly fitted parts. Your hand supplies the energy to use hand tools. See **Fig. 2-3.**

Fig. 2-3 Hand tools are the most basic tools. *What supplies the energy for hand tools?*

Power Tools Power tools are driven by electric or pneumatic motors. A **pneumatic motor** is a motor that is powered by air pressure. This pressure is created by an air compressor. Tools driven by pneumatic motors should be lubricated daily with oil. The air compressor should be drained of air at the end of each day.

You can often work more quickly with power tools than with hand tools. However, power tools are usually not as useful for performing sensitive operations or for making delicate adjustments. In many cases, a power tool is the only practical tool to use. For example, power tools are best suited for quickly removing nuts and bolts or for unthreading long-threaded fasteners. See **Fig. 2-4.** Power tools sometimes give better access to a vehicle part.

Fig. 2-4 Power tools are best suited for certain tasks. *What are two types of motors that drive power tools?*

Storing and Maintaining Tools

Keep your tools clean, organized, and in good working condition.

- Clean hand tools after every use.
- Remove oil and grease from tools before storing.
- Store tools properly.

Tools left lying on the floor are a safety hazard, causing someone to slip or trip. Technicians who store their tools carelessly will waste time looking for the right tool. Properly storing tools in tool chests and other appropriate containers will protect them from impact, abrasion, and corrosion.

Table 2-A identifies and describes the basic hand tools usually required for employment as an automotive technician. Before applying for a job, a technician should have all the tools in this table. He or she should know how to properly use each tool.

Images courtesy of Snap-on Tools Company, LLC, www.snapon.com

Table 2-A	INDIVIDUAL HAND TOOLS	
Tool	**Description**	**The Job**
Wrenches	• Long-handled tools with fixed or adjustable jaws. • A 1/4″–1″ USC set and a 7 mm–19 mm metric set will handle most jobs. The measurement given is the width of the jaw opening. Purchase in sets of open-end, box, and combination wrenches.	• Use to turn bolts, nuts, and screws.
❶ **Allen Wrench** Stock #: AWM110DHK	• Small L-shaped or T-shaped six-sided bar. Sometimes the bar has a six-pointed star shape. • A complete set should include standard 0.05″–3/8″, as well as metric 2 mm, 8 mm, 10 mm, and 12 mm. • Allen wrenches are available in sizes ranging from 3/32″–5/8″ and from 2 mm to 19 mm.	• Use to turn cap screws that have an internal hex turning configuration.
❷ **Combination Wrench** Stock #: SOEXM710	• Has a box on one end and is open on the other. • The two ends are usually the same size. • The most common box-wrench has 12 notches or "points" in the head. A six-point box wrench holds better on a nut or bolt but needs a greater swing. • Provides the flexibility of a box on one end and an open wrench on the other. • A complete set should include standard 1/4″–1 1/4″ and metric 7 mm–24 mm.	• Designed for a wide variety of work. • A 15° angle on the open end allows use when a minimum of wrench-swing space is available. • Because of its weak jaws, the open end should not be used on extremely tight nuts or bolts. • Use the box end for loosening extremely tight nuts or bolts.

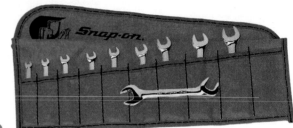

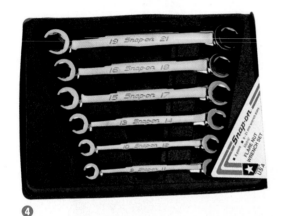

Images courtesy of Snap-on Tools Company, LLC, www.snapon.com

Table 2-A	INDIVIDUAL HAND TOOLS (continued)	
Tool	**Description**	**The Job**
❸ **Crowfoot Wrench Set** Stock #: 210FRHM	• Consists of a set of crowfoot drives and holders or extension bars. • Specialized open- and box-end wrenches that are turned with a socket handle. • The drives have slots to accept the holders or extension bars. • Available in standard and metric sizes.	• Use with an extension bar to turn nuts and bolts in hard-to-reach locations. • Use with torque wrenches when there is no other way to access a fastener head.
❹ **Flare-Nut (Tubing) Wrench** Stock #: RXFMS606B	• Special type of combination or box-end wrench. • The ends of the flare-nut wrench are thicker than those on other wrenches. This helps prevent slipping and rounding off the points on soft-metal tube fittings. • A complete set should include 3/8″–3/4″ standard and 10 mm–17 mm metric sizes.	• Use to attach or remove a flare nut or tubing nut from brake lines. • Use to grip the jamb nuts on fittings. • The flare nut pattern, with its hex box opening, is especially useful for air conditioning work where tubing terminates on flare nuts.
❺ **Ignition Wrench Set** Stock #: DSM810K	• Open-ended wrench with a 15° offset on one end and a 60° offset on the other end. • Sizes range from 1/8″ to 3/8″ and from 3.2 mm to 11 mm.	• Use for turning small nuts for ignition system adjustments. Used on contact point distributor ignitions. Distributorless systems do not have these components.
❻ **Torque Wrench** Stock #: BRUTUS3R250D	• Includes a gauge that measures force expressed in units of distance and weight. • A complete set should include a 1/4″ drive (10–250 lb-in), a 3/8″ drive (5–75 lb-ft), and a 1/2″ drive (50–250 lb-ft). • Torque wrenches are available in 1/4″, 3/8″, and 1/2″ drives.	• Use when fastening pressure is critical to sealing or operation.

Images courtesy of Snap-on Tools Company, LLC, www.snapon.com

Table 2-A	INDIVIDUAL HAND TOOLS (continued)	
Tool	**Description**	**The Job**
Socket Sets	• These are probably the most widely used tools in a service center. • A socket wrench has two basic parts—a detachable socket and a ratchet handle.	• Use to increase the speed for removing or installing bolts or nuts.
⑦ Socket Stock #: 114TMPB	• Cylinder-shaped, extended box-end tool that is placed on the ratchet handle. • Sockets are available in 6-point, 8-point, or the standard 12-point socket. Both regular-depth sockets and deep sockets are available. • The drive end of the sockets come in four sizes: 1/4″, 3/8″, 1/2″ and 3/4″. • Sizes range from 1/4″–1-1/8″ and from 2 mm–24 mm.	• Use 6-point socket if a bolt head or nut has rounded corners or excessive resistance to turning. • Use 8-point socket for turning square heads such as drain plugs, fill plugs, and pipe plugs. • Use 12-point socket to turn a bolt or nut in tight spots.
⑧ Flexible Socket Set Stock #: 209FUMY	• Specialized socket that incorporates a universal swivel joint as part of the socket, eliminating the need for a separate universal joint connector. • Available in various metric and standard sizes (10 mm to 19 mm set pictured).	• Allows you to turn a nut or bolt while holding the driver at an angle.
⑨ Flex/Universal-Type Socket Set Stock #: 206SFSUM	• Specialized socket that incorporates a universal swivel joint as part of the socket, eliminating the need for a separate universal joint connector. • Available in various metric and standard sizes (10 mm to 17 mm set pictured).	• Allows you to turn a nut or bolt while holding the driver at an angle.
⑩ Flexhead Ratchet Stock #: FCF936	• Ratchet with tilting head.	• Use to provide leverage and allow quick ratchet removal or tightening. • Use to provide leverage in spaces where ratchet head must be off axis with handle in order to turn.
⑪ Speed Handle Stock #: F4LBK	• Bar with socket attachment point on one end and offset handle on other end.	• Use for rapid tightening or loosening of nuts and bolts where little torque is required.

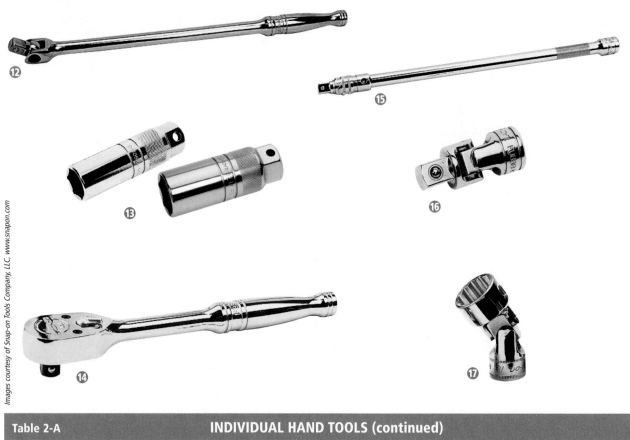

Images courtesy of Snap-on Tools Company, LLC, www.snapon.com

Table 2-A	INDIVIDUAL HAND TOOLS (continued)	
Tool	**Description**	**The Job**
⑫ **Flex Handle (Breaker Bar)** Stock #: F12LA	• Solid bar with flexible socket attachment point on one end.	• Use for applying torque (usually when loosening a bolt or nut) beyond what a standard ratchet can handle without breaking.
⑬ **Spark Plug Socket** Stock #: S9704KR Stock #: S9706KA	• A special deep socket that has a rubber insert. • Size are 5/8" and 13/16".	• Use for removing and installing spark plugs.
⑭ **Ratchet** Stock #: F936	• Connects to a socket and provides the leverage and ratchet mechanism for turning nuts and bolts. • Has a mechanism that permits free motion in one direction but lockup in the other. Select the direction for lockup by moving the reversing lever on the ratchet handle.	• Use to provide leverage and to allow quick ratchet removal or tightening.
⑮ **Extension** Stock #: FXKL11	• Fits into the ratchet handle at one end and receives a socket at the other end. • A complete set should include 3", 5", and 10" extensions.	• Allows you to reach with a ratchet otherwise unreachable nuts or bolts.
⑯ **Universal Joint** Stock #: FU80B	• Connecting piece with a swivel. • Connects to the driver at one end and the socket at the other end.	• Allows you to turn a nut or bolt while holding the drive at an angle.
⑰ **Flexible Socket** Stock #: FUM13A	• A standard socket with a universal joint. • Available in sizes from 3/8" to 3/4"; metric sizes available from 10 mm to 19mm. • Also called a universal socket.	• Allows you to turn nuts or bolts while holding the driver at an angle.

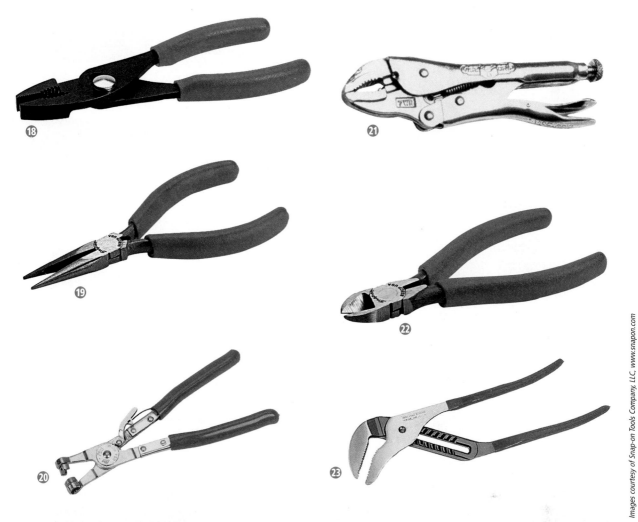

Images courtesy of Snap-on Tools Company, LLC, www.snapon.com

Table 2-A	INDIVIDUAL HAND TOOLS (continued)	
Tool	**Description**	**The Job**
Pliers	• Hand tools with a pair of adjustable pivoted jaws.	• Use for cutting, crimping, bending, or gripping.
⑱ **6″ Combination Pliers** Stock #: 46ACP	• Standard pliers that can be adjusted to hold various sizes of items.	• Provide great versatility.
⑲ **6″ Needle-Nose Pliers** Stock #: 95BCP	• Pliers that have long narrow gripping area.	• Use for holding or positioning small parts and when there is minimum space for maneuvering the plier head.
⑳ **Hose-Clamp Pliers** Stock #: HCP10	• Have special teeth for holding hose clamps. • There are two types—locking and nonlocking.	• Use to remove hose clamps.
㉑ **Locking-Jaw Pliers** Stock #: VP7WR	• Have locking jaws that are adjusted by turning a screw at the end of one handle. • Have a release lever on one of the handles.	• Use when you need a vise-like grip on the part being held or turned.
㉒ **Side-Cutting Pliers** Stock #: 85BCP	• Often called "side cutters" or "diagonals."	• Use for cutting thin sections of rod or wire or removing cotter pins.
㉓ **Slip-Joint (Water-Pump) Pliers** Stock #: CHN480	• Tongue and groove pliers.	• Use for various gripping jobs.

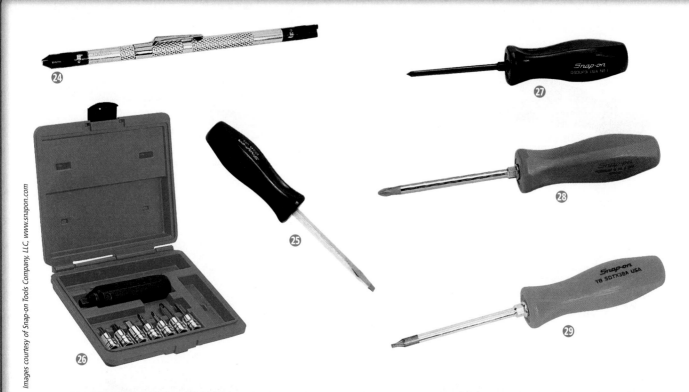

Images courtesy of Snap-on Tools Company, LLC, www.snapon.com

Table 2-A	**INDIVIDUAL HAND TOOLS (continued)**	
Tool	**Description**	**The Job**
Screwdrivers	• Made in a variety of sizes, shapes, and special-purpose designs. • Hand-held turning devices that can be equipped with a wide variety of head or drive configurations.	• Use for driving or turning screws.
㉔ **Screw Starter** Stock #: GA199A	• Tool for holding either a Phillips or standard screw. • Spring-loaded steel bits grip screw-slot wall.	• Use to grasp a screw to more easily start the screw in a threaded hole.
㉕ **Single-Blade Screwdriver** Stock #: SDD44	• Has a single blade that fits into the slot of a screw head. • A complete set should include a Stubby, a 6", a 9", a 12", and offset screwdrivers.	• Use for turning slotted-head screws.
㉖ **Impact-Driver Screwdriver** Stock #: 208EPIT	• A hand-held hex-shaped screwdriver that is approximately 6" long. • Uses the impact of a hammer blow to seat a driver blade in a screw and turn it with great momentary force.	• Use for removing a screw that is "frozen" in its thread.
㉗ **Phillips-Head Screwdriver** Stock #: GSDDP31	• Has two crossing blades that fit into a similarly shaped screw slot. • A complete set should include a Stubby #1 and #2; a 6" #1 and #2; a 12" #3, and an Offset #2.	• Use for turning Phillips-head screws.
㉘ **POZIDRIV® Screwdriver** Stock #: SDDZ42A	• The walls on POZIDRIV® tips are not as tapered as on Phillips tips and have wedges for a tight fit. • A complete set should include a #1, #2, #3, and #4.	• Use for turning POZIDRIV® screws.
㉙ **Torx® Head Screwdriver** Stock #: SDTX38AO	• A complete set should include the following: T-8 through T-60.	• Use for turning Torx® head screws.

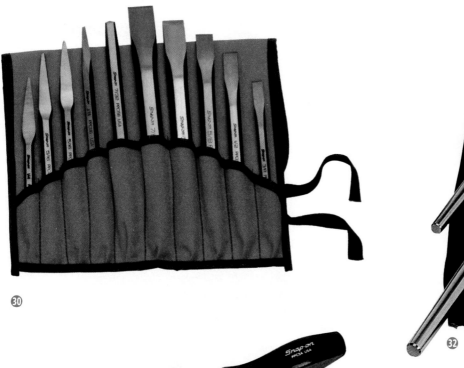

Images courtesy of Snap-on Tools Company, LLC, www.snapon.com

Table 2-A	**INDIVIDUAL HAND TOOLS (continued)**	
Tool	**Description**	**The Job**
Chisels and Punches	• A chisel is a cutting tool with a single cutting edge. • Chisels are available in a variety of shapes and sizes. • Chisels are made with tough steel alloys.	• Use chisels for cutting and shearing. • Use punches to drive round objects, such as pins that are tightly fitted in precision holes.
⑳ Chisel Stock #: PPC100AK	• A set should include a 5/16" cape chisel and a 3/8" and a 3/4" cold chisel.	• Use to cut off damaged or rusted nuts, bolts, and rivet heads.
㉛ Chisel Holder Stock #: PPC5A	• Has two basic parts. One is a doughnut-shaped part that is placed around the chisel. The other is a plastic handle that is attached to the doughnut. The handle is turned to tighten the doughnut around the chisel.	• Use to protect your hand and to get a strong grip on the chisel.
㉜ Punch Stock #: PPB20AK	• A set should include a center punch; a brass drift punch; 1/8", 3/16", 1/4" and 5/16" pin punches; and 3/8", 1/2", and 5/8" taper punches.	• Use a center punch to mark the spot where a hole is to be drilled. • Use a pin punch after marking the spot with a center punch. It will provide a more stable starting point for the drill bit. • Use a brass punch to avoid damaging the surface of the part being driven. • Use punches to knock out rivets and pins or to align parts for assembly.

Images courtesy of Snap-on Tools Company, LLC, www.snapon.com

Table 2-A	INDIVIDUAL HAND TOOLS (continued)	
Tool	**Description**	**The Job**
Hammers and Prying Tools	• A hammer consists of a weighted striking head and a wooden, composite, or plastic handle.	• Use hammers for striking. • Use prying tools for leveraging or separating parts.
㉝ 16-oz Ball Peen Hammer Stock #: BPN16B	• Most commonly used hammer in an automotive service center. • Has a flat face on one end of the head and a round end on the other.	• Use the flat end for general striking of objects. • Use the round end for shaping metal parts or rounding rivets.
㉞ Brass Hammer Stock #: HBR15	• Hammer head is made of brass to prevent steel parts from chipping when struck. • The relatively soft head is designed to accept the energy of the blow. This protects the surface being struck.	• Use for striking parts you wish to protect from being marred.
㉟ Dead-Blow Mallet Stock #: HSPD16	• Designed to deliver impact with a minimum of rebound. • Combination steel and soft face. • Has a hollow head partially filled with small metal shot.	• Use to reduce bounce-back of hammer head.
㊱ Plastic-Tip Hammer Stock #: HBPT24	• Plastic surface prevents damage to item being struck.	• Use when only light blows are required and when protecting the striking surface from being marred.
㊲ Rolling-Head Pry Bar Stock #: 7030A	• Has a pry bar with a 90° bent head. • Also known as a lady foot.	• Use when leverage is needed for jobs such as tightening pulleys or separating tightly fitted assemblies.
㊳ Rubber Mallet Stock #: BF620C	• Hammer head is made of solid rubber.	• Use when striking easily marred surfaces.
㊴ Screwdriver-type Pry Bar Stock #: SPB704AY	• A long shank made of hardened alloys with a plastic handle. • Range in size from 8″ to 24″.	• Use for removing and aligning parts.

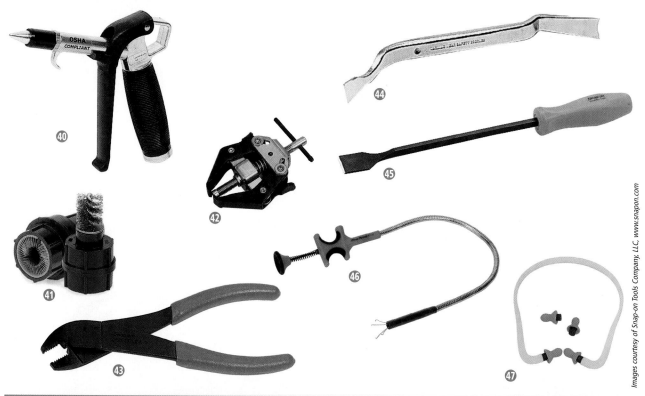

Images courtesy of Snap-on Tools Company, LLC, www.snapon.com

Table 2-A	INDIVIDUAL HAND TOOLS (continued)	
Tool	**Description**	**The Job**
Miscellaneous Tools	• All other hand tools that are used in the automotive repair facility.	• Uses include vehicle support, vehicle charging, grinding, and protection.
40 **Compressed-Air Blowgun (meeting OSHA requirements)** Stock #: JT30	• Connects to an air hose. • Brings air to small tip for high pressure. • Has a shut-off valve to stop flow of air.	• Use to direct compressed air at parts to dry or clean them.
41 **Battery Post Cleaner** Stock #: BTC3A	• Fine wire or scraper. • Reamer encased in a holder.	• Use for cleaning battery posts and terminals.
42 **Battery Terminal Puller** Stock #: GA486A	• Jaws engage below battery terminal with a center screw to lift the battery terminal.	• Use to remove battery terminals.
43 **Battery Terminal Pliers** Stock #: 208BCP	• Compact parrot-nose pliers with especially strong gripping power.	• Use to remove battery terminals.
44 **Brake Spoon** Stock #: B1461	• A wide-blade tool similar to a flat pry bar. • Approximately 12" long.	• Use to adjust drum brakes.
45 **Carbon Scraper (1")** Stock #: CSA14CO	• Carbon blade has special sharpened angles that won't gouge metal surfaces.	• Use to remove carbon and other debris from metal parts.
46 **Claw-Type Pickup Tool** Stock #: DPTC24	• A mechanical finger on a flexible section that is operated by a button that opens and closes the jaws.	• Use for picking up small objects in tight spaces.
47 **Ear Protection** Stock #: YA1160	• Something to cover or insert in ears.	• Use to protect ears from loud or piercing noises.

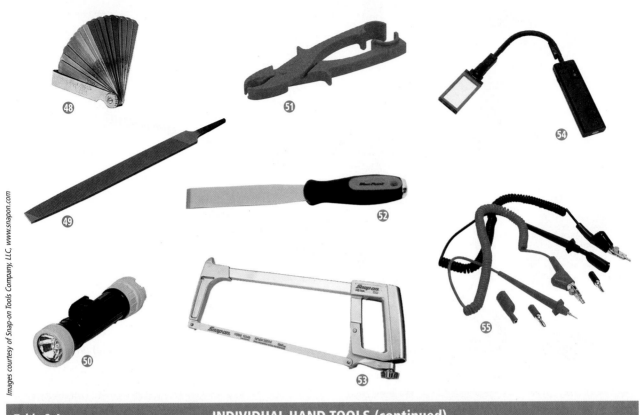

Images courtesy of Snap-on Tools Company, LLC, www.snapon.com

Table 2-A	INDIVIDUAL HAND TOOLS (continued)	
Tool	**Description**	**The Job**
48 **Feeler Gauge (Blade Type) Set** Stock #: FB325A	• A set of precision-thickness metal blades. • Complete set should include a set of standard feeler gauges, 0.002"– 0.040", and a set of metric feeler gauges, 0.006 mm–0.070 mm.	• Use for adjusting spark plug gap to prescribed measurement. • Used to measure small gaps.
49 **File** Stock #: 10FMK	• On a coarse file, there are only a few cutting edges per inch. On a fine file, the cutting edges are close together. • Set of files should include a coarse 6" and 12," a fine 6" and 12," a half-round 12", and a round 6" and 12".	• Use for removing burrs and cuts, smoothing sharp edges, and reducing and shaping metal.
50 **Flashlight** Stock #: ECF35	• Standard battery-operated, hand-held flashlight.	• Use instead of a utility light.
51 **Fuse Puller** Stock #: FZ7A	• Tool for gripping and removing blade- and glass-type fuses.	• Use to remove fuses.
52 **Gasket Scraper (1")** Stock #: PKLR53	• A 1"-wide blade connected to a handle.	• Use to remove gaskets or carbon and other debris from parts.
53 **Hacksaw** Stock #: HS18A	• An adjustable metal frame that holds a steel saw blade. • Blade is replaceable and has from 14 to 32 teeth per inch.	• Use for making a smooth cut in metal or hard plastics.
54 **Inspection Mirror** Stock #: YA5160A	• Small mirror with a telescoping handle.	• Use to inspect areas that would not otherwise be visible.
55 **Jumper-Wire Set (with adapter)** Stock #: TL3	• A wire lead with a terminal or probe on each end.	• Use to bypass and test circuits.

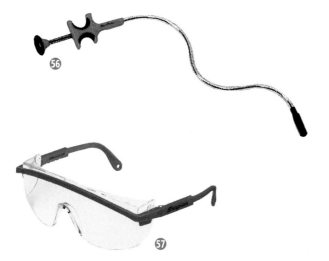

Images courtesy of Snap-on Tools Company, LLC, www.snapon.com

Table 2-A	INDIVIDUAL HAND TOOLS (continued)	
Tool	**Description**	**The Job**
㊏ **Magnetic Pickup Tool** Stock #: DPTM24	• Consists of a magnet hinged to the end of a rod. • Most magnetic pickup tools can be adjusted for length and swiveled to reach into otherwise inaccessible areas.	• Use for retrieving dropped metal parts from hard-to-reach locations.
㊐ **Safety Glasses (meeting OSHA requirements)** Stock #: GLASS1R	• Made with top and side protection and shatter-proof lenses.	• Use to protect eyes from flying debris.
㊑ **Test Light (12 V)** Stock #: CT2	• Has a probe on one end and an encased lightbulb on the other.	• Use for testing circuits and locating shorts, grounds, and open circuits up to 12 volts.
㊒ **Wire Brush** Stock #: AC241A	• Wire brush either connected to a handle or incorporated into a wheel for use on power-driven equipment.	• Use to clean surfaces.

SECTION 1 KNOWLEDGE CHECK

1. Why must automotive technicians know how to use a wide variety of tools?

2. Explain the phrase "no risk is acceptable" as it refers to automotive repair.

3. Why must a technician know a tool's capabilities and limits?

4. List the general difference in the way hand tools and power tools work.

5. What are torque wrenches and when are they used?

ASE TEST PREP

6. Technician A has decided to use a wrench to turn a bolt head. Technician B has decided to use a pair of pliers. Who is correct?
   ⓐ Technician A.
   ⓑ Technician B.
   ⓒ Both Technician A and Technician B.
   ⓓ Neither Technician A nor Technician B.

● Section 2
General Workplace Equipment

Objectives:
- Identify general workplace equipment.
- Demonstrate the correct use of general workplace equipment.

Vocabulary:
- general workplace equipment
- operator's manual

Automotive technicians usually supply their own hand tools. The employer usually supplies the stationary equipment. **General workplace equipment** is equipment that is shared by many technicians and used for a variety of tasks.

These tasks include hoisting cars off a shop floor, cleaning and surfacing parts, and analyzing performance defects. Some general equipment, such as holding fixtures and calibrating devices, is highly specialized for certain operations or for use on specific cars. See **Fig. 2-5.** Other equipment, like cleaning tanks and hydraulic presses, is more general. It is used for many different tasks and on many types of vehicles.

Jack Holtel

Fig. 2-5 Many automotive service centers require using stationary workplace equipment, such as a hoist.

Using General Workplace Equipment

General equipment can be more difficult to learn to use. Some equipment, like electronic diagnostic devices, is routinely upgraded. As a result, technicians need training to operate the equipment effectively.

There is one aspect of automotive work that new technicians can find confusing. There are often many different ways to do the same job. Different kinds of equipment will sometimes provide similar results. For example, special equipment can surface brake drums either by grinding them or by cutting them. Each method has advantages and disadvantages.

A manufacturer may recommend or require one specific procedure or piece of equipment when several others might also seem appropriate. As a result, you need to know more than just what a piece of equipment can do. You also need to know how it works, as well as its strengths and weaknesses. It is also important to know the applications for which the equipment is recommended or required. The **operator's manual** specifies procedures for the proper use and maintenance of the equipment.

Table 2-B identifies and describes the general tools and equipment required in a well-equipped automotive workplace. These tools and equipment are generally not considered to be individual hand tools. All tools and equipment should meet OSHA requirements.

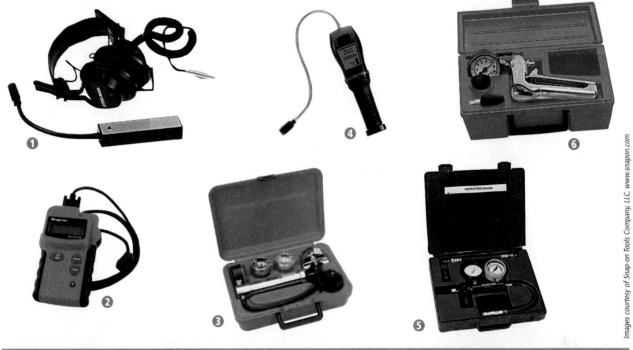

Table 2-B	GENERAL WORKPLACE EQUIPMENT	
Tool	**Description**	**The Job**
Diagnostic Tools	• Tools that diagnose various vehicle conditions.	• Uses include locating abnormal noises, checking leaks, and gathering data from the vehicle.
❶ Automotive Stethoscope (electronic recommended) Stock #: YA6500	• Consists of a headset connected to a hollow flexible tube that is attached to a sound-amplification probe. • An electronic stethoscope is preferred.	• Use to listen to very specific areas in cars to find abnormal noises.
❷ Scan Tool (OBDII) or Personal Computer (PC) Stock #: EESC307B	• Either a handheld computer scan tool or a personal computer with interface capability for on-board diagnostics. • CAN capability recommended.	• Use to gather data from the various electronic functions of a car and sensors.
❸ Cooling System Pressure Tester and Adapters Stock #: SVTS262B	• A handheld pump to pressurize radiator and cap.	• Use to determine the ability of a cooling system to hold pressure. • Use to check for antifreeze leaks.
❹ Cooling-Combustion Gas Detector (recommended) Stock #: ACT8080A	• Electronic device that employs a chemical reaction to identify combustion gases in a vehicle's cooling system.	• Use to analyze cooling systems.
❺ Cylinder Leakage Tester Stock #: EEPV309A	• Kit used with air compressor to test leakage on gasoline and diesel engines. • Consists of a neoprene hose, air gauge, and an adapter on each end of the hose. One end connects to the air supply. The other end threads into the cylinder chamber.	• Use as a test to measure ability to hold air. • Use to locate worn rings, defective valves, a cracked cylinder, or a leaky head gasket.
❻ Hand-Held Vacuum Pump Stock #: SVT270P	• A hand-held pump, with a gauge, used to create a vacuum, usually by pumping action.	• Use to simulate engine vacuum to check various vacuum-operated and calibrated devices on automobiles.

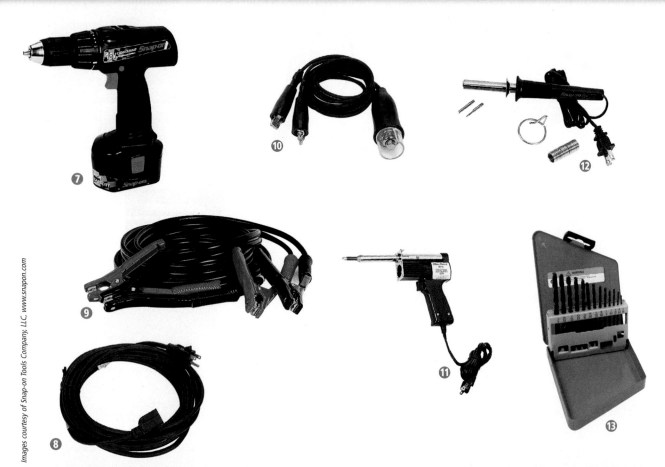

Images courtesy of Snap-on Tools Company, LLC, www.snapon.com

Table 2-B	GENERAL WORKPLACE EQUIPMENT (continued)	
Tool	**Description**	**The Job**
Electrical Tools	• Tools that require electricity for operation.	• Uses include drilling, jump starting, and soldering.
⑦ Drill Stock #: CDR3850	• 3/8" variable speed, reversible and 1/2" variable speed, reversible.	• Use for heavy-duty drilling.
⑧ Extension Cord Stock #: EC267B	• 12- or 16- gauge 3-conductor electrical cord with ground plug.	• Use for electrical equipment that has a cord too short to reach an electrical outlet.
⑨ Jumper Cables Stock #: BC20500	• Cables with clamps on both ends.	• Use to jump start a vehicle with a dead battery, from either the battery of another vehicle or from a stationary battery.
⑩ Remote Starter Switch Stock #: MT302A	• Two wires with clamps on each end, connected to a switch.	• Use to crank an engine or start it without turning the ignition key.
⑪ Soldering Gun Stock #: R490	• A pistol-looking tool with a heating element.	• Use to melt solder to solder electrical connections.
⑫ Soldering Iron (Pencil Tip) Stock #: R25A	• A pencil-looking tool with a heating element.	• Use to melt solder to solder electrical connections.
⑬ Twist-Drill Set 1/64"–1/2" Stock #: DB113C	• A hand-held air or electric motor or a drill press drives the drill bit. • The three major parts of a drill bit are the shank, body, and cutting head. The grooves along the body carry the removed chips out of the hole.	• Use for drilling holes in metal or other materials.

Images courtesy of Snap-on Tools Company, LLC, www.snapon.com

Table 2-B	GENERAL WORKPLACE EQUIPMENT (continued)	
Tool	**Description**	**The Job**
Miscellaneous Tools	• All other tools that are used in the automotive repair facility.	• Uses include vehicle support, vehicle charging, grinding, and protection.
⑭ **Axle Stands (Safety Stands)** Stock #: YA874B	• Strong steel stands that have a center post that can be adjusted for height.	• Use to safely support a vehicle so you can work under it.
⑮ **Battery Charger** Stock #: EEBC302A	• A converter box that changes 120-volt current to 6-volt, 12-volt, or 24-volt current.	• Use for charging vehicle batteries.
⑯ **Battery/Starter/ Charging System Tester** Stock #: EECS304B1B	• Handheld, computerized diagnostic tool with two permanent test leads.	• Use for performing automated tests to diagnose a battery. • Can detect the full range of battery failure modes including bad cells, sulfation, internal shorting, and other chemical and physical failures.
⑰ **Bearing Packer (hand operated)** Stock #: YA742	• Cup, usually transparent, filled with grease between two plastic cones.	• Lubricates a bearing with new grease.
⑱ **Belt-Tension Gauge** Stock #: AS4395A	• Spring-loaded gauge that shows pounds per square inch and fits over the belt.	• Use to measure the tightness of a belt.
⑲ **Bench or Pedestal Grinder**	• A grinding wheel attached to an electric motor.	• Use for grinding steel.
⑳ **Constant Velocity (CV) Universal Joint Service Tools** Stock #: FBG1 Stock #: YA3080 Stock #: YA3050 Stock #: CV9040	• Requires a boot-installation tool and boot-clamp pliers or crimping ring.	• Use to remove, repair, or install CV joints.

Images courtesy of Snap-on Tools Company, LLC, www.snapon.com

Table 2-B	GENERAL WORKPLACE EQUIPMENT (continued)	
Tool	**Description**	**The Job**
21 **Coolant Tester** Stock #: AF109	• Floating ball type hydrometer.	• Use for testing propylene glycol antifreeze solutions.
22 **Creeper** Stock #: JC26C	• Four swivel wheels attached to a flat board with a padded headrest.	• Use to move around under a vehicle.
23 **Digital Multimeter with Various Lead Sets** Stock #: EEDM512CK	• Digital continuity meter reading volts and amps.	• Use to check electrical voltage.
24 **Drain Pans**	• Plastic or steel containers.	• Use to catch liquids such as antifreeze or oil.
25 **Electric Heat Gun** Stock #: ETB1410	• Six temperature settings with LED indicator. • Two speed control switch. • Temperature range of 92°F to 1200°F [33°C to 649°C]. • 120VAC power requirement.	• Use for removing pinstriping or decals. • Use for drying body filler and epoxy and shrink tubing.
26 **Engine Coolant Recovery Equipment (or Recycler or Coolant Disposal Contract Service)** Stock #: RADPLUSA	• A suction pump connected to a storage tank. • The alternative is a contract with a recycler or coolant disposal service.	• Use for removing and storing antifreeze.
27 **Face Shield** Stock #: GA224B	• Transparent plastic shield to cover face. • Held on head by adjustable strap.	• Use to protect eyes from splashing chemicals or flying debris.
28 **Fender Cover** Stock #: JCK7D	• Plastic material or cloth that fits over fenders.	• Use to protect body of vehicle from scratches and other damage while working on it.

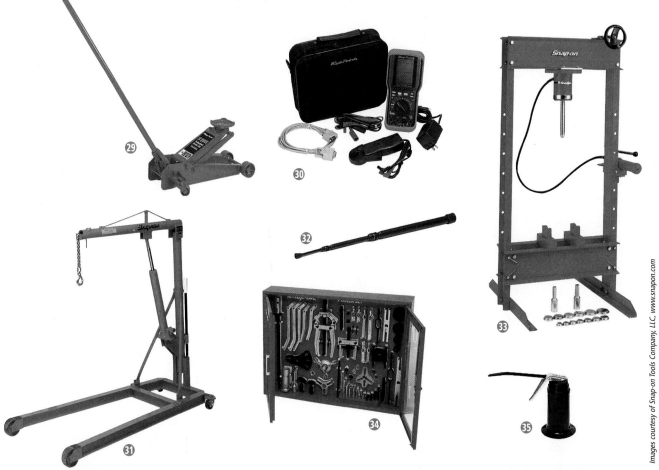

Images courtesy of Snap-on Tools Company, LLC, www.snapon.com

Table 2-B	GENERAL WORKPLACE EQUIPMENT (continued)	
Tool	**Description**	**The Job**
㉙ **Floor Jack (1-1/2 Ton Minimum)** Stock #: YA642B	• A steel arm raised by a hydraulic cylinder.	• Use to jack up a vehicle.
㉚ **Graphing Multimeter (GMM) Digital Storage Oscilloscope (DSO)** Stock #: MT599AK	• Computerized diagnostic tool that displays signal waveforms in addition to standard voltage, amperage, and resistance values. • Accessories include test lead set with alligator clips, inductive pick-up, and software.	• Use for validating OBD-II sensors and components.
㉛ **Hoist**	• Large piston-driven device used to lift heavy items.	• Use to remove engines.
㉜ **Hood Prop** Stock #: YA4590	• Telescoping steel tubing sections with locking levers on each section. • Working range of 18 1/2″ to 46 3/4″.	• Use for propping the hood of any car or truck.
㉝ **Hydraulic Press with Adapters (25 Ton)** Stock #: CG770HY	• Vertically oriented press that accepts items to be pressed together by hydraulic pressure.	• Use to press together parts that require more than normal pressure to join; used, for example, to place bearings.
㉞ **Master Puller Set** Stock #: CJ2000SB	• Assortment of pulling tools for a wide range of tasks.	• Use to remove hubs, bearings, pulleys, and so forth.
㉟ **Oil Can—Pump Type** Stock #: OC5A	• Stores small amount of oil and has a mechanism for pumping the oil from the can.	• Use to oil hinges, latches, and other parts that require lubrication.

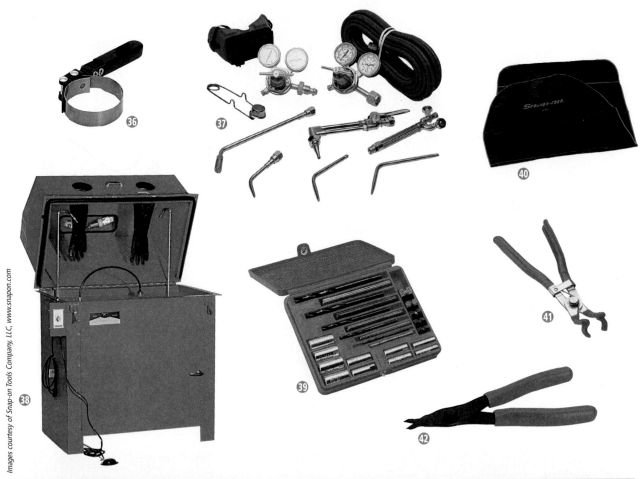

Images courtesy of Snap-on Tools Company, LLC, www.snapon.com

Table 2-B	GENERAL WORKPLACE EQUIPMENT (continued)	
Tool	**Description**	**The Job**
36 **Oil Filter Wrench** Stock #: GA333B	• A strap or cup that fits and tightens around a filter.	• Use for removing or installing oil filters.
37 **Oxy-Acetylene Torch** Stock #: WE200	• Tool that mixes oxygen and acetylene to produce a strong flame.	• Use to cut or braze metal.
38 **Parts Cleaning Tank (nonsolvent-based cleanser suggested)** Stock #: PBC42A	• Sink-like tank used for cleaning various parts in a cold liquid solvent.	• Use gloves to protect your hands from harsh chemicals. • Use to remove dirt, grease, and adhesives from gaskets or other parts.
39 **Screw Extractor Set** Stock #: E1020	• Drill-bit set used to extract broken screws and bolts.	• Use to remove broken screws and bolts.
40 **Seat Cover** Stock #: Seatcover1	• Piece of plastic, cloth, or paper designed to fit over seats.	• Use to protect vehicle seats from grease, tears, and other damage while working on vehicle.
41 **Spark Plug Boot Puller** Stock #: YA824B	• Special type of pliers with a unique grabbing end that is designed to fit over spark plug wire boot.	• Use to remove stubborn spark plug wires.
42 **Snap-Ring Pliers** Stock #: SRPC3800	• Have sharp, pointed tips. • Internal and external available.	• Use external for installing and removing special clips called snap rings. • Use internal to hold a bearing in a housing.

Images courtesy of Snap-on Tools Company, LLC, www.snapon.com

Table 2-B	GENERAL WORKPLACE EQUIPMENT (continued)	
Tool	**Description**	**The Job**
㊸ **Tap and Die Set**	• Made of very hard steel alloy that is strong enough to rethread nuts or bolts. • Available in standard and metric.	• Use tap to cut internal threads in holes. • Use die to cut external threads on bolts, studs, or rods.
㊹ **Temperature Sensing Device** Stock #: TEMP3A	• Temperature probe connected to digital readout.	• Use for verifying the temperature of components operating within the given range of the tool.
㊺ **Thread Repair Kit** Stock #: RTD48	• Rethreading taps and dies renew existing threads, clean dirty threads, and straighten damaged threads. • Includes thread restorer files. • Not for hardened threads or cutting new threads.	• Use to repair threads.
㊻ **Tire Inflator Chuck** Stock #: GA356	• Adapter that connects to air-compressor hose allowing air to be added to tires.	• Use to add air to tires.
㊼ **Trouble/Work Lights (Fluorescent Preferred)** Stock #: ECU4250A	• Electrical light.	• Use to light a wide area. • Because they produce less heat, fluorescent lights should always be used when working near gas tanks or with substances that could become dangerous with the addition of heat.
㊽ **Tube Quick-Disconnect Tool Set** Stock #: YA7244A	• Removal tool for quick disconnect tube fittings with push-lock connectors.	• Use to disconnect air-conditioning, transmission, and fuel lines.
㊾ **Tubing Bender** Stock #: TBS200A	• Special tool used for bending copper, brass, or steel tubing. • There are various kinds of tubing benders.	• Use for bending tubing.
㊿ **Tubing Cutter/Flaring Set (Double-Lap and ISO)** Stock #: TC28C	• A cutting wheel and feed mechanism that is adjustable to fit over tubing.	• Use to fit over tubing and cut the tubing.

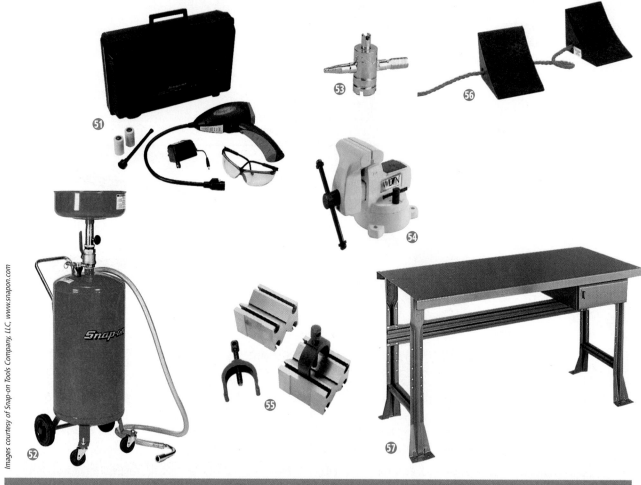

Images courtesy of Snap-on Tools Company, LLC, www.snapon.com

Table 2-B	GENERAL WORKPLACE EQUIPMENT (continued)	
Tool	**Description**	**The Job**
51 **Ultraviolet Leak Detection Device** Stock #: ACT780	• Probe tool with ultraviolet light.	• Use for detecting leaks in refrigerant, exhaust, and air induction systems. This may involve the use of UV reactive dies. Probe may also have electronic sensor for detecting certain types of gases.
52 **Used-Oil Receptacle with Extension Neck and Funnel** Stock #: YA777	• A receptacle with an adjustable telescopic tube that has a funnel at its top.	• Use to collect oil.
53 **Valve-Core Removing Tool** Stock #: GA143A	• Convenient guide that slips into the tire-valve stem.	• Use to remove or install valve-stem core.
54 **Vise** Stock #: WV1560VIS	• A steel or cast-iron tool used for holding parts. • The five basic parts of a vise are the handle, jaws, anvil, base, and position-adjustment bar.	• Use to free both hands for working on parts that require cutting, drilling, hammering, or gluing.
55 **V-Blocks**	• A steel block with a V-shape machined into it.	• Use to hold parts for precision measuring.
56 **Wheel Chocks** Stock #: YA9020	• A block of wood or rubber.	• Use to keep vehicle from rolling.
57 **Workbench** Stock #: EQG2223K5	• Stable metal or wooden tables on which work can be performed.	• Use for working on components that require assembly or disassembly.

Images courtesy of Snap-on Tools Company, LLC, www.snapon.com

Table 2-B	GENERAL WORKPLACE EQUIPMENT (continued)	
Tool	**Description**	**The Job**
Pneumatic Tools	• Tools that are powered by compressed air.	• Use for a variety of tasks that would take much longer using hand tools.
58 **Air Chisel Set with Various Bits** Stock #: PHG3050CH4	• Series of special chisel bits designed to be used with pneumatic tools. • Chisels include the following: flat chisel, sitting chisel, bent-end chisel, curved flat chisel, scraper, double-blade panel cutter, and muffler cutters.	• Use to speed up chiseling projects such as chiseling off rivets, chiseling off mufflers, or disconnecting ball joints.
59 **Air Compressor and Hoses** Stock #: BF180	• Supplies compressed air for many uses.	• Use for running air tools.
60 **Air Pressure Regulator** Stock #: BF1400	• A moisture trap that supplies clean dry air at constant pressure.	• Use to regulate air pressure.
61 **Air Ratchet (3/8″ Drive)** Stock #: AT702	• A ratchet set powered by compressed air.	• Use to quickly remove bolts.
62 **Impact Socket**	• Made of exceptionally strong metal to absorb extra torque. • A basic set includes a 3/8″ drive and a 1/2″ drive. Also available in metric.	• Use to remove stubborn bolts.
63 **Impact Wrench** Stock #: AT360	• A basic set includes both a 1/2″ drive and a 3/8″ drive.	• Designed for quick loosening or tightening of hard-to-turn nuts and bolts.

SECTION 2 KNOWLEDGE CHECK

1. Why is it usually more difficult to learn to use general workplace equipment than it is to learn to use hand tools?

2. Why is it important for technicians to know the specific uses for each item of general equipment?

3. What is a cooling-combustion gas detector?

4. What tool is used to check electrical voltage?

5. Name two items that can help protect a vehicle while it is being serviced.

ASE TEST PREP

6. Technician A says a soldering gun should be used to solder electrical connections. Technician B says a soldering gun should not be used to solder electrical connections. Who is correct?

   ⓐ Technician A.
   ⓑ Technician B.
   ⓒ Both Technician A and Technician B.
   ⓓ Neither Technician A nor Technician B.

Section 3
Measuring Systems and Tools

Objectives:

- Explain the relationship among weight, volume, and linear measurements in the metric system.
- Convert measurements from USC to SI and SI to USC.

Vocabulary:

- **System of International Units (SI)**
- **Celsius**

Measuring Systems

There is a need to take a wide variety of measurements in an automotive facility. Sometimes, such as in the measuring of the inside or outside dimension of a cylinder, the measurement must be accurate to one thousandth of an inch. Other times, such as for measuring a length of tubing, the measurement need not be so precise.

It is necessary to make many kinds of measurements to detect if parts are worn or damaged. They also identify parts that are out of adjustment or out of spec, and by how much. Sometimes technicians measure engine vacuum or power, generator output, or battery voltage. Alignment specialists measure angles in the front-suspension system. But for most service work, technicians measure length, diameter, or clearance. They might, for example, measure the bore, or diameter, of the engine's cylinders.

The SI System

Measurements can be made in the metric system or in the United States Customary (USC) system. The metric system is also known as the System of International Units (SI). The **System of International Units (SI)** is a system of measurement that uses meters, liters, and grams. See **Fig. 2-6.**

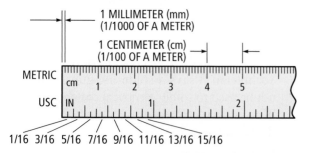

1 MILLIMETER (mm)
(1/1000 OF A METER)

1 CENTIMETER (cm)
(1/100 OF A METER)

METRIC

USC

1/16 3/16 5/16 7/16 9/16 11/16 13/16 15/16

Fig. 2-6 Ruler marked in both the metric and USC system.

The SI System The SI system is used for the measurements in all imported cars and most cars made in the United States. The SI system is based on multiples of ten, just like the monetary system in the United States. In the United States, ten pennies equal one dime, and ten dimes equal one dollar. Similarly, in the SI system, 10 mm equal 1 centimeter (cm), 10 cm equal 1 decimeter (dm), and 10 dm equal 1 meter (m). One thousand meters equal 1 kilometer (km), which is 0.62 mile. See **Table 2-C.**

Table 2-C	SI METRIC AND CUSTOMARY UNITS	
Type of Measurement	**SI Metric Unit**	**Approximate Size of Customary Unit**
1. Length and distance	a. meter [m] b. centimeter [cm] c. millimeter [mm] d. kilometer [km]	a. 1.1 yard b. 0.4 inch c. 0.04 inch d. 0.6 mile
2. Mass or weight	a. gram [g] b. kilogram [kg]	a. 1/28 ounce b. 2.2 pounds
3. Volume (liquid)	a. milliliter [mL or ml] b. liter [L]	a. 1/5 teaspoon b. 1.06 quart
4. Temperature	a. degrees Celsius [°C]	a. $1.8 \times °C + 32 = °F$
5. Pressure	a. 1 kilopascal [kPa]	a. 0.145 psi (pounds per square inch)
6. Energy	a. 1 kilojoule [kJ]	a. 0.239 Calories

Each type of measurement (such as length, volume, weight) is represented by a specific metric unit. The three basic metric measurements are:

- Meter (m) for length.
- Liter (L) for volume.
- Gram (g) for weight.

Each of these units (meter, liter, and gram) is called a stem unit. A stem unit is made larger or smaller by the addition of a prefix. The only stem unit that does not use prefixes is **Celsius,** the unit by which temperature is measured in degrees. Prefixes such as milli, centi, deci, and kilo have special meanings.

Table 2-D	METRIC UNITS			
Prefix	Stem	Results	Abbreviation	Size in USC units
milli	meter	millimeter (1/1000 of a meter)	mm	very small fraction of an inch
centi	meter	centimeter (1/100 of a meter)	cm	about 0.4 inch
kilo	meter	kilometer (1000 meters)	km	about 0.6 mile
mega	meter	megameter (a million meters)	Mm	more than 1 million yards
milli	gram	milligram (1/1000 of a gram)	mg	very small fraction of an ounce
centi	gram	centigram (1/100 of a gram)	cg	a small fraction of an ounce
kilo	gram	kilogram (1000 grams)	kg	about 2.2 pounds
mega	gram	megagram (a million grams, or a metric ton)	Mg	about 2200 pounds
milli	liter	milliliter (1/1000 of a liter)	ml	very small fraction of an ounce

For example:
- Kilo means 1000 (one thousand).
- Deci means 0.10 (one-tenth).
- Centi means 0.01 (one-hundredth).
- Milli means 0.001 (one-thousandth).

Table 2-D shows how a prefix added to a stem unit, a base unit, changes the value.

Weight and Volume The metric unit of weight is the gram. It is the weight of 1 cubic centimeter (cc) of water. See **Fig. 2-7**. One thousand grams is 1 kilogram (kg). This is equal to 1000 cc.

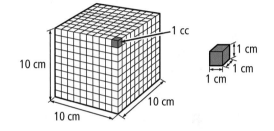

Fig. 2-7 A liter is 1000 cubic centimeters. *A gram equals the weight of how many cubic centimeters of water?*

Table 2-E	CONVERTING FRACTIONS OF AN INCH				
Inches					
Fraction	Decimal	mm	Fraction	Decimal	mm
1/64	0.0156	0.3969	31/64	0.4844	12.3031
1/32	0.0312	0.7938	1/2	0.5000	12.7000
3/64	0.0469	1.1906	33/64	0.5156	13.0969
1/16	0.0625	1.5875	17/32	0.5312	13.4938
5/64	0.0781	1.9844	35/64	0.5469	13.8906
3/32	0.0938	2.3812	9/16	0.5625	14.2875
7/64	0.1094	2.7781	37/64	0.5781	14.6844
1/8	0.1250	3.1750	19/32	0.5938	15.0812
9/64	0.1406	3.5719	11/16	0.6875	17.4625
5/32	0.1562	3.9688	45/64	0.7031	17.8594
11/64	0.1719	4.3656	23/32	0.7188	18.2562
3/16	0.1875	4.7625	47/64	0.7344	18.6531
13/64	0.2031	5.1594	3/4	0.7500	19.0500
7/32	0.2188	5.5562	49/64	0.7656	19.4469
15/64	0.2344	5.9531	25/32	0.7812	19.8438
1/4	0.2500	6.3500	51/64	0.7969	20.2406
23/64	0.3594	9.1281	13/16	0.8125	20.6375
3/8	0.3750	9.5250	53/64	0.8281	21.0344
25/64	0.3906	9.9219	27/32	0.8438	21.4312
13/32	0.4062	10.3188	55/64	0.8594	21.8281
27/64	0.4219	10.7156	7/8	0.8750	22.2250
7/16	0.4375	11.1125	57/64	0.8906	22.6219
29/64	0.4531	11.5094	29/32	0.9062	23.0188
15/32	0.4688	11.9062	59/64	0.9219	23.4156

The metric unit of volume for fluid, or liquid, measurements is the liter (L). It is slightly larger than a quart. The liter is the volume of a cube that measures 10 cm on a side (or 1000 cc). This is the same measurement for weight. One liter of water weighs 1 kg [1000 g]. One kg equals 2.2 pounds.

The USC System

Making small measurements in the USC system often requires dealing with fractions of an inch such as 1/4, 1/8, 1/16, 1/32, and 1/64. Sometimes these may not be small enough. Many automotive measurements are in thousandths and sometimes ten-thousandths of an inch. For example, 1/64 inch is 0.0156 inch. A bearing clearance may be 0.002 inch. To convert fractions of an inch into decimal fractions, technicians may need a table of decimal equivalents. **Table 2-E.**

Converting Measurements

Sometimes technicians must convert USC measurements to SI measurements. At other times they need to convert SI measurements to USC measurements. **Table 2-F** will help in these conversions.

Measurement Tools

A wide variety of tools are available for measuring and calibrating. To calibrate means to adjust precisely for a specific function. Some measuring tools, such as a tape measure, are used to make approximate measurements. Other measuring tools, such as a micrometer, can precisely make measurements as small as 0.0001″ (one ten-thousandth of an inch). See **Fig. 2-8.**

Table 2-G describes some of the basic measurement tools used in the automotive workplace.

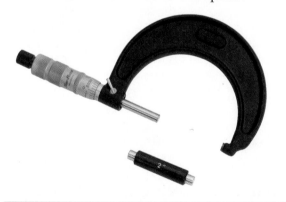

Fig. 2-8 A micrometer is a precision measuring tool.

Table 2-F	CONVERTING MEASUREMENTS	
To Change Customary	**To Metric**	**Multiply By**
Inches	Millimeters	25.400
Inches	Centimeters	2.540
Feet	Meters	0.305
Yards	Meters	0.914
Miles	Kilometers	1.609
Square inches	Square centimeters	6.451
Ounces (U.S. liquid)	Milliliters	29.573
Pints	Liters	0.473
Quarts (U.S. liquid)	Liters	0.946
Gallons (U.S. liquid)	Liters	3.785
Pounds	Kilograms	0.454
Short tons (2,000 lbs)	Metric tons	0.900
Miles per hour	Kilometers per hour	1.609
Pounds per square inch	Kilopascals	6.895
Miles per gallon	Kilometers per liter	0.425
Degrees Fahrenheit	Degrees Celsius	$(°F - 32) \div 1.8$
To Change Metric	**To Customary**	**Multiply By**
Millimeters	Inches	0.039
Centimeters	Inches	0.394
Meters	Feet	3.280
Meters	Yards	1.094
Kilometers	Miles	0.621
Square centimeters	Square inches	0.155
Milliliters	Fluid ounces	0.034
Liters	Pints	2.113
Liters	Quarts	1.057
Liters	Gallons (U.S. liquid)	0.264
Kilograms	Pounds	2.205
Metric tons	Short tons (2,000 lbs)	1.102
Kilometers per hour	Miles per hour	0.621
Kilopascals	Pounds per square inch	0.145
Kilometers per liter	Miles per gallon	2.354
Degrees Celsius	Degrees Fahrenheit	$(°C \times 1.8) + 32$

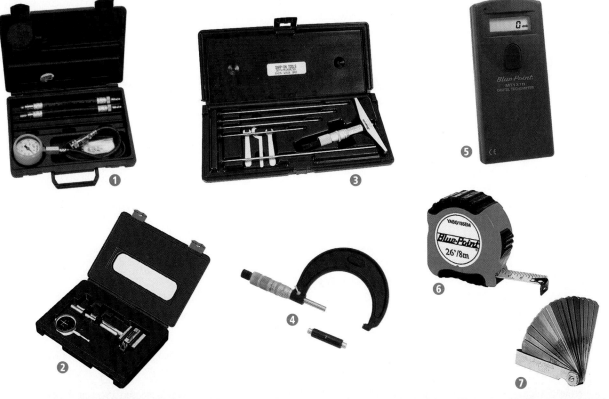

Images courtesy of Snap-on Tools Company, LLC, www.snapon.com

Table 2-G	MEASUREMENT TOOLS	
Tool	**Description**	**The Job**
❶ Compression Tester Stock #: MT308M	• Pressure gauge with hose that can be connected to cylinder spark plug hole.	• Use to measure the pressure in the engine cylinder at top dead center of the compression stroke.
❷ Dial Indicator with Flex Arm and Clamp Base Stock #: GA3645	• Has a dial face and a needle to register measurement. • The needle moves in relation to movement of a movable arm or plunger. • As the plunger moves, the needle shows the distance or variation.	• Readings may be in thousandths of an inch or hundredths of a millimeter. • Measures end-play in shafts or gears by pushing the plunger against the part to be measured until the needle moves.
❸ Depth Gauge Stock #: MICDEPTH6	• A type of micrometer. • Consists of a ratchet stop, thimble, barrel, base, and measuring rod.	• Use to measure the depth of grooves or holes.
❹ Outside Micrometer Stock #: MICB3A	• Hand-held precision measuring instrument. • Has a frame and a movable spindle with precision screw threads. • Available to measure in USC or SI. • A complete USC set includes the following dimensions in outside type: 0.1", 1"–2", 2"–3", 4"–5".	• Use to accurately make linear measurements as small as one-thousandth or one ten-thousandth of an inch. • Outside micrometer is designed to measure the outside diameter of cylindrical forms.
❺ Tachometer Stock #: MT137D	• Hand-held digital tachometer.	• Use to measure engine rpm.
❻ Tape Measure Stock #: YASG155EM	• Available to measure in USC and SI measurements.	• Use to make approximate measurements.
❼ Thickness Gauges Stock #: FB325A	• Strips or blades of metal of various thicknesses. • Most are made of steel; however, some are made of nonmagnetic metals such as brass.	• Also called feeler gauges. • Use to measure small gaps or distances such as the clearance between two parts.

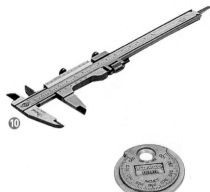

Table 2-G	MEASUREMENT TOOLS (continued)	
Tool	**Description**	**The Job**
⑧ **Tire Pressure Gauge** Stock #: GA246	• There are various types of tire-pressure gauges. They all measure the amount of air in a tire.	• Use to measure air pressure in tires.
⑨ **Vacuum Gauge** Stock #: EEPV311A	• Measures vacuum in inches of mercury.	• Use to measure vacuum and small pressures, such as engine vacuum.
⑩ **Vernier Calipers** Stock #: CM6421	• Has a movable scale that runs parallel to a fixed scale. • Available to measure in either one-thousandths of an inch or one-hundredths of a millimeter. • Measures standard distances of 0″ to 6″. Metric calipers measure metric distances from 0 mm to 125 mm. • Use to make quick and reasonably accurate measurements of small distances between surfaces.	• Can be used to measure the diameter of a rod. • Can be used to take inside or outside measurements.
⑪ **Spark Plug Gap Gauge** Stock #: FB361A	• Measures the air gap on spark plugs.	• Use to measure spark plug gaps. • The specified gauge should fit into the gap snugly, without binding.

SECTION 3 KNOWLEDGE CHECK

1. Give examples of two types of measurements a technician might make while working on a vehicle.

2. What do SI and USC stand for?

3. Which measurement system is used for all imported cars and most cars made in the United States?

4. List the basic metric measurement units for length, volume, and weight.

5. Why is it a good idea to have SI and USC conversion charts in an automotive workplace?

ASE TEST PREP

6. In the metric system the prefix kilo means:
   ⓐ One-tenth.
   ⓑ One-thousandth.
   ⓒ Ten.
   ⓓ One thousand.

● Section 4
Fasteners, Gaskets, and Sealants

Objectives:
- Describe the functions of gaskets and where they are used.
- List the three purposes of thread dressings.
- Describe typical uses of aerobic sealant and anaerobic sealant.

Vocabulary:
- screw thread
- pitch
- setscrew
- antiseize compound
- thread-locking compound

Characteristics of Fasteners

There are many different ways to hold parts together. Fasteners, such as nuts and bolts, and sealants, such as epoxy and RTV, are used to hold parts together. Sometimes gaskets are placed between two flat metal surfaces to make up for small irregularities in the metals. Otherwise, the result might be a leakage of air or liquid.

Fasteners hold automotive parts together. Screws, nuts, bolts (screws with hex heads), and studs (bolt-like fasteners with no head on either end) are examples of fasteners. Most fasteners are removable so the assembly can be taken apart. Many fastenerss are single use. Once removed, they must be discarded.

There are also more permanent ways of fastening parts together. This is usually done through soldering and welding.

Fastener Strength Groups

Both nuts and bolts are available in different strength classifications. These are identified as SAE grades. Fastener strength is most important for the fasteners that secure critical parts.

In the standard and metric measurement systems, bolts are marked on their heads. Nuts bear similar markings as indentations on one of their end faces. For example, three radial marks on a bolt head indicate a medium carbon steel, quenched and tempered (SAE Grade 5). Six radial marks indicate the strongest common threaded fasteners (SAE Grade 8). See **Fig. 2-9.**

Beyond that there are designations like S for "super." However, that is beyond the needs of most automotive applications. Bolts with unmarked heads have low strength. They should not be used in any critical application.

The strength of metric bolts is identified by a number on the head of the bolt. Strength can range from 4.6 (low strength) to 10.9 (very high strength). The strength noted is tensile strength. This is the amount of stress a bolt can take without breaking.

Screw Threads

A **screw thread** is a fastener that has a spiral ridge, or screw thread, on its surface. Threads can be internal (as on a nut) or external (as on a bolt or stud). Screws are manufactured with either SI or USC screw threads. SI and USC threads are not interchangeable. An SI screw will not fit a USC nut or vice versa. Some vehicles have metric (SI) fasteners. Others have USC fasteners. Some have both.

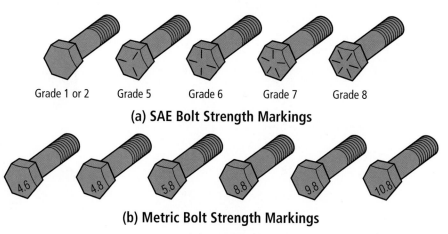

Grade 1 or 2   Grade 5   Grade 6   Grade 7   Grade 8
(a) SAE Bolt Strength Markings

4.6   4.8   5.8   8.8   9.8   10.8
(b) Metric Bolt Strength Markings

Fig. 2-9 Bolt strength markings. Standard radial bolt strength markings **(a)**. Metric numeric bolt strength markings **(b)**. *What is tensile strength?*

Complete Thread Designation

Bolts are identified by all of the factors noted above. A common bolt designation might be 1/4-20×2, Grade 5. This means that the bolt has a 1/4″ diameter shank, has 20 threads per inch, is 2″ long, with Grade 5 strength. A metric bolt might be designated M12×1.75×25. This means that the bolt has a 12-mm shank diameter, 1.75 mm between threads, and is 25 mm long.

Bolt Standards There are many standards for the manufacture of bolts. You may have placed a socket on a bolt only to find that it was slightly too large or small to properly turn the bolt. In this case, you may have encountered a difference in manufacturing standards. Three major systems of standards govern the manufacture of bolts: ISO (International Standards Organization), ANSI (American National Standards Institute), and JIS (Japanese Industrial Standard).

The ISO standard uses the metric system to identify bolt size. The ANSI standard uses U.S. customary measurements to identify bolt size. The JIS standard uses the metric system, but the heads on these bolts are smaller than those in ISO and ANSI of the same size thread. Bolt diameters and head sizes are shown in **Table 2-H.**

It is important to keep on hand the proper tools needed for working with all standardized bolts. Before tightening or loosening a bolt, make sure you are using the proper tool. It should fit snugly and securely, but not so tightly that it must be forced onto the bolt head. Apply torque to the bolt by pulling the tool, not by pushing it.

Fastener Size

Threaded fasteners are classified by length, pitch, series, and class. Fasteners are available in a wide variety of lengths and diameters. The length of a bolt or screw is the distance from the bottom of its head to the end of its threads. See **Fig. 2-10.**

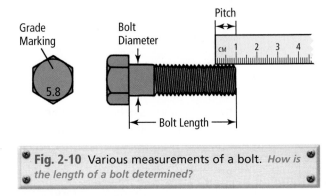

Fig. 2-10 Various measurements of a bolt. *How is the length of a bolt determined?*

Fastener Pitch

To determine the size of a fastener, you must measure the fastener's pitch. **Pitch** is the length from a point on a fastener thread to a corresponding point on the next thread. Thread pitch is calculated by dividing one inch by the number of threads per inch. Threaded fasteners can have several common pitches. These are UNC (coarse thread), UNF (fine thread), and UNEF (extra fine thread). See **Fig. 2-11.**

Table 2-H	BOLT DIAMETERS AND HEAD SIZES	
Bolt Diameter	**Head/Wrench Size**	
	ANSI/ISO	JIS
4	7	7
5	8	8
6	10	10
7	–	–
8	13	12
10	16	14
12	18	17
14	21	19
16	24	22
18	–	–
20	30	–

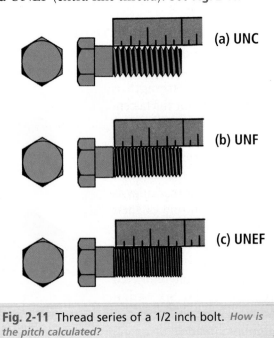

(a) UNC

(b) UNF

(c) UNEF

Fig. 2-11 Thread series of a 1/2 inch bolt. *How is the pitch calculated?*

It is important to know exactly what thread pitch you need. Attempting to mate fasteners of different pitches will strip the threads of one or both parts. Different pitches in threaded holes, nuts, studs, or bolts may be difficult to determine by eye.

TECH TIP Finding Pitch. Use a known metal bolt to match thread pitch to an unknown bolt if you do not have a gauge.

The same wrench will fit the turning heads of different fasteners with different thread pitches. Wrenches are designated by head size, not by bolt shank or nut bore diameter. Studs often have different thread pitches at either end. A thread-pitch gauge will help determine which fasteners will work in different situations. See **Fig 2-12**.

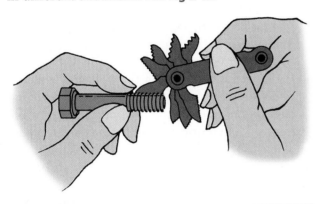

Fig. 2-12 Using a thread-pitch gauge. *What is a thread-pitch gauge used to determine?*

Nuts and Lock Washers

Figure 2-13 shows several nuts, including the following:
- The hex nut which is the most common nut in the automotive service center.
- The slotted hex and the castle nut, which are used with a cotter pin.
- The acorn nut which covers the end of a screw or bolt. This gives the assembly a neat appearance.
- The speed nut, which has little holding power. However, it can be quickly installed by pushing it over the threads. The speed nut provides a light clamping force when fast assembly is needed.

A lock washer placed under a nut or bolt head helps lock the fastener in place. The sharp edges of the lock washer bite into the metal. This helps prevent the nut or bolt from turning.

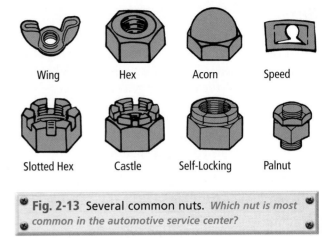

Fig. 2-13 Several common nuts. *Which nut is most common in the automotive service center?*

Other Fasteners

Many other types of non-threaded fasteners are used in automobiles. Some are used for special purposes.

Snap Rings

Snap rings are used to secure or locate the ends of shafts. There are two types of snap rings (external and internal). See **Fig 2-14**. External snap rings fit on shafts to prevent gears or collars from sliding on the shaft. Internal snap rings fit in housings to keep shafts or other parts in position.

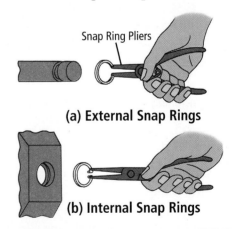

Fig. 2-14 There are two types of snap rings. *How do their functions differ?*

Thread Inserts

Damaged or worn threads can sometimes be replaced by installing a thread insert in a threaded hole. To install one type of thread insert:
- Drill out the old threads.
- Rethread the hole with the special thread-cutting tool or the tap from a thread repair kit.
- Install the thread insert in the tapped hole.

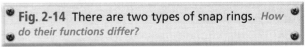

Setscrews

A **setscrew** is a threaded fastener that secures a collar or gear on a shaft. Setscrews are usually loosened or tightened using an allen wrench. Tightening the screw "sets" the collar or gear into place.

Self-Tapping Screws

Self-tapping screws are screws that cut their own threads when turned into drilled holes.

Rivets

Rivets are metal pins used to fasten parts together. One end has a head. After placing the rivet, use a driver (or hammer and rivet set) to form a head on the other end. To remove a rivet, cut off the rivet head with a chisel and hammer. Then use a punch and hammer to drive the rivet out of the hole.

Rivets are used when there is little likelihood that they will ever have to be removed for routine maintenance and repair. A blind hole is a hole where you cannot reach the end to form a head. Blind, or "pop," rivets are used in blind holes. See **Fig 2-15**.

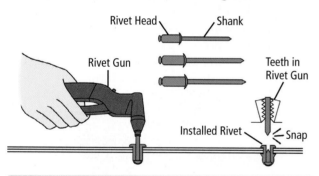

Fig. 2-15 Installing a blind rivet. The teeth inside the rivet gun pull the shank through the rivet head. *The shank snaps when the rivet is tight.*

There are many other specialized fasteners, and new ones are being invented. It is important for automotive technicians to know the characteristics of each type of fastener. Technicians should also master any special procedures or techniques needed to work with these fasteners.

Removing a Broken Bolt

A bolt that is broken below the surface can be drilled and removed with a screw extractor. The following is a general procedure:

1. Create a flat surface on the top of the broken bolt with a die grinder or a pin punch and hammer.

2. Use a center punch and hammer to make a dimple in the exact center of the broken bolt. This will locate the drill bit and prevent it from wandering from the center.

3. Determine the appropriate size screw extractor for the bolt and the proper size drill bit for that screw extractor. This information is usually provided in the extractor kit or marked on the side of the extractor.

4. Use a sharp drill bit and a slow speed (500 rpm or lower). Apply penetrating oil for lubrication and cooling and drill a hole through the broken bolt centerline. Be careful to drill a straight hole. If possible use a left-hand drill bit. This will put torque on the bolt in a left-hand direction. This may screw the broken bolt out.

5. Insert the screw extractor in the hole. Use the correct wrench or driver to turn it counterclockwise. It should wedge in the hole and begin to loosen the bolt. Some extractors must be driven into the hole with a hammer to lock them in place. Take care not to break the extractor. It is made of very hard steel and cannot be drilled out.

6. If the extractor turns in the bolt and will not remove it, try drilling the bolt out. Use several drill bits to enlarge the hole in stages until the minor diameter of the bolt threads are reached. Then use a pick or awl to try to remove the remaining bolt threads. If this is successful, chase and reuse the original threads.

7. If the above is not successful, the next option is to drill the hole to accommodate a tap the size of the original bolt and tap new threads. Other options would be to drill the hole oversize and tap it for the next size bolt or install a thread insert.

If the bolt is broken above the surface, apply penetrating oil. Then tap the bolt with a hammer to work oil into the threads. Try to remove the bolt with locking pliers or a stud remover. An alternate approach is to weld a flat washer to the bolt. Then weld a nut to the washer. A wire welder will allow better control of heat. Heat from the welding helps loosen the bolt. Then back out the bolt with a wrench.

If an extractor or a tap becomes broken in the fastener, take the part to a facility with a plasma cutter or an electrical discharge machine (EDM). This equipment will disintegrate the broken component until it crumbles. The threads and the hole in the original part should remain undamaged.

Restoring Threads

Thread chasers or re-thread taps and dies are available for chasing out damaged threads and removing nicks and burrs without undercutting good threads. Internal threads are restored with a re-thread tap. External threads are restored with a re-thread die. External threads may also be restored with a file thread restorer called a thread file. This is done by overlapping several good threads and filing the damaged ones.

Repairing Internal Threads

Damaged component threads must be repaired before other reconditioning is done. It is common to find thread damage on aluminum cylinder heads. Inspect spark plug holes and other holes for damage including dirty, worn, or stripped threads.

Several methods are used to repair thread damage. Cleaning the threads with a thread-chasing tap may be all that is required. If a thread is badly damaged or worn, it will need to be repaired by installing a thread insert. A thread repair kit contains threaded inserts and associated tools. A threaded insert is a metal device used to replace damaged threads.

When installing a threaded insert, drill the hole with the damaged threads to a size specified for the thread insert. Cut (tap) oversized threads into the hole using a thread cutting tap. Then thread the insert into the new threads. See **Fig. 2-16.** The insert has outer threads that fit into the threads in an oversize hole. The inner threads of the insert are the same as the original threads. Make sure the top of the insert is below the top surface of the hole.

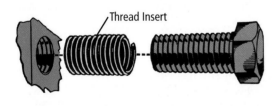
Thread Insert

Fig. 2-16 A thread insert is used when the original threads on a fastener are damaged or worn. *How is a thread insert installed?*

Follow the instructions provided with the thread repair kit. Some thread repair inserts are machined inserts. They are secured by staking the top edges of the insert into the surrounding metal of the damaged thread hole. Another type of thread insert is a coil of stainless steel that is threaded into position with a special tool. It requires the removal of a tang

after the insert is in flush position. The simplest thread insert is installed flush to the part surface with a simple bolt. Immediately upon installation, anaerobic adhesive, which hardens in the absence of air, will lock and seal the insert in place.

Thread Dressings

Many threaded-fastener applications require specific thread dressings. These dressings lubricate, lock, or seal threads. Often, some of these purposes are combined, as in compounds that both seal and lock threads.

Thread Lubrication

Sometimes it is necessary to install a steel bolt in an aluminum part such as a cylinder head or engine block. Before doing so, coat the bolt threads with an antiseize compound. See **Fig. 2-17.** An **antiseize compound** is a lubricant that prevents bolt threads from locking or seizing. Removing seized bolts may damage or pull out the aluminum threads. Coating the bolt threads with antiseize compound helps prevent this.

ANTISEIZE Compound

Fig. 2-17 Applying antiseize compound to the threads of a bolt. *When is it critical to use antiseize compound?*

Lubricating fastener threads is critical when the fasteners are to be torqued. Torque is a measurement of force expressed in units of distance and weight, such as "foot/pounds" or "Newton/meters." Where fastening pressure is critical to sealing or operation, bolt torque will be specified. For example, engine head bolts are torqued to a certain specification. This guarantees even and correct clamping pressure on an engine's head gasket between the head and block.

Torque value specifications assume that threads have been treated with an antiseize compound. To work effectively, an antiseize compound should be brushed onto the threads of at least one member of a threaded fastener pair. It should also be brushed onto the underside of the head of a bolt or nut that is being torqued. This is because there is as much friction on the underside as on the threads.

Thread-locking Compounds

A **thread-locking compound** is a compound used to prevent threaded fasteners from loosening. They are specified in many critical automotive applications. They are available as a liquid or a paste.

Thread-locking compounds are applied by dripping or rubbing the compound onto one member of a threaded pair. Most of these compounds are of the anaerobic type. See **Fig. 2-18**. Anaerobic compounds can harden in the absence of air. They can harden, or "cure," in the spaces between tightened threads. Once cured, the compounds prevent unthreading by conforming to the space between the threads. Thus, they prevent motion.

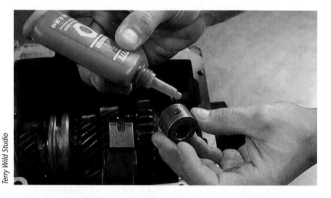

Terry Wild Studio

Fig. 2-18 Applying an anaerobic thread-locking compound to the outside of a bushing. *When must a primer be used prior to applying a thread-locking compound?*

Thread-lockers work only in clean, grease-free environments. Some thread-lockers will not cure without a "primer." The primer must be applied to the threads before the thread-locker is applied to the threads. Primers also speed the cure times for anaerobic sealants. They are sometimes applied for that reason.

Thread-lockers come in different grades. Always use the thread-locker grade specified for the strength of the locking action that is required. Milder grades of thread-locking compounds can be undone by heating the parts that they lock to. Heat the parts at a relatively low temperature, such as 400°F [205°C].

Simple thread sealants are sometimes used where threads are used to seal liquids and gases. They come in various form (pastes, liquids, caulks, tapes, and sprays). Sealants sometimes require a curing period before parts can be put back into service.

Gaskets and Sealants

Many types of gaskets and sealants are used in automobiles. When using any type of sealant, follow safety rules for handling. These materials may cause injury or pollute the environment if not handled properly. One of the most important gaskets is the head gasket, which seals between the cylinder head and the cylinder block. See **Fig. 2-19**.

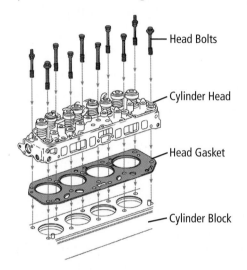

General Motors Corporation

Head Bolts

Cylinder Head

Head Gasket

Cylinder Block

Fig. 2-19 A head gasket is placed between the cylinder head and the cylinder block to seal the joint.

Preformed Gaskets

A **gasket** is a thin layer of soft material such as paper, cork, rubber, copper, synthetic material, or a combination of these. The gasket is preformed or precut to the desired shape and thickness. Clamping a gasket between two flat surfaces makes a tight seal.

The clamping force that results from the tightening of the fasteners squeezes the gasket. The soft material then fills any small irregularities in the mating surfaces. This prevents leakage of fluid, vacuum, or pressure from the joint. Holes through the gasket allow it to seal in fuel, oil, or coolant. The gasket material keeps dirt, water, and air out of the passages. Sometimes the gasket serves as a shim to take up space.

Formed-in-Place Gaskets

Some gaskets are formed in place. This is done by squeezing a bead of plastic gasket material or sealant from a tube onto one of the mating surfaces. Typical surfaces include valve covers, thermostat housings, water pumps, and differential covers. When using sealants always follow the manufacturer's instructions.

There are two kinds of plastic gasket material. Aerobic sealant hardens in the presence of air. It is sometimes referred to as room-temperature vulcanizing (RTV) sealant. This is a silicone-rubber sealant. It vulcanizes, or cures, at room temperature when exposed to air.

RTV sealant can be used with or without a preformed gasket. RTV sealant can be used on a surface that flexes or vibrates slightly, such as on an engine valve cover. Never use RTV sealant around parts with high temperatures and pressures, such as head gaskets. Clean the mating surfaces thoroughly before applying the sealant. It will not seal to dirty, greasy, or oily surfaces.

Anaerobic sealant material hardens in the absence of air. One way to remove the air is to squeeze the material between two surfaces. Such material can be used as an adhesive, a sealer, and a locking cement. It also serves as a chemical thread-locker on bolts, nuts, screws, and bushings.

Unlike aerobic sealant, anaerobic material should not be used on parts that flex. Anaerobic and aerobic sealants each have their own uses. The two should not be used interchangeably.

Welding

For some procedures, an oxy-acetylene torch must be used to heat and cut metal. In doing this, you need to follow strict safety procedures.

- Wear safety goggles or a face shield.
- Wear suitable protective clothing.
- Follow all safety rules when working with an oxy-acetylene torch.

Safety First **Welding Training** Never operate oxy-acetylene equipment without proper prior training and assessment on oxy-acetylene equipment from a qualified instructor. For welding safety information, refer to ANSI Z49.1: (or the current edition), Safety in Welding, Cutting, and Allied Processes.

The general procedure is as follows.

1. Write up the repair order.
2. Ensure that the proper personal protective equipment is being used and that appropriate safety precautions are being followed.
3. Install the appropriate cutting/heating tip on the torch.
4. Set the pressure on the regulators depending on the thickness of the metal to be cut and the tip size. Always consult the manufacturer's recommendations for your particular torch.
5. Mark the cutting line with chalk.
6. Place the part to be cut on a metal workbench so the cutting line clears the edge of the workbench.
7. Light the torch and adjust the flame.
8. Start the cut at the edge of the part to be cut.
9. Heat the metal to a bright red.
10. Gradually press down on the oxygen pressure lever and move the torch forward.
11. After the cut has been completed, turn the valves off at the tanks and return the pressure regulators to zero.

SECTION 4 KNOWLEDGE CHECK

1. Name three types of automotive fasteners.

2. Why is it important to classify nuts and bolts by strength?

3. What is the purpose of an antiseize compound?

4. What is the difference between a preformed gasket and a formed-in-place gasket?

5. Why is it important to thoroughly clean an area before applying a thread-locker or a sealant?

ASE TEST PREP

6. Technician A and Technician B are discussing what they need to do to install a steel bolt into an aluminum cylinder head. Technician A says they need to coat the bolt threads with an antiseize compound. Technician B says that would prevent the bolt threads from locking. Who is correct?

    ⓐ Technician A.

    ⓑ Technician B.

    ⓒ Both Technician A and Technician B.

    ⓓ Neither Technician A nor Technician B.

CHAPTER 2 REVIEW

Key Points

Addresses NATEF program guidelines for individual hand tools and general service center tools and equipment.

- Today's automotive technician must be familiar with a wide variety of tools and equipment.
- Ownership of a basic tool kit is often required for employment.
- The metric system is based on multiples of ten.
- Automotive technicians must convert measurements between standard, or USC, (United States Customary) and metric, or SI (System of International Units), and vice versa.
- Many threaded-fastener applications require specific thread dressings.
- Gaskets are used to create a seal between two flat surfaces. One example is the head gasket, which seals the cylinder head and the cylinder block.
- An aerobic sealant hardens in the presence of air. An anaerobic sealant hardens in the absence of air.

Review Questions

1. What tool is best suited for turning nut or bolt heads—pliers or a wrench? Why?
2. Name at least three tools that are used for calibrating.
3. Explain what technicians should know about proper use of tools and equipment.
4. Explain the relationship among linear measurements, weights, and volume in the metric system.
5. Connecting-rod-bearing clearance for an imported car engine is given as 0.51 mm. What is this in the USC system?
6. What is the function of a gasket? Name four surfaces that use formed-in-place gaskets.
7. What are the three purposes of thread dressings?
8. Define anaerobic sealant and aerobic sealant and name their typical uses.
9. **Critical Thinking** What type of sealant should be used on a brake hose?

TECHNOLOGY

Tools for Hybrids

Different tasks may require different tools. This is especially true when it comes to servicing new technologies such as those in hybrid vehicles. As a service technician, part of your job will be to familiarize yourself with new tools. You also need to know how to use the tools properly. You should acquire complete and accurate training in their use. You should be able to demonstrate the correct use of these tools to other technicians.

Hybrid vehicles have a high-voltage (HV) battery system. This system is used to power the electric drive motors as well as other electrical devices on the vehicle. Special tools are needed to properly and safely service the HV battery system and high-voltage components. The tools and equipment discussed here are among those used in servicing hybrid vehicles.

Insulated Gloves. Technicians must wear special insulated high-voltage gloves when working around the high-voltage battery system. Such gloves should be rated at 1,000 volts or higher. They must be in excellent condition. They should be lab-certified every six months.

Factory Scan Tool. A factory scan tool is needed. For many service procedures, an aftermarket scan tool cannot be used.

Insulated Tools. Technicians must use tools that are insulated against high voltage. These tools are needed to service the high-voltage system.

Specialized Tools. Hybrid vehicles require a number of specialized tools. For example, one hybrid requires a special high-pressure hydraulic tool for brake pad replacement. Another manufacturer requires a battery lifting device. Another requires a special tool to remove and replace the electric motor.

Use vehicle service manuals to identify the tools you will need. Experienced service technicians can also help you determine which tools to use when working on hybrid vehicles.

AUTOMOTIVE SERVICE EXCELLENCE
TEST PREP

Answering the following practice questions will help you prepare for the ASE certification tests.

1. A starter set of hand tools costs about:
   - ⓐ $500.
   - ⓑ $2,000.
   - ⓒ $3,000.
   - ⓓ $5,000.

2. Pneumatic motors are powered by:
   - ⓐ Electricity.
   - ⓑ Solar power.
   - ⓒ Air pressure.
   - ⓓ Water pressure.

3. Technician A says that you should clean hand tools after every use. Technician B says that you should remove oil and grease from hand tools before storing them. Who is correct?
   - ⓐ Technician A.
   - ⓑ Technician B.
   - ⓒ Both Technician A and Technician B.
   - ⓓ Neither Technician A nor Technician B.

4. Technician A says that an impact wrench requires a special type of socket. Technician B says that any standard socket is appropriate for use with the tool. Who is correct?
   - ⓐ Technician A.
   - ⓑ Technician B.
   - ⓒ Both Technician A and Technician B.
   - ⓓ Neither Technician A nor Technician B.

5. Technician A says that a bolt with three lines on its head is a grade three bolt. Technician B says that a bolt with three lines on its head is a grade six bolt. Who is correct?
   - ⓐ Technician A.
   - ⓑ Technician B.
   - ⓒ Both Technician A and Technician B.
   - ⓓ Neither Technician A nor Technician B.

6. Two service technicians are discussing the best way to thread a rod. Technician A says they should use a tap and die set. Technician B says they should use a thread repair insert kit. Who is correct?
   - ⓐ Technician A.
   - ⓑ Technician B.
   - ⓒ Both Technician A and Technician B.
   - ⓓ Neither Technician A nor Technician B.

7. What device is placed under a nut or bolt head to help hold a fastener in place?
   - ⓐ Speed nut.
   - ⓑ Rivet.
   - ⓒ Snap ring.
   - ⓓ Lock washer.

8. Torque value specifications for bolts assume that the threads are:
   - ⓐ coated with antiseize compound.
   - ⓑ coated with thread locking compound.
   - ⓒ coated with oil.
   - ⓓ uncoated.

9. Two service technicians are discussing the best way to make a very accurate measurement of a cylinder. Technician A says they should use a depth gauge. Technician B says they should use a dial indicator. Who is correct?
   - ⓐ Technician A.
   - ⓑ Technician B.
   - ⓒ Both Technician A and Technician B.
   - ⓓ Neither Technician A nor Technician B.

10. Two service technicians are discussing the best way to remove an engine from an automobile. Technician A says they should use a jack. Technician B says they should use a hoist. Who is correct?
    - ⓐ Technician A.
    - ⓑ Technician B.
    - ⓒ Both Technician A and Technician B.
    - ⓓ Neither Technician A nor Technician B.

Automotive Safety Practices

Section 1
General Workplace Safety

Section 2
Personal Safety Practices

Section 3
Tool and Equipment Safety

SAFETY FIRST
KEEP THIS AREA CLEAN

DANGER
LOCKOUT EQUIPMENT BEFORE SERVICING

CAUTION
WATCH YOUR STEP

DANGER
SAFETY GLASSES REQUIRED IN THIS AREA

DANGER
NO SMOKING TURN OFF ENGINE

RESTRICTED AREA
AUTHORIZED PERSONNEL ONLY

Customer's Concern

The service bay that you usually occupy is being used by your manager to offer personalized service to a long-time customer. So, when Brian Beckman arrives for his exhaust repair appointment, you pull his car into your co-worker Jake's bay.

After examining the exhaust system, you realize the bolts and brackets are badly corroded. You will need a torch to cut and remove the damaged section of exhaust pipe. After getting the oxy-acetylene kit into position, you adjust the valves to supply correct proportions of oxygen and acetylene, and then you prepare to ignite the torch. Just as you strike the flint, you realize something has gone terribly wrong. A flame shoots across the floor and quickly engulfs a pile of dirty towels. Commotion fills the service center.

Technician's Challenge

As the service technician, you need to find answers to these questions:

1. How can you get the fire under control? After shutting the oxy-acetylene unit down, what can you do? Where is the fire extinguisher?

2. Was anyone injured? If so, what can you do to help? Will the first aid kit suffice, or do emergency personnel need to be called?

3. Was this accident avoidable? What could Jake do differently to keep his service bay safe and orderly? Where should used towels be stored?

4. Could this have happened in your bay? What will you do differently if you need to use a co-worker's bay in the future?

Section 1
General Workplace Safety

Objectives:

- Recognize hazardous materials and wastes and proper methods for their disposal.
- Identify the types of safety information posted in an automotive service center.

Vocabulary:

- Occupational Safety and Health Administration (OSHA)
- hazardous materials
- Environmental Protection Agency (EPA)
- fire emergency plan
- spontaneous combustion
- material safety data sheet (MSDS)

OSHA

Safety means protecting yourself and others from danger and possible injury. Just as important, technicians must look out for the safety of others around them. Safety must be the first priority of every employee in the automotive workplace.

In 2003, more than 5,500 workers in the United States died due to job-related accidents. Nearly 3.4 million workers were disabled. The estimated number of cases of occupational disease was 269,500. The **Occupational Safety and Health Administration** (**OSHA**) was created in 1971 to deal with safety hazards. OSHA's purpose is:

> "To assure safe and healthful working conditions for working men and women . . . by authorizing enforcement of the standards developed under the [Occupational Safety and Health] Act . . . by providing for research, information, education and training in the field of occupational safety and health . . . ."

All employees must comply with all OSHA regulations. Observance of OSHA regulations and standards has helped make the workplace safer. See **Fig. 3-1.**

Fig. 3-1 Observance of OSHA standards has helped reduce on-the-job injuries.

Workplace Precautions

Most hazards are due to careless work habits or unsafe working conditions. Not wearing proper protective equipment, not practicing safe work procedures, and abusing chemicals and other substances are unsafe acts. Ninety-eight percent of all accidents are caused by unsafe acts or unsafe conditions.

Safety First

Regulations All workplace practices must be in accordance with federal, state, and local regulations. Diagnostic and repair tasks must be accomplished in accordance with the manufacturer's recommended procedures.

Ladders Ladders are sometimes used in the repair facility and parts room. Because they are not used frequently, they may not be maintained properly. To prevent accidents, inspect ladders before each use. Maintain them on a regular basis.

Always use the right ladder for the job. Never use a metal ladder near electric wires. Shock and electrocution can occur if the ladder contacts the wires.

Exit Doors and Aisles Keep areas around exit doors and aisles leading to exits free of obstructions. Clearly identify aisleways with safety tape or other approved material. During evacuation, a blocked exit could result in death.

Fig. 3-2 All automotive bay pits and floor openings must be covered or guarded when not in use.

Floors Slips and falls are a common cause of injuries. Prevent these by keeping floors clean and slip resistant. Contain and clean up all spills and leaks immediately. Cover or guard all pits and floor openings. See **Fig. 3-2**. Provide aisle space and keep it clear, especially around machinery. Keep all workspaces clean, orderly, and well lit. This will make it easier to complete repairs safely.

Ventilation Repair facilities must have an exhaust evacuation system for use on running vehicles. See **Fig. 3-3**. It is a hazard if a vehicle is running without being connected to the evacuation system. Exhaust gas contains carbon monoxide (CO) and other poisonous materials. CO is a colorless, odorless, tasteless, and poisonous gas. In just three minutes, an engine running in a closed one-car garage can produce enough CO to cause death. A small amount of CO can cause nausea and headaches.

Exhaust Evacuation System

Fig. 3-3 Automotive repair facilities must have a working exhaust evacuation system for use on running vehicles.

Safety First

Carbon Monoxide Carbon monoxide is a poisonous gas. It is invisible, it has no odor, and it has no taste. Avoid working on vehicles in enclosed, unventilated spaces while a vehicle's engine is running. Make sure all engine exhaust is properly and completely vented from the workspace. To further reduce the possibility of carbon monoxide poisoning, be sure that your workspace is properly ventilated.

Symptoms of carbon monoxide poisoning include drowsiness, dizziness, headache, and nausea.

Hazardous Materials and Wastes

Many products used on vehicles and workplace equipment contain hazardous materials. The waste from these products might also be hazardous waste. **Hazardous materials** and wastes are materials that pose a danger to human health and the environment. The "Right to Know" law, enforced by OSHA, requires that employers tell employees about the dangers of hazardous materials in their facilities.

EPA Many laws have been written to protect people from hazardous materials. The **Environmental Protection Agency (EPA)** is a government agency. It requires facilities to keep track of, handle, and dispose of hazardous materials properly. It develops and enforces regulations protecting the land, air, and water. The EPA sets standards that directly affect the manufacturing workplace. These standards govern internal air quality and the disposal of hazardous materials. Identifying learning opportunities in environmental laws and technology helps improve safety and ensure compliance with EPA regulations. See **Fig 3-4**.

Fig. 3-4 The regulations of the EPA protect the natural environment as well as workplace personnel.

Hazardous materials and wastes can cause illness or death. They affect humans, animals, and plants. They may cause long-term damage if released into the environment. Common automotive hazardous materials and wastes include:

- Batteries and battery acid.
- Used oil.
- Some used transmission fluid.
- Used coolant.
- Brake fluid.
- Solvent.
- Carburetor cleaner.

It is in the best interest of every repair facility to prevent pollution and the buildup of hazardous wastes. Methods include:

- Preventing spills on the floor by using different drain pans for different fluids. Use an oil drain pan for oil and a coolant drain pan for coolant.
- Using floor soaps and solvents that are biodegradable or easily decomposed by bacteria.
- Recycling and/or disposing of all hazardous wastes including fluids, greases, and lubricants. Dispose of all wastes according to state or federal regulations.

Fire Safety

One of the most serious hazards in automotive workplaces is fire. Flammable and combustible substances, such as gasoline and solvents, can easily catch fire or cause an explosion. It is actually the vapors that catch fire. If materials are handled properly, fires and explosions can be avoided. Every automotive employee needs to be aware of fire safety issues, preventive measures, and how to respond in emergency situations.

Fire Extinguishers A fire extinguisher is a portable container filled with a fire retardant material. It can be discharged to put out small fires. There are different extinguishers for different types of fires.

Table 3-A shows various fires and the type of extinguisher to use for each. You should be able to locate the fire extinguishers in the repair facility. Be sure to have the right type of extinguisher on hand. Learn how to use it correctly. Once used, fire extinguishers must be recharged.

Table 3-A	Using Fire Extinguishers		
Class of Fire		**Type of Flammable Material**	**Type of Fire Extinguisher to Use**
Class A		Wood, paper, cloth, plastic	Class A Class A:B
Class B		Grease, oil, chemicals	Class A:B Class A:B:C
Class C		Electrical cords, switches, wiring	Class A:C Class B:C
Class D		Combustible switches, wiring, metals, iron	Class D
Class K		Fires in cooking appliances involving combustible vegetable or animal oils and fats	Class K

Fire Emergency Plan Every workplace should have a fire emergency plan. A **fire emergency plan** includes the location of fire exits, where employees should meet outside, and what is expected of each person. Technicians should know what is expected of them in case of a fire.

Fire Prevention Follow these simple rules to prevent fires and explosions:

- Do not smoke around gasoline or other flammable liquids.
- Immediately wipe up any spills, especially flammable and combustible liquids.
- Leaking or spilled gasoline quickly vaporizes. Keep workplace doors open and the ventilation system running. Follow workplace rules for disposal, as gasoline is a hazardous material.
- If working on a vehicle that is leaking gasoline, exercise caution. Follow workplace rules for catching and disposing of the gasoline. Avoid tasks that could cause sparks, such as connecting a test light to the battery.
- Store no more than five gallons [19 L] of gasoline in an approved safety container. Never store gasoline in a glass container. The glass could break. An explosion and fire could result.
- When removing or replacing flammable or combustible liquids, use only an OSHA-approved container or portable holding tank. The tank stores the liquid safely. Ground wires prevent sparks that might jump between the tank or hose and the vehicle.
- When pumping a flammable liquid from one container to another, make sure that both containers are electrically grounded. Connect both containers using a grounding wire. This prevents static electricity from causing a spark.
- Store all flammables and combustibles in a fire-resistant cabinet. See **Fig. 3-5.**

- Oily rags can catch fire without a spark or flame. This is called spontaneous combustion. **Spontaneous combustion** is fire caused by chemical reactions with no spark. To prevent this, always store rags containing oil, grease, paint, or solvent in a fireproof safety container with a tightly fitted lid. The lid will prevent air from reaching the rags. See **Fig. 3-6.**
- Use caution when using a grinding wheel. Flying sparks can catch clothes and other materials on fire.

Fig. 3-6 Store used rags with oil, grease, or solvents in an OSHA-approved waste can. *Why is a lid required for this can?*

Sears Industrial Sales

TECH TIP **Disposing of Wastes.** Dispose of automotive wastes properly. Burn used oil in a waste oil burner. You might also place the oil in a drum or container labeled "Used Oil." Recycle coolant or place it in a drum labeled "Waste or Used Coolant." Store workplace rags used to clean up oil, grease, solvents, or gasoline in a metal container with a lid. Dispose of other hazardous materials according to federal and/or state regulations.

Safety Notices

Accidents are often caused by carelessness and inattention. They can also be caused by using damaged tools or the incorrect tool. Chemicals and substances can impair a person's judgment. It is important that you are aware of the layout of your facility. This will help you react well in an emergency. The term facility layout means the location of work benches, equipment, special tools, vehicle lifts, storage areas, and sources of compressed air and water.

Fig. 3-5 Store flammable and combustible liquids in fire-resistant cabinets. *What materials in the automotive workplace might be stored in a fire-resistant cabinet?*

Snap-on Tools

OSHA requires automotive service facilities to post certain information, including:
- An OSHA Job Safety and Health Protection poster.
- Emergency telephone numbers.
- Signs indicating exits and fire extinguishers.
- The ingredients of containers holding hazardous materials.

OSHA requires that an accident form be completed after each accident. Employers must advise employees of the location of accident forms. Employers are also required to inform employees of the location of all material safety data sheets (MSDS) covering the hazardous chemicals and substances in the building.

A **material safety data sheet (MSDS)** is an information sheet that identifies chemicals and their components. The sheet also lists possible health and safety problems and describes safe use of the chemical.

Posted safety signs are designed to maintain a safe and healthy workplace. See **Fig. 3-7.** Other federal, state, and local agencies may require additional postings or employee notifications. Standard colors are used to identify various physical hazards. Red is used for "danger" signs, and to identify fire protection equipment. Yellow means caution. Orange indicates warning. It identifies hazardous equipment or hazardous parts of a machine. Be aware of the location of exits, where chemicals and flammables are stored, and when personal protective equipment should be worn. Also note the recommended evacuation routes for fires, tornadoes, and hurricanes.

Auditory alerts can also help maintain a safe workplace. Auditory alerts are sounds that are used to caution people in the area. For example, vehicles such as forklifts emit a distinct sound when driven in reverse. A warning sound alerts others in the area

Fig. 3-7 Examples of safety signs posted in an automotive repair facility.

that the forklift is in operation. Flashing lights sometimes accompany these auditory alerts.

Evacuation Routes

All evacuation routes, including aisles and exits, must be clearly marked. The routes should be used when evacuation of an area is required. Emergencies or natural events such as tornadoes, hurricanes, or earthquakes may cause an evacuation.

Lockout/Tagout

Lockout/tagout is an OSHA procedure required in all workplaces. This procedure is designed to prevent electrical equipment from being started while being repaired or maintained. With lockout/tagout, all of the necessary switches must be opened, locked out, and tagged. Any person that may be involved with a piece of equipment must be trained on this procedure.

SECTION 1 KNOWLEDGE CHECK

1. What are the most common types of injuries encountered in the workplace?

2. Why must hazardous materials be used, stored, and disposed of properly?

3. What are the four classes of fire?

4. What is spontaneous combustion?

5. What is a lockout/tagout procedure?

ASE TEST PREP

6. Technician A says that a Class A fire would involve combustibles such as wood, paper, and cloth. Technician B says that a Class A fire involves electrical equipment such as motors and switches. Who is correct?
   ⓐ Technician A.
   ⓑ Technician B.
   ⓒ Both Technician A and Technician B.
   ⓓ Neither Technician A nor Technician B.

Section 2
Personal Safety Practices

Objectives:
- Identify personal protective equipment for use in the automotive repair facility.
- Identify ways in which attention to ergonomics can reduce workplace injuries.

Vocabulary:
- personal protective equipment (PPE)
- National Institute for Occupational Safety and Health (NIOSH)
- ergonomics

Personal Protective Equipment

Automotive technicians can follow a variety of personal safety practices to help ensure a safe workplace. Following these basic rules of safety will help to make the automotive service center a safe and enjoyable place to work.

Vehicles and automotive equipment, tools, and chemicals can create hazardous situations for a technician. Everyone should be protected from workplace hazards, hazardous work procedures, and substances that can cause injury or illness. Technicians must use personal protective equipment. **Personal protective equipment (PPE)** is equipment worn by workers to protect against hazards in the environment. Typical automotive PPE includes:
- Safety glasses, goggles, and face shields.
- Steel-toed boots and shoes with skid-resistant soles.
- Gloves.
- Respirators.
- Protective sleeves.
- Ear plugs and earmuffs.
- Bump hats.

Automotive employers must provide the correct PPE for technicians. Employers must also provide training on the proper use, fit, and care of most required PPE. It is the technician's responsibility to wear PPE.

Eye Protection

Approximately 1,000 eye injuries occur every day in the workplace. Three out of five workers injured in this way are not wearing eye protection at the time of the accident. Seventy percent of eye injuries result from flying or falling objects or sparks striking the eye. Another 20 percent of the eye injuries are caused by contact with chemicals. These accidents can occur in an automotive workplace. Wear protective eye devices to prevent injury. See **Fig. 3-8.** Wear a face shield with glasses or goggles when operating machinery. Technicians' eyes can be harmed by:
- Dust thrown off by grinding.
- Welding sparks.
- Small particles produced when chiseling and hammering.
- Radiation from welding.
- Air-conditioning refrigerant.
- Paints, thinners, and solvents.

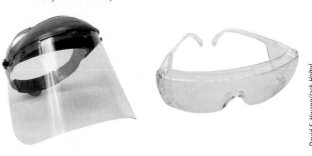

David S. Hwang/Jack Holtel

Fig. 3-8 Some types of eye protection available. *What protection should you use when grinding?*

Foot Protection

Accidents account for thousands of disabling foot injuries each year. Automobile engines and automotive parts and equipment are heavy. Service area floors are sometimes slippery. Steel-toed shoes will protect feet from heavy objects. See **Fig 3-9.** Footwear must meet OSHA's standards (ANSI Z 41.1) for impact resistance. This standard should be marked on the shoe label. Slip-resistant soles will offer protection from slips and falls.

David S. Hwang

Fig. 3-9 Steel-toed shoes. *What other type of PPE should you wear when working under a vehicle?*

Hand and Arm Protection

Some of the most common injuries in the automotive workplace are cuts to the hands. Such cuts can be dangerous. Many chemicals and hazardous wastes can cause injury and illness when absorbed through the skin. Some of these chemicals and materials are:

• Used oil, carburetor cleaner, some used coolant, and many solvents, paints, and thinners that contain carcinogens and substances that irritate or injure skin.
• Welding produces sparks and flying metal particles that can injure skin.
• Hot coolant can burn skin.
• Battery electrolyte contains acid that can irritate or burn skin.

Wear gloves to prevent injury to your hands. There are different gloves for different situations. When gloves cannot be worn, such as around moving machinery, use barrier creams. Barrier creams can help protect hands from harsh chemicals and other substances.

Technicians routinely work near very hot objects. Repairing exhaust systems or changing oil can expose bare arms to very hot conditions. Technicians should wear protective sleeves to prevent burns. See **Fig. 3-10**.

Lung Protection

Some brake linings contain asbestos. Exposure to airborne brake dust or asbestos fibers is extremely hazardous. Exposure to asbestos fibers can cause several disabling diseases. These diseases include asbestosis and gastrointestinal cancer. Technicians should exercise caution when working around asbestos.

• When handling containers of asbestos dust or other asbestos waste, wear a NIOSH-approved respirator. See **Fig. 3-11**. **NIOSH** is the **National Institute for Occupational Safety and Health.** NIOSH tests and certifies respirators and other items of safety equipment.

Terry Wild Studio

Fig. 3-11 A NIOSH-approved respirator. *What safety concerns are associated with asbestos?*

• Use a barrier cream on hands along with the standard PPE.
• Never use an air hose to blow dust from a brake assembly. Remove brake dust by one of the two approved methods. Use a wet wash-recycle system to capture the dust. You might also use a high-efficiency particulate air (HEPA) filter vacuum system.
• Wash hands after brake work to prevent the transfer of asbestos fibers to food.

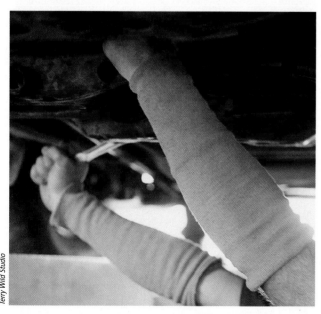

Terry Wild Studio

Fig. 3-10 Protective sleeves help prevent burns to bare arms. *What are some situations in which a protective sleeve might be beneficial?*

Head and Ear Protection

Bump hats will protect a technician's head from hot exhaust systems and sharp protruding objects. These hats also protect against grease, water, dirt, and sparks.

Some automotive tools and equipment, such as air-operated tools and high-speed drills, are very noisy. At certain levels and over a period of time, such noise can cause permanent hearing loss.

Pay attention to noise levels. There are decibel meters available to check the noise level. Wear ear plugs or muffs when appropriate. See **Fig. 3-12.**

Jack Holtel

Fig. 3-12 Examples of ear protection. *In what automotive repair situations should ear protection equipment be worn?*

Ergonomics

Ergonomics is the study of workplace design. It studies the tools used, the lighting, and the type of movements required by the employee on the job. Repetitive motions, forceful exertions, vibration, and sustained or awkward postures can cause arm and hand injuries. Common automotive injuries caused by ergonomic stresses are carpal tunnel syndrome, tendonitis, and back injuries.

Preventing Arm and Hand Injuries

Whenever possible, use tools that do the twisting for you, such as automatic screwdrivers or electric drills. If using a tool that produces excessive vibrations, wear gloves or put rubber sleeves on the tool. Make sure that the tool fits your hand properly. Use the tool in the correct way. See **Fig. 3-13.**

Counterclockwise

Fig. 3-13 Holding tools correctly can prevent serious injury. Never push a wrench. Always pull it. *What safety precaution can be taken when using tools that vibrate excessively?*

Preventing Back Injuries

Automotive repair work requires twisting, bending, and heavy lifting. These actions frequently cause back problems. Lift with your legs and keep your back straight. Always ask for help if an object is too heavy. See **Fig. 3-14.**

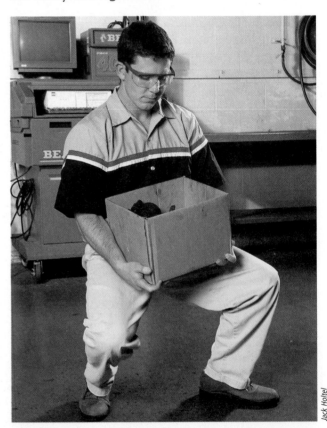

Jack Holtel

Fig. 3-14 Technicians should lift heavy objects in the workplace using the correct lifting procedures. *What is the correct lifting procedure?*

Emergency Response to Injuries

The only way to prevent accidents and injuries is to follow safety rules and regulations. Every year thousands of accidents and injuries occur in automotive repair workplaces. There are also numerous deaths. The most common injuries are lacerations, cuts, slips, falls, eye injuries, strains, hernias, and back injuries.

If someone is injured, notify your supervisor at once. Every repair facility must have a set procedure for emergencies. Every person should know this procedure. If possible, a trained person should be available to give first aid. Everyone in the facility should be able to locate the posted emergency phone numbers, evacuation routes, first aid kits, eyewash stations, and safety showers. See **Fig. 3-15**.

Terry Wild Studio

FIRST AID

Fig. 3-15 First aid kit. *What precautions must be taken when responding to an emergency?*

Emergencies call for fast action. Remember the following when responding to an emergency:

- If chemicals enter the eyes, flush immediately. See the MSDS for the substance.
- Think twice before giving any first aid. If the injured person is bleeding, special precautions must be taken. Improperly moving a person with a serious injury could worsen the injury.
- Cardiopulmonary resuscitation (CPR) is a procedure designed to restore a victim's breathing and heartbeat. It requires special training. Technicians who are not trained in the proper procedure should find someone who is trained.

Avoiding Bloodborne Pathogens

A pathogen is something that causes a disease. Bloodborne pathogens are microorganisms such as the hepatitis B virus and the HIV virus, which causes AIDS. Pathogens are found in the blood of people infected with the virus. The chance of being exposed to these diseases on the job is small. However, it is important to think before reacting when someone is bleeding.

It is easy to prevent exposure. Avoid contact with blood or other bodily fluids. First aid kits contain gloves for protection. Do not give first aid to a person unless you have been trained on how to avoid bloodborne pathogens.

SECTION 2 KNOWLEDGE CHECK

1. What eye protection should be worn when operating machinery?

2. Where should the OSHA standard for impact resistance be found on a shoe?

3. What precautions should be taken if using a tool that produces excessive vibrations?

4. List two pieces of PPE and describe the use of each one.

5. What are some common injuries caused by ergonomic stresses in the automotive workplace?

ASE TEST PREP

6. Technician A says that a wrench should never be pulled but should always be pushed. Technician B says that a wrench should never be pushed but should always be pulled. Who is correct?
   - ⓐ Technician A.
   - ⓑ Technician B.
   - ⓒ Both Technician A and Technician B.
   - ⓓ Neither Technician A nor Technician B.

Section 3
Tool and Equipment Safety

Objectives:
- Use hand and power tools in a safe manner.
- Demonstrate a knowledge of fire protection and safety techniques.

Vocabulary:
- **pneumatic tool**
- **lift point**
- **transmission jack**

Hand Tools

Automotive technicians use many different types of equipment and tools. It is important to learn how to safely use every tool and piece of equipment in the workplace.

Misuse and improper maintenance pose the greatest hazard in using hand tools. Observe the following when using hand tools:
- Keep hand tools clean and in good condition. Greasy and oily tools are difficult to hold and use.
- Wipe tools clean before and after each use.

Fig. 3-16 The correct use of tools. *What might affect what tools are easier and safer for you to use?*

- Use a hand tool only for the task for which it was designed. For example, use a screwdriver only for turning screws.
- Always wear safety glasses or goggles when using hand and power tools. This prevents chips and particles from flying into your eyes.
- Use hand tools correctly. For example, you should pull a wrench rather than push it. See **Fig. 3-16**.
- Do not use a hardened hammer or punch on a hardened surface. Hardened steel is brittle and can shatter from heavy blows. Slivers may fly out and cut a hand or enter an eye.
- Never use a tool that is in poor condition, such as a hammer with a broken or cracked handle. Do not use chisels and punches with mushroomed heads and broken or bent wrenches.
- Do not use a screwdriver on a part that is being handheld. The screwdriver can slip and hit the hand. This is a common cause of injury.

Electric Power Tools

There are a number of hazards when using power tools. Observe the following safety practices when using power tools:
- Use only power tools that have been properly grounded or double insulated.
- Make sure that all extension cords are the three-wire grounded type.
- Make sure the three-pronged plug is used in a grounded receptacle. See **Fig. 3-17**.
- Make sure that all power tools are equipped with a constant pressure switch that cannot be locked in the on position. This will prevent a dropped tool from continuing to run, possibly causing injury.

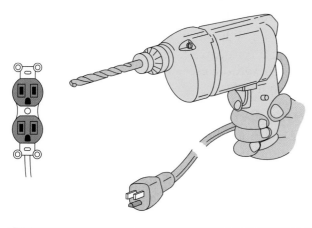

Courtesy Hunter Engineering Company

Fig. 3-17 An electric drill with a three-pronged plug. *What is the function of the third prong?*

- Avoid accidental startups by keeping fingers off the start switch when carrying a tool.
- Secure work with clamps or a vise. This will free both hands to operate the tool.
- Keep electrical cords away from oil and sharp edges.
- Make sure that all electrical cords are free of frays or breaks in the insulation.
- Disconnect power tools when not in use, before servicing, and when changing accessories such as bits and cutters. This will prevent a sudden, hazardous start-up.
- Keep tools as sharp and clean as possible for best performance.
- Wear the appropriate PPE, such as safety glasses and a face shield.
- Do not wear loose clothing, ties, or jewelry that can become caught in moving machinery.
- Do not wear gloves while operating power tools or equipment that rotates. Gloves can get caught in the moving parts.
- Do not stand in water while working on equipment. Electrical shock could occur.

Machine Guards

Machine guards are important safety devices. Always make sure the machine guard is in place when working on grinders and wire and abrasive wheels. Always use the hood guard with a dynamic (spin) tire balancer. See **Fig. 3-18.**

Power presses can create enormous pressure on parts in addition to producing sparks, dust, and flying chips. Under such pressure, bearings can burst open and shoot off at high speed. Be sure machine

Fig. 3-18 When in use, the machine guard must be down to prevent injury to the technician. Here the machine guard is shown directly behind the wheel.

guards are in place. In addition, wear PPE such as face shields with goggles and gloves when using machines with machine guards.

Pneumatic Tools

A **pneumatic tool** is a tool that is powered by compressed air. These tools include:
- Impact wrenches for removing and tightening nuts and bolts.
- Grinders for removing sharp edges and burrs, or finishing rough surfaces.
- Cutting tools for removing rusted parts like exhaust systems.
- Blowguns for cleaning parts and removing debris.

Check the operator's manual for the correct working air pressure. Uncontrolled or unregulated compressed air can move loose particles and debris at high speed. These particles can cause serious personal injury, especially to the eyes and exposed skin.

The proper use of compressed air is extremely important. When using pneumatic tools, always follow these suggested safety procedures.

- When using a blowgun, always wear the correct PPE, such as safety glasses or goggles, and a face shield. See **Fig. 3-19**. Always direct the airflow away from you.

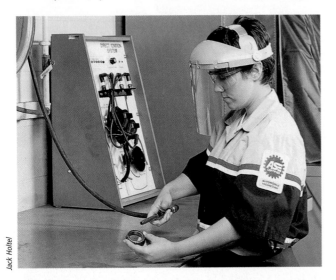

Jack Holtel

Fig. 3-19 A blowgun is used to blow parts dry or clean. Always wear safety glasses or goggles and a face shield when operating a blowgun. *Why are safety glasses and a face shield important?*

- Always carry a pneumatic tool by its frame or handle. Do not carry the tool by the attached compressed air hose.
- Make sure all pneumatic tools are securely attached to the compressed air line.
- Never use a pneumatic tool, such as a blowgun, to remove debris from your clothing or your body.
- When using compressed air to clean and dry a part such as a ball bearing, avoid spinning the part. A spinning part can eject debris or material remaining from the cleaning process. Use a brush or vacuum system to remove as much debris from the part as possible.
- Securely position a pneumatic tool before operating it. Many of these tools operate at high speed or under high pressure. Incorrect placement may result in component damage or personal injury.

Properly maintain compressors to keep contaminants out of the system and hoses. Proper maintenance prevents air hoses from breaking. A broken air hose can cause air and particles to blow into the workplace at high speed.

Routinely check air hoses for leaks and damage. Repair immediately. Lockout and bleed the system before any repair. This will prevent accidental start-up and the escape of pressurized air from a broken hose.

Drive Belts and Pulleys

Air compressors have pulleys and drive belts. Pay close attention when using these machines. It is easy to get your fingers caught in moving drive belts and pulleys. Be sure that guards have been placed over any pulleys and drive belts.

Fans can also injure fingers and hands. Keep your hands away from fans. Some fans can come on with the engine and ignition turned off. Always electrically disconnect a fan before beginning any repair job.

Lifts, Jacks, and Safety Stands

The safe use of lifts, floor jacks, and safety stands can prevent many unnecessary accidents. These devices should be properly placed at designated lift points. A **lift point** is a place on the vehicle frame where a lift, floor jack, or safety stand can be placed. Lift points are designated by the manufacturer.

Many of these accidents are caused by:
- Vehicles placed incorrectly on a lift or floor jack.
- Failure of a floor jack or lift to support the vehicle's weight.
- Vehicles slipping from a floor jack due to vehicle movement or imbalance.
- Incorrect placement of, or failure to use, safety stands.
- Placing a floor jack or safety stand at a lift point other than the designated vehicle lift points.

Vehicle Lifts

Always use the manufacturer's recommended lift points when lifting a vehicle. Use of any other point can cause damage to the vehicle or the vehicle could slip off the lift. **Figure 3-20** shows the lift points for one type of vehicle. Check each vehicle's service manual for the correct points.

When using a lift, observe these safety tips. Also, always refer to the lift manufacturer's manual for specific information.
- Only trained technicians should operate a lift.
- Keep the lift area free of oil, grease, and other debris.
- Never overload a lift. Check each lift's maximum weight capacity.

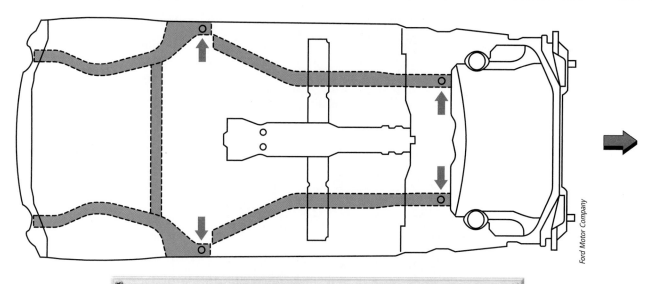

Ford Motor Company

Fig. 3-20 When using a lift, make sure the vehicle is positioned at the lift points recommended by the manufacturer. The lift points here are shown in red. *Why is it important to use the lift points noted by the manufacturer?*

- Never operate a lift with anyone inside the vehicle.
- Never lift a vehicle while someone is working under it.
- When driving a vehicle onto a lift, never hit or run over lift arms, adapters, or axle supports. This could damage the lift and the vehicle.
- If working under a vehicle, make sure the lift has been raised high enough to engage the locking device.
- Before lowering the lift, clear away all tools, trays, and other equipment from under the vehicle.

Floor Jacks and Safety Stands

When using a floor jack, position it properly under the vehicle. See **Fig. 3-21**. Do not allow the jack to slip out! Always put safety stands in place before going under a vehicle. See **Fig. 3-22**. When using safety stands, place the stands and the vehicle on a flat area of the floor where the vehicle weight cannot make the stands sink.

Fig. 3-22 Never go under a vehicle supported by a floor jack unless safety stands are in place. Place safety stands at the lift points recommended by the manufacturer. *Why is it important to place the stands and the vehicle on a flat, hard surface?*

Jack Holtel

Fig. 3-21 A floor jack properly lifting a vehicle. *What safety precaution do you see in this photo?*

Terry Wild Studio

Fig. 3-23 When using a hoist, make sure the load rating of the hoist can support the weight of the load.

Hoists

A hoist is used to pick up and move heavy objects. For example, technicians use a hoist to remove an engine from a vehicle. See **Fig. 3-23**.

Verify that the hoist has the correct load rating for the load. If the load is too heavy or held too far from the body of the hoist, the hoist can fall over. To help prevent this, use an appropriate sling or chain. The bolts attaching the chain to the object must be strong, tight, and threaded well into the object. This will allow lifting without tearing out the threads. When moving a load with a hoist, keep the load close to the body of the hoist to keep the hoist stable.

Transmission Jacks

A **transmission jack** is a jack that is used to support a transmission when it is serviced or replaced. Removing a transmission changes a vehicle's center of gravity. The vehicle will be easier to control if it is on a lift or hoist supporting the wheels.

Electrical Safety

While most vehicles use 12 volts, automotive workplaces use 110 and 220 volts. These voltages and the amperages involved are dangerous. They can cause burns and death. Practice these electrical safety habits when working in the workplace:

- Never use your fingers or bare hands to determine whether a circuit is live.
- Always replace a circuit breaker or fuse with a circuit breaker or fuse of the same capacity.
- Place "Out of Order" signs on equipment that is defective.
- Consider every electrical wire to be live until it is positively known it is dead.
- To prevent sparks from broken bulbs, use a fluorescent tube drop light. If a bulb cage light is used, always use a shatterproof bulb. See **Fig. 3-24**.

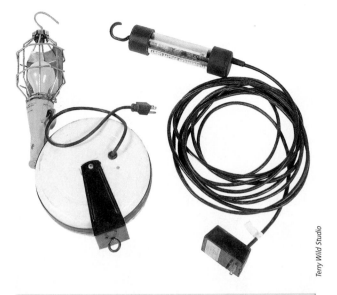

Terry Wild Studio

Fig. 3-24 Two types of drop lights. *Why is the fluorescent drop light safer?*

Welding Safety

Only trained workers should weld or cut with a torch. Head, eye, face, and body protection must be worn when welding or cutting.

Welding uses compressed gases. This presents other safety issues. OSHA has strict regulations for the storage of compressed gases. Technicians must be properly trained before working with compressed gases.

Compressed Gases

Compressed gases include oxygen and acetylene. Cylinders containing these gases must be stored upright, capped, and chained in approved racks. See **Fig. 3-25**. There must be at least 20 feet [6 m] or a solid barrier wall between stored oxygen cylinders and stored acetylene cylinders.

To prevent fire or explosion, store cylinders away from room heaters or other heat sources. Never store cylinders in unventilated lockers or closets. Never use cylinders as supports or rollers to move an object. The cylinder could explode.

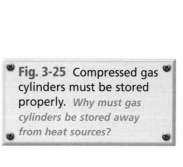

Fig. 3-25 Compressed gas cylinders must be stored properly. *Why must gas cylinders be stored away from heat sources?*

David S. Hwang

SECTION 3 KNOWLEDGE CHECK

1. What PPE should be worn when using all hand and power tools?

2. Why should all power tools be equipped with a constant pressure switch?

3. Name four types of pneumatic tools and their uses.

4. Name three pieces of equipment that require machine guards when operating.

5. What safety tips need to be followed when using a lift?

6. What tool is used to support a vehicle after it has been lifted to the correct height by a floor jack?

7. What tool is used to lift the engine from a vehicle?

ASE TEST PREP

8. Technician A says that pneumatic tools include impact wrenches, grinders, cutting tools, and blowguns. Technician B says that pneumatic tools include only impact wrenches. Who is correct?
   - ⓐ Technician A.
   - ⓑ Technician B.
   - ⓒ Both Technician A and Technician B.
   - ⓓ Neither Technician A nor Technician B.

9. Technician A says that stored oxygen and acetylene cylinders must have a solid barrier wall or at least 6 m [20 ft] of space between them. Technician B says that this is unnecessary and that oxygen and acetylene cylinders can be stored together. Who is correct?
   - ⓐ Technician A.
   - ⓑ Technician B.
   - ⓒ Both Technician A and Technician B.
   - ⓓ Neither Technician A nor Technician B.

CHAPTER 3 REVIEW

Key Points

Addresses NATEF program guidelines for automotive safety practices, including the work environment and the storage, handling, and use of hazardous materials.

- OSHA was created to establish standards and procedures that help decrease accidents, injuries, and deaths in the workplace.
- Hazardous wastes in the automotive repair facility should be properly disposed of to avoid danger to human health.
- Every employer is required to post certain safety information for its employees.
- Personal protective equipment can prevent exposure to hazards in the workplace.
- It is important to learn how to safely use every tool and piece of equipment.
- It is important for all employees to know emergency procedures.
- Safe work habits can prevent many accidents, injuries, and even deaths.

Review Questions

1. Who is responsible for complying with OSHA?
2. Identify several automotive hazardous materials and wastes and how to properly dispose of them.
3. Name three types of safety information employers are required to post for their employees.
4. Name three items of personal protective equipment and their uses in the automotive repair facility.
5. List three safety concerns when using hand tools.
6. What are several hazards technicians must be aware of when using power tools?
7. List three items that should be included in a fire emergency plan.
8. **Critical Thinking** Why do you think it might be important that CPR training be given to all employees?
9. **Critical Thinking** What substances used in the automotive workplace must have MSDS available?

HYBRID TECHNOLOGY

Safety Precautions

Procedures performed on a hybrid vehicle require special safety precautions. The procedures discussed here may not be specific to current models. Refer to the manufacturer's service manual and service bulletins, in print and online.

One of the most dangerous systems on a hybrid is the high-voltage battery system. This system includes the motor, battery pack, controls, and wiring harness. High-voltage power cables in hybrid vehicles are orange. Do not handle these harnesses without wearing high-voltage-approved insulated gloves. The gloves must be in excellent condition.

Always shut off a hybrid vehicle's high-voltage system before working around the engine, motor, battery pack, or high-voltage harness. Refer to the manufacturer's service manual for correct shut-off procedures.

Observe all safety precautions regarding the use of the key. Place the key where it will not be reinserted while the vehicle is being worked on.

The gasoline engine may start and stop at any time while the READY indicator is on. Always check the READY indicator status to verify whether the vehicle is on or shut off.

On Honda hybrids a shut-off switch is on the intelligent power unit (IPU). On the Toyota Prius the high-voltage system is disarmed by removing the service plug located in the rear of the trunk on the driver's side. Do not remove the service plug before you have insulated yourself against possible electrical shock. Wear high-voltage approved insulated gloves. Toyota recommends you carry the service plug in your pocket while working on the system. This will prevent a technician from reinstalling it while you are working on the system.

Toyota also recommends that you wait five minutes after pulling the service plug before working on the vehicle. This will allow capacitor discharge.

AUTOMOTIVE SERVICE EXCELLENCE
TEST PREP

Answering the following practice questions will help you prepare for the ASE certification tests.

1. OSHA was created to:

   ⓐ assure safe and healthful working conditions for working men and women.

   ⓑ authorize enforcement of the standards developed under the Act.

   ⓒ provide research, information, education, and training in the field of occupational safety and health.

   ⓓ All of the above.

2. Technician A says that carbon monoxide poisoning can occur in a workplace with poor ventilation. Technician B says opening windows will always prevent carbon monoxide poisoning. Who is correct?

   ⓐ Technician A.

   ⓑ Technician B.

   ⓒ Both Technician A and Technician B.

   ⓓ Neither Technician A nor Technician B.

3. Technician A says the "Right to Know" law applies only to large automotive workplaces. Technician B says having access to a material safety data sheet is required by the "Right to Know" law. Who is correct?

   ⓐ Technician A.

   ⓑ Technician B.

   ⓒ Both Technician A and Technician B.

   ⓓ Neither Technician A nor Technician B.

4. Examples of PPE include:

   ⓐ respirators.

   ⓑ steel-toed shoes with skid-resistant soles.

   ⓒ safety glasses, goggles, and face shields.

   ⓓ All of the above.

5. Technician A says MSDS list possible health and safety problems of a chemical. Technician B says MSDS identify chemicals and their components. Who is correct?

   ⓐ Technician A.

   ⓑ Technician B.

   ⓒ Both Technician A and Technician B.

   ⓓ Neither Technician A nor Technician B.

6. Which of the following is a good safety practice for power tool use?

   ⓐ Keep fingers on the START switch when carrying a tool.

   ⓑ Make sure the three-pronged plug is used in a grounded receptacle.

   ⓒ Use power tools that have a constant pressure switch that can be locked in the ON position.

   ⓓ All of the above.

7. Technician A says safety stands must always be used with a floor jack. Technician B says the floor jack can be used alone. Who is correct?

   ⓐ Technician A.

   ⓑ Technician B.

   ⓒ Both Technician A and Technician B.

   ⓓ Neither Technician A nor Technician B.

8. Used gasoline-soaked rags should be:

   ⓐ thrown into the trash.

   ⓑ stored in a fireproof container with a lid.

   ⓒ stored in an open fireproof container.

   ⓓ burned immediately.

9. Technician A says that lockout/tagout is used only on construction sites. Technician B says that any person involved with a machine has to be trained on the lockout/tagout procedures used in the facility. Who is correct?

   ⓐ Technician A.

   ⓑ Technician B.

   ⓒ Both Technician A and Technician B.

   ⓓ Neither Technician A nor Technician B.

10. Which of the following are automotive service facilities not required to post for employees?

    ⓐ MSDS covering all of the hazardous chemicals and substances in the building.

    ⓑ Signs indicating exits and hazardous substances.

    ⓒ Emergency telephone numbers.

    ⓓ The location of the nearest fire hydrant.

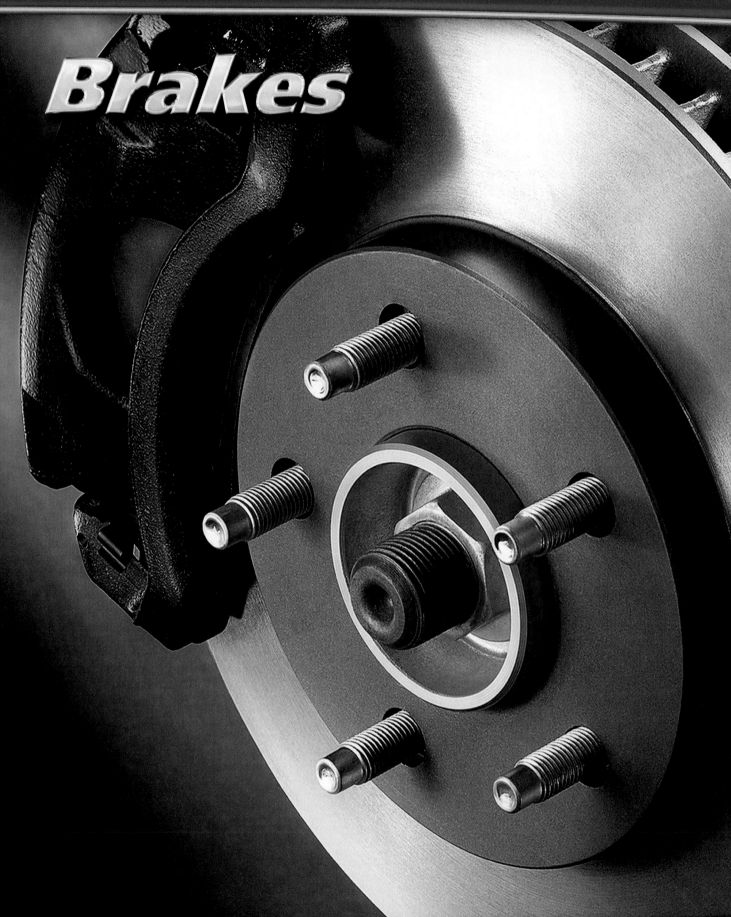

Brakes

Chapter 1
Brake System Operation

Chapter 2
Diagnosing & Repairing
the Hydraulic System

Chapter 3
Diagnosing & Repairing
Drum Brakes

Chapter 4
Diagnosing & Repairing
Disc Brakes

Chapter 5
Diagnosing & Repairing
Power Boosters

Chapter 6
Diagnosing & Repairing
Parking Brakes

Chapter 7
Diagnosing & Repairing
Antilock Brakes

Brake System Operation

Section 1
Brake Systems

Section 2
Service Brake System

Section 3
Brake Fluid

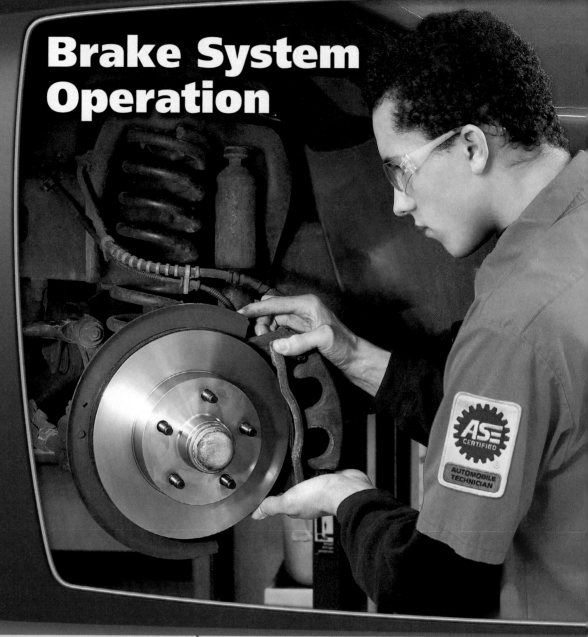

Customer's Concern

The brake system is one of the most important systems in a motor vehicle. Safe vehicle operation depends upon its effective and efficient operation. Without it, a driver has no way of slowing or stopping a moving vehicle.

Understanding the basic principles used in brake systems helps technicians diagnose and solve braking problems. A qualified brake technician can easily respond to the following questions. What important roles does friction play in service brakes and parking brakes? How do the principles of hydraulics relate to braking? What are the major components of a braking system? What is the difference between drum brakes and disc brakes? How are dual brakes split? Does the vehicle have an antilock brake system (ABS)?

Technician's Challenge

As the service technician, you need to find answers to these questions:

1. What happens within the braking system when a driver applies pressure to the brake pedal? What force ultimately stops a vehicle?

2. How does the master cylinder convert mechanical force from the brake pedal to hydraulic pressure at the wheel brakes?

3. What role does brake fluid play in the braking system? Why is brake fluid stability so important? What does the DOT have to do with brake fluid?

● Section 1
Brake Systems

Objectives:
- Identify the two basic types of wheel brakes.
- Explain how friction provides braking action in a motor vehicle.

Vocabulary:
- parking brakes
- friction
- static friction
- kinetic friction

Types of Brakes

All vehicles must have brakes. Without brakes, there is no way to safely slow or stop a moving vehicle. Most vehicles have two types of brakes–service brakes and parking brakes.

Service Brakes

Service brakes are the primary braking system. Force applied to the service brake pedal is converted to hydraulic pressure by the master cylinder. This pressure is transferred through the service braking system until it reaches the wheel brakes. Here, brake force is applied to the vehicle's wheels, causing the vehicle to slow or stop.

Figure 1-1 shows the major components (parts) of a vehicle's service brake system.

- The master cylinder serves as the brake fluid reservoir for the service brakes and converts mechanical force to hydraulic pressure for the braking system.
- The brake hoses/lines carry brake fluid under pressure from the master cylinder to the wheel brakes.
- The disc brakes include rotors and disc pads, which transfer brake force to the vehicle's wheels.
- The drum brakes include drums and brake shoes, which transfer brake force to the vehicle's wheels.
- The power brake booster supplies the increased forces needed by the brakes. The booster does this without requiring increased brake pedal pressure.
- The brake pedal activates the master cylinder.

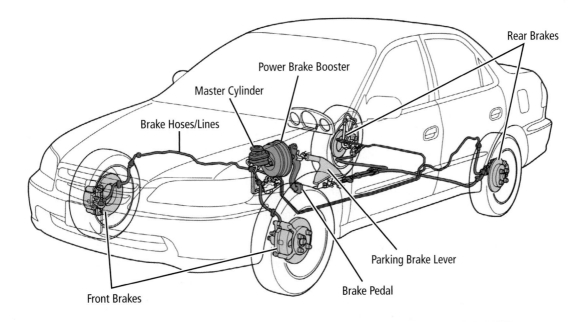

Rear Brakes

Power Brake Booster

Master Cylinder

Brake Hoses/Lines

Parking Brake Lever

Brake Pedal

Front Brakes

American Honda/Corp PR

Fig. 1-1 The major components in a typical braking system. *What are the differences between service brakes and parking brakes?*

Parking Brakes

Although sometimes mistakenly called emergency brakes, **parking brakes** are brakes that are used to keep a parked vehicle from moving. They are usually on the rear wheels and are mechanically operated.

Friction and Braking

Friction and braking are closely related in vehicles. Without friction, there would be no braking. **Friction** is the resistance to motion between two objects or surfaces that touch. Friction varies by the amount

Excellence in Science

Friction Stops!

A good driver's braking skills allow the brakes to stop the vehicle. Unfortunately, if a driver locks his wheels and skids, the brakes cannot do their job. Then the friction between the tires and the road must stop the vehicle. The stopping distance is much greater in a skid. The driver also has little control of steering with locked wheels.

Let's examine an unfortunate situation. Two older pickup trucks are traveling down the free-way at 55 mph [88 kph]. The trucks are identical except that one truck is fully loaded and the other is empty. Suddenly several deer step onto the roadway, right into the path of the trucks! The drivers see the deer immediately

and overreact. Each slams on his brakes at exactly the same instant and locks the wheels on his truck.

Under normal braking conditions more energy will be required to stop the fully loaded truck than the empty truck. The loaded truck would normally require a greater stopping distance. The two trucks with the locked brakes in this example have the same tire surface area in contact with the road, but they differ in weight. Under these conditions will the lighter truck still be able to stop in a shorter distance? Does the weight of the truck make a difference if the truck is skidding?

Apply It!

Experimenting with Friction

Meets NATEF Science Standards for friction and deceleration.

Materials and Equipment
• Three large metal flat washers
• Small piece of double-faced tape
• Ruler or other straightedge

Fig. A

1. Tape two of the washers together with the double-faced tape. No tape should touch the bottom surface of the stack. This stack represents the heavy, loaded truck. The single washer represents the lighter, empty truck.

2. Place the ruler on a smooth, level surface.

3. Put the single washer and the double washer side-by-side, touching the straight edge of the ruler. **Fig. A.**

4. Quickly shove and retract the ruler to set the washers in motion. Which one stops first?

Results and Analysis As you should have observed, the stopping distances of the objects are not dependent on their weight. Why?

Explanation The force of friction stops the trucks and washers. The amount of friction is proportional to the weight of the object. Each truck's kinetic energy of motion is also proportional to its mass. You might expect that the double washer would take longer to stop because of its greater kinetic energy. However, twice the mass results in twice the frictional stopping force. Finally, doubling the amount of friction causes the double washers to stop in exactly the same distance as the single washer. The single washer has half the kinetic energy but also half the frictional stopping force.

of force (often referred to as the load) between the surfaces. Friction also varies by the roughness of the surfaces and the materials from which the objects are made. For instance, there is more friction between a piece of sandpaper and a block of wood than between an ice cube and a countertop.

A lubricant between the objects can reduce friction. Water between the melting ice cube and the countertop allows the ice cube to move with less friction. Similarly, wet brakes will not stop a vehicle as effectively as dry brakes.

Without friction, no moving object would slow down or stop. A toy top, once set spinning, would continue to spin. It is the friction between the top, the surface it spins on, and the air around it that slows it down.

Another example is the space shuttle as it reenters Earth's atmosphere. Friction between the shuttle's surface and the atmosphere reduces the shuttle's speed. The reduction in speed creates massive amounts of heat. Friction slows the space shuttle from an orbital speed of about 18,000 mph [28,800 kph] to a landing speed of about 500 mph [800 kph].

There are two types of friction: static friction and kinetic friction. See **Fig. 1-2.**

Static Friction

Static means "at rest." **Static friction** is the resistance between objects that are in contact but at rest. Parking brakes are an example of static friction at work. Friction between the brake lining and the brake drum or rotor keeps the wheels from moving. Friction between the vehicle's tires and the pavement keeps the vehicle from sliding.

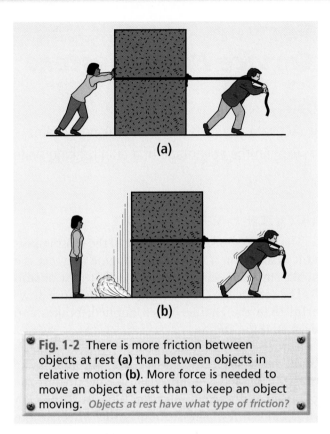

(a)

(b)

Fig. 1-2 There is more friction between objects at rest **(a)** than between objects in relative motion **(b)**. More force is needed to move an object at rest than to keep an object moving. *Objects at rest have what type of friction?*

Kinetic Friction

Kinetic means "in motion." The resistance between objects that are in contact and in relative motion is called **kinetic friction.**

Like the space shuttle, vehicles on Earth use kinetic friction to change their motion into heat energy. Friction between the moving and nonmoving parts of the service brakes creates heat.

As the vehicle slows and stops, kinetic energy is changed to heat energy. The brakes pass this heat to the air and other wheel parts.

SECTION 1 KNOWLEDGE CHECK

1. What are the two basic types of wheel brakes?

2. What is a master cylinder?

3. What carries brake fluid to the wheel brakes?

4. What is needed to stop any moving object?

5. What is static friction?

6. Is there more or less friction between two objects at rest than between objects in relative motion?

ASE TEST PREP

7. Two service technicians are discussing a car's primary braking system. They are talking about its:
   ⓐ parking brake system.
   ⓑ air brake system.
   ⓒ service brake system.
   ⓓ emergency brake system.

Section 2
Service Brake System

Objectives:
- Activate a vehicle's service braking system.
- Explain the advantage of a dual braking system.

Vocabulary:
- **disc brakes**
- **drum brakes**
- **dual-braking system**

Service Brake Action

The service brake system is one of the most important systems on a vehicle. The engine may get the vehicle moving, but it is the brakes that slow or stop it. The service brakes are designed to be more powerful than the engine. When applied, brakes can even stall the engine.

Service brakes, those operated by the vehicle's brake pedal, have two basic parts. The first is the master cylinder. The brake master cylinder is the part that applies hydraulic (fluid) pressure through the brake lines. The second is the wheel brake mechanisms. These are located at each of the vehicle's wheels. They are activated by hydraulic pressure.

Two types of service brakes are used on vehicles. **Disc brakes** use hydraulic pressure to clamp brake pads against a rotating disc called a brake rotor. See **Fig. 1-3. Drum brakes** use hydraulic pressure to press brake shoes against the inside of a rotating brake drum. See **Fig. 1-4.**

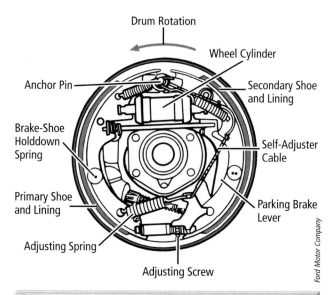

Ford Motor Company

Fig. 1-4 Drum brakes have shoes that push against the inside of a rotating drum. *What type of friction is at work here?*

Disc brakes have pads that clamp against a rotating rotor. Hand-operated bicycle brakes work in a similar way.

Drum brakes have shoes that press against the inside of the rotating brake drum. Early bicycle coaster brakes worked this way.

Pushing the vehicle's service brake pedal forces fluid through the braking system lines and hoses. The pressure of this fluid activates the brakes. The brake shoes and brake pads are stationary. The drums and rotors are moving. Kinetic friction between the brake shoes and drums, or brake pads and rotors, slows and then stops wheel rotation. Friction between the tires and the road stops the vehicle.

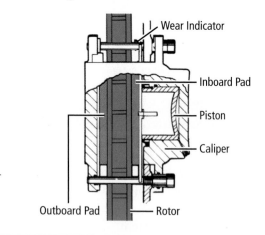

Robert Bosch Corp.

Fig. 1-3 Disc brake pads clamp around a rotating rotor to slow the vehicle. *What is created as a result of the braking action?*

The service brakes can be applied hard enough to lock the wheels (stop them from rotating). When brakes are locked, they no longer convert the vehicle's motion into heat. Success in stopping a vehicle then depends entirely on the kinetic friction between the tires and the road. If the kinetic friction is not great enough, the tires lose their grip on the road and the vehicle begins to skid.

The best braking performance occurs just before the tires begin to lose traction. This is the principle of antilock brakes.

Dual-Braking Systems

A **dual-braking system** has a dual-piston master cylinder, two fluid reservoirs, and two separate hydraulic systems. One hydraulic system controls the brakes of two wheels. The other hydraulic system controls the remaining two wheels. This arrangement provides additional safety. If one system fails, the other system continues to work.

The first dual-braking systems separated the front brakes from the rear brakes. More recent dual-braking systems are separated diagonally. Each system on a diagonally split system controls one front brake and one rear brake. See **Fig. 1-5**.

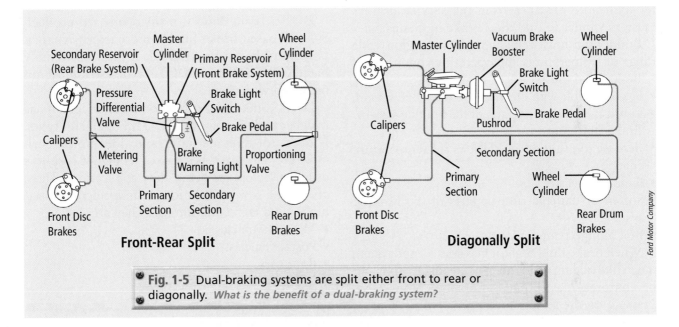

Fig. 1-5 Dual-braking systems are split either front to rear or diagonally. *What is the benefit of a dual-braking system?*

SECTION 2 KNOWLEDGE CHECK

1. Which type of service brakes use brake shoes?

2. What happens when a vehicle's service brake pedal is pushed?

3. What is the principle of antilock brakes?

4. Why are vehicles required to have dual-braking systems?

5. How are dual-braking systems split?

6. Which type of dual-braking system controls one front brake and one rear brake?

ASE TEST PREP

7. Technician A and Technician B are discussing the dual-braking system of a brand new front wheel drive car. Technician A says it is more likely that the brakes will be separated from front to rear. Technician B says it is more likely that they will be separated diagonally. Who is correct?

   ⓐ Technician A.

   ⓑ Technician B.

   ⓒ Both Technician A and Technician B.

   ⓓ Neither Technician A nor Technician B.

Section 3
Brake Fluid

Objectives:

B8 • Select, handle, store, and fill brake fluids to proper level.
   • Safely support a vehicle for brake servicing.

Vocabulary:
• **brake fluid**
• **brake pedal fade**

Brake Fluid Properties

Brake fluid is a liquid specially formulated to be used in hydraulic brake systems. It is used to transfer hydraulic pressure from the service brake's master cylinder to the wheel brake mechanisms.

Brake fluid must remain stable through a wide range of temperatures and operating conditions.
Brake fluid must:
• Be compatible with the metals in the brake system.
• Lubricate the moving parts of the braking system.
 Brake fluid must not:
• Become too thin or too thick as the temperature changes.
• Evaporate easily.
• Soften or damage rubber parts of the braking system.
• Boil at high temperatures.

When brake fluid boils, it becomes a vapor (gas), much like boiling water turns to steam. A vapor can be compressed; a liquid cannot be compressed. Pressing on the service brake pedal will compress the vapor in the hydraulic lines instead of transferring the pressure through the fluid. This can lead to partial or complete braking system failure, sometimes called **brake pedal fade**. In fact, vapor in the hydraulic braking system is the primary reason for brake pedal fade.

Brake Fluid Types The Society of Automotive Engineers (SAE) and the DOT have standards for brake fluid. The DOT specification is typically the one referred to. The three currently approved types are DOT 3, DOT 4, and DOT 5. The higher the number, the more strict the specifications, especially for the boiling point.

TECH TIP **Proper Brake Fluids.** Always follow the manufacturer's specifications. A vehicle's warranty may be voided if incorrect or incompatible brake fluids are used.

Both DOT 3 and DOT 4 brake fluid types are polyglycol-based. These are the most commonly used. They are inexpensive and compatible with most service brake systems.

DOT 5 brake fluid is a silicone-based product. Silicone-based brake fluid is more expensive than polyglycol-based brake fluid. It does not readily blend with DOT 3 and DOT 4 types, so it must not be mixed with them.

DOT 5 brake fluid offers some advantages. It has a higher boiling point than DOT 3 or DOT 4 types. It does not damage paint and does not absorb moisture. However, because of its higher cost, it is usually used only in heavy-duty applications. There are only a few applications where silicone-based brake fluid is in common use. They are:
• Military vehicles.
• Postal vehicles.
• Race cars.
• Motorcycles.

Safety First **Fluid Damage** DOT 3 and DOT 4 brake fluids are also strong paint solvents that can damage a vehicle's finish. Take care to avoid spilling these fluids on painted surfaces. Clean a spill immediately, using nonabrasive (nonscratching) soap and water.

Water in Brake Fluid The major disadvantage of polyglycol-based brake fluid is that it absorbs moisture. Because water boils at 212°F [100°C] and DOT 3 brake fluid boils at 401°F [205°C], any moisture in the brake fluid lowers its boiling point. Lowering the boiling point of brake fluid increases the chance of having vapor in the braking system.

Moisture gets into brake fluid through damaged seals and loose or faulty connections on the master cylinder. Moisture also enters through damaged brake hoses and seals on wheel cylinders and calipers.

After containers of brake fluid have been opened, they must be kept tightly capped when not in use. Brake fluid should not be stored for a long period of time. The longer it is stored, the more moisture it can absorb.

Brake Fluid Contamination Always ensure that the manufacturer's brake fluid is installed. If improper brake fluid is added, it could cause brake failure.

Pour brake fluid directly into the master cylinder reservoir from a sealed and clean container. This will decrease the chance of brake fluid contamination. It is important to keep dust and dirt out of the master cylinder reservoir. Never add anything but brake fluid to the reservoir. Petroleum products are particularly dangerous. They cause rubber parts to soften, swell, and fail. This could result in complete brake failure.

Installing Brake Fluid

As the disc brakes wear, the fluid level in the reservoir will drop. A leak in the system will also cause the fluid level to be low. If the level gets too low, there is a possibility that air can get into the hydraulic system. To prevent this, the fluid level must be kept above the minimum level at all times. See **Fig. 1-6.** Additionally, whenever the hydraulic system is serviced, the brake fluid will have to be replenished.

To install brake fluid in the master cylinder reservoir, do the following:

1. Clean all dirt and grease from the cap (or cover) with a clean shop rag as shown in **Fig. 1-7(a).**
2. Remove the cover by unscrewing the cap or prying off the wire bale with a screwdriver.

3. With the cover off, carefully pour fresh brake fluid into the reservoir until the level reaches the full or maximum mark. See **Fig. 1-7(b).**
4. If there is a screen in the reservoir, inspect it for any debris. If needed, clean the screen.
5. Replace the cap or cover. Secure it snugly, but do not over-tighten.

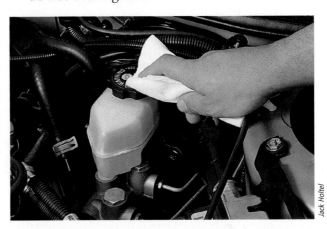

Fig. 1-7(a) Clean the master cylinder reservoir cap before unscrewing it. *Why is this important?*

Fig. 1-7(b) Always use fresh brake fluid from an unopened container. *What could happen if dirt or debris was in the brake fluid?*

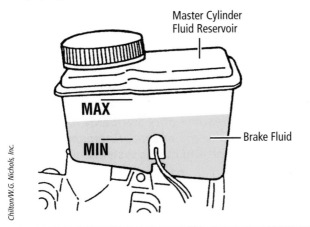

Master Cylinder
Fluid Reservoir

MAX

MIN

Brake Fluid

Fig. 1-6 The brake fluid level should be above the MIN mark on the reservoir. Do not overfill. *What might cause the fluid level to become critically low?*

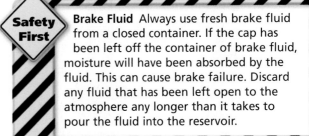

Safety First

Brake Fluid Always use fresh brake fluid from a closed container. If the cap has been left off the container of brake fluid, moisture will have been absorbed by the fluid. This can cause brake failure. Discard any fluid that has been left open to the atmosphere any longer than it takes to pour the fluid into the reservoir.

Brake Service Safety

Proper service procedures are vital to a technician's safety. Safety procedures, both personal and material, must always be observed.

Vehicle Support

Servicing wheel brake components requires lifting the vehicle. Portable floor jacks are designed only for lifting a vehicle. They cannot safely support a vehicle. Lift a vehicle with a floor jack. Then support the vehicle with safety stands.

When lifting a vehicle with a hydraulic or electric hoist, be sure to properly position the lift blocks under the vehicle's intended lift points. If you are unsure about the location of the vehicle's lift points, refer to its service manual. See **Fig. 1-8**. Make sure the hoist's safety support mechanism is engaged before working under the vehicle.

Brake Dust and Chemical Safety

Brake linings were once made of asbestos. Asbestos is a health hazard. It is no longer used for brakes on cars and light trucks. However, asbestos-lined brake shoes may still be in use on older vehicles. Therefore, do not use compressed air to blow brake dust from a brake assembly. Instead, use an aqueous brake cleaner as shown in **Fig. 1-9**.

Excellence in Math

Converting Temperatures

Vapor lock, overheated brakes, boiling radiators, and overheated engines all involve heat and temperature changes.

Most service manuals show temperatures in both degrees Celsius and degrees Fahrenheit. However, you will sometimes need to convert temperature readings from one system to the other. You could use thermometers that give temperatures both in degrees Celsius (°C) and degrees Fahrenheit (°F). **Fig. A.** But it's often easier to convert a temperature mathematically.

Refer to **Fig. A.** Look at the temperature difference between the boiling point and the freezing point of water. The change in Fahrenheit temperature from 212°F to 32°F corresponds to a change in Celsius from 100°C to 0°C.

The rate of change in Fahrenheit to Celsius is:

$$\frac{212 - 32}{100 - 0} = \frac{180}{100} = 1.8$$

For each increase of 1.8° Fahrenheit (1.8°F), there is an increase of 1° Celsius (1°C). Note that 0°C equals 32°F.

To convert Celsius temperatures to Fahrenheit temperatures, use this formula:

$$F = 1.8\,C + 32$$

The rate of change in Celsius to Fahrenheit is:

$$\frac{100 - 0}{212 - 32} = \frac{100}{180} = \frac{5}{9} = 0.556$$

For each increase of 5°C there is an increase of 9°F. Note that 32°F corresponds to 0°C.

To convert Fahrenheit temperatures to Celsius temperatures, you can use this formula:

$$C = \frac{5}{9}(F - 32) \text{ or } C = 0.556(F - 32)$$

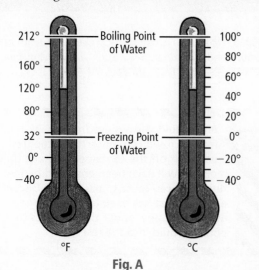

212° — Boiling Point — 100°
of Water
160° — — 80°
120° — — 60°
— — 40°
80° — — 20°
32° — Freezing Point — 0°
of Water
0° — — −20°
−40° — — −40°

°F   °C

Fig. A

Apply It!

Meets NATEF Mathematics Standards for using formulas to convert measurements between English and metric systems.

1. What is 98.6°F in °C?

2. DOT 3 brake fluid boils at 401°F. What is the equivalent temperature on the Celsius scale?

3. What is the Fahrenheit equivalent temperature for 40°C?

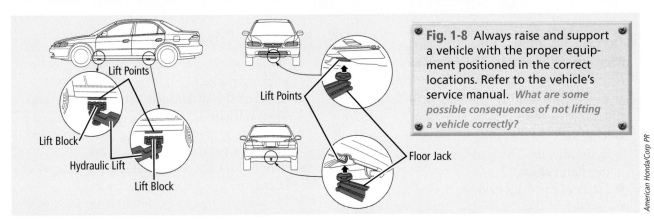

Fig. 1-8 Always raise and support a vehicle with the proper equipment positioned in the correct locations. Refer to the vehicle's service manual. *What are some possible consequences of not lifting a vehicle correctly?*

American Honda/Corp PR

Safety First   **Dust Prevention** When servicing wheel brakes, avoid creating potentially harmful brake lining dust.

When cleaning brake components, use an approved solvent, preferably in a brake washer. Spray solvents are also acceptable. Do not:
• Grind or scrape brake shoes or pads.
• Sand or file brake shoes or pads.
• Remove brake dust with compressed air or a brush.
   When using cleaning solvents:
• Wear goggles, especially when spraying solvents.
• If you get any brake fluid or other chemicals in your eyes, rinse them immediately with clean water.
• Always make sure there is adequate ventilation.
• Avoid breathing chemical vapors.
• Wear protective clothing such as aprons and gloves.

• Wash immediately after exposure to chemicals, including brake fluid.
• Change any clothes that get chemicals on them.

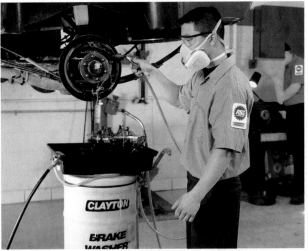

Jack Holtel

Fig. 1-9 Using an aqueous brake cleaner will help prevent brake dust from escaping into the environment. *What is the potential danger of brake dust?*

SECTION 3 KNOWLEDGE CHECK

1. What is brake fluid?

2. Identify at least two brake fluid properties.

3. Why is it a problem if brake fluid boils?

4. What are two advantages of DOT 5 brake fluid?

5. What are the steps to installing brake fluid?

6. What can be used to support a vehicle during service?

ASE TEST PREP

7. The most commonly used brake fluids are:
   ⓐ DOT 3 and DOT 5.
   ⓑ DOT 3 and DOT 4.
   ⓒ DOT 4 and DOT 5.
   ⓓ DOT 5 and DOT 6.

8. DOT 3 and DOT 4 brake fluids are:
   ⓐ water-based.
   ⓑ silicone-based.
   ⓒ polyglycol-based.
   ⓓ water- and polyglycol-based.

Key Points

Meets the following NATEF Standards for Brakes: describing brake functions and principles; selecting, handling, storing, and installing brake fluids.

- The service braking system is activated hydraulically. The parking brake is activated mechanically.
- Friction provides braking action in a vehicle.
- Service brakes have two main components: the master cylinder and the wheel brake mechanisms.
- The two basic types of service brakes are drum and disc.
- Dual-braking systems can be identified by the number of separate fluid reservoirs in the master cylinder.
- Brake fluids are chosen on the basis of intended use.
- A vehicle must be safely supported for brake servicing.

Review Questions

1. Which wheels are usually controlled by the parking brake?
2. Explain the difference between static and kinetic friction.
3. Which type of service brake can be compared to hand-operated bicycle brakes?
4. When does the best braking performance occur?
5. How many hydraulic systems are used in a dual-braking system?
6. What is a common cause of brake pedal fade?
7. Why is it important to use fresh brake fluid?
8. Why should you not use compressed air to clean dust from brakes?
9. Critical Thinking Consider the dangers of working with cleaning solvents. Identify at least three safety practices for using such solvents.
10. Critical Thinking When using a hydraulic lift, where should the lift blocks be placed?

Excellence in Communication

Taking Notes

Taking notes is a life skill. The ability to take good notes can be useful to you in many situations. You can use this skill when listening to a person describe how to do a procedure. You can take notes when you want to buy an item. For example, you can organize information from magazines, catalogs, and advertisements. Your notes will help you compare prices and features and make a wise decision.

A successful technician learns how to take notes to identify new parts or systems. Good notes will help you learn a procedure you are doing for the first time. There is often a blank page for notes in service manuals. In this text, you will read about new components and systems. Take notes on the material so you have a reference for study.

Often, important terms are printed in *italics* or **boldfaced** type. These print types signal you to take note of them. Using the titles of chapters and sections is a good way to organize your notes.

Apply It!

Meets NATEF Communications Standards for study habits and note-taking.

1. Read through this chapter.
2. As you read, look for **boldfaced** words and phrases.
3. Write down and define or explain each term.
4. Make these terms part of your notes for this chapter.

AUTOMOTIVE SERVICE EXCELLENCE
TEST PREP

Answering the following practice questions will help you prepare for the ASE certification tests.

1. One of the main functions of a master cylinder is to:

   ⓐ boost braking power by supplying increased force.

   ⓑ convert hydraulic pressure to mechanical force.

   ⓒ convert mechanical force to hydraulic pressure.

   ⓓ remove impurities from brake fluid.

2. Technician A says that a power brake booster supplies increased forces needed by the brakes without increased pedal pressure. Technician B says that increased pedal pressure is required. Who is correct?

   ⓐ Technician A.

   ⓑ Technician B.

   ⓒ Both Technician A and Technician B.

   ⓓ Neither Technician A nor Technician B.

3. The two types of friction are:

   ⓐ static friction and resistance friction.

   ⓑ static friction and kinetic friction.

   ⓒ heat friction and kinetic friction.

   ⓓ stable friction and dynamic friction.

4. Technician A says that the service brakes are designed to be more powerful than the vehicle's engine and can even stall the engine when applied. Technician B says that the service brakes are not more powerful than the vehicle's engine and cannot stall the engine when applied. Who is correct?

   ⓐ Technician A.

   ⓑ Technician B.

   ⓒ Both Technician A and Technician B.

   ⓓ Neither Technician A nor Technician B.

5. Which characteristic is desirable in brake fluid?

   ⓐ Evaporates easily.

   ⓑ Boils at high temperatures.

   ⓒ Does not absorb moisture.

   ⓓ Thins as temperature increases.

6. The DOT specification for brakes has a single number at the end. Which of the following brake fluids has the strictest specification, especially regarding boiling point?

   ⓐ DOT 3.

   ⓑ DOT 4.

   ⓒ DOT 5.

   ⓓ They all have the same specification.

7. Brake fluids are polyglycol based or silicon based. The types must not be mixed. Which of the following is silicone-based?

   ⓐ DOT 3.

   ⓑ DOT 4.

   ⓒ DOT 5.

   ⓓ All of the above.

8. Technician A says that a low brake fluid level may cause air to enter the hydraulic system. Technician B says that the fluid level drops as the disc brakes wear. Who is correct?

   ⓐ Technician A.

   ⓑ Technician B.

   ⓒ Both Technician A and Technician B.

   ⓓ Neither Technician A nor Technician B.

9. Technician A says that brake fluid must not be stored for a long period of time. Technician B says that the longer brake fluid is stored the more moisture it can absorb. Who is correct?

   ⓐ Technician A.

   ⓑ Technician B.

   ⓒ Both Technician A and Technician B.

   ⓓ Neither Technician A nor Technician B.

10. Technician A says that in cleaning brake components a spray solvent is not acceptable. Technician B says that brakes can only be cleaned by using an approved solvent in a brake washer. Who is correct?

    ⓐ Technician A.

    ⓑ Technician B.

    ⓒ Both Technician A and Technician B.

    ⓓ Neither Technician A nor Technician B.

Section 1
Hydraulics

Section 2
Brake Master
Cylinder

Section 3
Brake System
Valves

Diagnosing & Repairing the Hydraulic System

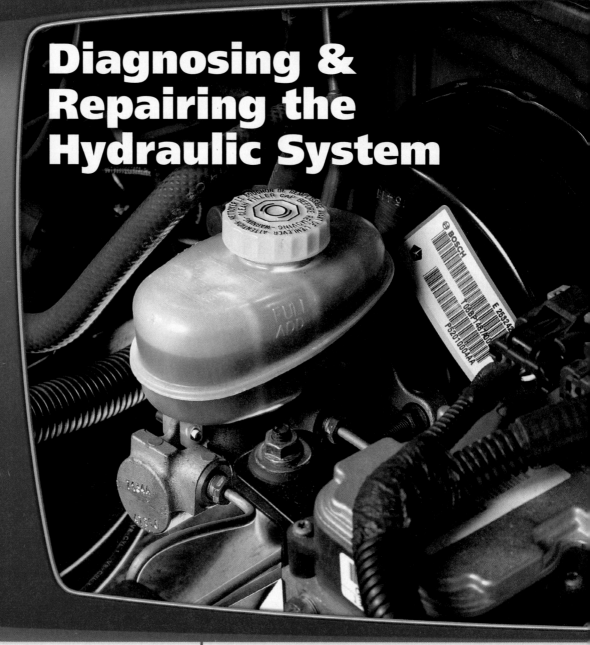

Customer's Concern

Juan Ortega is obviously distressed. He was driving his father's car in heavy traffic when he briefly lost control of the steering. Your service center was the closest facility he could find. He needs your help.

After taking a moment to regain his composure, Juan explains that he was slowly approaching a traffic light and preparing to stop. As he lightly pressed on the brake pedal, he heard a strange squealing noise coming from the front end of the vehicle. At the same time, he realized he could no longer steer the car. Once Juan took his foot off the brake pedal, the squealing stopped. Steering was restored. He made it safely through the intersection.

Technician's Challenge

As the service technician, you need to find answers to these questions:

1. Before asking questions and investigating the automotive problem, what can you do to help Juan?

2. Slamming on the brakes would undoubtedly cause steering loss, but why would Juan lose steering control when only lightly applying the brakes?

3. Are faulty brake components to blame for the squealing noise, or could the noise (and the steering loss) be caused by the tires skidding on the pavement?

Section 1
Hydraulics

Objectives:
- Describe how hydraulics is used to transfer motion.
- Describe how hydraulics is used to transfer force.

Vocabulary:
- hydraulics
- hydraulic pressure
- Pascal's law

Properties of Hydraulics

Hydraulics is the process of applying pressure to a liquid to transfer force or motion. The pressure applied to a liquid to create the force is called **hydraulic pressure.** Hydraulics represents the application of **Pascal's law.** Developed by the French mathematician Blaise Pascal, this law states that when there is an increase in pressure at any point in a confined liquid, there is an equal increase in pressure at every other point in the container. In automotive technology, the principles of Pascal's law are essential in diagnosing pressure concerns in the braking system. In an automotive brake system, hydraulic pressure creates the force to move the brake shoes or pads into contact with the brake drums or rotors.

A gas that is compressed has a smaller volume. Gas can be compressed by applying pressure to it. Liquids cannot be compressed. See **Fig. 2-1.** That is why hydraulic pressure is used to transmit motion and force in an automotive brake system. All the pressure applied to the liquid is transferred as motion and force.

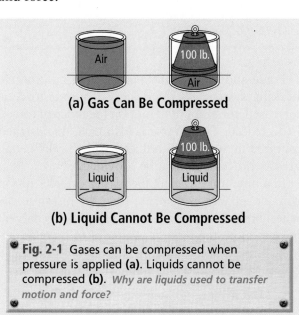

(a) Gas Can Be Compressed

(b) Liquid Cannot Be Compressed

Fig. 2-1 Gases can be compressed when pressure is applied **(a)**. Liquids cannot be compressed **(b)**. *Why are liquids used to transfer motion and force?*

The Transfer of Motion

An apply, or input, piston and an output piston are shown in the same cylinder in **Fig. 2-2.** There is liquid between the pistons. When enough pressure is applied to move the apply piston 8 inches [203 mm], the output piston moves the same distance and in the same direction.

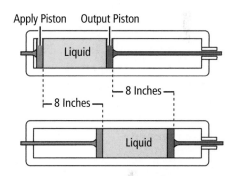

Fig. 2-2 A liquid can transmit both force and motion. When the apply piston is moved, the output piston moves the same distance.

The two pistons need not be in the same cylinder. A tube can be used to transfer hydraulic pressure from one cylinder to another as shown in **Fig. 2-3.**

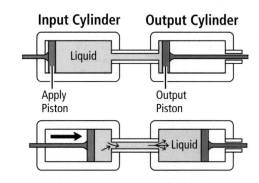

Fig. 2-3 A liquid can transmit motion and force through a tube from one cylinder to another. *Does the length of the connecting tube change the amount of movement of the output piston?*

In automotive brake systems, the input cylinder is called the master cylinder. The output, or remote, cylinders are the vehicle's wheel cylinders or calipers.

Applying force to the apply piston transfers hydraulic pressure through the connecting tube to the remote cylinder. Pressure in the remote cylinder forces the output piston to move. If the master cylinder and a wheel cylinder are the same diameter, the amount of force and movement is the same in both cylinders. Neither the length nor the diameter of the tube connecting the two cylinders affects the amount of movement of the output piston.

The Transfer of Force

When force is applied to an enclosed liquid, the pressure created by the force is transmitted equally in all directions. In **Fig. 2-4**, the piston has a surface area of 1 square inch [6.45 cm²]. A force of 100 pounds is applied to the piston. The piston therefore is applying 100 pounds per square inch (psi) [690 kPa] pressure to the liquid. Notice that all gauges show the same pressure.

The size of the piston is a factor in the amount of pressure applied to the fluid. If the surface area of the piston is doubled and the force applied is the same, half the pressure results.

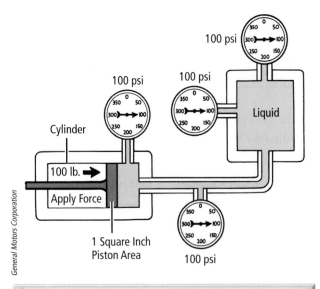

General Motors Corporation

Fig. 2-4 The pressure of a liquid is the same throughout the system. *What do you think the gauges would read if there were two tubes leading from the cylinder?*

In a system with more than one remote cylinder, the applied force is equally distributed to each cylinder. The output force of the remote cylinders will differ from each other, however, if the remote cylinder pistons are of varying sizes.

A remote cylinder with a piston half the size of the input piston delivers only half the force. A remote cylinder with the same size piston delivers the same amount of force. A remote cylinder with a piston twice the size of the input piston delivers twice the force. In other words, the larger the output piston, the greater the output force. See **Fig. 2-5**. This difference in applied force and output force is why light brake pedal pressure can stop a heavy car.

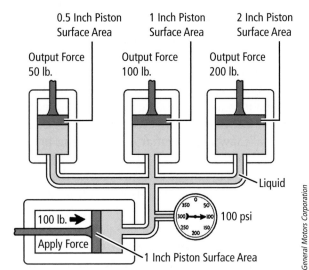

General Motors Corporation

Fig. 2-5 The force created by the apply piston is called system pressure. The output force of each remote cylinder depends upon the output piston's surface area. *What would the output force be if the output piston had a surface area of 4 square inches [25.8 cm²]?*

Force and motion are related in an automotive braking system. As the designed output force is increased, the amount of motion (distance of travel) is decreased. The reverse is also true. As designed required input force is reduced at the brake pedal, greater movement must be provided.

In a disc brake system, the master cylinder piston is much smaller in diameter than the piston in the wheel brake caliper. This means the brake pedal will have to move the master cylinder piston a relatively long distance. Being larger, the caliper piston will move only a short distance but will have increased force.

Excellence in Math

Calculating Hydraulic Pressure

You can calculate the pressure in a hydraulic brake system using the formula:

$$P = \frac{F}{A}$$

P is the pressure in pounds per square inch (psi). F is the mechanical force applied to a piston in pounds (lb). A is the surface area of the piston in square inches (in^2).

Here's an example. A mechanical force of 100 pounds is applied to the brake pedal pushrod. This force is transferred onto a master cylinder piston with a surface area of 2 square inches. What is the pressure in the braking system?

$$P = \frac{F}{A} = \frac{100 \text{ lb}}{2 \text{ in}^2} = 50 \text{ psi}$$

What is the pressure if the same force is applied to a master cylinder piston with twice the surface area?

$$P = \frac{F}{A} = \frac{100 \text{ lb}}{4 \text{ in}^2} = 25 \text{ psi}$$

Some manufacturers' specifications show pressure measured in the metric unit kPa, or kilopascals. You can convert pressure measured in psi to the metric form by remembering that:

$$1 \text{ psi} = 6.9 \text{ kPa}$$

To convert the pressure in the first example, use the formula:

$$50 \text{ psi} \times 6.9 = 345 \text{ kPa}$$

Apply It!

Meets NATEF Mathematics Standards for manipulating algebraic equations, using symbols, equivalent forms, and converting between the English and metric systems.

1. You need to calculate the pressure in a hydraulic brake system. What is the pressure in the system if a force of 100 pounds is applied to a piston with an area of 0.5 square inches? Give your answer in psi and kPa.

2. How would you calculate the force needed to produce a pressure when you know the surface area of the piston?
   Rearrange the equation $P = \frac{F}{A}$ to find F.

3. How much force must be applied to a piston with a surface area of 0.25 square inches to create a pressure of 160 psi?

SECTION 1 KNOWLEDGE CHECK

1. Define Pascal's law.

2. Why is liquid used between pistons rather than a solid connection?

3. Does an apply piston need to be in the same cylinder as the output piston?

4. How is hydraulic system pressure calculated?

5. What is the force created by the apply piston called?

6. Explain how light brake pedal pressure can stop a heavy car.

ASE TEST PREP

7. Technician A says brake fluid transmits motion. Technician B says brake fluid transmits force. Who is correct?
   ⓐ Technician A.
   ⓑ Technician B.
   ⓒ Both Technician A and Technician B.
   ⓓ Neither Technician A nor Technician B.

● *Section 2*
Brake Master Cylinder

Objectives:

B3 ● Check master cylinder for internal and external leaks and proper operation.

B4 ● Remove, bench bleed, and reinstall master cylinder.

B6 ● Inspect brake lines, flexible hoses, and fittings for leaks, dents, kinks, rust, cracks, bulging or wear; tighten loose fittings and supports.

B7 ● Fabricate and/or install brake lines (double flare and ISO types); replace hoses, fittings, and supports as needed.

B1 ● Diagnose pressure concerns in the brake system using hydraulic principles (Pascal's law).

B2 ● Measure brake pedal height; determine necessary action.

E5 ● Measure and adjust master cylinder pushrod length.

Vocabulary:
● **brake master cylinder**
● **brake lines**

Types of Master Cylinders

The **brake master cylinder** is a device that converts the force applied to the pedal into hydraulic pressure. It provides pressurized fluid to the remote cylinders. In an automobile the remote cylinders that activate the drum brakes are called the wheel cylinders. The cylinders that activate the disc brakes are called calipers.

Integral Master Cylinder

An integral master cylinder is a one-piece, cast-iron component with a dual reservoir. See **Fig 2-6**. It is called an integral master cylinder because the fluid reservoirs are integrated into the master cylinder assembly. This type of master cylinder is still found on some older large cars and light trucks.

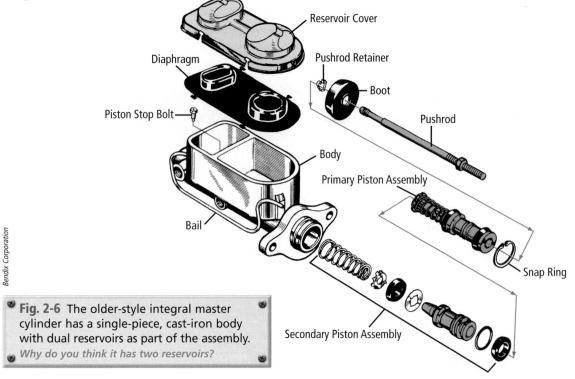

Bendix Corporation

Reservoir Cover

Diaphragm

Pushrod Retainer

Boot

Piston Stop Bolt

Pushrod

Body

Primary Piston Assembly

Bail

Snap Ring

Secondary Piston Assembly

Fig. 2-6 The older-style integral master cylinder has a single-piece, cast-iron body with dual reservoirs as part of the assembly. *Why do you think it has two reservoirs?*

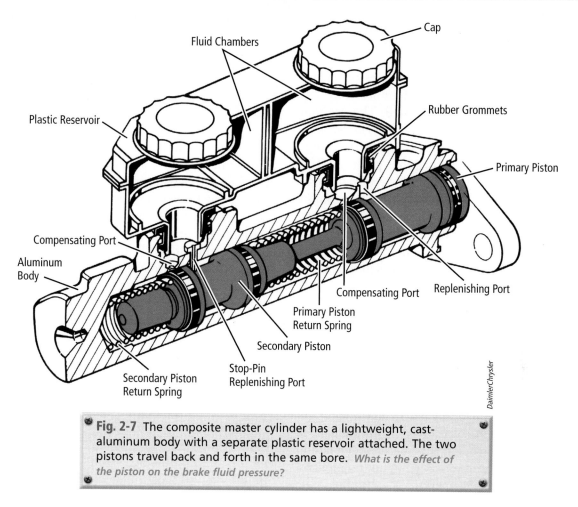

Fluid Chambers

Cap

Plastic Reservoir

Rubber Grommets

Primary Piston

Compensating Port

Aluminum Body

Compensating Port

Replenishing Port

Primary Piston Return Spring

Secondary Piston

Secondary Piston Return Spring

Stop-Pin Replenishing Port

DaimlerChrysler

Fig. 2-7 The composite master cylinder has a lightweight, cast-aluminum body with a separate plastic reservoir attached. The two pistons travel back and forth in the same bore. *What is the effect of the piston on the brake fluid pressure?*

Composite Master Cylinder

Most vehicles now have composite master cylinder assemblies. The master cylinder is made of cast aluminum. A plastic reservoir, holding the brake fluid, is attached directly to the master cylinder with rubber grommets that maintain a tight seal. See **Fig. 2-7**.

Master Cylinder Operation

A master cylinder converts mechanical brake pedal force into hydraulic pressure. Both integral and composite master cylinders work in the same way. The cylinder bore is filled with brake fluid. When the driver presses the brake pedal, the piston inside the bore moves forward. The force of the piston acting on the fluid transfers pressure to the wheel cylinders. When the driver releases the brake pedal, a spring moves the piston back to its original position. As the piston moves back, piston force and resulting fluid pressure are removed.

In a dual master cylinder, two pistons move back and forth in the same bore. See **Fig. 2-7**. The space in front of each piston is the fluid chamber. It is kept full by the reservoir above it.

There are two openings at the bottom of each reservoir. The openings toward the front are the compensating ports. These ports are open to the reservoir so fluid can enter and leave the high-pressure chambers. The openings toward the rear are the replenishing ports. These ports are open to the reservoir so fluid can keep the low-pressure chambers filled.

Safety First

Master Cylinder Reservoir Always replenish the master cylinder reservoir to the proper level with fresh brake fluid from a sealed container. Brake fluid attracts moisture from the air. Moisture in the brake system can cause rust. Rust particles in the fluid can wear away at the rubber seals. Look for leaks or excessively worn brake pads.

When the brakes are applied, the piston cup (seal) moves past the compensating port and seals it off from the bore. The cup seals the chamber and piston so fluid cannot flow into the low-pressure chamber.

As the piston continues its forward travel, fluid pressure builds. Pressure is transferred through the brake lines to the wheel cylinders.

The replenishing port fills the low-pressure chamber behind the piston. If this chamber were left empty, a vacuum would be created. The vacuum would try to pull the piston back. See **Fig. 2-8(a).**

When the brake pedal is released, return springs move the pistons to their original position. The pistons move faster than the fluid can return through the lines. This motion creates a partial vacuum in the high-pressure chamber. The piston cup allows fluid to flow from the low-pressure chamber into the high-pressure chamber. The fluid flows around the piston cup or through small holes in the piston as shown in **Fig. 2-8(b).**

Quick-Takeup Master Cylinders

This master cylinder design is used on disc brake systems with low-drag calipers. The calipers used in low-drag disc brake systems have special seals. These seals quickly pull the piston back into the bore.

In a low-drag disc brake system, there is a relatively large gap between the brake pads and the rotor. As a result, it takes a lot of fluid to move the caliper pistons the greater distance. The caliper pistons must travel the distance quickly but not require any excessive brake pedal travel.

> **TECH TIP** **Clean Brake Fluid.** Always clean off the master cylinder reservoir cover before removing it. This will prevent dirt from getting into the brake fluid. Also, always use fresh brake fluid when filling the master cylinder.

In the quick-takeup master cylinder, the primary piston operates in a step-bore cylinder. This is a cylinder with two different diameters. See **Fig. 2-9.**

When the brakes are first applied, fluid from the large-diameter low-pressure bore flows past the cup (seal) into the primary high-pressure chamber. This large amount of fluid quickly applies the brakes connected to the primary chamber. The fluid action also forces the secondary piston to quickly apply the brakes connected to the secondary chamber.

The quick-takeup design supplies a large amount of fluid with relatively short brake pedal travel. Both chambers are supplied with more fluid than is needed to apply the brakes. A quick-takeup valve opens as the pressure builds and allows the excess fluid to flow back into the reservoir.

Some master cylinders have a fluid-level sensor that illuminates a warning light on the instrument panel when the fluid level drops too low.

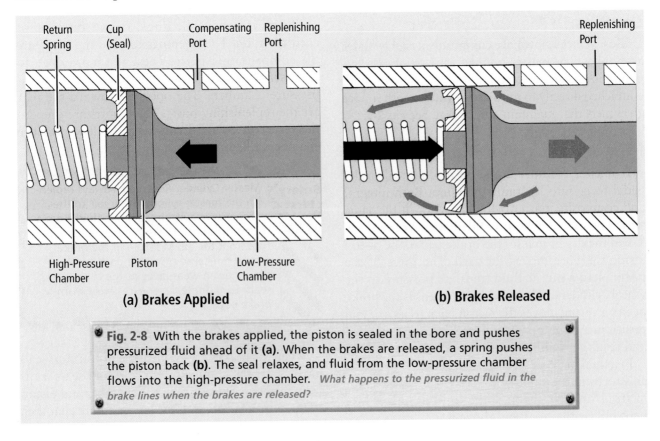

(a) **Brakes Applied**

(b) **Brakes Released**

Fig. 2-8 With the brakes applied, the piston is sealed in the bore and pushes pressurized fluid ahead of it **(a)**. When the brakes are released, a spring pushes the piston back **(b)**. The seal relaxes, and fluid from the low-pressure chamber flows into the high-pressure chamber. *What happens to the pressurized fluid in the brake lines when the brakes are released?*

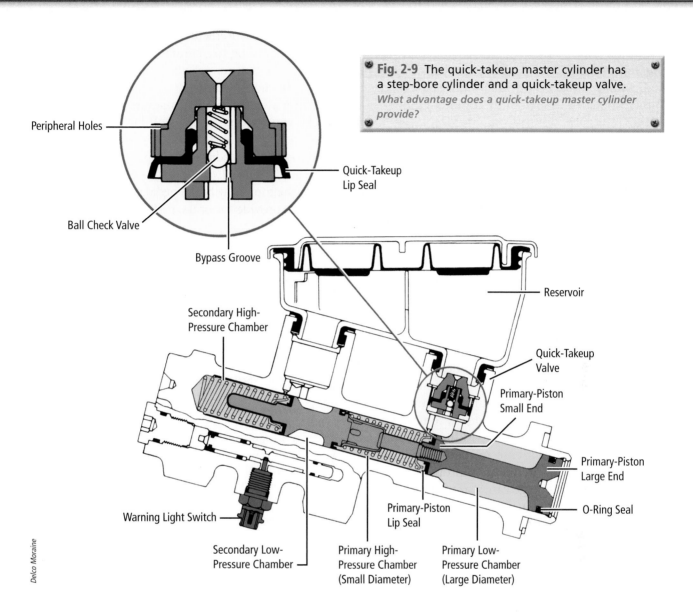

Peripheral Holes

Ball Check Valve

Bypass Groove

Quick-Takeup Lip Seal

Secondary High-Pressure Chamber

Reservoir

Quick-Takeup Valve

Primary-Piston Small End

Primary-Piston Large End

O-Ring Seal

Warning Light Switch

Secondary Low-Pressure Chamber

Primary-Piston Lip Seal

Primary High-Pressure Chamber (Small Diameter)

Primary Low-Pressure Chamber (Large Diameter)

Delco Moraine

Fig. 2-9 The quick-takeup master cylinder has a step-bore cylinder and a quick-takeup valve. *What advantage does a quick-takeup master cylinder provide?*

Master Cylinder Diagnosis

If the brake fluid reservoir is low, inspect the master cylinder for leaks. External fluid leaks cause a partial brake failure when fluid is lost. Internal leaks in the master cylinder cause brake failures with no loss of brake fluid. External fluid leaks can occur anywhere in the brake system including the master cylinder, but internal leaks with no fluid loss occur only within the master cylinder. Check the master cylinder booster mount, vacuum check valve, vacuum supply hose, or the rear master cylinder seal. It may be necessary to unbolt the master cylinder from the power booster. Refer to the manufacturer's manual for specific procedures.

The dual master cylinder has greatly enhanced safety by providing a partial brake system when a hydraulic leak occurs. However, a very dangerous condition may exist if the master cylinder itself develops an internal leak or a fluid bypass condition. This occurs if pressurized brake fluid leaks past the internal piston cups and returns to the reservoir while the brakes are applied. This will allow the brake pedal to go all the way to the floor intermittently or on each application. This condition can be caused by excessive wear of the cylinder bore and rubber cups or by damage caused by brake fluid contamination. Petroleum products or mineral oil contamination will cause the rubber cups to swell and become distorted so that they can no longer provide a good seal. Moisture or water contamination can cause iron parts to rust or aluminum parts to corrode and score the seals.

A leaking master cylinder creates a dangerous condition that should be corrected by replacing the master cylinder and flushing the brake system. Caliper and wheel cylinders should also be serviced if the problem was caused by contamination.

 Safety First **Brake Fluid Contamination** Many vehicle manufacturers now suggest that the brake system be properly flushed with new fluid at periodic intervals to help eliminate fluid contamination.

Brake Drag

If the brakes drag on only one wheel, the cause is usually a hardware problem at that wheel only. If the brakes on two wheels or on all wheels lock up or drag after the brake system has warmed up during normal use, the cause may be a defective master cylinder. If the master cylinder's compensating ports are plugged by debris or swollen rubber primary cups, brake fluid cannot return to the master cylinder reservoir. Instead, it becomes trapped in the brake system. The trapped fluid expands as the system heats up with use and causes application of the brakes in that circuit. An improperly adjusted or binding brake linkage can also trap fluid in the system by keeping the master cylinder pistons from completely returning to the released position.

To diagnose this problem, drive the vehicle to warm up the brake fluid and verify the complaint. Then place the vehicle on a lift, and turn each wheel by hand to verify drag. Loosen the master cylinder retaining fasteners at the booster or bulkhead, and pull the master cylinder straight forward to remove any force from the linkage. If this causes the brake drag to disappear, the linkage is improperly adjusted or binding. If the brakes still drag, loosen the brake lines at the master cylinder to relieve fluid pressure and retighten. If this causes the brake drag to disappear, the master cylinder is defective. It needs to be replaced.

Brake Pedal Height Adjustment
Many manufacturers do not provide for linkage adjustments. In those systems, a problem is usually due to a binding linkage condition. Some manufacturers include an adjustable pedal stop or stop light switch to adjust brake pedal height. Some manufacturers provide an adjustable brake pedal push rod to adjust brake pedal free play.

Pedal height and free play can be measured by placing a ruler between the brake pedal pad and the vehicle floor. Pressing the pedal lightly with a finger will allow measurement of free play. Adjust pedal linkage according to manufacturer's specifications.

If a manufacturer specifies a brake pedal height, the height should be adjusted according to the manufacturer's instructions. To adjust the brake pedal height, you may need to back off the stop light switch adjustment and adjust the length of the brake booster push rod. Then readjust the stop light switch. Brake pedal height is usually measured from the vehicle floor pan to the top of the brake pedal pad. Not all manufacturers provide for brake pedal height adjustment.

Power Brake Booster Push Rod Adjustment
Some manufacturers provide for an adjustment of a power brake booster push rod to the master cylinder. A gauge provided by the manufacturer is usually needed to make this adjustment. Push rod adjustments are usually needed only after inappropriate adjustments have been made in an attempt to solve other problems.

 TECH TIP **Driver Adjustable Pedals.** Do not confuse the service adjustment of pedal linkage with driver adjustable pedals. This is a new power accessory that works much like a power seat. It allows the driver to adjust the height of all pedals from the floor by the touch of an electrical switch. This feature, along with tilt steering columns and adjustable seats, aids in driver comfort.

Master Cylinder Bench Bleed

Bench bleed the master cylinder as follows:

1. Remove the master cylinder, using the manufacturer's service manual procedures. Some master cylinders can be "bench bled" prior to installation.
2. Mount the master cylinder in a vise, with the reservoir attached.
3. Attach the bleed lines to outlet ports in the master cylinder.
4. Run the bleed lines to a clean catch container that contains clean brake fluid.
5. Place the catch container below the level of the master cylinder outlet ports.
6. Fill the master cylinder reservoir with the clean brake fluid.
7. Using a wooden dowel, slowly push the master cylinder primary and secondary pistons. This compresses and drives air from the master cylinder.
8. Be sure fluid in the reservoir is maintained at the full level.

9. Repeat Step 7 several times until there are no more air bubbles in the fluid that moved to the catch container.
10. Remove the bleed tubes and cap the outlet ports.
11. Replace the reservoir filler cap.
12. Remove the master cylinder from the vise and reinstall according to the manufacturer's recommended procedures.

Brake Lines

Brake lines are the tubes and hoses that carry the brake fluid from the master cylinder to the wheel cylinders and calipers. There are two types of brake lines: rigid and flexible. Rigid lines run from the master cylinder to a connection point near the wheel brake. Flexible lines run from the connection point to the wheel cylinder or caliper.

Rigid brake lines are made of steel. Copper or brass tubing is too soft to safely handle the fluid pressure.

Replacement rigid brake lines are available as straight tubing or preformed (with all the required bends) to fit a particular vehicle model. In all cases the ends are flared to provide leakproof connections. A double flare looks like the bell of a trumpet bent back over itself. The International Standards Organization (ISO) flare resembles a bubble. See **Fig. 2-10.** Connections are made with fittings called flare nuts.

Special tools are used to make the flares. Technicians must be careful when forming the flares. Any damaged or cracked flares must be cut off and new ones formed. For this reason it is better to install tubing that has been "factory" (previously) flared. It comes in many lengths, and new flare nuts are included. When possible, use preformed brake lines. Replace brake lines, fittings, or supports as needed.

A vehicle's chassis and suspension move in relative motion to each other. To allow for this relative motion, there must be a flexible brake line between the chassis and the wheel brakes. Brake hoses made of rubber allow suspension movement. To prevent these hoses from bursting under high pressure, they are made of three layers:
• A flexible inner tubing.
• Reinforcement of braided fabric.
• Outer tubing for protection.

The fitting on one end of the brake hose fits the flared fitting and flare nut of a steel brake line. The other end of the brake hose has a threaded fitting or a banjo fitting sealed with copper sealing washers. See **Fig. 2-11.** Inspect rubber brake hoses at the brake line connection. Hoses should be free of cracks, dry rot, bulging, or other damage. Replace hoses, fittings, or supports as needed.

ISO Style Tubing Flare

ISO Flare Tube Nut

Tube — Seat

DaimlerChrysler

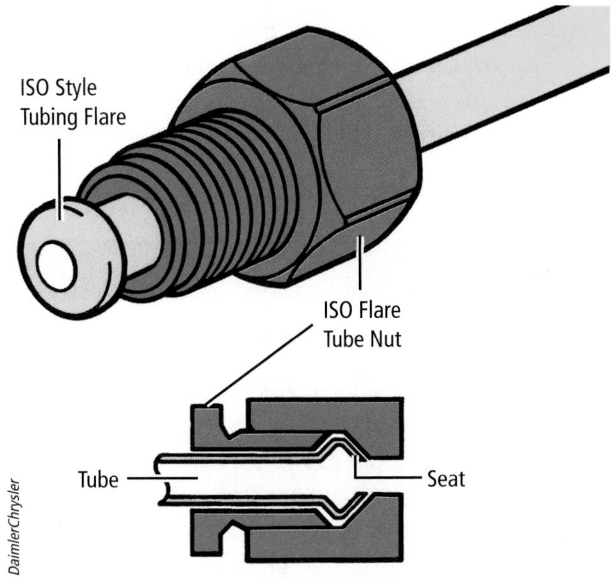

Fig. 2-10 The International Standards Organization (ISO) flare resembles a bubble. This flare has become the worldwide standard. *Why are the ends of brake lines flared?*

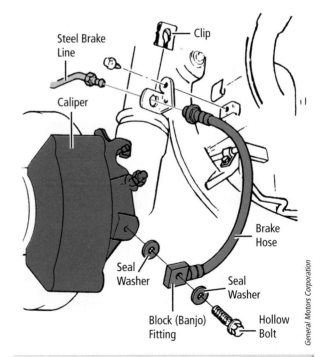

Steel Brake Line

Clip

Caliper

Brake Hose

Seal Washer

Seal Washer

Block (Banjo) Fitting

Hollow Bolt

General Motors Corporation

Fig. 2-11 A flexible brake hose connects the stationary, rigid brake line and the movable parts of the vehicle such as the caliper. *Why can rigid lines not be used throughout?*

Hydraulic Circuits

Early brake systems had a single hydraulic circuit with a single-piston master cylinder. In 1967 the U.S. Department of Transportation mandated dual master cylinders for all vehicles. The use of dual master cylinders in dual hydraulic circuit brake systems decreases the number of brake system failures. If one circuit fails, partial braking is still available. Only very rarely do both brake circuits fail at the same time. Dual-circuit brake systems are either front-rear split or diagonally split.

Front-Rear Split Systems

Front-rear split systems are found mostly on rear-wheel-drive (RWD) vehicles with front disc brakes and rear drum brakes. One circuit serves the front brakes; the other circuit serves the rear brakes. See **Fig. 2-12(a)**.

Front-wheel-drive (FWD) vehicles have much more weight in the front than in the rear. Therefore, the front brakes must provide up to 85 percent of the braking. If a FWD vehicle has a front-rear split system and the front half fails, the rear brakes may not be able to stop the car effectively.

Diagonally Split Systems

In a diagonally split system, the left front and right rear wheels share one hydraulic circuit and the right front and left rear wheels share the other. See **Fig. 2-12(b)**. Should there be a failure in one circuit, the other circuit can still provide stopping power.

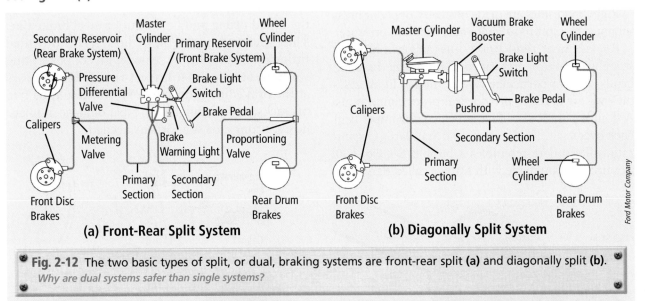

(a) Front-Rear Split System

(b) Diagonally Split System

Ford Motor Company

Fig. 2-12 The two basic types of split, or dual, braking systems are front-rear split **(a)** and diagonally split **(b)**. *Why are dual systems safer than single systems?*

SECTION 2 KNOWLEDGE CHECK

1. Name the remote cylinders that activate drum brakes and disc brakes, respectively.

2. How should brake pedal height be measured?

3. Explain the process for bench bleeding a master cylinder.

4. Which type of brake line flare has become the worldwide standard?

5. Why are diagonally split brake systems most effective for front-wheel-drive vehicles?

ASE TEST PREP

6. Technician A says a quick-takeup master cylinder allows the fluid to return quickly when the brakes are released. Technician B says quick-takeup master cylinders are used on low-drag brake systems. Who is correct?

   ⓐ Technician A.

   ⓑ Technician B.

   ⓒ Both Technician A and Technician B.

   ⓓ Neither Technician A nor Technician B.

● Section 3
Brake System Valves

Objectives:

B9 ● Inspect, test, and/or replace metering (hold-off), proportioning (balance), pressure differential, and combination valves.

B10 ● Inspect, test, and adjust height (load) sensing proportioning valve.

B12 ● Bleed (manual, pressure, vacuum or surge) brake system.

B13 ● Flush hydraulic system.

Vocabulary:

● **metering valve**
● **pressure differential valve**
● **proportioning valve**
● **residual pressure check valve**
● **brake bleeding**

Types of Control Valves

There are typically five types of control valves in automotive braking systems:
• Metering valves.
• Pressure differential valves.
• Proportioning valves.
• Residual pressure check valves.
• Combination valves.

Metering Valve

Most vehicles that have front disc and rear drum brakes are equipped with metering valves. See **Fig. 2-13**. The **metering valve** is the valve that controls, or delays, the flow of brake fluid to the front brakes.

The rear drum brakes take longer to respond than the front disc brakes. The metering valve ensures that front disc brakes do not act before the rear drum brakes. The delay is long enough to allow the drum brakes time to react. This delay is particularly necessary during light braking and on slick road surfaces.

Metering valves are not usually found on FWD cars that have diagonally split brake systems. Vehicles with similar type brakes (front and rear) may not need a metering valve. Brakes of the same type front and rear generally require the same amount of time to apply.

Pressure Differential Valve

In a dual system, a **pressure differential valve** is the valve that senses the pressure in each circuit. See **Fig. 2-13**. The valve piston stays centered as long as the hydraulic pressure in both circuits is balanced.

If the pressure drops in either circuit, the piston moves away from center. This movement triggers a switch that turns on the brake warning light. The warning light indicates a partial failure of the braking system. Refer to the manufacturer's manual for specific diagnosis and test procedures.

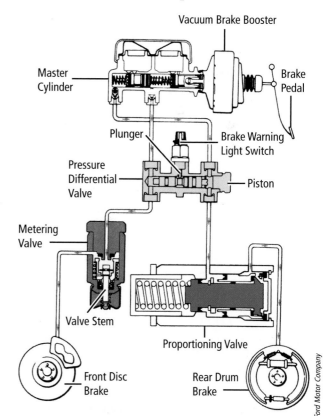

Ford Motor Company

Fig. 2-13 Control valves used on a typical front disc brake and rear drum brake system. *What is the purpose of a pressure differential valve?*

Proportioning Valve

A **proportioning valve** is a valve that reduces the amount of braking force at the rear wheels on front disc and rear drum brakes systems. During hard braking, forward momentum shifts the vehicle weight toward the front. The weight shift requires less braking force at the rear wheels. Too much braking force at the rear could cause the rear wheels to lock up.

The proportioning valve has no effect on braking force during normal braking. However, during hard braking the proportioning valve reduces the amount of pressure to the rear brakes once the pressure reaches a certain point. This is called the split point. See **Fig. 2-14**.

A proportioning valve should not be confused with a metering valve. A proportioning valve regulates braking force to the rear wheels. A metering valve delays fluid flow to the front brakes.

Proportioning valves are most commonly found in the master cylinder outlets. In some vehicles they are found in the brake lines near the rear brakes. If the vehicle has a problem with either front or rear brake lockup under normal braking, inspect the proportioning valve. Diagnose and test the valve, using the manufacturer's recommended procedures. Clean, adjust, or replace as needed.

Some light-duty trucks have load-sensing proportioning valves. See **Fig. 2-15**. The load-sensing proportioning valves adjust the pressure to the rear brakes according to changes in the load. The valves sense vehicle load by measuring the distance between the truck bed and the axle. As the load increases, the distance decreases. The heavier the load, the greater the pressure supplied to the rear brakes. Inspect the load-sensing proportioning valves. Diagnose and test per manufacturer's recommended procedures. Clean, adjust, or replace as needed. Inspect the linkage or spring actuator of the valve for free movement. Binding or restriction could keep it from operating properly.

Vehicles with antilock brake systems (ABS) usually do not have load-sensing proportioning valves. The ABS prevents wheel lockup.

> **TECH TIP** **Servicing Hydraulic Components.** When servicing or replacing components in the brake hydraulic system, keep dirt and moisture out of the hydraulic lines. Whenever you disconnect a line, cover the open end with a piece of tape or a rubber or plastic cap.

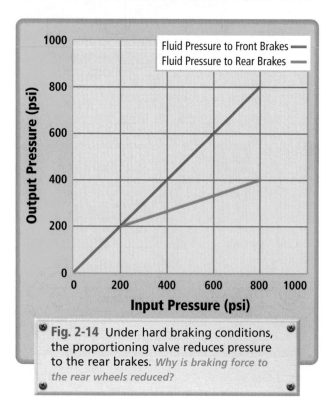

Fig. 2-14 Under hard braking conditions, the proportioning valve reduces pressure to the rear brakes. *Why is braking force to the rear wheels reduced?*

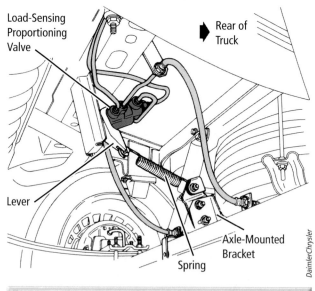

Fig. 2-15 Depending on the distance between the truck bed and the axle, the load-sensing proportioning valve controls the hydraulic pressure to the rear brakes. *Why does a vehicle with a heavier load require more braking force at the rear wheels?*

Residual Pressure Check Valve

Some master cylinders, used mainly with drum brakes, have a residual pressure check valve in the outlet port. The **residual pressure check valve** is a valve that maintains a residual pressure of about 6–18 psi [41–124 kPa] in the brake lines. The residual pressure keeps the seals in the wheel cylinders expanded. The expanded seals prevent air from leaking past them due to the sudden drop in pressure when the brakes are released.

Check valves are not used in disc brake circuits. Disc brakes do not usually use return springs. A check valve would allow pressure buildup and cause brake drag.

Generally, residual pressure check valves have not been used in brake systems since the 1970s. Instead, the wheel cylinders have cup expanders behind the seals to prevent fluid from leaking past them.

Combination Valve

Many vehicles with front disc and rear drum brakes have a three-function combination valve. See **Fig. 2-16**. This valve combines the pressure differential valve, metering valve, and proportioning valve into one unit. Two-function combination valves combine either the proportioning valve or the metering valve with the pressure differential valve.

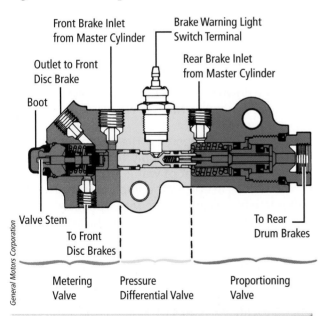

Front Brake Inlet from Master Cylinder

Brake Warning Light Switch Terminal

Outlet to Front Disc Brake

Rear Brake Inlet from Master Cylinder

Boot

Valve Stem

To Front Disc Brakes

To Rear Drum Brakes

Metering Valve

Pressure Differential Valve

Proportioning Valve

General Motors Corporation

Fig. 2-16 The combination valve combines the metering valve, pressure differential valve, and proportioning valve in one assembly. *Do all combination valves combine three valves into one assembly?*

Bleeding a Hydraulic Braking System

Servicing or replacing components in a hydraulic braking system usually allows air to enter the brake system. Air, like any gas, is compressible. In the system the trapped air acts like a cushion, creating a soft brake pedal feel and an unsafe condition. All trapped air must be bled out.

Water may also enter the hydraulic system through small pores in the flexible brake lines. Contaminated fluid should be flushed out periodically. **Brake bleeding** is the process of flushing air or contaminated fluid from the braking system. There are three basic methods. They are manual bleeding, pressure bleeding, and vacuum bleeding.

Manual Bleeding

Manual bleeding requires an assistant to operate the brake pedal from inside the vehicle. When the brakes are pumped, pressure is created by the master cylinder. The pressure pumps the fluid and air out of the system through the bleeder valves on each wheel. To manually bleed hydraulic brakes (non-antilock brake system), do the following:

1. With the engine and ignition OFF, pump the brake pedal several times. This will expel any remaining vacuum in the power brake booster.
2. Remove the master cylinder reservoir cover. Fill the reservoir to the full level. Place the cover loosely over the opening.
3. Pour a little brake fluid into a catch container. The bleeder hose must be submerged in the fluid during the bleeding process. The bleeder hose must be clear tubing. This will allow you to more easily see the air bubbles being expelled from the brake system.
4. The bleeding process sequence depends on the braking system. For a front-rear split, the sequence is right rear wheel, left rear wheel, right front wheel, and left front wheel. For a diagonally split, the sequence is right rear, left front, left rear, and right front.
5. Always check and, if needed, refill the master cylinder reservoir with fluid after bleeding each caliper or wheel cylinder. Refill more often if needed.
6. Loosen the bleeder valve at the wheel to be bled. Then, tighten it just enough to allow it to be easily loosened and tightened.

Excellence **in Science**

Using Hydraulics to Multiply Force

For centuries, people have used fluids to do work. But it was not until Blaise Pascal (1623–1662) studied fluids under pressure that the relationship between fluids and pressure was understood. The *Pa* in the metric system pressure unit kPa (kilopascal) derives from Pascal's name.

In this activity you will make a simple hydraulic system and show how it multiplies forces.

Apply It!

Make a Hydraulic Lift

Meets NATEF Science Standards for transferring force in a hydraulic system.

Materials and Equipment
- 1 strong balloon
- Large rubber bands
- 6-foot length of plastic tubing with about ½-inch inside diameter
- Measuring cup or baby bottle marked in fluid ounces
- Funnel to fit the tubing
- Thin, lightweight board about one square foot
- Four small blocks of wood about 1-inch thick
- A 12-ounce weight

1. Fill the balloon with as little water as possible. Do not inflate or stretch the balloon. Add just enough water to remove any trapped air.

2. Using a rubber band, tightly seal the mouth of the balloon over one end of the tubing.

3. Hang the other end of the tubing so the balloon lies flat on the floor.

4. Gently balance the board on the balloon with your hands. Don't press down. Notice that the weight will force some water up into the tube.

5. Use the blocks to support the four corners of the board.

6. Add water to the tube until the board just begins to rise off the blocks. Your hydraulic lift system is now ready for testing.

7. Put a 12-ounce weight at the center of the board.

8. Fill the measuring cup or baby bottle with water.

9. Using the funnel, slowly pour water into the tube until the board just begins to lift.

10. Write down how many ounces of water you poured into the tube. It wasn't nearly 12 ounces, was it?

Here's what is happening. The weight of the water you added is the apply force, or input force. A small amount of water at the bottom of the tube is acting as the apply piston. The balloon, which is in contact with the board, is the output piston. The difference in the areas of these two "pistons" is multiplying the force.

7. Install one end of the clear tubing over the bleeder valve. Leave room for a wrench to fit over the flats of the valve. Place the other end of the tubing into the catch container. Make sure the end is near the bottom and submerged. See **Fig. 2-17.**

8. Have an assistant slowly press the brake pedal down as far as possible. Ask the assistant to hold the pedal in the down position.

9. While the assistant holds the pedal down, open the bleeder valve enough to allow fluid to flow through the tubing and into the catch container. Watch for air bubbles to come out of the tube. The fluid flow will slow down in a few seconds.

When the air bubbles stop, tighten the bleeder valve. Have your assistant remove his or her foot from the brake pedal.

10. Repeat Steps 8 and 9 until no air bubbles can be seen coming from the tube. Then, securely tighten the bleeder valve. Remove the tube and container. Move on to the next caliper or wheel cylinder.

11. Check and, if needed, add brake fluid to the master cylinder reservoir.

12. Repeat Steps 6 through 11 for each caliper or wheel cylinder. Do this in the sequence required by the type of system.

13. After bleeding all four calipers and/or wheel cylinders, check and, if needed, add brake fluid to the master cylinder reservoir. Secure the master cylinder reservoir cover.

14. Check the brake operation. The brake pedal should stop firmly when pressed down. If the brakes feel spongy, repeat the bleeding procedure.

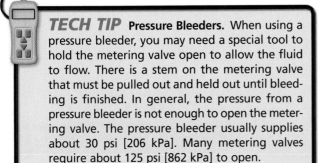

TECH TIP Pressure Bleeders. When using a pressure bleeder, you may need a special tool to hold the metering valve open to allow the fluid to flow. There is a stem on the metering valve that must be pulled out and held out until bleeding is finished. In general, the pressure from a pressure bleeder is not enough to open the metering valve. The pressure bleeder usually supplies about 30 psi [206 kPa]. Many metering valves require about 125 psi [862 kPa] to open.

Pressure Bleeding

Pressure bleeding, also called power bleeding, is the most popular method. The pressure bleeder is filled with brake fluid, attached to the master cylinder, and pressurized with shop air. The pressure bleeder provides the pressure normally provided by the master cylinder. See **Fig. 2-17**. Every pressure bleeder works differently. Follow the procedures in the manufacturer's manual.

Vacuum Bleeding

A single technician using a hand-held vacuum pump and appropriate adapter can do vacuum bleeding. The vacuum pump is used to draw fluid and trapped air from the system at the bleeder valves. Vacuum bleeding may not work on systems that do not have cup expanders. This method will not work on rear calipers with stroking seals. Refer to the vehicle's manual for determining whether this method is appropriate and for specific directions.

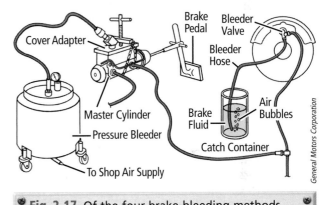

Fig. 2-17 Of the four brake-bleeding methods, pressure bleeding is the most common. *What are some of the disadvantages of the other methods?*

SECTION 3 KNOWLEDGE CHECK

1. What senses the pressure in each brake-system circuit?

2. What is the difference between a proportioning valve and a metering valve?

3. Two-function and three-function combination valves may combine which types of brake-system valves, respectively?

4. What process is used to flush air or contaminated fluid from the brake system?

5. Name the three types of bleeding that may be used to flush the brake system.

ASE TEST PREP

6. Technician A says a two-function combination valve combines the proportioning valve and the metering valve into one component. Technician B says a two-function combination valve combines either the proportioning valve or the metering valve with the pressure-differential valve. Who is correct?

ⓐ Technician A.

ⓑ Technician B.

ⓒ Both Technician A and Technician B.

ⓓ Neither Technician A nor Technician B.

CHAPTER 2 REVIEW

Key Points

Meets the following NATEF Standard for Brakes: bleeding brake systems.

- Hydraulic pressure creates the force needed to operate an automotive braking system.
- The master cylinder contains pistons that act on the brake fluid to transfer pressure to the wheel cylinders.
- Braking system components are connected by rigid and flexible brake lines.
- Technicians must use special tools to make brake line flares. Any cracked or damaged flares must be cut off and new ones formed.
- Dual-circuit brake systems are either front-rear split or diagonally split.
- Some braking system control valves delay the arrival of brake pressure at the wheel brakes. Others limit the amount of fluid pressure.
- Brake bleeding flushes air and contaminated brake fluid out of a braking system.
- The most popular method of bleeding brakes is pressure bleeding, or power bleeding.

Review Questions

1. Define hydraulics.
2. What creates the force to make brake shoes or pads come into contact with brake drums or rotors?
3. In what direction is force transmitted when it is applied to an enclosed liquid?
4. In a quick-takeup master cylinder, the primary piston operates in what type of cylinder?
5. Rigid brake lines are made from what type of metal?
6. What type of line is used between a vehicle's chassis and its wheel brakes? Why?
7. Why are flexible brake lines made of three layers?
8. Explain the purpose of load-sensing proportioning valves.
9. **Critical Thinking** Explain how load-sensing proportioning valves sense load changes?
10. **Critical Thinking** Explain how to manually bleed hydraulic brakes.

Excellence in Communication

"Reading" Your Customer

As a technician, you need to be able to "read" your customer. Often, you can learn more from customers' actions than from what they say. Take, for instance, the driver who plays his radio loudly as he drives in. He might say that he just noticed the noise. You might guess that the noise has been there for a while. The music may have been too loud for him to notice the noise.

Assuming that this driver has not been as attentive as he could have been may help you as you begin to diagnose the problem.

If a vehicle is clean, you may guess that the customer also pays attention to mechanical problems. If the vehicle is not well cared for, you may draw different conclusions. However, you need to be cautious when making such guesses. You are working with clues, not hard facts.

Apply It!

Meets NATEF Communication Standards for using and evaluating verbal and nonverbal cues.

Reread the "Customer's Concern" at the beginning of the chapter. Look for clues that tell you something about the customer.

1. What does the condition of the customer's car suggest to you about him?
2. What does his obvious distress suggest to you about him?
3. What can you learn about him from the complaint he makes?
4. What do you think the problem could be? Base your answer on what he has said and what you seem to know about him.

AUTOMOTIVE SERVICE EXCELLENCE
TEST PREP

Answering the following practice questions will help you prepare for the ASE certification tests.

1. Technician A says that gas can be compressed but liquids cannot be compressed. Technician B says that neither gas nor liquids can be compressed. Who is correct?

   ⓐ Technician A.

   ⓑ Technician B.

   ⓒ Both Technician A and Technician B.

   ⓓ Neither Technician A nor Technician B.

2. Technician A says that a solid connection can transfer force through the lines of a hydraulic system. Technician B says that a solid connection cannot transfer force through the lines of a hydraulic system. Who is correct?

   ⓐ Technician A.

   ⓑ Technician B.

   ⓒ Both Technician A and Technician B.

   ⓓ Neither Technician A nor Technician B.

3. All of the following are true about a master cylinder's operation except:

   ⓐ its piston compresses the brake fluid.

   ⓑ it provides pressure to the wheel cylinders.

   ⓒ it changes mechanical force to hydraulic pressure.

   ⓓ both integral and composite master cylinders work in the same way.

4. Technician A says that an integral master cylinder is a one-piece cast-iron component. Technician B says that an integral master cylinder has a plastic reservoir attached directly to the master cylinder. Who is correct?

   ⓐ Technician A.

   ⓑ Technician B.

   ⓒ Both Technician A and Technician B.

   ⓓ Neither Technician A nor Technician B.

5. The openings towards the front of the master cylinder reservoir are called:

   ⓐ replenishing ports.

   ⓑ feeding ports.

   ⓒ compensating ports.

   ⓓ balancing ports.

6. Technician A says that, in the low-drag brake system, there is a relatively large gap between the brake pads and the rotor. Technician B says that gap is relatively small. Who is correct?

   ⓐ Technician A.

   ⓑ Technician B.

   ⓒ Both Technician A and Technician B.

   ⓓ Neither Technician A nor Technician B.

7. The brake pedal goes all the way to the floor on each application. The most likely cause is:

   ⓐ excessive wear of the cylinder bore.

   ⓑ damage due to contaminated brake fluid.

   ⓒ swollen and distorted rubber cups.

   ⓓ all of the above.

8. Technician A says that adjustments to the power brake booster pushrod to the master cylinder usually require a manufacturer-provided gauge. Technician B says that such a gauge is not needed. Who is correct?

   ⓐ Technician A.

   ⓑ Technician B.

   ⓒ Both Technician A and Technician B.

   ⓓ Neither Technician A nor Technician B.

9. Metering valves are usually found on:

   ⓐ FWD cars that have diagonally split brake systems.

   ⓑ vehicles with drum brakes front and rear.

   ⓒ vehicles with disc brakes front and rear.

   ⓓ vehicles with front disc brakes and rear drum brakes.

10. For a front-rear split system, the brake bleeding sequence is:

   ⓐ left front wheel, right rear wheel, left rear wheel, right front wheel.

   ⓑ right rear wheel, right front wheel, left rear wheel, left front wheel.

   ⓒ left front wheel, left rear wheel, right front wheel, right rear wheel.

   ⓓ right rear wheel, left rear wheel, right front wheel, left front wheel.

Section 1
Drum Brake
Operation

Section 2
Diagnosing Drum
Brakes

Section 3
Servicing Drum
Brakes

Diagnosing & Repairing Drum Brakes

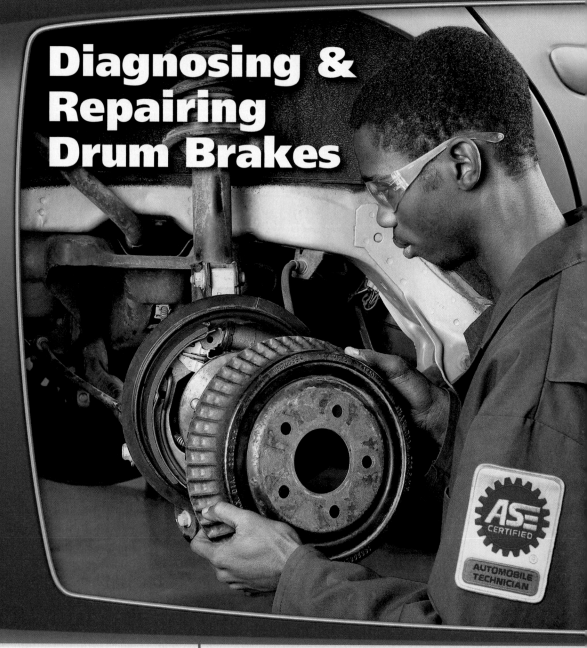

Customer's Concern

Joan Jason bought her full-size van new six years ago. She has been the only driver of the vehicle since then. The van's brakes have never been serviced. However, Joan says she's never had any problems until recently. Joan remembers that the problem started right after her nephew changed the oil the week before.

Whenever Joan applies the brakes, she says the van veers to the right. She has to steer to the left to keep her van on the road. Joan believes her nephew may have damaged the brakes in her van during the last oil change. Before she accuses her nephew of damaging her brakes, Joan wants you to diagnose the problem to find out what's really wrong and what caused the problem.

Technician's Challenge

As the service technician, you need to find answers to these questions:

1. Can you think of anything that Joan's nephew could have done to cause the van to pull to the right when braking?

2. Aside from brake-related problems, are there any other possible causes that may be to blame for the van's veering to the right when the brakes are applied?

3. What brake-related malfunctions may cause a vehicle to pull toward one side or another when the brakes are applied?

● Section 1
Drum Brake Operation

Objectives:
- Describe drum brake construction.
- Diagnose drum brake problems.
- Describe drum brake operation.
- Explain how to manually adjust drum brake self-adjusters.

Vocabulary:
- backing plate
- brake shoe
- brake hardware
- wheel cylinder
- leading-trailing drum brakes
- duo-servo drum brakes
- drum brake self-adjuster

Drum Brake Construction

Drum brakes use hydraulic pressure to press brake shoes against the inside of a rotating brake drum. Most current vehicles have drum brakes only on their rear wheels. See **Fig. 3-1.** They provide less than 40 percent of the overall braking effort for front-engine, rear-wheel drive cars and only about 20 percent for front-wheel drive cars. Older cars had drum brakes on all four wheels.

Hydraulic pistons activate drum brakes. The drum brakes are retracted by spring tension. They can also be engaged mechanically. For this reason, they are widely used as the mechanisms for parking brakes.

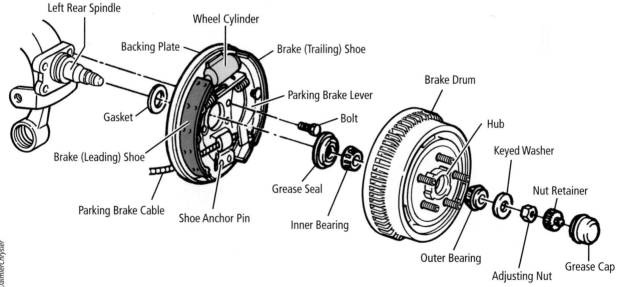

DaimlerChrysler

Fig. 3-1 Exploded view of a leading-trailing drum brake commonly found on front-wheel drive cars. Only about 20 percent of the braking is done by the rear drum brakes. *Why are self-adjusters necessary on drum brakes?*

The brake assembly attaches through the backing plate to an axle housing or a strut-spindle assembly. The **backing plate** is the metal plate on which many of the drum brake components are mounted. A metal brake drum encloses these components and provides a friction surface for the brake shoes. Two curved brake shoes are pushed outward against the inside of the brake drum. Friction between the shoes and the drum acts to slow or stop drum and wheel rotation.

A wheel cylinder provides the hydraulic force required to push the brake shoes against the drum. Brake hardware consists of return springs, hold-down springs, pins, and a self-adjuster. This hardware attaches the various components to the backing plate or to each other. When working properly, a self-adjuster assembly keeps the brakes correctly adjusted at all times.

Backing Plate

The backing plate bolts to the axle housing or spindle. The rest of the brake components are attached to the backing plate. See **Fig. 3-2.**

The backing plate has raised metal pads. The brake shoes ride on these pads. These pads cannot have any grooves in them; they must remain smooth.

There are several holes in the backing plate. These are for mounting the wheel cylinder and hold-down pins. Some vehicle models have a hole through which the brakes can be adjusted.

The backing plate helps to keep road debris from entering the drum brake assembly.

The backing plate must be firmly attached to the axle housing and must not be bent or otherwise damaged. A damaged backing plate can cause the brakes to malfunction.

Safety First — **Brake Shoe Linings** Do not allow the brake shoe linings to wear down to the rivets on riveted shoes. The rivets will grind grooves into the brake drum surface. Machining may not be able to remove these grooves. You will then need to replace the drum.

Brake Shoes

Brake shoes are made of metal, usually steel. See **Fig. 3-3.** The friction material, called the brake lining, is attached to the shoe by rivets or adhesives. Cemented linings are often called bonded linings. Together, the lining and shoe assembly are referred to as the **brake shoe.**

Drum brakes use friction between the drum and brake shoe to slow the motion of the vehicle. This friction creates enormous amounts of heat. The resulting high temperatures limit the materials suitable for brake shoe linings.

On older vehicles brake shoes were lined with asbestos fiber. Less hazardous materials are now used for linings. The linings are usually made of a semimetallic material or fiberglass. The friction material must be able to withstand the heat produced during braking.

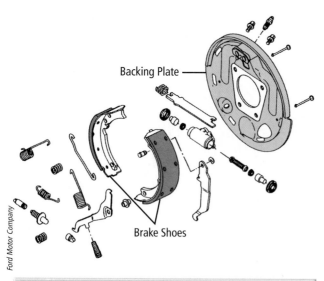

Ford Motor Company

Backing Plate

Brake Shoes

Fig. 3-2 The backing plate serves as a mounting point for the brake hardware and brake shoes. *What would happen if the backing plate were damaged?*

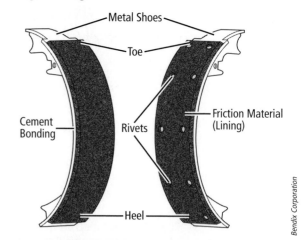

Bendix Corporation

Metal Shoes

Toe

Cement Bonding

Rivets

Friction Material (Lining)

Heel

Fig. 3-3 Rivets or adhesives are used to attach the lining to the metal shoe. *What might happen if the lining wears down to expose the rivets?*

Brake Hardware

The assorted small parts that attach to the shoes are known as **brake hardware**. See **Fig. 3-4**. This hardware includes springs, pins, cups, and clips that hold the drum brake assembly together.

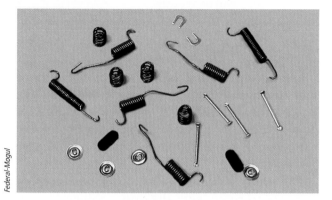

Federal-Mogul

Fig. 3-4 The hardware consists of the springs, pins, cups, and other small pieces that hold the shoes to the backing plate and retract the brakes when they are released. *Why should hardware be replaced with every job?*

Pin and cup assemblies hold the brake shoes against the backing plate. The pins pass through the backing plate, through the brake shoe and holddown spring, and lock to the cup. The cups can be unlocked from the pins by rotating one-quarter turn in either direction.

Return springs return the shoe to the anchor pin when the brakes are released.

Wheel Cylinders

The **wheel cylinder** converts the hydraulic pressure from the master cylinder into mechanical movement. When the driver pushes the brake pedal, brake fluid is forced out of the master cylinder through the brake lines to the wheel cylinder. See **Fig. 3-5**.

A wheel cylinder has two pistons. There are seals or cups on each piston. There is also a spring between the two pistons. See **Fig. 3-6**. As the pressure increases, the pistons overcome the brake shoe return springs. This causes the pistons to push the shoes outward into contact with the drum.

Early-model vehicles with four-wheel drum brakes usually had larger pistons in the front wheel cylinders than in the rear ones. This was necessary due to the greater braking force required on the front wheels. Braking transfers more of the vehicle's weight to the front wheels.

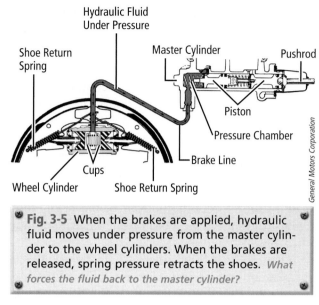

General Motors Corporation

Fig. 3-5 When the brakes are applied, hydraulic fluid moves under pressure from the master cylinder to the wheel cylinders. When the brakes are released, spring pressure retracts the shoes. *What forces the fluid back to the master cylinder?*

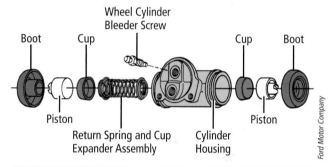

Ford Motor Company

Fig. 3-6 Wheel cylinders convert hydraulic pressure into mechanical movement. *Why are the front wheel cylinder pistons larger on some vehicles with four-wheel drum brakes?*

Types of Drum Brakes

There are two types of drum brakes: leading-trailing or non-servo, and duo-servo. **Leading-trailing drum brakes** are brakes in which the action of one shoe does not affect the other shoe. **Duo-servo drum brakes** are brakes in which the action of one shoe reinforces the action of the other shoe.

Leading-trailing drum brakes are used on the rear wheels of some front-wheel drive vehicles. Duo-servo drum brakes are usually found on the rear wheels of rear-wheel drive vehicles.

Leading-Trailing Drum Brakes

In the leading-trailing (non-servo) drum brake system, the tops of the brake shoes rest against the wheel cylinder. See **Fig. 3-7(a)**. The bottoms of the brake shoes rest against a fixed anchor. Depressing the brake pedal overcomes the return spring tension and causes the wheel cylinder pistons to move the tops of the brake shoes outward against the drums. Friction between the forward, or leading, brake shoe and the drum causes the leading shoe to try to rotate with the drum. This self-energizing action of the leading shoe forces the bottom of the brake shoe against the anchor pin. As a result, the leading shoe does most of the braking.

When the rear, or trailing, brake shoe contacts the drum, the rotation tries to force the brake shoe away from the drum. There is no self-energizing action. Therefore, the trailing shoe usually wears less than the leading shoe. When the vehicle is moving backwards, the brake shoes switch jobs and the rear brake shoe does most of the braking. This is because the rear brake shoe is now the leading shoe. The front brake shoe is now the trailing shoe.

The leading-trailing brake is less self-energizing and more dependent on the force supplied by the wheel cylinder.

TECH TIP **Brake Shoe Linings.** The brake shoe linings may be the same length on both shoes, but there may be a difference in their lining materials. If the brake shoes are marked, do not install them in the wrong locations. Brake function will be reduced.

Duo-Servo Drum Brakes

In duo-servo drum brakes, the tops of the brake shoes rest against a single anchor pin. See **Fig. 3-7 (b)**. The bottoms of the brake shoes are linked by a floating adjuster assembly. When the brakes are applied, the wheel cylinders force the shoes out against the drum.

The primary (forward) shoe contacts the drum and tries to rotate with the drum, pulling the top of the shoe away from the anchor pin. This causes the bottom of the shoe to transfer force through the adjuster assembly to the rear (secondary) brake shoe. This, in turn, forces the secondary shoe harder against the drum.

In duo-servo brakes, the self-energizing action of both shoes makes total braking force greater than the amount supplied by the wheel cylinder.

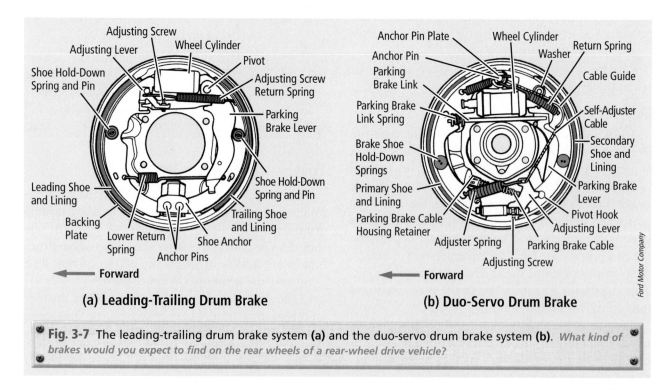

(a) Leading-Trailing Drum Brake

(b) Duo-Servo Drum Brake

Ford Motor Company

Fig. 3-7 The leading-trailing drum brake system **(a)** and the duo-servo drum brake system **(b)**. *What kind of brakes would you expect to find on the rear wheels of a rear-wheel drive vehicle?*

TECH TIP **Length of Lining.** You can usually identify the brake shoes in a duo-servo brake system. The primary (forward) shoes will usually have a shorter lining than the secondary (rearward) shoes. The lining is longer on the secondary shoe because it does more of the braking than the primary shoe.

Drum-Brake Self-Adjusters

A **drum-brake self-adjuster** is a device on drum brakes that compensates for lining wear by automatically adjusting the shoe-to-drum clearance. This adjustment prevents the brake pedal from getting lower and lower during normal use. The two types of self-adjusters are the one-shot and the incremental.

One-Shot Adjusters The one-shot adjuster makes a single adjustment once the clearance between the lining and drum reaches a predetermined gap. At this point, no additional adjustments can be made. The shoes must be replaced and the self-adjuster reset.

Incremental Adjusters Figure 3-8 shows an incremental adjuster. The incremental adjuster moves the shoes outward whenever the gap is large enough to turn the adjusting screw. On some vehicles, adjustment occurs when the vehicle is braked while moving either forward or rearward.

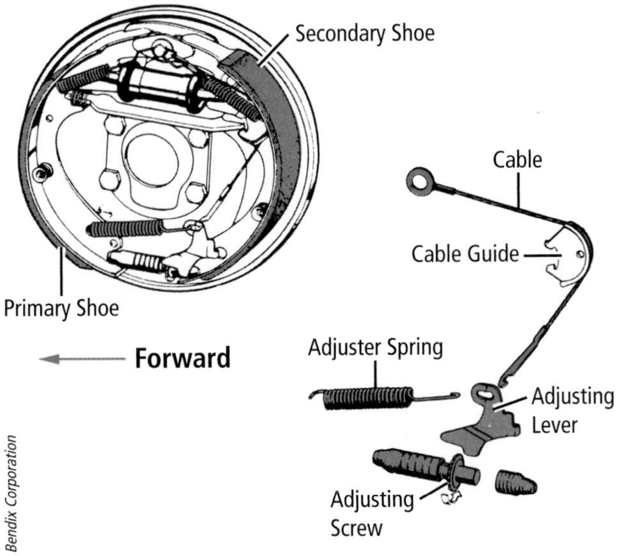

Secondary Shoe

Cable

Cable Guide

Primary Shoe

← **Forward**

Adjuster Spring

Adjusting Lever

Adjusting Screw

Bendix Corporation

Fig. 3-8 Some incremental adjusters have a cable and some have levers. The cable is attached to the secondary shoe, and the lever moves the star wheel in a ratcheting action. *What might happen if the self-adjuster does not work correctly?*

On other vehicles, adjustment occurs only when the vehicle is braked while moving rearward. And on yet other vehicles, particularly Asian imports, the brakes are adjusted whenever the parking brake is applied.

Safety First **Parking Brake Use** Remind drivers to use their parking brakes regularly if that is the method used to keep their brakes adjusted correctly. Parking brakes that are not used regularly could freeze up.

An incremental self-adjuster is attached to the secondary shoe of a duo-servo brake. The adjusting lever attaches to the self-adjuster cable that passes around a cable guide and fastens to the anchor pin. The brakes are adjusted each time they are applied while the vehicle is moving backward. Friction forces the upper end of the primary shoe against the anchor pin. The wheel cylinder forces the upper end of the secondary shoe downward and away from the anchor pin. This causes the cable to pull the adjusting lever upward.

If the brake linings have worn enough, the lever passes over and engages the end of a new tooth on the adjusting wheel. This wheel is commonly called the star wheel. The incremental-adjuster assembly is a one-way, ratcheting mechanism.

When the brakes are released, the adjuster spring pulls the adjusting lever downward. This turns the tooth and slightly lengthens the adjusting screw. The brake shoes move closer to the drum.

TECH TIP **Adjusting Screws.** The adjusting screws on cable-type adjusters are right hand and left hand. If they are reversed, the screws retract the shoes instead of expanding them. If unsure about which side an adjuster goes on, pull the end cap from the adjuster. It will be marked right or left on the end of the adjusting screw.

Excellence in Science

Inertia and Friction

Inertia is not really a force that prevents your car from moving. It is the result of gravity, which holds the car to the earth, and friction, which results from the contact between the tires and the road surface. A force must be exerted to overcome that inertia. Even with a force, the friction will remain, tending to slow the car as the force is applied.

Friction is also produced when two pieces of metal move in contact with each other. We know that oil is a key lubricant in reducing that friction. The reason lies in its molecular structure. Motor oil and the other products resulting from the fractional distillation of crude oil are made up of specific hydrocarbons (molecules of hydrogen and carbon). When oil is applied to engine parts that are in contact with each other, the microscopic particles of oil line up between them. The outer layers of the oil molecules cling to the metal pieces. The others line up in the layers between the pieces.

The result of this lubrication is that the only friction resulting from the movement of the metal parts is in the rubbing together of the oil molecules. This is different from the friction that would have been produced by the metal pieces moving in direct contact.

Apply It!

Direct Contact

Meets NATEF Science Standards for motion and lubrication.

Materials and Equipment
- A wooden surface (wood desktop)
- Two books
- 4 round pencils

1. Push the book along the surface of the desk.
2. Add the second book on top of the other book.
3. Try pushing two books across the surface.
4. Place 4 round pencils under the books.
5. Now try pushing the two books.
6. What happens? Explain why.

SECTION 1 KNOWLEDGE CHECK

1. What is the metal plate on which many of the drum brake components are mounted?

2. What is brake hardware?

3. Explain the role of wheel cylinder pistons in braking.

4. Explain the difference between leading-trailing drum brakes and duo-servo drum brakes.

5. What is the purpose of a self-adjuster?

6. Explain the difference between a one-shot adjuster and an incremental adjuster.

ASE TEST PREP

7. Technician A says brake hardware is attached to the backing plate. Technician B says the backing plate keeps road debris from entering the drum brake assembly. Who is correct?
   - ⓐ Technician A.
   - ⓑ Technician B.
   - ⓒ Both Technician A and Technician B.
   - ⓓ Neither Technician A nor Technician B.

Section 2
Diagnosing Drum Brakes

Objectives:

A2 • Identify and interpret brake system concern.

B5 • Diagnose poor stopping, pulling or dragging concerns caused by malfunctions in the hydraulic system; determine necessary action.

C1 • Diagnose poor stopping, noise, vibration, pulling, grabbing, dragging or pedal pulsation concerns.

Vocabulary:
• brake grabbing
• brake pedal free play

Dragging, Pulling, or Grabbing Brakes

When a vehicle with a brake problem comes in, talk to the owner. Ask him or her questions about the problem. Listen carefully to what the owner says. It is important to fully understand the problem before you begin your diagnosis. Once you have the facts and understand the complaint, you can begin to consider possible causes. See **Table 3-A.**

After identifying the possible causes, test each of them, beginning with the most likely ones. Continue to eliminate possible causes until the problem is found.

To correct the problem, you may need to repair, adjust, or replace a component. Or, you may only need to bleed the braking system.

Safety First

Brake Dust Use caution when working around brake dust. When working on brakes, you must:

• Wear safety glasses at all times.

• Use an approved brake washer or aerosol cleaner to remove brake dust. Never use an air hose to blow out the dust.

• Wear a respirator to avoid breathing airborne brake dust. Treat all brakes as though they have asbestos linings.

• Dispose of brake dust in a sealed container in accordance with hazardous waste laws.

• Wash your hands after performing brake service and do not wear your work clothes home.

One Brake Drags

When one brake drags, it indicates that the shoes are not pulling back from the drum. The following are some causes for this.

• Wheel cylinder piston stuck in the applied position.
• Weak or broken brake return springs.
• Loose wheel bearings that cause the drum to wobble.
• Backing plate is bent or damaged, and the shoes are hanging up.
• Brake adjuster is overextended.
• Damaged brake hose.
• Seized parking brake cable.

Rear Brakes Drag

The parking brakes may not release completely if they are over adjusted or if the cables are corroded. Also, the brakes can drag if the parking brake pedal or lever does not return to the full release position.

All Brakes Drag

When all brakes are dragging, it is because the fluid is still under pressure. There are several reasons fluid pressure will remain in the system.

• Master cylinder piston not returning far enough to uncover the compensating port.
• Mineral oil in the system caused by topping off the master cylinder with automatic transmission fluid, engine oil, or power steering fluid, which will swell the rubber seals.
• Improperly adjusted master cylinder pushrod.

Table 3-A	DRUM-BRAKE DIAGNOSIS	
Complaint	**Possible Cause**	**Check or Correction**
1. Pedal goes to floor, loss of pedal reserve	a. Linkage or shoes out of adjustment or damaged b. Brake linings worn c. Lack of brake fluid d. Air in hydraulic system e. Defective master cylinder	a. Check and repair linkage or adjusters b. Replace c. Add fluid, bleed system d. Add fluid, bleed system e. Repair or replace
2. One brake drags	a. Shoes out of adjustment b. Clogged brake line c. Wheel cylinder defective d. Weak or broken return spring e. Loose wheel bearing	a. Adjust b. Clear or replace c. Repair or replace d. Replace e. Adjust or replace
3. All brakes drag	a. Incorrect linkage adjustment b. Defective master cylinder c. Mineral oil in system	a. Adjust b. Repair or replace c. Replace damaged rubber parts; flush, fill, and bleed system
4. Pulls to one side when braking	a. Oil on brake linings b. Brake fluid on brake linings c. Brake shoes out of adjustment d. Tires not uniformly inflated e. Brake line clogged f. Defective wheel cylinder g. Backing plate loose h. Mismatched linings	a. Replace linings and oil seals; avoid overlubrication b. Replace linings; repair or replace wheel cylinder c. Adjust d. Adjust tire pressure e. Clear or replace line f. Repair or replace g. Tighten h. Install matched linings
5. Soft or spongy pedal	a. Air in hydraulic system b. Brake shoes out of adjustment c. Defective master cylinder d. Loose connections or damaged brake line e. Loss of brake fluid	a. Add fluid, bleed system b. Adjust c. Repair or replace d. Tighten connections, replace line e. See item 9, below
6. Poor braking requiring excessive pedal force	a. Brake linings wet with water b. Shoes out of adjustment c. Brake linings hot d. Brake linings burned e. Brake drum glazed f. Power brake inoperative g. Wheel cylinder pistons stuck	a. Allow to dry b. Adjust c. Allow to cool d. Replace e. Refinish or replace f. Repair or replace g. Repair or replace
7. Brakes grab	a. Shoes out of adjustment b. Wrong linings c. Brake fluid, oil, or grease on lining d. Drums scored e. Backing plate loose f. Power brake booster defective	a. Adjust b. Install correct linings c. Replace shoes and repair leaks d. Refinish or replace drums e. Tighten f. Repair or replace
8. Noisy brakes	a. Linings worn, shoes warped, or rivets loose b. Drums worn or rough c. Loose parts	a. Replace shoes b. Refinish or replace c. Tighten
9. Loss of brake fluid	a. Master cylinder or wheel cylinder leaks b. Loose connectors, damaged brake line **NOTE: After repair, add brake fluid and bleed system**	a. Repair or replace b. Tighten connections, replace line
10. Brakes do not self-adjust	a. Adjusting screw stuck b. Adjusting lever does not engage adjusting wheel c. Adjuster incorrectly installed	a. Free and clean b. Repair or replace adjuster c. Install correctly
11. Brake warning light comes on while braking	a. One section of hydraulic system has failed b. Pressure differential valve defective	a. Inspect and repair b. Replace
12. Pedal pulsation or vibration	a. Loose wheel bearings b. Wheel or tire problems c. Broken or weak brake return springs d. Debris in or on brake drums or shoes e. Out of round drums	a. Adjust b. Inspect wheel for damage; test wheel and tire balance c. Replace springs d. Clean and machine brake drum; replace brake shoes e. Machine or replace

Pulls to One Side When Braking

When a vehicle pulls to one side when braking, the brakes on that side of the vehicle are defective. However, it is also possible that the brakes on the opposite side of the vehicle are not working. If one side is not working, the vehicle will pull to the side that is working. Verify normal brake operation on the opposite side of the vehicle to help isolate the problem. A pull to one side could be caused by:

• Linings contaminated with oil or grease.
• Brakes that are out of adjustment.
• A defective automatic brake adjuster.
• A faulty or leaking wheel cylinder.
• A restricted hydraulic brake line.

Brakes Grab

Brake grabbing is a condition in which the brakes apply more quickly than expected compared to the amount of pedal effort applied. Some causes include:

• Linings contaminated with grease or oil.
• An inoperative proportioning valve.
• Shoes out of adjustment.
• A leaking wheel cylinder.
• A loose backing plate.

Replace contaminated linings. Always check grease seals to ensure they are not leaking. A loose backing plate, where it bolts to the axle housing, allows the shoes to twist in the drum. Inspect backing plates any time brake work is being performed.

Brake Pedal Symptoms

Many brake complaints are related to the way the brake pedal feels. In fact, this may be the first symptom of a brake problem.

Brake Pedal Free Play

Brake pedal free play is the amount of pedal movement before the pushrod touches the piston inside the master cylinder. Without the correct amount of free play, the brake pedal will not return fully and the brakes may not fully release. There should be at least one-quarter to one-half inch of free play at the brake pedal. See **Fig. 3-9**. The master cylinder pushrod may need adjusting or something may be interfering with pedal travel.

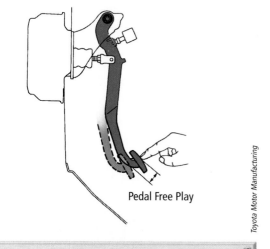

Pedal Free Play

Toyota Motor Manufacturing

Fig. 3-9 With the engine off, pump the brakes a couple of times to remove the vacuum from the booster. Measure the brake pedal free play. It should be one-quarter to one-half inch. *What might happen if there is no free play?*

Soft or Spongy Pedal

A soft or spongy pedal is usually the result of air in the hydraulic system. See **Fig. 3-10**. This is because air is compressible and liquids are not. Check for the following:

• Low fluid level in the master cylinder.
• Plugged air vents in the master cylinder cover or cap.
• Residual pressure check valve failure.

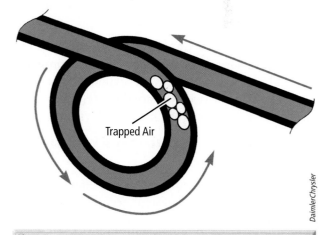

Trapped Air

DaimlerChrysler

Fig. 3-10 Air trapped in the hydraulic system is a major cause of soft or spongy pedal. *Why does trapped air cause this problem?*

Low Fluid Level in Master Cylinder Air, instead of fluid, may enter the system when the pedal is stroked if the master cylinder is low on fluid. Check for fluid leaks and add fluid. Then bleed the hydraulic system. **Figure 3-11** shows a typical master cylinder fluid reservoir.

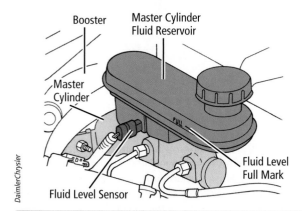

Fig. 3-11 Keep the master cylinder fluid reservoir at the "Full" mark. Clean off any dirt or other foreign matter from the cover before opening the brake fluid reservoir. Dirt in the fluid reservoir can damage the seals and lead to brake system failure.

Plugged Air Vents in Master Cylinder Cover/ Cap Plugged air vents in the cover or cap can cause a partial vacuum in the master cylinder. This may allow air to bypass the primary cup. Eliminate this condition by clearing the vent and bleeding the hydraulic system of any trapped air.

Residual Pressure Check Valve Failure If the residual pressure check valve does not hold pressure, air can be sucked past the wheel cylinder cups when the brakes are released. Replace the residual pressure check valve and bleed the hydraulic system.

Poor Braking Requiring Excessive Pedal Force

Poor braking requiring excessive pedal force can be a temporary or a persistent condition. Some of its causes are:
- Obstruction of the brake pedal.
- Pinched brake lines.
- Defective power booster.
- Defective vacuum check valve for power booster.
- Low engine vacuum.
- Glazed linings or brake drums.
- Wet brakes.
- Overheated brakes.

Power booster failure will cause a very hard pedal and reduced braking power. Such failure can result from insufficient vacuum from the engine or a defective vacuum check valve.

Driving through deep water can cause temporary brake fade until the brakes dry off. Excessively long intervals of braking create high temperatures that may burn or char the brake lining. Overheating can also glaze the brake drum. When this happens, the low friction surface between the lining and the drum will lead to poor braking. Replace the brake shoes, wheel cylinders (if necessary), and brake hardware. Machine or replace the brake drum.

Brakes Do Not Self-Adjust

If the self-adjusters do not work, pedal travel will be excessive. Reasons self-adjusters may not work include:
- Driver seldom applies brakes in reverse.
- Driver seldom applies parking brake.
- Self-adjuster screws (star wheels) are on wrong sides of vehicle or frozen in place.
- Teeth on star wheel are rounded off.
- Adjuster cable is worn or stretched.

Always check the brake hardware and replace any worn items when doing a brake job. If the adjuster assembly is installed backwards, it will not function. Check all adjuster parts.

Pedal Pulsation or Vibration

Pedal pulsation is when the brake pedal feels as if it is pushing back against the driver's foot when the brakes are applied. This is normal on vehicles with antilock brakes. When the brakes are applied suddenly, such as in a panic situation, the brake pedal will lightly pulsate as the antilock feature is engaged. This is not normal with any other brake system. In a brake system with drum brakes, pulsation can be caused by:
- Loose wheel bearings.
- Wheel or tire problems.
- Broken or weak brake return springs.
- Debris in or on the brake drum or shoes.
- Warped or out-of-round drums.

Loose Wheel Bearings If the wheel bearings are not adjusted to the manufacturer's specifications, pulsation can result at the brake pedal. Refer to the vehicle service manual for the specific adjustments.

Excellence in Math

Measuring Out-of-Round Brake Drums

Courtney Leruchi says the brakes on her car are pulsating. You suspect the brake drums may be out of round.

The brake specifications give an 11.000″ drum diameter with a maximum allowance of 11.090″ diameter. You will resurface, or machine, the drum to a maximum of 11.060″, leaving 0.030″ for further wear.

You use a brake drum micrometer to measure the inside diameter at points 90° apart. What action would you recommend if the smallest diameter measurement is 11.018″ and the largest diameter measurement is 11.028″?

Write a sentence stating how much the drum is out of round. Explain your recommendation to the customer. Support your answer mathematically.

You find the difference between the largest and smallest measurements of diameter:

$11.028″ − 11.018″ = 0.010″.$

The drum is 0.010″ out of round.

The maximum brake drum diameter desired is 11.060″. So the diameter available to work with is

$11.060″ − 11.018″ = 0.042″$

Because there is enough metal to work with, you can use a brake drum lathe to remove up to 0.021″ of metal. Note that removing 0.021″ around the entire drum would increase the diameter by 0.042″.

In practice, a technician would probably remove just enough metal to make the drum round. Then he or she would check to make sure the inside diameter was acceptable.

Apply It!

Meets NATEF Mathematics Standards for using multiplication and division and working with tolerance specifications.

The customer was so pleased with your explanation that she recommended you to her brother. His vehicle has an 8.640″ drum diameter with a maximum allowance of 8.730″ diameter.

1. What action would you recommend if two measurements 90° apart are 8.648″ and 8.674″, respectively?

2. Write a sentence stating how much the drum is out of round.

3. Explain your recommendation to the customer. Support your answer mathematically.

Wheel and Tire Problems Use a wheel balancer to check the wheel runout for bent, cracked, or loose wheels. Check tires for tread separation or sidewall damage. Check wheel-and-tire assembly balance.

Broken or Weak Brake Return Springs Inspect the brake springs and shoes. Springs not retracting the brake shoes properly may cause pulsation. Shoes may have glazed areas. Replace the brake springs and hardware. Clean or replace brake shoes as needed.

Debris in or on the Brake Drum or Shoes Inspect the brake shoes and drum. Warped or out-of-round drums, embedded material, or other foreign substances can cause high spots, resulting in brake pedal pulsation. Clean and machine the brake drum if within the manufacturer's specifications. Replace the brake shoes if damaged or contaminated.

Fluid Leaks, Noise, and Warning Lights

Among these symptoms, noisy brakes and a lit warning light are the most obvious. The detection of fluid leaks can sometimes require careful inspection.

Loss of Brake Fluid

A leak will cause loss of brake fluid. A leak can occur anywhere in the hydraulic system. Look for wet spots around connected components or brake lines. Pay particular attention to the following:

- Brake lines and component connections.
- Brake hoses and their connections.
- Master cylinder.
- Wheel cylinders.
- Calipers.

Leaks at most components, connections, and lines are obvious. Check the vacuum supply to the booster. See **Fig. 3-12**. Although there may be moisture where the master cylinder meets the vacuum booster, the fluid will often leak into the booster. It may also leak into the vacuum line leading from it.

Noisy Brakes

Brake system noise results from the vibration of brake system components. Noise sources include:

- Excessively worn linings.
- Warped shoes.
- Threaded drums.
- Loose hardware.
- Loose backing plate.

Linings that are worn to the rivets or the steel backing and are touching the drum will make a grinding or scraping noise. Any loose parts in the

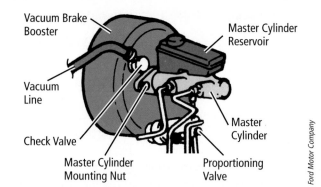

Vacuum Brake Booster

Master Cylinder Reservoir

Vacuum Line

Check Valve

Master Cylinder Mounting Nut

Master Cylinder

Proportioning Valve

Ford Motor Company

Fig. 3-12 A leak will sometimes be apparent where the master cylinder bolts to the booster. Frequently, however, the fluid enters the booster itself. *Where else might you find brake fluid leaking from a master cylinder?*

drum brake system can make noise when the brakes are applied. A bent backing plate will give a high-pitched noise as the drum rotates.

A drum may have spiral grooves from improper machining. These act as threads. The linings may ride up the grooves to the end. They will make a clunk as they return to their original position.

Brake Warning Light Comes On While Braking

In split brake systems, the pressure differential valve turns on the brake warning light if fluid pressure is lost in one-half of the system. Locate the problem, which is likely a leak, and repair it. Refer to the vehicle's service manual for instructions on resetting the pressure differential valve if necessary.

SECTION 2 KNOWLEDGE CHECK

1. What are the shoes failing to do when one brake drags?

2. Define brake pedal free play.

3. Name at least one source of brake system noise.

4. What complaint may be caused by wet brake linings?

5. Explain brake grabbing.

6. Which brake system complaint is normal with antilock brakes, but not with other brake systems?

ASE TEST PREP

7. Glazing of the brake drum friction surfaces is caused by:

   ⓐ excessive use.

   ⓑ overheating.

   ⓒ defective brake hardware.

   ⓓ improper machining.

● *Section 3*
Servicing Drum Brakes

Objectives:

C2 ● Remove, clean (using proper safety procedures), inspect, and measure brake drums.

C3 ● Refinish brake drum.

C4 ● Remove, clean, and inspect brake shoes, springs, pins, clips, levers, adjusters/self-adjusters, other related brake hardware, and backing support plates; lubricate and reassemble.

C5 ● Remove, inspect, and install wheel cylinders.

C6 ● Pre-adjust brake shoes and parking brake before installing brake drums or drum/hub assemblies and wheel bearings.

C7 ● Install wheel, torque lug nuts, and make final checks and adjustments.

Vocabulary:
● **star wheel**
● **brake spoon**
● **brake drum micrometer**
● **discard diameter**

Drum Brake Self-Adjusters

Few vehicles come without self-adjusters. These vehicles require periodic adjustment to keep the shoes in close proximity to the drums.

Brakes with self-adjusters should need adjustment only after servicing of brake shoes or drums. However, if the vehicle needs only an adjustment of the drum brake system, perform the adjustment as follows:

• Manually adjust brake self-adjusters by turning the adjuster's star wheel. The **star wheel** is an adjusting nut with indexing arms. These arms allow positive and accurate rotation. See **Fig. 3-13**. Most duo-servo brakes have a slot, or knockout, in the backing plate or drum through which you can access the star wheel.

• Turn the star wheel using a brake adjusting tool called a **brake spoon**. Turning the star wheel in one direction will move the shoes closer to the drum. Turning the star wheel in the opposite direction will move the shoes away from the drum. The correct direction for shortening or lengthening the adjuster varies from vehicle to vehicle. Refer to the vehicle's service manual for additional information.

• Complete the adjustment by making several alternating forward and reverse stops with the vehicle.

• If adjustment requires use of the parking brake, apply and release it several times—sometimes up to 50 cycles may be required.

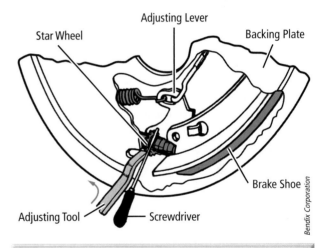

Star Wheel Adjusting Lever Backing Plate

Brake Shoe

Adjusting Tool Screwdriver

Bendix Corporation

Fig. 3-13 Use a screwdriver to push the adjuster lever away from the star wheel and turn it in the direction opposite to its normal rotation. *Why are drums occasionally difficult to remove?*

Brake Drums

Sometimes the only brake service needed will be brake adjustment. There will be many more cases, though, in which you will need to remove the brake drum to access the brake shoes and brake hardware.

Drum brake servicing requires a series of steps. The brake drum must be removed, cleaned and inspected, measured, and machined.

Removing the Brake Drum

To remove brake drums refer to the vehicle's service manual. In general, do the following:
- Raise the car and install safety equipment if using a jack stand.
- Loosen and remove the wheel cover, if there is one.
- Loosen and remove the wheel.
- Remove the brake drum from the drum brake system assembly.

Difficult-to-Remove Brake Drum A ridge of rust on the lip of the brake drum or excessive drum wear can make drum removal difficult. You may need to back off the brake adjuster before removing the drum. Back off the adjuster by turning the star wheel backwards. Access the star wheel through a slot in the rear of the backing plate.

Cleaning and Inspecting Brake Drums

Clean the brake drum with a clean shop towel using cleaning solvent or denatured alcohol. Inspect the cleaned brake drum for the following defects, shown in **Fig. 3-14**:
- Scoring—scratches or grooves in the drum's machined brake surface.
- Hard spots—areas of the machined brake surface that have not worn down with the rest of the machined surface.
- Bell mouthing—drum brake surface shows evidence of excessive wear toward the drum's rim.

- Barreling—machined brake surface is no longer flat and shows evidence of having greater wear toward the center of the brake drum's machined surface.
- Threads—brake drum's machined surface has the appearance of being threaded; results from improper machining.

Measuring Brake Drums

Measure the diameter of the drum, using a **brake drum micrometer.** This is a micrometer specially adapted to the measurement of brake drums. See **Fig. 3-15**. If the damage is not extensive, the drums can be machined. In machining brake drums, a brake lathe removes metal to restore the drum's braking surface.

If the drum is worn or scored too deeply, it must be replaced. The **discard diameter,** which is the maximum allowable diameter, is cast into the drum.

DaimlerChrysler

Fig. 3-15 Measuring the inside diameter of a brake drum.

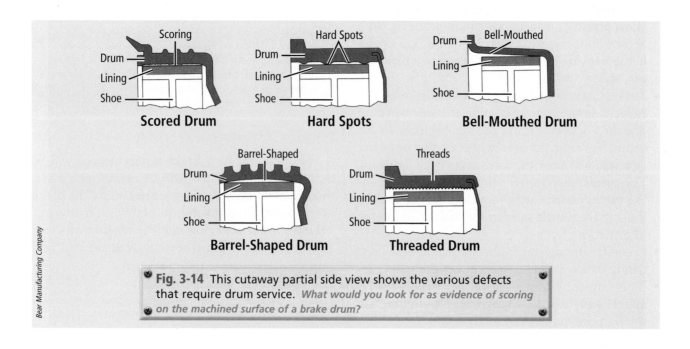

Scored Drum **Hard Spots** **Bell-Mouthed Drum**

Barrel-Shaped Drum **Threaded Drum**

Bear Manufacturing Company

Fig. 3-14 This cutaway partial side view shows the various defects that require drum service. *What would you look for as evidence of scoring on the machined surface of a brake drum?*

Safety First Cleaning and Inspecting Brake Drums Use caution when working around brake dust. Wear safety glasses. Wear a respirator to avoid breathing brake dust. Dispose of dust in a sealed container in accordance with hazardous waste laws. Wash your hands after servicing brake drums and do not wear your work clothes home.

Machining Brake Drums

To machine, or refinish, the brake drum, perform the following steps. (Follow the brake lathe manufacturer's instructions when using the lathe.)

1. Determine the maximum diameter for the machined surface of the brake drum. (The value is cast into the body of the brake drum.)
2. Measure the inside diameter of the brake drum using a brake drum micrometer or measuring calipers.
3. Calculate the amount of material that can be safely removed from the drum's machined surface.
4. Mount the brake drum on the brake lathe.
5. Machine the brake drum, being careful not to remove too much material.
6. Remove the brake drum from the lathe.
7. Clean the brake drum by wiping the machined surface with cleaning solvent and a clean rag. This will remove metal dust left in the drum. If not removed, the dust will be forced into the lining on the first brake application.
8. Remeasure to make sure brake drum is within specifications.

Brake Shoes

Inspect brake shoes for minimum thickness. If necessary, remove and replace.

Inspecting Brake Shoes

Replace brake shoes when their lining wears down below minimum thickness. Replace with new shoes or relined shoes. Relined brake shoes are recycled shoes with new friction material attached.

Inspect the entire wheel brake mechanism, paying particular attention to brake lining wear. Before removing the brake hardware, note where all the parts belong. Install brake shoes in the forward or rearward position as designed. There may be differences between the shoes, even if they look the same.

Follow the manufacturer's instructions for replacement of shoes. See **Fig. 3-16.**

Terry Wild Studio

Fig. 3-16 Replacing brake shoes on a rear drum-brake system. *Which replacement shoe is installed in the leading shoe position?*

Removing Brake Shoes

1. Remove the return springs from the backing plate.
2. Unhook the return springs from the brake shoes.
3. Remove the retainer pins and cups holding the shoes to the backing plate.
4. Remove the brake shoes from the backing plate.
5. Remove the self-adjuster.
6. Be sure to note the mounting orientation of the self-adjuster.

Wheel Cylinders

Wheel cylinder service requires removal and inspection of the wheel cylinder. A new wheel cylinder may need to be installed.

TECH TIP Wheel Cylinders. Rebuilding wheel cylinders was once a common service operation. Today it is rarely done. Many wheel cylinders in current use are made of aluminum and cannot be honed. While cast iron wheel cylinders can still be rebuilt, this is not cost effective. It can also place more liability on the service facility and the technician should the part fail. Today it is far more common to replace wheel cylinders.

Removing a Wheel Cylinder

To remove the wheel cylinder:
1. Remove the wheel and brake drum.
2. Remove brake shoes and brake hardware.
3. Disconnect the brake line from the wheel cylinder.
4. Plug the end of the brake line with a rubber vacuum line plug to keep out dirt.
5. Loosen and remove the attaching bolts or retainer clip.
6. Remove the wheel cylinder for servicing.
7. Inspect the wheel cylinder bore for wear or scoring. A leaking wheel cylinder with deep scores should be replaced. Leaking wheel cylinders with no serious damage may often be rebuilt.

Installing a Wheel Cylinder

Install a new or serviced wheel cylinder by following the removal instructions in reverse order.

The hydraulic system must be bled following any servicing or replacement of a wheel cylinder.

Inspecting, Installing, and Adjusting Brakes

The final steps of drum brake service are critical. They depend on careful inspection, installation, and adjustment of brake system components.

Inspecting Hardware

If possible, replace all brake hardware when servicing drum brakes. If this is not possible, then:
1. Carefully inspect the brake hardware for damage.
2. Replace any damaged components.
3. Disassemble the self-adjuster and clean it thoroughly.
4. Lubricate the threads on the self-adjuster with high-temperature grease. See **Fig. 3-17**.

Fig. 3-17 After cleaning the self-adjuster, lubricate the threads. Use a high-temperature grease.

5. Reassemble the self-adjuster and wipe off any excess lubricating grease.
6. The brake hardware is ready for reassembly.

Installing Brake Shoes

1. Reattach the brake shoes to the backing plate using the pin, spring, and cup assemblies.
2. Install the parking brake hardware.
3. Install the self-adjuster.
4. Attach the brake shoe return and hold-down springs. See **Fig. 3-18**.

Fig. 3-18 Attach the brake shoe return and hold-down springs between the shoes and the anchor pin. *Why should all brake hardware be replaced?*

Adjusting Brake Shoes

If a brake shoe adjusting gauge is not available, manually adjust the brake shoes.

Brake Shoe Adjusting Gauge Use a brake shoe adjusting gauge to adjust the brake shoes. This gauge can be used only before the brake drum is reinstalled.

When using a brake shoe adjusting gauge, measure the drum and adjust the shoes to match its diameter. See **Fig. 3-19**. Any additional adjustment, if required, can be made after the wheels are installed by accessing the star wheel through the backing plate.

TECH TIP **Star Wheel Adjustment.** You may not need to adjust the star wheel if a brake shoe adjusting gauge is used.

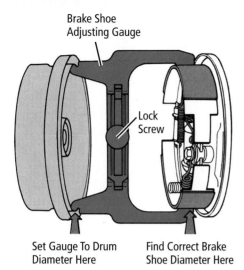

Brake Shoe Adjusting Gauge

Lock Screw

Set Gauge To Drum Diameter Here

Find Correct Brake Shoe Diameter Here

Ford Motor Company

Fig. 3-19 Use a brake shoe adjusting gauge to set the preliminary clearance or adjustment. *Why is a brake shoe adjustment gauge used?*

Manual Brake Shoe Adjustments Manually fit the brake shoes to the drum when no gauge is available as follows:

1. Extend the self-adjuster a small amount.
2. Place the brake drum over the shoes.
3. Continue to extend the self-adjuster and fit the drum until the shoes lightly brush the drum during installation.
4. You are now ready to install the brake drum.

Installing Brake Drums

Be sure you have repaired or replaced and correctly reinstalled all wheel brake hardware before proceeding with brake drum installation.

To install a new or machined brake drum, perform the following steps:

1. Install the drum over the wheel brake assembly.
2. Be sure that the drum is free to move.
3. Install the wheel. Tighten and torque the wheel nuts, following manufacturer's instructions. For more information on tightening and torquing the wheel nuts refer to "Wheel Fasteners" on SS-517.
4. Reinstall the wheel cover, if there is one.
5. Test the brakes. If they are too tight, back off the star wheel on the self-adjuster.
6. Remove all tools from beneath the vehicle.
7. Remove the jack stands or other safety hardware from beneath the vehicle.
8. Lower the car to the ground.
9. Use the correct method to activate the vehicle's self-adjuster. Repeat activation of the self-adjuster until you are satisfied that the brakes are properly adjusted.
10. Test drive the vehicle to ensure the brakes are working properly.

Safety First

Road Test Before performing a road test, be sure to obtain written permissions from appropriate authorities.

SECTION 3 KNOWLEDGE CHECK

1. What is a brake spoon?
2. What does a technician look for when inspecting a brake drum?
3. What is the purpose of a brake lathe?
4. When must brake shoes be replaced?
5. Explain how to install brake shoes.
6. Explain how to manually adjust brake shoes when no adjusting gauge is available.
7. What type of tool should be used to push the caliper piston back into the cylinder bore?
8. What resource should be consulted for information on tightening and torquing wheel nuts?

ASE TEST PREP

9. Technician A says the return springs should be replaced with every brake job. Technician B says the return springs will become weak if they are overheated. Who is correct?
   ⓐ Technician A.
   ⓑ Technician B.
   ⓒ Both Technician A and Technician B.
   ⓓ Neither Technician A nor Technician B.

CHAPTER 3 REVIEW

Key Points

Meets the following NATEF Standards for Brakes: diagnosing and servicing drum brakes and master cylinders.

- Most current vehicles have drum brakes only on their rear wheels.
- Drum brakes have two metal shoes lined with friction material. The shoes are pushed against the inside of the brake drum during braking.
- There are two types of drum brakes: leading trailing or non-servo, and duo-servo.
- Leading-trailing drum brakes are used on the rear wheels of front-wheel drive vehicles.
- Duo-servo drum brakes are usually found on the rear wheels of rear-wheel drive vehicles.
- A drum brake diagnosis table can be used to identify potential problems with brake systems.
- Self-adjusters can be manually adjusted by using a brake "spoon" tool to turn the star wheel.
- Wheel cylinders can be serviced on or off the vehicle. They can also be replaced.
- Brake drums can be machined to remove minor defects.

Review Questions

1. What rides on the raised metal pads of a drum brake backing plate?
2. What brake system part converts hydraulic pressure into mechanical movement?
3. What type of drum brakes allow the tops of brake shoes to rest against a single anchor pin?
4. What may cause a brake warning light to come on?
5. If the brakes on one side of a vehicle are not working, the vehicle will pull in which direction?
6. Describe what a technician should do when checking for brake fluid leaks.
7. Which system must be bled after servicing or replacing a wheel cylinder?
8. Explain how to use a brake shoe adjusting gauge.
9. **Critical Thinking** What may cause pedal pulsation or vibration in a drum brake system?
10. **Critical Thinking** What will a driver notice if self-adjusters are not working?

Excellence in Communication

Reading Exploded Views

Often, a technician has to "look" into a vehicle's system. A vehicle has many parts. They may be stacked one on top of another, as in an engine. Many small parts cannot be seen inside large components or assemblies. Even some large components cannot be seen clearly on the vehicle.

Service manuals and books provide pictures that allow the technician to see into an assembled system. These pictures are called exploded views. Exploded view diagrams can clarify information that would be very difficult to explain using only words. These views show all pieces of a system. Even very small pieces such as O-rings, springs, nuts, screws, and bolts are shown. The picture indicates how the parts fit together to form components. Some of these parts may fit inside each other when the component is assembled.

The technician can refer to exploded view diagrams when disassembling or reassembling vehicle systems and components. Every part may be identified by name and/or part number. The technician can use the part name or number to order replacements.

Apply It!

Meets NATEF Communications Standards for adapting reading strategies and comprehending written information.

1. Study **Fig. 3-6** until you understand how the parts of a wheel cylinder fit together.

2. Write a sentence describing the assembly.

3. Did you find it difficult to describe how the parts fit together? Explain.

AUTOMOTIVE SERVICE EXCELLENCE
TEST PREP

Answering the following practice questions will help you prepare for the ASE certification tests.

1. Technician A says that on some vehicles incremental adjusters operate when the vehicle is braked while moving either frontward or rearward. Technician B says that on some imports from Asia the brakes are adjusted whenever the parking brake is applied. Who is correct?

    ⓐ Technician A.
    ⓑ Technician B.
    ⓒ Both Technician A and Technician B.
    ⓓ Neither Technician A nor Technician B.

2. When all brakes drag, which of the following would be the most likely cause?

    ⓐ Weak or broken brake return springs.
    ⓑ Master cylinder not returning far enough to uncover the compensating port.
    ⓒ Damaged brake hose.
    ⓓ Seized parking brake cable.

3. Technician A says that when the brakes pull to one side when braking, the most likely cause is wet brakes. Technician B says that the cause is a defective automatic brake adjuster. Who is correct?

    ⓐ Technician A.
    ⓑ Technician B.
    ⓒ Both Technician A and Technician B.
    ⓓ Neither Technician A nor Technician B.

4. A vehicle has poor braking requiring excessive pedal force. Technician A says that this can be caused by a worn or stretched adjuster cable. Technician B says that this can be caused by low engine vacuum. Who is correct?

    ⓐ Technician A.
    ⓑ Technician B.
    ⓒ Both Technician A and Technician B.
    ⓓ Neither Technician A nor Technician B.

5. A self-adjuster may not work if the driver:

    ⓐ often applies the brakes in reverse.
    ⓑ often applies the parking brake.
    ⓒ seldom applies the parking brake.
    ⓓ fails to check brake fluid level.

6. In a split brake system, the pressure differential valve turns on the brake warning light if fluid pressure is lost in:

    ⓐ one-tenth of the system.
    ⓑ one-quarter of the system.
    ⓒ one-half of the system.
    ⓓ two-thirds of the system.

7. A drum brake surface with excessive wear toward the drum's rim shows evidence of:

    ⓐ barreling.
    ⓑ hard spots.
    ⓒ bell mouthing.
    ⓓ threads.

8. Technician A says that a leaking wheel cylinder with deep scores should be replaced. Technician B says that a leaking wheel cylinder with no serious damage may often be rebuilt. Who is correct?

    ⓐ Technician A.
    ⓑ Technician B.
    ⓒ Both Technician A and Technician B.
    ⓓ Neither Technician A nor Technician B.

9. If the drum brake self-adjuster has been disassembled and cleaned, its threads should:

    ⓐ not be lubricated.
    ⓑ be lubricated with machine oil.
    ⓒ be lubricated with motor oil.
    ⓓ be lubricated with high-temperature grease.

10. Technician A says that the brake shoe adjusting gauge can be used after the brake drum has been reinstalled. Technician B says that the brake shoe adjusting gauge can be used only before the brake drum is reinstalled. Who is correct?

    ⓐ Technician A.
    ⓑ Technician B.
    ⓒ Both Technician A and Technician B.
    ⓓ Neither Technician A nor Technician B.

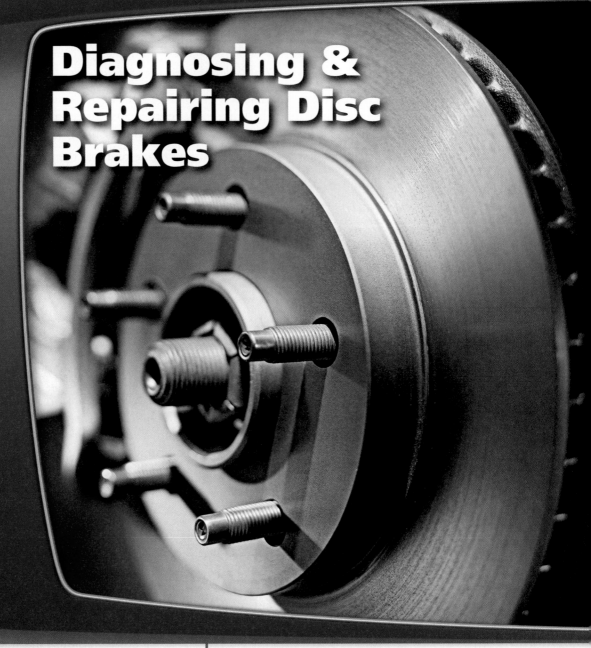

Diagnosing & Repairing Disc Brakes

Section 1
Disc Brake
Construction
and Operation

Section 2
Disc Brake
Diagnosis

Section 3
Disc Brake
Service

Customer's Concern

Stacy Thompson was on her way to a job interview in a neighboring state when her car started to shake. The shaking was so bad that she thought a back wheel was going to fall off of her car. She has only a few hours to make it to her interview. She needs your help quickly.

After asking Stacy a few questions, you learn that her car didn't just start shaking as she was driving down the highway. In fact, she had noticed the problem more than a week before when she suddenly hit the brakes to avoid hitting a squirrel. "The brake pedal seemed to push back against my foot, and the steering wheel sort of shook or vibrated," she said.

On a short test drive around the service center parking lot, you recognize brake pedal pulsations.

Technician's Challenge

As the service technician, you need to find answers to these questions:

1. Are the brake pedal pulsations due to brake system problems? Could any other automotive defect cause brake pedal pulsations?

2. After considering the potential causes of Stacy's automotive problem, which causes should you examine first? Which should you exclude first?

3. Once you determine what is causing the brake pulsations, how will you correct the problem and get Stacy back on the road to her interview?

● Section 1

Disc Brake Construction and Operation

Objectives:
- Describe disc brake construction.
- Describe disc brake operation.

Vocabulary:
- brake pads
- rotors
- calipers
- caliper mounting brackets
- fixed caliper disc brakes
- floating caliper disc brakes
- sliding caliper disc brakes
- disc brake wear indicators

Disc Brake Construction

Disc brakes use hydraulic pressure to clamp brake pads against a rotating disc called a brake rotor. Most vehicles have front-wheel disc brakes. Rear-wheel brakes can be either disc or drum. Disc brakes are engaged by hydraulic pressure. Parking brakes on vehicles with four-wheel disc brakes are activated by a mechanical system. Some systems mechanically activate the calipers. Other systems use a small drum brake inside the rotor to serve as the parking brake.

Disc brakes use friction between the rotor and brake pads to convert vehicle motion into heat. As with drum brakes, great amounts of heat are produced during braking. This high heat limits the types of materials that can be used for brake pads. Unlike drum brakes, however, disc brakes release heat quickly. Some rotor designs are better suited than others for releasing heat.

Disc brake systems have four major parts. These are the:
- **Brake pads,** which are friction surfaces that convert motion into heat.
- **Rotors,** which are metal discs supported by the suspension. They are clamped by the calipers, slowing the wheel rotation. This slows and stops the vehicle.
- **Calipers,** which are housings that contain the pistons and the brake pads. Connected to the hydraulic system, the calipers hold the brake pads so they can straddle the rotor.
- **Caliper mounting brackets,** which hold the calipers in place.

Disc brakes are constructed so the friction surfaces are external and in contact with the air flowing under the vehicle. This makes them more effective than drum brakes. On drum brakes, friction surfaces are enclosed in the drum and covered by the backing plate. This makes it harder to dispel the heat generated during braking. This is one reason disc brakes are more effective in making repeated stops. Disc brakes are easier to service, due to their simpler design.

Brake Pads

Brake pads are the parts of disc brake systems that convert vehicle motion into heat. They are flat steel plates with friction material, called linings, attached by rivets or adhesive. The pads are in the caliper housing. They are pushed against each side of the rotor by the caliper piston(s). Linings are made from non-asbestos, semimetallic, or ceramic materials on late-model vehicles. Caution: Some replacement pads for older vehicles may have some asbestos content.

When the brakes are applied, the pads generate high braking forces on both sides of the brake rotor. Because both sides of the rotor are exposed to the cooling air, heat can be rapidly removed from the rotor. This allows repeated stops without brake fade.

When the brakes are applied, the vehicle weight transfers toward the front of the vehicle. Because of this weight transfer, the front brakes do more work than the rear brakes.

Brakes must be able to handle the vehicle's weight. The way a vehicle is built decides how much weight is on the front wheels. Due to weight distribution in rear-wheel drive automobiles, about 60 percent of braking is handled by the front disc brakes and 40 percent by the rear brakes.

Front-wheel-drive vehicles have their drivetrains mounted over the front wheels. This results in about 80 percent of the braking effort being handled by the front disc brakes. The rear brakes provide only 20 percent of the braking effort.

Rotors

Rotors are disc-shaped devices made from cast iron or sintered iron. They have flat friction surfaces machined onto both sides. They are attached to the spindles or hubs and rotate on the wheel bearings.

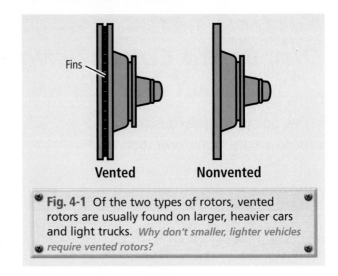

Fig. 4-1 Of the two types of rotors, vented rotors are usually found on larger, heavier cars and light trucks. *Why don't smaller, lighter vehicles require vented rotors?*

There are two type of rotors:

- Vented rotors have fins in the space between their machined surfaces. These fins allow air to pass through the rotor. This airflow helps carry away excess heat built up during braking. Vented rotors are used on heavier vehicles that produce large amounts of heat during braking. See **Fig. 4-1**.

- Nonvented rotors are solid metal with no air vents to aid in heat removal. Nonvented rotors are used mainly on smaller vehicles where brake overheating is not a serious problem. See **Fig. 4-1**.

Calipers

Calipers are housings that contain the pistons and the brake pads. See **Fig. 4-2**. They convert hydraulic pressure from the master cylinder into linear motion. Each caliper includes a housing with one, two, or four cylinder bores. Each cylinder bore has a single piston.

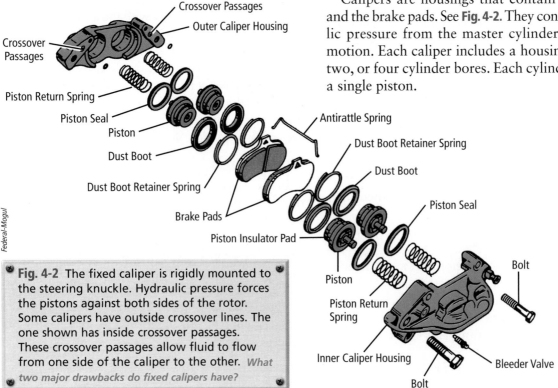

Federal-Mogul

Fig. 4-2 The fixed caliper is rigidly mounted to the steering knuckle. Hydraulic pressure forces the pistons against both sides of the rotor. Some calipers have outside crossover lines. The one shown has inside crossover passages. These crossover passages allow fluid to flow from one side of the caliper to the other. *What two major drawbacks do fixed calipers have?*

When the driver presses the brake pedal, brake fluid is forced out of the master cylinder through the brake lines and into the calipers. Fixed calipers have two sides, an inboard side and an outboard side. There are pistons in each half. Fluid passes between the caliper halves—either through outside crossover lines or through inside passages. Hydraulic pressure from the master cylinder forces pistons in both halves of the caliper to push the pads against the rotor. This provides the desired braking action. Floating or sliding calipers use only one piston. They allow caliper movement to equalize force to both sides of the rotors.

Disc Brake Operation

The operation of a disc brake depends on its caliper arrangement. The three types of disc brakes are:
• Fixed caliper disc brakes.
• Floating caliper disc brakes.
• Sliding caliper disc brakes.

Fixed Caliper Disc Brakes

Fixed caliper disc brakes are disc brakes that use a caliper that is fixed in position and cannot move. The caliper has pistons on both sides of the rotor, in both the inboard and outboard caliper halves. There may be two or four pistons in each caliper as shown in **Fig. 4-2.**

Two major drawbacks of fixed caliper designs are their high costs to manufacture and to repair. These drawbacks result from the complexity of fixed caliper designs.

Floating Caliper Disc Brakes

Floating caliper disc brakes are disc brakes that use a caliper that is free to move sideways on bushings and guide pins. A support bracket is mounted to the spindle or steering knuckle. The caliper housing is mounted to the support bracket. Floating caliper disc brakes have only one piston. This piston is on the inboard side of the caliper. See **Fig. 4-3.**

The piston applies direct pressure to the inboard pad. As the inboard pad contacts the rotor, it forces the caliper to slide along the pins. This pulls the outboard pad against the rotor.

The actual movement of floating calipers on the guide pins when brakes are applied is very small. When the brakes are applied, the caliper grips the rotor. It relaxes upon release of the brake pedal. The brake pads stay at zero clearance to the rotor. See **Fig. 4-4.**

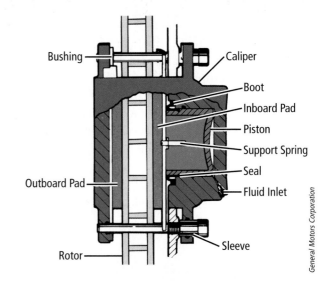

General Motors Corporation

Fig. 4-3 Construction of a floating caliper disc brake, which has only one piston. When pressure is applied, the outboard pad is forced against the rotor. *Is the piston in a floating caliper on the inboard side or on the outboard side of the caliper?*

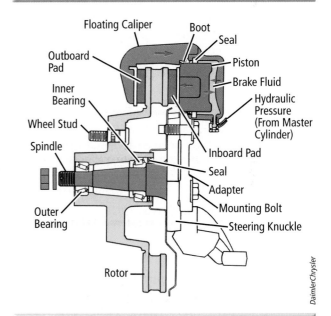

DaimlerChrysler

Fig. 4-4 The red arrows show the movement of floating calipers. *What is the normal clearance between the rotor and the brake pads when the brakes are at rest?*

TECH TIP **Guide Pins.** The guide pins must be clean to allow free movement of the caliper along the pins. If the movement is not free, the result can be uneven wearing of the pads. This could result in uneven braking of the vehicle. Clean or replace the guide pins when servicing floating caliper disc brakes. Remember to grease the guide pins when installing them.

Sliding Caliper Disc Brakes

In operation, sliding calipers are similar to floating calipers. The difference is in the way the caliper is mounted and moved. **Sliding caliper disc brakes** use a caliper that is held in place by a retainer, a spring, and a bolt. There are no guide pins. Sliding calipers slide on mating surfaces. These surfaces are machined onto both the caliper and the mounting bracket. See **Fig. 4-5.**

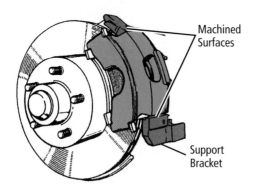

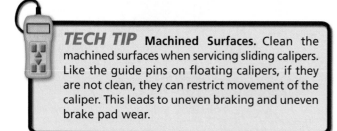

Fig. 4-5 The sliding caliper's machined surfaces move along the machined surfaces of the support bracket. *What must be kept clean to allow free movement of the caliper?*

TECH TIP **Machined Surfaces.** Clean the machined surfaces when servicing sliding calipers. Like the guide pins on floating calipers, if they are not clean, they can restrict movement of the caliper. This leads to uneven braking and uneven brake pad wear.

Self-Adjusting Disc Brakes

Disc brakes will self-adjust. They automatically adjust for brake pad wear. The caliper's cylinder bore has a rectangular groove with a square-cut seal. This seal fits tightly around the piston. The seal provides a barrier between the piston and the caliper bore. This barrier keeps brake fluid from leaking. A dust boot on the open end of the caliper bore keeps out dirt and water.

When the brakes are applied, the piston moves toward the rotor. This causes the square-cut seal to deflect slightly. The seal continues to grip the piston. When the brakes are released, the square-cut seal acts to pull the piston back into the bore and away from the rotor. This small movement keeps the pads at zero clearance with the rotors.

As the pads wear, the piston travel when the brakes are applied becomes greater than the amount the seal can deflect. When this happens, the piston slides outward through the seal and assumes a new position. See **Fig. 4-6.** This moves the pads closer to the rotor and adjusts for brake pad wear.

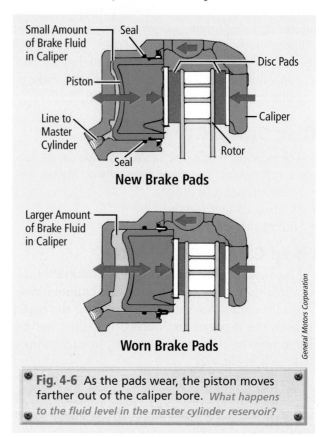

New Brake Pads

Worn Brake Pads

General Motors Corporation

Fig. 4-6 As the pads wear, the piston moves farther out of the caliper bore. *What happens to the fluid level in the master cylinder reservoir?*

Brake fluid from the master cylinder fills the additional space behind the piston in the caliper bore. This lowers the fluid level in the master cylinder. This is why a disc brake reservoir is larger than a drum brake reservoir.

The shape of the seal groove in the caliper determines how far the seal travels with the piston. The amount of seal deflection also determines how far the piston retracts into the caliper bore. On a low drag caliper, the seal groove in the caliper's bore is cut at a small angle. This design allows the seal more movement.

Greater movement allows the seal to deflect farther when the brakes are applied. See **Fig. 4-7(a).** It also permits them to retract more when they are released. See **Fig. 4-7(b).**

This increased piston movement allows the brake pads to be pulled farther from the rotors. As a result, when the brakes are released, the pads do not drag against the rotor. Dragging pads would waste energy and increase fuel consumption.

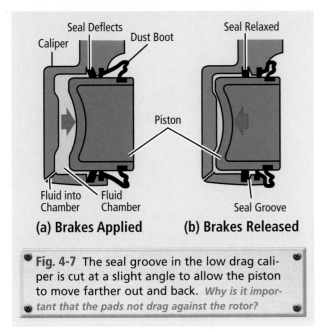

(a) Brakes Applied   (b) Brakes Released

Fig. 4-7 The seal groove in the low drag caliper is cut at a slight angle to allow the piston to move farther out and back. *Why is it important that the pads not drag against the rotor?*

The greater piston movement of low drag calipers requires more brake fluid movement into and out of the master cylinder. As a result, systems with low drag calipers require the use of quick take-up master cylinders.

In design and operation, the low-drag caliper is similar to other calipers, with the exception of the square-cut seal and groove.

Disc Brake Wear Indicators

Disc brake wear indicators are devices that alert the driver to the need for brake service. They are found on some disc brake pads. Ignoring the warning and continuing to use worn pads may cause costly damage to the rotors. There are two types of wear indicators: mechanical and electrical.

Mechanical Wear Indicators Mechanical wear indicators are attached to the metal part of the pad. As the lining wears down, the wear indicator rubs against the rotor, making a high-pitched sound. This tells the driver to have the brakes serviced. See **Fig. 4-8**.

Electrical Wear Indicators Disc pads with electrical wear indicators have buried sensor wires. When the pads wear down far enough, these sensor wires contact the metal rotor. The metal rotor conducts the current across the sensor wires. This turns on the warning light on the dash.

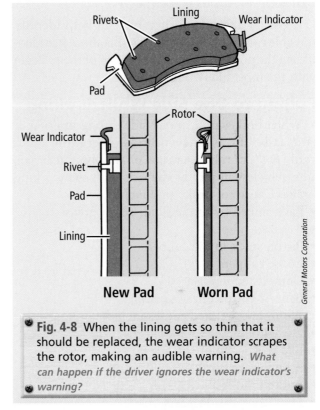

New Pad   Worn Pad

General Motors Corporation

Fig. 4-8 When the lining gets so thin that it should be replaced, the wear indicator scrapes the rotor, making an audible warning. *What can happen if the driver ignores the wear indicator's warning?*

SECTION 1 KNOWLEDGE CHECK

1. What are the four major parts of a disc brake system?

2. What makes disc brakes more effective than drum brakes?

3. What are vented rotors? When are they used?

4. What two brake system parts are housed by calipers?

5. Name the three types of disc brakes.

6. What is the purpose of disc brake wear indicators?

ASE TEST PREP

7. Technician A says sliding calipers are mounted with guide pins. Technician B says the floating calipers slide on machine surfaces. Who is correct?
   - ⓐ Technician A.
   - ⓑ Technician B.
   - ⓒ Both Technician A and Technician B.
   - ⓓ Neither Technician A nor Technician B.

● Section 2
Disc Brake Diagnosis

Objectives:

A2 ● Identify and interpret brake system concern.

D1 ● Diagnose poor stopping, noise, vibration, pulling, grabbing, dragging or pedal pulsation concerns.

Vocabulary:
● **rotor runout**
● **pedal pulsation**

General Complaints

A disc brake diagnosis table can help identify possible causes of disc brake complaints. After identifying the possible causes, check each of them. Begin with the most likely. See **Table 4-A.**

Pulling to One Side While Braking

When brakes pull to one side during braking, it is usually due to uneven brake operation. First, verify proper brake operation on the opposite brake. The vehicle will pull to the side with the working brake. Causes of brake pull include:
• Pads ruined by brake fluid, oil, or grease.
• A seized caliper.
• Piston stuck in the caliper.
• Loose caliper.
• Unmatched linings.
• Bent or warped brake pad(s).
  Non-brake-related causes include:
• Low tire pressure.
• Bad wheel alignment.
• Broken rear spring.
• Broken shocks.
• Loose suspension parts.

Front Disc Brakes Grabbing

If the front brakes grab (and the rear drum brakes are in good condition), the causes may be:
• Incorrect brake pad lining.
• Defective surface finish on rotor.
• Contaminated brake pad lining.

On vehicles with rear drum brakes, a defective metering valve can allow the front brakes to grab. The metering valve is designed to hold off hydraulic pressure to the front disc brakes until the rear brakes have overcome the return spring tension.

Failing to Release

Disc brakes might fail to release due to:
• Brake pedal binding.
• Master cylinder pushrod out of adjustment.

• Incorrect stoplight switch adjustment.
• Caliper piston not retracting properly.
• Parking brake out of adjustment.
• Hydraulic lines (pipes, hoses, banjo bolts) restricted.

Excessive Pedal Travel

Excessive pedal travel exists when the piston must travel farther than normal. Excessive pedal travel indicates the need for a greater volume of brake fluid to compensate. Causes include:
• Excessive rotor runout knocking the pistons back into their bores. **Rotor runout** is a term used to describe the wobble of the brake rotor. See **Fig. 4-9.**
• Loose calipers.
• A damaged piston seal in the caliper.
• Rear caliper parking brake out of adjustment.
• Floating or sliding caliper not moving freely.

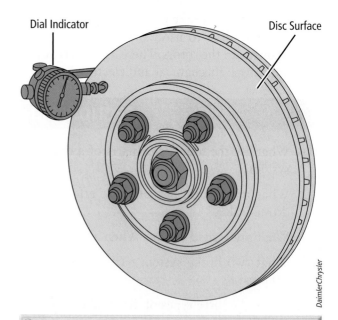

Dial Indicator   Disc Surface

DaimlerChrysler

Fig. 4-9 Runout can knock the piston back into the bore. *What are some of the symptoms of excessive runout?*

Table 4-A	DIAGNOSING DISC BRAKES	
Complaint	**Possible Cause**	**Check or Correction**
1. Excessive pedal travel	a. Excessive rotor runout b. Air in hydraulic system c. Low brake fluid d. Bent brake pad and lining or loose insulators e. Loose wheel bearing f. Damaged piston seal in caliper g. Power brake inoperative h. Failure of one section of hydraulic system i. Caliper parking brake out of adjustment j. Loose calipers k. Floating or sliding caliper not moving freely	a. Refinish or replace rotor b. Bleed brakes c. Fill, inspect, repair, and bleed system d. Inspect and replace e. Adjust or replace f. Replace g. Repair or replace h. Inspect and repair; check brake warning light i. Inspect rear calipers; repair j. Tighten retaining bolts k. Inspect, clean, repair, or replace guide pins or slides
2. Pedal pulsations or vibrations	a. Excessive rotor runout (wobble) b. Rotor out of parallel (uneven rotor thickness) c. Loose wheel bearings d. Tight caliper slides e. Wheel and tire vibration	a. Refinish or replace rotor b. Refinish or replace rotor c. Adjust or replace d. Free and repair e. Diagnose vibration
3. Excessive pedal force, grabbing, uneven braking	a. Power brake booster defective b. Brake fluid, oil, or grease on lining c. Linings worn or glazed d. Wrong lining e. Piston stuck in caliper f. Failure of one section of hydraulic system	a. Repair or replace b. Repair leakage; replace pads c. Replace pads d. Install correct lining e. Service or replace caliper f. Inspect and repair; check brake warning light
4. Pulls to one side while braking	a. Brake fluid, oil, or grease on linings b. Seized caliper c. Piston stuck in caliper d. Incorrect tire pressure e. Bent or warped brake pads f. Incorrect wheel alignment g. Broken rear spring h. Restricted line or hose i. Unmatched linings j. Loose caliper k. Loose suspension parts l. Broken shocks	a. Repair leakage, replace pads b. Service or replace caliper c. Service or replace caliper d. Adjust e. Replace f. Align g. Replace h. Repair or replace i. Replace j. Tighten k. Tighten l. Replace shocks
5. Brake noise	a. Typical of some disc brakes	a. Not detrimental, no action required. Often eliminated when driver increases or decreases brake-pedal force slightly
• Frequent or continuous squeal	a. Brake pad loose on caliper b. Worn or missing parts c. Improper clearance on rear disc brakes d. Rotor scored or improperly machined e. Antisqueal compound not applied to pads f. Brake pad lining is glazed g. Rivets loose in brake pad	a. Clinch brake pad tabs to caliper b. Check for damaged or missing antirattle springs, antisqueal shims or insulators, or worn caliper guide pins and bushings c. Check clearance between rotor and lining d. Remachine or replace rotor e. Remove and apply antisqueal compound to back of pads f. Inspect rotor; replace pads g. Replace brake pads
• Occasional squeal	a. Typical of many disc brakes	a. Not detrimental, no action required. Explain to driver the occasional squeal cannot always be eliminated
• Scraping	a. Disc rubbing caliper b. Loose wheel bearing c. Worn lining; wear sensor scraping on disc d. Improper assembly	a. Remove rust or mud from caliper; tighten caliper bolts b. Adjust or replace c. Inspect disc; replace pads d. Assemble properly
• Rattle at low speed	a. Pads loose on caliper b. Loose antirattle clips c. Loose attaching hardware	a. Clinch pad tabs to caliper; install new pads b. Adjust or tighten clips c. Tighten attaching hardware
• Groan when slowly releasing brakes (creep groan)	a. Brake pads loose on caliper	a. Clinch brake pad tabs to caliper; install new brake pads

Table 4-A	DIAGNOSING DISC BRAKES (continued)	
Complaint	**Possible Cause**	**Check or Correction**
6. Brakes fail to release	a. Power brake booster defective b. Brake pedal binding c. Master cylinder push rod improperly adjusted d. Driver rides pedal e. Incorrect stoplight switch adjustment f. Caliper piston not retracting g. Speed control switch improperly adjusted h. Incorrect parking brake adjustment i. Restricted pipes, hoses, or banjo bolts	a. Repair or replace b. Free and repair c. Adjust d. Notify driver e. Adjust f. Service or replace g. Adjust h. Adjust i. Repair
7. Fluid leaking from caliper	a. Damaged or worn piston seal b. Scores or corrosion on piston or in caliper bore c. Defective caliper seal d. Loose brake line fitting e. Damaged copper sealing washer on banjo bolt	a. Replace b. Service caliper c. Rebuild or replace caliper d. Tighten fitting or replace brake line e. Replace copper sealing washer
8. Front disc brakes grab (rear drum brakes do not)	a. Defective metering valve b. Incorrect brake pad linings c. Improper surface finish on rotor d. Contaminated brake pad linings	a. Replace b. Replace c. Refinish rotor d. Replace
9. No braking with pedal fully depressed	a. Piston pushed back in caliper b. Leak in hydraulic system c. Damaged piston seal d. Air in hydraulic system e. Leak past primary cup in master cylinder f. Low fluid in reservoir	a. Pump brake pedal; check brake pad position b. Repair c. Replace d. Add fluid; bleed system e. Service or replace master cylinder f. Add fluid
10. Fluid level low in master cylinder	a. Leaks b. Worn linings	a. Repair; add fluid; bleed system b. Replace
11. Warning light comes on while braking	a. One section of hydraulic system has failed b. Pressure differential valve defective	a. Check both sections; replace b. Replace
12. Caliper parking brake will not hold vehicle	a. Improper parking brake cable adjustment b. Defective rear actuators c. Ineffective rear lining d. Defective parking brake pedal assembly	a. Adjust b. Adjust, repair c. Inspect and replace d. Repair
13. Caliper parking brake will not release	a. Improper cable adjustment b. Vacuum release system inoperative	a. Adjust b. Repair

Pedal Pulsations

A **pedal pulsation** is a throbbing or vibration of the pedal. Pedal pulsations are often due to:

- A rotor with excessive runout.
- A rotor that is out of parallel (uneven rotor thickness).
- Loose wheel bearings.
- Tire and wheel vibration.

Uneven rotor thickness knocks the pistons back into their bores. This motion is carried through the brake fluid, back to the master cylinder, and then to the pedal. Often these problems can be corrected by machining or replacing the rotor.

Pedal pulsations are normal on some ABS brakes. Pulsations are noticeable only when ABS brakes are activated in emergency or panic stops.

Excessive Pedal Force, Grabbing, and Uneven Braking

Excessive pedal force, grabbing, and uneven braking are usually caused by a problem with the power brake booster. They could also result from:

- Contaminated pads (brake fluid, grease, and oil).
- Worn or glazed pads.
- The wrong pads.
- Piston stuck in the caliper.
- Worn, glazed, or scored rotor. See **Fig. 4-10**.

Terry Wild Studio

Fig. 4-10 A worn or scored rotor will not produce the friction needed for good braking. *How might this be corrected?*

If the rotor is worn, scored, or glazed, check rotor thickness with a micrometer to see if it can be machined on a lathe. If the rotor is not thick enough to machine, replace it. Replace glazed pads at the same time. Always service both sides of the vehicle, even if the condition is only on one wheel. This will help eliminate uneven braking. Check for problems in the hydraulic system.

No Braking with Pedal Fully Depressed

No braking with the pedal fully depressed may be caused by the piston (and thus the pads) being too far from the rotor after servicing. It may take more than several pumps to extend the pistons. It may also be the result of low brake fluid in the master cylinder reservoir.

Fluid Leaking from Caliper

Visible brake fluid on the caliper indicates a leak. This may be caused by:
• A defective piston seal.
• A scored or pitted piston.
• A loose brake line fitting.
• A damaged copper sealing washer on a banjo bolt.

Low Fluid Level in Master Cylinder

Low fluid level in the master cylinder is usually due to worn brake pads. As the pistons move farther out of the caliper bore, the fluid level drops. Check the hydraulic system for leaks, as well.

Safety First

Fluid Use Never put oil, transmission fluid, or power steering fluid in the brake system. It will damage the rubber parts and can lead to brake fluid leaks and eventual brake failure.

TECH TIP **Low Fluid Level in Master Cylinder.** When the fluid level is low in the master cylinder and there are no visible leaks, remove the vacuum hose from the booster. Check for visible signs of brake fluid in the hose. The leak may be in the rear seal of the master cylinder. This could allow fluid to be drawn into the booster and through the vacuum hose into the engine. Loosen the bolts holding the master cylinder to the power booster. Look for wet areas between the master cylinder and the booster. If fluid is escaping from the rear of the master cylinder, the master cylinder must be replaced. Most master cylinder cores are returned for remanufactured or new units.

Noise

Brake noise indicates vibration of brake parts. Some occasional noises are normal. High humidity or using a very light touch on the brake pedal when applying the brakes can cause brake squeal. Another cause of brake squeal is use of a hard brake pad compound. Other noises may indicate brake problems.

Scraping Sounds Scraping sounds may be caused by:
• The caliper contacting the rotor.
• Brake pad worn down to the metal backing.
• Mechanical wear indicators rubbing the rotor.

Rattling Noises Rattling noises may be caused by:
• Loose antirattle clips.
• Loose attaching hardware.
• Loose pads.
Some non-disc brake related causes include loose wheel bearings and debris or rust between the rotors and splash shields.

Constant Squealing A constant brake squeal may be the result of:

- Pads loose in the caliper.
- Worn or missing antirattle springs, guide pins, or bushings.
- Loose or missing antisqueal shims. See **Fig. 4-11.**
- Loose pad lining attachment rivets.
- Scored or improperly machined rotor.
- Antisqueal compound not on backs of pads.
- Glazed pads.

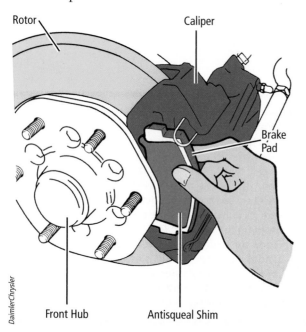

DaimlerChrysler

Rotor   Caliper

Brake Pad

Front Hub   Antisqueal Shim

Fig. 4-11 An antisqueal shim or compound can sometimes control brake squeal. *Name two non-disc brake related causes of brake noise.*

TECH TIP **Antisqueal Compound.** Antisqueal compound can be placed on the metal backing of brake pads to eliminate some squealing noises. Do not apply coating to the friction surface of the pads.

Brake Warning Light On

If the brake warning light comes on while braking, there may be unequal pressure between the two hydraulic braking circuits. This could mean that one side of the hydraulic system has failed. It may also indicate that the pressure differential valve is not working correctly.

Parking Brake Complaints

Parking brake adjustment is important, especially on vehicles with rear disc brakes.

Caliper Parking Brake Not Holding If the parking brake is not holding the vehicle, inspect the parking brake cable or assembly for proper operation. If the vehicle has four-wheel disc brakes, refer to the vehicle's service manual for the correct procedure to adjust the parking brakes.

Caliper Parking Brake Not Releasing When the parking brake does not release properly, check the parking brake cable adjustment. Inspect the cable for rust, which may cause binding. Some vehicles have a parking brake vacuum release system. Check to see that it is working correctly.

SECTION 2 KNOWLEDGE CHECK

1. Why shouldn't a driver be concerned with occasional disc brake squealing?

2. What may cause a caliper parking brake's failure to hold a vehicle?

3. What will the driver hear when brake pads become loose on the calipers?

4. What does brake noise indicate?

5. What may cause disc brake scraping sounds?

6. What may be used to control brake squeal?

7. Improperly measured and adjusted master cylinder pushrod length may lead to what brake system complication?

ASE TEST PREP

8. Why are shims or brake compound placed on the back of disc brake pads?
   - ❶ To attach the brake pads to the caliper piston.
   - ❷ To help reduce disc brake noise.
   - ❸ To hold the brake pads in the proper position.
   - ❹ To stop brake fluid leaks at the caliper piston.

● Section 3
Disc Brake Service

Objectives:

D4 ● Remove, clean, and inspect pads and retaining hardware.

D11 ● Adjust calipers equipped with an integrated parking brake system.

D2 ● Remove caliper assembly from mountings; clean and inspect for leaks and damage to caliper housing.

D5 ● Disassemble and clean caliper assembly; inspect parts for wear, rust, scoring, and damage; replace seal, boot, and damaged or worn parts.

D12 ● Install wheel, torque lug nuts, and make final checks and adjustments.

D3 ● Clean and inspect caliper mounting and slides for wear and damage.

D6 ● Reassemble, lubricate, and reinstall caliper, pads, and related hardware; seat pads, and inspect for leaks.

F8 ● Inspect and replace wheel studs.

D7 ● Clean, inspect, and measure rotor with a dial indicator and a micrometer; follow manufacturer's recommendations in determining need to machine or replace.

D8 ● Remove and reinstall rotor.

D9 ● Refinish rotor on vehicle.

D10 ● Refinish rotor off vehicle.

Vocabulary:

● **scores**
● **honing**
● **on-car brake lathe**
● **nondirectional finish**

Disc Brake Pad and Caliper Service

Check the brake pads first. They may be the only problem. Always check the vehicle service manual before doing any repair work. The procedures outlined here represent only one possible method.

You can usually replace the pads in fixed calipers without removing the calipers from the vehicle. Only the wheel will need to be removed. On floating or sliding calipers, however, you must remove the wheel and caliper to replace the pads.

> **Safety First** **Dust Mask/Respirator** Do not use pressurized air to clean disc brake calipers and pads. Breathing brake dust is a health hazard. Always wear a dust mask or respirator when servicing brakes.

Inspecting Disc Brake Pads

Disc brake pad inspection requires removing the vehicle's wheel. Inspect pad surface for signs of glazing, cracking, or other problems. Replace pads if they are worn to minimum thickness or if the pads on the same wheel have uneven wear. If wear is uneven, inspect slides, guides, and pistons of the caliper for binding.

Inspect the brake pads as follows:

1. Use a hoist or other device to safely raise the vehicle. Place safety stands under the vehicle.
2. Remove the lug nuts holding the wheel to the axle or hubs. Remove the wheel.
3. Check pads for even wear. Uneven wear indicates a problem with the caliper. Refer to the vehicle service manual for minimum thickness. If the manual does not specify minimum thickness, compare the thickness to that of a new pad.

4. Inspect brake pad retaining hardware. Repair or replace as necessary.

5. If pads appear to be more than about 75 percent worn, replace them and reinstall the wheel. If pads do not need to be replaced, reinstall the wheel.

6. Remove safety stands and lower the vehicle to the ground.

7. Verify that the brakes work normally. Then remove the vehicle from the hoist.

8. Road test the vehicle.

Safety First **Road Tests** Before performing a road test, be sure to obtain written permissions from appropriate authorities.

Replacing Disc Brake Pads

Before removing and installing disc brake pads, open the bleeder valve as you are retracting the caliper piston.

Replacing Disc Brake Pads (Fixed Calipers) Before installing new disc brake pads, coat the back of the pads with the antisqueal compound. Do this 15–20 minutes before you expect to install them to allow the antisqueal compound to dry. Remove the old brake pads as follows:

1. Remove and discard one-half to two-thirds of the fluid from the master cylinder.

2. Use a hoist or other device to safely raise the vehicle. Place safety stands under the vehicle.

3. Remove the lug nuts holding the wheel to the axle or hub. Remove the wheel.

4. Remove the brake pad retaining bolts or pins from the caliper housing.

5. To prevent damage to hydraulic components, loosen the brake caliper bleeder valve to release brake fluid pressure created during the brake piston retraction process. Close the valve after the process has been completed.

6. Use a piston retraction tool to push the caliper pistons back into the cylinder bore. This is necessary to make room for the thicker replacement brake pads.

7. Remove the brake pads.

8. Coat the metal sides of the replacement disc pads with antisqueal compound or install new shims.

9. Install the new pads with the linings toward the friction surface of the rotor.

10. Reinstall the brake pad retaining bolts or pins in the caliper housing.

11. Bleed the brake system after the brake pad replacement has been completed.

12. Reinstall the wheel.

13. Remove the safety stands and lower the vehicle to the ground.

14. Pump the brake pedal several times to displace the caliper pistons and verify that the brakes operate normally.

15. Top off the fluid in the master cylinder.

16. Remove the vehicle from the hoist.

17. Test drive the vehicle.

Safety First **Road Tests** Before performing a road test, be sure to obtain written permissions from appropriate authorities.

Removing and Replacing Disc Brake Pads and Calipers (Floating or Sliding Calipers)

Before removing the disc brake calipers, remove and discard one-half to two-thirds of the fluid from the master cylinder reservoir. This prevents the fluid from overflowing when the caliper pistons are pushed back into their bores.

Remove a floating disc brake caliper as follows:

1. Use a hoist or other device to safely raise the vehicle. Install safety stands under the vehicle.

2. Remove the lug nuts holding the wheel to the axle or hub. Remove the wheel.

3. Use a piston retraction tool or a C-clamp to force the pistons back into the bore of the caliper. See **Fig. 4-12**. Back the pistons and disc brake pads away from the rotor to make caliper removal easier.

4. Remove the two caliper guide pins or mounting bolts and positioners. On sliding-type calipers, remove the bolt, retainer key, and flat spring.

5. Remove the caliper. Support or hang the caliper to the vehicle frame with a piece of wire. Never allow the caliper to hang by the hose as this may do internal damage to the hose.

TECH TIP **Supporting the Caliper.** Support the caliper with wire. Without stretching the brake hose, attach one end of a piece of wire to a strong suspension member. Do not let the caliper hang from the brake hose. The hose might be damaged.

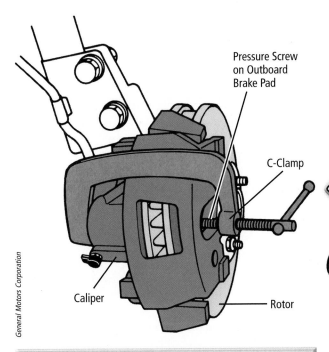

General Motors Corporation

Pressure Screw
on Outboard
Brake Pad

C-Clamp

Caliper

Rotor

Fig. 4-12 Use a retraction tool or a C-clamp to force the piston back into the caliper bore. *Why is it necessary to push the caliper piston(s) back into the bore?*

6. Remove the brake pads, support spring, and outer bushings from the caliper. Discard the bushings. Slide the inner bushings off the guide pin and discard them.
7. Inspect the caliper for wear and damage.
8. Inspect the caliper mounting bracket, slides, and guide pins. Slides and guide pins must be rust-free, smooth, and undamaged. Repair or replace as necessary.
9. Inspect the rotor for damage.
10. Clean all disc brake components. Lubricate caliper slide and guide parts with special brake caliper lubricant. Do not get brake caliper lubricant on the rotor friction surface or on the brake pads.
11. Install the new disc brake pad with the spring clip on the inboard pad. Install the outboard pad.
12. Install the caliper containing the new pads over the rotor. Install new bushings on the guide pins. Using the appropriate hardware, secure the caliper. If necessary, bend the ears (tabs) of the outboard pad to remove any play or rattle.
13. Add fresh brake fluid. Gently pump the brakes until the pedal comes up. Recheck the brake fluid in the reservoir. Add fluid, if necessary.

14. Reinstall the wheel. Tighten and torque the wheel nuts, following manufacturer's instructions. For more information on tightening and torquing the wheel nuts, refer to "Wheel Fasteners" on SS-517.
15. Remove the safety stands and lower the vehicle to the ground.
16. Test drive the vehicle.

Safety First **Road Tests** Before performing a road test, be sure to obtain written permissions from appropriate authorities.

TECH TIP **Burnishing.** New linings must be burnished for the best stopping performance. Burnishing burns off the glaze on the brake linings and smooths them. Make several brake applications (not panic stops) from about 50 mph [80 km/h]. Gently apply the brakes at first, increasing brake pedal pressure as the vehicle slows. The vehicle does not need to come to a complete stop. Resume driving, leaving a minute or two between brake applications.

Repairing Disc Brake Calipers

Perform caliper service if the caliper shows signs of damage or fluid leakage. If the caliper is damaged beyond repair, replace it. The damage that can occur in caliper assemblies includes:

• Scratches, pits, and scoring on the piston or cylinder bore surfaces.
• Damaged square-cut seals.
• Damaged dust boots.
• Damaged cylinder grooves.
• Damaged or leaking bleeder valves.

Scoring is serious damage to the piston surface or the inside surface of the cylinder bore. **Scores** are grooves or deep scratches on the piston's surface. Scoring is caused by debris or metal-to-metal contact. If you cannot remove damage to these surfaces by honing the cylinder bore or by polishing the piston, replace the caliper. Otherwise, perform service on the caliper as follows:

1. After removing the pads, remove the brake hose. Do not damage or lose the copper washers. To prevent brake fluid from leaking, cap or plug the brake hose.

2. Loosen and retighten the bleeder valve on the caliper to verify that the threads are not damaged or seized. If the bleeder valve breaks off, replace the caliper.

3. Take the caliper to the workbench to remove the piston. Place several shop towels against the outboard side of the caliper to cushion it. Carefully use air pressure at the hose inlet to force the piston out of the caliper. See **Fig. 4-13.**

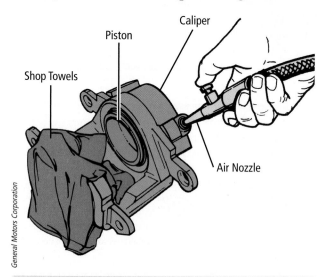

General Motors Corporation

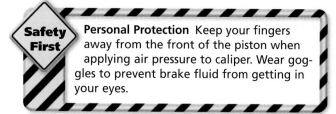

Fig. 4-13 Place shop towels in front of the piston to cushion it. *What could happen if the piston were damaged?*

Safety First **Personal Protection** Keep your fingers away from the front of the piston when applying air pressure to caliper. Wear goggles to prevent brake fluid from getting in your eyes.

4. Do not drop or damage the piston. Damage to the piston could cause brake fluid leaks after reassembly.

5. After removing the piston, remove the dust boot. Using a plastic or wooden stick, take the square-cut piston seal out of the cylinder bore. Be very careful not to damage the seal groove. Damage to the seal groove can lead to brake fluid leaks and damage to the new square-cut seal. See **Fig. 4-14.**

6. Clean the caliper housing and pistons in brake cleaning fluid. Make sure the square-cut seal groove and cylinder bore are clean.

7. Examine the piston for scratches, pits, or scoring. The piston surface rides on the square-cut seal. If the seal is damaged, it can cause a leak.

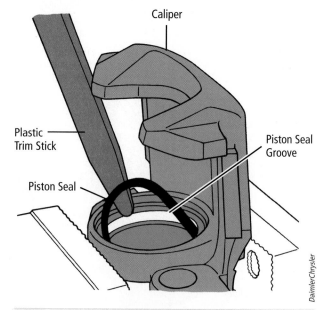

DaimlerChrysler

Fig. 4-14 To avoid damage to the seal groove, remove the piston seal with a plastic or wooden stick. *What might happen if the seal groove is damaged?*

8. Inspect the caliper bore for pitting, corrosion, or roughness. Small imperfections can be honed out.

9. Hone the caliper's cylinder bore to remove imperfections. **Honing** is the process of smoothing with abrasives. See **Fig. 4-15.** If honing cannot repair the bore, replace the caliper.

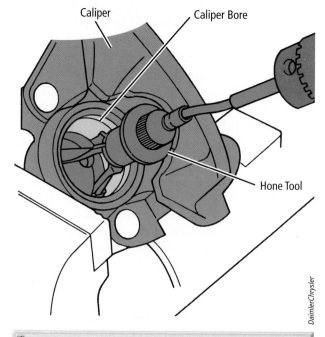

DaimlerChrysler

Fig. 4-15 Minor imperfections can be removed with light honing. *What solvent should be used to clean the bore after honing?*

10. Clean the caliper, including the cylinder bore. Install the square-cut seal in the seal groove in the cylinder bore. Verify that the seal is not twisted or rolled. An improperly installed square-cut seal can cause the caliper to leak brake fluid.

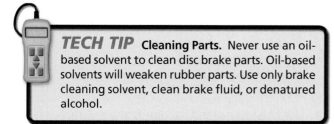

TECH TIP **Cleaning Parts.** Never use an oil-based solvent to clean disc brake parts. Oil-based solvents will weaken rubber parts. Use only brake cleaning solvent, clean brake fluid, or denatured alcohol.

11. Coat the piston with clean brake fluid. Assemble the new boot onto the piston.
12. Push the piston into the bore until it bottoms out in the bore.
13. Position the boot in the caliper counterbore and install the boot in the counterbore using the appropriate tool (see vehicle's service manual).
14. Slide the new inboard pad into place. See **Fig. 4-16.** Be sure to use the proper brake pad. Some brake pads are specific to the inboard or outboard side. Install the outboard pad.
15. Install the caliper on the vehicle. Follow the instructions in "Removing and Replacing Disc Brake Pads and Calipers (Floating or Sliding Calipers)."

Push Pad Downward Until It Lies Flat

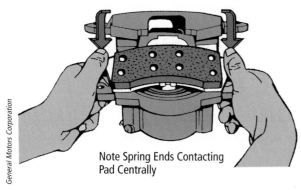

General Motors Corporation

Note Spring Ends Contacting Pad Centrally

Fig. 4-16 Inboard pad installation. *Why is it important to install the inboard pad on the inboard side?*

Disc Brake Rotor Service

Rotor service follows removal of the caliper and pads. First you need to measure the rotor's thickness. This determines if there is enough material to allow machining and still have the rotor within the vehicle manufacturer's specifications.

Measuring Disc Brake Rotors

A rotor should be evaluated while it is still on the vehicle.

1. Use a micrometer to measure the thickness of the rotor in several places around the rotor.
2. Compare the smallest measurement to the minimum thickness allowed for the rotor. The minimum thickness for the rotor is stamped into the rotor. See **Fig. 4-17.**
3. Compare the thickness measurements around the rotor. If the variation is more than 0.0005 inch, the friction surfaces of the rotor are not parallel with each other. This is a test for parallelism.
4. Measure runout by first adjusting the wheel bearing to zero end play. Then mount a dial indicator. Rotate the rotor and measure the runout as it turns. Maximum allowable lateral runout is usually about 0.004 to 0.005 inch [0.10–0.13 mm]. If runout is excessive, replace the rotor.
5. If a rotor has smooth friction surfaces (not scored or damaged) and is within parallelism, runout, and minimum thickness specifications, it can remain in service. Readjust wheel bearing to specifications.
6. Minor scoring, runout, or parallelism can be corrected by machining. Proceed with rotor machining only if the measurements indicate enough material thickness remains to safely allow machining.
7. If the rotor does not have enough thickness to allow machining, it must be replaced. A rotor that is machined below its minimum thickness can fail during use.

Terry Wild Studio

Fig. 4-17 The rotor must be discarded if it is beyond the minimum thickness after machining. *What is the minimum thickness of this rotor?*

Excellence in Science

Graphing Deceleration

One day on a clean dry street, you make an abrupt stop for a traffic light. The antilock brake system does its job and the car stops quickly and safely. You wonder, "What is the relationship between speed and stopping distance?"

When you stop a vehicle, its kinetic energy of motion is converted to heat. Friction stops the car. The brake rotors become warm. The equation for finding the stopping distance, x, at a certain speed, v, is:

$$x = \frac{v^2}{(2g\mu_s)}$$

In the denominator, g is the acceleration of gravity (32 ft per second per second) and μ_s is the coefficient of static friction.

The coefficient of static friction is used because the stopping distance is the shortest when the tires do not skid. The coefficient of static friction between rubber and dry concrete is approximately 0.60.

The table shows the minimum stopping distance for various initial speeds. The stopping distance of a vehicle moving 20 mph [32 kph] is four times the distance for a vehicle moving 10 mph [16 kph]. Doubling the speed usually quadruples the stopping distance. You can understand how quickly stopping distance increases with speed by plotting a graph.

Apply It!

Meets NATEF Science Standards for using graphs and describing the role of friction in deceleration.

1. Use a sheet of standard graph paper. Graph the information in the table. Label the horizontal axis "Speed in mph." Mark speed values of 0, 10, 20, 30, 40, 50, and 60 on the horizontal axis.

2. Near the left edge of the page, label the verticle axis "Stopping Distance in Feet". Mark distance values of 0, 20, 40, 60, 80, 100, 120, and 140 on the verticle axis.

3. Plot the values in the table on your graph.

STOPPING DISTANCE AND VEHICLE SPEED	
Speed (mph)	**Stopping Distance (ft)**
0	0.0
10	5.6
20	22.4
30	50.4
40	89.6
50	140.0
60	201.6

4. Design a safe experiment to verify the values in the table.

Removing Disc Brake Rotors

After removing the caliper, remove the rotor as follows:

1. Remove the dust cap, cotter pin, hex nut, and thrust washer holding the rotor to the spindle assembly. (On front-wheel-drive and rear disc brakes, there may be a retaining screw holding the rotor to the hub assembly. It may be possible to remove the screw and the rotor without removing the hub and bearings from the vehicle.)

2. Remove the rotor and wheel bearings (inner and outer) from the spindle. See **Fig. 4-18.**

3. Remove the inner and outer wheel bearings from the rotor. Then clean the rotor with brake solvent. The rotor must be clean before you can inspect it for damage.

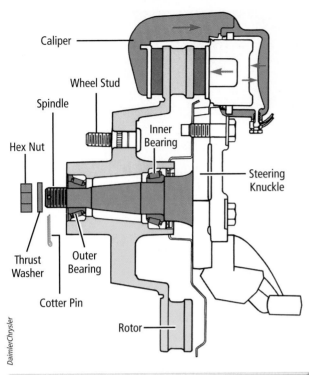

DaimlerChrysler

Caliper

Wheel Stud

Spindle

Hex Nut

Inner Bearing

Steering Knuckle

Thrust Washer

Outer Bearing

Cotter Pin

Rotor

Fig. 4-18 Wheel bearings are positioned on each side of the rotor to support smooth rotation of the rotor. *Why do you need to clean the rotor after removal?*

Inspecting and Replacing Wheel Studs

Refer to the vehicle service manual for specifications and special procedures. Then inspect and replace the wheel studs as follows:

1. Make sure that you follow all procedures in the appropriate service manual.
2. Raise and support the vehicle.
3. Remove the wheel and tire assembly.
4. Inspect the wheel studs for damage.
5. If any wheel studs need to be replaced, remove the brake caliper and properly hang or support it.
6. Remove the rotor, using proper procedures.
7. Select an appropriate size deep-well impact socket that the head of the stud will pass through.
8. Place the socket on a hard surface, such as a large vise or anvil. Have someone hold the rotor on top of the socket, with the head of the stud centered in the socket opening.

9. From the top of the rotor hub, use a soft punch and large hammer to drive the damaged stud through the socket. The socket supports the rotor hub around the stud to prevent the hub from being warped or bent. If available, a hydraulic press can be used instead of the punch and hammer.
10. Turn the rotor and hub assembly over, and support the front side with the stud hole centered on the socket.
11. Use a soft punch and hammer to drive the new stud through the hole until the head of the stud is seated against the rotor hub.
12. Service bearings and seal as necessary. Replace the rotor, caliper, wheel, and related parts as necessary.
13. Properly torque wheel studs.

Machining Disc Brake Rotors

If the rotors have only surface scoring, they may not require additional service. However, if the scoring is deep, or if the rotor has lateral runout, lack of parallelism, or a taper, it must be machined.

You can perform machining using a standard brake lathe or an on-car brake lathe. An **on-car brake lathe** is a device used to perform brake rotor machining on the vehicle.

Machined rotors must have a nondirectional finish. A **nondirectional finish** is a finish that does not have machining grooves. If not applied, the brakes may "walk" during use and cause brake noise.

Most car manufacturers suggest using an on-car brake lathe. See **Fig. 4-19.**

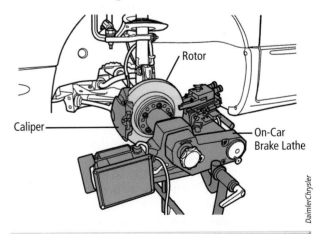

Rotor

Caliper

On-Car Brake Lathe

DaimlerChrysler

Fig. 4-19 Use an on-car brake lathe to restore the rotor to its original condition. *What is the advantage of using an on-car brake lathe?*

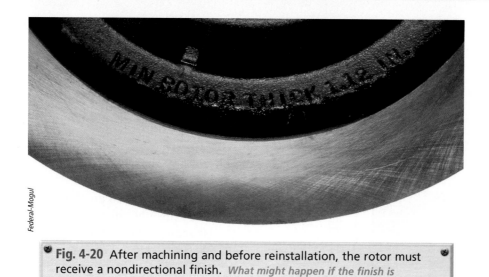

Federal-Mogul

Fig. 4-20 After machining and before reinstallation, the rotor must receive a nondirectional finish. *What might happen if the finish is not correct?*

On-Car Brake Lathe Perform disc-brake rotor machining with an on-car brake lathe as follows:

1. Attach the on-car brake lathe to the wheel brake assembly. Follow the instructions given in the on-car brake lathe manual.
2. Machine the rotor according to the manual.
3. After machining, the rotor must have a nondirectional finish put on it before it is returned to service. Many brake lathes have the ability to apply a nondirectional finish. See **Fig. 4-20.** Remove the on-car lathe.
4. Thoroughly clean the wheel brake assembly, using brake solvent or denatured alcohol.
5. Check the rotor for thickness. Use a micrometer to measure rotor thickness to determine that the rotor has not been machined beyond minimum thickness.
6. Replace any components that were removed in order to install the on-car lathe.

TECH TIP **Rotor Surface Finish.** Carefully inspect the rotor's surface finish. If machining grooves are left in the surface, the pads will follow those grooves and "walk" until they can go no farther. They will then make a noise as they snap back to their original position. The pads will also wear prematurely.

Standard Brake Lathe Perform brake rotor machining with a standard brake lathe as follows:

1. Mount the rotor on the brake lathe. Follow the instructions given in the brake lathe manual.

2. Machine the rotor according to the brake lathe manual.
3. Check the rotor for thickness. Use a micrometer to measure rotor thickness to determine that the rotor has not been machined beyond minimum thickness.

TECH TIP **Bearing Lubrication.** Clean the bearings and inspect them for damage. They should be free of pits and color. If a slight blue color is evident, install new bearings. If they are not damaged, lubricate them with wheel-bearing grease and install them in the rotor.

Installing Disc Brake Rotors

After you have machined and cleaned the rotor, reinstall it as follows:

1. Pack the bearings (if appropriate) with wheel-bearing grease. Install the inner bearing and a new seal in the rotor hub.
2. Place the rotor on the vehicle. (On front-wheel-drive vehicles or those with rear disc brakes, replace the retaining screw when installing the rotor on the hub.)
3. Install the outer bearing. Then install the thrust washer and spindle retaining nut. Snug the nut down.
4. Tighten and torque the spindle retaining nut and adjust bearing preload to the value given by the vehicle service manual.
5. Install the cotter pin and bend the tabs to hold it in place. Install the dust cap.

Excellence in Math

Measuring Brake Rotors

The disc brakes on an automobile need to be serviced. You suspect the rotors are the problem. You will measure the thickness of the rotor at six points. Then you can decide if the rotor is still thick enough to be machined. If it is thick enough, you will check the lateral runout. You will also use the measurements to decide if the thickness variation (parallelism) is within tolerance limits.

You find the following brake rotor information in the service manual:

Original Thickness	1.27″	32.200 mm
Minimum Wear Thickness	1.25″	31.700 mm
Discard Thickness	1.21″	30.700 mm
Maximum Lateral Runout	0.003″	0.080 mm
Parallelism Tolerance	0.0005″	0.013 mm
(Allowable Thickness Variation)		

You start with the left front brake. You use metric measurements for your calculations.

Lateral runout is 0.075 mm, and the six measurements for parallelism are 32.000 mm, 31.850 mm, 31.882 mm, 32.000 mm, 31.916 mm, and 31.997 mm.

You first make a quick mental estimate to see if the rotor should be discarded. Because the smallest measurement of the rotor's thickness is greater than the discard thickness (30.700 mm), you do not have to discard the rotor.

The lateral runout of 0.075 mm is less than 0.080 mm and is within tolerance limits. You now check the measurements for parallelism. You find that:

32.000 mm − 31.850 mm = 0.150 mm
and 0.150 mm > 0.013 mm

Because the variation is greater than allowed, you decide to machine, or refinish, the rotor.

Apply It!

Meets NATEF Mathematics Standards for mentally comparing tolerances and understanding conditional solutions.

You look at the right front brake and make the following measurements: 32.140 mm, 32.135 mm, 32.140 mm, 32.138 mm, 32.139 mm and 32.140 mm. Lateral runout is 0.015 mm.

1. Make a quick mental estimate to see whether the rotor will have to be discarded because it is too thin.

2. If the rotor can be reused, determine whether the lateral runout measurement is within tolerance limits.

3. Determine whether the rotor needs to be refinished.

SECTION 3 KNOWLEDGE CHECK

1. When should brake pads be replaced?

2. What kind of damage can occur in caliper assemblies?

3. What type of socket is used in replacing wheel studs?

4. How can you determine whether enough material is present on a rotor to machine?

5. How can you test for parallelism?

6. Name the two device(s) used to machine rotors.

ASE TEST PREP

7. Technician A says rotors must have a non-directional finish on the machined surface. Technician B says the rotor must be discarded if it is beyond the minimum thickness. Who is correct?

   ⓐ Technician A.

   ⓑ Technician B.

   ⓒ Both Technician A and Technician B.

   ⓓ Neither Technician A nor Technician B.

CHAPTER 4 REVIEW

Key Points

Meets the following NATEF Standards for Brakes: diagnosis, service, and repair of disc brake calipers, brake pads, rotors, and master cylinder.

- Disc brakes use friction between the rotor and the brake pads to reduce the motion of the vehicle.
- Disc brake systems have four major parts: mounting brackets, calipers, brake pads, and rotors.
- Vented rotors are used on heavier vehicles. Nonvented rotors are used mainly on smaller vehicles.
- Disc brake problems can include noisy brakes, pulling, grabbing, and pedal pulsation.
- Brake pad inspection should include inspecting for uneven wear and signs of glazing, cracking, or other problems.
- Caliper service is performed if an inspection of the caliper indicates damage or signs of fluid leakage.
- A rotor's thickness should be measured while the rotor is on the vehicle.
- Disc brake rotor defects, such as grooves, can sometimes be removed by machining.

Review Questions

1. What are the advantages of low drag calipers?
2. Describe burnishing.
3. Explain the difference between fixed caliper disc brakes, floating caliper disc brakes, and sliding caliper disc brakes.
4. What is rotor runout?
5. Define honing.
6. How is runout measured?
7. Explain how to remove a rotor.
8. What is scoring?
9. **Critical Thinking** A nondirectional finish is free of machine grooves. Explain why machined rotors must have it.
10. **Critical Thinking** Disc brake reservoirs are larger than drum brake reservoirs. Explain why.

Excellence in Communication

Reading Diagrams

Diagrams are visual representations of written words. The purpose of the "pictures" is to make clear how parts fit together or function. Many complex components or systems cannot be easily described in words alone.

Sometimes people who do not like to read will try to understand a subject using only visual information. However, they may have problems because the picture may not tell the whole story. A written explanation may be necessary to understand how a system functions.

You need to be able to "read" a diagram as well as the text that applies to it. The written words tell you much of what you need to know. The diagram lets you "see" what the words are describing. Using these two tools together, you may more easily understand what you need to know about the function or construction of the part or system.

Apply It!

Meets NATEF Communications Standards for reading strategies.

1. Refer to **Fig. 4-3** and **Fig. 4-4**. Read the section on calipers and the text that applies to these figures.
2. Referring only to the above figures, explain how the floating calipers disc brake is assembled and how it operates.
3. Did you read information in the text that helped you understand the diagrams? Explain.

AUTOMOTIVE SERVICE EXCELLENCE
TEST PREP

Answering the following practice questions will help you prepare for the ASE certification tests.

1. Technician A says that vented rotors are used mainly in heavier vehicles. Technician B says that vented rotors are used mainly in smaller vehicles. Who is correct?

   ⓐ Technician A.
   ⓑ Technician B.
   ⓒ Both Technician A and Technician B.
   ⓓ Neither Technician A nor Technician B.

2. There are three types of disc brake calipers. They are:

   ⓐ stable caliper, fixed caliper, and floating caliper.
   ⓑ stable caliper, fixed caliper, and sliding caliper.
   ⓒ fixed caliper, floating caliper, and sliding caliper.
   ⓓ fixed caliper, sliding caliper, and pin caliper.

3. The front disc brakes are grabbing. The most likely cause is:

   ⓐ a loose caliper.
   ⓑ low tire pressure.
   ⓒ broken shocks.
   ⓓ contaminated brake pad lining.

4. Technician A says that a likely cause for a brake failing to release is that the caliper piston is not retracting properly. Technician B says that a likely cause is that the pads are ruined by brake fluid, oil, or grease. Who is correct?

   ⓐ Technician A.
   ⓑ Technician B.
   ⓒ Both Technician A and Technician B.
   ⓓ Neither Technician A nor Technician B.

5. Pedal pulsations are sometimes related to rotor problems. What is the likely cause?

   ⓐ A rotor with excessive runout.
   ⓑ A rotor that is out of parallel.
   ⓒ A rotor that has uneven thickness.
   ⓓ All of the above.

6. Technician A says that a rotor mounted on a lathe for refinishing off the vehicle is automatically finished to the correct thickness. Technician B says that the thickness of the rotor needs to be checked with a micrometer to make sure it has not been machined beyond its minimum thickness. Who is correct?

   ⓐ Technician A.
   ⓑ Technician B.
   ⓒ Both Technician A and Technician B.
   ⓓ Neither Technician A nor Technician B.

7. A vehicle needs to have the brake pads replaced. There is a floating caliper brake assembly. Technician A says that the pads can be removed without removing the wheel and calipers. Technician B says that the wheel and caliper must be removed to replace the pads. Who is correct?

   ⓐ Technician A.
   ⓑ Technician B.
   ⓒ Both Technician A and Technician B.
   ⓓ Neither Technician A nor Technician B.

8. Uneven wear on a brake pad most likely indicates a problem with:

   ⓐ the wheel cylinder.
   ⓑ the brake pad retaining hardware.
   ⓒ the caliper.
   ⓓ brake pad retaining bolts.

9. Maximum allowable runout on a disc brake rotor is usually about:

   ⓐ 0.004 to 0.005 inch.
   ⓑ 0.006 to 0.007 inch.
   ⓒ 0.008 to 0.009 inch.
   ⓓ 0.010 to 0.011 inch.

10. If machined rotors have a directional finish:

   ⓐ the rotors will not be parallel.
   ⓑ the rotors will fail.
   ⓒ the brakes may grab.
   ⓓ the brakes may make noise.

Section 1
Power Boosters

Section 2
Diagnosing Power Boosters

Diagnosing & Repairing Power Boosters

Customer's Concern

Dave Kelly always performs his own routine automotive service. He's familiar with the procedures for checking, changing, and replenishing brake fluid. He's familiar with the causes of brake squeal, pedal pulsation, and other common brake complaints. However, the problem he's experiencing now has him stumped.

Last night, when Dave headed home from work, he noticed it was increasingly difficult to apply the brakes when he needed to stop. He says that even when he basically stands on the brake pedal, it doesn't move much. He wonders if the brake pedal or input rod is wedged against another part. You explain to Dave that his problem is more likely related to the brake booster. He gives you permission to begin diagnostic work.

Technician's Challenge

As the service technician, you need to find answers to these questions:

1. How old is Dave's car? When were the brakes last serviced? Is the car equipped with a vacuum booster or hydraulic booster?

2. Could Dave's rigid brake pedal be caused by anything other than a faulty power booster? Is there any chance of the brake pedal or input rod being "wedged" against another part?

3. If the booster is to blame, what is wrong? How can you determine whether it is storing vacuum or hydraulic pressure correctly?

● *Section 1*
Power Boosters

Objectives:

- Identify the two basic types of brake power boosters.
- Explain the operation of a vacuum assisted brake booster.
- Explain the operation of a hydraulically assisted brake power booster.
- Identify the purpose of the accumulator.

Vocabulary:

- **vacuum booster**
- **power piston**
- **control valve**
- **spool valve**
- **accumulator**

Types of Power Boosters

Disc brakes require more braking force than drum brakes. The added force is needed because drum brakes are self-energizing while disc brakes are not. Power boosters were designed to provide the additional force. Power boosters are also called power-assist units.

Power boosters are mounted between the brake pedal lever and the master cylinder on the engine side of the vehicle's bulkhead. A bulkhead is a metal partition that separates vehicle compartments. Power boosters supply the increased force needed by the brakes without requiring increased brake pedal pressure. There are two basic types of power boosters: vacuum assisted and hydraulically assisted.

Vacuum assisted designs can be single diaphragm or tandem (dual) diaphragm. These units include those that are hydraulically assisted (hydro-boost) and those that are electrohydraulically assisted (Powermaster™).

Vacuum Boosters

The **vacuum booster** is a device that uses vacuum to supply additional energy to boost brake application pressures. See **Fig. 5-1**. This allows the driver to apply the brakes with less force on the brake pedal. The vacuum can be supplied by the engine's intake manifold or by a separate vacuum pump, or both.

Vacuum Supply

During operation a gasoline engine draws in air through the carburetor or throttle body. This creates a vacuum in the intake manifold. This vacuum can be used for many purposes. One is to supply vacuum to the power brake booster.

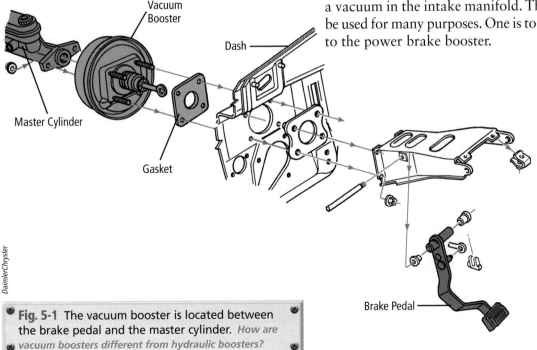

DaimlerChrysler

Vacuum Booster

Dash

Master Cylinder

Gasket

Brake Pedal

Fig. 5-1 The vacuum booster is located between the brake pedal and the master cylinder. *How are vacuum boosters different from hydraulic boosters?*

Manifold vacuum is highest at idle and lowest at wide-open throttle. To prevent these changes from affecting the amount of vacuum available to the booster, vacuum is often stored in a reservoir. See **Fig. 5-2.**

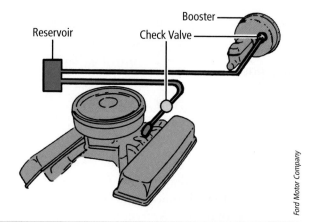

Reservoir
Booster
Check Valve

Ford Motor Company

Fig. 5-2 The engine supplies vacuum for the booster. A reservoir holds a small supply of vacuum for emergencies. *When is manifold vacuum highest— when the engine is at idle or at wide-open throttle?*

A check valve is installed between the manifold and reservoir (or in the reservoir). It keeps the vacuum from flowing in the opposite direction under low manifold vacuum conditions.

The vacuum check valve at the booster maintains vacuum inside the booster housing. Vacuum storage is important because, should the engine stall, power boost remains available for at least one brake application. It may be enough for two or three applications.

The brakes will still work even after all vacuum has been used. The difference is that the driver will have to push harder on the brake pedal.

Vacuum boosters rely on a pressure differential across a diaphragm to multiply the force coming from the brake pedal. The diaphragm is suspended between two chambers of the booster housing. When the system is at rest, the vacuum on each side of the diaphragm is the same. When the driver presses the brake pedal, atmospheric pressure enters the side nearest the pedal. This raises the pressure on the pedal side of the diaphragm.

Because there is vacuum on the master-cylinder side of the diaphragm, the diaphragm moves in the direction of the vacuum. It applies boosted pressure to the master cylinder's primary piston.

There are two types of vacuum boosters, the single diaphragm and the tandem (dual) diaphragm.

Single-Diaphragm Vacuum Boosters

The vacuum booster housing is a steel canister. It is separated into two chambers by a flexible rubber diaphragm. The diaphragm is positioned between two pushrods. One pushrod extends from the rear of the booster through the bulkhead and attaches to the brake pedal lever. A second pushrod extends out the front of the power booster and makes contact with the primary piston located inside the master cylinder. See **Fig. 5-3.**

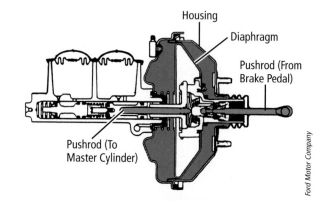

Housing
Diaphragm
Pushrod (From Brake Pedal)
Pushrod (To Master Cylinder)

Ford Motor Company

Fig. 5-3 The diaphragm is positioned between the brake pedal pushrod and the master cylinder pushrod. *What does the pushrod extending from the rear of the booster attach to?*

The pushrod connected to the brake pedal is attached to the power piston. The **power piston** is the interface between the front and rear pushrods. The power piston is attached to, or suspended from, the diaphragm, shown in **Fig. 5-4.**

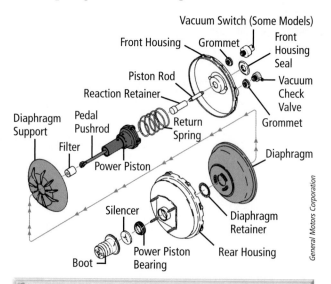

Vacuum Switch (Some Models)
Front Housing
Grommet
Front Housing Seal
Piston Rod
Vacuum Check Valve
Reaction Retainer
Grommet
Diaphragm Support
Pedal Pushrod
Return Spring
Diaphragm
Filter
Power Piston
Silencer
Diaphragm Retainer
Boot
Power Piston Bearing
Rear Housing

General Motors Corporation

Fig. 5-4 An exploded view of a typical vacuum booster. *What part of the power booster is the power piston suspended from?*

Excellence in Math

Brake Pedal Ratios

You have learned that the brake hydraulic system increases both pressure and braking force. However, there is another force multiplier—the brake pedal ratio. In the figures below, the brake pedal ratios are B to A or B/A. The brake pedal ratio is the ratio of the lengths of the lever arms on the pedal assembly. The brake pedal ratio for **Fig. A** is 3 to 1 or 9″ divided by 3″. The brake pedal ratio for **Fig. B** is 5 to 1 or 10″ divided by 2″.

The mechanical advantage supplied by the brake pedal assembly is determined by the brake pedal ratio. The ratio chosen depends on whether the brake system is equipped with a power booster. If a booster is present, the pedal assembly does not need to increase the force as much.

A driver applies a force of 50 lb [23 kg] to the unboosted brake pedal. **Fig. B**. The force on the master cylinder pushrod will be:

50 lb × 10″/2″ = 250 lb

Apply It!

Meets NATEF Mathematics and Science Standards for levers and ratios.

1. The driver applies the same 50 lb. of force to the pedal of the power brake system. **Fig. A**. What is the force on the master cylinder pushrod?

2. How much additional force must be provided by the booster to create the same brake input force as in the unboosted system?

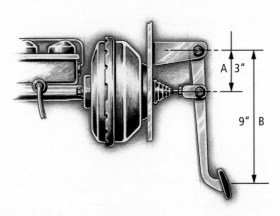

A | 3″

9″ | B

B:A = 3:1

Fig. A Brake pedal ratio for a power assisted brake.

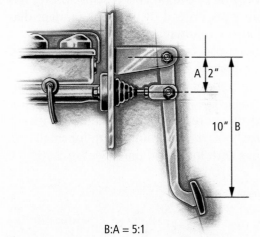

A | 2″

10″ | B

B:A = 5:1

Fig. B Brake pedal ratio for a brake without power assist.

Inside the power piston is a control valve. The **control valve** is a valve that regulates the flow of atmospheric pressure and vacuum to the two separate chambers in the booster.

The control valve has two ports. One port (the vacuum valve) is normally open, allowing vacuum to enter the rear chamber. The second port (the air valve) is normally closed. It opens when the driver pushes the brake pedal. It allows air, at atmospheric pressure, to enter the rear chamber. At the same time, the vacuum valve to the rear chamber closes. This creates a pressure differential between the two chambers. The high-pressure side forces the diaphragm and power piston to move the pushrod toward the master cylinder. When the driver stops pushing the pedal, both valves close. This is the "hold" position.

When the driver releases the pedal, the air valve closes and the vacuum valve opens. The vacuum equalizes on both sides of the diaphragm. A spring on the front of the diaphragm helps push the brake pedal back to its rest position.

When brakes are applied, air rushing into the rear chamber would normally make an undesirable hissing noise. Filters installed on the inlet side of the booster prevent this. The filters also keep dirt out of the booster.

A rubber reaction disc and a reaction piston are located at the end of the brake pedal pushrod. These discs provide brake "feel" feedback to the driver. See **Fig. 5-5(a)**.

As the driver presses on the brake pedal, the reaction disc compresses slightly. At the same time, the master-cylinder pushrod presses on the reaction piston in the opposite direction. Because there is an equal and opposite reaction for every action, the driver gets a good pedal feel.

Tandem (Dual) Diaphragm Vacuum Boosters

Some vehicles are equipped with tandem diaphragm vacuum boosters. This type of booster has two diaphragms instead of one. The tandem diaphragm has the following advantages:

• It doubles the surface area to provide more boost. This is important for some heavier vehicles.
• The same amount of diaphragm area (and boost) can be achieved with a smaller diameter booster housing. Or, more boost can be achieved with the same size booster. This is important for small cars and those with low hood lines. See **Fig. 5-5(b)**.

Hydraulic Boosters

In the early days of emission controls, engines were designed with camshafts that had long overlaps. Coupled with the retarded ignition timing specifications, these engines developed little useful vacuum. There was concern that vacuum boosters may be inadequate. To meet this concern, another source of brake boost was developed—the hydraulic booster.

Unlike vacuum boost, hydraulic boost is constant even if the engine is under load. This is because the boost pressure is obtained from the power steering pump. The power steering pump is driven by an engine belt and delivers a constant source of pressure. These booster systems are known as mechanical-hydraulic, or hydraulically assisted. They use mechanical and hydraulic systems in combination. More recent hydraulic booster systems are powered by electric pumps. These hydraulic booster systems are known as electrohydraulically assisted systems.

Bendix hydraulically assisted power brakes were first used on GM cars. The booster is located between the master cylinder and bulkhead (similar to a vacuum booster). The booster receives high pressure fluid from the power steering pump by way of a high pressure hose. Two more lines lead from the booster. One high pressure line runs to the steering gear. One low pressure line runs back to the power steering reservoir as shown in **Fig. 5-6**.

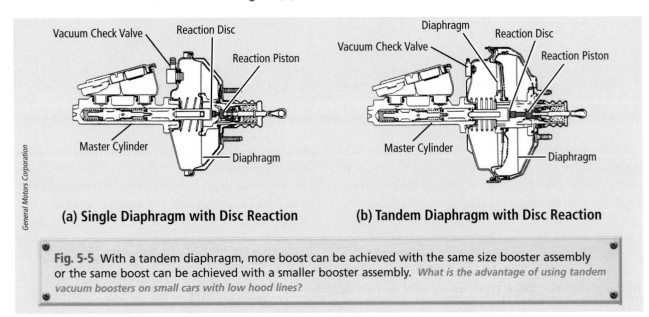

General Motors Corporation

(a) Single Diaphragm with Disc Reaction

(b) Tandem Diaphragm with Disc Reaction

Fig. 5-5 With a tandem diaphragm, more boost can be achieved with the same size booster assembly or the same boost can be achieved with a smaller booster assembly. *What is the advantage of using tandem vacuum boosters on small cars with low hood lines?*

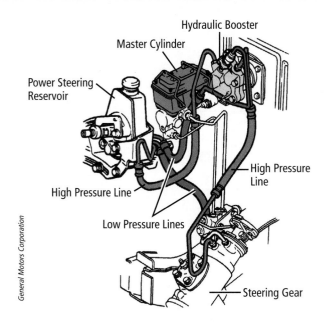

General Motors Corporation

Safety First

Depressurizing Any hydraulic boost system should be depressurized before disconnecting any lines from the system. Failure to do this could result in hydraulic fluid being sprayed into the eyes or onto the skin. Always wear safety glasses.

Hydraulically Assisted Boosters

The main components of the hydraulically assisted system are the lever, spool valve, master cylinder pushrod, input rod, and power piston.

The **spool valve** is a valve that shuttles back and forth to open and close ports for the pressurized power steering fluid. It resembles a spool that carries sewing thread.

When the driver applies the brakes, the input rod moves a lever forward against the power piston. It also moves the spool valve forward, closing the return port to the power steering pump.

Figure 5-7 shows a spool valve. As the pressure increases, the spool valve is pushed forward. As it moves, high pressure fluid flows through the spool valve into the boost chamber. The power piston pulls the lever forward with it. This increases the brake application force.

When the driver releases the brakes, a spring opens the spool valve. The fluid goes from the power steering pump to the steering gear. See **Fig. 5-8.**

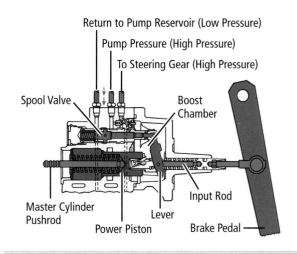

General Motors Corporation

Fig. 5-7 When the spool valve moves forward, the flow of power steering fluid is closed off to the steering gear and the power steering pump return line. Fluid flows through the spool valve, into the boost chamber, and helps move the power piston. *What are the main components inside the hydraulically assisted booster?*

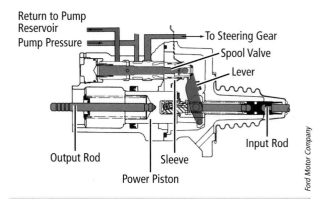

Ford Motor Company

Fig. 5-8 When the brakes are released, the fluid bypasses the booster and goes directly to the steering gear. *What device is used to open the spool valve?*

The hydraulically assisted system includes an accumulator. This provides pressure to the booster in case the engine stalls or the power steering belt breaks.

An **accumulator** is a device that stores fluid under pressure. A strong spring or pressurized nitrogen gas provides the pressure. The accumulator stores enough pressure for one or two brake applications. After that the brakes will behave like brakes without power assist. Power steering fluid should be changed routinely on vehicles with hydraulically assisted power brakes.

Electrohydraulically Assisted Boosters

The electrohydraulically assisted booster operates very much like the hydraulically assisted system, with one major exception. Instead of using the power steering pump to supply hydraulic pressure, it uses a separate hydraulic pump driven by an electric motor. See **Fig. 5-9.**

Electrohydraulically assisted boosters use brake fluid from the master cylinder reservoir rather than power steering fluid. There are several advantages to electrohydraulically assisted boosters. They are less complex, smaller, and the pump needs to run only when there is a demand. Electrohydraulically assisted boosters are also well suited for use on antilock brake systems.

Like hydraulically assisted systems, electrohydraulically assisted systems have an accumulator to store fluid under pressure. Inside the accumulator, a diaphragm separates the brake fluid from the section filled with high pressure nitrogen. The electrohydraulically assisted booster receives its pressure boost from the accumulator. A pressure switch turns the electric pump on and off at proper pressure levels. This keeps the accumulator charged.

Safety First — **Fluid Use** Power steering fluid should be added only to the power steering pump. Adding power steering fluid to the master cylinder is a very dangerous mistake that could lead to total brake failure.

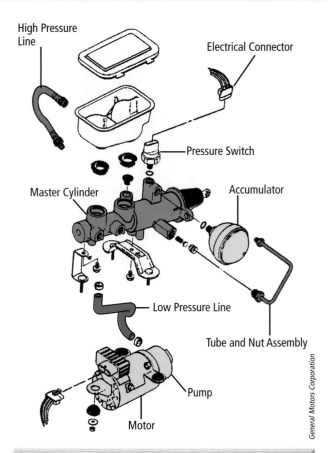

High Pressure Line

Electrical Connector

Pressure Switch

Master Cylinder

Accumulator

Low Pressure Line

Tube and Nut Assembly

Pump

Motor

General Motors Corporation

Fig. 5-9 The electrohydraulically assisted booster uses hydraulic pressure supplied by a pump driven by an electric motor. *How is the electrohydraulically assisted booster different from the hydraulically assisted booster?*

SECTION 1 KNOWLEDGE CHECK

1. When a vacuum booster system is at rest, what happens to the vacuum on either side of the diaphragm?

2. What is the purpose of the control valve?

3. Why do vacuum boosters contain filters?

4. What are the main components of a hydraulically assisted booster?

5. What is the purpose of an accumulator in a hydraulically assisted booster?

6. What are some of the advantages to electrohydraulically assisted boosters?

ASE TEST PREP

7. Technician A says some vacuum boosters have a single diaphragm. Technician B says tandem vacuum boosters have two diaphragms. Who is correct?
   - ⓐ Technician A.
   - ⓑ Technician B.
   - ⓒ Both Technician A and Technician B.
   - ⓓ Neither Technician A nor Technician B.

● Section 2
Diagnosing Power Boosters

Objectives:

E1 ● Test pedal free travel with and without engine running; check power assist operation.

E2 ● Check vacuum supply (manifold or auxiliary pump) to vacuum-type power booster.

E3 ● Inspect the vacuum-type power booster unit for vacuum leaks; inspect the check valve for proper operation.

E4 ● Inspect and test hydraulically assisted power brake system for leaks and proper operation.

Vocabulary:
● field-serviceable part
● vacuum storage system

Diagnosing Vacuum Boosters

Brake boosters are generally not serviced. When they stop working, they are replaced as a unit. No field-serviceable parts are available, except for the vacuum check valve. A **field-serviceable part** is a part that can be repaired.

Generally, the only symptom of a vacuum booster problem is a hard brake pedal. This is when the driver must use extra effort to stop the car.

Testing Vacuum Booster Operation

To test vacuum booster operation, do the following:

1. Start the engine and let it idle. Apply and release the brakes several times.
2. Turn the engine off. Apply and release the brake pedal until the pedal gets hard to push. Press down on the brake pedal and start the engine. The pedal should move down a small amount. If it does not, the booster is not working.

There are several possible causes. To isolate the failure, inspect the:

● Vacuum check valve(s) for restrictions or leaks.
● Vacuum supply lines and reservoirs (if present) for leaks.
● Vacuum supply hose for soft spots that could collapse during use and restrict flow.

If the vacuum check valves, reservoir (if present), or the vacuum supply hose are defective, replace them. Otherwise, you must replace the entire vacuum booster.

Testing Vacuum Storage System Operation

The **vacuum storage system** stores engine vacuum in the booster. To test the vacuum storage system, start the engine and run it at a medium idle. Turn off the engine and wait for about five minutes. Press down on the brake pedal. It should provide one or two soft applications before it gets hard to push. If it does, the vacuum storage system is operating normally. See **Fig. 5-10**.

If the pedal is hard to push during the first and second applications of the test, vacuum is not being stored in the vacuum system. If this is the case the check valve(s), hose(s), reservoir (if used), or booster is leaking.

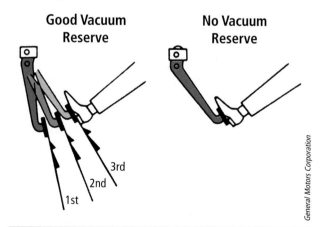

Good Vacuum Reserve   **No Vacuum Reserve**

3rd
2nd
1st

General Motors Corporation

Fig. 5-10 Testing the vacuum storage system. *How many soft applications should you get after pressing the brake pedal?*

Excellence in Science

Levers Multiply Force

Sarah is driving down the highway at cruising speed. She puts her foot on the brake pedal to stop her car. What happens? The car slows to a controlled stop. How can a person apply enough force to stop a heavy vehicle?

The driver receives a mechanical assist and a power assist from the brake system. The brake pedal attaches to a lever that provides the mechanical assist. Let's investigate the mechanical advantage of a lever.

Apply It!

Demonstrating Mechanical Advantage

Meets NATEF Science Standards for levers and force.

Materials and Equipment
- Yardstick
- 1.0 or 1.5 liter unopened bottle of water
- Two short lengths of string or fishing line
- Spring scale
- C-clamp

1. Tie one end of a string tightly around the top of the water bottle. Tie the other end into a loop. Hang the loop on the scale. Record the weight of the bottle as F_1.

2. Set up the experiment as shown below. Clamp one end of the yardstick to a table. Slide the loop of the string attached to the water bottle along the yardstick to the middle of the stick. Keep the bottle supported from below until Step 5.

3. Record the distance in inches from the edge of the table to the bottle's attachment point, as L_1.

4. Tie the other string into a loop. Use the loop to attach the scale near the end of the yardstick as shown.

5. Pull up on the scale until the yardstick just barely supports the hanging bottle. Then measure on the scale the force needed to just support the water bottle. Record this force as F_2.

6. Measure and record the distance from the end of the table to the point where the scale is attached. Record this as L_2.

7. Calculate the ratio of $F_1:F_2$. This is the mechanical advantage of the lever.

8. Calculate the ratio of $L_2:L_1$. How does this ratio compare to the mechanical advantage of the previous step?

Results and Analysis You should have discovered that the mechanical advantage of a lever is the same as the ratio of the distances, or $F_1:F_2 = L_2:L_1$.

Check this by sliding the water bottle to several other points along the yardstick and repeating Steps 5–8. If you slide the bottle toward the table, the mechanical advantage increases. Half the force is required. Slide the bottle toward the spring scale and the mechanical advantage decreases. The scale will show that the force, F_2, increases.

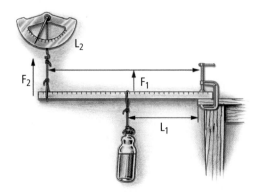

Diagnosing Hydraulically Assisted Boosters

As with vacuum boosters, the only symptom of a hydraulically assisted booster problem is a hard brake pedal.

Testing Hydraulically Assisted Booster Operation

To check hydraulically assisted booster operation, do the following:

1. Start the engine.
2. With the engine running, apply the brakes several times.
3. Turn the engine off. Apply the brakes several more times until the pedal gets hard to push.
4. Keep your foot pressed down on the pedal and start the engine. If the booster is working properly, the pedal will fall a small amount and then push back against your foot. If the pedal does not fall, the booster is not working.

If a hydraulically assisted booster is not working, check the following:

• Check the power steering pump belt.
• Check the power steering fluid level.
• Inspect all hoses and connections for fluid leaks.

If everything checks out and power steering has normal power assist, the booster is defective. You must replace it as a unit.

TECH TIP **Power Steering Pump Belts.** It is possible for the power steering pump belt to come off or break. If this happens, both power steering and hydraulically assisted power brakes will continue to work but will lose power assist.

Testing Hydraulic Pressure Storage System Operation

To test the hydraulic pressure storage system, do the following:

1. Start the engine and let it idle.
2. Turn the steering wheel from lock to lock several times.
3. Apply the brakes a few times. This allows the accumulator to charge with fluid.
4. Shut off the engine and allow the car to sit.
5. After about 30 minutes, apply the brakes.
6. If the system is working normally and the accumulator is holding a charge, you should get one or two assisted brake applications before the pedal gets hard to push. If the pedal is hard to push on the first application, the accumulator is leaking.

Safety First **Brake Pad Dust** Avoid inhaling brake pad dust. It can be hazardous to your health. Never use an air hose or brush to clean any brake assembly. Use an OSHA-approved vacuum cleaner.

SECTION 2 KNOWLEDGE CHECK

1. What is a field-serviceable part?
2. Explain how to test the operation of a vacuum booster.
3. What should be inspected if a vacuum booster is not working?
4. What is the purpose of the vacuum storage system?
5. Explain how to test the vacuum storage system.
6. What will a driver notice if a vehicle has a brake booster problem?

ASE TEST PREP

7. A car equipped with a brake booster has a very hard brake pedal with the engine running. What should be checked?
   ⓐ The parking brake.
   ⓑ Electrical supply to the pump.
   ⓒ The power steering pump belt.
   ⓓ The vacuum check valve.

CHAPTER 5 REVIEW

Key Points

Meets the following NATEF Standards for Brakes: diagnosis and repair of power boosters.

- Power assist systems supply the increased forces needed by brakes without requiring increased brake pedal pressure.
- Vacuum boosters use a pressure differential across a diaphragm to boost brake pedal force.
- The vacuum storage system should store enough vacuum for one or two brake applications with the engine turned off.
- Hydraulic boosters control the flow of pressurized fluid to boost brake pedal force.
- The main components of the hydro-boost system are the lever, spool valve, master cylinder pushrod, input rod, and piston.
- A hard brake pedal when the vehicle's engine is running may indicate hydro-boost booster failure.
- Applying the brakes and turning the wheel lock to lock during the hydraulic pressure storage test allows the accumulator to charge with fluid.

Review Questions

1. What is a power piston?
2. Why is a check valve installed between the manifold and the reservoir that stores vacuum?
3. If all of the vacuum is used, how will the driver apply the brakes?
4. Why are hydraulic boosters considered more effective than vacuum boosters?
5. What is a spool valve?
6. What happens to the brakes once the hydro-boost system's accumulator is empty?
7. What should you check first if a hydraulically assisted booster is not working?
8. How long must the engine be off when testing hydraulic pressure storage system pressure?
9. **Critical Thinking** A tandem diaphragm vacuum booster offers several advantages. Name one.
10. **Critical Thinking** Why apply the brakes and turn the wheel lock to lock when testing the hydraulic pressure storage system?

Excellence in Communication

Recording Information

Note taking is an informal method used to record information. You can write in a form you can easily understand. You don't need to use complete sentences. However, you should write neatly and spell words correctly so you can share your notes with others if necessary. Taking notes as a form of communication can be especially helpful in diagnosing a vehicle's problem.

You should take notes during a discussion with a customer about a vehicle's problem. Listen carefully. Write down what you believe are the customer's important observations. Include observations of your own.

Using these notes and your own knowledge, you can start to eliminate unlikely causes. You can also jot down ideas for testing to diagnose the problem.

Apply It!

Meets NATEF Communications Standards for taking notes and organizing and editing information.

Reread the "Customer's Concern" at the beginning of this chapter. Assume you are the technician.

1. On a sheet of paper, take notes on Mr. Kelly's observations about brake failure in his vehicle.
2. Note what you have observed.
3. Next to Mr. Kelly's observations and your own, write down what you think may be causing the brake failure. Also note the causes you think you can eliminate and why.

AUTOMOTIVE SERVICE EXCELLENCE
TEST PREP

Answering the following practice questions will help you prepare for the ASE certification tests.

1. Engine vacuum constantly changes. To keep these changes from affecting the amount of vacuum available to the booster, vacuum is often stored in a reservoir. At what stage of engine operation is manifold vacuum highest?

   ⓐ Wide-open throttle.

   ⓑ Deceleration.

   ⓒ Idle.

   ⓓ Downshifting.

2. A vacuum booster housing is a steel canister with two chambers separated by:

   ⓐ the power piston.

   ⓑ a rubber diaphragm.

   ⓒ a spool valve.

   ⓓ a reaction disc.

3. Compared with hydraulically assisted boosters, electrohydraulically assisted boosters:

   ⓐ are more complex.

   ⓑ are larger.

   ⓒ have a pump that needs to run only when there is a demand.

   ⓓ have a pump that runs continuously.

4. Technician A says that hydraulic boost is constant because the boost pressure is obtained from the power steering pump. Technician B says that hydraulic boost is constant even if the engine is under load. Who is correct?

   ⓐ Technician A.

   ⓑ Technician B.

   ⓒ Both Technician A and Technician B.

   ⓓ Neither Technician A nor Technician B.

5. The main components of the hydraulically assisted system are:

   ⓐ the lever, master cylinder pushrod, and power piston.

   ⓑ the spool valve and power piston.

   ⓒ the lever, spool valve, master cylinder pushrod, input rod, and power piston.

   ⓓ the lever, spool valve, and power piston.

6. Technician A says that the pressure in an accumulator can be provided by a strong spring. Technician B says that the pressure can be provided by pressurized air. Who is correct?

   ⓐ Technician A.

   ⓑ Technician B.

   ⓒ Both Technician A and Technician B.

   ⓓ Neither Technician A nor Technician B.

7. Technician A says that if the brake pedal provides one or two soft applications before it gets hard to push, the vacuum storage system is defective. Technician B says that this indicates that the vacuum storage system is operating normally. Who is correct?

   ⓐ Technician A.

   ⓑ Technician B.

   ⓒ Both Technician A and Technician B.

   ⓓ Neither Technician A nor Technician B.

8. A symptom of a vacuum booster problem is:

   ⓐ soft brake pedal.

   ⓑ no brakes.

   ⓒ hard brake pedal.

   ⓓ brakes fail to release.

9. The accumulator stores brake fluid under pressure. After two or three brake applications in quick succession:

   ⓐ there is no pressure and no braking.

   ⓑ the brakes act as if there is no power assist.

   ⓒ the brake pedal is soft.

   ⓓ the accumulator quickly repressurizes.

10. A hydraulically assisted booster is not working. You find no problem with the hoses and connections. If the power steering has normal power assist:

   ⓐ the booster is serviceable.

   ⓑ the power steering pump is defective.

   ⓒ the booster is defective and must be replaced as a unit.

   ⓓ the booster can be repaired.

Section 1
Parking Brake
Basics

Section 2
Parking Brake
Controls, Diagnosis,
and Repair

Diagnosing & Repairing Parking Brakes

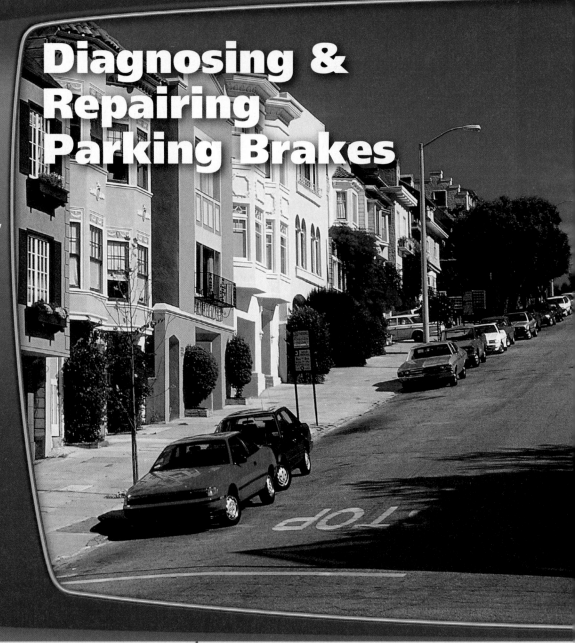

Customer's Concern

Rico Nunez says the brake warning light in his car has been glowing for several days. He hasn't noticed any problems with the brakes. In fact, he says the car stops better than ever. However, he has noticed two problems that seem strangely coincidental to the brake warning light glowing. The car is hesitant in accelerating. Also, he's been stopping for gas more frequently.

Rico asks you to take the car for a test drive. As you put the manual transmission in gear, you immediately notice that the car requires excessive throttle to move. Your first hunch is that the parking brake is engaged. That would explain the hesitant acceleration as well as the poor fuel mileage. However, the parking brake lever is in the released position.

Technician's Challenge

As the service technician, you need to find answers to these questions:

1. Has Rico been using his parking brake more or less than usual? When he applied the parking brake the last time, did he notice anything unusual when he engaged or released it?

2. If the parking brake lever is in the released position, how could the parking brake still be to blame for Rico's problems?

3. Once the problem is diagnosed and repaired, how can you ensure that Rico doesn't again have this problem with his car? What sort of maintenance will you suggest for the car's parking brake?

Section 1
Parking Brake Basics

Objectives:

- Identify the two types of parking brake systems.
- Inspect the parking brake warning light system.
- List the components of a parking brake system.
- **C6** Pre-adjust brake shoes and parking brake before installing brake drums or drum/hub assemblies and wheel bearings.

Vocabulary:

- integral parking brake
- auxiliary parking brake

Parking Brake Components

The parking brake is designed to hold a parked vehicle stationary. It relies on static friction to keep the wheels from turning. In some cases, a parking brake uses the wheel brake components of the service brake system. In other cases, the parking brake is totally separate.

Unlike service brakes, parking brakes are not operated by a hydraulic system. Parking brakes have a mechanical operating system.

Braking Mechanisms

Most parking brakes use the existing rear drum brake shoes, or rear disc pads, of the vehicle's wheel brake mechanism. Many vehicles, such as the Corvette, use a separate set of drum brakes. In these vehicles the parking brake shoes are applied independently of the rear disc brakes.

The two types of parking brake systems are integral parking brakes and auxiliary parking brakes. The **integral parking brake** is a parking brake that uses the same brake shoes or pads as the service brakes. The **auxiliary parking brake** is a parking brake that uses a separate set of brake linings.

Actuating Mechanisms

Two kinds of actuating mechanisms are used on parking brakes. Some systems use pedals. Other systems use hand levers. Most parking brake systems use cables to carry motion from the brake pedal or hand lever to the braking mechanism.

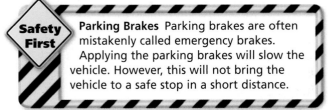

Safety First
Parking Brakes Parking brakes are often mistakenly called emergency brakes. Applying the parking brakes will slow the vehicle. However, this will not bring the vehicle to a safe stop in a short distance.

Brake Warning Lights

All parking brakes have a warning light switch that closes when the parking brakes are applied. See **Fig. 6-1**. When the switch closes, a red light on the instrument panel glows. It is usually the same light that glows if there is a service brake failure. The light warns the driver that the parking brakes are on.

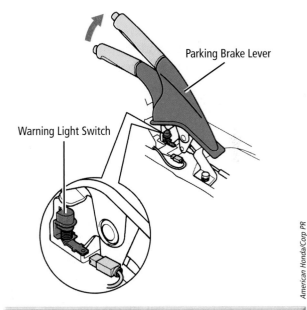

Parking Brake Lever

Warning Light Switch

American Honda/Corp PR

Fig. 6-1 Parking brake warning light switch on a vehicle with a hand lever brake. *What is the purpose of the warning light switch?*

If the brake warning light stays on when the parking brake hand lever or pedal is not applied, verify that the lever or pedal is returning fully to the released position. Also check the switch at the parking brake hand lever or pedal. Adjust and service as needed. If this light will not turn on and it is not burned out, check and repair the electrical circuit. Refer to the vehicle service manual.

Parking Brake Construction and Operation

Three basic types of parking brake systems are commonly used on vehicles:

- Rear drum integral parking brake assemblies.
- Rear disc integral parking brake assemblies.
- Auxiliary parking brake assemblies.

Rear Drum Integral Parking Brakes

Rear drum brake assemblies are integral systems. This means they use the same brake shoes and drums as the service brakes.

This is the most common system. It is also very reliable. Drum brakes make good parking brakes because of their superb static friction. The service brake shoes double as parking brakes.

Rear Drum Integral Parking Brake Construction Rear drum brakes with integrated parking brake capability have additional brake hardware. This hardware consists of the parking brake cable, parking brake lever, and parking brake link. See **Fig. 6-2.**

Rear Drum Integral Parking Brake Operation The parking brake is activated when the driver presses the parking brake pedal or pulls the parking brake hand lever. This pulls the parking brake cable, activating the mechanical parking brake components in the rear wheel brake assembly.

When the parking brake hand lever or pedal pulls the parking brake cable, it pivots the brake lever. This forces the rear brake shoe into contact with the drum. At the same time, the parking brake link pushes forward. This forces the front brake shoe into contact with the drum, applying the parking brakes. See **Fig. 6-3.**

Because most rear drum brakes have the duo-servo design, any forward movement of the car increases the application effort of the brakes. In reverse, however, rotation of the drum tends to decrease the holding power of the parking brakes.

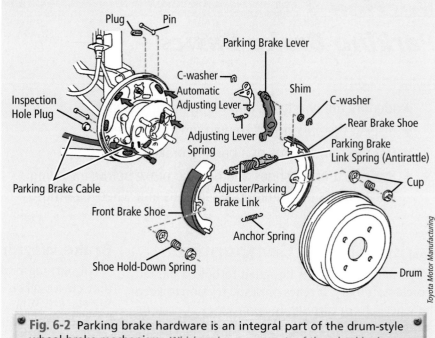

Fig. 6-2 Parking brake hardware is an integral part of the drum-style wheel brake mechanism. *Which major components of the wheel brake mechanism shown are specific to the parking brake system?*

Toyota Motor Manufacturing

TECH TIP **Applying the Parking Brake.** The parking brake can be applied using only a pedal or hand lever. However, it is best to press and hold the service brake pedal and then apply the parking brakes. This puts the linings in place without placing undo stress on the parking brake cable, which could eventually be damaged.

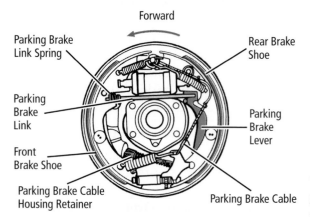

Ford Motor Company

Fig. 6-3 A duo-servo drum brake. Applying the parking brake transmits force mechanically through the parking brake cable. This mechanical force actuates the parking brake lever. This pivots and forces the front and rear brake shoes against the drum. *Which component of the parking brake hardware transfers motion from the brake lever to the forward brake shoe?*

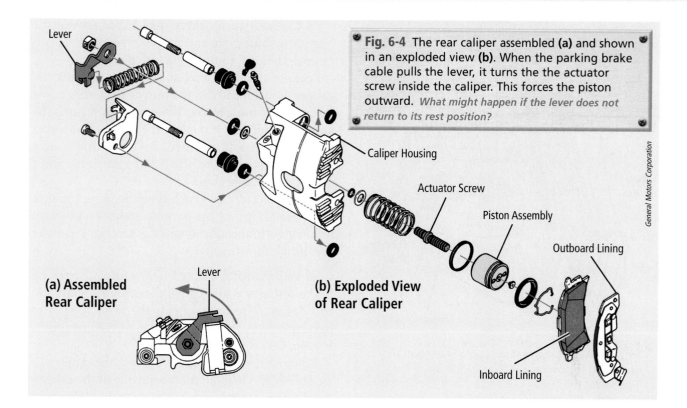

General Motors Corporation

Fig. 6-4 The rear caliper assembled **(a)** and shown in an exploded view **(b)**. When the parking brake cable pulls the lever, it turns the the actuator screw inside the caliper. This forces the piston outward. *What might happen if the lever does not return to its rest position?*

Lever

Caliper Housing

Actuator Screw

Piston Assembly

Outboard Lining

(a) Assembled Rear Caliper

Lever

(b) Exploded View of Rear Caliper

Inboard Lining

Rear Disc Integral Parking Brakes

Cars equipped with rear disc brakes and floating calipers often use the service brake pads for the parking brake function. Three basic types of mechanisms are used to mechanically actuate the parking brakes:

- Screw-nut-cone.
- Ball-ramp.
- Cam-rod.

Screw-Nut-Cone Parking Brakes Screw-nut-cone parking brakes are common on General Motors vehicles. This parking brake mechanism is also used to keep the rear disc brakes adjusted.

When the driver applies the parking brake, the cable pulls a lever on the outside of the caliper housing. The lever turns the actuator screw inside the caliper. A nut follows the threads of the screw and jams into the clutch surface of the caliper piston. See **Fig. 6-4.**

The piston cannot turn because it is locked into place by tabs on the inboard brake pad. Because the piston cannot turn, it is forced to move outward. As it moves outward, it forces the piston against the brake pad, which contacts the rotor. The parking brake is released by removing tension from the parking brake cable.

After servicing screw-nut-cone rear calipers, the technician must cycle the parking brakes as many times as necessary to relocate the pads close to the rotor. This is the only way to move the nut along the screw threads sufficiently to set the initial brake adjustment. The screw-nut-cone parking brake piston assembly is nonserviceable.

TECH TIP **Use the Parking Brake.** Advise the vehicle owner to use the parking brake regularly. This is necessary to keep the brakes properly adjusted. It will also help to keep the parking brake mechanism operating correctly. When not used for long periods of time, parts may seize and cause the parking brake to not properly apply or release.

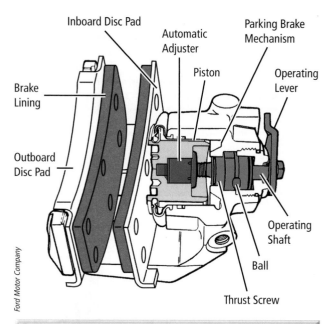

Inboard Disc Pad
Automatic Adjuster
Piston
Parking Brake Mechanism
Operating Lever
Brake Lining
Outboard Disc Pad
Operating Shaft
Ball
Thrust Screw

Ford Motor Company

Fig. 6-5 A ball-ramp caliper assembly. When the operating lever moves, the balls ride up ramps. This forces the piston out and against the inboard disc pad. *What happens when the parking brake mechanism turns the nut inside the caliper piston?*

Ball-Ramp Parking Brakes The ball-ramp parking brake design is commonly used on Ford vehicles. Ball-ramp mechanisms are one-way clutches.

When the parking brake is applied, the cable pulls a lever on the outside of the caliper. The lever is attached to the operating shaft, which has an end plate. See **Fig. 6-5.**

As the lever turns, three steel balls between the operating shaft plate and thrust screw plate ride up ramps. They try to push the two plates apart.

Because the operating shaft face is against the caliper housing, it cannot move. As a result, the thrust screw must move. When it does, it turns the automatic adjuster nut inside the piston. This forces the caliper piston outward. As the piston moves outward, it pushes the brake pad against the rotor and applies the brakes.

Brakes are adjusted each time the service brakes are applied. Cycling the parking brake several times following a brake job, however, is necessary to make the initial adjustment.

Cam-Rod Parking Brakes The cam-rod parking brake actuator is also called the eccentric shaft and rod design. The operation is the same. Cam-rod parking brakes are more common on Asian imports. See **Fig. 6-6.**

When the parking brake is applied, the cable pulls an arm (lever) located on the outside of the caliper. As the arm moves, it turns the parking lever cam assembly or eccentric shaft. The cam assembly or eccentric shaft pushes on a rod positioned between the cam and the actuator. As the rod pushes on the actuator, the actuator pushes on the piston. The piston then pushes the brake pads against the rotor.

Springs push the rod back when the parking brake is released. Like the screw-nut-cone design, the brakes are adjusted whenever the parking brakes are applied.

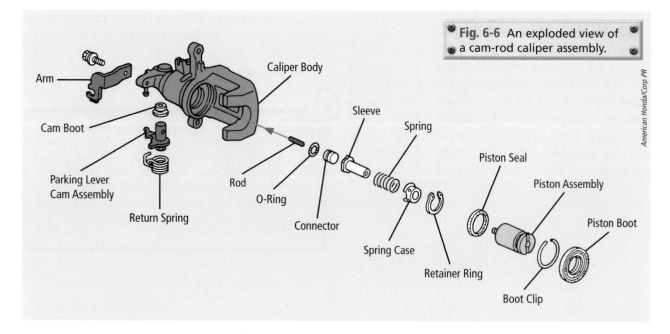

Fig. 6-6 An exploded view of a cam-rod caliper assembly.

American Honda/Corp PR

Arm
Caliper Body
Sleeve
Spring
Piston Seal
Cam Boot
Parking Lever Cam Assembly
Return Spring
Rod
O-Ring
Connector
Spring Case
Retainer Ring
Piston Assembly
Piston Boot
Boot Clip

Excellence in Science

Levers in Braking Systems

Cables play an important part in parking brake systems. They "pull" on the integral or auxiliary pads or shoes to set the parking brakes. Can cables also "push"? At first glance, the question may seem strange. How can a flexible cable push?

In this activity you will make a working cable brake system. Using a bicycle caliper brake, you will show that the answer to the above questions depends on the path of the cable.

Apply It!

Testing a Brake Cable

Meets NATEF Science Standards for understanding energy, force, and levers.

Materials and Equipment
• Flat board, about 8″ wide and 24″ long [20 cm x 60 cm] • Bicycle handlebar brake lever assembly • Bicycle front brake cable • Bicycle side-pull brake caliper assembly	• 6″ [15 cm] piece of wooden dowel or broomstick, the same diameter as a bicycle handlebar • Nails or screws to fasten the dowel to the board

1. Clamp the brake lever to the dowel. Fasten the dowel to the board with screws or nails. **Fig. A.**

2. Drill two holes in the board at positions X and Y. The center shaft of the caliper assembly must fit tightly into each hole (see illustrations).

3. Put the center shaft of the brake caliper assembly into hole X. **Fig. A.**

4. Cut the cable sheath and cable so that the cable will run in a straight line between the lever and the caliper. Thread the cable. Install the cable so that the caliper is slightly closed. **Fig. A.**

5. Push the brake lever down. Notice which part of the caliper moves. Hold the part that does not move with your fingers while you push the lever down. Do you feel that part trying to move?

6. Move the caliper to position Y. **Fig. B.** Press the lever down. What parts of the caliper move? Try holding one part of the caliper still. Observe what happens. Then hold the other part of the caliper. What happens?

Results and Analysis

This experiment demonstrates that a cable system can sometimes both pull on one part and push on another part. Look at **Figs. A** and **B**. What changed to allow the cable system to "push?" What special conditions are needed for a cable to act this way?

Notice the similarity between the bicycle brake mechanism and the disc brakes on a vehicle. Which do you think came first? Research the history of bicycle technology to find when caliper-rim brakes were first used.

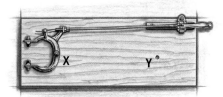

Fig. A

Fig. B

Auxiliary Parking Brakes

A growing number of vehicles with rear disc brakes use auxiliary drum brakes for parking only. This system used to be most common on systems with fixed calipers. However, it is now being used on systems with floating calipers as well.

Auxiliary Parking Brake Construction On a caliper system with an auxiliary parking brake, the rotor is shaped like a hat. The service brakes contact the brim of the hat. The parking brake is applied to the inside crown of the hat. See **Fig. 6-7.**

The parking brake is simply a drum brake with a set of small shoes. The small shoes have soft linings with a high coefficient of friction. Even so, the soft linings will not wear out if properly used. This is because they provide only static friction.

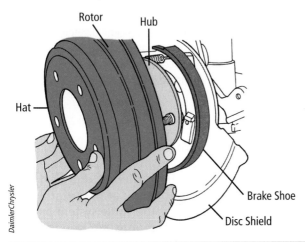

DaimlerChrysler

Fig. 6-7 The auxiliary drum parking brake consists of small brake shoes that act on the "hat" section of the rear brake rotor. *Why do the soft shoe linings not wear out if properly used?*

Auxiliary Parking Brake Operation Most designs have two brake shoes. There is an adjuster screw at the bottom and a cam at the top where the shoes meet. When the parking brake is applied, a lever rotates the cam. This forces the shoes apart and against the drum.

General Motors uses a single shoe that is almost a circle. An actuator at the bottom expands this circular shoe, or band, whenever the parking brake is applied. Adjustments are made at the parking brake cable. See **Fig. 6-8.**

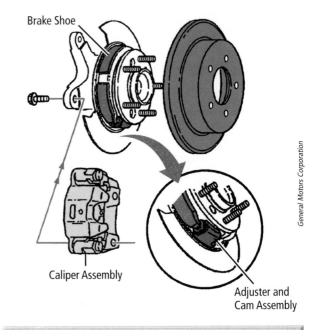

General Motors Corporation

Fig. 6-8 This parking brake is a single, nearly circular band with sections of friction material bonded to it. There is an adjuster with an actuating cam at the bottom. *Where are single-shoe parking brake adjustments made?*

SECTION 1 KNOWLEDGE CHECK

1. Explain the difference between integral and auxiliary parking brakes.

2. What type of mechanism is the parking brake pedal or lever?

3. Why should the service brake pedal be pressed when applying the parking brake?

4. Which type of parking brake is most common on Asian imports?

5. What does the rotor of an auxiliary parking brake resemble?

ASE TEST PREP

6. Technician A says the auxiliary parking brake shoes have a low coefficient of friction. Technician B says auxiliary parking brake shoes wear rapidly. Who is correct?

    ⓐ Technician A.

    ⓑ Technician B.

    ⓒ Both Technician A and Technician B.

    ⓓ Neither Technician A nor Technician B.

● *Section 2*
Parking Brake Controls, Diagnosis, and Repair

Objectives:
- Identify the mechanical components in parking brake controls.
- Describe the operation of a parking brake hand lever.
- **F4** Check parking brake operation.
- **F3** Check parking brake cables and components for wear, rusting, binding, and corrosion; clean, lubricate, or replace as needed.

Vocabulary:
- **parking brake equalizer**
- **pawl**
- **interference nut**
- **jam nut**
- **transfer cable**

Mechanical Components

Parking brake controls consist of connected mechanical components. Components typically include the following:
- A hand lever or pedal activates the parking brake.
- Cables to transfer force and motion from the parking brake hand lever or pedal to the parking brake mechanism at the wheels.
- A parking brake equalizer that distributes forces evenly. The **parking brake equalizer** is a device that balances the braking forces so that both rear brakes are applied evenly.

Parking Brake Hand Levers

Parking brake hand lever assemblies are simple ratchets with a pawl. A **pawl** is a ratchet tooth that is used to lock a device. The pawl engages the teeth of the stationary ratchet stop. When the hand lever is engaged, it pulls the parking brake cable. See **Fig. 6-9**.

A release button on the end of the hand lever is pushed to release the parking brake. This disengages the pawl. The hand lever can be returned to the rest position. The cable should then become slack.

Parking Brake Pedals

Parking brake pedal mechanisms operate on the same ratchet principle as hand lever mechanisms. Pressing the brake pedal causes the ratchet to engage. See **Fig. 6-10**.

In some cases the brake is released by pulling on a handle. In others the brake is released by pressing the pedal a second time. Some systems use a vacuum actuator to automatically release the brakes when the car is put in gear.

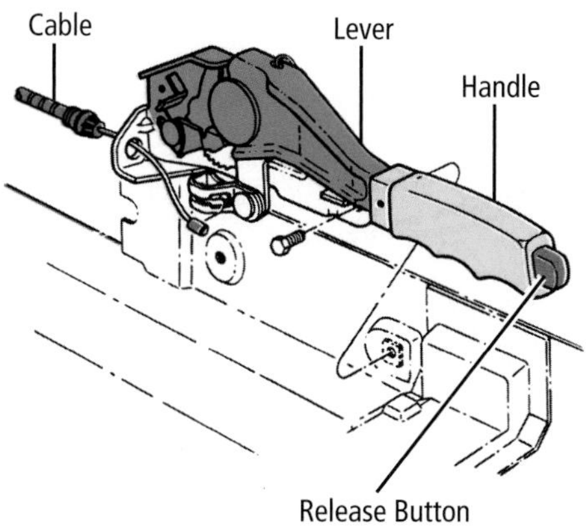

Cable   Lever

Handle

General Motors Corporation

Release Button

Fig. 6-9 Most parking brake hand levers have a simple ratchet and pawl design. *How are the parking brakes released?*

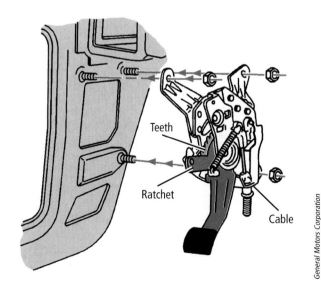

Teeth

Ratchet

Cable

General Motors Corporation

Fig. 6-10 Pedal-activated parking brakes also use a ratchet mechanism. *How are pedal-activated brakes released?*

Parking Brake Linkage

The parking brake linkage that connects the pedal or hand lever to the rear brakes is usually a cable. In the past, rods were used on some vehicles. They are still used on some trucks.

The cable is a braided wire rope covered with a metal or plastic sleeve. Most cars have at least two cables. The first leads from the parking brake pedal or hand lever to the equalizer. Another cable runs between the rear wheel brakes and through the equalizer.

Unless the parking brakes are used on a regular basis, the cables may rust. When this happens, the cable may not move in its housing. Cables should be lubricated occasionally to prevent corrosion.

If a cable seizes, each of the cables may be replaced individually. Do not attempt to repair a failed brake cable.

Parking Brake Equalizer

There are several different types of parking brake equalizers. The most common equalizer is a crescent-shaped cable guide attached to a threaded stud. The threaded stud provides tensioning adjustments for the parking brake cable assembly. See **Fig. 6-11**.

Parking Brake Complaints

There are two ways parking brakes can fail:
• The brakes can fail to hold.
• The brakes can fail to release.

Parking Brake Fails to Hold

If the brake fails to hold, the service brakes could be malfunctioning. The linings can be excessively worn or out of adjustment. Grease or oil on the linings can also cause failure.

If the service brakes are acceptable, the parking brake cable may need to be adjusted.

Parking Brake Fails to Release

If the parking brake fails to release, it is often due to a corroded cable. Many motorists, especially those who have cars with automatic transmissions, do not use their parking brake regularly. Unless the driver uses the parking brake regularly, corrosion can build up in the cable housing. Parking brake cables should be lubricated on a yearly basis. Apply lube spray at the cable housing and at the parking brake hand lever or pedal. Work the parking brake hand lever or pedal several times to move the spray lube down and through the cable.

Applying the brake creates enough force to move the cable. But when the brake is released, the return springs may not be strong enough to overcome the friction in the cable. Frayed cables can also hang up and fail to release.

Fig. 6-11 The parking brake linkage consists of cables, connectors, and guides. *Can the equalizer mechanism be used to adjust the parking brake cable assembly?*

DaimlerChrysler

Cable Guide
Equalizer
Threaded Stud
Adjuster Nut
Intermediate Cable
Cable Connector
Right Rear Cable
Boot
FWD
Retainer Hook
Cable Guide
Front Cable
Connector
Cable Guide
Cable Connector
Bracket
Left Rear Cable

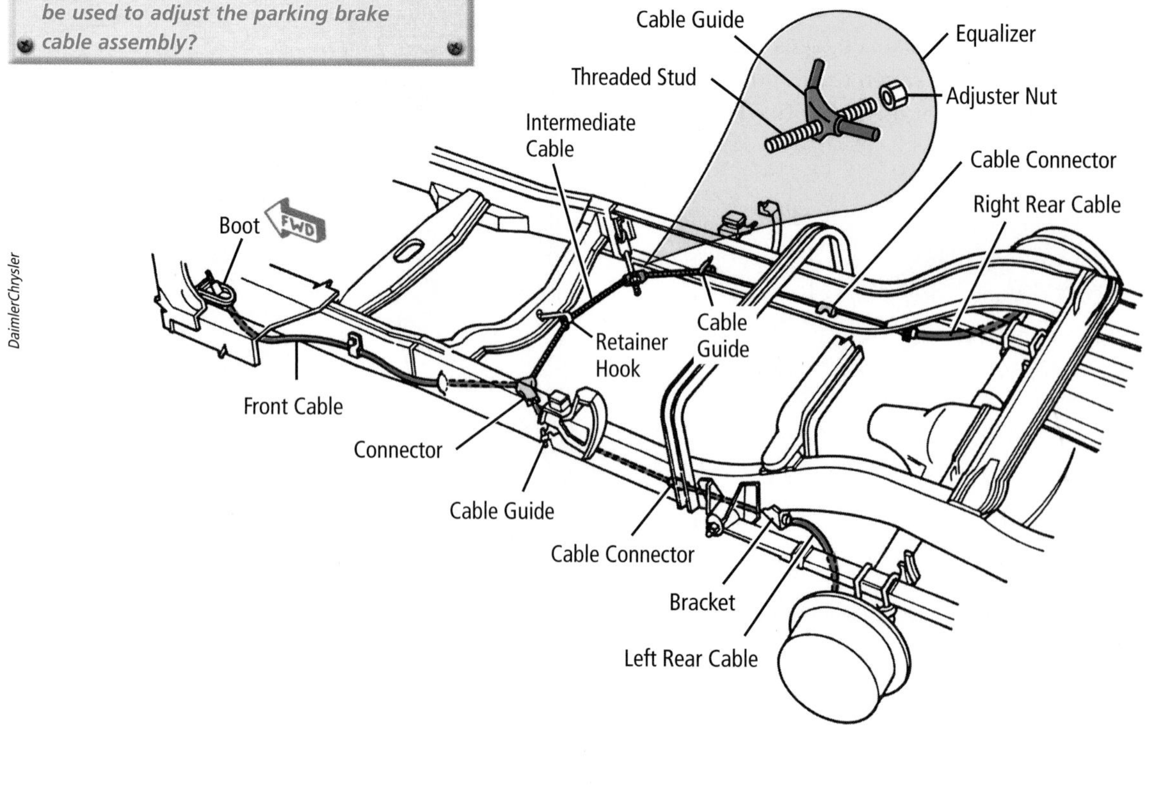

On cars with rear-caliper parking brakes, the cables could be overadjusted. The levers should travel fully to the stops (bosses) on the caliper housing when the brakes are released.

Often the brake warning light on the instrument panel will glow if the brakes do not fully release. The cause is usually a hand lever or pedal that does not fully retract or a bad brake warning light switch.

Parking Brake Repair

Parking brake repair involves adjusting and replacing cables and auxiliary parking brake shoes.

Adjusting Parking Brake Cables

Cables will stretch over time with use. Their effective length can be adjusted. Some cable adjusters are under the car, at the equalizer. Others are at the parking brake hand lever. On some systems there is an interference nut. An **interference nut** is a self-locking nut that will not loosen. On others there is a jam nut. A **jam nut** is a second nut that is tightened against the adjusting nut to keep it from moving.

Most lever-actuated cables are adjusted at the lever itself. Adjust by tightening a nut or turning an adjustment screw.

Replacing Parking Brake Cables

Replacing parking brake cables is straightforward. Most cables have a ball or barrel connector on the ends. This slips through a slot and seats in the component to which it connects.

TECH TIP **Do Not Twist the Cable.** If the cable is twisted, it can be damaged and may fail prematurely. To prevent twisting while adjusting, hold the cable's adjustment rod with a pair of locking pliers.

Replacing the Primary (Front) Cable To replace the primary cable:
1. Loosen the adjuster at the equalizer until there is sufficient slack to remove the cable from the equalizer. See **Fig. 6-12**.
2. Remove the cable from the equalizer and then remove it from the pedal assembly or hand lever inside the car. See **Fig. 6-13**.
3. Install the new cable by performing these steps in reverse order.

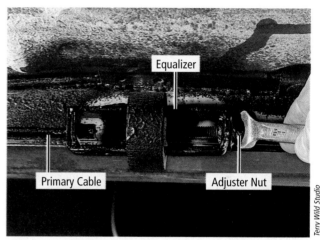

Equalizer

Primary Cable

Adjuster Nut

Terry Wild Studio

Fig. 6-12 At a point in front of the equalizer, hold the cable with a wrench. Then loosen the adjuster nut with another wrench. *How is the primary cable connected to the equalizer?*

Parking Brake Pedal

Terry Wild Studio

Fig. 6-13 The front cable (not visible) attaches to the brake pedal near the firewall and floorboard. *Where is the other end of the front cable attached?*

Replacing the Transfer (Rear) Cable(s) The **transfer cable** is a cable that runs between the rear wheels or from the equalizer to each rear wheel. This cable is generally replaced from under the car. To replace the transfer cable:

1. Disconnect the cable(s) from the equalizer. See **Fig. 6-14**.
2. Remove the cable(s) from the brackets. See **Fig. 6-15**.
3. Once the cable(s) is free of the equalizer and brackets, it can be removed from the brake shoe or caliper actuator levers.

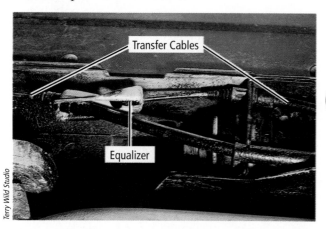

Fig. 6-14 The transfer cables attach to the equalizer. *What is the purpose of the equalizer?*

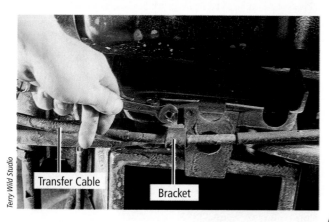

Fig. 6-15 Brackets support the transfer cables as they are being routed to the rear brakes.

Most transfer cables are held to the backing plate with fingers. These fingers must be compressed before the cable can be removed from the backing plate. Install the replacement cable by performing these steps in reverse order. See **Fig. 6-16**.

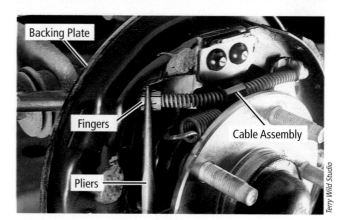

Fig. 6-16 Squeeze the fingers when removing the transfer cable from the backing plate. *How is the transfer cable accessed for replacement?*

TECH TIP **Compressing Cable Fingers.** A useful trick for compressing the cable fingers is to use a small, worm-type hose clamp. Place the clamp around the cable fingers and then tighten by turning the screw.

Auxiliary Parking Brake Shoes

Auxiliary parking brake shoes, like service drum brakes, need to be adjusted.

Adjusting To adjust auxiliary shoes, turn a star wheel as you would when adjusting service drum brakes. There is usually an access hole in the rotor shield.

Replacing Parking brake shoe replacement is similar to service brake shoe replacement. Check the vehicle service manual for specific instructions.

In general, the auxiliary parking brake shoes are much smaller than normal drum brake shoes. They are attached to the backing plate in a similar manner. Pins pass through the steel web of the shoe. The shoe is held in place by a spring.

TECH TIP **Cable Maintenance.** Parking brake cables transmit the force applied by a lever or foot pedal to the brakes at the wheels. Hanging under the vehicle, they are subject to road debris and water. Since the cable is made of woven steel wire, it can rust. A buildup of rust inside the cable housing may prevent the cable from moving. To prevent this, the parking brake cable should occasionally be lubricated with light oil where it enters the cable housing.

Excellence in Math

Parking on a Hill

What keeps a car from sliding when parked on a steep incline?

The drawing below shows an incline with an angle, *z*. The rise, or height, of the incline is labeled *y*. The run, or horizontal distance, is labeled *x*.

The *slope* is the ratio of rise (*y*) to run (*x*) or *y/x*. The car will slip when the slope on which it is parked is greater than the value of the coefficient of static friction. A typical coefficient of static friction for rubber tires on dry concrete is 0.60.

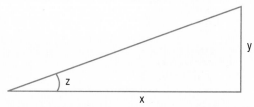

For example if the angle, *z*, is 5° with a run of 150 ft, the rise is 13.12 ft. The ratio of rise to run is:

$$\frac{y}{x} = \frac{13.12}{150} = 0.0875$$

A vehicle on a 5° slope will not slip if the coefficient of static friction is greater than 0.0875. The table shows the rise for a run of 150 feet, with angles of incline between 0° and 45°.

Apply It!

Meets NATEF Mathematics Standards for interpreting tables and using angles and geometric figures.

The table shows rise and run for angles of incline between 0° and 45°.

1. Calculate the ratio of rise to run for the entries in the table.

2. The coefficient of static friction for rubber tires on dry concrete is 0.60. Analyze the ratios you have calculated. Determine the approximate angle at which a vehicle will begin to slip.

3. Assume that the street is wet. The coefficent of static friction for rubber tires on a wet street is only about 0.20. At what angle will the vehicle begin to slide?

Angle (z)	Rise (y)	Run (x)	y / x
0	0	150	0.0
5	13.12	150	0.0875
10	26.45	150	
15	40.19	150	
20	54.60	150	
25	69.95	150	
30	86.60	150	
35	105.03	150	
40	125.86	150	
45	150.00	150	

SECTION 2 KNOWLEDGE CHECK

1. Name the three basic mechanical components of a parking brake.

2. What is the most common type of parking brake equalizer?

3. What may happen if a parking brake cable is corroded?

4. Explain how to adjust auxiliary parking brake shoes.

ASE TEST PREP

5. Technician A says the parking brakes may not hold if there is grease on the linings. Technician B says the brakes may not hold if the linings are excessively worn. Who is correct?

   ⓐ Technician A.

   ⓑ Technician B.

   ⓒ Both Technician A and Technician B.

   ⓓ Neither Technician A nor Technician B.

CHAPTER 6 REVIEW

Key Points

Meets the following NATEF Standards for Brakes: inspection and servicing of parking brakes and the parking brake warning light system.

- There are two basic types of parking brake systems: one uses the same brake shoes or pads as the service brakes; the other uses a separate set of brake linings.
- In some cases, parking brakes use components from the service brake system. In other cases, the parking brakes have separate components.
- The parking brake warning light system warns the driver that the parking brake is on.
- Screw-nut-cone parking brakes are common on General Motors vehicles. Ball-ramp parking brakes are used on Ford vehicles. Cam-rod parking brakes are more common on Asian imports.
- Parking brake hand lever assemblies are simple ratchets with a pawl.
- Parking brake pedal mechanisms operate on the same ratchet principle as hand lever mechanisms.
- Servicing parking brakes includes cable adjustment and replacement.
- Parking brake failure is usually due to corroded, worn, or out-of-adjustment cables.

Review Questions

1. What are the two types of actuating mechanisms used on parking brakes?
2. What causes the brake warning light to glow?
3. Name the three types of parking brake assemblies used on vehicles.
4. What motion tends to decrease the holding power of rear drum parking brakes?
5. What must a technician do after servicing screw-nut-cone rear calipers?
6. What type of parking brake would you most likely find on a Ford sedan?
7. What is another name for the cam-rod parking brake actuator?
8. What is a jam nut?
9. (Critical Thinking) The linings of an auxiliary parking brake are soft. Why won't they wear out if the parking brake is properly used?
10. (Critical Thinking) There are several reasons why a parking brake may fail to hold. Name one.

Excellence in Communication

Remember—Safety First

Safety is important to both the customer and the technician. If you, as the technician, are not careful, you may harm yourself or your customer. And you may do serious damage to your customer's vehicle.

An action as simple as using old brake fluid that has been contaminated with water can cause brakes to fail. Using the wrong fluid or not checking the fluid level properly can also lead to problems. To assure personal safety and proper service of your customer's car—read!

Technicians must always look for visual clues. Sometimes a manual will warn you about specific service products. Sometimes, the label on a can or package will tell all. When you read the *Safety First* features in this chapter, you will be given specific information. Stay on the alert for safety information about all products and procedures that you use.

Apply It!

Meets NATEF Communications Standards for collecting, evaluating, and using information.

Read the *Safety First* features in this chapter.

1. Where could you find this information and other similar warnings?
2. Make a list of sources that warn or advise about the products used in servicing a vehicle.
3. Keep a list of specific warnings that you find as you service cars.
4. Use this list as an on-the-job resource.

AUTOMOTIVE SERVICE EXCELLENCE
TEST PREP

Answering the following practice questions will help you prepare for the ASE certification tests.

1. Parking brakes differ from service brakes. Which of the following is a difference?

   ⓐ Parking brakes rely on kinetic friction.
   ⓑ Parking brakes do not use the wheel brake component of the service brake system.
   ⓒ Parking brakes are operated by a mechanical operating system.
   ⓓ Parking brakes do not use any components of the service brake system.

2. The best parking brakes are:

   ⓐ disc brakes.
   ⓑ drum brakes.
   ⓒ ABS brakes.
   ⓓ power-boosted brakes.

3. A mechanism used to mechanically actuate parking brakes is a:

   ⓐ screw-nut-cone mechanism.
   ⓑ socket mechanism.
   ⓒ flexible link mechanism.
   ⓓ hydraulic mechanism.

4. Technician A says that most auxiliary parking brake designs have one brake shoe. Technician B says that most auxiliary parking brake designs have two brake shoes. Who is correct?

   ⓐ Technician A.
   ⓑ Technician B.
   ⓒ Both Technician A and Technician B.
   ⓓ Neither Technician A nor Technician B.

5. Technician A says that if a parking brake cable seizes that it must be replaced. Technician B says that a seized parking brake cable can be repaired. Who is correct?

   ⓐ Technician A.
   ⓑ Technician B.
   ⓒ Both Technician A and Technician B.
   ⓓ Neither Technician A nor Technician B.

6. The parking brake fails to hold. The service brakes have been checked and are found to be acceptable. What should be done?

   ⓐ Adjust the parking brake cable.
   ⓑ Lubricate the parking brake cable.
   ⓒ Replace the parking brake cable.
   ⓓ Advise driver to use the parking brake more regularly.

7. Parking brake hand levers are released by:

   ⓐ depressing a button on the hand lever.
   ⓑ depressing the brake pedal.
   ⓒ pulling the release handle.
   ⓓ backing the car a short distance.

8. Parking brake cables stretch over time. How can their effective length be adjusted?

   ⓐ Through the cable adjuster at the equalizer.
   ⓑ Through the cable adjuster at the parking brake hand lever.
   ⓒ By means of an interference nut.
   ⓓ All of the above.

9. Technician A says that auxiliary parking brake shoes are generally much smaller than normal drum brake shoes. Technician B says that normal drum brake shoes are generally much smaller than auxiliary parking brake shoes. Who is correct?

   ⓐ Technician A.
   ⓑ Technician B.
   ⓒ Both Technician A and Technician B.
   ⓓ Neither Technician A nor Technician B.

10. Technician A says that most transfer cables are held to the backing plate with fingers. Technician B says that most transfer cables are held to the backing plate with a nut and a bolt. Who is correct?

    ⓐ Technician A.
    ⓑ Technician B.
    ⓒ Both Technician A and Technician B.
    ⓓ Neither Technician A nor Technician B.

Section 1
Antilock Brake
System Operation

Section 2
Antilock Brake
Diagnosis and
Repair

Section 3
Controlling Torque

Diagnosing & Repairing Antilock Brakes

Customer's Concern

Anna Takchawee was driving her new sedan through a thunderstorm yesterday. As she came out of a sharp curve, two cars collided in front of her. When she hit the brakes, she braced herself for a collision and steered toward the shoulder. She was able to bring the car safely to a full stop. She was grateful that her antilock brakes enabled her to steer past the accident scene and safely stop her car.

Since Anna's near miss, the brake and ABS lights have been glowing on her dashboard. Knowing another accident may be looming around the next corner, she wants to be sure her ABS is working properly. Anna was assigned to your service team when she purchased her new car at your dealership.

Technician's Challenge

As the service technician, you need to find answers to these questions:

1. Is this the first time Anna has activated the ABS on her new car? Did the warning lights ever glow prior to yesterday?

2. What is your first step in diagnosing an ABS problem? How might a scan tool help you diagnose Anna's problem?

3. Why is safety so important when working with ABS? Once you've diagnosed the problem, how can you safely prepare to remove a system part?

● Section 1
Antilock Brake System Operation

Objectives:

● Describe how an antilock brake system (ABS) works.
● Describe the differences between integral ABS and nonintegral ABS.
● Identify the three main ABS channel configurations.
● Identify the wheels controlled by each of the three main ABS channel configurations.

Vocabulary:

● antilock brake system (ABS)
● wheel speed sensor
● tone wheel
● integral braking system
● nonintegral braking system
● ABS channel
● wheel lockup

Benefits of an Antilock Brake System

An **antilock brake system (ABS)** is a system on motor vehicles that prevents the wheels from locking during braking. This system improves the driver's ability to control the vehicle while braking in panic stops or in emergencies. Stopping a vehicle quickly on a slick road can be dangerous. Tires skid when they lose traction on the road surface. This loss of traction happens when the driver applies the brakes so hard that the wheels "lock." Wheel lock means that the wheels stop rotating.

Wheel lock occurs when the force (speed) of the vehicle is greater than the friction between the tires and road surface. Wheels that are locked begin to skid. This breaks traction at the road surface.

A friction rating of a road surface depends on the construction of the road. Gravel has a very low friction rating. Dry asphalt has a high friction rating. Water on an asphalt road decreases its friction rating. When the friction rating of a road surface goes down, the stopping distance of a vehicle on that surface goes up. The stopping distance of a vehicle depends on the:
• Speed of the vehicle.
• Type and condition of tires.
• Driver's use of the vehicle's brakes.
• Road condition (dry, wet, snow, gravel).

Vehicle design also affects braking action. You need to consider whether the vehicle has the engine in the front or rear. You also need to consider whether it has rear-wheel drive, front-wheel drive, or four-wheel drive.

ABS was first developed in the United States for aircraft. Vehicle manufacturers adapted the system first for heavy-duty trucks and later for passenger vehicles.

Manufacturers soon realized the benefits of equipping vehicles such as vans and pickup trucks with ABS. These vehicles are harder to stop safely. Even the simpler and less expensive rear-wheel ABS greatly improved their stopping power.

ABS is based on the concept of braking while maintaining control. When a driver brakes and the wheels lock, the wheels skid. Because the wheels are not rotating, the driver cannot steer the vehicle. ABS allows the driver to brake the vehicle up to the point of wheel lockup. Thus, ABS allows the driver to decelerate, or slow down, and still steer the vehicle.

ABS benefits the average driver. In a panic situation, the average driver lacks the vehicle handling skills to apply the brakes to the point just prior to lockup.

During a skid, an experienced driver can pump the brakes and steer into the skid. This may help minimize a bad situation. ABS provides a better way to maintain vehicle steering and stopping control. ABS prevents the brakes from locking the wheels, regardless of most road conditions.

ABS helps drivers cope with the ability of rear wheels to maintain traction. A truck without ABS is designed to stop efficiently when fully loaded. It relies on the proportioning valve to balance front-to-rear braking effect. When the truck is empty and the vehicle's traction is low, the rear wheels may tend to slide.

Figure 7-1 shows a vehicle equipped with all-wheel ABS. A manufacturer's decision to equip a vehicle with only rear-wheel ABS or all-wheel ABS depends on the vehicle's design. It also depends on how much

the customer is willing to pay for the option. More expensive vehicles are likely to have the more sophisticated ABS systems. These can include yaw sensing (sensing that the vehicle is sliding or spinning), deceleration sensing, and traction control (discussed later in this chapter).

The Role of Sensors

On most vehicles ABS provides normal braking action during regular braking. However, during hard braking ABS prevents wheel lockup. ABS functions whether the vehicle is being driven on snow, ice, gravel, or even wet leaves. ABS allows the brakes to slow the vehicle until the wheels are near lockup and the tires are starting to slide.

When wheel lockup is detected, ABS takes over. It stops further application of hydraulic brake pressure to the locking wheel. The brake fluid pressure is reduced, or even released, depending on the situation. This allows the wheel to resume rolling. Brake pressure is then reapplied, and the process starts over. The ABS process is similar to the rapid pumping action of the brakes. However, with ABS the process is done more quickly and with greater precision. Each wheel is controlled individually by the ABS control module.

Safety First

ABS Drivers new to ABS must learn the differences between ABS and standard brakes to realize their full benefit. With ABS, hard braking or panic stops will cause rapid pulsing, or modulation, of the brake pressure. Drivers will likely feel this through the brake pedal. Drivers describe this as if the brake pedal is "kicking" the driver's foot away from the pedal. Drivers need to know that this is normal with ABS. They should continue to apply the brakes and steer the vehicle as required to avoid an accident.

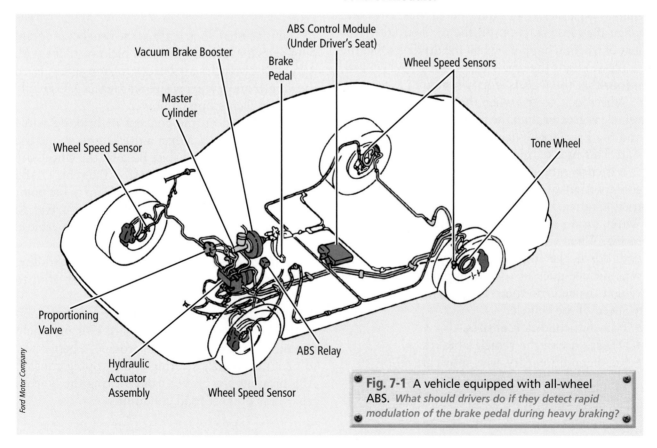

Vacuum Brake Booster

ABS Control Module (Under Driver's Seat)

Brake Pedal

Wheel Speed Sensors

Master Cylinder

Wheel Speed Sensor

Tone Wheel

Proportioning Valve

Hydraulic Actuator Assembly

Wheel Speed Sensor

ABS Relay

Ford Motor Company

Fig. 7-1 A vehicle equipped with all-wheel ABS. *What should drivers do if they detect rapid modulation of the brake pedal during heavy braking?*

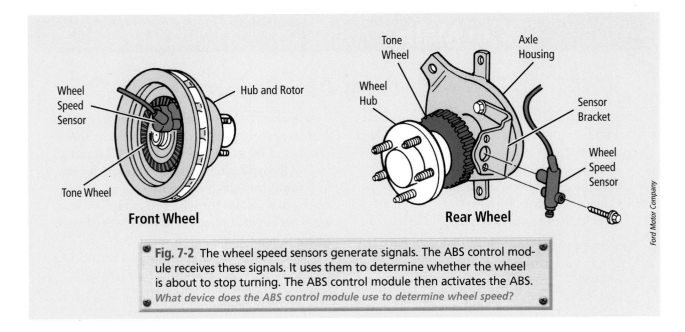

Front Wheel

Rear Wheel

Ford Motor Company

Fig. 7-2 The wheel speed sensors generate signals. The ABS control module receives these signals. It uses them to determine whether the wheel is about to stop turning. The ABS control module then activates the ABS.
What device does the ABS control module use to determine wheel speed?

Rapidly pumping the brake pedal will adjust the hydraulic brake pressure to all wheels at the same time. But with ABS a single wheel or a combination of all four may be controlled. The ABS rapidly pumps the brakes to keep the rate of wheel deceleration below the point at which the wheels lock.

The **wheel speed sensor** is a device that inputs wheel speed to the ABS control module. There are wheel speed sensors at each wheel. They continuously monitor wheel rotation speed. For each ABS-controlled wheel, a built-in toothed **tone wheel,** or reluctor wheel, rotates as part of the vehicle's wheel. See **Fig. 7-2.** The teeth of the tone wheel pass through the wheel speed sensor's magnetic field. This causes a voltage signal that is sent to the ABS system.

The wheel speed sensor consists of a permanent magnet and a winding. This sensor is a permanent magnet sensor. The rotating toothed tone wheel is near the stationary wheel speed sensor. The sensor generates an alternating current (AC) signal as each tooth passes through the magnetic field of the wheel speed sensor. The AC signal is sent to the ABS control module through a shielded cable. The control module uses the signals to measure each wheel's speed.

ABS takes action when the brake light switch signals the control module that the brake pedal has been depressed. The control module action is based on wheel sensor input information and information stored in the on-board computer. The control module may determine that one or more wheels is nearing a locked condition. It then signals the hydraulic actuator. The actuator reduces, or modulates, brake pressure to the slowing wheel(s). This action prevents wheel lockup.

Integral and Nonintegral Antilock Brake Systems

There are two types of ABS systems—integral and nonintegral (or nonintegrated). In an **integral braking system,** the brake booster, master cylinder, pump, accumulator, and pressure modulator may be combined as a single unit. Servicing an integral system can be more costly. Its components are more expensive. These units are not in wide use on current models.

A **nonintegral braking system** uses traditional brake system components, such as the master cylinder and brake booster. The ABS components include the ABS control module and hydraulic actuator. This is the most widely used unit today.

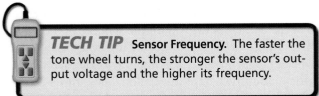

TECH TIP **Sensor Frequency.** The faster the tone wheel turns, the stronger the sensor's output voltage and the higher its frequency.

Excellence **in Math**

Interpreting ABS Graphs

An antilock brake system (ABS) prevents lockup by monitoring the speed of each wheel compared to the vehicle speed.

To prevent lockup, the computer may:
- Reduce braking pressure.
- Increase braking pressure.
- Hold the pressure constant.

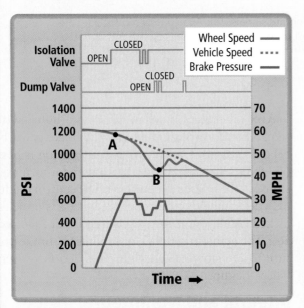

The computer does these three things by controlling the isolation and dump valves in the brake hydraulic system. Look at the graph of wheel speed, vehicle speed, and brake pressures. The dotted line represents overall vehicle speed. Under optimum conditions the wheel speed and the vehicle speed should remain the same.

At point A the wheel speed has begun to decrease more quickly than the vehicle speed. The wheel starts to lockup. The ABS starts to control the hydraulic pressure to prevent lockup. At Point B the ABS has begun to overcome the lockup and allows the wheel to continue rotating. This begins to bring the wheel speed back where it belongs.

The ABS computer is programmed to calculate the *slip ratio*. This ratio can be written as:

$$\frac{\text{vehicle speed} - \text{wheel speed}}{\text{vehicle speed}} \times 100$$

This ratio (a fraction) is usually shown as a percentage by multiplying it by 100. The size of the slip ratio determines how the ABS controls the valves. The ideal slip ratio is zero. This means that vehicle speed and wheel speed are the same.

Apply It!

Meets NATEF Mathematics Standards for interpreting and using graphs.

1. Follow the horizontal lines to the speed scale on the right of the graph. Estimate the speeds indicated there.

2. Calculate the slip ratio at Point B. Use the slip ratio formula given above.

3. Did the ABS keep the slip ratio at less than 30 percent as it was programmed to do?

If the brake fluid reservoir is low, follow these steps:
1. Inspect the brake system for leaks.
2. Inspect the brake pads for wear.
3. Refer to the vehicle service manual to correct any problem in the brake system. Add brake fluid that meets the vehicle manufacturer's specifications. Follow the procedure described in the vehicle manual. In an ABS, do not add brake fluid without first checking the system for other problems. Some ABS systems require special procedures to check or adjust fluid levels.

Understanding ABS Channels

An **ABS channel** is a hydraulic line from the ABS actuator to the wheel. Antilock brake systems come in a variety of forms. Some operate on only the rear wheels. Some operate on all the wheels. Some activate a pair of wheels together and the other two wheels independently. Still others activate each wheel independently. These are called one-, three-, and four-channel systems.

One-Channel ABS

The one-channel ABS has ABS only on the rear wheels. For economy and simplicity, many vans and pickup trucks have only rear-wheel ABS. In some cases these rear-wheel antilock systems (GM and DaimlerChrysler's RWAL) or rear antilock brake systems (Ford's RABS) control both rear wheels at the same time. See **Fig. 7-3**.

Safety First | **RWAL or RABS Braking** During braking with RWAL or RABS, the front brakes can still lock. If the front brakes lock, the driver will be unable to steer the vehicle.

Wheel lockup occurs when braking causes tires to lose traction, resulting in skidding. Wheel lockup is sensed either at the differential carrier or, as in GM, at the transmission output shaft. In these systems, hydraulic application of ABS affects control of both rear wheels together. A single hydraulic brake line supplies pressure to both rear-wheel cylinders. See **Fig. 7-4**.

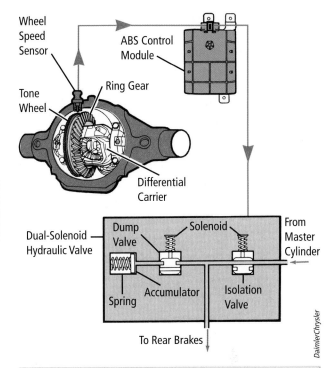

DaimlerChrysler

Fig. 7-4 The wheel speed sensor for the rear-wheel antilock brakes on many Dodge and Ford trucks is mounted in the differential carrier. *What is the advantage of one-channel ABS if the vehicle can experience longer stopping distances?*

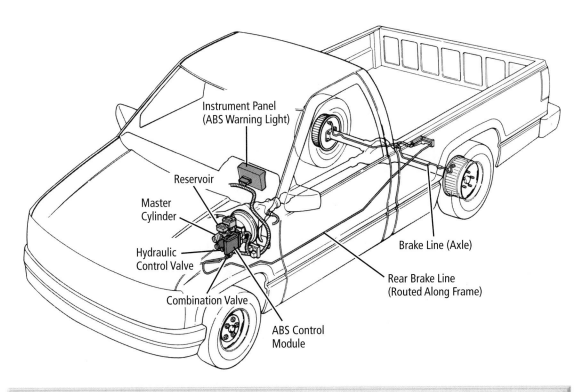

General Motors Corporation

Fig. 7-3 The RWAL system is found on some GM and Dodge trucks. *Are the rear wheels controlled individually or together?*

A vehicle equipped with one-channel ABS may have longer stopping distances when ABS is active. However, ABS reduces the possibility of vehicle spinout due to rear-wheel lockup.

A comparison of the front and rear brake pressures in this situation can be shown. See **Fig. 7-5.** First the isolation valve closes. This prevents any increase in pressure from reaching the rear brakes.

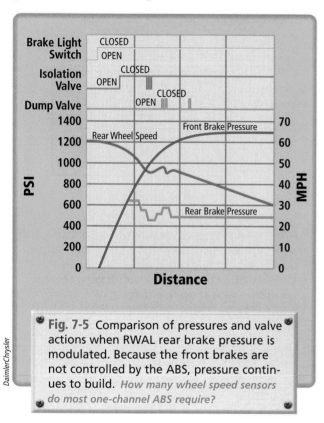

DaimlerChrysler

Fig. 7-5 Comparison of pressures and valve actions when RWAL rear brake pressure is modulated. Because the front brakes are not controlled by the ABS, pressure continues to build. *How many wheel speed sensors do most one-channel ABS require?*

If additional modulation is needed, the control module briefly opens the dump valve. This relieves the pressure in the rear brakes by allowing fluid to flow from the brake circuit into the accumulator.

Three-Channel ABS

In three-channel ABS, both front wheels of the vehicle are independently controlled. If either front wheel nears lockup, the ABS can control only that wheel. This allows for improved braking and steering control. A single circuit controls both rear wheels at the same time.

The three-channel ABS combines the advantage of the rear-wheel-only system with the addition of independent lock-up control of the front wheels.

Four-Channel ABS

A vehicle with four-wheel independent ABS control is equipped with a four-channel ABS. This system improves steering control at the front and slide prevention at the rear. It also paves the way for traction control systems. These systems rely on many of the ABS components.

In a three- or four-channel ABS system, solenoids in the system close or open one or more of the brake hydraulic circuits. Solenoids will either hold or release hydraulic pressure to one or more of the wheel brakes. This depends on which wheels are about to lock up.

SECTION 1 KNOWLEDGE CHECK

1. Describe what happens when ABS takes over vehicle braking.

2. Explain the difference between an integral and nonintegral ABS system.

3. Define an ABS channel.

4. Which wheels does an ABS one-channel system serve?

5. Explain how the wheels in a three-channel ABS system are controlled.

6. Which type of ABS system improves steering and prevents rear-wheel slide?

ASE TEST PREP

7. Technician A says a three-channel ABS combines the lower cost of an RWAL system with the added benefits of better steering control. Technician B says a three-channel ABS has a separate brake circuit to each rear wheel and a common circuit for the front wheels. Who is correct?

   ⓐ Technician A.

   ⓑ Technician B.

   ⓒ Both Technician A and Technician B.

   ⓓ Neither Technician A nor Technician B.

● Section 2
Antilock Brake Diagnosis and Repair

Objectives:

- ● Determine whether the ABS warning light is functioning normally.
- **G1** ● Identify and inspect antilock brake system (ABS) components.
- **G3** ● Diagnose antilock brake system (ABS) electronic control(s) and components using self-diagnosis and/or recommended test equipment.
- **G2** ● Diagnose poor stopping, wheel lockup, abnormal pedal feel or pulsation, and noise concerns caused by the antilock brake system (ABS).
- **G4** ● Depressurize high-pressure components of the antilock brake system (ABS).
- **G6** ● Remove and install antilock brake system (ABS) electrical/electronic and hydraulic components.
- **G8** ● Diagnose antilock brake system (ABS) braking concerns caused by vehicle modifications (tire size, curb height, final drive ratio, etc.).
- **G5** ● Bleed the antilock brake system's (ABS) front and rear hydraulic circuits.
- **G7** ● Test, diagnose and service ABS speed sensors, toothed ring (tone wheel), and circuits using a graphing multimeter (GMM)/digital storage oscilloscope (DSO) (includes output signal, resistance, shorts to voltage/ground, and frequency data).

Vocabulary:

- ● **deceleration sensor**
- ● **lateral acceleration sensor**
- ● **antilock warning light**
- ● **ABS diagnostic connector**

Antilock Brake System Control Module

There are several components in an antilock brake system. Some components supply information to the ABS control module. Other components receive commands from the control module. Still others respond to hydraulic activity in the system. See **Fig. 7-6.**

The brain of the ABS is the control module. Like any electronic control module, it receives input data, processes it, and provides output data signals, or commands.

Input data comes from sensors. The ABS control module takes the data and reviews the data stored in its memory. The module then decides when and how action should be taken.

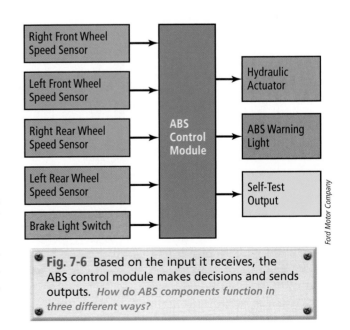

Fig. 7-6 Based on the input it receives, the ABS control module makes decisions and sends outputs. *How do ABS components function in three different ways?*

The control module changes output data to signals. These signals are sent to actuators. These actuators include the hydraulic control unit, the pump, and the brake and ABS lights in the instrument cluster. The control module decides which wheels should be ABS-controlled under a variety of driving conditions. These driving conditions include:

• Hard braking.
• Hard cornering.
• Driving with four-wheel drive engaged.

The control module also initiates a self-diagnosis each time the vehicle is started. Depending on the vehicle, this self-test occurs between 5 and 25 mph [8–40 kph]. If the control module determines, after reviewing its stored data, that operating conditions are outside of specifications, it shuts down the ABS. The module then turns on the ABS warning light. It also stores a diagnostic trouble code (DTC). This DTC can be retrieved later by a technician.

Hydraulic Components

Hydraulic components pressurize the fluid within the ABS system. These components are controlled by various sensors and actuators.

Pump, Accumulator, and Reservoir

The integral ABS must have high pressure available to be able to go into action. The pump builds up a reserve of brake fluid pressure. This reserve is stored in the accumulator. When accumulator brake fluid pressure drops to approximately 1,500 psi [10,343 kPa], a low-pressure switch turns on the pump. This rebuilds the pressure reserve.

A high-pressure switch shuts off the pump at around 2,500 psi [17,238 kPa]. Repeated braking can use up the high pressure in the accumulator. If this happens, the driver can still brake normally. However, the brake pedal will require greater than normal force.

In many nonintegral systems, brake fluid vented from the wheel circuits is stored in a reservoir. This is separate from the one on the master cylinder. The reservoir is not pressurized.

The next time the brakes are applied, the motorized pump pressurizes the fluid. The pump sends the fluid back to the master cylinder.

Hydraulic Actuator

In RWAL systems the ABS control module signals the ABS relay to power the hydraulic actuator. Either a two- or three-position flow control valve in the hydraulic actuator controls pressure to both rear wheels.

Check the vehicle service manual for the proper tires and gearing if the vehicle continues to set a DTC.

In a three-channel system, each wheel may have a wheel speed sensor. Although each front wheel brake is controlled individually by the actuator, a single three-position solenoid controls the pressure to both rear brakes. See **Fig. 7-7**.

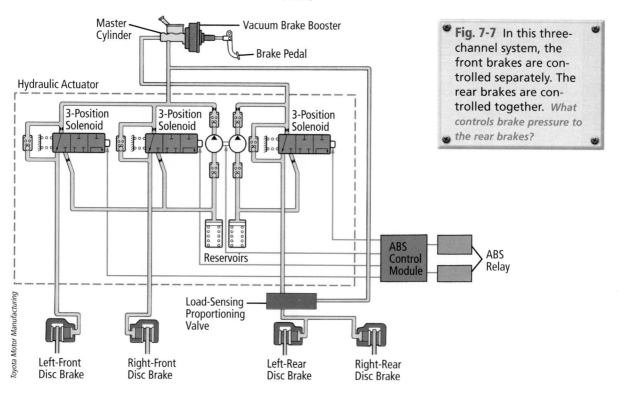

Master Cylinder — Vacuum Brake Booster — Brake Pedal

Hydraulic Actuator

3-Position Solenoid

Reservoirs

Load-Sensing Proportioning Valve

ABS Control Module — ABS Relay

Left-Front Disc Brake — Right-Front Disc Brake — Left-Rear Disc Brake — Right-Rear Disc Brake

Toyota Motor Manufacturing

Fig. 7-7 In this three-channel system, the front brakes are controlled separately. The rear brakes are controlled together. *What controls brake pressure to the rear brakes?*

During normal braking, operating the brake pedal causes a normal increase of brake pressure at each wheel. See **Fig. 7-8(a).** This changes when the system determines that a wheel lockup is about to occur. The ABS control module signals the solenoid valve in the hydraulic unit to close the spring-loaded check ball (right check ball). This prevents additional pressure from entering the brake line to the wheel. Instead of increasing with further application of the brakes, hydraulic pressure is held constant. This is the hold-pressure position. See **Fig. 7-8(b).**

If the wheel still tends to slow down too fast or lock up, the ABS goes into the reduce-pressure position. See **Fig. 7-8(c).** The ABS control module signals the solenoid valve to move the other check ball (left check ball) to open a passage that allows fluid to flow back from the wheel brake line to the reservoir in the hydraulic unit.

During ABS operation, this apply-hold-release cycling action causes the brake pedal to pulsate. This happens very rapidly and feels like a vibration. Under certain conditions with some systems, the solenoid valves can also allow the brake fluid pressure to increase.

Fig. 7-8 During normal brake operation, fluid flow is normal and ABS is not activated **(a).** If the wheel is decelerating and near lockup, pressure to the wheel is held **(b).** If wheel lockup is imminent, the fluid pressure is reduced **(c).**
What happens when the ABS control module signals the solenoid valve to close the right check ball?

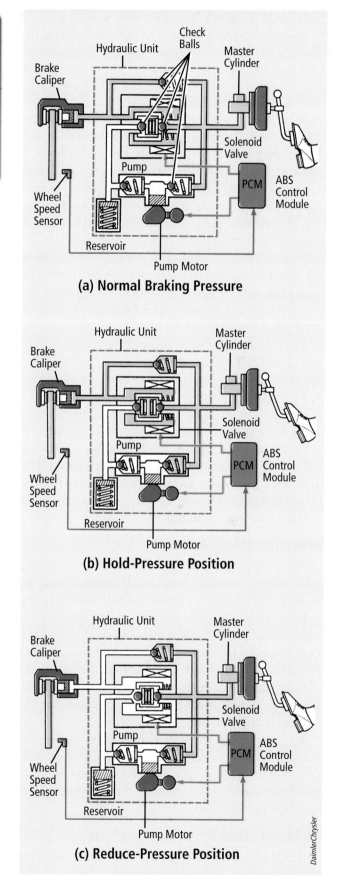

(a) Normal Braking Pressure

(b) Hold-Pressure Position

(c) Reduce-Pressure Position

DaimlerChrysler

Sensors and Warning Lights

Sensors relay information to the control module. The control module acts on this input to control braking.

Speed Sensors

In the GM RWAL system, a sensor at the output shaft of the transmission generates the speed signal. The signal is routed to the digital ratio adapter controller (DRAC). There it is converted to a digital signal for the ABS control module. DRAC output signals are also routed to the cruise control module, the powertrain control module (PCM), and the instrument panel cluster (for the speedometer).

The ABS control module continuously monitors the speed of the wheels (or driveshaft or differential ring gear with RWAL). As long as all wheels are turning at about the same speed during a hard stop, the ABS control module takes no action.

The ABS is sensitive. It can be affected by a number of factors:

- Mismatched or badly worn tires in the same set.
- The mounting of larger- or smaller-than-stock tires. This will upset the preprogrammed functions of the ABS. Such tire conditions could cause dissimilar wheel speed signals. These signals can confuse the ABS control module, causing it to set a DTC.
- If the vehicle uses a tone wheel mounted in the rear differential, changing the gear ratio can upset the ABS control module.

Deceleration Sensor

Some vehicles have an additional input to the ABS control module. The **deceleration sensor,** or G-sensor, tells the control module whether the vehicle is moving or stopped.

If a vehicle were on ice, pressing the brake pedal could cause a four-wheel lockup condition. Signals from the wheel speed sensors would mistakenly indicate that the vehicle had stopped. However, the G-sensor signals the ABS control module that the vehicle is still moving.

By comparing incoming data from the wheel sensors and the G-sensor, the ABS control module senses that all four wheels have stopped turning, but the vehicle is still moving. As a result, ABS is immediately enabled.

Lateral Acceleration Sensor

The **lateral acceleration sensor** senses hard cornering during braking. At least one manufacturer uses such a sensor in the ABS. Mercury switches or a Hall-effect lateral accelerometer detect high G-forces during moderate to hard turns. The sensor provides input to the ABS control module.

The result is that the ABS is enabled for better braking control—even under less-than-lockup conditions. This includes conditions such as braking on a curved exit ramp, where wheel lockup could cause the vehicle to slide or spin.

> **Safety First**
>
> **ABS Braking** Without adequate training, drivers may be caught off guard by ABS pedal pulsations. Drivers might momentarily release the brake pedal. This will disengage ABS and increase the stopping distance. The pulsations can occur as rapidly as eighteen times per second. This is much faster than even a professional driver can pump the brakes. Practice forcing the ABS to operate under controlled conditions, such as in a vacant parking lot. With ABS activated, practice steering the vehicle as if to avoid hitting an object. A big advantage of ABS is that steering remains possible during hard braking. Drivers must remember the limits of their vehicles. Drivers should avoid a false sense of security with ABS. Yet they should remember to do more than panic and "stand on the brakes."

ABS Warning Light

Many vehicles with antilock brake systems have a yellow or amber **antilock warning light** on their instrument panels. The warning light includes the symbols and letters (ABS). See **Fig. 7-9.** The light glows during a self-test when the vehicle is started. It also glows if the ABS control module detects trouble in the antilock brake system. The light may also turn on to indicate that the antilock system is activated. In certain systems, DTCs stored by the ABS control module may be retrieved using the ABS warning light. The warning light can "blink out" the DTC in timed flashes. The flash sequence corresponds to a DTC listed in the vehicle service manual.

Brake Warning Light

The fluid reservoir that is part of the hydraulic unit includes a low-fluid level sensor. If the brake fluid is low, the sensor turns on a red instrument panel warning light or low brake fluid display.

The red brake warning light will glow if there is low pressure in any section of the brake hydraulic system. This could be due to low brake fluid caused by normal brake pad wear. It could also be caused by a leak or rupture in the system. Both lights will glow briefly during the self-test of the ABS.

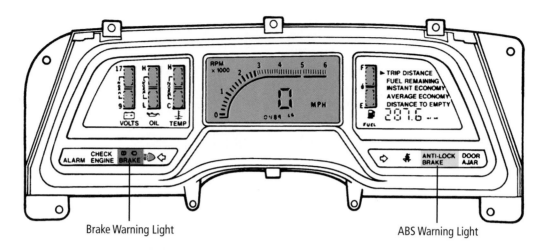

Brake Warning Light

ABS Warning Light

Ford Motor Company

Fig. 7-9 The antilock warning light may indicate a malfunction that the ABS is active, and/or DTCs. *What is different about the warning light when it is indicating DTCs versus indicating that there is a malfunction or that the ABS is active?*

Four-Wheel-Drive Switch

For handling reasons, ABS on four-wheel-drive vehicles is disabled when the vehicle is in four-wheel drive. Only those vehicles that use a viscous-clutch differential can use ABS while in four-wheel drive.

ABS is also disabled if the limited-slip front differential locks the front wheels together. The wheels are effectively locked through the drive train. In this situation the ABS cannot operate properly.

Diagnosing and Repairing Antilock Brakes

Only service personnel trained on the specific ABS should attempt to repair that system. The removal and installation of antilock brake system (ABS) electrical/electronic and hydraulic components should be done only by trained personnel following manufacturer's instructions. Hydraulic fluid pressures in ABS systems are extremely high. Improper servicing procedures can result in personal injury and material damage. When servicing an ABS, consult the vehicle service manual. The designs of these complex systems vary from one vehicle manufacturer to another.

Safety First

ABS Hydraulic System The ABS hydraulic system may be under extreme pressure, even when the vehicle is not running. Technicians must take extreme care when servicing the hydraulic system.

Diagnosing Antilock Brakes

Technicians must understand the function of each ABS component. Only then is it possible to determine whether a component is malfunctioning. Diagnosis can be made using the ABS control module and the **ABS diagnostic connector.** See **Fig. 7-10.** The diagnostic connector allows technicians to access the control module using a scan tool designed for the vehicle being serviced. The scan tool "reads" the DTCs stored in the control module. The DTCs provide the information needed to find problems in the ABS circuit. The technician should also be aware that some ABS braking concerns can be caused by a vehicle modification such as tire size or final drive ratio. The diagnosis should consider these as possible causes.

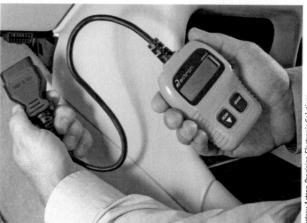

Courtesy Actron Precision Electronic Solutions

Fig. 7-10 Technicians use a scan tool to read the DTCs stored in the ABS control module. *What is the function of the diagnostic connector?*

ABS Diagnostic Connector There are many different styles of ABS diagnostic connectors in vehicles equipped with antilock brakes. The ABS diagnostic connector is the point at which the scan tool is connected. The scan tool provides the data readout on the status of the ABS system. Each connector is designed to interface with a product-specific scan tool to troubleshoot ABS. The ABS diagnostic connectors are under the dash, behind the glove box, under the hood, or under the seat.

Beginning with the 1996 model year, all ABS data are routed through the 16-pin data link connector (DLC). The DLC connector provides access to vehicle information, operating conditions, and diagnostic information.

Testing and Diagnosing ABS Speed Sensors

Refer to the vehicle service manual for specifications and general procedures. Then test and diagnose the ABS speed sensors as follows.

1. Make sure that you follow all procedures in the appropriate service manual.
2. Have your instructor test-drive the vehicle. Before test-driving the vehicle, note whether the red Brake or the amber ABS warning lamp is on. If the red Brake lamp is on, there is a hydraulic problem that must be corrected. If the amber ABS warning lamp is on, the ABS is not functional. Note that the illumination of the red Brake lamp may indicate reduced braking ability.
3. If the amber ABS warning lamp remains lighted, it indicates a problem in the ABS system.
4. Following manufacturer's instructions, use a proper diagnostic scanner to obtain diagnostic trouble codes (DTCs) to determine the nature of the failure.
5. If DTCs indicate problems in the speed sensors, properly raise the vehicle on a lift and do a visual inspection. Wheels may have to be removed.
6. Look for visual indications of damage to wiring, sensors, or toothed reluctor rings (tone wheels) at each vehicle wheel or at transmission or final drive. See **Fig. 7-11**.
7. Follow manufacturer's instructions to connect a graphing multimeter (GMM) or a digital storage oscilloscope (DSO) to wiring leads of the speed sensor located at a connector near the sensor.

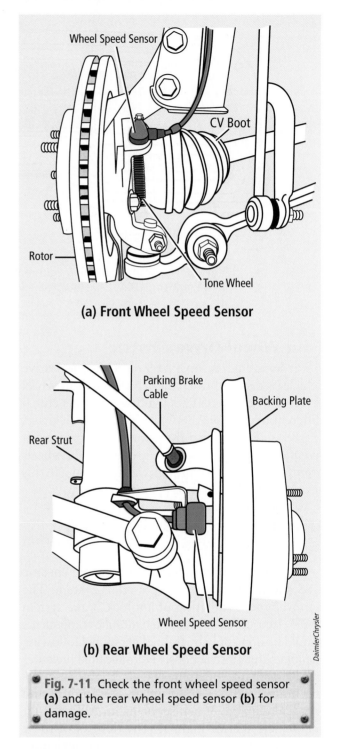

(a) Front Wheel Speed Sensor

(b) Rear Wheel Speed Sensor

Fig. 7-11 Check the front wheel speed sensor **(a)** and the rear wheel speed sensor **(b)** for damage.

8. Check for a visual indication on the meter of the voltage produced as you turn the related wheel. You may want to compare signals between different sensors.
9. If there is no voltage signal, check continuity between both conductors to the sensor. The resistance value between these two wires must be within manufacturer's specifications. If not, there may be a short or an open circuit in the sensor.

10. Check between one of the leads to the sensor and a good ground. Continuity indicates a grounded sensor.
11. Visually inspect the tone wheel for damaged or missing teeth. See **Fig. 7-11(a)**.
12. If there is an adjustment of the sensor, verify proper adjustment.
13. If no problems are found at the speed sensors, the GMM or DSO may be used to check other circuits of the ABS system. Be sure to follow manufacturer's instructions.

Safety First **ABS System Pressure** Antilock brake systems have very high system pressures. Follow the procedure to "bleed down" the system pressure before attempting any repair requiring the removal of any system part. Improper repair could result in ABS malfunction. This could lead to injury to the vehicle occupants or to property damage. Always consult the service manual before doing any work on an ABS-equipped vehicle.

Bleeding Antilock Brakes

The procedure for bleeding antilock brakes may not totally purge air from the valves. Some vehicles require a special scan tool to perform a complete brake bleed. Refer to the vehicle service manual for specific procedures before bleeding the brakes. General guidelines for bleeding nonintegral antilock brakes are as follows:

- With the engine and ignition OFF, pump the brake pedal several times. This will expel any vacuum remaining in the power brake booster.
- Remove the master cylinder reservoir cover. Fill the reservoir to the full level. Place the cover loosely over the opening.
- Pour a little brake fluid into a catch container— enough to submerge the end of the clear tubing during the bleeding process. This makes it easier to see the air bubbles being expelled from the brake system. See **Fig. 7-12**.
- The bleeding process sequence depends on whether the brake system is rear-split or diagonally split. With a front-rear split system, the sequence is right rear, left rear, right front, left front. With a diagonally split system, the sequence depends on the split. Always check the vehicle service manual for the correct order.

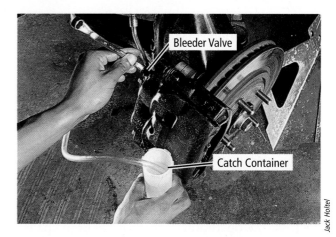

Bleeder Valve

Catch Container

Jack Holtel

Fig. 7-12 When bleeding brakes, use clear tubing between the bleeder valve and the catch container. *Why is it important to use clear tubing?*

- When bleeding brakes, check the brake fluid level in the master cylinder reservoir. If needed, refill the reservoir after completion of the bleeding of a caliper or wheel cylinder. Refill more often if needed.

Safety First **Wear Safety Glasses** When bleeding the brake system, wear safety glasses. Brake fluid at high pressure may come out of the bleeder screws when they are opened.

- Loosen the bleeder valve on the wheel to be bled. Then tighten it only enough that it can be loosened and tightened easily.
- Install one end of the clear tubing over the bleeder valve. Leave room for a wrench to fit over the flats of the valve. Place the other end of the tubing into the catch container so the end is submerged near the bottom.
- Have an assistant pump the brake pedal twice and hold the pedal down. Open the bleeder valve and allow fluid and air to escape. Close the bleeder valve just before the fluid stops flowing. Have your assistant release the pedal, pump twice, and then hold the pedal down. Open the bleeder again and release more fluid and air. Continue this operation until there are no more air bubbles in the fluid.

- Securely tighten the bleeder valve. Remove the tube and container. Move on to the next caliper or wheel cylinder.
- If needed, add brake fluid to the master cylinder reservoir.
- Repeat the five steps above for the remaining calipers or wheel cylinders in the sequence specified.
- After bleeding all four calipers or wheel cylinders, top off the fluid level in the master cylinder reservoir.
- Secure the master cylinder reservoir cover.
- Check the operation of the brakes. Brake pedal travel should be normal. The pedal should be firm when depressed, not spongy.
- Test drive the vehicle.

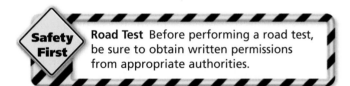

Safety First **Road Test** Before performing a road test, be sure to obtain written permissions from appropriate authorities.

 HYBRID **TECHNOLOGY**

Regenerative Braking

The ABS system in a hybrid saves energy in various ways. When a car's brakes are applied, energy is spent. To capture this energy, hybrid automobiles use a regenerative braking system.

A regenerative system is a system that is designed to capture and use energy that would otherwise be lost. In this system, the brakes are linked to a generator. This generator uses the kinetic energy, or the energy of the vehicle's motion, to recharge the battery. This recharging occurs whenever the brakes are applied. Without such a system, this energy would be lost, as it is in conventional vehicles. See **Fig. A**.

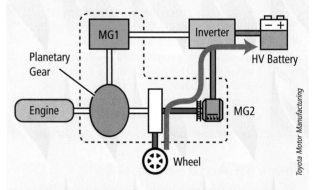

Toyota Motor Manufacturing

Fig. A When the vehicle is decelerating, kinetic energy from the wheels is recovered. It is converted into electrical energy and used to recharge the HV battery.

SECTION 2 KNOWLEDGE CHECK

1. What prompts the control module to decide which wheels should be ABS controlled?

2. Explain the hold-pressure position.

3. What factors may adversely affect the ABS system?

4. What is the purpose of the deceleration sensor or G-sensor?

5. What is the purpose of a lateral acceleration sensor?

6. What is the purpose of an ABS diagnostic connector?

ASE TEST PREP

7. Technician A says a lateral acceleration sensor tells the ABS control module that the vehicle is in a hard-cornering maneuver. Technician B says the lateral acceleration sensor tells the ABS control module the vehicle's forward velocity. Who is correct?

ⓐ Technician A.

ⓑ Technician B.

ⓒ Both Technician A and Technician B.

ⓓ Neither Technician A nor Technician B.

Section 3
Controlling Torque

Objectives:

G9 • Identify traction control/vehicle stability control system components.

• Describe the purpose and operating principles of traction control systems (TCS).

Vocabulary:
• **understeer**
• **oversteer**

Traction Control

When a wheel is given more torque than it can transfer to the road, the tire loses traction and spins. This occurs most often during heavy acceleration or on slippery surfaces. To prevent wheel spin, some vehicles with ABS also incorporate a traction control system (TCS).

ABS components can also control wheel spin. As a result, many high-end cars come equipped with ABS and TCS. See **Fig. 7-13**. When a wheel is about to spin, the TCS, using ABS components, applies the brake only at that wheel. This slows the wheel so that wheel spin does not occur.

If a driver accelerates on a slippery surface, the TCS helps avoid wheel spin. This helps prevent momentary loss of vehicle control. It also reduces tire wear. With additional electronics it can also avoid loss of traction from "drag torque" when downshifting.

An ABS and a TCS share some components, such as wheel speed sensors and hydraulic actuators. A combined ABS and TCS control module is called an antilock brake system-traction control module (ABS-TCS).

With TCS, when engine torque causes a drive wheel to break loose and spin, the ABS causes brake pressure to be applied to that wheel. This slows the wheel to prevent wheel spin.

If braking alone does not prevent wheel spin, the ABS control module calls for reduced engine speed and torque. It does this by signaling the powertrain control module (PCM). The PCM receives the request for less torque and retards ignition timing. If this does not stop wheel spin, the amount of fuel delivered to the engine is reduced.

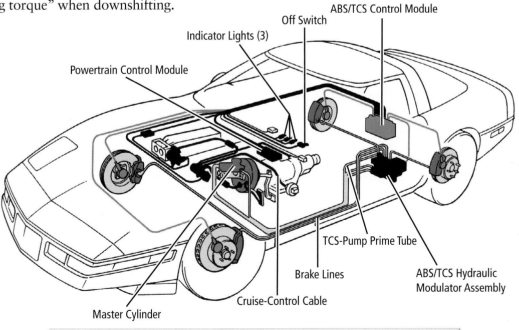

General Motors Corporation

Fig. 7-13 A vehicle with an ABS and a traction control system (TCS).
What is the purpose of a TCS?

Excellence in Science

Converting Kinetic Energy

A moving vehicle has kinetic energy. Kinetic energy is the energy of motion. The amount of kinetic energy depends on the mass and speed of the vehicle.

To stop a vehicle, this energy must be dissipated or dispersed. It must be changed into another form as quickly and efficiently as possible. This energy conversion is made by the braking system. The brakes convert kinetic energy into heat. They use the friction of the brake shoes or pads on the drums or discs.

A locked wheel and a skidding tire are certainly not the best ways to convert kinetic energy into heat. The heat created by the friction begins to melt the tire. Sliding on melting rubber, the tire has a very low coefficient of friction.

The ABS is designed to keep as much of the friction as possible inside the brakes, not on the road. The friction is as high as possible in the brakes. The kinetic energy of the vehicle goes into heating the brake drums or discs, not the tires and pavement.

Apply It!

Converting Energy to Heat

Meets NATEF Science Standards for understanding kinetic energy, friction, and heat.

Materials and Equipment
- Rubber wheel from a toy car, with its axle (a nail will do)
- Strip of coarse sandpaper
- Flat surface; such as a table with a tablecloth

To understand the conversion of kinetic energy into heat, try the following experiment. As you perform this experiment, try to keep the downward pressure on the wheel even and equal in each step.

1. Hold the wheel and its axle so that the wheel can easily turn. Roll the wheel across the flat surface. The very small force needed to do this comes from the low coefficient of rolling friction. This is why a vehicle, without braking, takes so long to coast to a stop.

2. Lock the wheel with your finger. Slide the wheel rapidly across the flat surface many times. The force needed depends on the coefficient of sliding friction. More force will be needed than in the previous step. Feel the wheel where it has been sliding. It's warm. This is the energy you supplied, converted to heat.

3. Roll the wheel across the flat surface while you hold the sandpaper very gently onto the top of the wheel. Let the sandpaper slide over the wheel. Do not let the wheel skid! This should require more force to turn the wheel on it axle. You have now moved the friction to where it is the greatest. You have spread the heat energy over the entire system.

4. Think carefully about what you have observed in this experiment. Do you see how an ABS is an energy manager for the conversion of kinetic energy into heat? Write a paragraph describing where the energy of a moving vehicle goes under the following conditions:

   - Coasting to a stop.
   - Locking up the brakes and skidding.
   - Making an emergency stop with ABS.

Vehicle Stability Control

An ABS can also improve vehicle handling and stability. An advanced stability control system can prevent tire skid and vehicle instability when cornering.

The heart of the system is a central processor that takes information from a number of sensors and then determines whether the car is in a stable or unstable state. By combining the data from ABS sensors (for wheel speed), steering angle sensors, yaw sensors (measuring the amount a car fishtails, or rotates around its vertical center axis), and lateral force sensors (measuring the amount of sideways g-force generated by the car), the central processing unit can actually detect when a vehicle is behaving in a way contrary to the driver's intentions.

If the processor does detect instability, such as a slide produced by a sudden swerve, it automatically applies light brake pressure to a select wheel (or wheels) to maintain or restore control. On some systems, engine torque is also automatically decreased to aid in the stabilizing process.

The most common types of slides are understeer and oversteer. **Understeer** is a condition in which the front of the car plows toward the outside of a turn without following the curve of the turn. See **Fig. 7-14(a)**. When the stability control system detects understeer, it applies light brake pressure to the inside rear wheel. This helps "tug" the front of the car back onto the intended line.

Oversteer is a condition in which the rear of the car fishtails toward the outside of a turn, increasing the chance of a spin. See **Fig. 7-14(b)**. To counteract such a situation, the stability system applies braking

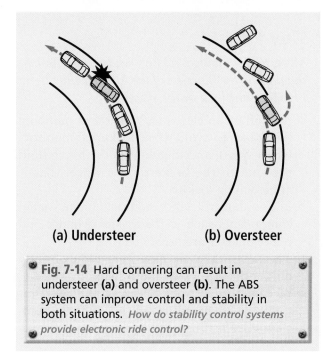

(a) Understeer   **(b) Oversteer**

Fig. 7-14 Hard cornering can result in understeer **(a)** and oversteer **(b)**. The ABS system can improve control and stability in both situations. *How do stability control systems provide electronic ride control?*

to the outside front wheel, bringing the rear end back in line.

On most vehicles, a warning light on the dashboard illuminates when the system is operating. These systems use the ABS/Stability hydraulic control unit for wheel braking.

The ABS may also use inputs from other motion and speed sensors to determine if the vehicle is under control. The stability controls are able to determine when a vehicle has reached its limit of directional change. The system can detect when a vehicle is about to skid out of control. The ABS may apply one or more of the wheel brakes to regain vehicle stability and directional control.

SECTION 3 KNOWLEDGE CHECK

1. When accelerating on a slippery surface, what equipment may help a driver avoid wheel spin?

2. What are two advantages of a traction control system?

3. How does TCS work when engine torque causes a drive wheel to spin?

4. If the wheels continue to spin after the PCM retards ignition timing, what happens?

5. What will the ABS do if it detects understeer?

6. What will the ABS do if it detects oversteer?

ASE TEST PREP

7. The ABS component that processes input signals, makes decisions, and outputs signals is the:
   ⓐ PCM.
   ⓑ ECM.
   ⓒ BCM.
   ⓓ ABS control module.

CHAPTER 7 REVIEW

Key Points

Meets the following NATEF Standards for Brakes: diagnosing the function of the ABS warning light; bleeding antilock brake systems.

- ABS offers an electronic method of pumping the brakes to avoid wheel lockup. It monitors wheel speed, and then lowers the brake fluid pressure to the brake on the wheel that is approaching lockup.
- In a nonintegral ABS, traditional brake system components such as the master cylinder and brake booster are used.
- The ABS brake warning light glows briefly during the self-test of the system.
- Bleeding an antilock brake system may not totally purge air from valves. Check the vehicle service manual. The use of a scanner may be required.
- A traction control system (TCS), which is a spinoff of ABS technology, prevents unwanted wheel spin.
- Some traction control systems can signal the PCM to reduce engine speed and torque.

Review Questions

1. Why does an empty truck have less braking control than a loaded truck?

2. What is yaw sensing?

3. Why is rapidly pumping the brake pedal less effective than ABS?

4. How does ABS affect normal braking?

5. Describe how the tone wheel influences ABS.

6. Which wheels have wheel speed sensors?

7. Name the three ABS channel configurations.

8. What is a DLC?

9. **Critical Thinking** Why would mounting larger- or smaller-than-stock tires on a vehicle affect the ABS?

10. **Critical Thinking** Explain how to bleed antilock brakes.

Excellence in Communication

Interpreting Technical Illustrations

Illustrations and diagrams of parts, components, and systems are very useful in an operator's manual. You have seen that an exploded view shows how the parts of a system fit together. The rear wheel in **Fig. 7-2** is an example of a simple exploded view illustration. You also need to know how a system is related to other automotive components, including the chassis. One excellent way to view these relationships is to use an outline or shadow to represent the vehicle or a specific section of it. **Fig. 7-1**. The whole system can be pictured within the outline or shadow. You can then see the relationship of a system to other components and the chassis. You can also see how parts of the system relate to each other.

An illustration can show clearly and simply an object that might be hard to explain in words.

Apply It!

Meets NATEF Communications Standards for using an operator's manual.

Refer to **Fig. 7-1**.

1. Follow the route of the hydraulic lines shown in yellow.

2. What color is used to show the ABS?

3. Where is the ABS control module?

4. How does an outline or shadow view differ from an exploded view?

AUTOMOTIVE SERVICE EXCELLENCE
TEST PREP

Answering the following practice questions will help you prepare for the ASE certification tests.

1. In a fully-loaded truck without ABS the front-to-rear braking effect is balanced by:
   - ⓐ the metering valve.
   - ⓑ the wheel speed sensors.
   - ⓒ the yaw sensor.
   - ⓓ the proportioning valve.

2. The one-channel ABS system known as RABS (rear antilock brake system) is used by:
   - ⓐ General Motors.
   - ⓑ DaimlerChrysler.
   - ⓒ Toyota.
   - ⓓ Ford.

3. In three-channel ABS:
   - ⓐ front wheels are not independently controlled.
   - ⓑ front wheels are controlled independently.
   - ⓒ two circuits control both rear wheels at the same time.
   - ⓓ three circuits control both rear wheels at the same time.

4. Technician A says that in a three- or four-channel ABS system, solenoids close or open one or more of the brake hydraulic circuits. Technician B says that the solenoids hold or release hydraulic pressure to one or more of the wheel brakes, depending on which wheels are about to lock up. Who is correct?
   - ⓐ Technician A.
   - ⓑ Technician B.
   - ⓒ Both Technician A and Technician B.
   - ⓓ Neither Technician A nor Technician B.

5. Technician A says that on many nonintegral systems the reservoir that stores brake fluid vented from the wheel circuits is not pressurized. Technician B says that this reservoir is pressurized. Who is correct?
   - ⓐ Technician A.
   - ⓑ Technician B.
   - ⓒ Both Technician A and Technician B.
   - ⓓ Neither Technician A nor Technician B.

6. The ABS control module self-test occurs:
   - ⓐ between 1 and 5 mph.
   - ⓑ between 5 and 25 mph.
   - ⓒ between 25 and 30 mph.
   - ⓓ between 30 and 50 mph.

7. Technician A says that in certain systems the ABS warning light can blink out a stored DTC in timed flashes. Technician B says that this flash sequence can be entered into the scan tool for reading. Who is correct?
   - ⓐ Technician A.
   - ⓑ Technician B.
   - ⓒ Both Technician A and Technician B.
   - ⓓ Neither Technician A nor Technician B.

8. Technician A says that the antilock warning light is red. Technician B says that this light may be yellow or amber. Who is correct?
   - ⓐ Technician A.
   - ⓑ Technician B.
   - ⓒ Both Technician A and Technician B.
   - ⓓ Neither Technician A nor Technician B.

9. If a vehicle with ABS were on ice, pressing the brake pedal could cause a four-wheel lockup. Signals from wheel speed sensors would mistakenly indicate that the vehicle had stopped. The ABS control module would receive a signal that the vehicle is still moving. This signal would be received from:
   - ⓐ the yaw sensor.
   - ⓑ the lateral acceleration sensor.
   - ⓒ the deceleration sensor.
   - ⓓ the steering angle sensor.

10. Technician A says that the amount a car fishtails is measured by the lateral force sensor. Technician B says it is measured by the yaw sensor. Who is correct?
    - ⓐ Technician A.
    - ⓑ Technician B.
    - ⓒ Both Technician A and Technician B.
    - ⓓ Neither Technician A nor Technician B.

Electrical & Electronic Systems

Chapter 1
Electrical System
Operation

Chapter 2
Diagnosing & Servicing
the Battery

Chapter 3
Diagnosing & Repairing
the Starting System

Chapter 4
Diagnosing & Repairing
the Charging System

Chapter 5
Diagnosing & Repairing
Lighting Systems

Chapter 6
Diagnosing & Repairing
Accessory and Safety
Systems

Section 1
The Nature of Electricity

Section 2
Electrical Automotive Components

Section 3
Reading and Testing Electrical Circuits

Section 4
Electronic Automotive Components

Electrical System Operation

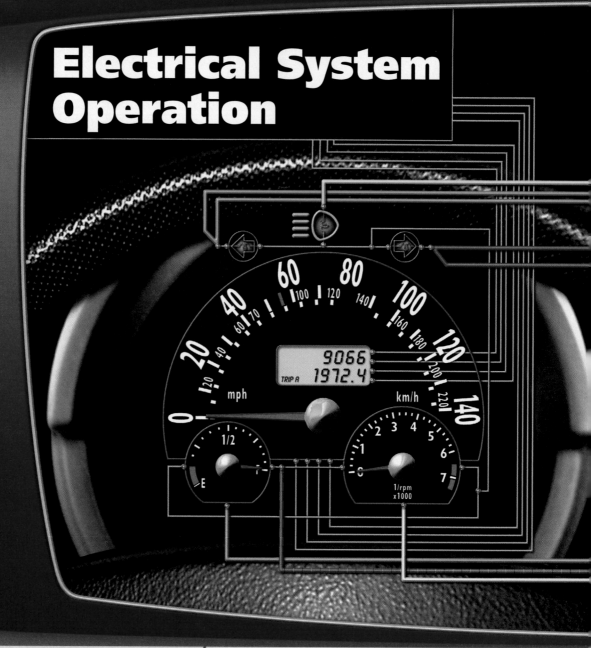

Customer's Concern

The automotive electrical system uses a generator and battery to supply electrical energy to the vehicle. Electrical and electronic circuits distribute and use the electrical energy to perform a variety of tasks. Electricity is used in powertrain control, cranking, lighting, safety, and convenience systems.

Today's technicians use logic probes, volt-ohm-meters, oscilloscopes, and other diagnostic tools to quickly identify automotive electrical system problems. These tools are helpful, but they are not substitutes for knowledge. Proper diagnosis and repair depend greatly upon a technician's understanding of how electricity is generated, stored, distributed, and used in a vehicle's electrical system.

Technician's Challenge

As the service technician, you need to find answers to these questions:

1. What part of a vehicle's electrical system is responsible for storing electricity and supplying it to other automotive systems as needed?

2. What do the symbols of a wiring diagram mean? How is a wiring diagram used to diagnose automotive electrical problems?

3. How are test lights, logic probes, volt-ohm-meters, and oscilloscopes used to diagnose automotive electrical problems?

● Section 1
The Nature of Electricity

Objectives:
- Describe how current flows through a conductor.
- Define the relationships between voltage, current, and resistance.
- **A5** Diagnose electrical/electronic integrity for series, parallel and series-parallel circuits using principles of electricity (Ohm's Law).

Vocabulary:
- conductor
- current flow
- insulator
- voltage
- direct current
- alternating current
- resistance
- series circuit
- parallel circuit
- Ohm's law

Understanding the Atom

Understanding electricity requires a basic knowledge of physics. Everything we see, touch, feel, or smell is composed of matter. All matter is made of atoms, and all atoms have an atomic structure.

The atomic structure of an atom includes three basic particles: protons, neutrons, and electrons. Protons and neutrons are found in the nucleus, at the center of the atom. Protons have a positive (+) electrical charge. Neutrons have no electrical charge. Electrons orbit the nucleus of an atom much like a planet orbits the sun. Electrons have a negative (−) electrical charge. See **Fig. 1-1.**

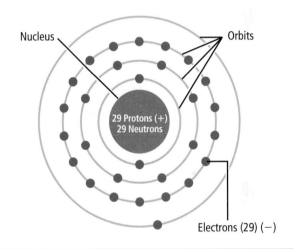

Fig. 1-2 A copper atom has 29 protons and 29 neutrons in its nucleus, and 29 electrons in orbit around the nucleus. *How many electrons are in the copper atom's outer shell?*

The atomic structure of the copper atom has 29 protons, 29 neutrons, and 29 electrons. The positive charge of the protons in the nucleus is exactly balanced by the negative charge of the electrons. Electrons circle the nucleus in different orbits, depending on their energy levels. These orbits are called shells.

The copper atom has two electrons in the shell closest to the nucleus. There are eight electrons in the second shell and 18 electrons in the third shell. That leaves one electron in the outer shell. See **Fig. 1-2.**

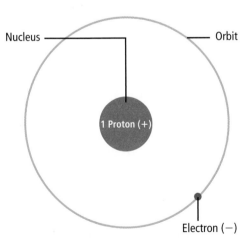

Fig. 1-1 The hydrogen atom has the simplest structure. It has a single proton in the nucleus and no neutrons. It has one electron in orbit around the nucleus. *Which particle has a positive charge? Which particle has a negative charge?*

The electron or electrons located in the outer shell are the important ones in the study of electricity. In the copper atom, the one electron in the outer shell is a "free" electron. Free electrons can move from one atom to another. Other electrons are held tightly by the nucleus and do not move.

Conductors

An electrical **conductor** is a material that contains free electrons and easily conducts electrical current. The movement of free electrons through a conductor creates current flow. **Current flow** is the movement of electrical energy through a conductor.

Several materials are used as conductors in motor vehicles.
- Copper is an excellent conductor used in automotive wiring systems.
- Iron and steel, although not as good as copper, are used in a vehicle's body and frame as electrical grounds.
- Tin and lead, used in solder connections, are also conductors but not quite as good as iron and steel.
- Gold and silver are good conductors. They are used in the microchips in a vehicle's computerized control systems.

Insulators

Some materials do not have free electrons in their atomic structure. They hold their electrons very tightly. Thus, they lack free electrons. Such a material, which is a poor electrical conductor, is called an **insulator**. See **Fig. 1-3**.

Fig. 1-3 The white material on these spark plugs is a ceramic material that is used as an insulator.
Why is an insulator a poor electrical conductor?

Three materials are commonly used as insulators in motor vehicles.
- Plastic is used as an insulator around wires and plugs.
- Rubber is used in insulating mounts for electrical equipment.
- Glass is used to insulate and enclose electrical components such as lightbulbs.

The Flow of Electricity

Traditional theory describes electricity as the flow of current from a positive source to a negative source. Electron flow theory describes electricity as the flow of electrons from a negative source to a positive source.

Both theories work well and are accepted by scientists. However, when using either theory, the complete set of rules for that theory must be used.

Voltage

Voltage is a measurement of the pressure that causes electrical energy (current) to flow. The flow of electrons through a wire is much like the flow of water through a pipe. A wire has free electrons that can flow. A pipe is filled with water that can flow. No movement takes place unless a force or pressure is applied. In the case of electrons, voltage supplies the pressure to cause electrical energy to flow. In the case of water, a force as basic as gravity can supply the pressure to cause water flow.

Voltage refers to the electromotive force (EMF) that moves electrons. Electrical pressure is measured in volts and uses the symbol E.

Current

Current flow is created when voltage moves electrons through a conductor. This flow is measured in amperes (symbol A). A flow of one ampere (or amp) means that many billions (6.25×10^{18}) of electrons are passing a defined point each second. This is a very large number. But the electrical charge of a single electron is extremely small.

There must be a complete circuit before current can flow. Even though a voltage may be present, current cannot flow unless there is a return path to the current source. There are two types of current, direct current (DC) and alternating current (AC).

Direct Current Current that flows in a single direction is called **direct current**. The direction of flow depends on the polarity of the applied voltage. Most automotive vehicles' electrical circuits use DC current.

Alternating Current Current that changes its direction of flow in a regular and predictable way is called **alternating current**. AC current moves back and forth in the circuit, reversing direction whenever the polarity of the applied voltage changes. The current in your house or apartment is AC.

Electrical power is measured in watts. Power is the rate of energy use in an electrical circuit. One watt is one amp of current flowing at one volt. In other words, power (or watts) is equal to amps times volts.

Resistance

Resistance is the opposition to current flow. The amount of resistance is measured in units called ohms. The symbol R or the Greek symbol Ω is used to represent resistance.

No material is a perfect conductor of electricity. Even copper, a very good conductor, has some resistance.

The resistance of a conductor depends on the:
• Type of material from which it is made.
• Size of the material (for example, wire gauge).
• Length of the conductor.
• Temperature of the conductor. The lower the temperature, the less the resistance.

Battery cables are made of copper, have a large size, and are short. At normal operating temperatures, battery cables have very low resistance.

Resistance can also be designed into a circuit using devices called resistors. They have limited conductivity.

Electrical Circuits

Several types of electrical circuits are found in automotive wiring. The type of circuit used depends on how and when the electrical components are supplied with power.

Series Circuits

In a **series circuit**, individual components are connected end to end to form a single path for current flow. See **Fig. 1-4(a)**. Because there is only one path, the same amount of current flows through every part of the circuit. In addition, any resistance added to or removed from the circuit affects the entire circuit.

Series circuits have two major disadvantages. First, when connected in series, each circuit has to have its own switch and protective device. This is impractical because of the number of components and wires that would be needed. A second disadvantage is that in a series circuit if one component is open, the entire circuit is disabled. For example, if all exterior lighting was connected in series and one lightbulb burned out, none of the other lights would light. For both of these reasons, most automotive circuits are connected in parallel. See **Fig. 1-4(b)**.

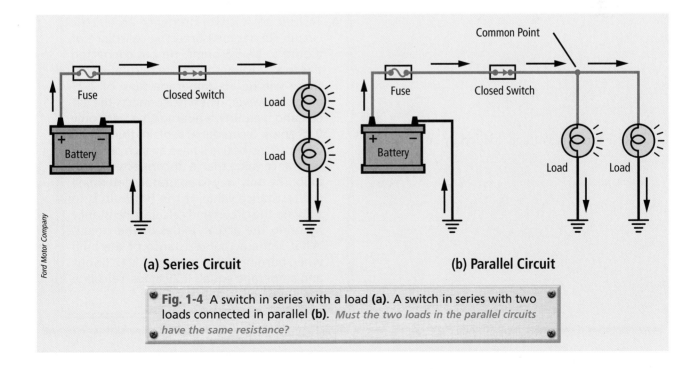

(a) **Series Circuit**   (b) **Parallel Circuit**

Fig. 1-4 A switch in series with a load **(a)**. A switch in series with two loads connected in parallel **(b)**. *Must the two loads in the parallel circuits have the same resistance?*

Ford Motor Company

Excellence in Math

Using Ohm's Law

Ohm's law states that, in a circuit, the electromotive force *(E)* is equal to the product of the current *(I)* and the resistance *(R)*. Electromotive force is often referred to as voltage.

As a formula, Ohm's law is written as $E = I \times R$. Use this formula to calculate the electromotive force, or voltage, in a circuit when the current and resistance are known.

The unit for voltage *(E)* is the volt *(V)*. The unit for current *(I)* is the ampere *(A)*. The unit for resistance *(R)* is the ohm (Ω).

If the current in a circuit is 15 A and the resistance is 0.4 Ω, what is the voltage?

Use $E = I \times R$, then $E = 15\,A \times 0.4\,\Omega = 6\,V$.

If voltage and current are known, what formula could you use to determine resistance?

You know that $E = I \times R$. If both sides of the equation are divided by the current *(I)*, the relationships between the voltage, current, and resistance will be preserved.

You will write:

$$E = I \times R$$

Then you will divide both sides by *I*:

$$\frac{E}{I} = \frac{I \times R}{I}$$

$$\frac{E}{I} = R$$

$$R = \frac{E}{I}$$

Resistance is voltage divided by current.

Apply It!

Meets NATEF Mathematics Standards for using symbols and converting formulas to equivalent forms.

1. If voltage and resistance are known, what formula could you apply to determine the current? Rewrite $E = I \times R$ in the form "$I = \underline{\quad}$."

2. A high-intensity discharge lamp needs a high initial voltage to jump the spark gap and start the lamp. A technician determines that the resistance of a particular lamp is 2,000 ohms and the current in the circuit when the lamp is first turned on is 10 amps. What is the voltage necessary to jump the spark gap?

3. If the voltage across a circuit is 12.4 volts and the resistance of that same circuit is 0.5 ohms, what is the current in that circuit? If the maximum load rating of the circuit is 22 amps, is the circuit operating normally? If not, how could the circuit be altered to bring it back to proper operating specifications?

4. Technician A is working with an electric circuit. He has measured the resistance of a bulb to be 5.5 ohms. He has connected this to a 12.6 volt source. He calculates that there will be an amperage flow of 2.29 amps. However, when he connects the circuit and measures amperage, he finds only 0.25 amps. Technician B explains that a bulb when active (hot) will have a much different resistance value than a disconnected (cold) bulb. The only way to accurately determine the resistance value of the hot bulb is to activate the circuit and calculate resistance by using the actual values of the circuit. What is the actual resistance of the bulb when burning? If voltage equals 12.6 volts and amperage equals 0.25 amps, calculate the working resistance.

Parallel Circuits

In a **parallel circuit**, two or more loads are connected in separate branches. In most cases the parallel branches are connected in series with a common switch and protective device. Equal voltage is applied to each branch of a parallel circuit. Current flow divides as it reaches the parallel path. The amount of current flowing through each branch depends on the resistance of that path only. Resistance in one branch of a parallel circuit does not affect current flowing through the other branches. Total current flow in a parallel circuit is equal to the sum of the current in each separate branch.

The backup light circuit is an example of a parallel circuit. Assuming that the bulbs are the same, an equal amount of current will flow through each bulb. The circuits for headlights, taillights, and turn signals are other examples of parallel circuits.

It is common to have both series and parallel connections in the same circuit. A backup light switch is wired in series with its fuse and in parallel with the two backup lights.

Ohm's Law

Ohm's law states that the three electrical values—voltage, current, and resistance—are mathematically related. This relationship is defined in Ohm's law. Ohm's law makes it possible to calculate any one of the three values if the other two values are known.

In Ohm's law, E = Voltage, I = Current, and R = Resistance.

- Voltage is equal to the current times the resistance ($E = I \times R$).
- Current is equal to the voltage divided by the resistance ($I = \frac{E}{R}$).
- Resistance is equal to the voltage divided by the current ($R = \frac{E}{I}$).

An Ohm's law pie chart can be used to find the unknown values. Covering the unknown value determines whether the other two values are multiplied or divided to find the unknown. See **Fig. 1-5**.

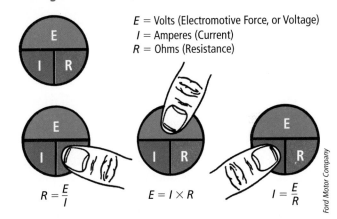

E = Volts (Electromotive Force, or Voltage)
I = Amperes (Current)
R = Ohms (Resistance)

$R = \frac{E}{I}$ $E = I \times R$ $I = \frac{E}{R}$

Ford Motor Company

Fig. 1-5 Ohm's law states the relationships between voltage, current, and resistance. *What is the voltage if the current is 2 amperes and the resistance is 100 ohms?*

SECTION 1 KNOWLEDGE CHECK

1. What is an electrical conductor?

2. Name three materials that are commonly used as insulators in motor vehicles.

3. What is the difference between the traditional and electron flow theories of electricity?

4. What term describes the measurement of pressure that causes current to flow?

5. What is created when voltage moves electrons through a conductor?

6. What affects the resistance of a conductor?

ASE TEST PREP

7. Technician A says that glass is commonly used to insulate and protect electric components. Technician B says that copper is commonly used to insulate and protect such components. Who is correct?

   ⓐ Technician A.

   ⓑ Technician B.

   ⓒ Both Technician A and Technician B.

   ⓓ Neither Technician A nor Technician B.

● Section 2
Electrical Automotive Components

Objectives:

A19 ● Repair wiring harness (including CAN/BUS systems).

A15 ● Inspect and test fusible links, circuit breakers, and fuses; determine necessary action.

A16 ● Inspect and test switches, connectors, relays, solid state devices, and wires of electrical/electronic circuits; perform necessary action.

A18 ● Repair connectors and terminal ends.

A17 ● Remove and replace terminal end from connector.

Vocabulary:
- generator
- photocell
- battery
- circuit boards
- fuse
- fusible link
- circuit breaker

Storing and Generating Electricity

The automotive electrical system produces and controls the flow of electricity. Electrical energy operates many systems, including the:

- Starting system.
- Computerized engine control system.
- Lighting system.
- Power accessories.
- Climate control system.
- Audio system.

The components that are used to control the flow of electricity include:

- A battery—stores electrical energy.
- A generator—generates electric current while the engine is running.
- Conductors—connect components in electrical circuits.
- Terminals (plug/unplug type)—allow wires and conductors to be connected or disconnected from a circuit.
- Connectors—keep terminals connected.
- Fuses and circuit breakers—protect electronic circuits from excessive current flow.
- Switches—used to open and close circuit paths.
- Loads—lights, motors, and other devices that use current flow to do useful work.
- Ground—path that returns electrical flow to the energy source.

Generator

The vehicle's **generator** is the device that converts mechanical energy into electrical energy.

Mechanical Generators A mechanical generator converts mechanical energy to electrical energy. The generator is driven by the engine. In operation, magnetic fields created in the rotor intercept the wires of the stator coil. This motion between the rotor magnetic field and the stator coil wires generates voltage. See Chapter 4, "Diagnosing & Repairing the Charging System," for more information.

Chemical Generators A chemical generator uses a chemical reaction to create current flow. Current flow is produced when a load device, such as a lightbulb, is placed in a circuit with a battery. With no device connected, the battery does not generate current flow. This is how batteries work. See Chapter 2, "Diagnosing & Servicing the Battery," for more information on batteries.

Photoelectric Converters A photoelectric converter, or **photocell**, uses light energy to create current flow. Photocells convert light into electricity. *Photo* means "light." Photocells are made of a special type of semiconductor. When light hits the semiconductor, it knocks electrons loose from the semiconductor. These free electrons comprise the current flow generated by a photocell.

Piezoelectric Converters Piezoelectric converters use physical pressure to create current flow. This method is used in piezoelectric sensors.

Battery

A **battery** is an electrochemical device that stores electric current. The battery supplies current to the starter and ignition system when a vehicle is started.

It can supply current to the electrical system when generator output is low. It maintains electronic memory circuits when the ignition is turned off.

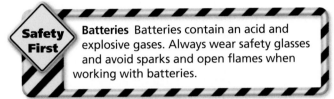

Safety First

Batteries Batteries contain an acid and explosive gases. Always wear safety glasses and avoid sparks and open flames when working with batteries.

Conducting Electricity

Electrical current is conducted through automotive systems by wires. It is also conducted by printed circuits.

Conductors

A material that conducts electrical current is called a conductor. Paths for current flow can be created in several ways.

Automotive Wire Most conductors are made of stranded copper wire covered with plastic insulation.

The size of the wire used is determined by the amount of current the wire will carry. The thickness of the insulation depends on the amount of voltage in the circuit.

Use of wire of the proper size is critical because current flow is sensitive to changes in resistance. For circuit repairs, both the wire gauge number and the wire length must be considered. The most common system for sizing wire is the American Wire Gauge (AWG) system. See **Table 1-A.**

Table 1-A	Wire Sizes
AWG Size (Gauge)	**Metric Size (mm²)**
20	0.5
18	0.8
16	1.0
14	2.0
12	3.0
10	5.0
8	8.0
6	13.0
4	19.0

Wire colors are indicated by alphabetical codes. The first code indicates the basic wire color. The second code indicates the color of the stripe.

The color codes are as follows:

BL = Blue	OR = Orange
BK = Black	PK = Pink
BR = Brown	RD = Red
DB = Dark Blue	TN = Tan
DG = Dark Green	VT = Violet
GY = Gray	WT = White
LB = Light Blue	YL = Yellow
LG = Light Green	

General-purpose vehicle wiring conducts about 15 volts and has thin insulation. Spark plug wires have thick insulation to keep the high voltage from arcing to ground.

Groups of wires bundled together form a wiring harness. A harness provides a convenient way to route and protect wires in a confined area. See **Fig. 1-6.**

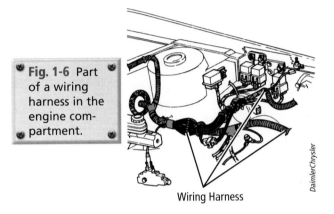

Fig. 1-6 Part of a wiring harness in the engine compartment.

DaimlerChrysler

Wiring Harness

Repairing a Wiring Harness To repair a wiring harness:

1. Using a wire stripper, strip approximately ¼″ of insulation from each wire.
2. Slip a piece of shrink wrap tubing over one end of the wire and slide it away from the area you will be soldering.
3. Using rosin core solder and a hot soldering iron, apply heat to the wire. Slowly allow the solder to flow into the strands of copper wire.
4. Complete the same procedure on the other wire.
5. Place both ends next to each other and apply heat with the soldering tip to the ends of wires. Allow the solder to flow together.
6. Test the joint for strength by tugging apart lightly at the joint.
7. Slide the shrink tubing over the joint. Apply heat from a hot air heat gun on the tubing to shrink it in place, forming a watertight, protective seal.
8. As each wire in the harness is repaired, try to stagger the area of repair. Multiple repairs in one spot can make it difficult to reinstall the convolute tubing over the harness when finished.

Printed Circuits Electronic circuits and dashboard wiring often use circuits printed on plastic boards. These printed circuits are called **circuit boards.** Printed circuits require less space and are more reliable than single wire connections.

Terminals

Terminals are mechanical stampings made of tin-coated brass or steel. One end of the terminal is crimped or soldered onto the end of a wire. The other end is designed to mate with a matching terminal to form a connection. The terminal is designed to make a good electrical connection that can be easily separated and reconnected. **Figure 1-7** shows examples of terminals and connectors.

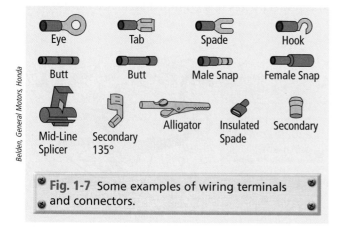

Belden, General Motors, Honda

Fig. 1-7 Some examples of wiring terminals and connectors.

Part of the terminal design is a clip that holds the connection tightly together. Bending or crimping terminals with pliers may destroy the clip and make an unreliable, intermittent connection. Loose or damaged terminals are a frequent cause of electrical failures. Always use an approved crimping tool such as the one shown in **Fig. 1-8.**

Fig. 1-8 Use a crimping tool to secure terminals and connectors to wires.

Connectors

Connectors are usually plastic-bodied connector blocks. They are used to connect and disconnect multiple wires. Connector blocks hold several male and/or female terminals. In this way entire wiring harnesses can be plugged together.

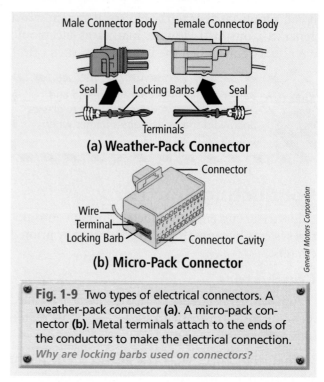

General Motors Corporation

(a) Weather-Pack Connector

(b) Micro-Pack Connector

Fig. 1-9 Two types of electrical connectors. A weather-pack connector **(a)**. A micro-pack connector **(b)**. Metal terminals attach to the ends of the conductors to make the electrical connection. *Why are locking barbs used on connectors?*

Connectors usually have rubber seals and outer coatings to protect the terminals. Connectors also have plastic locking barbs to secure the connector block halves together. This prevents mechanical strain on the terminals. See **Fig. 1-9.**

Connector Service and Repair The following is the general procedure for connector service and repair.

1. Locate the secondary terminal lock. It is generally in the rear, the side, or the front of the connector. The lock is often red, blue, or gray.
2. Remove the secondary lock. This can usually be done with a small screwdriver or a special tool.
3. Remove the terminal by disengaging the primary lock. Determine the terminal part number or family.
4. Obtain the appropriate removal tool by referring to the appropriate cross-reference book.
5. Locate the area in the front of the connector where the removal tool is to be inserted. Insert the tool next to the terminal where the primary lock is located. Never insert the tool in the mating end of the terminal. Inserting the tool in the terminal itself will damage the terminal and create a loose connection between mating terminals.
6. Position the terminal by using the attached wire. For push-to-seat terminals, slide the terminal forward. For pull-to-seat terminals, slide the terminal rearward. This movement allows the lock tang to disengage from the lock shoulder.

7. Flex the primary lock tang, whether it is part of the connector or part of the terminal, by lightly prying it with the removal tool selected.

8. Gently remove the terminal from the connector by pulling or pushing on the wire connected to the terminal.

TECH TIP **Terminal Removal Tools.** When using terminal removal tools, use only light pressure to flex the primary locks. If great force is needed to release the locks, you may be using the wrong tool.

Controlling Electricity

The flow of electrical current is controlled by a number of devices. These include circuit breakers, switches, and load devices.

Fuses, Fusible Links, and Circuit Breakers

Fuses, fusible links, and circuit breakers are safety devices used to protect vehicle electrical systems. Electrical shorts and defective electrical components can quickly create high current flow. If the current is too high, circuits, components, or wiring will be damaged. These safety devices work by opening the circuit to stop current flow.

Fuses Fuses contain a metallic element in a glass or plastic package. See **Fig. 1-10.** A **fuse** is a safety device that contains an element that is calibrated to melt when the current level in the circuit exceeds the fuse rating. Typical automotive fuse ratings include 3, 5, 10, and 20 amps. Three kinds of blade-type fuses are commonly used. These are the standard blade type, the high-current blade type, and the miniature blade type. Blade-type fuses have a specific amperage rating. They are color-coded and permanently marked to show the manufacturer's name, the amperage rating, and the voltage rating. Two slots in the fuse body allow checks for voltage drop, available voltage, or continuity.

When the fuse element melts (blows), the circuit opens. This quickly stops current flow and prevents damage. A fuse is a one-time use device that must be replaced after the fault is corrected.

Maxi fuses are larger in size. Maxi fuses have a longer time delay before protecting the circuit against over-amperage. These fuses are designed to handle the sudden surge of amperage in certain circuits, such as a motor circuit.

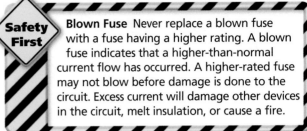

Safety First **Blown Fuse** Never replace a blown fuse with a fuse having a higher rating. A blown fuse indicates that a higher-than-normal current flow has occurred. A higher-rated fuse may not blow before damage is done to the circuit. Excess current will damage other devices in the circuit, melt insulation, or cause a fire.

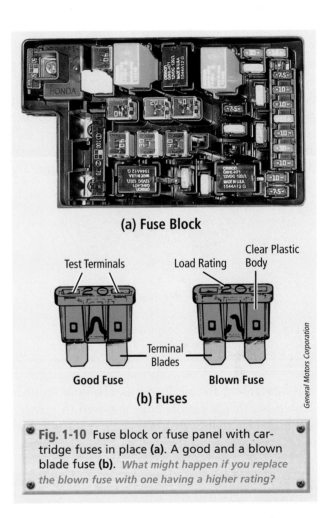

(a) Fuse Block

Test Terminals — Load Rating — Clear Plastic Body

Terminal Blades

Good Fuse **Blown Fuse**

(b) Fuses

General Motors Corporation

Fig. 1-10 Fuse block or fuse panel with cartridge fuses in place **(a)**. A good and a blown blade fuse **(b)**. *What might happen if you replace the blown fuse with one having a higher rating?*

Fusible Link A **fusible link** is a short length of insulated wire connected in the circuit. Typically it is four gauge sizes smaller than the wires it is protecting. Like a fuse, it is designed to melt when current flow exceeds the rating for the circuit. Unlike a fuse, it may not show visible signs of having blown. Check its continuity with a digital multimeter.

Some fusible links are easily replaced, similar to a cartridge or blade fuse. Others are permanently installed as a part of the wiring harness.

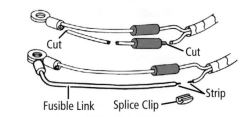

General Motors Corporation

Cut
Cut
Strip
Fusible Link   Splice Clip

Fig. 1-11 This fusible link is part of the wiring harness. The splice should be covered with shrink wrap. *Why is the fusible link connection soldered?*

To replace a fusible link, cut it out as shown at the top of **Fig. 1-11**. Strip the insulation. Splice the wires with a splice clip and solder in the new fusible link. See **Fig. 1-12**. Soldering the connection provides a strong permanent connection. Tape should not be used in a repair. Shrink wrap should be used to properly seal an electrical wiring repair to ensure it will not corrode due to exposure to water or other contaminates.

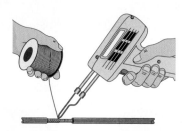

Fig. 1-12 Soldering a new fusible link. *Why should shrink wrap be used?*

Replacement fusible links may be color-coded. Brown and black fusible links are used to protect 10- and 12-gauge wires, respectively. Green and orange are used to protect 14- and 16-gauge wires,

respectively. The size and location of fusible links are in the vehicle's electrical and wiring diagrams.

Circuit Breakers A **circuit breaker** opens the circuit when it detects high current flow. See **Fig. 1-13**. A circuit breaker is a reusable device. A manual circuit breaker must be reset by hand. An automatic circuit breaker resets itself when the bimetal strip cools.

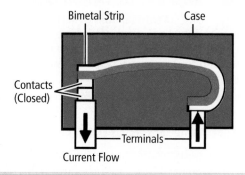

Bimetal Strip   Case
Contacts (Closed)
Terminals
Current Flow

DaimlerChrysler

Fig. 1-13 Circuit breaker construction. *Why are circuit breakers not considered one-time devices?*

Switches

Manually activated switches are activated by the driver. Position switches are turned on or off by the movement of some part of the vehicle. The switch that controls the interior lights when a door is opened or closed is a position switch.

Load Devices

A load device is a component that uses electrical energy for useful work. For example, a motor converts electrical energy into rotary motion. Solenoids use electrical energy to create back and forth motion, such as that needed for a door lock actuator.

SECTION 2 KNOWLEDGE CHECK

1. Name three automotive systems that operate on electrical energy.

2. What device supplies current to maintain electronic memory circuits when the ignition is turned off?

3. What is the difference between a photoelectric converter and a piezoelectric converter?

4. What instrument is used to check the continuity in a fusible link?

ASE TEST PREP

5. Technician A says that in removing a terminal end from a connector, the removal tool should never be inserted in the mating end of the terminal. Technician B says the tool should be inserted in the mating end of the terminal. Who is correct?

ⓐ Technician A.

ⓑ Technician B.

ⓒ Both Technician A and Technician B.

ⓓ Neither Technician A nor Technician B.

● Section 3
Reading and Testing Electrical Circuits

Objectives:

A6 ● Use wiring diagrams during diagnosis of electrical circuit problems.

A8 ● Check electrical circuits with a test light; determine necessary action.

A7 ● Demonstrate the proper use of a digital multimeter (DMM) during diagnosis of electrical circuit problems.

A9 ● Measure source voltage and perform voltage drop tests in electrical/electronic circuits using a voltmeter; determine necessary action.

A11 ● Check continuity and measure resistance in electrical/ electronic circuits and components using an ohmmeter; determine necessary action.

H9 ● Diagnose body electronic system circuits using a scan tool; determine necessary action.

H10 ● Check for module communication (LAN/CAN/BUS) errors using a scan tool.

A12 ● Check electrical circuits using fused jumper wires; determine necessary action.

A13 ● Locate shorts, grounds, opens, and resistance problems in electrical/electronic circuits; determine necessary action.

A2 ● Identify and interpret electrical/electronic system concern; determine necessary action.

A20 ● Perform solder repair of electrical wiring.

Vocabulary:
- **wiring diagram**
- **multimeter**
- **polarity**
- **electronic circuit tester**
- **scan tool**
- **oscilloscope**
- **jumper wire**
- **open circuit**
- **short circuit**

Wiring Diagrams

Electrical devices are shown in wiring diagrams as symbols. A **wiring diagram** is a drawing that shows the wires, connectors, and load devices in an electrical circuit. See **Fig. 1-14**. A wiring diagram, sometimes called a schematic, shows where the components are connected in the circuit. Wiring diagrams do not show what components actually look like or where they are located on the vehicle.

 TECH TIP **Finding Current Flow Direction.** In many wiring diagrams, the current is assumed to flow from the power source at the top of the diagram to the ground at the bottom.

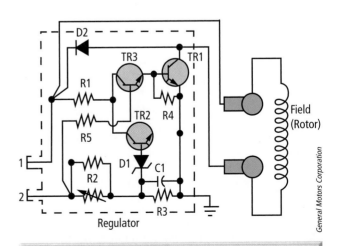

Fig. 1-14 A wiring diagram of an electronic voltage regulator.

General Motors Corporation

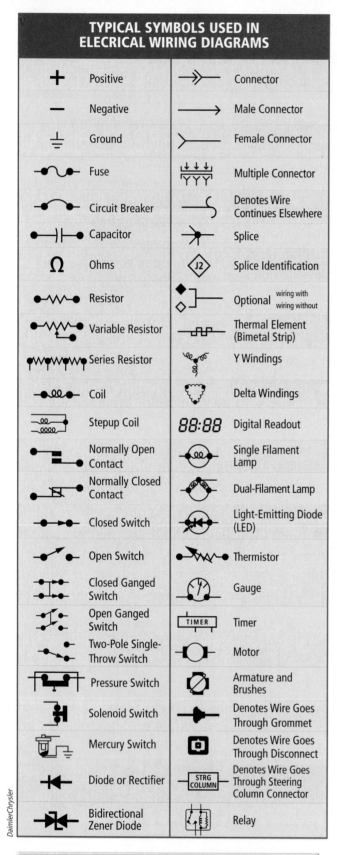

TYPICAL SYMBOLS USED IN ELECRICAL WIRING DIAGRAMS

Symbol	Name	Symbol	Name
+	Positive		Connector
–	Negative		Male Connector
	Ground		Female Connector
	Fuse		Multiple Connector
	Circuit Breaker		Denotes Wire Continues Elsewhere
	Capacitor		Splice
Ω	Ohms	J2	Splice Identification
	Resistor		Optional (wiring with / wiring without)
	Variable Resistor		Thermal Element (Bimetal Strip)
	Series Resistor		Y Windings
	Coil		Delta Windings
	Stepup Coil	88:88	Digital Readout
	Normally Open Contact		Single Filament Lamp
	Normally Closed Contact		Dual-Filament Lamp
	Closed Switch		Light-Emitting Diode (LED)
	Open Switch		Thermistor
	Closed Ganged Switch		Gauge
	Open Ganged Switch	TIMER	Timer
	Two-Pole Single-Throw Switch		Motor
	Pressure Switch		Armature and Brushes
	Solenoid Switch		Denotes Wire Goes Through Grommet
	Mercury Switch		Denotes Wire Goes Through Disconnect
	Diode or Rectifier	STRG COLUMN	Denotes Wire Goes Through Steering Column Connector
	Bidirectional Zener Diode		Relay

DaimlerChrysler

Fig. 1-15 Some of the more common symbols used in electrical wiring diagrams. *Why are symbols used?*

Electrical Symbols

Electrical symbols are much like the icons used on personal computer displays. The symbols represent components. Symbols used by different manufacturers are similar but not necessarily identical. Charts are usually included in the vehicle service manual to explain each symbol. See **Fig. 1-15**. Symbols for complicated or unique subassemblies may be shown as a block diagram. See **Fig. 1-16**.

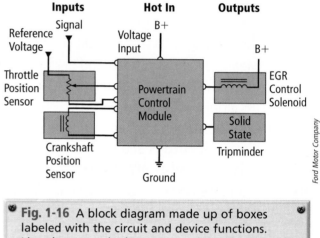

Ford Motor Company

Fig. 1-16 A block diagram made up of boxes labeled with the circuit and device functions. Lines between the boxes represent the wiring that connects the devices. *When are block diagrams used?*

Electrical Test Equipment

A variety of electrical test and measurement equipment is available to technicians. This equipment can be used to isolate the cause of electrical problems. General-purpose testers measure voltage, current, and resistance. Special-purpose testers may read engine trouble codes or display spark signal waveforms or other unique information.

Volt-Ohm-Meters

Volt-ohm-meters (VOMs) are the most common general-purpose testers used by a technician. They are also called multimeters because they perform multiple functions. A **multimeter** measures voltage, current, and resistance. Many models have additional features, such as diode testing and frequency measurement.

A typical multimeter has two test leads with metal probes or test clips on the end. The leads must be connected to the proper terminals (jacks) on the front of the meter. The positive test lead is usually red. The negative lead is usually black. The leads are used to connect the meter to a circuit or to a component to make specific measurements. The leads should be connected with the correct polarity. **Polarity** is the quality of an electronic component or circuit that determines the direction of current flow.

Digital volt-ohm-meters (DVOMs) display readings numerically. The DVOM is capable of reading DC and AC voltage, pulse-width-modulated signals, amperage, and resistance. The voltmeter on a DVOM has very high impedance (resistance), usually at least 10 million ohms (10 megohms). With high impedance, the current flow through the voltmeter will be very low and the effect of the meter on the circuit will be minimal. High impedance meters protect circuit components and ensure accurate readings while measurements are being made. Use only digital meters when testing electronic components and circuits. See **Fig. 1-17.** A DVOM should be used to check for voltage or continuity. In rare instances a test light may be used.

Fluke Corporation

Fig. 1-17 A typical digital multimeter. *What unit is used to signify resistance?*

Test Lights

Circuit-powered test lights are powered by the circuit being tested. They have two test leads; one lead connects to ground, and the other has a probe tip. A 12-volt bulb is connected between the ground lead and the probe tip. See **Fig. 1-18.**

If the test probe contacts a 12-volt source, the bulb lights. Circuit-powered test lights can indicate whether voltage is available at a connection or test point.

Safety First **Test Lights** Do not use test lights on electronic equipment. Power from the test light could damage sensitive electrical components. Always disconnect the vehicle battery or isolate any device or lead before checking it.

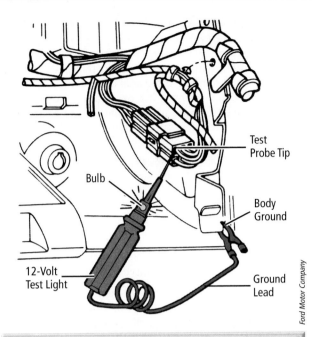

Ford Motor Company

Fig. 1-18 A circuit-powered test light. Voltage from the circuit being tested powers a 12-volt test light. *If the light does not operate when testing a circuit, what conclusion can you draw?*

Logic Probes

Logic probes are sometimes called electronic circuit testers. An **electronic circuit tester** is a device that is used to safely test electronic circuits. They use light-emitting diodes (LEDs), either singly or in combination, to display test results. Logic probes do not display values. The LEDs only indicate the presence of voltage, resistance, or polarity at the test point. See **Fig. 1-19.**

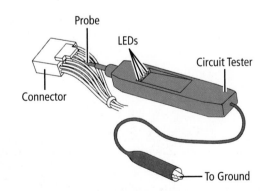

General Motors Corporation

Fig. 1-19 Logic probes have small light-emitting diodes (LEDs) that glow individually or in combination to indicate voltage, resistance, or polarity. *Could a logic probe be used to measure the presence of a voltage at a test point on a printed circuit?*

Scan Tools

A **scan tool,** also called a scanner, is an electronic instrument that is used to read a vehicle's data stream and diagnostic trouble codes. Many computerized systems in the automobile have self-diagnostic capabilities. The system computer can test circuits to determine those that are not working correctly. The computer (PCM) stores a diagnostic trouble code (DTC) for all circuits that fail the test. A diagnostic trouble code is a code that identifies a system or component malfunction. Scan tools can give a direct digital readout of these stored trouble codes. See **Fig. 1-20.**

Most scanners allow you to read data while the vehicle is operating. The scanner is connected to a data link connector (DLC). Scan tools are now capable of detecting network CAN/BUS problems. A fault code will be generated when a problem exists. Diagnosis is accomplished by using the scan tool to detect trouble codes. The proper diagnosis flow chart is then consulted to isolate the concern.

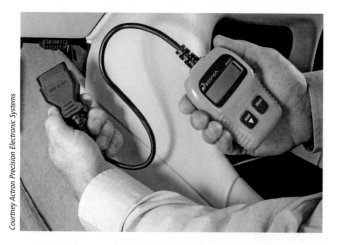

Courtesy Actron Precision Electronic Systems

Fig. 1-20 A scan tool retrieves trouble codes through a diagnostic connector. *What device stores trouble codes that are read out using scan tools?*

Oscilloscopes

An **oscilloscope** is an instrument that displays voltage changes within a certain time period. Many voltages found in the automobile are not simply AC or DC. The voltages associated with fuel injectors and ignition coils have unique waveforms. If a component is not operating correctly, the waveform will change. Analyzing a waveform can aid in diagnosing electrical problems. See **Fig. 1-21.** A lab scope is a hand-held digital graphing multimeter (DGMM). It can be used to diagnose a possible problem in an electronic system by monitoring signals at the input and output of each system block. Check that each block is operating as expected and is correctly linked to the next block.

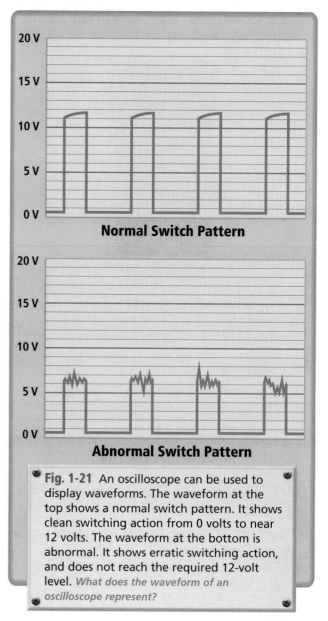

Normal Switch Pattern

Abnormal Switch Pattern

Fig. 1-21 An oscilloscope can be used to display waveforms. The waveform at the top shows a normal switch pattern. It shows clean switching action from 0 volts to near 12 volts. The waveform at the bottom is abnormal. It shows erratic switching action, and does not reach the required 12-volt level. *What does the waveform of an oscilloscope represent?*

Jumper Wire

A **jumper wire** is a short piece of wire used as a temporary connection between two points in a circuit. It may have alligator clips or other terminals on each end. Some jumper wires include a fuse or circuit breaker. A fused jumper wire of no more than 10 amps should be used. Jumper wires should be used only to bypass non-resistive components such as switches and wires. Do not use a jumper wire to bypass circuit protection devices or load components such as lightbulbs or motors. See **Fig. 1-22**.

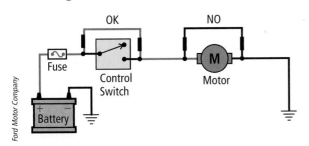

Fig. 1-22 Correct and incorrect use of a jumper wire. *What will happen if a jumper wire is connected across a load device?*

Safety First | **Jumper Wires** Never use jumper wires to bypass load components such as motors, solenoids, or lightbulbs. Using jumper wires will cause excess current to flow through the circuit. Excess current will damage other components in the circuit and may be high enough to melt insulation or cause a fire. If in doubt, use only a fused jumper wire. This type of jumper wire has a fuse to protect against excessive current.

Electrical Circuit Problems

Troubleshooting an electrical circuit begins with knowing how the circuit should work. A wiring diagram is a guide to a current flow path. In addition to the wiring diagram, troubleshooting charts and basic system checks are available in the vehicle service manual.

Circuit and wiring problems are most likely to occur at connection locations. Check ground and wiring harness connections, and make sure the terminals are tightly connected to the wire and are not damaged or corroded.

There are several basic steps to good electrical troubleshooting.
1. Verify the customer complaint. (Identify the problem you need to solve.)
2. Based on the verified symptoms, make a preliminary diagnosis about what part of the system or what component is not working correctly.
3. Use the vehicle service manual and your technical knowledge to determine how the system is supposed to function.
4. Carefully inspect the affected system for damage or obvious causes of the problem.
5. Make sure that all of the conditions are met for the system to operate.
6. Perform tests to see whether the problem is in the component or the circuit.

Open Circuit

An **open circuit** is an incomplete circuit that occurs when the electrical path is broken. Common causes of an open circuit are a burned-out fuse or lightbulb, a broken wire, or a defective switch. An open circuit stops current flow and prevents operation of devices in the circuit, as shown in **Fig. 1-23**. A jumper wire can be used to locate an open circuit. As an example, if a circuit does not work when the switch is turned on, connect a jumper wire from the battery side of the switch to the load side. If the circuit now works, the switch is defective. Open circuits can also be found by visually inspecting wiring and connectors and by testing a circuit for voltage with a voltmeter or test light. An ohmmeter or self-powered test light can be used to test parts of a circuit and individual components for continuity.

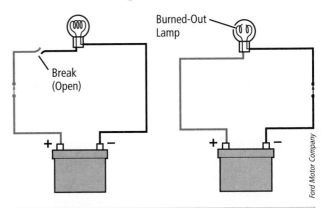

Fig. 1-23 An open circuit is a break in the current flow path. Causes include a broken wire or a burned-out lamp. *Name two devices used to test for open circuits.*

Measuring Circuit Resistance

You can use Ohm's law to calculate the current and voltage in an automotive circuit. This will help you diagnose problems. However, unless you are careful, the values you calculate may not be correct.

Some circuits need to be analyzed before applying Ohm's law. Here's a simple example. The lamp filament of a 3496 replacement lamp for brakelights and taillights will measure about 0.6 ohms. Ohm's law predicts a current of about 20 amps:

$$\frac{12 \text{ volts}}{0.6 \text{ ohms}} = 20 \text{ amps}$$

But when the light is on, the filament glows brightly and becomes very hot. When this happens the resistance increases. The bright filament will actually be about 5 ohms. It will draw about 2.4 amps.

Power is the rate at which electrical energy is delivered to the circuit. The watt is the basic unit of power. The metal base of the lamp will show a 27-watt rating for the lamp. You can use the power formula to estimate the current drawn when the lamp is on.

$$P = E \times I \text{ or } I = \frac{P}{E}, \text{ where } P \text{ is the wattage}$$

So, $\frac{27 \text{ watts}}{12 \text{ volts}} = 2.25 \text{ amps}$

Use Ohm's law to estimate the actual resistance of the lamp in operation. You will find that the resistance is about 5 ohms.

Here is what happens. Before you apply Ohm's law to a working circuit, think about whether the current flow will cause anything to change. In our example, it did. Current flow through the filament increased its resistance. The "cold" resistance measured with the DVOM is the incorrect value to use in Ohm's law.

Assume that you measure the resistance of a motor with a DVOM. If you then use that measured resistance to estimate the current drawn in operation, you will be misled.

Some parts of a motor have a different resistance when the motor is spinning. That makes the actual resistance less than expected. During operation, the rotating armature of a motor generates a small countervoltage. Countervoltages have the opposite polarity to applied (battery) voltage. In an operating motor, battery voltage must overcome not only the resistance of the circuit, but the countervoltage as well. For this reason, using only a resistance measurement to calculate current flow in a motor circuit will lead to incorrect answers.

Apply It!

Applying Ohm's Law

Meets NATEF Science Standards for Ohm's law and the relationship of heat and resistance in electrical systems.

A 55-watt headlight measures about 0.5 ohms when cold.

1. Use the power formula to estimate the current this light will draw when turned on.

2. Use Ohm's law to estimate the light's "hot" resistance.

Results and Analysis

This problem gives another example of the importance of understanding the construction and operation of the components and circuits you work on.

Remember that Ohm's law applies *only* to loads that do not change their resistance under any condition. Wires, connectors, switches, and relay contacts should behave as predicted by Ohm's law. Always ask yourself, "Does the circuit I am testing contain a lamp or a motor that may alter the reading?"

Short Circuit

A **short circuit** occurs when two (or more) conductors touch each other where no connection is intended. In most cases, the insulation has been damaged. As a result, the bare wires come in contact with each other. A "short to power," or "wire-to-wire," short occurs when a conductor that is not powered comes in contact with one that is. This problem causes circuits to work when they are not turned on. For example, a short to power between horn wiring and turn signal wiring could cause the horn to sound when the turn signals are used. A short circuit in a coil of wire, such as a relay or solenoid, will bypass part of the normal resistance of the circuit, causing excessive current flow. This type of short circuit frequently causes a fuse to burn out or a circuit breaker to cycle on and off.

To locate a short circuit in wiring, note the unintended operation of a circuit. Use a wiring diagram to determine where the problem is most likely to occur. Inspect wires and wiring harnesses for physical damage. Short circuits can be found by measuring resistance or current draw. If the resistance is lower or the current draw is higher than specified, a short circuit is indicated. See **Fig. 1-24.**

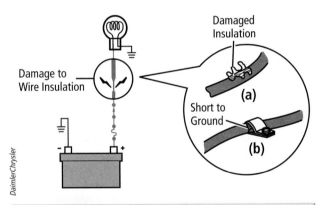

Damage to Wire Insulation

Damaged Insulation

Short to Ground

(a)

(b)

DaimlerChrysler

Fig. 1-24 Damaged insulation can lead to short circuits **(a)** and unwanted ground connections **(b)**. *What is another name for a short to power?*

Grounded Circuit

Most automotive circuits are connected to "ground" as the return circuit to the battery and generator. When an unintended ground connection occurs, the circuit cannot operate normally. Unintended grounds are usually "copper to iron" connections. These are caused by damage to wire insulation. For example, a powered wire (copper) touches a metal surface of the engine, body, or chassis (usually iron). Current in the circuit returns to the battery or generator at that point instead

of flowing through the intended load. The result is usually an open fuse or circuit breaker and no system operation. This problem is often referred to as a "short to ground." A short to voltage and a short to ground are not the same. The causes and testing procedures for each are different.

To test for unwanted ground connections, turn off the power. Disconnect any intentional grounds. Use a self-powered test light or ohmmeter to check for continuity between the conductor and a nearby clean metal surface. If there is continuity, the circuit is grounded.

Excessive Circuit Resistance

The components in an electrical circuit that use energy also resist the flow of current. For example, the filament in a light bulb is a resistor. As such, the filament restricts the flow of current in the circuit. The balance between resistance and current flow and voltage in a circuit is described by Ohm's law: $E = I \times R$ (voltage equals current times resistance).

Excessive resistance in a circuit is a common cause of electrical and electronic system failures. It occurs when a circuit has more resistance than intended. It may be caused by:

• Loose or dirty connections.
• Undersized wires or cables.
• Broken strands of wire.
• Excessive heat buildup.
• Burned switch contacts.
• Excessively long wires.

TECH TIP **Excessive Resistance** If the resistance in a circuit is increased by loose connections, corrosion, or other problems, then current flow naturally decreases. Reduced current flow means that components in the circuit will not have the amount of current that they need to function normally. The problem is caused by excessive resistance in the circuit, not by malfunctioning components.

Excessive resistance causes a circuit to operate at less than normal efficiency. For example, a rusted ground connection in the headlight circuit may cause one headlight to be dim.

Excessive resistance is found by measuring voltage drop. Connect a DVOM across the portion for the circuit to be tested. Operate the circuit so that there is current flow. If the voltage drop is higher than specified for that circuit, the resistance is higher than normal.

Solder Repair of Wiring

A wire in a harness or in a bus circuit must be repaired with rosin core solder and shrink wrap. Care must be taken with bus circuits because the wires are normally twisted together to reduce electromagnetic interference. The wires must be twisted to specification after they are repaired. Also, because system resistance is critical for proper operation, soldering is the only method of repair to use on these circuits. The following is a general procedure for performing the solder repair of wiring.

1. Refer to the vehicle service manual for specifications and general service procedures.
2. Disconnect the negative battery terminal before making electrical repairs.
3. Locate the damaged wire. Open up the wiring harness as necessary to inspect and gain access to the damaged wire.
4. Determine the extent of the damage. If the damage is only a broken or cut wire, it can usually be properly spliced.
5. Use a wire stripper to remove ¼″ of insulation from each end of the wire. Slip a 1½″ length of heat-shrink insulation up one wire. Place each bare end of the wire into a solder-type butt splice connector. Crimp each end of the connector with a terminal crimping tool.
6. Use a soldering gun to heat the connector. Touch each end of the connector or the center opening, if present, with a piece of rosin core solder. The hot wire in the terminal should absorb the melting solder. Use just enough solder to create a good bond.
7. Allow the connector to cool. Then slip the heat shrink tubing over the connector in a centered position. Use a heat gun to heat the tubing, causing it to shrink to a waterproof seal.
8. Another way to create a wire splice is to bare each end of the wire ½″ and twist the wires together. Heat the bare wires with a solder gun, and touch a piece of rosin core solder to the wire. Use enough solder to make a good connection. Allow the bare wire ends to absorb a small amount of the solder. Let the solder cool. Then bend the twisted wires back against the side of the wire. Use shrink wrap tubing to cover the splice. Use a heat gun to heat the tubing to shrink it to a waterproof seal.
9. To replace a damaged section of wire, use a proper length of equal size wire. Cut out the damaged section of wire and make two splices.
10. To splice numerous wires in a wiring harness, stagger the splices 1½″ apart. Use shrink-wrap tubing to individually insulate each splice. Cover all wires with shrink-wrap tubing. Use a heat gun to heat the tubing, causing it to shrink to a waterproof seal.
11. Solder-type terminals may be installed on wire ends by using a procedure similar to that used to make a splice.

Safety First

Soldering The rosin in solder releases fumes that are harmful to eyes and lungs. Always solder in a well-ventilated area. Wear eye protection. Be careful when working with hot solder. Wash your hands after soldering.

SECTION 3 KNOWLEDGE CHECK

1. In wiring diagrams, how should you assume current flows?
2. What is the symbol for ohms?
3. What are test lights used for?
4. What measures voltage, current, and resistance?
5. What is a jumper wire?
6. What are some common causes of an open circuit?

ASE TEST PREP

7. Technician A says that in electrical diagrams the symbols used by different manufacturers represent components. Technician B says that the symbols used by different manufacturers are similar but not necessarily identical. Who is correct?
   - ⓐ Technician A.
   - ⓑ Technician B.
   - ⓒ Both Technician A and Technician B.
   - ⓓ Neither Technician A nor Technician B.

● Section 4
Electronic Automotive Components

Objectives:
- Identify the function of a diode.
- Identify the function of a thermistor.
- Safely handle electronic automotive components.

Vocabulary:
- diode
- clamping diode
- zener diode
- thermistor

Uses of Semiconductors

The term "electricity" is normally used to describe the flow of electrons through conducting materials such as copper, silver, and iron. The term "electronics" deals with the behavior and effects of electrons and with electronic devices.

Electronic devices used to depend on vacuum tubes, which were little more than modified incandescent lightbulbs. In the mid-1900s vacuum-tube technology was gradually replaced with solid-state technology. In solid-state devices, current passes through solid components such as transistors instead of through a glass tube filled with inert gas. Transistors are also known as semiconductors. **Figure 1-25** shows some typical solid-state devices.

Pure silicon is neither a good conductor nor a good insulator. Semiconductors are manufactured by adding small amounts of certain elements to a thin silicon wafer, or "chip." The process of adding these elements is called "doping." One side of the chip is doped so that extra electrons will be present. The extra electrons make this layer of silicon negative. The other side of the chip is doped with a different element, causing fewer electrons to be present. This side will be positive.

Doping creates a positive (P) and a negative (N) layer on the same silicon chip. The two layers are known as a "PN junction." This is the basis for a diode, a common component of electronic circuits. A **diode** is a solid-state electronic device that allows the passage of an electric current in one direction only.

The basic PN junction can be combined in various ways to produce many electronic devices. Two of the more common uses of PN junctions are in light-emitting diodes (LEDs) and transistors. Silicon chips can be designed to control the flow of electrons in simple and complex circuits. Thousands of tiny electronic devices can be combined on a single silicon wafer to form an integrated circuit (IC). These ICs are used in circuits such as powertrain control modules (PCMs), radios, electronic climate controls, and antilock brake control modules.

Solid-State Components

A number of solid-state components can be made using combinations of the basic PN junction. Among the more common devices are diodes, zener diodes, light-emitting diodes, transistors, and thermistors.

Diodes

Diodes are one-way electronic check valves for current. A **diode** allows conventional current flow (+ to −) only in the direction of the arrow in its symbol.

A diode "turns on" and conducts only when the correct voltage is applied to its terminals. If the applied voltage is too low or of the wrong polarity, the diode blocks current. Diodes can be tested with the DIODE TEST position on a DVOM. Connect the test leads to the diode and observe the meter. Reverse the leads and test again. The diode should conduct in one direction only. Diodes are commonly used as rectifiers. Six diodes are used in an automotive generator to rectify (change) AC to DC.

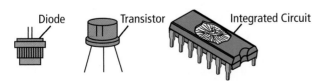

Diode   Transistor   Integrated Circuit

Fig. 1-25 These typical solid-state devices, shown here much enlarged, are a diode, a transistor, and an integrated circuit. *What is the function of each of these devices?*

Another common use for a diode is to prevent voltage spikes (momentary high-voltage surges). Voltage spikes can damage other electronic components. In this case a diode is connected in parallel with a winding. When current flow through the winding stops, a high voltage is induced in the winding. This voltage can damage the module that controls the circuit. The diode provides a path to use up the unwanted voltage without having the voltage go through the module. Used in this way, the diode is called a **clamping diode** because it "clamps down" on induced voltage spikes. See **Fig. 1-26**.

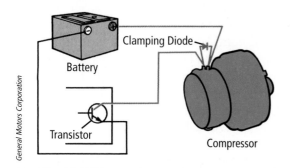

General Motors Corporation

Fig. 1-26 A clamping diode protects against surge voltage. *How is the diode connected?*

Zener Diodes

Zener diodes are a special type of diode. A **zener diode** is a diode that has been doped so that it is able to conduct current in a reverse direction without being damaged. The zener diode symbol is similar to that of a regular diode except for the small lines added to the vertical line representing the cathode. See **Fig. 1-27**. Zener diodes are most often used as voltage sensors. Electronic voltage regulators use a zener diode to determine when voltage regulation occurs.

General Motors Corporation

Fig. 1-27 Diodes can be represented in several ways. The third symbol from the left is a zener diode. *In which direction will conventional current flow through a diode?*

Light-Emitting Diodes

Light-emitting diodes (LEDs) are similar to regular diodes except they are designed to give off light. They are produced by doping a silicon chip with different elements to produce red, green, orange, yellow, or blue light. There is a small lens on the diode housing to make the light visible. An LED is commonly depicted as a diode with arrows pointing away from it. This indicates that light is being given off.

LEDs can be made very small and use very little current. They are used as indicating lamps on dash displays and in optical-type sensor circuits. Large LEDs have been used as stop lamps in some late model cars.

Transistors

Transistors are also constructed from layers of P and N material. They have three terminal connections instead of two. There are several types of transistors, all operating in a somewhat similar manner. See **Fig. 1-28**. A transistor is often used as an electronic switch or relay. When the transistor is off, no current can flow. When the correct voltage is applied to a control circuit, the transistor turns on and conducts current.

With no moving parts, the transistor can be used as a high-speed switch, turning a circuit on and off thousands of times per second. A transistor can also be used as an amplifier. When a transistor is used in this way, a small amount of control current regulates a much larger amount of output current.

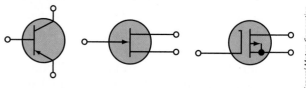

General Motors Corporation

Fig. 1-28 Several different symbols are used to indicate a transistor. *Transistor operation is similar to what electrical device?*

Thermistors

A **thermistor** is a small solid-state device used for temperature sensing. The resistance of a thermistor may change from a few ohms to several million ohms as temperature changes. Thermistors are used as engine coolant temperature (ECT) sensors and intake air temperature (IAT) sensors. They also provide temperature compensation in electronic voltage regulators. One symbol for a thermistor is the sawtooth resistor symbol with an arrow drawn through it. Also used is the resistor symbol with the letter *T* next to it.

Handling Solid-State Components

High temperatures, physical impact, high voltage, reverse polarity, and static electricity may damage solid-state components. High temperature problems are minimized by mounting electronic components on an aluminum housing. This protects the electronic components from heat-related damage. In some cases special heat-transfer grease must be used between a component and the surface on which it is mounted.

The chips in electronic components are fragile. Avoid striking or dropping components containing solid-state circuits.

In general, electronic circuits are designed to operate within the voltage range produced by the vehicle's electrical system. Take care to avoid creating high-voltage spikes while working on the vehicle. High voltage in the electrical system may be caused by:

• Disconnecting a component or its wiring while the circuit is in operation.
• Disconnecting the battery while the engine is running.
• Improper use of a battery charger.

Damage to electronic components is frequently caused by reversed polarity connections. Make sure the cables are connected correctly when installing a battery, using jumper cables, or charging a battery.

A form of static electricity known as electrostatic discharge (ESD) can damage some electronic modules.

The static energy builds up during normal work activities such as sliding across a car seat. ESD can damage a module without the technician's knowledge. Circuits containing modules that may be damaged by ESD are marked with a special symbol. See **Fig. 1-29**.

To avoid damaging ESD sensitive modules, follow these steps:

• Read and follow the directions in the service manual and on packaging.
• Leave a new module in its protective packaging until ready for installation.
• Do not touch any terminals on the module.
• Before handling a module, touch a nonsensitive metal surface on the vehicle. This will discharge any static voltage present.
• Anti-ESD wrist straps and work mats are available. Use them when recommended.

General Motors Corporation

Fig. 1-29 A warning label for circuits containing components that may be damaged by electrostatic discharge. *What is another name for electrostatic discharge?*

SECTION 4 KNOWLEDGE CHECK

1. What is the process of adding small amounts of certain elements to a thin silicon wafer, or chip?

2. What are the two layers created by doping called?

3. What is a diode?

4. Name three solid-state components that can be made using combinations of the basic PN junction.

5. What do the diodes in an automotive generator rectify or change?

6. Identify the function of a thermistor.

ASE TEST PREP

7. Technician A says that a transistor can be used as an amplifier. Technician B says that a transistor can be used as a high-speed switch. Who is correct?
   a Technician A.
   b Technician B.
   c Both Technician A and Technician B.
   d Neither Technician A nor Technician B.

CHAPTER 1 REVIEW

Key Points

Meets the following NATEF Standards for Electrical/Electronic Systems: using wiring diagrams; checking and measuring electrical circuits.

- All matter is made of atoms. Atoms have three components—protons, neutrons, and electrons.
- Electrical current is carried through a conductor by "free" electrons.
- Ohm's law defines the relationships among voltage, current, and resistance.
- Ohm's law states that the voltage in a circuit is equal to the current multiplied by the resistance: $E = I \times R$.
- Wiring harness repair requires the correct application of shrink tubing.
- Fuses, fusible links, and circuit breakers protect electrical circuits by opening if excessive current occurs.
- Wiring diagrams show how circuit components are connected.
- Volt-ohm-meters, test lights, scan testers, and oscilloscopes are used to test electrical circuits.
- Electronic modules can be damaged by electrostatic discharge (ESD).

Review Questions

1. Name three electrical conductors that may be used in motor vehicles.
2. What type of current changes its direction of flow back and forth in the circuit as polarity of the applied voltage changes?
3. What is the resistance if the voltage is 12 and the current is 2 amperes?
4. What is the Ohm's Law formula for finding voltage?
5. What is a device used to convert mechanical energy into electrical energy?
6. What is a VOM?
7. What devices enable technicians to get a direct digital readout of stored trouble codes?
8. What kind of diode may be used to prevent voltage spikes?
9. What is ESD?
10. **Critical Thinking** What is the purpose of touching a nonsensitive metal surface on the vehicle before handling an ESD sensitive module?

Excellence in Communication

Using Electrical Symbols

Symbols are often used as shortcuts for words, things, or ideas. We understand symbols when we learn what they mean. We know what a stop sign or a yield sign means without reading the words. There is general agreement among people as to what a particular symbol means. This is one reason symbols are usually so easily understood. The symbols used in schematic wiring diagrams are different.

Schematic wiring diagrams, or circuit diagrams, use symbols to indicate the components of electrical circuits. When you consult a vehicle service manual to read a schematic wiring diagram, be aware that not all manufacturers use the same symbols. You may need to find the chart of electrical symbols used in the manual if you see a symbol with which you are not familiar.

Apply It!

Meets NATEF Communications Standards for using text resources to gather data.

Study **Figs. 1-14** and **1-15** in this chapter.

1. On a sheet of paper, make a comparison chart of three electrical symbols. Draw the symbols for a single filament lamp or load, an open switch, and a ground, as shown in each of the figures.

2. Compare the versions for each electrical component. Write down your observations based on your drawings of these symbols.

3. Check two service manuals, either print versions or online. Do the symbols used in their schematic diagrams differ from the ones you have drawn?

AUTOMOTIVE SERVICE EXCELLENCE
TEST PREP

Answering the following practice questions will help you prepare for the ASE certification tests.

1. An example of a good electrical conductor is:
   a gold.
   b plastic.
   c wood.
   d rubber.

2. Technician A says that glass is a good insulator. Technician B says that lead is a good insulator. Who is correct?
   a Technician A.
   b Technician B.
   c Both Technician A and Technician B.
   d Neither Technician A nor Technician B.

3. Two symbols that can be used to represent resistance are:
   a ® and √.
   b £ and ¥.
   c R and Ω.
   d Σ and Δ.

4. Technician A says that the resistance of a conductor depends on the type of material used and the size of that material. Technician B says that the resistance of a conductor depends on the length and temperature of the conductor. Who is correct?
   a Technician A.
   b Technician B.
   c Both Technician A and Technician B.
   d Neither Technician A nor Technician B.

5. Technician A says that most conductors are made of stranded carbon filaments covered with a fiberglass insulator. Technician B says that most conductors are made of stranded copper wire covered with plastic insulation. Who is correct?
   a Technician A.
   b Technician B.
   c Both Technician A and Technician B.
   d Neither Technician A nor Technician B.

6. The automotive generator turns mechanical energy into:
   a kinetic energy.
   b potential energy.
   c chemical energy.
   d electrical energy.

7. What are the advantages of using a printed circuit?
   a They are large and require more space than single wire connections.
   b They operate only one device at a time.
   c They can be replaced.
   d They require less space and are more reliable than single wire connections.

8. Technician A says that logic probes provide more information and can be used in a wider variety of applications. Technician B says that digital multimeters provide more information and can be used in wider variety of applications. Who is correct?
   a Technician A.
   b Technician B.
   c Both Technician A and Technician B.
   d Neither Technician A nor Technician B.

9. Which tool can be used to read a vehicle's diagnostic trouble code (DTC)?
   a Oscilloscope.
   b Digital multimeter.
   c Scan tool.
   d Logic probe.

10. Technician A says that the repair area for each wire should be staggered in harness repair. Technician B says that multiple repairs in one spot can make it difficult to reinstall the convolute tubing over the harness when finished. Who is correct?
    a Technician A.
    b Technician B.
    c Both Technician A and Technician B.
    d Neither Technician A nor Technician B.

2

Diagnosing & Servicing the Battery

Section 1
Automotive Batteries

Section 2
Battery Inspection and Testing

Section 3
Battery Servicing

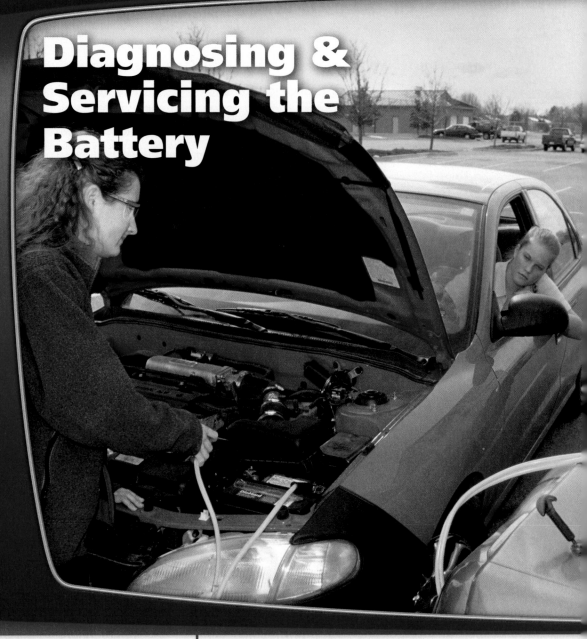

Customer's Concern

Adam Chambers is a regular customer at your service center. So, you are not surprised when he shows up a little over two months after his last oil change. What is somewhat surprising is the fact that he left his car running in front of the shop.

Adam admits he is a little afraid to turn the ignition off today. His neighbor, Steve, had to help him get his car started this morning. Adam does not know much about automotive electrical systems, but Steve said his battery was fully charged. Rather than using the jumper cables, Steve simply disconnected and then reconnected the battery cables. The car started right away.

Adam says he would hate to get stranded somewhere. He wants you to take a closer look.

Technician's Challenge

As the service technician, you need to find answers to these questions:

1. How could Steve tell that the battery was fully charged? Are there any tips you can share with Adam about examining his battery's charge?

2. Why would disconnecting and reconnecting the battery cables assist in starting Adam's car? Was there a faulty connection?

3. What can prevent a battery's charge from flowing freely through the terminal posts and battery cables? How can you correct the problem?

Section 1
Automotive Batteries

Objectives:
- Explain the purpose of the automotive battery.
- Explain the construction of the automotive battery.

Vocabulary:
- key-off load
- electrolyte
- cold-cranking amps (CCA)
- reserve capacity
- terminal voltage

Purpose of the Battery

The automotive battery stores electrical energy in chemical form. The automotive battery:
- Stores the electrical energy needed to operate the starter, ignition system, and fuel system during cranking.
- Supplies "key-off" power for lights and accessories.
- Supplies the power needed to operate various key-off loads. A **key-off load** is a device that draws current even when all switches are turned off. Examples are computer and radio memory circuits. Key-off loads are sometimes referred to as parasitic drains.
- Provides some of the power for electrical loads during normal operation. This is necessary when the load exceeds the generator's output.
- Serves as a load regulator to dampen transient voltages that occur in the electrical system. These voltage spikes might otherwise damage sensitive electrical and electronic components.

Battery Construction

Three types of automotive batteries are in use today: lead-antimony, lead-calcium, and recombination. Antimony and calcium are elements. When they are added to lead, the resulting combination is an alloy that improves the electrical properties of the battery. The addition of these alloys also adds strength. Recombination batteries channel the gas so that it does not vent out of the battery. This process helps keep the electrolyte concentration at the optimum level. For any battery, be sure to consult the service information.

Automotive batteries use lead and acid to store energy in chemical form. The chemicals used in the battery determine how much voltage it will produce.

The amount of lead and acid in the battery determines the amount of energy (current) the battery can store. Drawing current out of the battery causes it to be discharged. An advantage of the lead-acid type of battery is that it may be recharged easily. Recharging restores the electrical energy lost during discharge.

Figure 2-1 shows the key parts of a typical automotive battery.
- The plastic case and cover serve as a container for the battery components.
- Vent caps cover cell openings. They are non-removable on maintenance-free batteries. Conventional batteries have removable vent caps. The vent allows the gases formed during battery operation to escape to the atmosphere.
- The active materials are lead peroxide and sponge lead pastes that become the positive and negative plates.

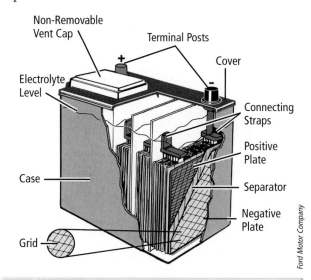

Non-Removable Vent Cap · Terminal Posts · Cover · Electrolyte Level · Connecting Straps · Positive Plate · Case · Separator · Negative Plate · Grid

Ford Motor Company

Fig. 2-1 Cutaway view of a maintenance-free battery. Major components are identified. *What two liquids make up the electrolyte?*

- The grid is the lead alloy framework that holds the active plate materials.
- Separators are porous insulators that are used to separate the plates while allowing the electrolyte to flow between the plates.
- An **electrolyte** is a compound that conducts an electrical current in a water solution. In an automotive battery, the electrolyte is a mixture of sulfuric acid and water.
- In each cell, connecting straps connect plates of the same polarity. They also connect the cells together to form the battery. The end straps are connected to the battery terminals. Connecting straps are made of a lead alloy.
- Terminal posts are the connection points for battery cables. Some batteries have top posts; others have threaded side terminals. Some have both.

Automotive batteries have six cells connected in series. Each cell produces about 2.1 volts. When connected in series, they produce 12.6 volts (6 × 2.1). Connected in series means the positive (+) strap of the first cell is connected to the negative (−) strap of the second cell. The "+" of the second cell is connected to the "−" of the third cell, and so on. The cell wall seals around the lead straps that connect the cells. This keeps each cell separate. The first negative and the last positive connecting straps are connected to the external battery terminals.

The plastic case of the battery separates the cells and supports the plates, connecting straps, and terminals. See **Fig. 2-2**. The case also holds the acid and water used as the electrolyte. Each cell is composed of a number of positive and negative plates. Typically there are nine to thirteen or more of each.

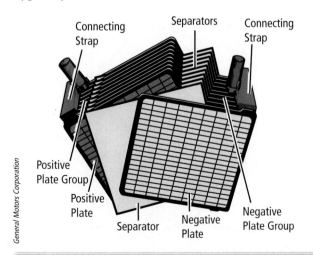

Fig. 2-2 Partially assembled battery components.
Why is it necessary to have separators between the positive and negative plates?

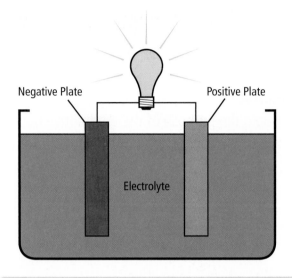

Fig. 2-3 Voltage is produced by the chemical reaction between the plates and the electrolyte.
What does the amount of current a battery can produce depend on?

The amount of current a battery can provide depends on the amount of plate material in contact with the electrolyte. See **Fig. 2-3**.

Battery plates are formed on a lead alloy grid. The grid structure supports the active plate materials of the battery. The positive plates are made of brown lead peroxide. Negative plates are composed of gray sponge lead. These materials are made into pastes. The pastes are pressed into and supported by the grid structure. Porous separators keep the plates from touching each other, while allowing the electrolyte to flow freely between the plates.

The electrolyte provides a conductive path for electron travel between the plates. In a fully charged battery, the electrolyte is approximately one-third sulfuric acid and two-thirds water. In a fully charged battery, the negative plates contain free electrons. A difference of potential exists between the positive and negative plates in each cell. When a load is connected to the battery, current flows to equalize the difference in potential between the plates.

Safety First

Sulfuric Acid Always wear safety glasses when working around batteries. Batteries contain sulfuric acid. Do not allow the acid to touch any part of your body or clothing. Use clean water to flush any area that comes in contact with battery acid. See a doctor if needed.

When current flows from the battery, a chemical reaction occurs between the electrolyte and the plates. As the battery discharges, the chemical reaction depletes the acid in the electrolyte. The electrolyte eventually becomes weaker because it contains a smaller amount of acid and a larger amount of water. A weak electrolyte cannot support a high level of current flow. The relationship between the amount of acid and water affects the density (specific gravity or weight) of the electrolyte. An electrolyte with a low density has a low level of acid. The density of the electrolyte provides an indication of the state-of-charge of the battery.

 **Safety First** **Metallic Objects** Batteries can produce very high current. Remove all jewelry, including watches, necklaces, and similar items before working around batteries. Remove or put tape over rings. Keep tools and other metallic objects that could cause an arc away from battery terminals.

Battery Operation

To produce current, a chemical reaction must occur between the electrolyte and the active plate materials. The plates are slowly converted to lead sulfate. The formation of lead sulfate releases electrons. These electrons make up the current that flows from the battery. When the battery is fully discharged, most of the acid has left the electrolyte and entered the plates. The electrolyte is now mostly water. As a result, discharged batteries can freeze and be permanently damaged in cold weather.

 Safety First **Charge Indicator** If the charge indicator (when used) is clear or yellow, do not charge the battery.

Automotive batteries are called secondary cells because, unlike some flashlight batteries (primary cells), they can be recharged. Charging reverses the chemical reaction of discharge by forcing electrons back into the battery. This converts the lead sulfate back into sulfuric acid and restores the plates to their original condition.

Part of the chemical reaction involved in charging a battery separates water into hydrogen and oxygen gases. In conventional batteries the hydrogen and oxygen gases escape through the vents and some

water is lost. In maintenance-free batteries these gases are collected and recombined, so less water is lost. The use of lead-calcium alloys to make grids and straps reduces the amount of hydrogen produced. This further reduces water loss in maintenance-free batteries.

 TECHNOLOGY

Hybrid Vehicle Auxiliary Battery

The hybrid vehicle auxiliary battery may be an absorbed glass mat (AGM) maintenance-free battery. Its electrolyte is trapped in separators to reduce the amount of hydrogen gas released when the battery is charged. The electrolyte cannot be replaced. This battery powers the hybrid vehicle's electrical systems in a manner similar to the powering of those in a conventional vehicle. The hybrid vehicle auxiliary battery may be located someplace other than under the hood.

Because of the many electrical and electronic components and computers in a hybrid vehicle, a higher than usual key-off parasitic drain may be normal. This may require that the battery be charged periodically or be disconnected if the vehicle is not driven for more than two weeks. Make sure all accessories are off, that all doors are properly closed, and that interior lights automatically turn off. Accessories or lights that are left on could quickly deplete the auxiliary battery.

The auxiliary battery is grounded to the metal chassis of the vehicle. This battery is very sensitive to high-voltage. Refer to the manufacturer's specifications before charging an AGM battery. When charging the auxiliary battery, use a battery charger approved for charging the AGM battery. Otherwise, damage to the battery may result.

Battery Management Systems

A battery management system protects the battery cells from out-of-tolerance operating conditions and offers individual cell protection. It also allows the automotive system to respond to external fault conditions by isolating the battery and addressing the cause of the fault. For example, a cooling fan might be turned on if the battery overheats. The battery management system has three main components: the battery monitoring unit (BMU), the battery control unit (BCU), and the CAN/BUS vehicle communications network.

Battery Performance

All batteries produce current through chemical reactions. These reactions are affected by temperature. As the battery gets colder, less current output is available. See **Fig. 2-4.**

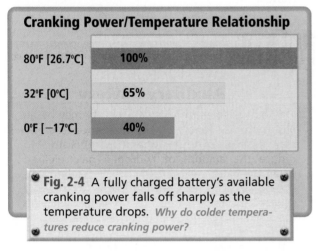

Cranking Power/Temperature Relationship

80°F [26.7°C]	100%
32°F [0°C]	65%
0°F [−17°C]	40%

Fig. 2-4 A fully charged battery's available cranking power falls off sharply as the temperature drops. *Why do colder temperatures reduce cranking power?*

Many batteries fail in cold weather because their reduced output is not enough to crank the engine. As the battery gets hotter, harmful reactions such as self-discharge and grid corrosion become a problem. Battery life is usually shorter in hot climates.

Poor maintenance and battery age also affect output. Batteries should be kept as fully charged as possible. A discharged battery means that lead sulfate remains on the plates (sulfation). Eventually the sulfate hardens, making charging difficult or impossible. When a battery is not held securely in the tray, material can shake from the plates and connections may crack. Such conditions will reduce battery capacity and life.

Even well-maintained batteries eventually fail. Common causes of failure are hard sulfation, shedding of plate material, grid corrosion, and shorting between plates. In many cases a combination of these problems causes battery failure.

A battery has a service life. The service life of a battery is usually indicated in months. Ratings of 48, 60, and 75 months are typical. Batteries that are at or near the end of their service life should be tested as a normal maintenance item.

Battery Ratings

Capacity ratings measure a battery's ability to supply current under specified conditions. The two most widely used ratings are cold-cranking amps and reserve capacity.

Cold-Cranking Amps (CCA)

The amount of current a fully charged battery can supply at 0°F [−17.8°C] for 30 seconds is known as **cold-cranking amps (CCA).** For example, let's look at a battery with a CCA rating of 400. The battery is able to supply 400 amps at 0°F (−17.8°C) for 30 seconds without the battery voltage falling below 7.2 volts. Most automotive batteries have CCA ratings between 400 and 1000 amps. This rating is especially important when cold starting is a concern.

TECH TIP **Battery Ratings.** Some batteries are also rated in cranking amps (CA). Because this test is made at 32°F [0°C], it results in higher ampere ratings than the CCA test. Do not confuse the CA and CCA ratings.

Reserve Capacity

The measure of how many minutes a battery can supply a load of 25 amps at 80°F [27°C] is known as **reserve capacity.** The minimum terminal voltage on this test is 10.5. Reserve capacity relates to how well the battery can handle key-off loads. A typical value for reserve capacities is 125 minutes. This means the battery can supply 25 amperes for 125 minutes at 80°F [27°C].

Table 2-A shows typical CCA and reserve capacities for batteries. It is not practical to convert from one of these rating systems to the other. Make sure any replacement battery has the minimum CCA and reserve capacity ratings specified by the vehicle's manufacturer.

Table 2-A	Battery Specifications	
Test Load Amps	**Cold-Cranking Amps**	**Reserve Capacity Minutes**
200	405	75
210	430	90
250	500	90
310	625	90
310	630	105
330	770	115
360	730	115

Excellence in Math

Applying Ohm's Law to Series Circuits

A 12-volt automotive battery has six cells. Each cell has a voltage of about 2 volts. When the cells are connected in series, the combined voltage is higher than the voltage of any single cell by itself. The total voltage in a series circuit is the sum of the individual voltages. The formula for the total voltage, V_T, of the 12-volt battery is:

$$V_T = V_1 + V_2 + V_3 + V_4 + V_5 + V_6$$

In general, the total resistance in a series circuit is the sum of the individual resistances. You can write the formula for the total resistance, R_T, in a series circuit if there are three individual resistors, R_1, R_2, and R_3, as:

$$R_T = R_1 + R_2 + R_3$$

Ohm's law still applies in a series circuit. The total resistance, R_T, and the total voltage, V_T, are used in the formula for the circuit.

$$V_T = I \times R_T$$

You can find R_T and the current if you know the voltage and the value of each resistance in a series circuit. Consider a series circuit with a 12-volt battery and three resistors, whose values are 1.0 Ω, 2.5 Ω, and 2.5 Ω.

First, find the total resistance:

$$R_T = 1.0 \text{ Ω} + 2.5 \text{ Ω} + 2.5 \text{ Ω} = 6 \text{ Ω}$$

Use Ohm's law to find the current.

$V = I \times R_T$. Thus:

$$I = \frac{V}{R_T} = \frac{12 V}{6 \text{ Ω}} = 2 \text{ amps}$$

Apply It!

Meets NATEF Mathematics Standards for calculating algebraic expressions using addition and division.

1. What is the total resistance and the current in a series circuit with a 6-volt battery and two resistances of 6 Ω and 4 Ω?

2. What is the current in a circuit with two 6-volt batteries and two resistances of 0.15 Ω and 0.35 Ω, all connected in series?

Terminal Voltage

The voltage measured across a battery under specified conditions is known as **terminal voltage.** The open circuit, or at rest, voltage of a fully charged battery is 12.6 volts. In use, however, the actual measured voltage will differ.

- During cranking, the voltage may drop to 10 volts or less, depending on load and temperature.
- With the engine running, charging-system voltage will usually be in the range of 13.5–15.0 volts, depending on temperature. Voltage outside this range usually means a charging system problem.

SECTION 1 KNOWLEDGE CHECK

1. What do automotive batteries use to store energy in chemical form?

2. Give an example of a parasitic drain.

3. Describe how battery cells are connected in a series.

4. What may cause a battery to fail?

5. What is a capacity rating?

6. What is reserve capacity?

ASE TEST PREP

7. Technician A says that each cell in an automotive battery produces about 1.5 volts. Technician B says that each cell in an automotive battery produces about 2.1 volts. Who is correct?
   - ⓐ Technician A.
   - ⓑ Technician B.
   - ⓒ Both Technician A and Technician B.
   - ⓓ Neither Technician A nor Technician B.

Section 2
Battery Inspection and Testing

Objectives:

B1 • Perform battery state-of-charge (conductance) test; determine necessary action.

B2 • Perform battery capacity test; confirm proper battery capacity for vehicle application; determine necessary action.

A14 • Measure and diagnose the cause(s) of excessive key-off battery drain (parasitic draw); determine necessary action.

Vocabulary:
• open-circuit voltage (OCV) test
• hydrometer
• specific gravity
• load test

Battery Inspection

Signs of possible battery problems can often be found by carefully inspecting the battery, battery tray and hold-down clamps, and cables. Inspect the following:

- Battery tray and hold-down clamps—make sure the battery is held securely in place.
- Case and cover—look for loose posts and cracks or other physical damage. Clean surfaces to prevent small leakage currents from occurring across dirt and moisture.
- Terminal connections—make sure they are clean and tight.
- Cables—replace if damaged. Make sure replacement cables are the correct wire gauge (diameter).
- Electrolyte level—on batteries with removable vent caps only, remove the vent caps. Add water to bring electrolyte to indicated level. Distilled water is preferred.

Safety First **Battery Safety** Remember that an automotive battery will emit hydrogen gas as it is being charged. It is very important to keep sparks and flames away from the battery.

Battery Testing

Several tests are available to determine a battery's condition. Batteries typically cannot be tested unless they are fully charged. A state-of-charge test, or conductance test, can determine whether a battery is fully charged. The easiest, most accurate way to determine the battery's state of charge is through use of an **open-circuit voltage (OCV) test.** A battery load test or an electronic battery test can determine whether a fully charged battery is good or bad.

Some batteries have a built-in hydrometer that can quickly indicate the battery's state of charge. However, built-in hydrometers sometimes fail and are not always accurate. A regular hydrometer can be used on batteries with removable vent caps.

The electrolyte in a fully charged battery is about one-third sulfuric acid and two-thirds water. As the battery discharges, the percentage of acid in the electrolyte decreases. The amount of acid in the electrolyte is an accurate measure of the battery's state of charge. Sulfuric acid is heavier or denser than water.

A **hydrometer** is an instrument that measures the density, or specific gravity, of a liquid. **Specific gravity** is the weight per unit volume of a substance compared with the weight per unit volume of water. A different type of hydrometer is used to test the anti-freeze protection of engine coolants.

Built-in Hydrometers

Some maintenance-free batteries have a built-in hydrometer called a charge indicator. This hydrometer has a small green ball in a cage at the bottom of a clear plastic tube. When the battery is adequately charged, the ball will float and appear as a green dot in the charge indicator. See **Fig. 2-5.** This does not necessarily mean that the battery is in good condition. It means only that the battery state of charge is acceptable. Only a load test or an electronic test can determine whether a battery is good or bad.

If the battery is discharged, the weaker electrolyte cannot float the green ball and the indicator will be dark. This means the battery must be charged and then tested. A clear or yellow indicator means the electrolyte level is too low, and the battery should be replaced. Do not attempt to test, charge, or jump-start a battery that is too low on electrolyte. It could explode.

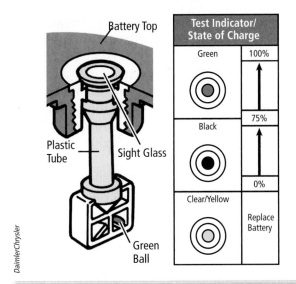

DaimlerChrysler

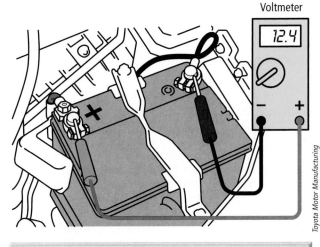

Toyota Motor Manufacturing

Fig. 2-5 Appearance of the charge indicator under various battery conditions. *What will be the color of the charge indicator if the battery is low on electrolyte?*

Fig. 2-6 Open-circuit voltage is measured with all lights and accessories off. *Why must all loads be removed before conducting this test?*

Some manufacturers use a slightly different color code for the built-in hydrometer. In these batteries, readings show:

- Green—a charge of 75 percent or more.
- Black—a charge between 50 percent and 75 percent.
- Red—a charge less than 50 percent.
- Yellow—a low electrolyte level.

Refer to the vehicle service manual for specific information.

Safety First

Battery Charge Keep the battery as fully charged as practical. A discharged battery may freeze at 20°F [−7°C]. A fully charged battery will not freeze at −75°F [−59°C]. Freezing water expands and may crack cell walls, damage plates, or break internal battery connections. Charging a frozen battery may produce explosive gases. The best way to keep a battery from freezing is to keep it adequately charged.

Open-Circuit Voltage (OCV) Test

An open-circuit voltage (OCV) test may be used to determine the state of charge of a battery. It is the only way to check the state of charge on a battery that does not have a built-in hydrometer or removable vent caps. Before making the OCV test, turn on the headlights for 3–5 minutes. This will remove any surface charge from the plates. The surface charge may also be removed by cranking

the engine for 15–30 seconds with the ignition disabled. Turn off all lights and accessories. Use a digital volt-ohm-meter (DVOM) to measure voltage at the battery terminals. See **Fig. 2-6**.

There is a relationship among specific gravity, OCV, and battery state of charge. **Figure 2-7** can be used to determine battery state of charge using OCV.

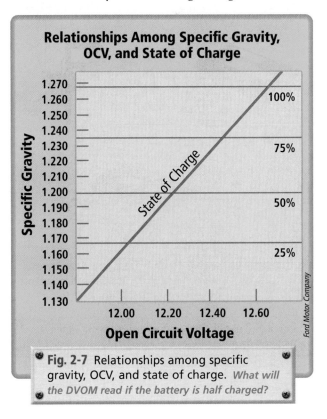

Ford Motor Company

Fig. 2-7 Relationships among specific gravity, OCV, and state of charge. *What will the DVOM read if the battery is half charged?*

Battery Load Test

The battery load test is also called the high-rate discharge test. The **load test** is a test that measures terminal voltage while the battery is supplying a large current for 15 seconds. The load used in the test is approximately what starter current draw would be at normal temperature. Typical load testers include a voltmeter, ammeter, and an adjustable carbon pile resistor. Adapters are often required when testing or charging side terminal batteries. See **Fig. 2-8.**

Safety First | **Load Testing** Load testing produces large amounts of heat inside the load tester. Testing a large battery may generate several thousand watts of power. This will cause the load resistance (carbon pile) to become very hot. Allow the tester to cool down before reuse.

The results of a battery load test are valid only when the battery is adequately charged. The battery is adequately charged only if one of the following occurs:
- The built-in charge indicator is green.
- The specific gravity reading (corrected for temperature, if needed) is at least 1.230.
- The OCV is at least 12.4 volts.

A battery that is not adequately charged will usually fail a load test. To perform a load test:
1. Make sure the load control is OFF.
2. Connect the tester as shown in the vehicle service manual or the tester instruction manual.
3. Remove the surface charge if the battery has been charged before the test is made. This can be done by turning on the headlights or cranking the engine.
4. Apply a load equal to one-half the CCA rating of the battery for 15 seconds. (Some batteries have the correct load value marked on a label or on the battery case.)
5. After 15 seconds, note the voltage and turn off the load.
6. Disconnect the tester.

If the voltage is 9.6 volts or higher, the battery is good. Battery temperature will affect the voltage reading. If the battery is not at room temperature or higher, use the temperature compensation chart found in the tester's instructions or in the vehicle service manual. See **Table 2-B.** If the voltage is less than noted for a given temperature, the battery is defective and should be replaced. Causes of a low or discharged battery are given in **Table 2-C.**

Table 2-B	Temperature Compensation		
Minimum Battery Voltage	Temperature	°F	°C
9.6		70	21
9.5		60	16
9.4		50	10
9.3		40	4
9.1		30	−1
8.9		20	−7
8.7		10	−12
8.5		0	−18

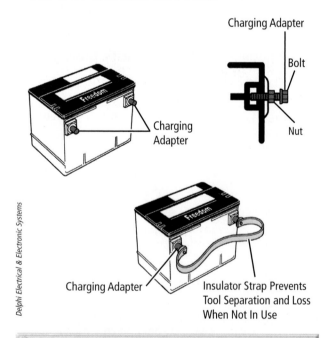

Charging Adapter

Bolt

Charging Adapter

Nut

Charging Adapter

Charging Adapter

Insulator Strap Prevents Tool Separation and Loss When Not In Use

Delphi Electrical & Electronic Systems

Fig. 2-8 Typical charging adapter tools. *When would it be necessary to use adapters?*

Table 2-C	Causes of Low or Discharged Battery
Drains on The Battery • Batteries being less than adequately charged when received • Extended storage of vehicle (self-discharge and parasitic loads) • Parasitic drains, such as drains caused by trunk or other lights that stay on	**Faulty Charging System** • Generator not supplying the required amperage to recharge the battery • Low charging voltage • Broken generator drive belt • Dirty or damaged wiring or connectors
Faulty Starter System • Excessive current draw from starter motor	**Owner Cause** • Extended cranking periods due to hard or no-start condition • Accessory left on, such as headlights or interior lights

State-of-Charge Testing

An electronic battery tester may also be used to determine battery condition, or state-of-charge. This is also called a conductance test. Many vehicle and battery manufacturers consider electronic battery testing the most accurate way to determine whether a battery is good or bad. They will warranty only those batteries tested by using an electronic battery/starting/charging system tester.

These testers are microprocessor controlled. The controller sends a low-voltage AC signal through the battery and measures the return pulse. The controller compares the returned signal to data in its memory to determine battery condition and state of charge. Electronic battery testers are reliable and easy to use. They can be used even if the battery is not adequately charged. They can also identify batteries with internal damage that may be dangerous to charge. Some electronic battery/starting/charging system testers will give the user a unique code that must be submitted with a battery warranty claim. This code informs the manufacturer that an electronic battery tester was used.

To perform an electronic battery test:
1. Turn off all electrical loads.
2. Make sure the test leads make good contact with the battery terminals.
3. Enter the battery's CCA rating in the display window.
4. Press the START button.

The results of the test will be displayed in a few seconds. See **Fig. 2-9.** Refer to the tester instruction manual for additional information.

Midtronics Inc.

Fig. 2-9 An electronic battery tester. A reading from an electronic battery tester is shown at the right. *What battery rating must be entered to conduct this test?*

Key-Off Loads (Parasitic Drains) Testing

An undercharged or dead battery may result from higher than normal key-off loads. These loads are also called parasitic drains. They represent the current needed to maintain memory circuits in devices such as computers, radios, and climate controls. On most vehicles, normal key-off drain will be less than 30–50 milliamps. The actual drain depends on the number of electronic devices on the vehicle.

Excellence in Science

Investigating Electrolytes

The electrical energy needed to start an automobile is stored in the battery in a chemical reaction. An automotive battery is an example of a wet-cell battery. Flashlight batteries are dry-cell batteries.

In a wet-cell battery, the cells contain plates of two different materials. In the automotive battery, these plates are lead (Pb) and lead peroxide (PbO_2). A liquid electrolyte surrounds the plates. The electrolyte in an automotive battery is a mixture of about one-third sulfuric acid (H_2SO_4) and two-thirds water (H_2O).

A battery is discharged by turning on the ignition switch or using electrical accessories. The electrolyte reacts with the lead and lead peroxide. This chemical reaction moves electrons from the electrolyte to the plates. Electricity is produced when electrons are moved from one place to another in a closed circuit.

- The lead plates attract sulfate ions from the sulfuric acid. An ion is a charged atom.
- Hydrogen ions in the electrolyte "pull" oxygen and its electrons from the oxygen in the lead peroxide and replace them with sulfate ions, making lead sulphate ($PbSO_4$).
- The oxygen ions combine with hydrogen ions from the sulfuric acid to make water.

Eventually both plates contain lead sulfate ($PbSO_4$). The chemical reaction stops. No electrons are moving, no electricity is produced.

When a battery is recharged, the chemical reactions are reversed.

- The sulfate ions leave the plates and combine with hydrogen ions from the water to make more sulfuric acid.
- The oxygen ions that are left behind are now attracted to the lead peroxide plate. The plates are lead and lead peroxide again.

Apply It!

Making a Wet-Cell Battery

Meets NATEF Science Standards for laboratory safety and electrochemical reactions in batteries.

Materials and Equipment
- Safety glasses and rubber gloves
- Diluted sulfuric acid
- DVOM

- Wet-cell battery kit available from scientific supply stores. (Kit contains plastic tumbler, holder for metal strips, and terminals for measuring volts and current)

- 6" piece of insulated copper wire with 1" insulation stripped from each end
- 2 strips of zinc
- 2 strips of copper

Safety First | **Personal Protective Equipment**
Sulfuric acid is corrosive. Wear safety glasses and rubber gloves during this experiment.

1. Fill the tumbler half-full with diluted sulfuric acid.

2. Place one zinc strip in the acid. Is there a clue that a chemical reaction is taking place? Remove and rinse the strip in water.

3. Repeat the above procedure with one of the copper strips. What did you observe?

4. Attach the copper wire between the terminals. Attach the copper strips in the holders.

5. Measure the voltage between the two terminals with the DVOM. What is the reading?

6. Replace the copper strips with zinc strips. Repeat the procedure. What is the reading?

7. Remove one of the zinc strips and rinse it in water. Replace it with a copper strip. Measure the voltage. What is the reading?

8. Connect the DVOM to measure current. Place the metal strips as far apart as possible. There should be a small measurable current flow.

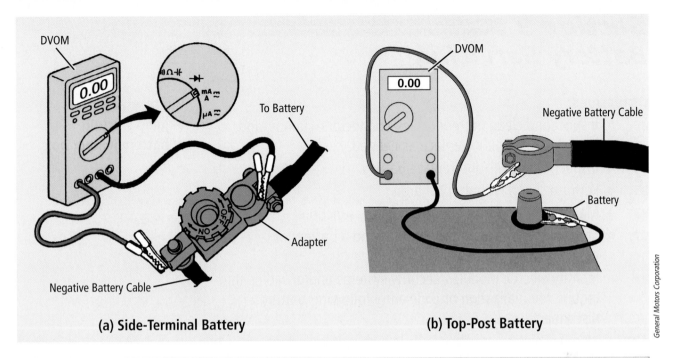

(a) Side-Terminal Battery   (b) Top-Post Battery

General Motors Corporation

Fig. 2-10 An adapter is needed when measuring parasitic drain on a side-terminal battery. The DVOM leads are connected to terminals on the adapter. *What DVOM scale is used to measure the key-off drain?*

Refer to the vehicle service manual for specifications. To measure parasitic drain:

1. Run the vehicle for a few minutes, making sure all electronic systems are turned on.
2. Turn off the ignition and all other switches. Make sure all lights are off and the doors are closed.
3. Without breaking the circuit, connect the highest ammeter scale of a DVOM between the negative battery terminal and the negative cable. On side-terminal batteries, this requires a test adapter. See **Fig. 2-10(a).**

4. On post-type batteries, hold the meter leads on the post and cable clamp. While maintaining this connection, carefully slide the clamp from the post. See **Fig. 2-10(b).** Change to the milliamp scale when the current flow is low enough to do so.

Very high parasitic drain is often caused by underhood, glovebox, or trunk lamps that do not shut off. If no obvious cause is found, follow instructions in the vehicle service manual to locate the cause of the high parasitic drain.

SECTION 2 KNOWLEDGE CHECK

1. When inspecting a battery, what should a technician look for at the terminal connections?

2. What can an open-circuit voltage (OCV) test determine?

3. Why shouldn't a battery that is too low on electrolyte be tested, charged, or jumped?

4. How long does the battery supply current while conducting a load test?

5. How can you tell if a battery is adequately charged?

6. What often causes high parasitic drain?

ASE TEST PREP

7. Technician A says that a hydrometer test can be made at any temperature and the readings obtained can be accepted as correct. Technician B says that this is true as long as corrections are made to the readings when needed. Who is correct?

   ⓐ Technician A.
   ⓑ Technician B.
   ⓒ Both Technician A and Technician B.
   ⓓ Neither Technician A nor Technician B.

Section 3
Battery Servicing

Objectives:

B6 • Inspect and clean battery cables, connectors, clamps, and hold-down; repair or replace as needed.

B4 • Inspect, clean, fill, and replace battery.

B5 • Perform slow/fast battery charge.

B3 • Maintain or restore electronic memory functions.

B7 • Start a vehicle using jumper cables and a battery or auxiliary power supply.

B9 • Identify electric modules, security systems and/or radios that require reinitialization or code entry following battery disconnect.

A21 • Identify location of hybrid vehicle high-voltage circuit disconnect (service plug) location and safety procedures.

B8 • Identify high-voltage of electric or hybrid electric vehicle and related safety precautions.

B10 • Identify hybrid vehicle auxiliary (12V) battery service, repair, and test procedures.

Vocabulary:
• **jump starting**
• **battery jumper box**

Battery Maintenance

All batteries, even maintenance-free ones, benefit from periodic checks.

Routine battery maintenance includes:
• Inspecting for physical damage and corrosion.
• Cleaning the battery, cable connections, and tray.
• Checking fluid level and topping off with distilled water.
• Testing.
• Charging when needed.
• Replacing if defective.

Battery Cleaning

Corrosion around the battery is caused by small amounts of acid that leave the cells in the escaping gases. Neutralize the acid with a mixture of baking soda and water. Flush clean with water. Do not allow the cleaning solution to enter the cell openings.

Cleaning a battery clamp or terminal requires a wire brush to remove corrosion and oxidation. Special brushes are available for this purpose. See **Fig. 2-11.** Cable-clamp bolts may corrode and become weakened. Corroded bolts should be replaced.

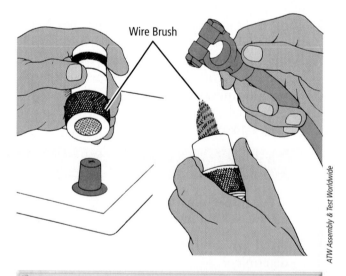

Wire Brush

ATW Assembly & Test Worldwide

Fig. 2-11 Using a battery terminal brush to clean the battery terminal posts and clamps. *Why is it important to clean the connections?*

To prevent corrosion, install chemically treated felt washers before reconnecting the battery cables. Protective spray coatings may be used after reconnecting battery cables. Lubricating grease is not recommended because it may soften and run off.

Clean the battery tray as necessary. Replace it if it is damaged. After removing any rust and corrosion, repaint the tray with rust-inhibiting paint. Be careful to avoid overspray that may damage or mar other surfaces. Replace hold-down brackets or bolts if they are damaged or missing.

Battery Charging

There are several methods for charging a battery. Slow charging uses a current of 3–10 amps and may take 24 hours or more. Medium charging is done with a charging current of 15–25 amps, usually for 3–5 hours. Fast charging uses a current of 30–50 amps for up to one hour. See **Fig. 2-12.**

> **Safety First** **Charging a Battery** Before disconnecting the battery, turn off all accessories and loads in the vehicle. Be careful to connect the battery charger leads to the correct battery terminals. The red cable should always go to the battery positive (+), and the black cable to the battery negative (−). Reverse polarity connections will damage sensitive electrical and electronic components.

Jack Holtel

Fig. 2-12 Battery charger connected to a battery in a vehicle. Disconnect the negative (ground) cable from the battery before connecting the charger cables. *Why is it important to disconnect the negative battery cable before connecting the battery charger?*

Normally, batteries are charged until they are three-fourths charged or more. Avoid overcharging by checking the state of charge frequently. Reduce the charge rate if the battery releases excessive gases or feels unusually warm to the touch. When charging a battery in the vehicle, disconnect the negative battery cable to avoid damaging sensitive electronic components. Never attempt to charge a battery that is frozen or that has a shorted cell.

A slow charge rate is best for the battery. The faster the charge rate, the greater the internal heating. Battery charging should always be done in a well-ventilated area.

Battery Replacement

The four common mistakes made during battery replacement are:
- Installation of a battery with too little capacity.
- Failure to properly secure the battery to the battery tray.
- Improper tightening and protection of the battery terminals.
- Dropping the battery.

Battery Removal

To remove a battery:
1. Identify the electric modules, security systems, and radios that require reinitialization or code entry following battery disconnect. Check the vehicle service manual for this information.
2. Connect a memory holder to the cigarette lighter receptacle. Memory holders use a small 9- or 12-volt battery to supply power to memory circuits while the vehicle battery is disconnected. This prevents the loss of stored information such as engine operating adjustments and radio and climate-control presets. Do not open doors or use any electrical devices in the vehicle while using the memory holder. The small batteries are not capable of supplying current for normal electrical loads.

> **Safety First** **Disconnecting a Battery** Before disconnecting a battery, turn off all electrical loads. This will prevent a spark from occurring when the cable is removed. Always remove the ground cable first. This prevents arcing if a wrench touches another metal surface while touching a battery terminal.

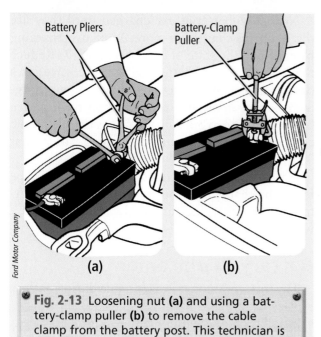

Battery Pliers

Battery-Clamp Puller

Ford Motor Company

(a)   (b)

Fig. 2-13 Loosening nut **(a)** and using a battery-clamp puller **(b)** to remove the cable clamp from the battery post. This technician is using battery pliers to hold the nut.

3. Remove the negative or ground cable from its battery terminal. Avoid damaging the posts when removing the cable clamps. Use cable pullers and battery pliers to prevent battery damage. See **Fig. 2-13**.
4. Remove the positive battery cable from the battery. Use the same method as for the negative cable.
5. Remove the battery hold-down clamps from the battery and the battery tray.
6. Carefully remove the battery from the battery tray. Use a clamp-type battery carrier if needed. See **Fig. 2-14**.

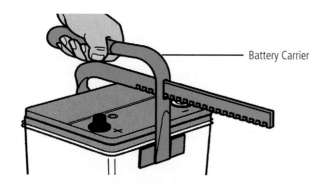

Battery Carrier

Fig. 2-14 A lifting tool makes it easier to remove batteries from tight spaces. *What holds the battery in the battery tray?*

TECH TIP **Battery Carrier.** Batteries can be heavy and difficult to remove. A clamp-type battery carrier may be helpful in removing the battery when clearances are small.

Safety First **Battery Spills** Batteries contain a sulfuric acid solution. Always keep a battery level when removing it. Corrosive acid can spill from the filler or vent caps if the battery is allowed to tip over. If the acid comes in contact with the skin, serious burns can result. Acid spills can damage paint and fabrics. Always flush or neutralize any acid spill to minimize any corrosive effects.

Battery Installation

Before installing a new battery, make sure you have the correct replacement. The size of new battery should be the same as the original. It should also have the same terminal arrangement. The CCA or reserve capacity rating should be the same or higher. The battery tray should be clean. The drain holes should be open. All mounting hardware should be in good condition. Clean, repair, or replace these items as needed. To install a battery:

1. Place the battery in the tray with the terminals in the proper position.
2. Install the battery hold-down clamps. Make sure they are secure.
3. To prevent corrosion, install chemically treated felt washers on both terminals.
4. Connect the positive battery cable. Tighten the clamp or bolt securely, but do not overtighten.
5. Connect the negative or ground cable. Tighten the clamp or bolt securely, but do not overtighten.
6. Disconnect the memory holder from the cigarette lighter.
7. Remove all tools and equipment from the vehicle.
8. Make sure the vehicle starts and runs normally.
9. Check the charging system dash indicator for normal operation.

Some vehicles have electronic modules, radios, and security systems with certain settings. These devices must be reinitialized after the recharged or replaced battery is installed. For some vehicles, the technician may need to erase the fault codes caused by the initial battery removal.

Battery Damage

The following will reduce battery capacity and life:

- Overcharging causes loss of electrolyte and damage to the plates and grids. Charge batteries as slowly as practical. Turn off the charger when the battery nears full charge. If overcharging occurs during normal operation, check the charging system.
- Hard sulfation occurs when the battery remains in a discharged condition for a month or more. The lead sulfate on the plates hardens, making it difficult or impossible to charge the battery. Sulfation is one of the leading causes of battery failure.
- Deep cycling occurs when a deep discharge and charge cycle is repeated often. This results in excessive shedding of active material from the plates. The material will settle to the bottom of the battery case, where it can short between plates.
- Freezing damage occurs when weak batteries freeze and damage the plates and possibly the case.
- Low electrolyte level allows uncovered area of plates to dry out.
- Excessive vibration is caused by the improper mounting of the battery to the case. The vibration causes internal damage to the plates and connectors.

Safety First

Hot Battery If you encounter a vehicle with a battery that is hot and spewing electrolyte, be very careful! Shut off the engine to prevent additional charging. Make sure the area around the car is well ventilated. Do not allow sparks or open flames near the battery. Stay away from the battery until it cools. This may take an hour or more. After the battery has cooled, check it for internal shorts. A battery with an internal short will fail a load test or an electronic battery test. If the battery tests okay, check the charging system.

Jump Starting

Jump starting is the process of starting the engine in one vehicle by connecting it to the battery in another vehicle. See **Fig. 2-15.** Jump starting can be a dangerous process if not done correctly. Whenever possible, check the condition of the bad battery before making any connections. Batteries that are completely discharged or low on electrolyte can explode. Avoid causing arcs when making the connections. If not done properly, the resulting sparks could ignite fuel vapors or battery gases. They can also damage the terminals or components where the arc occurs.

Safety First

Jump Starting a Battery Connecting batteries for jump starting can create dangerous voltage and current surges. These surges can permanently damage expensive electronic components in the vehicle. Always observe proper polarity and connection practices when jump starting. Batteries contain explosive hydrogen gas and corrosive acid. Always protect your eyes and exposed skin.

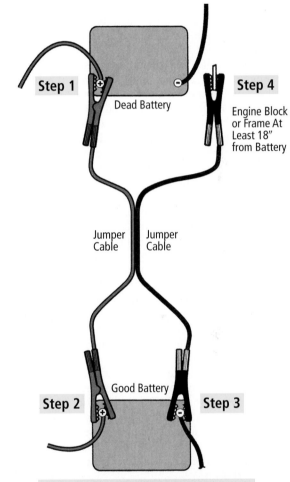

General Motors Corporation

Fig. 2-15 The four basic steps in connecting jump starting cables. **Step 1:** Connect the (+) cable to the (+) terminal of the dead battery. **Step 2:** Connect the opposite end of the (+) cable to the (+) terminal of the good battery. **Step 3:** Connect the (–) cable to the (–) terminal of the good battery. **Step 4:** Connect the opposite end of the (–) cable to a good ground connection away from the battery in the vehicle with the dead battery.

TECHNOLOGY

High-Voltage in Hybrids

Refer to the appropriate service manual. The hybrid system high-voltage wire insulation, connectors, terminal insulating boots, and safety disconnects are orange or orange-red in color. Both high-voltage power cables are isolated from the metal chassis. Thus, there is no possibility of shock by touching the metal chassis.

Before servicing or working on any hybrid vehicle, be sure to turn off the hybrid system. Turn off the key or keep the remote key fob at least fifteen feet from the vehicle to prevent the engine from starting unexpectedly. If planned work is more than routine maintenance or the work will be near the high-voltage wiring or components, disconnect the auxiliary 12-volt battery negative cable. Then wait more than five minutes. This will allow the computer's backup power supply capacitors to discharge and safely power down the various computers.

If the high-voltage battery pack or any high-voltage component is going to be serviced or removed, follow manufacturer's recommendations for disconnecting and isolating the high-voltage battery from the power cables. Wait at least fifteen minutes before checking for the possibility of high voltage being present. Follow the manufacturer's procedure for checking for any remaining voltage. The voltage should be 0 volts. A high-voltage battery pack is shown in **Fig. A**.

In performing service work close to high-voltage wiring or components identified by their orange color, observe all manufacturer safety precautions. Careless handling of high-voltage components can cause severe electrical shock and burns or even fatal electrocution. Safety precautions include:
- Always wear suitable eye protection
- Wear special high-voltage protective gloves.
- Tools may have to be wrapped in vinyl.
- Place insulating material under the high-voltage battery pack when it is placed on the workbench.
- Observe manufacturer procedures when working with high-voltage batteries.

Fig. A A hybrid high-voltage battery pack.
What color are high-voltage wires?

Some vehicles may have convenient connection points under the hood for both positive and negative terminals. See **Fig. 2-16.** Using these terminals keeps dangerous sparks away from the battery.

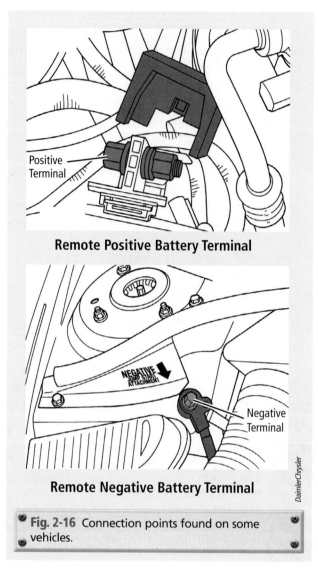

Remote Positive Battery Terminal

Remote Negative Battery Terminal

Fig. 2-16 Connection points found on some vehicles.

If you must jump start a vehicle, use extreme caution. Follow the instructions in the vehicle owner's manual. Be sure to follow all safety precautions.
- Wear safety goggles.
- Avoid sparks and open flames.
- Do not allow the vehicles to touch. If the vehicles touch, a ground connection may be made.

The jump starting procedure requires a set of jumper cables of adequate wire gauge (diameter). Always connect cables in the proper sequence, observing correct polarity.

1. Make sure both vehicles have a 12-volt negative ground electrical system.

2. Make sure the vehicles are not touching each other.

3. Set the parking brakes on both vehicles. Place transmissions in PARK or NEUTRAL.

4. Turn off all lights and accessories. This will avoid accidental damage to these components.

5. Connect one end of the red positive (+) cable to the positive terminal of the dead battery.

6. Connect the other end of the positive (+) cable to the positive (+) terminal of the good battery.

7. Connect one end of the black negative (−) cable to the negative (−) terminal of the good battery.

8. Connect the other end of the negative (−) cable to the engine block or frame of the vehicle with the dead battery. To avoid the danger of sparks igniting battery gases, make sure this connection is at least 18″ [46 cm] from the dead battery.

9. Start the vehicle with the good battery. Turn on the blower motor of the vehicle with the good battery. This helps to prevent potential voltage surges, which can damage sensitive electronic systems.

10. Attempt to start the engine of the vehicle with the dead battery. To avoid starter damage, do not crank the engine longer than 30 seconds at a time.

11. After the engine starts, remove the jumper cables in reverse order. Do not allow the positive and negative cables to touch. Do not allow the positive cable to touch the surface of any vehicle.

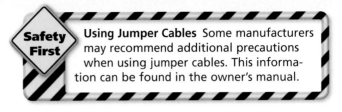

Safety First

Using Jumper Cables Some manufacturers may recommend additional precautions when using jumper cables. This information can be found in the owner's manual.

Using a Battery Jumper Box

Many shops use a battery jumper box instead of jumper cables. A **battery jumper box** is a portable power pack used for jump starting vehicles. See **Fig. 2-17**. The jumper-box cables are connected in the same way as jumper cables. Connect the red positive lead to the battery positive terminal. Connect the black negative lead to a clean ground connection at least 18″ [46 cm] from the battery.

Jack Holtel

Fig. 2-17 A battery jumper box may be more convenient to use than jumper cables. *How are the cables connected?*

SECTION 3 KNOWLEDGE CHECK

1. What common household product is mixed with water to neutralize acid around the battery?

2. Name the steps involved in routine battery maintenance.

3. What is a memory holder?

4. Explain how to install a new battery.

5. Name two dangerous aspects of jump starting.

6. How should a battery jumper box be connected?

ASE TEST PREP

7. Technician A says that hybrid vehicle high-voltage battery safety disconnects are yellow. Technician B says that the hybrid vehicle high-voltage battery terminal insulating boots are orange or orange-red. Who is correct?

   ⓐ Technician A.

   ⓑ Technician B.

   ⓒ Both Technician A and Technician B.

   ⓓ Neither Technician A nor Technician B.

CHAPTER 2 REVIEW

Key Points

Meets the following NATEF Standards for Electrical/Electronic Systems: inspecting batteries; performing battery state-of-charge and load tests.

- The primary components of an automotive battery are the case, cover, vent caps, plates, separators, electrolyte, and terminals.
- A battery operates by storing electrical energy in chemical form.
- A battery hydrometer, built-in hydrometer, or open circuit voltage test can be used to determine battery state of charge.
- A load test or a battery load or electronic battery test can be used to determine battery condition.
- When replacing a battery, a memory holder prevents loss of stored information in memory.
- Strict safety precautions must be followed when servicing the battery system of a hybrid vehicle.
- Jump starting is the process of starting the engine in one vehicle by using the battery in another vehicle.

Review Questions

1. Name the key parts of a typical automotive battery.
2. Name at least three purposes of the automotive battery.
3. What takes place during charging to restore battery function?
4. What happens to battery power as temperature drops?
5. What is the amount of current a fully charged battery can supply at 0°F for 30 seconds?
6. What is a hydrometer?
7. When reading a built-in hydrometer, what does the color green mean?
8. What would a load test reading of 9.4 at 70°F indicate?
9. **Critical Thinking** Consider the battery cleaning process. What should be used to clean battery clamps and terminal posts?
10. **Critical Thinking** Consider the battery replacement process. Name the four common mistakes made during battery replacement.

Excellence in Communication

Writing a Memo

A memo is an informal written note containing information, directions, or suggestions. A memo usually begins with four lines of information:

DATE: (date when you write the memo)

TO: (person receiving the memo)

FROM: (person sending the memo)

RE: (subject of the memo)

Information you should put in a memo includes:
- The customer's complaint.
- The vehicle's symptoms.
- What you have done, including diagnostic tests, repairs, or adjustments.
- Your recommendations.

In a memo, include all the information you think is necessary. However, the memo should be as short and clear as possible. It will become an important part of a vehicle's repair file.

Apply It!

Meets NATEF Communications Standards for organizing written information and adapting style and structure for a written report.

1. Reread the "Customer's Concern" at the beginning of the chapter. Assume you are the technician who checked out the vehicle.

2. Write a sample memo to the service writer. In your memo include:
   - The DATE, TO, FROM, and RE lines. Make up a name for the service writer.
   - All the details you think he or she will need to identify the vehicle. Include its mileage, make, model, year, and VIN.
   - The warranty information for the battery.
   - What you have done to check out the vehicle.
   - Your conclusions and recommendations.

AUTOMOTIVE SERVICE EXCELLENCE
TEST PREP

Answering the following practice questions will help you prepare for the ASE certification tests.

1. Which type of automotive battery has removable vent caps?

   ⓐ Maintenance free.

   ⓑ Conventional.

   ⓒ Lead-rhodium.

   ⓓ Lithium-ion.

2. Technician A says that the plate separators in a battery are insulators. Technician B says that the plate separators are porous and allow the electrolyte to flow between the plates. Who is correct?

   ⓐ Technician A.

   ⓑ Technician B.

   ⓒ Both Technician A and Technician B.

   ⓓ Neither Technician A nor Technician B.

3. How many individual cells does an automotive battery contain?

   ⓐ 2.

   ⓑ 1.

   ⓒ 8.

   ⓓ 6.

4. Technician A says that the cells in an automotive battery are connected in series. Technician B says that the cells in an automotive battery are connected in parallel. Who is correct?

   ⓐ Technician A.

   ⓑ Technician B.

   ⓒ Both Technician A and Technician B.

   ⓓ Neither Technician A nor Technician B.

5. Technician A says that excessive key-off loads cannot result in a dead battery. Technician B says that key-off loads are so small that they can have no effect on a battery. Who is correct?

   ⓐ Technician A.

   ⓑ Technician B.

   ⓒ Both Technician A and Technician B.

   ⓓ Neither Technician A nor Technician B.

6. What is a normal key-off load?

   ⓐ 3–5 amps.

   ⓑ 30–50 amps.

   ⓒ 0.3–0.5 amps.

   ⓓ 0.03–0.05 amps.

7. Which of the following is considered to be the most accurate test of a battery's state of charge?

   ⓐ Open-circuit voltage test.

   ⓑ High-rate discharge test.

   ⓒ Conductance test.

   ⓓ Battery load test.

8. Technician A says that if planned work on a hybrid vehicle is more than routine maintenance, the auxiliary 12-volt battery negative cable must be disconnected. Technician B says that this cable must be disconnected only if work will be near high-voltage wiring. Who is correct?

   ⓐ Technician A.

   ⓑ Technician B.

   ⓒ Both Technician A and Technician B.

   ⓓ Neither Technician A nor Technician B.

9. A memory holder should be plugged in:

   ⓐ after the battery has been removed for servicing.

   ⓑ before the battery is removed for servicing.

   ⓒ when all the lights and accessories are running.

   ⓓ at all times.

10. Technician A says that vehicles should be in contact while jump starting. Technician B says that the negative cable should be connected to the engine block or frame on the vehicle with the dead battery. Who is correct?

    ⓐ Technician A.

    ⓑ Technician B.

    ⓒ Both Technician A and Technician B.

    ⓓ Neither Technician A nor Technician B.

Diagnosing & Repairing the Starting System

Section 1
The Starter

Section 2
Diagnosing the Starting System

Customer's Concern

As the owner of a mobile automotive service business, you are used to frequent calls from stranded drivers. On this cold winter evening, you are called to the nearly deserted parking lot of a local dentist's office. Dr. Erin O'Connor returned to her office and telephoned you when her vehicle would not start for her commute home.

As you sit in the driver's seat and turn the key, you recognize the slow cranking noises that usually indicate some sort of starting system problem. Dr. O'Connor says the car has started slowly for a few months, but it usually starts after a few turns of the ignition key. After several unsuccessful attempts this evening, she decided it was time to call for service.

Technician's Challenge

As the service technician, you need to find answers to these questions:

1. When was the last time Dr. O'Connor had her car serviced? Was the battery tested and fully charged at that time?

2. What could be causing the starting problems? Could the battery be dead? Is the starter to blame? Could the weather affect the starting system?

3. How will you correct the problem? Is a jump start necessary? Will you install a new battery? Does the car need a new starter?

● Section 1
The Starter

Objectives:
- Explain the operation of a starting system.
- Identify the major internal components of a starter.
- Explain the function of an overrunning clutch.
- Explain the purpose of the ring gear and pinion.

Vocabulary:
- **starter**
- **starter relay**
- **starter solenoid**
- **armature**
- **commutator**
- **electromagnetic field**
- **overrunning clutch**
- **gear ratio**

The Starter and the Starting System

The vehicle starting system provides an efficient and reliable method to crank an engine. An internal combustion engine needs air, fuel, and an ignition source to operate. The engine crankshaft must rotate to draw in and compress an air/fuel mixture in the engine's cylinders. The starting system converts electrical energy from the battery into mechanical energy from the starter. This energy is then used to crank the engine.

The major parts of the typical starting system are:
- Battery—an electrical storage device and the source of current for the starting system.
- Ignition switch—the main control device for the starting system.
- **Starter**—a high-torque electric motor that cranks the engine.
- **Starter relay**—an electrical device that opens or closes a circuit in response to a voltage signal.
- **Starter solenoid**—an electromechanical device that, when connected to an electrical source such as a battery, produces a mechanical movement. Some systems use both a relay and a solenoid.
- PARK/NEUTRAL position switch—a switch that prevents the starter relay or solenoid from closing when the vehicle is in gear.

These parts are used in two separate electrical circuits, a high-current motor circuit (red) and a low-current control circuit (blue). See **Fig. 3-1**. The high current needed to operate the starter (150 amps or more) requires a heavy-gauge cable. It is not practical or safe to route this high-current circuit through the ignition switch and dashboard. Instead, the ignition switch controls a circuit that supplies low current to the starter relay or solenoid. The contacts of the relay or solenoid control the high-current path to the starter. When the contacts close, the starter connects directly to the battery.

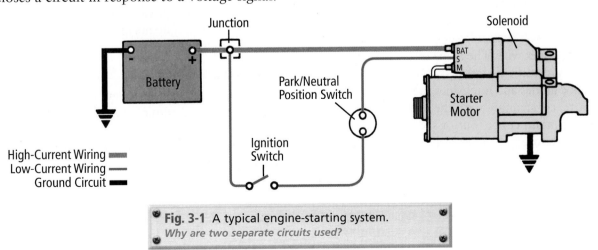

Junction

Solenoid

BAT
S
M

Battery

Park/Neutral
Position Switch

Starter
Motor

High-Current Wiring
Low-Current Wiring
Ground Circuit

Ignition
Switch

General Motors Corporation

Fig. 3-1 A typical engine-starting system.
Why are two separate circuits used?

A PARK/NEUTRAL position switch in the low-current circuit controls starter operation. This switch prevents the relay or solenoid from operating with the vehicle in gear. The gear selector of an automatic transmission must be in PARK or NEUTRAL. A clutch-pedal operated switch is used with a manual transmission.

The battery is the source of electric current to operate the starter. The low- and high-current circuits control where and when the current flows. The starter converts this current into the mechanical torque (turning power) needed to crank the engine.

With the ignition switch in the start position, low current flows from the battery. It flows through the ignition switch and the PARK/NEUTRAL position switch to the starter relay or solenoid. This closes the contacts in the relay or solenoid and completes a high-current path from the battery to the starter. With current applied, the starter cranks the engine.

Crankshaft rotation brings air and fuel into the engine's cylinders. A high-voltage spark, created at the spark plugs, ignites the air/fuel mixture in the cylinders. Power from the burning fuel in the cylinders provides the energy to maintain engine operation.

Starter Construction

A starter is a high-torque electric motor that converts electrical energy from the battery into mechanical energy to crank the engine. Advances in technology have changed the construction of some starters. Their new design makes them smaller, lighter, and more powerful. They require less current by using permanent magnets instead of field coils. They use internal gear reduction to increase cranking torque.

Field Coil Starter

A field coil starter contains two basic assemblies: an armature and field coils. See **Fig. 3-2**. The field coils are mounted in the starter housing. An electromagnet consists of a soft iron pole shoe (core) wrapped with a coil of copper wire. The field coil is an electromagnet that produces a stationary magnetic field. The pole shoe guides and intensifies the magnetic field so that it reacts strongly with the armature. Field coil starters contain either four or six field coils.

The **armature** is the part of the starter that rotates. It contains many individual windings (coils). A nonconducting material electrically separates the coils. Current flowing through the coils creates magnetic fields. A laminated iron core increases the strength of the magnetic fields in the armature.

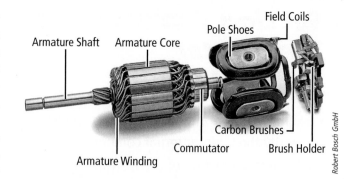

Robert Bosch GmbH

Armature Shaft · Armature Core · Pole Shoes · Field Coils · Carbon Brushes · Commutator · Brush Holder · Armature Winding

Fig. 3-2 Components of the field coil starter: armature shaft, armature winding, armature core, commutator, pole shoes, field coils, carbon brushes, and brush holder.

Tech Tip **Electrical Connections.** Poor electrical connections to the starter or the engine block are often a source of trouble. Poor connections create resistance to current flow through the circuits of the starting system. Low-current flow results in poor cranking performance. Battery terminals may develop a layer of corrosion. Remember to check all cable connections. Terminals must be clean and tight.

The armature mounts on a shaft located inside the starter housing. Bearings support the armature at each end. The smaller the space between the armature and the field magnets, the stronger the magnetic reaction. However, the armature must be able to rotate freely without touching the field magnets.

The **commutator** is a series of copper segments placed side by side to form a ring around the armature shaft. Nonconducting material separates each segment. Two segments, appropriately placed, connect to each end of a coil in the armature. As the armature rotates, carbon brushes ride against the commutator segments and supply current to the armature coils.

Permanent Magnet Starter

Many starters use permanent magnets. A permanent magnet is a ceramic magnetic material. It does not require current flow through a field coil to create its magnetic field. Permanent magnets replace the electromagnetics.

Starter Operation

Electric motors work on the principle of electromagnetism. Electromagnetism occurs when current flowing through a conductor creates an electromagnetic field. An **electromagnetic field** is the space around an electromagnet that is filled with invisible lines of force. The strength of the field depends on the amount of current flow and the number of wires in the coil. Placing an iron core inside the coil also increases field strength.

A basic law of magnetism states that like magnetic poles repel, unlike magnetic poles attract. In a field coil starter, current passing through the field coils creates an electromagnetic field. See **Fig. 3-3**. The same current passes through one brush, into the commutator segment, through the armature coil, out through the other segment, and through another brush to ground.

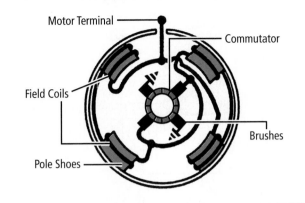

Fig. 3-3 The starter has four field coils, four brushes, and multiple armature windings. *What component is not needed on a permanent magnet starter?*

> **Safety First** **Metallic Objects** When checking cable connections, remove all rings, watches, and jewelry. Severe burns can result if high current is shorted to ground through metallic objects.

Current passing through the armature coils creates another electromagnetic field. As the armature rotates, the brushes and the commutator reverse the direction of the current flow in the armature coils. Reversing the direction of current in each coil reverses the direction of the magnetic field. The magnetic fields in the armature are attracted and repelled by the magnetic field created by the field coils. The action of the magnetic fields makes the armature rotate.

In a permanent magnet starter, current flows only through the armature windings. The permanent magnets provide the stationary magnetic field. The magnetic fields in the armature are attracted and repelled by the magnetic fields created by the permanent magnets.

> **Safety First** **Shorts** A short or short to ground in the high-current circuit can result in a fire and severe vehicle damage.

High current flows to the starter only when the ignition switch is in the START position. As long as current flow exists, the armature continues to rotate. When the ignition switch returns to the run position,

the contacts of the starter relay or solenoid open. No current flows to the starter. Without current flow, the starter armature stops rotating. The starter stops cranking the engine.

Solenoid Starter

The solenoid in a solenoid-operated starter has two functions. See **Fig. 3-4**. It closes the high-current contacts connecting the battery to the starter. It also moves the starter pinion gear assembly into mesh with the ring gear. The ring gear is located on the flywheel or drive plate of the engine. The low-current control circuit energizes the coils of the solenoid.

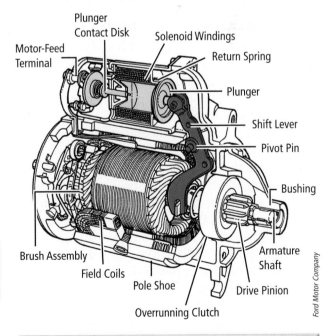

Fig. 3-4 Cutaway view of a solenoid starter. *What are the two functions of the solenoid?*

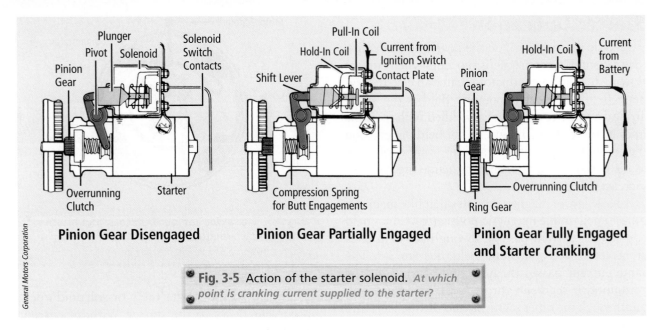

Pinion Gear Disengaged

Pinion Gear Partially Engaged

Pinion Gear Fully Engaged and Starter Cranking

Fig. 3-5 Action of the starter solenoid. *At which point is cranking current supplied to the starter?*

The magnetic field that is created in the starter solenoid coil pulls the plunger into the solenoid. See **Fig. 3-5.** The end of the shift lever, attached to the plunger, moves in the same direction. As the plunger moves, the shift lever moves the pinion gear assembly on the armature shaft toward the ring gear. Electrical contacts at the base of the plunger close when the pinion and ring gears fully mesh. The closed contacts provide a current path between the battery and the starter. The starter begins to crank the engine.

Relay and Solenoid Starters

Some manufacturers use both a relay and a solenoid. See **Fig. 3-6.** Low current applied to the relay coil pulls the relay plunger into the center of the coil. Contacts on the relay plunger connect low current to the solenoid coil.

Low current applied to the solenoid coil energizes the solenoid. The energized coil pulls the solenoid plunger into the center of the solenoid coil. Electrical contacts connected to the base of the solenoid plunger close when the pinion and ring gear mesh. The closed contacts provide a high current path between the battery and the starter.

Typical service problems with relays and solenoids may include burned or pitted contacts and binding of the plunger assembly. Defective relays and solenoids are replaced. A chattering or buzzing from a relay, solenoid, or starter is an indication of low battery current or high resistance in the circuit.

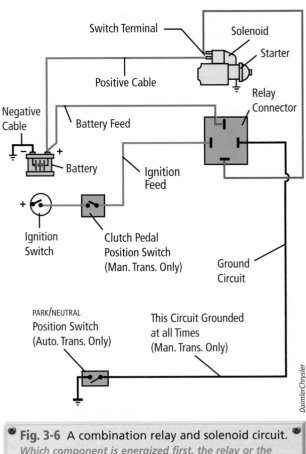

Fig. 3-6 A combination relay and solenoid circuit. *Which component is energized first, the relay or the solenoid?*

Excellence in Science

Demonstrating Magnetism

An engine's starting system—battery, solenoid, and starter—uses electricity and magnetic force. Electric current flows through the coils of the solenoid. This creates a magnetic field that produces movement that closes contacts to complete a circuit. The current from the battery can now crank the engine.

But how does a solenoid work?

When electric current flows through a wire, it creates a magnetic field around the wire. **Figure A** shows current flowing through a single loop, or coil, of wire. The small blue arrows show the direction of the magnetic field. Note that the lines of magnetic force all flow in the same direction in the center of the wire loop. That's where the field is concentrated.

If you wind the wire into a coil of many loops to make a solenoid, the magnetic fields are added together. The more loops in a solenoid's coil, the stronger its magnetic field. An iron core in the coil's center will increase magnetic strength.

When the solenoid is energized, magnetic forces will attract or repel this core, or plunger, causing movement. This movement will close contacts in the starter circuit.

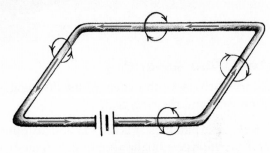

Fig. A

Apply It!

Constructing an Electromagnet

Meets NATEF Science Standards for electrical circuitry, grounding, voltage, current, resistance, and magnetism.

Materials and Equipment
- Digital multimeter
- No. 36 copper wire (plain enamel magnet wire), 25–30' [8–9 m]
- DC power supply: regulated and fused, low voltage, variable (0–12 volts, 0.5 amps)
- Magnetic compass
- Coil core: a large iron nail or steel bolt
- Insulating tape

1. Wrap a layer of insulating tape around the coil core. Wind the insulated magnet wire around the coil core in closely spaced turns. Avoid overlapping the windings.

2. Tape the first and last turn to the coil core. Strip the insulation from each end of the wire.

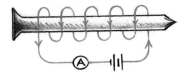

3. Make sure the power supply is turned off. Connect a digital multimeter, Ⓐ, in series with the coil and the power supply. Set the multimeter to measure current.

4. Hold a compass near the end of the coil. What happens?

5. Turn on the power supply. Repeat Step 4 with the voltage set at 1 volt. Observe the magnetic force of the electromagnet on the compass needle.

6. Reverse and increase the current. Observe. What happens to the compass needle?

Robert Bosch GmbH

Fig. 3-7 The pinion gear meshes with and drives the ring gear. *Where is the ring gear located?*

Pinion Gear

Ring Gear

Starter Drive Assembly

The starter drive assembly engages and disengages the pinion gear and the ring gear.

Pinion Gear The pinion gear is the smallest gear in a gear set. The pinion gear on the armature shaft meshes with the larger ring gear on the flywheel or drive plate of the engine. See **Fig. 3-7**. The ring gear has about fifteen times as many teeth as the pinion gear. The pinion gear must rotate fifteen times to rotate the ring gear one time. If the starter operates at 3,000 rpm, it will crank the engine at 200 rpm.

Overrunning Clutch The **overrunning clutch** prevents the engine from driving the starter. See **Fig. 3-8**. As the engine starts, its speed may rapidly increase to 2,000 rpm or higher. If the pinion gear remained engaged with the ring gear, the starter's armature would rotate at 30,000 rpm! The armature would break apart at such speed. The overrunning clutch transmits torque only in one direction. It rotates freely in the opposite direction, preventing armature damage.

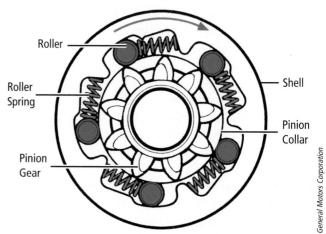

Roller

Roller Spring

Pinion Gear

Shell

Pinion Collar

General Motors Corporation

Fig. 3-8 A cutaway view of an overrunning clutch with pinion gear. Note the notches in the shell. *What makes the overrunning clutch unlock?*

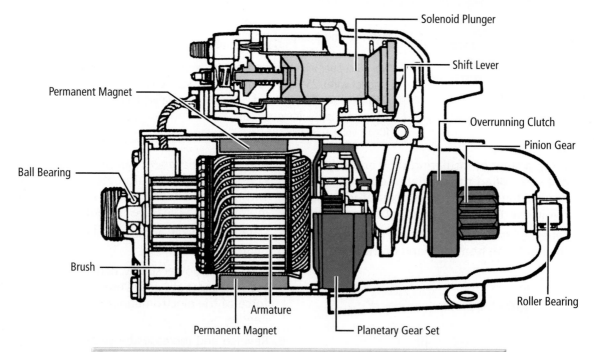

Solenoid Plunger

Shift Lever

Permanent Magnet

Overrunning Clutch

Pinion Gear

Ball Bearing

Brush

Armature

Planetary Gear Set

Permanent Magnet

Roller Bearing

General Motors Corporation

Fig. 3-9 A cutaway view of a permanent magnet starter with internal gear reduction. *Why does this starter have a gear ratio of 45:1?*

During starter operation, rotation of the armature forces the rollers into the small end of the notches in the clutch shell. This action locks the clutch to transmit cranking torque to the engine. As the engine starts, ring gear rotation turns the pinion and clutch shell faster than the armature. The roller springs force the rollers into the large end of the shell notches. The overrunning clutch unlocks, removing cranking torque, allowing the pinion gear to spin freely until it disengages.

Gear Reduction and Cranking Torque The forces of friction and compression require high torque to crank the engine. Torque is affected by starter design and by the gear ratio between the pinion and the ring gear. A **gear ratio** expresses the number of rotations one gear must make to rotate a driven gear one time. If the starter connects directly to the crankshaft, the gear ratio is 1:1. A direct connection does not supply enough torque to crank the engine.

TECH TIP **Pinion Gear Teeth.** Check the pinion gear for broken or chipped teeth before installing the starter. Improper alignment of the pinion to the ring gear may be the cause of such damage, and a shim may be required.

Gear reduction increases starter torque by increasing the gear ratio. In our example starter, the pinion gear and ring gear form an external reduction gear set. The pinion gear must rotate fifteen times to rotate the ring gear one time, for a ratio of 15:1.

Some starters use a combination of internal and external gear reduction to increase torque. See **Fig. 3-9.** Internal gear reduction is supplied by planetary gears. See **Fig. 3-10.** External gear reduction is supplied by the starter pinion gear and the engine ring gear. The combination of internal and external gear reduction provides a much higher gear ratio, for example 45:1. The pinion gear must rotate forty-five times to rotate the ring gear one revolution.

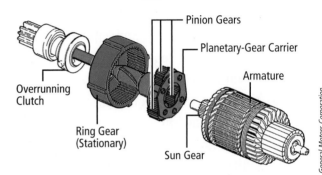

Pinion Gears

Planetary-Gear Carrier

Armature

Overrunning Clutch

Ring Gear (Stationary)

Sun Gear

General Motors Corporation

Fig. 3-10 An exploded view of a starter using planetary gear reduction. *Why is gear reduction used?*

SECTION 1 KNOWLEDGE CHECK

1. Name the six major parts of the typical starting system.

2. What does the starter do?

3. What is an armature?

4. What are the two functions of a solenoid in a solenoid-operated starter?

5. How many times must a pinion gear rotate to rotate the ring gear once?

6. Why would a starter use a combination of internal and external gear reduction?

ASE TEST PREP

7. Technician A says that the source of current for the starting system is the starter. Technician B says that the source of current for the starting system is the battery. Who is correct?

ⓐ Technician A.

ⓑ Technician B.

ⓒ Both Technician A and Technician B.

ⓓ Neither Technician A nor Technician B.

Section 2
Diagnosing the Starting System

Objectives:

A16 ● Inspect and test switches, connectors, relays, solenoid, solid state devices, and wires of electrical/electronic circuits; perform necessary action.

A9 ● Measure source voltage and perform voltage drop tests in electrical/electronic circuits using a voltmeter; determine necessary action.

A13 ● Locate shorts, grounds, opens, and resistance problems in electrical/electronic circuits; determine necessary action.

C6 ● Differentiate between electrical and engine mechanical problems that cause a slow-crank or no-crank condition.

C1 ● Perform starter current draw tests; determine necessary action.

C2 ● Perform starter circuit voltage drop tests; determine necessary action.

C5 ● Inspect and test switches, connectors, and wires of starter control circuits; perform necessary action.

C3 ● Inspect and test starter relays and solenoids; determine necessary action.

C4 ● Remove and install starter in a vehicle.

Vocabulary:
● **cranking voltage/ current draw test**
● **voltage drop test**

Starting System Tests

The three basic starting system complaints are:
● The engine does not crank.
● The engine cranks slowly but does not start.
● The starter operates but does not crank the engine.

Many starting system problems are diagnosed by looking and listening when cranking the engine. See **Table 3-A.**
● Does the relay or solenoid chatter?
● Do the headlights or interior lights dim heavily or go out?
● Does the engine crank at a normal speed?

Cranking Voltage/Current Draw Test

The **cranking voltage/current draw test** measures battery voltage and current during engine cranking. See **Fig. 3-11.** Make sure the battery is fully charged

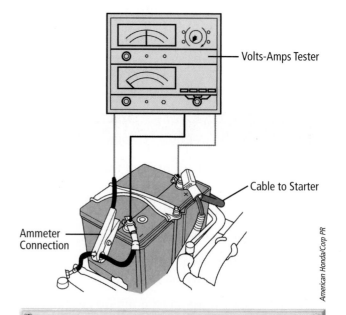

Volts-Amps Tester

Cable to Starter

Ammeter Connection

American Honda/Corp PR

Fig. 3-11 The cranking voltage/current draw test measures battery voltage and current during engine cranking. *Why must the ignition or fuel system be disabled?*

Table 3-A	DIAGNOSING THE STARTING SYSTEM	
Complaint	**Possible Cause**	**Check or Correction**
1. No cranking, lights stay bright	**a.** Open circuit in ignition switch **b.** Open circuit in starter **c.** Open in control circuit **d.** Open fusible link	**a.** Check switch contacts and connections **b.** Check commutator, brushes, and connections **c.** Check solenoid or relay, switch, and connections **d.** Correct condition causing link to blow; replace link
2. No cranking, lights dim heavily	**a.** Trouble in engine **b.** Battery low **c.** Very low temperature **d.** Frozen armature bearing, short in starter	**a.** Check engine to find trouble **b.** Check, recharge, or replace battery **c.** Battery must be fully charged, with engine, wiring circuits, and starter in good condition **d.** Repair or replace starter
3. No cranking, lights dim slightly	**a.** Faulty or slipping drive **b.** Excessive resistance or open circuit in starter	**a.** Replace parts **b.** Clean commutator; replace brushes; repair poor connections
4. No cranking, lights go out	**a.** Poor connections, probably at battery	**a.** Clean cable clamp and terminal; tighten clamp
5. No cranking, no lights	**a.** Battery dead **b.** Open circuit	**a.** Recharge or replace battery **b.** Clean and tighten connections; replace wiring
6. Engine cranks slowly but does not start	**a.** Battery run down **b.** Very low temperature **c.** Starter defective **d.** Undersized battery cables or battery **e.** Mechanical trouble in engine **f.** Battery has run down trying to start vehicle	**a.** Check, recharge, or replace battery **b.** Battery must be fully charged, with engine, wiring circuits, and starter in good condition **c.** Repair or replace starter **d.** Install cables or battery of adequate size **e.** Check engine **f.** See item 8
7. Engine cranks at normal speed, but does not start	**a.** Ignition system defective **b.** Fuel system defective **c.** Air leaks in intake system **d.** Engine defective	**a.** Make spark test; check timing and ignition system **b.** Check fuel pump, fuel line, or fuel delivery system **c.** Tighten mountings and fittings; replace gaskets as needed **d.** Check compression, valve timing, etc.
8. Relay or solenoid chatters	**a.** Relay or solenoid defective **b.** Low battery **c.** Burned relay or solenoid contacts	**a.** Replace relay or solenoid **b.** Charge battery **c.** Replace relay or solenoid
9. Pinion disengages slowly after starting	**a.** Sticking solenoid plunger **b.** Overrunning clutch sticks on armature shaft **c.** Overrunning clutch defective **d.** Shift lever return spring weak	**a.** Repair or replace solenoid **b.** Clean armature shaft and clutch sleeve **c.** Replace clutch **d.** Repair or replace starter
10. Unusual noises	**a.** High-pitched whine during cranking (before engine starts) **b.** High-pitched whine after engine starts as ignition key is released **c.** Loud buzzing or siren sound after engine starts **d.** Rumble, growl, or knock after engine starts, and starter is coasting to a stop	**a.** Too much clearance between pinion gear and ring gear **b.** Too little clearance between pinion gear and ring gear **c.** Defective overrunning clutch **d.** Bent or unbalanced armature

before beginning the test. Low cranking voltage may indicate a bad battery, bad starter, or poor cable connections. To perform the test:

1. Disable the ignition or fuel system to prevent starting. Refer to the manufacturer's service manual.
2. Connect a voltmeter across the battery terminals.
3. Connect the ammeter current probe around the cable to the starter.
4. Turn the ignition switch to the START position.
5. Crank the engine 5–10 seconds and note the voltage and current readings.
6. Release the ignition switch.
   Cranking voltage is normal if:
   • The voltage reading is 9 volts or higher at 70°F [21°C].
   • The engine cranks normally.

Cranking voltage is not normal if:
• The voltage is below 9 volts.
Cranking current is normal if:
• The current draw is between 140–200 amps.
The readings vary with starter size, engine size, and engine compression ratio. Consult the manufacturer's service manual for specified values. Readings higher or lower than specified may indicate a faulty starter. If abnormal results are obtained:
• Check for resistance in the high-current circuit, the electrical cables, battery terminals, and ground connections. In testing the battery, use an electronic battery/starting/charging system tester.

Voltage Drop Test

The **voltage drop test** checks for high resistance across a cable, component, or connection. This test is performed while cranking the engine. Resistance reduces voltage. A voltage drop across any component reduces the available cranking voltage. See **Fig. 3-12.** Normal voltage drop readings should be less than 0.5 volts. Excessive voltage drop indicates high resistance at the point of measurement. Resistance may be due to loose or damaged connections, undersized cables, or burned contacts. Consult the manufacturer's service manual for specified values.

To perform the voltage drop test:
1. Disable the ignition or fuel system. Refer to the manufacturer's service manual.
2. Connect the voltmeter leads across each cable, switch, component, and connection in the circuit.
3. Hold the ignition switch to the START position.
4. Note the voltage reading across each component.
5. Compare with manufacturer's specifications.

Excellence in Math

Calculating Resistance

Mr. Jackson's truck does not start. You turn on the headlights, and they appear normal. When you try to crank the engine, it turns over slowly. You check the battery connections, and they feel solid, even though there is a layer of corrosion. Because the headlights burned brightly, you feel the battery is okay.

You suspect the problem is excessive resistance somewhere in the circuit. This could be caused by a loose or corroded connection. You decide to perform a voltage drop test for excessive resistance. You will measure the voltage drop across each connection while trying to start the engine. Then you decide to calculate the resistance and the power loss at each connection.

You perform the voltage drop test by measuring the voltage between the battery terminal post and the cable clamp while cranking the engine. You also connect an ammeter clamp around the cable to the starter. With a cranking current of 150 amps, you measure 1 volt between the terminal post and the cable clamp.

You calculate the resistance across that connection by using Ohm's law.

$$R = \frac{E}{I} = \frac{1 \text{ volt}}{150 \text{ amps}} = 0.006 \text{ ohms}$$

You can calculate the power being lost in the connection by using the formula:

Power $= I \times E = 1 \times 150 = 150$ watts

This 150 watts of power will appear as heat in the resistance of the connection. This heat may further deteriorate the already poor connection. The heat is power that did not reach the starter. It may be part of the reason for the engine's slow cranking.

Apply It!

Meets NATEF Mathematics Standards for formulas, decimals, symbols, estimating, and determining exact values.

When you test the same connection in a van, you measure a voltage drop of 0.15 volts for a 150–amp starting current.

1. Use the measured voltage for the van to calculate the resistance across the connection. Compare your result for the van with the calculated resistance for Mr. Jackson's truck.

2. Check the instructions for the voltage drop test in this chapter. Which vehicle's voltage drop reading indicates excessive resistance?

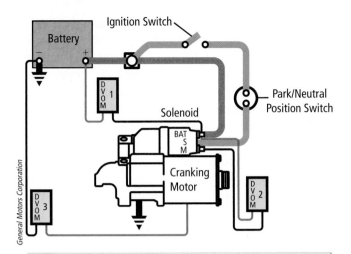

General Motors Corporation

Fig. 3-12 The voltage drop test checks for excessive voltage drop across each component. *Why is current flow needed to make voltage checks?*

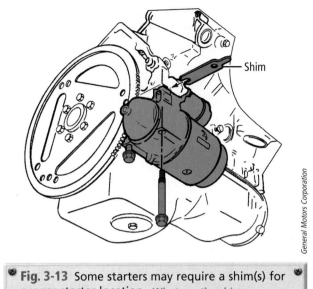

General Motors Corporation

Fig. 3-13 Some starters may require a shim(s) for proper starter location. *What are the shims used for?*

Starter No-Load Bench Test

A starter no-load bench test can be made on some starters after the starter has been removed from the vehicle. To remove the starter:

1. Disconnect the negative battery cable.
2. Raise the vehicle if necessary. Use wheel blocks and jackstands to prevent the vehicle from falling.
3. Disconnect any braces, shields, or parts that interfere with removal.
4. Disconnect the wiring from the starter.
5. Support the starter.
6. Remove the mounting bolts.
7. Notice the location and number of any shims between the starter and the engine. The shims determine the clearance between the pinion and the ring gear. See **Fig. 3-13.** Failure to replace shims may result in improper meshing of the gears.
8. Remove the starter from the vehicle.

To replace the starter, hold it in the proper position. Reinstall any shims that were in place when the starter was removed. Install and tighten starter mounting bolts. Connect the solenoid wires, and then reconnect the negative battery cable.

The no-load test checks for normal armature speed and current draw when a specified voltage is applied.

The test requires the following:
- An ammeter, a voltmeter, or a combination volt-amps tester (VAT).
- A remote starter switch.
- A battery.
- A carbon pile to adjust voltage to the starter (may be part of the VAT).

To perform the starter no-load bench test:
1. Connect the components. See **Fig. 3-14.**
2. Close the remote starter switch.
3. Adjust the carbon pile to obtain the manufacturer's specified no-load voltage.
4. Note the current flow and listen for normal armature rotation.
5. Compare the readings with those found in the manufacturer's specifications. Possible test results:
   - Rated current draw and speed indicate normal operation.

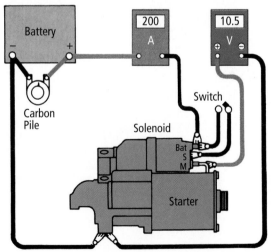

General Motors Corporation

Fig. 3-14 The electrical connections for a starter no-load bench test. *What do the results of the test indicate?*

- Low speed and high-current draw indicate internal friction or shorted armature.
- No speed with high-current draw indicates a grounded component or frozen armature.
- No speed with no current draw indicates an open circuit in the starter or solenoid.

Testing Relays and Solenoids

Failure of an engine to crank when the key is turned to START may be due to a defective relay or solenoid. If no movement of the relay or solenoid plunger can be detected, follow these steps:

- Make sure the battery is good and properly charged.
- Inspect the battery cables and wiring to the starter for damage.
- Make sure the PARK/NEUTRAL position switch is closed. (The shift lever must be in PARK or NEUTRAL or the clutch pedal fully depressed.)
- Have someone attempt to crank the engine. Use a DVOM to check for voltage at the switch (S) terminal of the relay or solenoid.
- If no voltage is present, check the wiring circuit to the switch terminal. This will include the ignition switch and the PARK/NEUTRAL position switch or clutch switch. Repair this circuit as needed.

- If voltage is present, but the plunger does not move, the relay or solenoid is defective. Check the relay winding with an ohmmeter. Disconnect the wire at the switch terminal. Connect one ohmmeter lead to the switch terminal. Connect the other to a bare metal surface on the relay. If the ohmmeter indicates an open circuit, replace the relay.
- A starter solenoid has two windings. Each must be checked separately. This is most easily done with the starter on the bench. Disconnect the heavy connector between the solenoid and the starter. Connect one ohmmeter lead to the switch (S) terminal. Connect the other to the terminal that was connected to the starter. See **Fig. 3-15(a)**. Next connect the ohmmeter leads from the "S" terminal to the solenoid case. See **Fig. 3-15(b)**. If either ohmmeter reading indicates an open circuit, replace the solenoid.

If the relay or solenoid plunger does move, but cranking is slow, the problem may be high resistance in the main cranking circuit. Measure voltage drop to determine whether high resistance is present. If the voltage drop across the relay or solenoid contacts is higher than specified (usually about 0.3 volt), replacement is required.

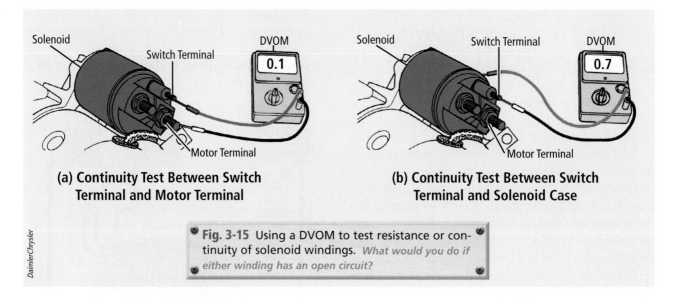

(a) Continuity Test Between Switch Terminal and Motor Terminal

(b) Continuity Test Between Switch Terminal and Solenoid Case

DaimlerChrysler

Fig. 3-15 Using a DVOM to test resistance or continuity of solenoid windings. *What would you do if either winding has an open circuit?*

Starter Service

Most starters are relatively maintenance-free. However, they may fail with use. Most service facilities install a new or remanufactured starter when service is needed. Rebuilding starters is not a common service practice. However, if replacement is not an option, it may be possible to rebuild a starter. See **Fig. 3-16.**

Major steps in rebuilding a starter may include the following:
- Replacing armature bearings and bushings.
- Testing the armature and field coils.
- Resurfacing the commutator.
- Replacing defective field coils.
- Replacing worn brushes.
- Replacing the overrunning clutch.
- Replacing electrical contacts in the solenoid.
- Lubricating the splines, shafts, and bearings.
- Checking the pinion clearance.
- Bench testing performance.

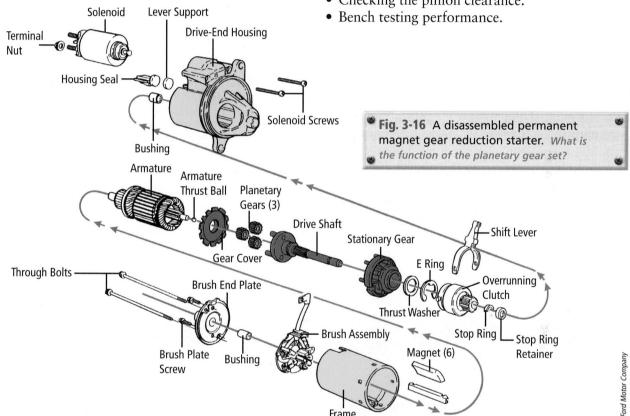

Fig. 3-16 A disassembled permanent magnet gear reduction starter. *What is the function of the planetary gear set?*

Ford Motor Company

SECTION 2 KNOWLEDGE CHECK

1. What are the three basic starting system complaints?

2. Name two reasons an engine may crank slowly but not start.

3. What may be the cause of a loud buzzing or siren sound after the engine starts?

4. What is a voltage drop test?

5. What is needed to perform a no-load bench test?

6. Explain how to perform a no-load bench test.

ASE TEST PREP

7. Technician A says that low cranking voltage can indicate a bad battery. Technician B says that low cranking voltage can indicate poor cable connections. Who is correct?
   ⓐ Technician A.
   ⓑ Technician B.
   ⓒ Both Technician A and Technician B.
   ⓓ Neither Technician A nor Technician B.

CHAPTER 3 REVIEW

Key Points

Meets the following NATEF Standards for Electrical/Electronic Systems: starter testing; starter removal and replacement.

- The battery supplies electrical current to the starter through the relay or solenoid contacts.
- Though similar in operation, field coil and permanent magnet starters differ in construction.
- The starter armature rotates because the magnetic field of the field coils or permanent magnets repels the magnetic field of the armature.
- The pinion gear and ring gear provide a gear ratio of 15:1.
- An overrunning clutch transmits starter torque in only one direction.
- Relay and solenoid windings can be checked with an ohmmeter.
- The cranking voltage/current draw test measures battery voltage and current during engine cranking.
- The voltage drop test checks for high resistance across a cable, component, or connection.

Review Questions

1. Describe a commutator.
2. What happens to the armature when the ignition switch returns to RUN?
3. What part prevents the engine from driving the starter?
4. What is the smallest gear in the gear set?
5. If a starter operates at 2250 rpm, at what rpm will it crank the engine?
6. What affects cranking torque?
7. What type of test measures battery voltage and current during engine cranking?
8. What are normal voltage drop readings?
9. **Critical Thinking** When performing a cranking voltage/current draw test, why should the ignition or fuel system be disabled?
10. **Critical Thinking** Explain how to check both starter solenoid windings.

Excellence in Communication

Ask the Right Questions

To determine a vehicle's problem you need information from your customer. The customer has firsthand knowledge about the vehicle's problem. To gather information from your customer, you need to ask the right questions. The answers to these questions will help you diagnose the vehicle's problem.

Successful technicians are skilled at asking questions that lead to the source of the problem. Specific questions related to Who, What, When, Where, and How should be the basis for your investigation. When you read the "Customer's Concern" at the beginning of this chapter, did you notice that you needed to find out when the vehicle does not start? You will need to ask questions, such as, "Does this happen all the time?" Finally, you will have enough information to begin your diagnosis.

Apply It!

Meets NATEF Communications Standards for speaking, verbal cues, and oral information.

Read again the "Customer's Concern" at the beginning of this chapter.

1. Make a list of questions you might ask the customer to help you diagnose the problem with her vehicle.
2. Share your list with your team members. Ask for their comments on your questions.
3. Make a list of key questions to ask customers. This will be a valuable resource for you on the job.

AUTOMOTIVE SERVICE EXCELLENCE
TEST PREP

Answering the following practice questions will help you prepare for the ASE certification tests.

1. The components of a field coil starter do not include which of the following:

   a a commutator.

   b field coils.

   c armature winding.

   d permanent magnet.

2. Technician A says that a commutator is a series of copper segments placed side by side to form a ring around the armature shaft. Technician B says this description actually refers to pole shoes. Who is correct?

   a Technician A.

   b Technician B.

   c Both Technician A and Technician B.

   d Neither Technician A nor Technician B.

3. Where does a starter's pinion gear connect to the engine?

   a Powertrain control module (PCM).

   b Flywheel.

   c Camshaft.

   d Timing chain.

4. Technician A says that the overrunning clutch is responsible for the proper gear ratio. Technician B says that the overrunning clutch keeps the engine from cranking the starter and destroying it. Who is correct?

   a Technician A.

   b Technician B.

   c Both Technician A and Technician B.

   d Neither Technician A nor Technician B.

5. If the pinion gear on a starter rotates 60 times to turn the flywheel 10 times, what is the gear ratio?

   a 10:1.

   b 10:6.

   c 6:1.

   d 8:3.

6. Technician A says that the starting system may be malfunctioning if the engine does not crank. Technician B says the starting system may be malfunctioning if the engine cranks slowly but does not start. Who is correct?

   a Technician A.

   b Technician B.

   c Both Technician A and Technician B.

   d Neither Technician A nor Technician B.

7. What should you do before performing a cranking voltage/current draw test?

   a Make sure the battery is fully charged.

   b Make sure the battery is fully discharged.

   c Remove the starter from the vehicle.

   d Connect a test light to the starter.

8. Technician A says that a voltage drop test checks the current flowing to the starter. Technician B says that a voltage drop test checks for high resistance across a cable, component, or connection. Who is correct?

   a Technician A.

   b Technician B.

   c Both Technician A and Technician B.

   d Neither Technician A nor Technician B.

9. Which of the following tools is not necessary to perform a starter no-load bench test?

   a Ammeter.

   b Voltmeter.

   c Combination volt-amps tester (VAT).

   d Oscilloscope.

10. Technician A says that the two starter windings must be checked separately. Technician B says that the two starter windings can be checked simultaneously. Who is correct?

   a Technician A.

   b Technician B.

   c Both Technician A and Technician B.

   d Neither Technician A nor Technician B.

Section 1
Charging System Components and Operation

Section 2
Charging System Testing and Service

Diagnosing & Repairing the Charging System

Customer's Concern

When you arrived to open the service center this morning, you were not-so-warmly greeted by Dave Murphy. Since having his SUV at your facility, he has noticed some strange noises coming through his radio speakers. Just last week, your technician, Janine, performed the manufacturer's suggested 75,000-mile service on Dave's vehicle.

The service records indicate that Janine performed a standard oil change, topped off vital fluids, replaced the serpentine belt, rotated the tires, tested the battery, changed the spark plugs, and installed a new air cleaner filter. At first glance, the records do not indicate a relation between last week's service visit and Dave's recent radio static. Unfortunately, that does not help Dave.

Technician's Challenge

As the service technician, you need to find answers to these questions:

1. What additional service, if any, did Janine perform on the SUV that may not have been included in the service records?

2. Could any of the recorded service tasks cause noise to filter through Dave's radio speakers? Are the noise and the recent service visit simply a coincidence?

3. Research the applicable vehicle and service information. What parts of the electrical or charging system could be to blame for the noise? How will you solve this problem?

Section 1
Charging System Components and Operation

Objectives:
- Identify the four main parts of the charging system.
- Explain how a generator works.

Vocabulary:
- rotor
- slip rings
- brush
- stator windings
- rectification
- voltage regulator

Charging System Components

The charging system supplies all current needed for vehicle operation, lights, and accessories while the engine is running. It should also supply enough current to keep the battery charged.

When the engine is not running, the battery alone supplies the current needed for cranking, ignition, fuel injection, and all other electrical loads. The battery also supplies current when the engine is running if electrical loads are higher than the generator output. If the generator fails, the battery is the only source of current.

The charging system includes a generator, voltage regulator, system wiring, and the battery. A gauge or warning light on the instrument panel allows the driver to monitor the system. See **Fig. 4-1.**

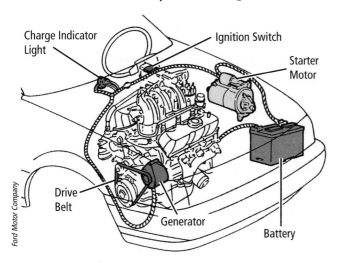

Fig. 4-1 A typical charging system. *Which parts shown are not part of the charging system?*

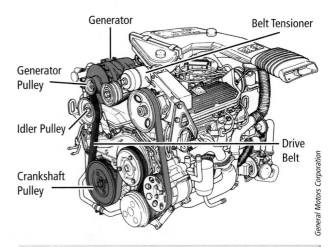

General Motors Corporation

Fig. 4-2 Generator mounting and drive-belt arrangement on an engine. Notice the difference in diameter between the crankshaft pulley and the generator pulley. *Why is it important that the generator rotor turn faster than the engine?*

Today's charging systems use an alternating current (AC) generator. At one time they were called alternators. Before the early 1960s most vehicles had direct current (DC) generators. DC generators are still found on older vehicles.

The engine supplies the mechanical energy to drive the generator. Serpentine belts (or the older V-belts) transfer power from the engine to the generator. See **Fig. 4-2.** These belts are made of rubber reinforced with fiberglass or nylon cords for strength. Idler, or tension, pulleys maintain a constant tension on the belt to prevent slippage under load.

The drive ratio between the pulleys is about 3:1 (three to one). This means the generator rotor turns three revolutions for one crankshaft revolution.

Excellence in Science

Demonstrating Generator Action

You are driving—and suddenly the generator fails. The charging system warning light comes on! What happens if you ignore these warnings? Eventually, the battery goes dead and the engine stops running! A dead battery with no generator to charge it cannot supply the voltage to run the engine. Your generator is necessary for continued vehicle operation.

A generator is basically the opposite of a starter motor. In a starter motor, a magnetic field and a coil (armature) convert current into a rotational torque that cranks the engine. In an automotive generator, a magnetic field and a coil (rotor) convert the torque of the engine into a voltage (and current) in another coil (stator). The voltage in the stator coil produces current flow in the charging system.

Here is a simple experiment you can do to demonstrate generator action.

Apply It!

Inducing a Current in a Coil

Meets NATEF Science Standards for generators.

Materials and Equipment
- 50 feet [15m] of 24-gauge insulated copper wire
- Multimeter with DC milliamp/microamp scale
- Ceramic block magnet (about 0.4″ × 0.9″ × 1.9″ [about 9 mm × 22 mm × 48 mm])
- Electrical tape

1. Set the multimeter on the most sensitive DC-current scale.

2. Loosely wind the wire around your hand in a coil of about 3″ [7.6 cm] in diameter. Lay the coil of wire flat on a table.

3. Wrap a length of tape around the right side of the coil to keep it wound. Wrap another length of tape around the left side of the coil.

4. Scrape about 1″ [2.5 cm] of the insulation from each end of the wire. Attach the multimeter leads to the ends of the wire.

5. Hold the magnet very near one side of the coil without moving it. Make sure the magnet is either face down or face up. Observe that no current is induced as long as the magnet is stationary.

6. Quickly move the magnet to the right. Note that a small amount of current is generated.

7. Stop the magnet. Notice that again no current is generated.

8. Move the magnet back to the left. Notice that current is generated, but the needle moves in the opposite direction.

The higher rotor speed allows the generator to supply electrical power even at low engine speeds. If the drive ratio was too high, the generator would self-destruct at high engine speeds.

Generator Construction

A generator works on the principle of electromagnetic induction. When a moving magnetic field cuts across stationary conductors, an electrical pressure (voltage) is induced in the conductors. This voltage will produce current flow if there is a complete circuit.

The amount of voltage induced in the conductors depends on three factors:
- The strength of the magnetic field.
- The number of stationary conductors.
- The speed at which the magnetic field cuts across the conductors.

Rotor Assembly The **rotor** is the part of the generator that is rotated by the drive belt. It creates the rotating magnetic field of the generator. At the center of a rotor is an iron shaft and core. The shaft is supported on both ends by bearings in the generator housing. Many loops (turns) of small wire are wound around the iron core. This winding is called the rotor field coil because current flow through the coil creates a magnetic field.

The ends of the rotor field coil windings are connected to the slip rings. **Slip rings** are a series of copper segments that allow current to flow through the field coil while it rotates. Small carbon brushes ride on the slip rings. A **brush** is a block of conducting material, such as carbon. It rests against the rotating ring to form a continuous electric circuit. These brushes connect the field circuit wiring to the field coil.

Soft iron pole pieces are assembled over the ends of the field coil. The iron core and pole pieces concentrate and direct the magnetic field produced by the field coil. A typical rotor may have six north and six south poles. When assembled, every other pole has the opposite magnetic polarity. See **Fig. 4-3**.

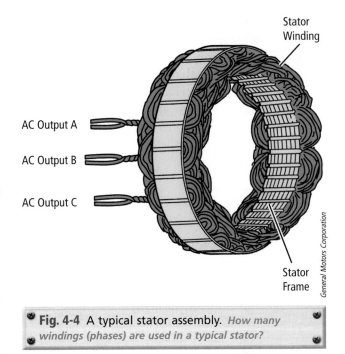

General Motors Corporation

Fig. 4-4 A typical stator assembly. *How many windings (phases) are used in a typical stator?*

Stator windings may be connected in two different ways. The wiring diagram for a wye-connected stator resembles the letter Y. The three windings have one common connection. The wiring diagram for a delta-connected stator is a triangle. In this case there is no common connection. However, pairs of windings are connected at three points. The two types of stators operate in the same manner. Three windings provide a stable voltage output from the generator. See **Fig. 4-5**.

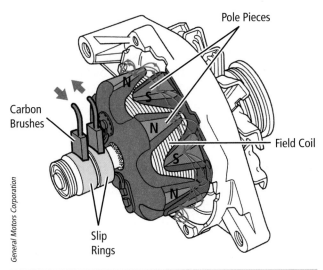

General Motors Corporation

Fig. 4-3 A typical generator rotor assembly. *What are the ends of the field-coil windings connected to?*

Stator Assembly The **stator windings** are the stationary conductors in a generator. The rotor spins inside the stator assembly. Stators usually have three separate windings, or phases. The three windings are equally spaced inside an iron core called the stator frame. See **Fig. 4-4**.

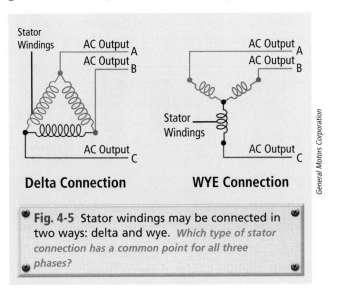

Delta Connection   **WYE Connection**

General Motors Corporation

Fig. 4-5 Stator windings may be connected in two ways: delta and wye. *Which type of stator connection has a common point for all three phases?*

Diodes Automotive vehicles operate on DC. The output of an AC generator must be rectified (changed) to DC. This is the job of the diode rectifier. A diode is an electrical device that allows current to flow in only one direction. See **Fig. 4-6.** By using two diodes per winding, the AC output of the stator winding is changed to DC. Diodes are either positive or negative, depending on the polarity of the current they conduct.

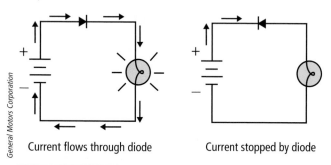

Current flows through diode   Current stopped by diode

General Motors Corporation

Fig. 4-6 A diode permits current flow in only one direction. *How many diodes are used for each winding?*

The three positive diodes are mounted in a small aluminum casting called the positive rectifier (diode) bridge. This bridge is connected to the output (BAT) terminal of the generator. A capacitor is also connected from the bridge to ground. It reduces radio noise and helps to smooth out the voltage pulses from the stator. Three negative diodes are mounted in the negative rectifier bridge. This bridge is grounded at the generator housing. The positive and negative rectifier bridges are assembled together as a unit but they are insulated from each other. See **Fig. 4-7.**

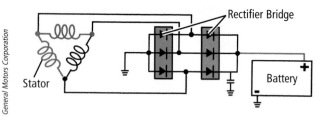

Rectifier Bridge

Stator   Battery

General Motors Corporation

Fig. 4-7 Stator connected to rectifier bridge (diodes). *What type of stator connection is shown?*

Generator Housing The generator housing consists of two aluminum end frames assembled together. The rotor, stator, diodes, bearings, and capacitor are located inside the generator housing. See **Fig. 4-8.**

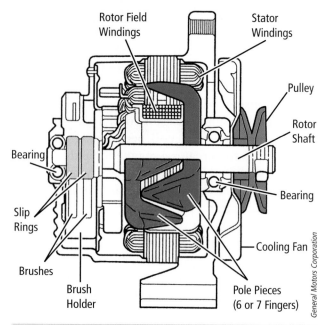

Rotor Field Windings — Stator Windings — Pulley — Rotor Shaft — Bearing — Cooling Fan — Pole Pieces (6 or 7 Fingers) — Bearing — Brushes — Brush Holder — Slip Rings

General Motors Corporation

Fig. 4-8 Cutaway view of a generator. Some components are not visible in this view. *How is the rotor shaft supported?*

Some generators have a voltage regulator located inside or on the back of the housing. The drive pulley and cooling fan are mounted on the rotor shaft at the drive end of the generator.

Generator terminals are located at the slip-ring end of the housing. The output (battery or BAT) terminal is connected by a fairly large wire that leads to the positive battery terminal. Other terminals are used for the field circuit and to monitor or control charging system operation.

Charging System Operation

The generator and voltage regulator work together to produce the current needed by the electrical system. The generator produces the output current. As with a bar magnet, the magnetic fields produced in the rotor of the generator have polarity (north and south). When the magnetic field is not cutting across a stator winding, no voltage is created. See the 0° point in **Fig. 4-9.** When the rotor moves so that a south pole nears one side of a stator winding, a north pole will near the other side of the same winding.

The magnetic fields will induce a voltage that rises from 0 to a maximum value. This happens at 90° of rotation. As the two magnetic poles move past this winding, the induced voltage falls back to 0. At 180° of rotation, no voltage is being induced. This is because the magnetic fields are not cutting across the stator winding in this position.

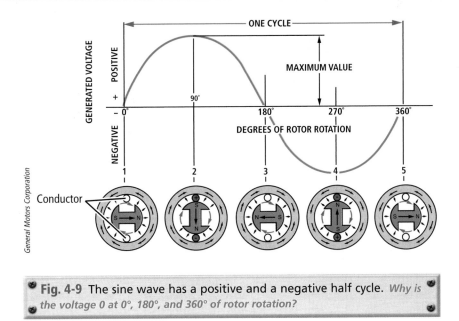

General Motors Corporation

Fig. 4-9 The sine wave has a positive and a negative half cycle. *Why is the voltage 0 at 0°, 180°, and 360° of rotor rotation?*

As rotation continues, the opposite poles will near the same stator winding. Now the pattern will be repeated. However, the induced voltage will be of the opposite polarity. The rotor has turned 270°. With one full revolution, the rotor is back at its starting point. The voltage is again at 0, as it was at 180°. Each movement of a pair of rotor poles past a stator winding will produce a sine wave (AC) voltage pattern.

Because the stator has three separate windings, it produces three separate sine waves or phases. These sine waves are spaced 120° apart. With this arrangement the voltage never drops to 0. As voltage from one phase begins to drop, voltage from the next phase is increasing to the peak value. See **Fig. 4-10.** This provides a more constant voltage output from the stator.

Rectifying AC Voltage

The AC voltage induced in the stator is changed to DC by the diode rectifier. This process is called **rectification.** The diodes allow current flow in one direction only. They route negative voltage pulses through the stator circuit. This ensures that all current at the output terminal flows in the same direction. Current induced in the stator windings is always AC. Current flowing from the output terminal is always DC. The diodes permit both halves of the sine wave to be used. This is called full-wave rectification.

By using 12 magnetic poles in the rotor, three-phase windings in the stator, and full-wave rectification, the output of the generator is almost a smooth DC voltage. The battery and a capacitor in the generator smooth out most of the remaining voltage ripple. See **Fig. 4-11.**

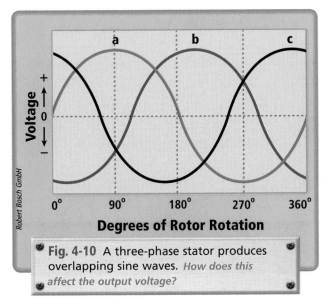

Robert Bosch GmbH

Fig. 4-10 A three-phase stator produces overlapping sine waves. *How does this affect the output voltage?*

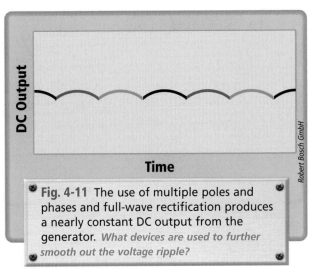

Robert Bosch GmbH

Fig. 4-11 The use of multiple poles and phases and full-wave rectification produces a nearly constant DC output from the generator. *What devices are used to further smooth out the voltage ripple?*

Excellence in Math

Analyzing Sine Waves

Refer to the graph in **Fig. 4-9**. Ask these questions to better understand the graph.

1. What is the initial voltage?

2. What is the voltage at 180° of rotor rotation? At 360°?

3. What is the polarity of the voltage values that are found between 0° and 180°?

4. What is the polarity of the voltage values that are found between 180° and 360°?

5. Would the voltage between 180° and 360° power a battery?

The answers:

1. The initial voltage is 0 V.

2. At 180° and 360°, the graph indicates the voltage is zero.

3. Between 0° and 180°, the voltage is positive.

4. The graph indicates the voltage is negative between 180° and 360°.

5. The voltage is negative. The voltage of the battery must be positive to be used.

Figure A shows the result of adding another waveform starting when the rotor rotation is at 120°.

Now, with the second waveform, there is a positive voltage at 180°. Which areas now represent positive voltage? Which represents a negative voltage?

The areas A and B represent positive voltage. Areas C, D, and E represent negative voltage.

Apply It!

Meets NATEF Mathematics Standards for interpreting graphs, understanding geometric figures, and drawing conclusions.

1. If a third waveform starts 120° after the second wave, the graph in **Fig. 4-10** would result. Is there a positive voltage corresponding to each degree of rotor rotation?

2. In addition, the voltage varies less. The voltage is kept closer to what value?

The graph shown in **Fig. B** illustrates the net effect of generating the three alternating waveforms. Note that the waves are examples of sine waves generated by a sine function. A complete analysis of a sine function requires the study of trigonometry, which is not covered in this text.

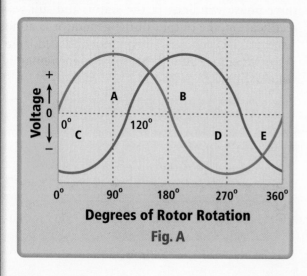

Fig. A

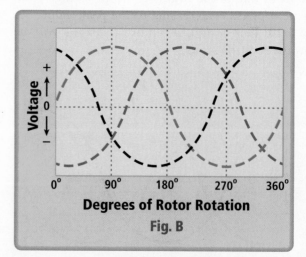

Fig. B

Temperature Compensation

The voltage required to charge a battery varies with battery temperature. It may take almost 16 volts to charge a very cold battery. When the battery is hot, the required voltage is much less. A temperature-sensitive resistor, called a thermistor, is used in most charging systems. It adjusts regulator voltage according to the underhood or battery temperature. The thermistor may be located in the voltage regulator or near the battery. The normal range of charging voltage is from about 13.5 volts (hot) to over 14.5 volts (cold).

Regulating the Generator

Generators can produce enough voltage to seriously damage the electrical system. Voltage output must be limited to prevent overcharging the battery and damaging electrical and electronic components. An electronic **voltage regulator** is a device used to control the generator output voltage. Voltage regulators can be mounted inside the generator, on the back of the generator, or under the hood. See **Fig. 4-12.** On some vehicles the voltage regulator is a part of the powertrain control module (PCM).

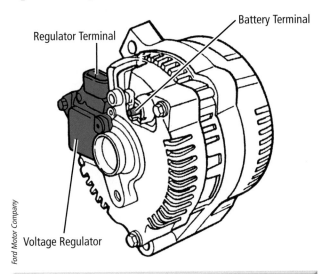

Fig. 4-12 A generator with the regulator mounted on the rear of the housing. *Name two other places the voltage regulator may be located.*

With the engine running, the voltage regulator senses charging system voltage. The normal range is from about 13.5 to 15.0 volts, depending on the underhood temperature. As long as the output is below this range, no regulation is required. When operating conditions cause generator output to reach

the maximum desired voltage, the regulator begins to control rotor field current. Regulating field current controls the strength of the rotor's magnetic field. Reducing field current reduces the strength of the magnetic field. With a weaker magnetic field, voltage output is reduced.

Electronic voltage regulators control field current with a transistor. See **Fig. 4-13.** Turning the transistor on and off very rapidly controls the amount of current flowing through the rotor.

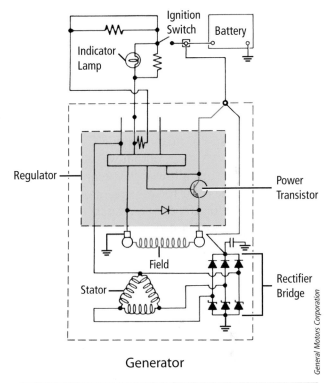

Fig. 4-13 Diagram of a generator with a built-in (integral) voltage regulator. The transistor in the regulator is in series with the field winding. *What is the purpose of the transistor?*

Some regulators control field current by varying the frequency of the current pulses to the rotor. Other regulators use a fixed frequency but vary the "on" time (duty cycle) of the current. In either case, the voltage regulator controls the generator's output by varying the amount of current flowing in the rotor coil.

With high engine speed and low electrical loads, the generator voltage tends to be too high. During these conditions rotor current flow can be on for as little as 10 percent of the time and off for 90 percent. Average field current is low.

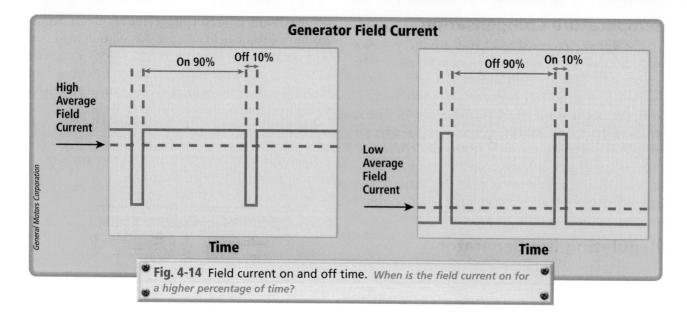

General Motors Corporation

Generator Field Current

On 90% Off 10%

High Average Field Current

Off 90% On 10%

Low Average Field Current

Time

Time

Fig. 4-14 Field current on and off time. *When is the field current on for a higher percentage of time?*

During low-speed, high-load conditions, the reverse is true. Voltage output will be less than the maximum allowed. Current will flow through the rotor for 90 percent of the time and be off for 10 percent. Average field current is high. See **Fig. 4-14.**

Instrument Panel Charge Indicators

Displays on the instrument panel inform the driver when the charging system is not operating normally. These indicators can also be helpful to the technician when diagnosing problems in the system.

Indicator Light

Some vehicles are equipped with a charging system indicator light. The light is operated by the difference between battery voltage and charging voltage. The charging indicator light should come on when the ignition switch is turned on. With the engine running, the lamp will go out if the generator is producing normal voltage output. If generator output is low or zero, the light will be on. On some vehicles the light will also be on if the voltage is higher than normal. The light cannot warn the driver if the voltage is within the normal range but generator current output is lower than it should be. Indicator lights have the advantage of being simple and easy to understand. See **Fig. 4-15.**

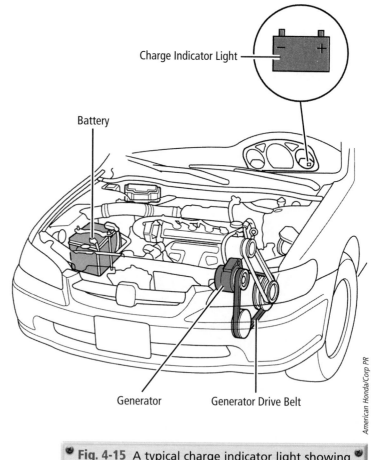

Charge Indicator Light

Battery

Generator   Generator Drive Belt

American Honda/Corp PR

Fig. 4-15 A typical charge indicator light showing the international charging system symbol. *What is the advantage of an indicator light over a meter?*

Some vehicles equipped with charge indicator lights also have a second warning system. The PCM monitors charging system voltage. It will turn on the malfunction indicator lamp (MIL) if certain charging system problems occur. (This lamp may be labeled CHECK ENGINE.) For example, the lamp is turned on and a diagnostic trouble code (DTC) is stored if system voltage is above 16.9 volts for more than 50 seconds. Lamp operation and diagnostic trouble code storage also occur for other charging system problems.

Voltmeter

An instrument panel voltmeter is connected so that it displays voltage in the electrical system. The voltmeter provides a more accurate reading of system activity than does an indicator light.

- With the key off, a dash voltmeter needle will be at the low end of the scale. The meter is not connected until the ignition switch is turned on.
- With the key on and engine off, the voltmeter needle indicates battery voltage. Normally this is between 12 and 13 volts.
- While the engine is cranking, the voltmeter needle may drop to 11 volts or less.
- With the engine running, the voltmeter needle indicates charging system voltage. The normal range is between 13.5 and 14.5 volts, depending on battery condition and underhood temperature. Some dash voltmeters do not display actual voltage. Instead, they show a range of low, normal, and high values.

TECH TIP **Warning Lights.** In some systems the indicator light will not turn on if the generator voltage is too high. In this case the warning light comes on only if the charging system is not producing normal voltage.

HYBRID TECHNOLOGY

Regenerative Braking System

Hybrids save energy in various ways. When a car's brakes are applied, energy is spent. To capture this energy, hybrid automobiles use a regenerative braking system. A regenerative system is a system that is designed to capture and use energy that would otherwise be lost. In this system, the brakes are linked to a generator. This generator uses the kinetic energy, or the energy of the vehicle's motion, to recharge the battery. This recharging occurs whenever the brakes are applied. Without such a system, this energy would be lost, as it is in conventional vehicles.

SECTION 1 KNOWLEDGE CHECK

1. Name the four parts of the charging system.

2. What is the principle on which a generator works?

3. Name the parts that are connected to the rotor field coil windings and allow current to flow through the field coil as it rotates.

4. Describe the two different ways that stator windings may be connected.

5. What makes up the generator housing?

6. What is a voltage regulator?

ASE TEST PREP

7. Technician A says that the stator usually has two different coils of wire. Technician B says that the stator usually has three different coils of wire. Who is correct?

   ⓐ Technician A.

   ⓑ Technician B.

   ⓒ Both Technician A and Technician B.

   ⓓ Neither Technician A nor Technician B.

● Section 2
Charging System Testing and Service

Objectives:

A9 ● Measure source voltage and perform voltage drop tests in electrical/electronic circuits using a voltmeter; determine necessary action.

A13 ● Locate shorts, grounds, opens, and resistance problems in electrical/electronic circuits; determine necessary action.

D3 ● Inspect and adjust, or replace generator (alternator) drive belts; pulleys, and tensioners; check pulley and belt alignment.

A10 ● Measure current flow in electrical/electronic circuits and components using an ammeter; determine necessary action.

D1 ● Perform charging system output test; determine necessary action.

D5 ● Perform charging circuit voltage drop tests; determine necessary action.

D2 ● Diagnose charging system for the cause of undercharge, no-charge, and overcharge conditions.

● Identify possible causes of charging system noise.

D4 ● Remove, inspect, and install generator (alternator).

● Bench test a generator.

Vocabulary:

● **charging voltage test**
● **charging current test**
● **voltage regulator test**
● **memory holder**
● **bench test**

Preliminary Checks

You should perform charging system testing and diagnosis in a logical order. Without a test sequence in mind, you may overlook important clues to system failures.

Before testing the charging system itself, make several checks to determine the overall condition of the charging circuit. Failure to make these checks prior to testing may cause misleading results during testing. Check the following:

1. Inspect the drive belt and check its tension.
2. Start the engine. Observe the charging system indicator on the instrument panel.
3. If the MIL is on, check for charging system related DTCs.
4. Inspect the battery and charging system cables, wires, and connections. Repair as needed.
5. Test the battery for condition and state of charge. Charge or replace if needed.

Check the generator drive-belt condition and tension before testing the output of the charging system. A worn or loose belt will slip, causing generator output to be lower than normal. A damaged belt may break, disabling the water pump, generator, and power steering pump. The air conditioning compressor and cooling fan may also be affected.

Replace any belts that are frayed, torn, or have parts of the V-ribs missing. See **Fig. 4-16**. Also replace belts that slip or squeal even after proper adjustments have been made. Replace V-belts if they are badly glazed (shiny) or worn. A worn belt rides on the bottom instead of the sides of a pulley. Ignore minor cracks on a serpentine drive belt. Cracks are normal and do not interfere with the proper operation of the belt. Belt dressings intended to improve the friction or grip of V-belts should not be used on serpentine belts.

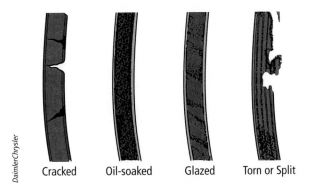

Cracked Oil-soaked Glazed Torn or Split

DaimlerChrysler

Fig. 4-16 A damaged serpentine belt. The cord structure in the belt gives it strength. The V-ribs give it contact area for gripping the pulleys. *What will happen if pieces of the V-ribs are missing?*

Common System Problems

Generator components most likely to fail are the bearings, brushes, and rectifiers. Poor connections in the generator or in the circuit wiring are also common causes of charging system failure.

Table 4-A identifies common charging system problems, possible causes, and suggested checks and corrections.

Checking Drive-Belt Tension

It takes several horsepower to drive a generator at maximum output. Even a good or new belt cannot transmit enough power if it slips due to insufficient tension. If belt tension is too high, there

Table 4-A	Diagnosing the Charging System	
Condition	**Possible Cause**	**Check or Correction**
1. Battery does not stay charged— engine starts okay	a. Battery defective b. Loose or worn generator belt c. Damaged or worn wiring or cables d. Generator defective e. Regulator defective f. Other electrical system malfunction	a. Test battery; replace if necessary b. Adjust or replace belt c. Repair as required d. Test and/or replace components as required e. Test; replace if necessary f. Check other systems for current draw; service as required
2. Generator noisy	a. Loose or worn generator belt b. Bent pulley flanges c. Generator defective d. Loose generator mounting	a. Adjust tension or replace belt b. Replace pulley c. Service or replace generator d. Tighten
3. Lights or fuses burn out frequently	a. Damaged or worn wiring b. Generator or regulator defective c. Battery defective	a. Service as required b. Test, service, and replace if necessary c. Test; replace if necessary
4. Charge indicator light flickers after engine starts or comes on while driving	a. Loose or worn generator belt b. Generator defective c. Field-circuit ground defective d. Regulator defective e. Light circuit wiring or connector defective	a. Adjust tension or replace b. Service or replace c. Service or replace wiring or connection d. Test; replace if necessary e. Repair as required
5. Charge indicator light flickers while driving	a. Loose or worn generator belt b. Loose or improper wiring connections c. Generator defective d. Regulator defective	a. Adjust tension or replace belt b. Service as required c. Service or replace d. Test; replace if necessary
6. Charge indicator meter shows discharge	a. Loose or worn generator belt b. Damaged or worn wiring (grounded or open between generator and battery) c. Field-circuit ground defective d. Generator defective e. Regulator defective f. Meter wiring or connections defective g. Damaged or defective meter h. Other electrical system malfunction	a. Adjust tension or replace belt b. Repair or replace wiring c. Repair or replace wiring d. Service or replace e. Test; replace if necessary f. Service as required g. Replace h. Service as required

will be higher than normal loads on the bearings of the parts being driven. This could cause early bearing failure. The best way to check belt tension is with a belt-tension gauge. This gauge measures the amount of belt deflection under a specified load.

Belt tension is adjusted by first loosening the mounting bolt and lock nut. See **Fig. 4-17**. The adjusting bolt is then adjusted to obtain the desired tension. Other vehicles are similar, but some do not use adjusting bolts. In vehicles without adjusting bolts, the tension is adjusted by carefully prying against the stator frame in the middle of the generator. Do not pry against the end frames. Refer to a service manual for specific adjustment procedures.

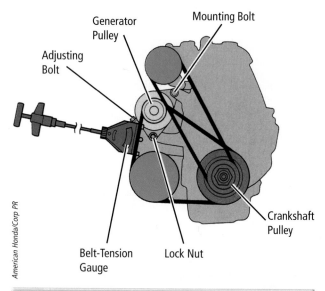

American Honda/Corp PR

Fig. 4-17 The belt-tension gauge measures belt deflection under specified loads. *Why is it important that the generator's drive belt be properly tensioned?*

Some vehicles use an automatic belt tensioner to keep the belt properly adjusted. See **Fig. 4-18**. In normal use, periodic belt-tension adjustments are not necessary. To remove the drive belt, you must release the tension applied by the tensioner. Tension is released by rotating against spring pressure. Check for free movement of the tensioner after the belt is replaced.

Charging System Tests

Four tests may be made to determine whether the charging system is operating normally. They are:

- Charging voltage test.
- Charging current test.
- Voltage regulator test.
- Voltage drop test.

Toyota Motor Manufacturing

Fig. 4-18 Automatic belt tensioners are used on some vehicles. *When is it necessary to release the tension from the belt?*

Charging Voltage Test

The **charging voltage test** determines whether generator voltage is within the normal range. It does not indicate whether generator current output is normal. It is a simple, quick test. To measure charging system voltage:

1. Connect a voltmeter to the battery terminals. See **Fig. 4-19**.
2. Start the engine and run it at about 2,500 rpm. Observe the voltage at the battery. It should be in the range of 13.5 to 14.5 volts, depending on temperature. Voltage may be higher if the charging system is very cold.
3. If the voltage is between 13.5 and 14.5, generator voltage output is normal. (Check current output if needed.)

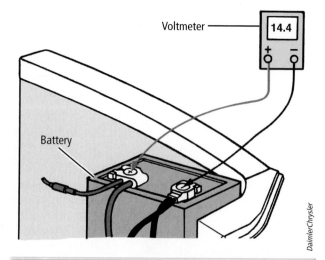

DaimlerChrysler

Fig. 4-19 The charging voltage test measures charging system voltage. *At what speed should the engine be running during this test?*

4. If the voltage is less than 13.5, generator voltage output may be low. Perform a current output test to verify that the generator is defective.

5. If the voltage is over 14.5 (at normal temperature), the voltage regulator is probably defective. In most cases, it is not practical to bench test a voltage regulator.

Charging Current Test

The **charging current test** measures the maximum current output of the generator at a specified voltage. It is the only test that can determine whether the current output is within the manufacturer's specifications. Measure charging system current output using a volts-ampere tester (VAT). See **Fig. 4-20**. This tester has a built-in carbon-pile load and inductive (clamp-on) ammeter lead.

To perform the charging current test:

1. Make sure the tester load control is turned off. Make sure that all switches are in the proper positions.

2. Connect the tester leads as follows: Connect the heavy load test leads and voltmeter leads to the proper battery terminal. (Voltmeter leads do not have to be connected if the voltmeter selector switch is placed on INTERNAL.)

Safety First | **Moving Parts** When working around a running engine, stay clear of moving belts, pulleys, and fans. Avoid hot exhaust manifolds. Equipment test leads can also be damaged by moving belts, pulleys, fans, and hot exhaust manifolds.

3. Clamp the inductive ammeter lead over the heavy wire connected to the BAT terminal on the generator. Make sure the arrow on the inductive pickup is pointed in the correct direction.

4. Start the engine and run it at about 2,500 rpm.

5. Turn the load control knob clockwise to get the maximum ammeter reading without the voltage dropping below 13.0 volts.

6. Turn off the load control as quickly as possible. The carbon-pile load will overheat if left on too long. Note that older analog testers have a carbon-pile load knob that is operated manually. On newer digital testers, such as the one pictured, there is no knob. This function is automatic once the tester is programmed.

Snap-on Diagnostics

Fig. 4-20 The VAT combines an ammeter, voltmeter, and load device into a single tester. *What is the inductive pick-up lead used for?*

7. The generator is good if the ammeter reading is within 15 amps of rated output. This value may be marked on the generator or found in the service manual.

8. If the output is low or zero, use a voltmeter to check whether the correct voltage is present at all generator wiring harness terminals. Refer to the service manual or wiring diagram for specified values. If the voltages are normal, remove the generator for bench testing or replacement.

TECH TIP Inductive Ammeter Lead. The ammeter lead may be clamped over either battery cable if necessary. If the ammeter is connected at the battery, all lights and accessories must be off when measuring current output.

Voltage Regulator Test

The VAT can also be used to check the voltage regulator. A **voltage regulator test** checks that the voltage regulator can keep the charging system at a predetermined voltage. If the generator current output is normal, check the charging voltage. With the engine still running under test conditions, note the ammeter reading. If the charge rate is less than 20 amps, read the voltmeter. This will be the regulated voltage. If the charge rate is above 20 amps, the generator may not be producing maximum voltage. In this case, charge the battery (with the generator or a charger) until the ammeter reads less than 20 amps during the test. Then read the voltmeter again.

Some generators can be tested with the voltage regulator bypassed. This will determine whether the generator or regulator is at fault. Bypassing the voltage regulator is known as "full fielding" the generator. The procedure requires either a voltage or ground connection to the proper field terminal, depending on the type of generator. See **Fig. 4-21**. If low generator output increases to normal when the regulator is bypassed, the regulator is defective.

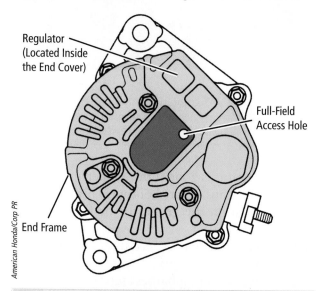

Fig. 4-21 A generator with an access hole for full fielding. A terminal inside the opening is connected to ground to bypass the voltage regulator. *Why is the full-fielding procedure used on some generators?*

Not all manufacturers recommend (or permit) full-field testing. With the regulator bypassed, there is no control over system voltage. If the voltage becomes too high, sensitive electronic components will be damaged. Refer to the charging system section of the service manual to determine whether and how full-field testing can be done on a generator.

Voltage Drop Test

Excessive resistance in the charging system is found by measuring voltage drop. Perform this test after performing the charging current and voltage regulator tests with a VAT. With the VAT still connected and the engine running, follow these steps:

1. Turn the voltmeter selector switch to the EXTERNAL 3 VOLT position.

2. Connect the positive voltmeter lead to the BAT terminal on the back of the generator. Connect the negative voltmeter lead to the positive battery terminal.

Safety First **Voltage Level** System damage may occur if voltage is allowed to exceed 16.5 on the full-field test.

3. Adjust engine speed so the ammeter reads between 10 and 20 amps. Read the voltmeter. This will be insulated-circuit voltage drop.
4. Move the positive voltmeter lead to the negative terminal of the battery. Move the negative voltmeter lead to the generator housing. Read the voltmeter. This will be ground-circuit voltage drop.

Check the manufacturer's specifications in the service manual. If voltage drop is higher than specified, there is excessive resistance in that circuit. Find and correct the problem.

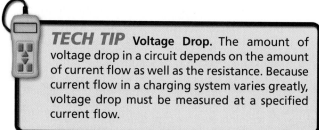

TECH TIP **Voltage Drop.** The amount of voltage drop in a circuit depends on the amount of current flow as well as the resistance. Because current flow in a charging system varies greatly, voltage drop must be measured at a specified current flow.

Charging System Diagnosis

Charging system problems can be caused by the generator, voltage regulator, or battery. Defective wiring, poor connections, and slipping drive belts can also cause problems. Batteries should be tested using an electronic battery/starting/charging system tester.

Undercharged Battery

An undercharged battery usually results in slow cranking. Possible causes for this problem include:
- Low generator current output.
- Low charging voltage.
- High resistance in the charging circuit.
- Lights or accessories used with engine off.
- Frequent short-trip driving.
- High key-off (parasitic) drain.
- Hard sulfation on battery plates.
- Use of high-current accessories added after the vehicle was manufactured.

If the battery and charging system are tested and are operating normally, check for the other possible causes of the undercharged battery.

Overcharged Battery

Overcharging the battery can produce dangerous hydrogen gas that may explode. Sulfuric acid vapors usually spew from battery vents during overcharging. If the overcharging is caused by high generator voltage, damage to the electrical system may occur. Possible causes of overcharging include:
- A defective voltage regulator.
- A grounded rotor coil (in some generators).
- A defective battery (shorted cell).
- High resistance in voltage regulator sensing circuit.

TECH TIP **Noisy Generator.** To determine whether the cause of a noisy generator is mechanical or electrical, disconnect the field circuit and start the engine. If the noise is gone, the problem is electrical.

Charging System Noise

Generator noise may result from either mechanical or electrical causes. Mechanical noise, such as grinding or metallic noises, may be caused by defective bearings, bent pulleys, defective belts, or bent cooling fan blades. Defective brushes and slip rings may also produce noise. Radio noise, such as static or whining, may be caused by a defective generator.

Removing the Generator

The generator and its wiring may be accessed from the top, bottom, or side of the engine compartment. You may need to remove parts or accessories to access the generator. Consult the service manual for specific instructions.

To remove the generator:
1. Connect a memory holder to the cigarette lighter receptacle. A **memory holder** is a memory protection device that prevents temporary failure of electronic components. On many vehicles, this receptacle is dead when the ignition is OFF. Be sure that the memory holder is connected to an auxiliary power source that is powered when the ignition is OFF.

Output Terminal Shorting The output (BAT) terminal on the generator is connected directly to the battery. Accidentally shorting this terminal to ground with tools or wires can cause very high current flow. This may result in serious burns as well as damage to the vehicle wiring. Always disconnect the negative battery cable before working on generator wiring.

Disconnections Do not disconnect charging system wiring or the battery while the generator is operating. Doing so may produce voltage spikes that could damage electronic components.

2. Disconnect the negative battery cable.
3. Disconnect and remove the wiring harness from the generator.
4. Release tension from the drive belt and remove it from the generator pulley.
5. Remove the lock bolt, mounting bolt, and adjusting bolt that mounts the generator. See **Fig. 4-22.**
6. Remove the generator from the vehicle.

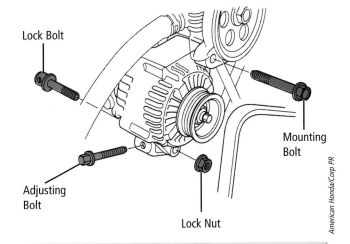

Lock Bolt

Mounting Bolt

Adjusting Bolt

Lock Nut

American Honda/Corp PR

Fig. 4-22 Generator removal. *When is it necessary to remove the wiring harness after removing the generator from its mounting?*

TECH TIP **Identifying Wires.** In some cases it may be necessary to identify individual wires before you remove them. This makes it easier to get the wires back on the correct terminal when reinstalling the generator.

Generator Bench Testing

A **bench test** is a test of a component that has been removed from the vehicle. To bench test a generator:
1. Clean the parts with a dry or slightly damp cloth. Do not place electrical parts in a cleaning tank.
2. Inspect the brushes, slip rings, and bearings.
3. Inspect and test the rotor and stator. Refer to the service manual for test procedures and specifications. See **Fig. 4-23.**

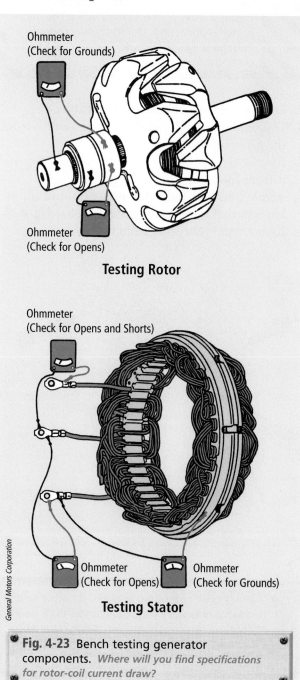

Ohmmeter
(Check for Grounds)

Ohmmeter
(Check for Opens)

Testing Rotor

Ohmmeter
(Check for Opens and Shorts)

Ohmmeter
(Check for Opens)

Ohmmeter
(Check for Grounds)

Testing Stator

General Motors Corporation

Fig. 4-23 Bench testing generator components. *Where will you find specifications for rotor-coil current draw?*

4. Check if the diodes can be easily disconnected from the stator. If so, they can be tested using the DIODE TEST position on a DVOM. Special testers are required if the diodes and stator cannot be separated.

TECH TIP **Installing the Regulator.** Regulators mounted inside or on the back of the generator and the rectifier (diode) bridge may require the use of heat-transfer grease during installation. Failure to do so may lead to early component failure.

Installing the Generator

Replacement generators may have a variety of output ratings, pulley types, voltage regulator calibrations, and mounting positions. Check part numbers to be sure you are installing the correct generator. Install the proper drive pulley on the generator if necessary. Follow the instructions in the service manual for pulley removal and installation.

To install a generator:
1. Connect the generator wiring harness first if necessary.
2. Position the generator in its mounting bracket.
3. Install the pivot and clamp bolts. Do not tighten.
4. Install the drive belt and place it over the pulley.
5. Allow the automatic tensioner to apply tension to the drive belt. If a tensioner is not used, adjust the belt using a tension gauge.
6. Tighten the pivot and clamp bolts using specified torque values from the vehicle service manual.
7. Connect any wires not previously connected.
8. Reconnect the negative battery cable.
9. Disconnect the memory holder.
10. Start the vehicle and verify proper charging system operation.

TECH TIP **Output Terminal Test.** Before reinstalling a generator that has been repaired, connect one ohmmeter lead to the output terminal and the other to the case. Then reverse the leads. If both readings are low, the output terminal is grounded.

TECHNOLOGY

Recharging by Braking

In traditional braking systems, when you press the brake the vehicle comes to a stop. This happens because the force applied to the pedal is transmitted through a hydraulic system to the brake pads or shoes. This force causes the pads or shoes to press against rotors or drums, creating friction. The friction created in this process serves to transform the vehicle's kinetic energy (motion) into heat. The heat produced dissipates into the atmosphere. The end result of the process is the vehicle coming to a stop.

In addition to the traditional braking system, some hybrid vehicles use a new technology that transforms some of the vehicle's kinetic energy into electrical energy. The electrical energy is used to recharge the battery. This is known as regenerative braking.

A regenerative braking system uses a motor generator connected to the drive axle. A motor generator can change electrical energy to kinetic energy (motion), and kinetic energy to electrical energy. When you step on the accelerator, current is sent to the motor generator. The supplied electricity is transformed to motion and used to drive the wheels. When you step on the brakes, the motor generator transforms the motion supplied by the wheels into electricity. This electricity is used to charge the battery, which will in turn supply power to the motor generator.

In addition to producing electricity when braking, the motor generator also helps the vehicle stop. When you press the brake the motor generator no longer drives the wheels. Instead, it functions as a mechanical load device. The force needed to drive the motor generator acts as resistance to the continued motion of the wheels and helps stop the vehicle.

In a regenerative braking system a generator is mechanically linked to the axle of a vehicle. While the vehicle is accelerating or coasting, the generator does not produce any electricity. Doing so would apply unnecessary load on the drive train and decrease fuel economy. Instead, the generator produces power only when the vehicle is braking. The motion of the axle drives the generator, producing electricity that is routed to an inverter and then to the battery, which stores the electrical energy for later use.

In addition to transforming kinetic energy into electrical energy, the generator has the added advantage (for the purpose of braking) to applying extra load to the wheels. This extra load increases the available braking horsepower while still using the same amount of hydraulic pressure. A small braking force produces a small amount of current in the generator and a small amount of resistance to continued forward motion. A large amount of braking force produces a large amount of current and large amount of resistance to forward motion.

SECTION 2 KNOWLEDGE CHECK

1. When should drive belts be replaced?

2. What happens if belt tension is too high?

3. Name the four tests used to determine whether the charging system is operating normally.

4. What happens when a battery is overcharged?

5. What is a memory holder?

6. Explain how to disassemble a generator.

7. What should you do first before installing a new generator?

8. What is a bench test?

9. What might radio noise such as static or whining indicate?

ASE TEST PREP

10. Technician A says that all manufacturers recommend full-field testing. Technician B says that not all manufacturers recommend full-field testing. Who is correct?
    - ⓐ Technician A.
    - ⓑ Technician B.
    - ⓒ Both Technician A and Technician B.
    - ⓓ Neither Technician A nor Technician B.

11. What type of device does a regenerative braking system use to charge the battery while braking?
    - ⓐ Solenoid.
    - ⓑ Compressor.
    - ⓒ Motor generator.
    - ⓓ Engine.

CHAPTER 4 REVIEW

Key Points

Meets the following NATEF Standards for Electrical/Electronic Systems: diagnosing charging system problems; inspecting and adjusting drive belts.

- Generators use electromagnetic induction to generate voltage.
- The major components inside a generator are the rotor, stator, and rectifier (diode) bridge.
- Diodes rectify AC voltage in the stator to DC voltage at the output terminal.
- On-the-vehicle charging system tests include the charging voltage test, charging current test, voltage regulator test, and voltage drop test.
- The only complete test of a generator is the current output test.
- Some generators can be tested for current output with the regulator bypassed.
- Checking and adjusting drive-belt tension is an important part of charging system service.
- Hybrid automobiles use a regenerative braking system to capture and use energy that would otherwise be lost.

Review Questions

1. What three factors determine the amount of voltage induced in the conductors?
2. What part of the generator is rotated by the drive belt?
3. What allows current to flow through the field coil while it rotates?
4. What is the process that changes AC voltage induced in the stator to DC voltage?
5. Explain temperature compensation in relation to battery charging.
6. What test determines whether a charging system is operating normally?
7. What test measures the maximum current output of the generator at a specified voltage?
8. What is the purpose of a voltage regulator test?
9. **Critical Thinking** What may happen if the charging system wiring or battery is disconnected while the generator is operating?
10. **Critical Thinking** What charging system problems may cause lights or fuses to burn out frequently?

Excellence in Communication

Using Electrical Schematics

Electrical schematics, or wiring diagrams, are the "road maps" for current flow through a circuit.

Being able to read an electrical schematic is vital to your job as an automotive technician. The electrical and electronic systems on a vehicle are becoming more complex every year. These changes result in new schematics.

These schematics are printed in service manuals and textbooks so that you can "read" the electrical paths. Technical terms are used to identify parts in schematics. Electrical symbols tell what is happening to the electrical current. You may encounter a symbol you do not recognize. Refer to the key in the book or manual for an explanation. Keys are usually provided to explain what the symbols represent.

Understanding these terms and symbols will help you successfully diagnose and solve vehicle problems.

Apply It!

Meets NATEF Communications Standards for comprehending and using written information to determine technical sequences.

Refer to **Fig. 4-13**. This figure shows the electrical schematic for a generator with a built-in voltage regulator.

1. On a sheet of paper, list the technical terms for the parts shown in **Fig. 4-13**. Explain the function of each part in a sentence.
2. Identify and draw the electrical symbols used in the figure. Explain what each one represents.
3. Follow the path of the electrical current from the generator to the battery.
4. Write a paragraph explaining this wiring diagram.

AUTOMOTIVE SERVICE EXCELLENCE
TEST PREP

Answering the following practice questions will help you prepare for the ASE certification tests.

1. What component is responsible for transferring power from the engine to the generator?
   - ⓐ Voltage regulator.
   - ⓑ Battery.
   - ⓒ Serpentine belt.
   - ⓓ System wiring.

2. Technician A says that the amount of voltage induced in the conductors of a generator depends on the strength and number of the conductors. Technician B says that the amount of voltage depends on the speed at which the magnetic field cuts across the conductors. Who is correct?
   - ⓐ Technician A.
   - ⓑ Technician B.
   - ⓒ Both Technician A and Technician B.
   - ⓓ Neither Technician A nor Technician B.

3. The purpose of a generator's slip rings is to:
   - ⓐ create a rotating magnetic field.
   - ⓑ connect the field circuit wiring to the field coil.
   - ⓒ induce a voltage in the generator's main conductors.
   - ⓓ allow current to flow through the rotating field coil.

4. At which two points in one rotation of the field coil will the induced voltage be equal to zero?
   - ⓐ 90° and 270°.
   - ⓑ 180° and 360°.
   - ⓒ 90° and 360°.
   - ⓓ 0° and 90°.

5. Technician A says that if the belt tension is too low it will not transmit enough power to drive the generator. Technician B says that if belt tension is too great the higher than normal loads may cause the bearings on the parts being driven to fail prematurely. Who is correct?
   - ⓐ Technician A.
   - ⓑ Technician B.
   - ⓒ Both Technician A and Technician B.
   - ⓓ Neither Technician A nor Technician B.

6. At what speed should the engine be running in order to conduct a charging voltage test?
   - ⓐ 1000 rpm.
   - ⓑ 1500 rpm.
   - ⓒ 2000 rpm.
   - ⓓ 2500 rpm.

7. Technician A says that when conducting a charging current test with an inductive ammeter connected at the battery, all lights and accessories must be off when measuring current output. Technician B disagrees and says that turning the lights and accessories off is unnecessary. Who is correct?
   - ⓐ Technician A.
   - ⓑ Technician B.
   - ⓒ Both Technician A and Technician B.
   - ⓓ Neither Technician A nor Technician B.

8. What result does an undercharged battery usually have on automotive systems?
   - ⓐ Produces dangerous levels of hydrogen.
   - ⓑ Engine cranks slowly.
   - ⓒ Produces excess voltage.
   - ⓓ Dome lights fail to light with door open.

9. Technician A says that the amount of voltage drop in a circuit depends on both the amount of current flow and resistance. Technician B says that because current flow in the charging system varies greatly, voltage drop must be measured at a specific current flow. Who is correct?
   - ⓐ Technician A.
   - ⓑ Technician B.
   - ⓒ Both Technician A and Technician B.
   - ⓓ Neither Technician A nor Technician B.

10. Which of the following is not a likely cause of an overcharged battery?
    - ⓐ Defective voltage regulator.
    - ⓑ Defective battery (shorted cell).
    - ⓒ High resistance in voltage regulator sensing circuit.
    - ⓓ Defective belt.

Section 1
Lighting Systems

Section 2
Instrument Panel
Displays

Section 3
Brake Warning
Lights, Switches,
and Sensors

Diagnosing & Repairing Lighting Systems

VOLVO
for life

Customer's Concern

Michelle Fusco says she is having trouble seeing road signs and lane markers at night. She changed the headlights on her old car after a police officer gave her a warning ticket for a burned-out headlight. Michelle replaced both headlights because her car has been around awhile and she figured they could use an upgrade. Now she says they are actually providing less light together than the one headlight provided alone.

When Michelle followed her friend home from softball practice last night, she noticed other drivers were flashing their lights at them. She assumed they were warning them about something ahead. The next day, Michelle's friend said, "Your lights were practically blinding me through my rearview mirror last night."

Technician's Challenge

As the service technician, you need to find answers to these questions:

1. Is Michelle experiencing any other problems related to the lighting system? Did she install the correct headlights for her car?

2. Could shining the headlights against a screen assist you in solving Michelle's headlight problem? Why or why not?

3. How will you solve this headlight problem? Will another set of headlights be needed? Can the existing set be adjusted?

● Section 1
Lighting Systems

Objectives:

E4 ● Identify system voltage and safety precautions associated with high intensity discharge headlights.

● Explain how the brake, turn signal, and hazard warning light circuits are wired.

E3 ● Inspect and diagnose incorrect turn signal or hazard light operation; perform necessary action.

E1 ● Diagnose the cause of brighter than normal, intermittent, dim, or no light operation; determine necessary action.

E2 ● Inspect, replace, and aim headlights and bulbs.

Vocabulary:
● **incandescent bulb**
● **halogen lamp**
● **high-intensity discharge (HID) lamp**
● **rheostat**

Light Sources

The lighting system conducts power to the exterior and interior lights on a vehicle.

Exterior lights generally include the head, parking, tail, side marker, and license plate lights. Separate circuits control the remaining exterior lights, including brake, turn signal, backup, and hazard warning lights. Daytime running lights (DRLs) are a separately controlled safety feature using the headlights. Fog light circuits have a separate on/off switch but may be powered through the headlight switch.

Interior lights include instrument panel lights, courtesy lights, and the dome/map light. Glove box, trunk, underhood, and vanity mirror lights are individually controlled.

All lights in a vehicle are electrically operated. Several different technologies are used to produce light.

Incandescent Bulbs

A bulb that uses a tungsten filament placed in a vacuum inside a glass bulb is known as an **incandescent bulb**. The filament is the small wire-like conductor inside the bulb. Current flowing through the filament causes it to glow white-hot and give off light and heat. The vacuum in the glass bulb prevents the filament from burning up due to the oxygen in air. These bulbs are typically used for side marker, license plate, and interior lights. See **Fig. 5-1**.

Some bulbs have two filaments sharing a common ground connection. Dual-filament bulbs are used in brake lights, taillights, and some headlights.

Turn Signal (3057NA)

Park Lamp (3156)

Turn Signal (3157)

Park Lamp (3156)

Park Lamp (1156)

Marker Lamp (194)

Interior Lamp (916)

Erick Dodge

Fig. 5-1 Several types of bulbs are used in automotive lighting systems. *What is a bulb filament?*

Excellence in Math

Calculating Wattage

The watt is the basic unit of power. Power is the rate at which electrical energy is delivered to a circuit. "How many watts?" is a question often asked about speakers, sound systems, hair dryers, and lightbulbs. A sound system may be rated at 20 watts and a hair dryer at 1,250 watts. Household bulbs may be rated at 40, 100, or 150 watts. Some automotive bulbs are rated at less than 5 watts.

Ohm's law states that voltage is the product of current and resistance. If you know two of the values, you can calculate the third. The power formula is related to Ohm's law. Use the power formula to calculate the current flow when a lamp is on. The power formula is stated as $P = E \times I$, where:

P = power in watts (W)

E = operating voltage

I = current in amperes

What is the power for a lightbulb with a voltage of 12.6 V and a current of 1.04 A?

$$P = E \times I$$

$$P = 12.6 \text{ V} \times 1.04 \text{ A} = 13.1 \text{ W}$$

Round wattage to tenths, voltage to tenths, and current to hundredths.

Rewrite the power formula in terms of the current. Solve for I.

Start with $P = E \times I$. Divide both sides by E:

$$\frac{P}{E} = \frac{E \times I}{E}$$

$$I = \frac{P}{E}$$

Calculate the current in a bulb where the voltage is 14.5 V and the power is 4.9 W:

$$I = \frac{P}{E} = \frac{4.9 \text{ W}}{14.5 \text{ V}} = 0.34 \text{ A}$$

A 1154 bulb has a double filament. The operating voltage is 6.4 V and the currents are 2.63 A and 0.75 A.

What are the power values for each filament? For the lower-current filament:

$$P = E \times I = 6.4 \text{ V} \times 0.75 \text{ A} = 4.8 \text{ W}$$

For the higher-current filament:

$$P = E \times I = 6.4 \text{ V} \times 2.63 \text{ A} = 16.8 \text{ W}$$

Apply It!

Meets NATEF Mathematics Standards for converting formulas to equivalent forms.

1. In a 1157 bulb, the wattage is 26.9 W and 7.6 W. The voltage is 12.6 V. What are the corresponding current values?

2. In a 1176 bulb, the voltage is 14.5 V and the currents are 1.34 A and 0.59 A. What are the corresponding wattages?

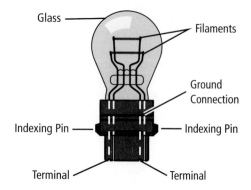

Glass — Filaments — Ground Connection — Indexing Pin — Indexing Pin — Terminal — Terminal

Fig. 5-2 Some automotive lightbulbs have dual filaments.

Each filament has its own terminal. This allows the unit to operate as two separate bulbs. See **Fig. 5-2.**

Gas-Filled Bulbs

Some lamps use a gas instead of a vacuum inside the bulb. The gas may protect the filament or be used in place of it. A **halogen lamp** is a bulb filled with halogen gas. Halogen is an inert (chemically inactive) gas. This protects the filament from burnout and allows it to operate at a higher temperature. The higher temperature of the filament changes the color and the intensity of the light. Halogen bulbs produce a whiter light. It is about 25 percent brighter than the light from a conventional lightbulb.

Mercury vapor or xenon gas is used in high-intensity discharge lamps. A **high-intensity discharge (HID) lamp** is a lamp in which light is produced when high voltage creates an arc between two electrodes. The light source (lamp) is also referred to as a burner. A device called a ballast module produces the high voltage required for HID operation. The ballast module may be a separate assembly or part of the lamp housing. HID lamps produce a slightly bluish light. It is several times brighter than the light from halogen bulbs. HID lamps have no filaments to break. They last much longer than conventional or halogen bulbs. See **Fig. 5-3**.

Safety First **Halogen Bulbs** Halogen bulbs get very hot and contain gas that is under pressure. They may explode if scratched or dropped. Wear eye protection when handling a halogen bulb. Allow the bulb to cool before removing it. Do not touch the glass bulb with your fingers or any oily cloth. Contaminants will get on the glass and reduce bulb life.

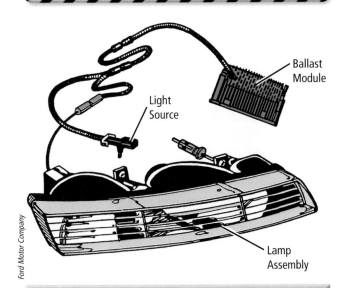

Ford Motor Company

Ballast Module

Light Source

Lamp Assembly

Fig. 5-3 High-intensity discharge (HID) lamps require a ballast module. *What does the ballast module do?*

Neon gas can also be used for vehicle lighting. Glass tubes filled with neon are energized by high voltage produced by a ballast device. The motion and energy of the neon gas produce light without the need for an internal arc or filament.

Neon-filled tubes are used in some brake lights because they light up quickly when energized. This gives drivers more time to react to the brake light signals.

Safety First **HID Lamps** Automobiles currently use a 12-volt electrical system for their headlamps. Xenon HID lighting systems require more than 20,000 volts to power the bulbs. When the bulbs are lit, they require only 12 volts. Because of the high voltage needed to get the xenon gas to emit light, ballasts are used to start the 20,000-volt arc. Probing or disconnecting the ballasts or their wiring while in operation can be extremely dangerous because of the high voltage present.

Light-Emitting Diodes

Light-emitting diodes (LEDs) are commonly used in automotive interior and exterior lighting. The most common LED color is red, which is used for brake lights and taillights. See **Fig. 5-4**.

LEDs are also used as instrument panel warning lamps. Having no filament, they are less likely to require replacement than conventional bulbs.

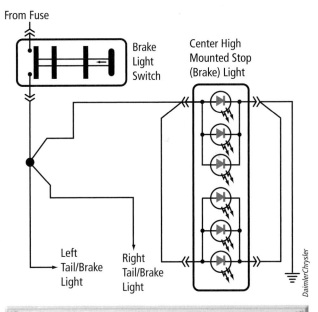

From Fuse

Brake Light Switch

Center High Mounted Stop (Brake) Light

Left Tail/Brake Light

Right Tail/Brake Light

DaimlerChrysler

Fig. 5-4 Some vehicles use light-emitting diodes (LEDs) for exterior lighting. *How does a technician know that this center high-mounted stop (brake) light (CHMSL) uses LEDs?*

Basic Lighting Circuits

For a lighting system to perform as intended, the driver must be able to control system operation. This is possible through the use of a circuit. The circuit may include switches, relays, and modules as well as the necessary lamps.

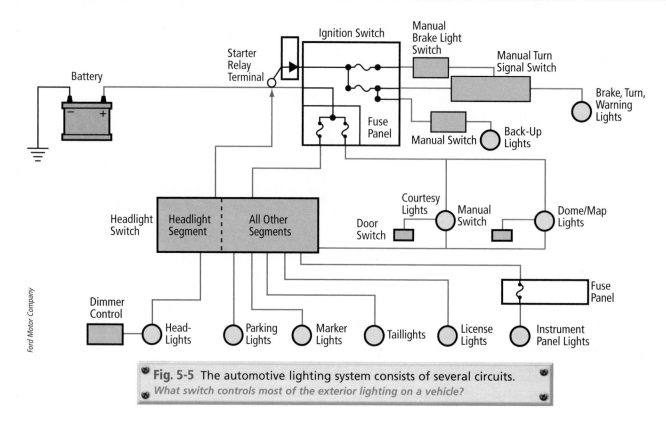

Ford Motor Company

Fig. 5-5 The automotive lighting system consists of several circuits. *What switch controls most of the exterior lighting on a vehicle?*

Headlight and Related Circuits

The headlight circuit controls the most often used exterior lighting on a vehicle. See **Fig. 5-5**. This circuit also controls instrument panel lighting. The major components of a basic headlight circuit are the:

- Headlight switch.
- Circuit protection device.
- Dimmer switch.
- Headlights.
- Front parking lights.
- Rear parking lights/taillights.
- Side marker lights.
- License plate light(s).

A typical headlight switch has three positions:

- OFF—all lights are off.
- PARK—headlights are off; all other lights are on.
- HEAD—all lights are on.

The headlight switch can be a push/pull, rocker, or rotary type of switch. When the exterior lights are on, the headlight switch also provides power to the instrument panel lights. A **rheostat** is a device that is used to vary the resistance in an electrical circuit. A rheostat is used to control the current flow through the panel light circuit. A rheostat is either part of the headlight switch or is mounted nearby.

Rotating the rheostat knob controls the brightness of the instrument panel lights. Full rotation of the rheostat in one direction closes a switch that turns on the vehicle's interior lights. See **Fig. 5-6**.

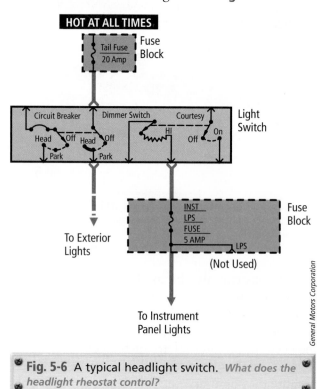

General Motors Corporation

Fig. 5-6 A typical headlight switch. *What does the headlight rheostat control?*

Many headlight switches have built-in circuit breakers to protect the headlight circuits against electrical overloads. A circuit breaker is used instead of a fuse or fusible link so that the headlights do not suddenly go out if an overload occurs. Instead, the headlights will pulse on and off, providing some road illumination. A circuit breaker protects only the headlight circuit. Fuses protect the other light circuits controlled by the headlight switch.

Some headlight circuits do not use circuit breakers. Instead, there is a separate fuse for each headlight. If one fuse burns out, the other light(s) are not affected.

A headlight dimmer switch is usually part of the multifunction switch on the steering column. The multifunction switch is used to select either high- or low-beam headlights. It may also control the windshield wipers and turn signals. When the high-beams are selected, a high-beam indicator lamp on the instrument panel is turned on. See **Fig. 5-7**. Some dimmer switches have a "flash to pass" feature. This circuit turns on the high-beam lights only while the switch is held in the flash to pass position. When the switch is released, the lights return to low beam.

A variety of headlight systems have been used in recent years. Sealed-beam headlights are either incandescent or halogen. They are either round or rectangular. They are used in two-headlight and

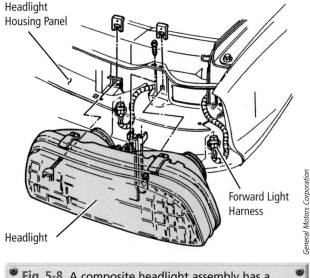

Headlight Housing Panel

Forward Light Harness

Headlight

General Motors Corporation

Fig. 5-8 A composite headlight assembly has a replaceable halogen or HID bulb. *What is another name for a composite headlight?*

four-headlight combinations. Sealed-beam bulbs contain the filament(s), reflectors, and lenses in one unit. They are identified as type-1 or type-2 bulbs, depending on the number of filaments used. Type-1 bulbs have one filament (either high- or low-beam). Type-2 bulbs have two filaments, one high beam and one low beam. The letter H or the word HALOGEN appears on the lenses of halogen sealed-beam units.

Many vehicles use composite (aerodynamic) headlights. These lights have a plastic housing that includes a reflector and lens. A replaceable halogen or HID bulb fits into the back of the housing. See **Fig. 5-8**.

The position of the headlights is adjustable. This allows proper placement of the light beam on the road in front of the vehicle.

Parking/Tail/License/Side Marker Lights

When the headlight switch is in the PARK or HEAD position, power is supplied to lights at the front, side, and rear of the vehicle. Some parking lights (front) and taillights (rear) use dual-filament bulbs. One filament is powered by the headlight switch for parking light and taillight operation. The second filament has less resistance. This permits more current flow, producing brighter light. This filament is used for brake light and turn signal light operation. The only connection between the headlights and the other exterior lights is the headlight switch. One or more fuses usually protect exterior light circuits.

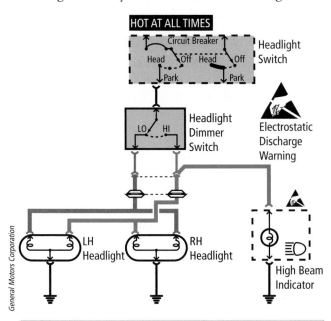

Fig. 5-7 The dimmer switch controls power to two separate sets of headlights. *What additional light comes on when the high-beam headlights are used?*

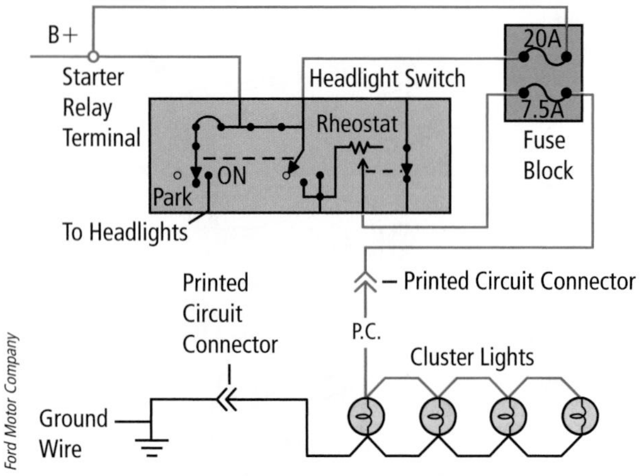

Ford Motor Company

Fig. 5-9 A diagram of instrument panel lights.
What controls the power to the instrument panel lights?

Instrument Panel Lighting

Turning on the headlight switch supplies power to the instrument panel lighting circuit. See **Fig. 5-9**. The panel lights illuminate the speedometer and other gauges, the radio, and the climate controls. In many applications this circuit is routed through the taillight fuse as well as the panel lights fuse. If the taillight fuse is burned out, the panel lights are also out. This should prompt the driver to get the necessary repairs. The panel light circuit is controlled by a rheostat in the headlight switch or mounted separately on the dash. The rheostat controls the brightness of the panel lights.

Interior/Courtesy Lights

Vehicle interior and courtesy lights are controlled by two different switches. When the instrument panel light rheostat is turned past its full brightness position, a switch closes to turn on the interior lights. The interior lights stay on until the rheostat switch is rotated out of the closed position. Door jamb switches also control interior lights. When any door on a vehicle is opened, a switch on the door jamb causes the interior lights to come on. The lights go out when all doors are closed. See **Fig. 5-10**.

Some vehicles have illuminated entry systems. This system uses an electronic module to turn on the interior lighting before the doors are opened. The system can be activated by lifting a door handle or by using a remote keyless entry transmitter. In most cases the module will turn off the interior lights gradually after the doors are closed.

Electronic Lighting Controls

Many lighting circuits use sensors, relays, and electronic modules to control some lighting functions.

Automatic Lighting Control

Several versions of automatic lighting control are in use. On some vehicles the exterior lights are controlled automatically, depending on the amount of light sensed by an ambient light sensor. This sensor is usually mounted on the top of the instrument panel. When the light level is high (daylight), the exterior lights remain off. As darkness approaches, the light sensor signals a module to turn on the exterior lights. The exterior lights can also be turned on at any time with the headlight switch.

Automatic Headlight Dimming

Some vehicles have circuits that use light sensors to signal the presence of oncoming traffic. If the high-beam headlights are on, a module switches the

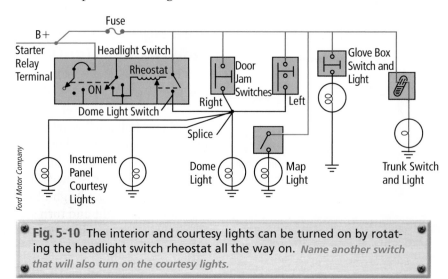

Ford Motor Company

Fig. 5-10 The interior and courtesy lights can be turned on by rotating the headlight switch rheostat all the way on. *Name another switch that will also turn on the courtesy lights.*

headlights to low beam when sufficient light strikes the sensor. The sensitivity of the circuit is usually adjusted with a rheostat on the instrument panel.

Lamp and Body Control Modules

Some vehicles use lamp modules or body control modules (BCMs) to control vehicle lighting. The module receives inputs from various switches and supplies power to the appropriate lights through a relay or solid state switch. Electronic modules are commonly used to control automatic exterior lighting, headlight off delay, and illuminated entry systems. See **Fig. 5-11**.

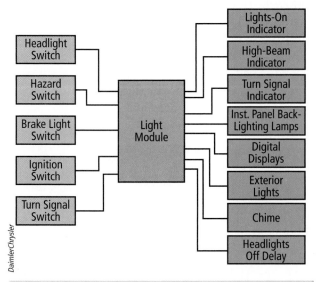

DaimlerChrysler

Fig. 5-11 Some vehicles use electronic modules to control lighting circuits. *Name two lighting functions that could be controlled by an electronic module.*

Daytime Running Lights

The daytime running lights (DRL) module turns on the headlights at a slightly reduced power during daytime. This safety feature makes the vehicle more visible. Operating the lights at reduced power in daylight increases the life of the bulb. Some DRL circuits use an ambient light sensor mounted on the instrument panel. When the ambient light sensor "sees" a lower light level, the module supplies normal power to the lights for nighttime driving.

In general, the headlights operate in the DRL mode when the ignition switch is on and the transmission is in gear. Some DRL circuits do not use light sensors. In such cases the headlights must be turned on manually for normal nighttime brightness. Other exterior lights, such as side marker and taillights, are not affected by DRL. They are controlled by the headlight switch.

Brake, Turn Signal, and Hazard Warning Lights

Brake, turn signal, and hazard warning lights are used to signal actions by the driver. They are not affected by headlight circuit operation. These circuits often share bulb filaments and wiring.

Brake Light Circuits

A switch operated by the brake pedal controls the brake lights. The brake light circuit includes lights on both sides at the rear of the vehicle and the center high-mounted stop (brake) light (CHMSL). The CHMSL is located at the rear of the vehicle at approximately driver's eye level for better visibility.

When the brakes are applied, the brake light switch closes, supplying current to the brake light bulbs. If the brake lights and turn signals share the same bulb filament, the brake light circuit passes through the turn signal switch. This makes it possible for the rear turn signal filament to flash even when the brake light circuit is activated.

Turn Signal Circuits

The turn signal circuit flashes lights on either side of the vehicle, signaling other drivers when the vehicle is turning. The circuit consists of the turn signal switch, flasher unit, turn signal bulbs (or filaments), and indicator lights. The flasher unit controls turn signal operation. A standard-duty flasher unit contains a set of normally closed electrical contacts, a bimetal element, and a heating element. See **Fig. 5-12**.

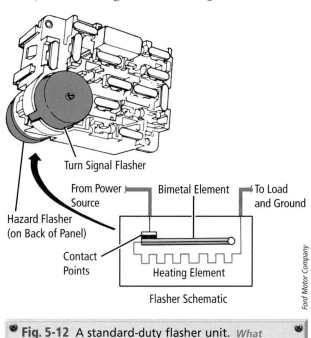

Ford Motor Company

Fig. 5-12 A standard-duty flasher unit. *What causes the contact points in the flasher to open?*

The flasher unit acts like a self-resetting circuit breaker. When the turn signal switch is moved to either the left- or right-turn position, the circuit is activated. Current flows through the contacts and heating coil of the flasher to the bulbs. Heat causes the bimetal arm to bend, opening the contacts. With the contacts open, current flow stops, causing the turn signal bulbs to go out. The bimetal element cools and returns to its original position, closing the contacts. As this process is repeated, the turn signal bulbs and the turn indicator bulb(s) on the instrument panel flash on and off.

With the standard-duty flasher, the flash rate depends on the amount of current flow in the circuit. A burned-out bulb or excessive resistance in the circuit decreases the flash rate. Connecting trailer lights to the vehicle increases the flash rate. The flash rate can also be affected by the use of incorrect bulbs. With a standard-duty flasher, an abnormal flash rate indicates a problem in the circuit. Continued use of a turn signal circuit with an increased flash rate could damage the flasher unit.

Flasher Units Heavy-duty flashers are available for vehicles wired for trailer pulling. This flasher has normally open contacts. Current flows through the heating element only when the circuit is first energized. Heat causes the bimetal element to close the contacts. The flash rate does not depend on the number of bulbs in the circuit. A disadvantage of a heavy-duty flasher is that the flash rate will not change if one or more bulbs are burned out.

Electronic Flashers Most vehicles use electronic flashers that have timing circuits to control power transistors. The transistor turns on and off at a uniform rate, regardless of the current flow in the circuit. A single electronic flasher unit may be used for both the turn signal and hazard warning circuits. In some applications the flasher function is included in the body control module or lighting module instead of being a separate assembly.

TECH TIP **Replacing Flasher Units.** Flasher units are calibrated for the number of bulbs in the circuit. When replacing a flasher unit, make sure to install the correct replacement part.

Hazard Warning Circuits

The hazard warning circuit flashes all of the turn signals and the dash indicator lamps at the same time. This circuit has its own ON/OFF switch, located on the steering column or on the instrument panel. A heavy-duty flasher is used due to the number of bulbs in the circuit.

Backup Light Circuit

The backup light circuit is controlled by the backup light switch. On vehicles with automatic transmissions, the backup light switch is part of the PARK/NEUTRAL position (P/NP) switch. Vehicles with manual transmissions use a switch operated by the shift linkage. When the transmission is in reverse, the switch is closed and the backup lights are turned on. If the backup lights are on when the transmission is not in reverse, the backup light switch is defective or out of adjustment. See **Fig. 5-13.**

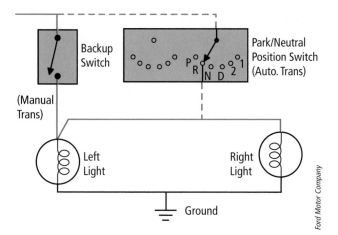

Fig. 5-13 The backup light circuit is controlled by a switch operated by the shift lever, or linkage. *What could cause the backup lights to be on in PARK or NEUTRAL?*

Diagnosing Lighting Problems

Bulbs are either turned on or burned out. When a light is dimmer than normal, it is because of a problem in the circuit. Brighter than normal bulb operation could be caused by high charging system voltage (all lights) or use of the wrong bulb. Intermittent light operation is almost always due to a loose or dirty connection in the circuit.

When diagnosing lighting problems, remember that lightbulbs are connected in parallel. If a light is out, check to see if other lights in the same circuit are on. If they are on, the power supply, circuit protection device, and switch for that circuit are working.

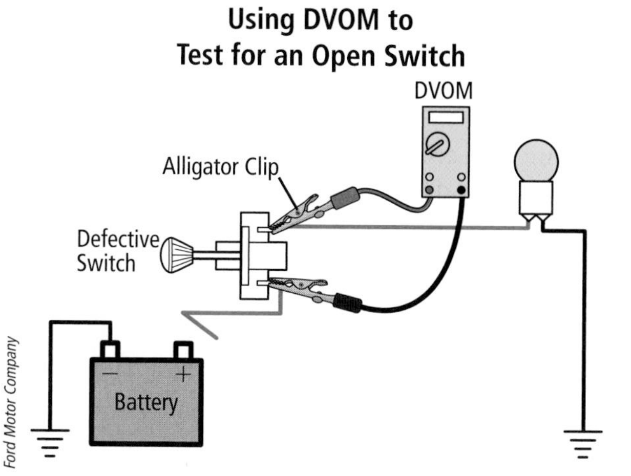

Using DVOM to Test for an Open Switch

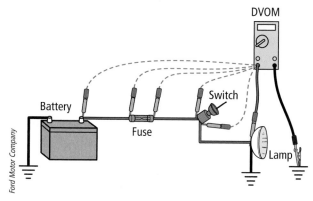

DVOM

Alligator Clip

Defective Switch

Battery

Ford Motor Company

Fig. 5-14 A DVOM can be used to check continuity.
What two types of electrical devices should not be bypassed with a jumper wire?

If an entire lighting circuit is not working, check the switch and circuit protection devices first. A DVOM can be used to test a switch. Set the DVOM to ohms. With the switch closed, there should be continuity (zero ohms) across the switch. See **Fig. 5-14**.

You can use a test light to test fuses without removing them from the fuse block. Before replacing a fuse, fusible link, or circuit breaker, check the circuit for shorts or grounds that may have caused an electrical overload. Repair the circuit before installing new parts.

If the switch and protection devices are good, use a DVOM to check for voltage at various points in the circuit until the problem has been found. See **Fig. 5-15**.

Determine Opens by Probing Succeeding Test Points in Hot Circuit

DVOM

Battery

Switch

Fuse

Lamp

Ford Motor Company

Fig. 5-15 You can use a DVOM to check an electrical circuit for voltage.

If only one light is out, remove and inspect the bulb and its socket. A burned-out bulb may be discolored or have a loose filament visible inside. Check the socket for corrosion and loose connections.

Many lighting problems are caused by a poor ground connection. This is a frequent cause of one or more dim lights. Some lightbulb sockets are connected directly to ground. Others require a ground wire connection. When working on lighting problems, make sure all ground connections are clean and tight.

Bulb Replacement Light assemblies and bulb replacement methods vary considerably among vehicles. If the procedure for bulb removal is not clear, refer to the vehicle service manual for instructions. The following suggestions may be helpful.

• Headlight bulb replacement is usually made through the rear of the light assembly. This may require the removal of trim pieces and/or the light housing to gain access to the bulb.
• Halogen headlight bulbs are removed after turning or releasing a retaining ring. See **Fig. 5-16**.
• Some fogging of the composite type of light assembly due to moisture is normal. Unless unusual conditions exist, the moisture escapes to the atmosphere through vents provided for that purpose.
• When replacing sealed-beam units, do not tamper with the headlight adjusting screws.

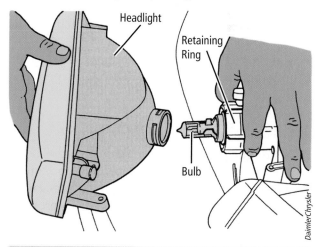

Headlight

Retaining Ring

Bulb

DaimlerChrysler

Fig. 5-16 A retaining ring must be rotated to remove the bulb from this headlight assembly.
What should you do if you are not sure how to safely remove a headlight bulb?

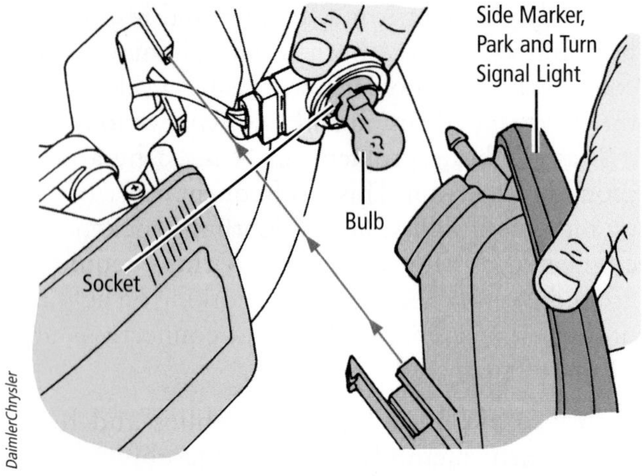

Side Marker, Park and Turn Signal Light

Bulb

Socket

DaimlerChrysler

Fig. 5-17 Some small bulbs can be removed from the rear of the light housing. *How is the bulb socket removed from the housing?*

- In some cases, you can replace small bulbs by first removing the light socket from the back of the light housing. Carefully turn the socket to release it before pulling it out. See **Fig. 5-17**.
- If you cannot remove the bulb socket from the housing, you will need to remove the lens from the light assembly to access the bulb.
- Some bulbs are removed from their sockets by pushing in and rotating the bulb. Other bulbs can be pulled straight out of the socket.
- Make sure to install the correct bulb. Bulb numbers are usually given in the owner's manual and vehicle service manual.
- Make sure the gaskets and seals around the light housing are in good condition and properly aligned.

Headlight Aiming

Headlight position is mechanically adjustable. The lights must be aimed to provide maximum visibility without blinding oncoming drivers. Headlights are aimed using the adjustment screws provided for that purpose.

Safety First **Heat Buildup** Do not operate the headlights with the aimers installed. Excessive heat buildup may damage the headlight lens.

Different methods of checking alignment are widely used. Each of the following methods is identified by the device it uses to aim the headlights. The methods are these:

- Aiming screen. This device is a 12-foot by 5-foot screen placed 25 feet from the vehicle. The focus of the headlamps on the screen is observed and used to adjust headlamp aim. See **Fig. 5-18**.
- Mechanical aimer. This is a mechanical device installed on the headlamps by means of suction cups. It determines the plane of the headlamp beam.
- Optical aimer. This device measures certain characteristics of the headlamp beam pattern. See **Fig. 5-19**.
- Photometric aimer. This device measures luminous intensity at selected points of the beam pattern.
- Vehicle-headlamp aiming device. This device is permanently installed on the vehicle and/or headlamp by the vehicle manufacturer to indicate the horizontal and vertical aim of the headlamps.

The screen method of aiming provides a screen (target) mounted on a wall at a specified height and distance from the front of the vehicle. With the vehicle properly positioned, the adjusting screws are turned until the headlight beam strikes the screen in the proper location.

TECH TIP **Headlight Aiming.** Verify proper headlight operation. Check headlight aim on low beam. If necessary, verify the adjustment on high beam.

The required dimensions and other specifications for this procedure are found in the vehicle service manual.

Another alignment method uses headlight aimers temporarily attached to the headlight assembly. The aimers must be installed so that the adjustment rods contact the aiming pads on the headlight assembly. Adapters are available for use with various types of lights. The headlight is adjusted to move a bubble level on the aimer to a specified position. Some vehicles have a bubble level built into the headlight assembly.

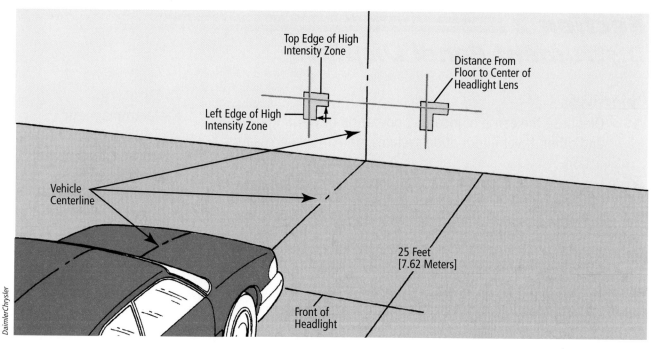

Top Edge of High Intensity Zone

Distance From Floor to Center of Headlight Lens

Left Edge of High Intensity Zone

Vehicle Centerline

25 Feet [7.62 Meters]

Front of Headlight

DaimlerChrysler

Fig. 5-18 Headlights can be aimed using the screen method. *What are the two important dimensions when placing a headlight aiming screen in front of a vehicle?*

Before checking headlight aim, make these preliminary checks:
• Vehicle must be on a level floor.
• Fuel tank level should be as specified in the vehicle service manual.
• Tires should be properly inflated.
• Luggage area should not be heavily loaded.
• If vehicle is regularly used to pull a trailer, this load should be simulated.

Courtesy Hopkins Manufacturing

Fig. 5-19 An optical headlight aimer.

SECTION 1 KNOWLEDGE CHECK

1. Name the three types of lightbulbs used on vehicles.

2. What part of a high-intensity discharge (HID) lamp produces the high voltage required for operation?

3. Name one advantage of LEDs.

4. What is a rheostat?

5. How is an ambient light sensor used in conjunction with daytime running lamps?

6. What is a CHMSL?

ASE TEST PREP

7. Technician A says all automotive lightbulbs have filaments. Technician B says that filaments are found only in incandescent bulbs. Who is correct?
   ⓐ Technician A.
   ⓑ Technician B.
   ⓒ Both Technician A and Technician B.
   ⓓ Neither Technician A nor Technician B.

Section 2
Instrument Panel Displays

Objectives:

F3 • Diagnose the cause of incorrect operation of warning devices and other driver information systems; determine necessary action.

F1 • Inspect and test gauges and gauge sending units for cause of intermittent, high, low, or no gauge readings; determine necessary action.

F2 • Inspect and test connectors, wires, and printed circuit boards of gauge circuits; determine necessary action.

F4 • Inspect and test sensors, connectors, and wires of electronic (digital) instrument circuits; determine necessary action.

Vocabulary:

- electromagnetic display
- vehicle speed sensor (VSS)
- liquid crystal display (LCD)

Types of Displays

Instrument panel displays provide important information concerning vehicle operating conditions. Gauges, lamps, and digital displays inform the driver about variables such as speed, oil pressure, and fuel level. Most of these displays are located in a section of the instrument panel known as the instrument cluster.

Driver information displays are divided into three basic types: electromagnetic (analog) displays, digital displays, and warning lamps. Most vehicles use both electromagnetic (analog) displays and warning lamps. Some vehicles use various combinations of the three types of displays.

Electromagnetic Displays

A gauge that uses electromagnetism to move an indicating needle (pointer) is known as an **electromagnetic display**. See **Fig. 5-20**. Magnetic coils in the

gauge unit are connected to a regulated voltage source. Ground for magnetic coils is through both the cluster ground connection and a variable resistance sending unit. The needle indicates the value of the condition being monitored. Electromagnetic gauges are also known as analog displays because the units indicated can vary between minimum and maximum values. Analog displays include temperature, fuel, and oil pressure gauges. See **Fig. 5-21**.

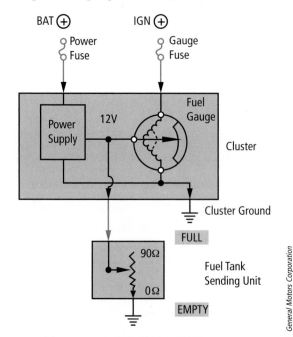

Fig. 5-21 A typical electromagnetic gauge circuit. *Where are the electromagnetic coils grounded?*

DaimlerChrysler

Fig. 5-20 An electromagnetic, or analog, information display. *Why are electromagnetic displays also called analog?*

General Motors Corporation

When the gauge is in operation, voltage is applied to the magnetic coils. The amount of current flow through the coils depends on the resistance of the sending unit. The gauge circuit is calibrated to make the indicating pointer read high or low, depending on the condition being measured. Electromagnetic gauge circuits differ in design and operation. Some gauges read high when the sending unit resistance is high. Other gauges read low under the same conditions.

In some applications sensor output will be connected to the powertrain control module (PCM) instead of the instrument cluster. In this way the PCM can route sensor information to other modules that require the same data. Refer to the vehicle service manual for information on sending unit circuits and gauge operation. You will need this information when diagnosing gauge problems.

Another analog display is the pointer-type speedometer. At one time speedometers were mechanically driven by a cable. Now most speedometers are electronically operated. As with other analog displays, the speedometer pointer is moved by electromagnetic fields. Instead of a variable resistance sending unit, the input signal for a speedometer comes from a vehicle speed sensor (VSS). A typical **vehicle speed sensor (VSS)** is a small AC signal generator driven by a shaft in the transmission. When the vehicle is moving, the VSS generates a voltage signal proportional to vehicle speed.

Electronic circuits in the cluster convert the VSS signal into a speed display and operate an odometer to record the distance traveled. See **Fig. 5-22**.

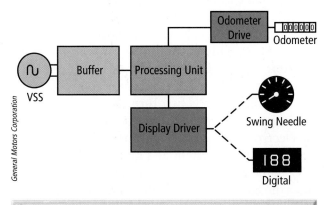

Fig. 5-22 A block diagram of a typical speedometer/odometer circuit. *What type of signal does this vehicle speed sensor (VSS) produce?*

Solid State Digital Displays

Several types of digital (graphic) images are used in instrument panel driver information systems. The information may be displayed as letters, numbers, or bar graphs. Electronically controlled solid state light segments create the desired images. Each segment in a multisegment display is a separate light source. Digital displays are controlled by a microprocessor known as a central processing unit (CPU) in the instrument cluster. Based on inputs from sending units, the CPU turns on the appropriate light segments to form letters, numbers, or bar graphs.

Light-Emitting Diodes

Light-emitting diodes (LEDs) are used in 7- or 11-segment displays to form letters and numbers. See **Fig. 5-23**. The segments in LEDs can also be arranged to form bar graphs.

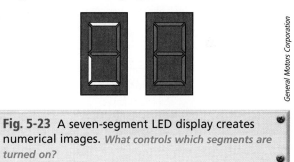

Fig. 5-23 A seven-segment LED display creates numerical images. *What controls which segments are turned on?*

Liquid Crystal Displays

A panel that is placed in front of an incandescent or halogen lightbulb is known as a **liquid crystal display (LCD)**. The LCD does not actually produce light. The LCD panel is a "sandwich" of a fluid between two layers of glass that have a conductive coating. Voltage signals from the CPU to the glass layers cause the fluid between the glass to either pass or block light from the bulb. The resulting light and dark segments form the images. See **Fig. 5-24**.

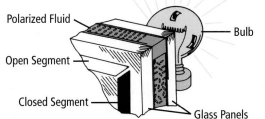

When Segment Opens, Light Passes Through

Polarized Fluid

Open Segment

Closed Segment

Bulb

Glass Panels

Fig. 5-24 Liquid crystal displays use a fluid to control the passage of light. *Why is a bulb used behind the LCD panel?*

LCD displays produce only black and white images. Color filters are often used in front of the display to produce a variety of colored images. In addition to instrument panel displays, LCDs are widely used in DVOMs, calculators, and gasoline pump displays.

Digital display circuits are similar to analog gauge circuits. See **Fig. 5-25.** Each variable to be displayed requires an input signal from a sending unit. In general, the same types of sensors are used for both analog and digital displays. While the sending units may look the same, they are not necessarily interchangeable. Always check part numbers when replacing components.

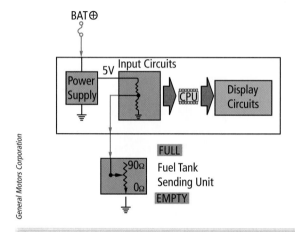

General Motors Corporation

Fig. 5-25 Digital display circuits are similar to analog gauge circuits. *Will this display read high or low if the sending unit lead wire is grounded?*

Digital odometers require a means of storing mileage data when the ignition switch is OFF. This information is stored in a nonvolatile random access memory (NVRAM) chip. As the vehicle is driven, accumulated mileage is stored in the NVRAM. When the ignition is shut off, the chip retains the information in its memory for display when the ignition is turned on again. If a new or rebuilt cluster is installed in a vehicle, the original NVRAM must be installed in the replacement unit.

Instrument Panel Warning Lights

Instrument panel warning lights are less expensive than analog gauges or electronic displays. A driver may be more likely to notice a warning light than to notice an unusual operating condition on a gauge or other display. Red, amber, green, and blue indicators are often used as instrument panel warning signals. Warning lights are usually either incandescent bulbs or LEDs. See **Table 5-A.**

Table 5-A	BULB INDICATORS	
Indicator	**Color**	**Bulb #/LED**
Battery	Red	LED
Brake	Red	LED
Air bag	Red	LED
Low Oil	Red	LED
Seatbelt	Red	LED
Temperature	Red	LED
Door Ajar	Red	LED
Decklid Ajar	Red	LED
High Beam	Blue	74
Turn Signals	Green	194
Cruise	Green	74
Trac On	Green	74
Trac Off	Amber	LED
Check Engine	Amber	LED
ABS	Amber	LED
Low Fuel	Amber	LED
Low Washer Fluid	Amber	LED
Illumination	Bluegreen	194

Warning lights require an input signal to operate correctly. The input signal is usually a simple switch. This can be on either the battery or ground side of the warning light.

In externally grounded warning circuits, voltage is supplied to the lights when the ignition switch is ON. When the grounding switch is closed, the light will be on. When the switch is opened, the light will go out. Some of these circuits also have a bulb test feature. When the ignition switch is turned and held just past the RUN position, the switch grounds the light circuit. This is the bulb test section of the ignition switch. The bulb test is used in circuits where the warning light does not come on when the ignition switch is first turned on.

The ground switch for some warning lights is in an electronic module. The module monitors the operation of the system and grounds the circuit to turn on the warning light when appropriate. In some cases the module will cycle the warning light on and off to signal specific conditions or trouble codes.

Safety First **IVRs** Some older vehicles have thermoelectric gauges that use instrument voltage regulators (IVRs). Grounding the sending unit lead wire on these vehicles may damage the gauge. Refer to the vehicle service manual.

Excellence **in Science**

Demonstrating an Electrical Ground

Many vehicle electrical systems use the frame or chassis as one conductor in the circuit. For example, both the parking brake and brake fluid level warning switches connect one side of the warning light to the chassis ground.

This arrangement is economical and reliable. Using the chassis as one conductor saves wire, weight, complexity, and cost. Because the switches are frequently far from the warning lights, putting the switches in the positive, or "hot," wire of the circuit would require twice as much wire and many extra connectors.

This type of circuit is easy to build for light testing circuits. The short circuit of a switch wire to ground causes a warning. However, it does not blow a fuse or cause damage. Also, the chassis is a very reliable conductor. It cannot easily break and create an open circuit.

Apply It!

Constructing a Grounded Circuit

Meets NATEF Science Standards for understanding electrical grounds and fuses.

Materials and Equipment
- 12-volt battery or power supply
- In-line automotive fuse assembly, 1 amp or less
- Small 12-volt lamp and socket assembly
- 3 normally open push-button switches
- About 10′ [3 m] of hookup wire
- Piece of wood, about 6″ × 24″ × 1″ thick [about 15 cm × 60 cm × 3 cm]
- Strip of sheet metal, about 2″ [5 cm] wide and as long as the board
- Sheet metal screws, ½″−¾″ [1 cm–2 cm]

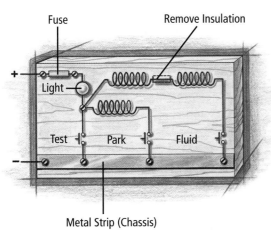

Metal Strip (Chassis)

1. Construct the circuit shown here. This circuit demonstrates the three reasons for using the chassis as the "ground return" part of the system. The coiled hookup wires represent the distance from the dashboard to the parking brake and fluid level sensor switches.

2. Test the circuit. Push the test switch to close it. Then release it. The warning light will come on, and then go off. This represents the light test when the vehicle is started.

3. Simulate the situation where the parking brake is set and the fluid level is low. Press and hold the parking brake and fluid-low switches one at a time. This situation signals trouble by lighting the warning light.

4. Remove the fuse. Then press and release the test switch. The warning light does not flash. This indicates a fault.

5. Replace the fuse. Now simulate a wire being shorted to ground. To do this, pull down and press the bare part of the fluid-low wire to the metal chassis strip. The warning light comes on to indicate a fault, but the fuse does not blow.

6. In this system, the fuse, light, and test switch are located near each other, as they are in a vehicle. The switches are located far away. Can you think of a vehicle electrical system in which the fuse and switch(es) are located together and the lights are far away?

Warning light circuits can also be internally grounded. In this case the ignition switch does not have to be in the circuit. Instead, a switch that controls the individual circuit is located between the battery and the light circuit. When the control switch is closed, the warning light comes on. The warning light stays on as long as the switch is on. Examples of this type of circuit include the high-beam indicator, hazard warning indicators, and seat belt warning light.

Diagnosing and Servicing Instrument Panel Displays

When diagnosing instrument panel display problems, note how many displays are affected. For example, if only one gauge, display, or lamp is out, it is unlikely that the problem is a fuse or common ground connection. Also determine whether the problem is failure to operate, intermittent operation, or an inaccurate display.

Gauges and Graphic Displays

If only one gauge or digital display fails to respond normally, refer to a wiring diagram to determine how the circuit is powered and grounded. An open circuit in the sending unit or its wiring can cause this problem. With the ignition switch ON, disconnect the lead wire at the sending unit. Observe the display while briefly touching the lead wire to a good ground connection. If the display changes when you do this, the sending unit is probably defective. If the display does not change, check the wiring between the sending unit and the instrument panel. Inspect the printed circuit board and connectors for damage. If the wiring is good, the gauge or display is defective.

When one gauge or display reads inaccurately, check for resistance in the sending unit circuit. You can use gauge testers to temporarily take the place of the sending unit. You can use them on both analog and digital displays. The tester has one or more rheostats that allow you to set specific resistance values as listed in the vehicle service manual. Connect the tester to the sending unit lead wire. Adjust the resistance as required. If the display is not as specified, the sending unit is probably defective. Replace defective analog gauges individually. Replace digital display modules as a unit. Stepper motor odometers and digital odometer memory chips must be removed from the defective unit and reinstalled in the replacement part.

Warning Lights

When warning lights fail to come on, check the fuse by observing if other lights on the same fuse are working. If the fuse is good, check the bulb if it is easily accessible. If the bulb is not easily accessible, it may be easier to check the circuit by applying voltage or ground. Refer to the vehicle service manual to determine whether the circuit is internally or externally grounded.

Depending on the circuit, use a jumper wire to apply voltage, or disconnect and ground the lead wire to the switch. If the light does not light, the bulb is probably defective. If the light does light, repair the wiring or replace the control switch as needed. If a warning light stays on all the time, check for a grounded wire to the switch or a defective switch.

SECTION 2 KNOWLEDGE CHECK

1. Name the three basic types of driver information displays.
2. What supplies the input signal for the speedometer needle?
3. What type of light is used to form letters, numbers, and bar graphs?
4. What do green instrument panel lights indicate?
5. What problems are unlikely if only one instrument panel gauge, display, or light is out?
6. What can be used to temporarily take the place of the sending unit?

ASE TEST PREP

7. Technician A says that the coils for electromagnetic gauges are grounded at the sending unit. Technician B says that the coils are grounded at the sending unit and at the cluster ground connection. Who is correct?
   a Technician A.
   b Technician B.
   c Both Technician A and Technician B.
   d Neither Technician A nor Technician B.

● Section 3
Brake Warning Lights, Switches, and Sensors

Objectives:
- Identify conditions under which the brake warning light may glow.
- Identify ways in which the ABS warning light is different from other brake warning lights.

Vocabulary:
- **low brake fluid level sensor**
- **electric brake pad wear indicator**

Activating Switches and Sensors

Brake system switches and sensors are activated either by driver input or system input.

The brake warning light is located in the instrument panel. When lit, it alerts the driver to a problem with one or more of the brake systems. It is usually a red light and it may display an icon or the word "brake." It may display both. See **Fig. 5-26.**

The brake warning light will come on briefly when the driver turns the ignition switch to the ON position. This is the bulb check. If the light is not glowing, the bulb may be burned out, the socket could be loose, or a fuse could be blown. Inspect and replace any damaged parts. Refer to the vehicle service manual.

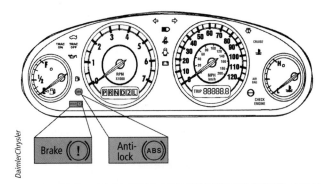

DaimlerChrysler

Fig. 5-26 The brake warning light will glow when there is a problem with the brake system or components. *How can you recognize the brake warning light?*

Safety First **Brake Warning Light** If the brake warning light does not come on with the ignition key in the run position, repair the light system immediately. In this failure mode, the driver will not be alerted to a potentially life-threatening vehicle condition.

The brake warning light may also glow under the following conditions:
- If the parking brake is set.
- If the fluid level in the master cylinder is low.
- If the pressure-differential switch senses a difference in pressure between two hydraulic circuits.

The antilock brake system (ABS) warning light is different from other brake warning lights. First, it is usually amber, not red. Second, it defaults to ON and must be turned off by the ABS control module.

When the ignition is turned to the ON position, the amber ABS light will glow to show that it is working. Once the ABS performs its automatic self-check, the ABS control module opens the circuit to the warning lamp and turns it off.

The ABS will not function when the ABS warning light is illuminated. The ABS warning light glows whenever there is an electrical or hydraulic malfunction of the ABS. The ABS system should be checked as soon as possible.

Brake Light Switches

All vehicles have at least one brake light switch. Some have more than one. Depressing the brake pedal activates the brake light switch. On some vehicles the only function of the brake light switch may be to turn on the brake lights. See **Fig. 5-27**.

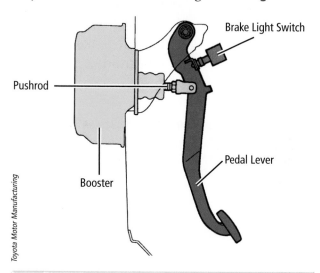

Toyota Motor Manufacturing

Fig. 5-27 Most vehicles have simple brake light switches. *Do some vehicles have more than one brake light switch?*

The brake light switch may also have multiple functions. It may be used to provide information to the ABS, the torque converter clutch, or the cruise control system. Many vehicles have additional independent switches for these purposes.

In older domestic vehicles, the brake light switch is usually wired into the same circuit as the turn signals and hazard flashers. This turns on the brake lights when the brakes are applied. The same filament is used for both brake lights and turn signals. Import vehicles and later-model domestic vehicles with amber rear turn-signal lights have separate circuits for rear turn signals and brake lights.

Parking Brake Switch

The parking brake switch closes to complete the brake warning light circuit to ground. It turns on the brake warning light whenever the parking brake is applied. The brake warning light may also remain on if the parking brake is not fully released. This alerts the driver to fully release the parking brake before proceeding. Not fully releasing the parking brake may allow it to drag. This can lead to serious overheating of the wheel brake mechanism and shorten brake pad life.

Brake Fluid Level Sensors

A **low brake fluid level sensor** is simply a float-operated switch. When the float drops because of low fluid level, the switch closes. When the switch closes, it completes the ground circuit and illuminates the brake warning light. This warning light alerts

HYBRID TECHNOLOGY

Hybrid Warning Lights

The warning lights in a hybrid vehicle are different from those in a conventional vehicle. See **Fig. A**. They include the following:

- Ready light. When the vehicle is turned to START, indicates that the vehicle is ready to drive.
- Output control warning light. Turns on when the HV (hybrid vehicle) battery charge is insufficient at R range or when there is an abnormal temperature rise in the HV battery. It may also light when the HV battery temperature is low.
- Master warning light. Turns on when a buzzer sounding; linked with the EMPS (electric motor-assisted power steering) malfunction warning light and the hybrid system malfunction warning light.
- Malfunction indicator light. Indicates a malfunction in the engine control system.
- Discharge warning light. Indicates a malfunction in the 12-volt charging system.
  - EMPS malfunction warning light. Indicates a malfunction in the EMPS system.
  - HV battery warning light. Indicates that the HV battery is discharged to the lower limit.
  - Hybrid system warning light. Indicates a malfunction in MG (motor generator) 1 and/or 2, HV battery, or HV ECU (engine control unit).

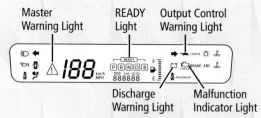

Master Warning Light   READY Light   Output Control Warning Light

Discharge Warning Light   Malfunction Indicator Light

Center Meter

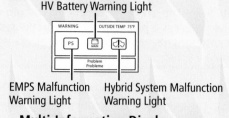

HV Battery Warning Light

EMPS Malfunction Warning Light   Hybrid System Malfunction Warning Light

Multi-Information Display

Toyota Motor Manufacturing

Fig. A A hybrid indicator and warning light system.

the driver that the brake fluid level in the master cylinder may be dangerously low. Most current vehicle models are equipped with such sensors. The sensor may be located in the side of the reservoir. It may be a part of the reservoir's cap.

On some vehicles, the warning lights receive battery power only after the voltage has passed through two fuses. Always check the fuses first if the warning lamp does not glow when the key is turned on. The wiring diagram also shows that the switches complete the ground side of the circuit to turn on the light. See **Fig. 5-28.**

Brake Wear Indicator Light

An **electric brake pad wear indicator** has a sensor wire molded into the pad lining. When the lining wears to a predetermined depth, a wire contacts the brake rotor.

The brake rotor, acting like a switch, completes the circuit to ground. This illuminates the brake-wear indicator light on the instrument panel. These indicators are in more expensive vehicles.

TECH TIP Checking Brake Warning Lights. On some vehicles equipped with daytime running lights (DRLs), the brake warning lamp circuit passes through the DRL control module. If the brake warning light will not go out, the problem could be in this control module.

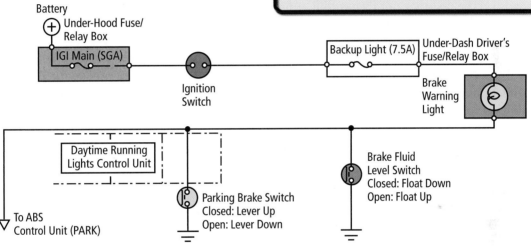

American Honda/Corp PR

Fig. 5-28 Wiring diagram for a Honda Accord brake warning light circuit. The switches usually complete the ground for the circuit. *What item should be checked first if the brake warning light does not glow when the key is turned on?*

SECTION 3 KNOWLEDGE CHECK

1. What may cause the brake warning light to remain off when the engine is started?

2. What may cause a brake warning light to glow?

3. What is the first indication of an ABS electrical or hydraulic malfunction?

4. What sensor activates the brake warning light when the brake fluid is low?

5. How do brake fluid level sensors work?

6. Explain how a brake-wear indicator light works.

ASE TEST PREP

7. Technician A says that if the red brake warning light does not come on when the key is turned to the ON position the cause may be a blown fuse. Technician B says that it could be a burned out bulb or a loose bulb socket. Who is correct?

ⓐ Technician A.

ⓑ Technician B.

ⓒ Both Technician A and Technician B.

ⓓ Neither Technician A nor Technician B.

CHAPTER 5 REVIEW

Key Points

Meets the following NATEF Standards for Electrical/Electronic Systems: inspecting, replacing, and aiming headlights; diagnosing incorrect turn signal operation.

- The headlight switch controls all regular exterior lighting.
- On vehicles with combination turn signal and brakelight bulbs, the brake light circuit goes through the turn signal switch.
- The flash rate for standard-duty flasher units depends on the amount of current flow in the circuit.
- Correct headlight aiming assures good visibility.
- The value displayed on an electromagnetic gauge depends on the resistance of the sending unit.
- Digital displays are controlled by a central processing unit (CPU).
- Warning light circuits may be switched at either the voltage or ground side of the circuit.
- The functions of the brake light switch can vary, in addition to turning on the brake lights.
- The brake warning light may be an indication that the parking brake has not been released.

Review Questions

1. What is a filament?
2. Explain how a high-intensity discharge (HID) lamp works.
3. Why are neon-filled tubes used in some brake lights?
4. Name the seven major components of a basic headlight circuit.
5. How does a multifunction switch relate to headlights?
6. What may cause a bulb to glow brighter than normal?
7. Explain the two methods used for headlight aiming.
8. What is the panel placed in front of an incandescent or halogen lightbulb?
9. What is a nonvolatile random access memory chip?
10. **Critical Thinking** Consider why only certain gases can be used in lightbulbs. Name the inert (chemically inactive) gas used in some lightbulbs.

Excellence in Communication

Recognizing Consequences

"Potentially life-threatening!" These are serious words. When a medical doctor speaks these words, they mean that a life might be ended by an illness. In an automotive context, these words are as serious as when they are spoken by a doctor. They, too, indicate a condition that could lead to the death of a driver, passenger, or pedestrian.

As a technician servicing a vehicle, you are responsible for the safety of the occupants of a vehicle. You need to read service manuals and safety bulletins very carefully. Keep your skills and knowledge up to date. Learn about new safety issues and new solutions by reading new information as it is released. You need to pay close attention to details. As a technician, you must accept the serious responsibilities of your job.

Apply It!

Meets NATEF Communications Standards for making inferences and predicting outcomes.

After re-reading Section 3, *Brake Warning Lights, Switches, and Sensors:*

1. Fold a sheet of notebook paper in half lengthwise. Head one half "Warnings." Head the other half "Consequences If Not Serviced."

2. List the "Warnings" given for the brake warning lights.

3. Study each warning. In the "Consequences" column, write the possible results if the warnings are ignored. Be sure to explain why some situations are or could become life-threatening.

AUTOMOTIVE SERVICE EXCELLENCE
TEST PREP

Answering the following practice questions will help you prepare for the ASE certification tests.

1. An incandescent bulb uses which type of filament?
   a Tungsten.
   b Steel.
   c Aluminum.
   d None of the above.

2. Technician A says that incandescent bulbs produce brighter, whiter light than halogen lamps. Technician B disagrees and says that halogen lamps produce light that is 25 percent brighter and whiter than incandescent bulbs. Who is correct?
   a Technician A.
   b Technician B.
   c Both Technician A and Technician B.
   d Neither Technician A nor Technician B.

3. What does a ballast module do?
   a Keeps the vehicle afloat when crossing high water.
   b Provides extra weight for braking.
   c Produces the initial charge to get a HID lamp to emit light.
   d Inflates the air bag.

4. Technician A says that LED lights are commonly used in automotive interior and exterior lighting. Technician B says that the most common LED color is red. Who is correct?
   a Technician A.
   b Technician B.
   c Both Technician A and Technician B.
   d Neither Technician A nor Technician B.

5. If the brake warning light comes on briefly when the engine is first started and then goes out this indicates:
   a low brake fluid pressure.
   b depleted vacuum reserve.
   c bulb check; everything is normal.
   d ABS module malfunction.

6. Electromagnetic displays are also called:
   a digital displays.
   b warning lamps.
   c absolute displays.
   d analog displays.

7. Technician A says that digital displays are controlled by micro processors known as central processing units (CPUs). Technician B says that digital displays can show letters, numbers, or bar graphs. Who is correct?
   a Technician A.
   b Technician B.
   c Both Technician A and Technician B.
   d Neither Technician A nor Technician B.

8. Instrument panel warning lights are usually lit by which type of device?
   a High-intensity discharge lamps.
   b Halogen lamps.
   c Incandescent lamps.
   d LCDs.

9. One gauge is no longer working in a customer's vehicle. Technician A says that the problem is a common fuse that is not functioning. Technician B says that the problem is likely to be a malfunction with the gauge itself or one of the sensors or sending units connected to that gauge. Who is correct?
   a Technician A.
   b Technician B.
   c Both Technician A and Technician B.
   d Neither Technician A nor Technician B.

10. Technician A says that the parking brake switch activates the ABS warning lamp. Technician B says that the switch does not activate any warning lamps. Who is correct?
    a Technician A.
    b Technician B.
    c Both Technician A and Technician B.
    d Neither Technician A nor Technician B.

Section 1
Accessory Motors
and Circuits

Section 2
Cruise Control
Systems

Section 3
Supplemental
Restraint Systems

Section 4
Horn Circuits

Diagnosing & Repairing Accessory and Safety Systems

Customer's Concern

Max Wellington just returned from a long vacation. He and his family drove his sedan over 3,200 miles. So, it's no surprise that Max is at your service center this morning for a lube, oil, and filter. But that's not all.

As the primary driver on the trip, Max relied heavily on the cruise control to ease leg strain. He said the cruise control system worked great for most of the trip. It was just in the last 500 miles that he noticed it wasn't maintaining the set speed. When he set the cruise at 65 mph, it would hold for a while then gradually lose speed. Max says, "Every 10 miles or so we'd lose about 5 miles per hour. I'd have to use the gas pedal to get back up to 65 and then reset the cruise."

Technician's Challenge

As the service technician, you need to find answers to these questions:

1. What is the first step in diagnosing Max's problem? Can a scan tool be used to read diagnostic trouble codes?

2. What could be causing the cruise control system to lose speed over time? Could the problem be related to the brake switches?

3. How might throttle linkage and vacuum relate to this problem? If there are no problems with throttle linkage and vacuum, what is defective?

● Section 1
Accessory Motors and Circuits

Objectives:

- Explain how small direct current (DC) motor circuits work.
- **G2** Diagnose incorrect wiper operation; diagnose wiper speed control and park problems; perform necessary action.
- **G3** Diagnose incorrect washer operation; perform necessary action.
- **H1** Diagnose incorrect operation of motor-driven accessory circuits; determine necessary action.
- **H9** Diagnose body electronic system circuits using a scan tool; determine necessary action.
- **H8** Remove and reinstall door panel.
- **H3** Diagnose incorrect electric lock operation; determine necessary action.

Vocabulary:

- **positive temperature coefficient (PTC) resistor**
- **park switch**

Permanent Magnet Motors

Small direct current (DC) motors are widely used to power automotive accessory systems. Most of these motors are permanent magnet (PM) type motors. The motor armature rotates inside a permanent magnetic field. Windshield wiper motors are examples of permanent magnet motors. Part of the operating circuit for some small motors may be in the body control module (BCM). The BCM uses inputs from a variety of sensors to control the operation of the motor.

Permanent magnet motors contain four major components: an armature, brushes, commutator, and the magnet(s). The brushes and commutator conduct current to the armature windings, creating an electromagnetic field. This magnetic field reacts with the permanent magnetic field, causing the armature to rotate. See **Fig. 6-1.** The armature shaft is connected either directly or through gears to the device to be operated.

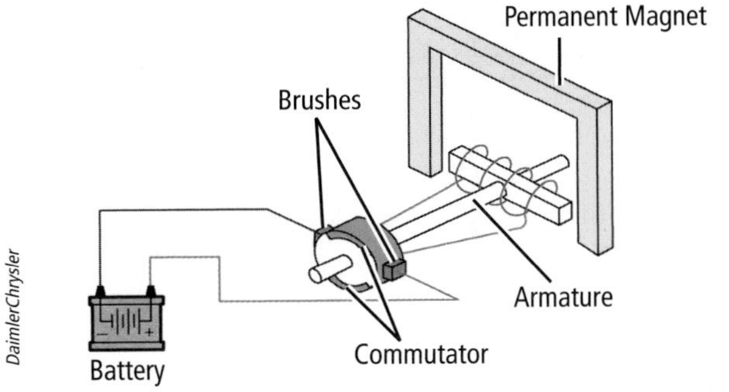

Small motor circuits often use two protection devices. A fuse or circuit breaker in the fuse panel protects the wiring. In addition, a self-resetting circuit breaker is located inside the motor. See **Fig. 6-2.** The circuit breaker in the motor can be either mechanically or electronically operated. Electronic circuit breakers are positive temperature coefficient resistors. A **positive temperature coefficient (PTC) resistor** is a solid state device that opens a circuit when an over-current condition occurs. Both types of circuit breaker reset when power to the motor is shut off.

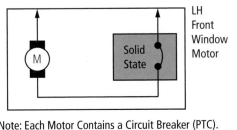

Note: Each Motor Contains a Circuit Breaker (PTC).
It Resets Only After Voltage Is Removed From the Motor.

General Motors Corporation

Fig. 6-2 An internal circuit breaker.

Accessory Motors

Accessory motors may be nonreversing or reversing. The type depends on whether the armature reverses the direction of current flow.

DaimlerChrysler

Permanent Magnet

Brushes

Armature

Commutator

Battery

Fig. 6-1 A typical permanent magnet (PM) motor.

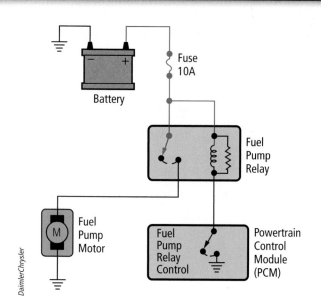

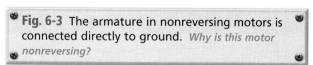

DaimlerChrysler

DaimlerChrysler

Fig. 6-3 The armature in nonreversing motors is connected directly to ground. *Why is this motor nonreversing?*

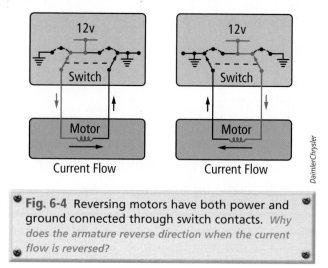

DaimlerChrysler

Fig. 6-4 Reversing motors have both power and ground connected through switch contacts. *Why does the armature reverse direction when the current flow is reversed?*

Nonreversing Motors

The polarity of an electromagnetic field depends on the direction of the current flow that creates the field. In a PM motor, the direction of armature rotation depends on the direction of current flow through the armature windings. When one brush of a motor is connected directly to ground, the motor is nonreversing. When power is applied, current always flows through the armature in the same direction. This means that the magnetic field always has the same polarity. The armature always rotates in the same direction. Nonreversing motors are used to operate such devices as fuel pumps, heater blowers, and windshield wipers. See **Fig. 6-3**.

Reversing Motors

If the direction of current flow through an armature is reversed, its magnetic polarity is also reversed. This causes the armature to rotate in the opposite direction. The armature in a reversing motor is not connected directly to ground. Instead, the circuit is wired through a control switch. One control switch contact provides power while another contact supplies a ground connection. The switch contacts may be "ganged" (connected together) so that they move at the same time. By

changing the position of the switch the direction of the current flow is changed. The armature can be made to rotate in either direction. Reversing motors are used to operate devices such as power windows, seats, and antennas. See **Fig. 6-4**.

Some vehicles with power windows have an "express down" feature for the driver's window only. When the driver's window switch is momentarily moved to the express position, the window will move all the way down without the switch being held. An electronic module controls the express down circuit. See **Fig. 6-5**. For safety reasons this express feature does not work when the window is being raised.

Fig. 6-5 Power windows use reversing motors to move the window up and down. *How does the circuit for the LH window differ from the RH window?*

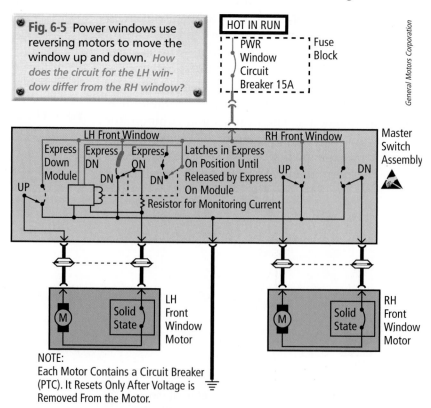

General Motors Corporation

NOTE:
Each Motor Contains a Circuit Breaker (PTC). It Resets Only After Voltage is Removed From the Motor.

Accessory Circuits

Some accessory circuits use more than one reversing-type motor. Power seat circuits, for example, use several motors, depending on the number of possible seat adjustments. See **Fig. 6-6.**

Windshield Wiper Circuits

Most windshield wiper circuits use nonreversing PM motors, designed for two-speed operation. They have three brushes instead of two. An insulated and a ground brush are located 180° apart on the commutator. A second insulated brush is located near the first. When the wiper switch completes the circuit to the first insulated brush, the wiper motor operates at normal speed. Moving the wiper switch to the HIGH position moves the circuit to the second insulated brush. This causes the motor to operate at high speed. The wiper motor assembly includes a gearbox and attached linkages that convert the rotary motion of the motor armature to the back-and-forth motion of the wiper arms.

Safety First — **Remove Jewelry** Never work on electrical circuits while wearing jewelry. The accidental shorting of voltage through a ring or watchband can result in serious burns.

The motor assembly also contains a park switch operated by a cam, relay, or both. The **park switch** is a switch that supplies power to the motor after the wiper switch is turned off. This allows the blades to travel to their normal park position at the base of the windshield before the motor stops. If the park switch does not close, the wiper blades stop where they are when the wiper switch is turned off. If the park switch contacts stick closed, the wipers do not stop when the wiper switch is turned off.

Many windshield wiper circuits contain an electronic module to provide pulse, or intermittent, operation. When the wiper switch is in the pulse position, a timing delay circuit controls the voltage to the module. Varying the position of the switch controls the amount of delay that occurs between wiper strokes.

TECH TIP **Avoiding Module Damage.** If the motor circuit includes an electronic module, use only a digital voltmeter when measuring voltage. Use caution when handling the module to avoid damage due to electrostatic discharge (ESD). Accidental shorting of circuits can result in permanent component damage.

Windshield Washer Circuits

Windshield washer circuits work in conjunction with the windshield wipers. A nonreversing PM motor drives the washer pump. The motor is controlled by a separate set of contacts in the wiper switch. In most cases when the washer circuit is activated, the wiper motor operates at low speed. The wiper completes several strokes after the washer shuts off, then returns to its previous status (operating or parked).

Heated Glass, Power Seats, and Mirrors

Heated Glass Diagnosis The rear defroster grid can be checked by using a digital multimeter to verify that voltage is present at each separate grid. A test light may be also used to verify that voltage is present. The switch can be diagnosed by using a digital multimeter.

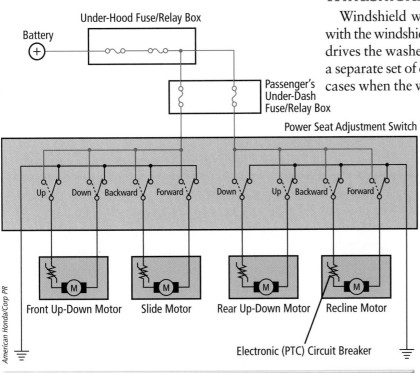

American Honda/Corp PR

Fig. 6-6 A wiring diagram for an eight-way power-seat circuit. *How many fuses and circuit breakers are used in this circuit?*

Excellence in Math

Using Metric Prefixes

You will frequently use metric measurements in your work. It is important to understand the metric system. With a little practice, you will be surprised at how easy and convenient it is to use this system.

Metric units for specific measurements such as length, pressure, resistance, voltage, and current are related to each other by factors of ten. Prefixes indicate how many multiplications or divisions by ten are involved. In the table, the most commonly used metric prefixes are unshaded.

As you know, multiplying by ten can be done by moving the decimal point to the right:

$$2 \text{ kg} = 2,000 \text{ g} = 2,000,000 \text{ mg}$$

Dividing by ten can be done by moving the decimal point to the left:

$$360 \text{ mm} = 36 \text{ cm} = 0.36 \text{ m}$$

You might choose to use any one of the three ways of expressing these measurements. Your choice would depend on the situation.

It is easier to use factors of ten than it is to use many of the factors found in the English (customary) system. Factors such as 12, 16, 36, 128, or 5280 are harder to remember and use in multiplication or division. Using metric prefixes, you can do the mathematics more easily in your head.

Prefix	Symbol	Factor
giga-	G	× 1,000,000,000
mega-	M	× 1,000,000
kilo-	k	× 1,000
hecto-	h	× 100
deca-	da	× 10
deci-	d	÷ 10
centi-	c	÷ 100
milli-	m	÷ 1,000
micro-	μ	÷ 1,000,000
nana-	n	÷ 1,000,000,000

Apply It!

Meets NATEF Mathematics Standards for understanding place values when using the metric system.

Convert the following to complete each statement.

1. 0.0005 A = __?__ mA = __?__ μA
2. 12 kΩ = __?__ Ω = __?__ MΩ
3. 36 km = __?__ m = __?__ mm
4. 0.0028 V = __?__ μV = __?__ mV
5. 120,000 Pa = __?__ kPa = __?__ Mpa

Which of the three ways of writing each number do you think would be easiest to use? Why? Remember they all represent the same value.

Power Seat Diagnosis A scan tool may be used to read codes and aid in diagnosing power seat issues. Before attempting any repair, verify seat operation. Diagnosis is possible by using a digital multimeter to measure voltage and check the continuity of switches, motors, and wiring.

Power Mirror Diagnosis A scan tool may be used to read codes and aid in diagnosing power mirror issues. Before attempting any repair, verify mirror operation. Diagnosis is possible by using a digital multimeter to measure voltage and check the continuity of switches, motors, and wiring.

Diagnosing Motor Circuits

Because all direct current motors use the same operating principles, the diagnostic techniques for all motor circuits are very similar. A wiring diagram for a typical windshield wiper and washer motor circuit is shown in **Fig. 6-7**. Before attempting to diagnose problems in the electrical circuit, make sure the motor is free to move. Check for mechanical interference that could prevent the motor from operating normally. If a wiper motor operates at only one speed, refer to a wiring diagram to determine the current path for the other brush circuit.

Checking the Ground Circuit

Nonreversing motors are usually grounded through their cases. Make sure the motor mounting bolts are clean and tight. A loose or corroded mounting bolt cannot provide a good ground connection. Reversing motors are grounded through a separate set of contacts in the control switch. With the switch in the operating position, measure voltage drop from the motor to a ground connection. A voltage drop of less than 0.5 volts is usually considered acceptable. If the voltage drop is higher, check the circuit for poor connections. If the ground connection is questionable, use a jumper wire to connect the motor case to a known good ground. If the motor operates with the jumper connected, the ground circuit is defective.

If the power source and ground circuit are good, the motor itself is usually defective. Most small motors are serviced by replacement only. Some replacement parts may be stocked for wiper motors. Check with a parts supplier for the availability of these parts.

Checking Power Source

Some motor circuits are powered only when the ignition switch is on. Other circuits are not controlled by the ignition switch (hot at all times). Make sure the ignition switch is in the correct position for the circuit you are working on. If the circuit has more than one switch controlling the motor, try all of the switches. If the motor can be operated from any switch, the power source and circuit protection devices are good. If the motor does not operate at all, check the fuse and circuit breaker. Circuit breakers that are inside a motor reset when the power source (control switch) is turned off. Check the circuit for an electrical overload before replacing an open fuse or circuit breaker. An overload may be caused by a motor that cannot rotate due to internal or external interference.

Some motor circuits use relays to connect both the power and ground side of the motor. In this case the control switches conduct only the low current used by the relay windings. With less current flow, there is less arcing at the switch contacts. The higher current flow required by the motor is conducted through the relay contacts.

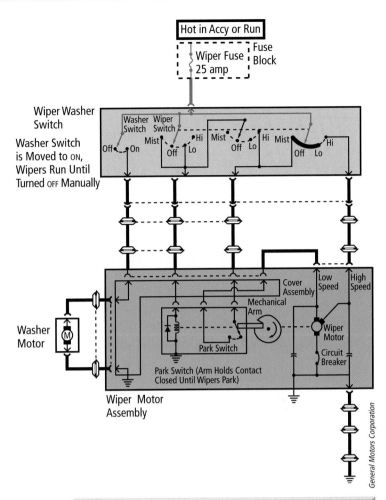

Fig. 6-7 Nonreversing permanent magnet windshield wiper and washer motors. *What two devices operate the park switch on the wiper motor?*

Use a voltmeter to check for voltage from the power source to the motor terminal when the switch is on. For reversing motors, you need to refer to a wiring diagram to determine which side of the circuit is powered for a given direction of movement. If there is no voltage at the motor, check the switch, connectors, and wiring for an open circuit. If the circuit uses relays, check for voltage to and from the relays while the circuit is activated. Check the relay windings for continuity with a voltmeter or ohmmeter. If voltage is present at the battery side of the motor, check the ground circuit.

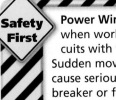

Safety First

Power Windows Use extreme caution when working with power window circuits with the door trim panel removed. Sudden movement of the window could cause serious injury. Removing the circuit breaker or fuse is advisable.

Electric Lock Diagnosis

To diagnose the electric lock:

1. Refer to appropriate vehicle service manual for specifications. Follow all procedures in manual.
2. Make sure the battery is in normal fully charged condition before testing circuits.
3. If all locks are inoperative, check circuit breakers or fuses and wiring to the doors. See **Fig. 6-8**.
4. If only one lock is inoperative, remove the door panel for access to the system. Disconnect the electrical connector from the door lock motor.
5. To lock the door, connect a 12-volt power source to the positive pin of the lock motor. Connect a ground wire to the other pin. To unlock the door, reverse the connections at the motor terminals.
6. If the lock does not work, replace the motor.
7. To test the door lock switch, remove it from its mounted position. Use an ohmmeter to check continuity in the Lock and Unlock positions.
8. If this test does not produce the desired result, replace the switch.

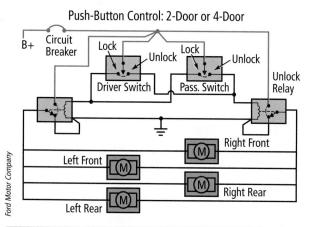

Push-Button Control: 2-Door or 4-Door

Ford Motor Company

Fig. 6-8 Some motor circuits use relays to control current to and from the motor.

Removing and Reinstalling a Door Panel

It may be necessary on occasion to remove a door panel to gain access to power lock or power window motors. General procedures for removing and reinstalling the door panel are as follows.

1. Make sure that you follow all procedures in the appropriate service manual.
2. Carefully inspect the door panel to locate and determine what hardware and fasteners will have to be removed.
3. If a manual window crank handle is present, remove it. You may have to remove a concealed clip with a wire hook.
4. Remove the inner door lock handle. It may sometimes be removed in a manner similar to the removal of the window crank handle.
5. Remove any screws that support the armrest. Trim plugs may conceal these screws. Sometimes a power window and lock control panel must be removed to access these screws.
6. Remove any power window and door lock control panels and disconnect the electrical wiring harness. You may also need to disconnect a wire to a courtesy light.
7. Use a trim panel remover to pry loose all retaining clips behind the panel around the edges of the panel.
8. Remove the door panel by lifting it upward and away from the door.
9. Be careful not to damage the vinyl moisture barrier behind the door panel. Make sure barrier is in place when installing the door panel.
10. After making repairs, reverse the order of the above instructions to install the door panel.

SECTION 1 KNOWLEDGE CHECK

1. Name an automotive part that may be powered by a permanent magnet type motor.
2. What part of a small motor uses inputs from a variety of sensors to control operation?
3. How does current flow in a nonreversing motor?
4. What supplies power to the windshield wiper motor after the wiper switch is turned off?
5. How would you test a door lock switch?

ASE TEST PREP

6. Technician A says that windshield wiper motors are nonreversing PM motors. Technician B says that most of these have three brushes instead of two. Who is correct?
   ⓐ Technician A.
   ⓑ Technician B.
   ⓒ Both Technician A and Technician B.
   ⓓ Neither Technician A nor Technician B.

Section 2
Cruise Control Systems

Objectives:

- Identify the major components of an electronic/vacuum cruise control system.
- **H4** Diagnose incorrect operation of cruise control systems; determine necessary action.

Vocabulary:
- **cruise control vacuum servo**
- **stepper motor**

Types of Cruise Control Systems

Cruise (speed) control systems are designed to reduce driver fatigue by maintaining a constant cruising speed. When engaged, the system controls throttle position to maintain the driver-selected vehicle speed. Two types of cruise control systems are currently in use: the electronic/vacuum operated system and the electronic system.

Electronic/Vacuum Systems

Electronic/vacuum cruise control systems use an electronic circuit to regulate vacuum to the cruise control vacuum servo. A **cruise control vacuum servo** is a device that uses a vacuum-operated diaphragm to hold the throttle linkage open. See **Fig. 6-9**. In addition to the diaphragm, the servo has an inlet and outlet valve and a servo position sensor. When the system is disengaged, a return spring closes the throttle.

Components The major components of an electronic/vacuum cruise control system are the:
- Electronic control unit.
- Cruise control switch.
- Vacuum servo.
- Brake (and clutch, if used) switch.
- Vacuum release valve.
- Throttle cable.
- Vehicle speed sensor (VSS) input.
- Manifold vacuum source.

On some vehicles the control unit is a self-contained module located under the instrument panel. Other vehicles have the control unit function built into the powertrain control module (PCM) or body control module (BCM).

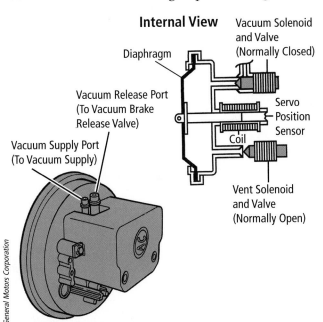

Internal View

Diaphragm
Vacuum Solenoid and Valve (Normally Closed)
Vacuum Release Port (To Vacuum Brake Release Valve)
Servo Position Sensor
Vacuum Supply Port (To Vacuum Supply)
Coil
Vent Solenoid and Valve (Normally Open)

General Motors Corporation

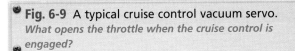

Fig. 6-9 A typical cruise control vacuum servo. *What opens the throttle when the cruise control is engaged?*

TECH TIP **Reading Cruise Control System Information.** When the cruise control circuit is in the PCM or BCM, diagnostic trouble codes (DTCs) and other cruise system information can be read in the data stream.

The cruise control switches are often part of a multifunction switch on the steering column. The switches may also be located on the steering wheel or on the instrument panel. The vacuum servo is located under the hood and is connected by a cable to the throttle linkage. The brake and clutch switches disengage cruise operation when the pedal is depressed. Applying the brakes disengages the system in two ways. A vacuum release valve and an electric release switch are mounted on the brake pedal bracket.

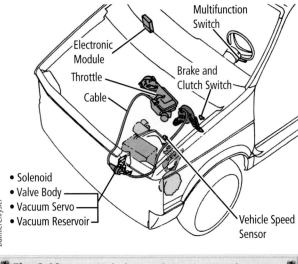

Multifunction Switch

Electronic Module

Throttle

Cable

Brake and Clutch Switch

- Solenoid
- Valve Body
- Vacuum Servo
- Vacuum Reservoir

Vehicle Speed Sensor

DaimlerChrysler

Fig. 6-10 A typical electronic/vacuum cruise control system. *How is the vacuum servo connected to the throttle lever?*

When the brake pedal is depressed, the vacuum release valve opens to vent the vacuum from the servo. At the same time, the electric release switch opens, electrically disconnecting the system. Two brake release devices are used as a safety feature. If either device fails, the other will still disengage the system. Vehicles with manual transmissions may use an electric release switch operated by the clutch pedal in addition to the two brake release devices. See **Fig. 6-10.**

When either the clutch pedal or brake pedal is depressed, the system is electrically disengaged.

System Operation The electronic module uses inputs from the cruise control switch, VSS, servo-position sensor, and brake/clutch release switches. See **Fig. 6-11.** In most cases four modes of operation are possible: cruise, coast, resume/accelerate, and tap up/tap down.

For safety reasons, the vehicle must be traveling above 25 mph [40 kph] to engage the system. When the vehicle slows below this point, the cruise control system automatically disengages.

With the cruise switch ON, momentarily pressing the set button activates the system. The control unit opens the vacuum inlet valve and closes the vent valve on the servo. As vacuum builds in the servo, the diaphragm moves the throttle to a position that maintains the selected cruising speed. When the speed is reached, the control unit closes the inlet valve. This seals the vacuum in the servo vacuum chamber and maintains the set speed.

If the vehicle speed begins to decrease (going uphill, for example), the controller opens the inlet valve to admit more vacuum. This causes the servo to open the throttle farther to maintain the set speed. When vehicle speed increases (going downhill), the vent valve is opened to release some vacuum. This causes the throttle to close slightly to prevent over-speeding. During operation the controller opens and closes the servo valves as needed. This provides the throttle opening required to maintain the desired vehicle speed.

If the SET button is held in, the vehicle decelerates until the button is released. The speed at which the button is released is the new set speed. On many systems, if the SET button is pushed in and released immediately, the set speed decreases by 1 mph [1.6 kph]. This is the "tap down" feature.

The RESUME/ACCEL (R/A) switch serves three purposes. If the brake or clutch switch has disengaged the cruise system, the R/A switch causes the system to resume the previous speed. The R/A function also restores the previous speed if the system was disengaged because vehicle speed dropped below 25 mph [40 kph]. The resume feature does not work if the cruise or ignition switches have been turned off. If the R/A switch is held in the ON position while in the cruise mode, the vehicle accelerates until the switch is released. Moving the R/A switch to ON and releasing it immediately increases the set speed by 1 mph [1.6 kph]. This is the "tap up" mode.

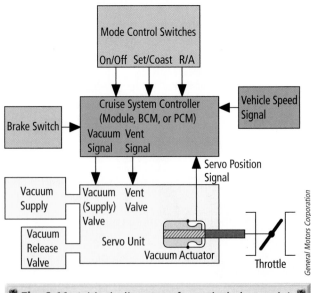

Mode Control Switches

On/Off Set/Coast R/A

Cruise System Controller (Module, BCM, or PCM)

Vacuum Vent Signal Signal

Brake Switch

Vehicle Speed Signal

Servo Position Signal

Vacuum Supply

Vacuum (Supply) Valve

Vent Valve

Vacuum Release Valve

Servo Unit

Vacuum Actuator

Throttle

General Motors Corporation

Fig. 6-11 A block diagram of a typical electronic/vacuum cruise control system. *What three input signals does the controller use to operate the system?*

Electronic Systems

Electronic (stepper motor) cruise control systems do not use a vacuum servo. Instead, an electronic controller and a stepper motor are combined into a single unit called a cruise control module. A **stepper motor** is a type of electric motor that is used to position a component very precisely. See **Fig. 6-12.** The stepper motor replaces the vacuum diaphragm. It opens the throttle to maintain the desired cruising speed. In some applications the control module is still referred to as a servo.

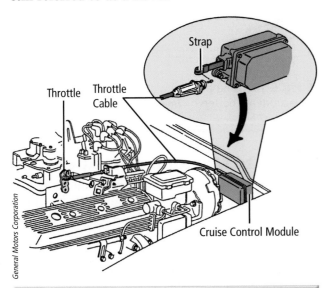

Fig. 6-12 A typical electronic (stepper motor) cruise control system. *What component in the cruise control module opens the throttle?*

Electronic System Components The cruise control module is located under the hood of the vehicle. In addition to the electronic controller and stepper motor, the module contains a solenoid-operated clutch and a drum gear and strap. See **Fig. 6-13.** The drum gear strap is connected to the throttle cable.

The cruise control switch and VSS are similar to those used for the electronic/vacuum cruise control system. Two brake electrical release switches are used. One switch serves as a backup for the other. A clutch electrical release switch is used on vehicles with manual transmissions.

System Operation As with other cruise control systems, vehicle speed must be above 25 mph [40 kph] for the circuit to engage. With the cruise switch ON, pressing the SET button activates the system. The cruise control module energizes the solenoid-operated clutch. This connects the drum gear and

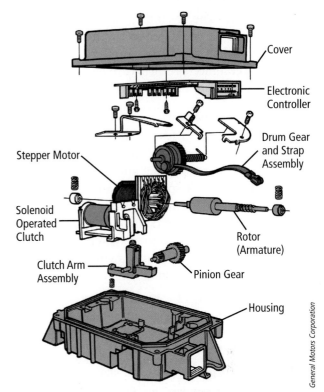

Fig. 6-13 The cruise control module contains the electronic controller, stepper motor, solenoid-operated clutch, and drum gear and strap. *What is the drum gear strap connected to?*

strap to the stepper motor rotor (armature). The control circuit moves the armature in small steps to open the throttle to the position that maintains the set speed. Stepper motor movement causes the drum and strap to open or close the throttle.

As soon as the brake, clutch, or cruise switch opens the electrical circuit, the clutch is disengaged. This disconnects the drum gear from the motor armature and allows a return spring to close the throttle. When the system is disengaged, the armature returns to the closed throttle position.

The coast, resume/accelerate, and tap up/tapdown modes of operation for this system are identical to that of the electronic/vacuum cruise control system.

Diagnosing and Repairing Cruise Control Systems

When diagnosing any cruise control problem, determine whether the control circuit is in the PCM or BCM. If so, use a scan tool to read any diagnostic trouble codes (DTCs) and other information related to the cruise control operation. Electronic testers are available for some cruise control systems.

They plug into the wiring harness between the controller and servo. Refer to the manufacturer's instructions when using such a tester.

The most common problems are failure to engage and failure to maintain a set speed.

Failure to Engage

If the cruise control system does not engage:

1. Check the cruise control fuse.
2. Inspect the system wiring and connections.
3. Check for a vehicle speed input to the controller.
4. Referring to a wiring diagram, check for the correct voltage at the controller and servo terminals as the cruise control switch is operated.
5. Check the brake (and clutch) switches for proper position and operation.

Safety First **Servo Solenoid Valves** Do not energize the servo solenoid valves with jumper wires while the engine is running. The engine over-speed condition that will result could cause severe engine damage.

The following checks apply to vacuum-operated systems only:

1. Start the engine. Check for vacuum at the vacuum line to the servo. Vacuum should be at least 10 in. [25 cm] of mercury at idle. See **Fig. 6-14**.
2. Check for leaks in vacuum release hose and valve.
3. Check the resistance of the servo solenoid windings. Refer to the vehicle service manual for specifications.
4. Check for a vacuum leak at the servo. (See the procedure below.) If the results of these checks are satisfactory, the controller is usually defective.

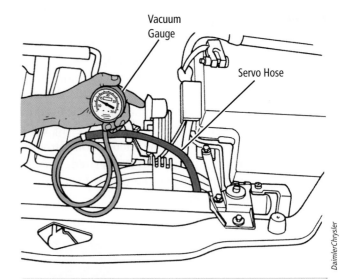

DaimlerChrysler

Fig. 6-14 Using a vacuum gauge to check for a vacuum at the servo. *How much vacuum should be present?*

Failure to Maintain a Set Speed

If the cruise system fails to maintain the set speed, check the throttle linkage adjustment. Refer to the vehicle service manual for the correct procedure. If the linkage adjustment is good, check for a vacuum leak at the servo. With the engine off, use jumper wires to energize the servo solenoid valves. Apply vacuum with a hand-held vacuum pump. If the servo fails to hold a vacuum, it must be replaced. If the linkage adjustment and servo are good, the controller is probably defective.

SECTION 2 KNOWLEDGE CHECK

1. What is a cruise control vacuum servo?
2. Which two switches disengage cruise operation?
3. Name the four modes of cruise control operation.
4. Explain what the control unit does when a car using cruise control begins climbing a hill.
5. What is a stepper motor?
6. What may cause a cruise control system's failure to maintain a set speed?

ASE TEST PREP

7. Technician A says that in an electronic/vacuum cruise control system the throttle linkage is held open by a permanent magnet motor. Technician B says that it is held open by a stepper motor. Who is correct?
   ⓐ Technician A.
   ⓑ Technician B.
   ⓒ Both Technician A and Technician B.
   ⓓ Neither Technician A nor Technician B.

Section 3
Supplemental Restraint Systems

Objectives:

- Identify the components of the supplemental restraint system.
- H5 • Diagnose supplemental restraint system (SRS) concerns; determine necessary action. (Note: Follow manufacturer's safety procedures to prevent accidental deployment.)
- H6 • Disarm and enable the airbag system for vehicle service.

Vocabulary:

- air bag
- inflator module
- air bag control module
- crash sensor

Air Bag Systems

Supplemental restraint systems (SRSs) are also called air bag systems. An **air bag** is a balloon-type passenger safety device that inflates automatically on vehicle impact. The original systems were designed to protect only the driver. In addition, the air bags inflated only if there was sufficient impact at the front of the vehicle. Newer systems also protect some passengers. They can be triggered by side as well as frontal impacts.

Air bag systems are intended to be used with seat belt restraints. An unbelted driver or passenger is not likely to receive maximum protection from the air bags. Even in relatively minor impacts, unbelted occupants have been seriously injured or killed by inflating air bags.

Air bag inflation (deployment) occurs when on-board sensors detect a sudden impact of sufficient severity. Current flow through an igniter circuit starts a chemical reaction in a solid propellant. The chemical reaction generates nitrogen gas that inflates the air bag. The gas is stored in a cylinder in the air bag module.

Components of Air Bag Systems

Most air bag systems use similar components, but the terminology is not standardized. Each manufacturer has unique terms for some system components.

Always refer to the service manual or training manual if you are unfamiliar with the components in the system you are working on. See **Fig. 6-15**.

Side air bags are mounted to the side of the seats, the roof, or the door. Used for side impact only, these bags will not deploy on frontal or rear impact. Also, each side operates independently. Therefore, the left-side air bag deploys upon left-side impact, the right-side air bag deploys on right-side impact. Rear airbags are used for rear passenger protection in the event of a frontal impact. A bag is deployed from the seat back to protect an adult's torso area.

Safety First **Inflator Module Circuit** Do not attempt to test the inflator module circuit with an ohmmeter or test light. The air bag may inflate, causing serious injury.

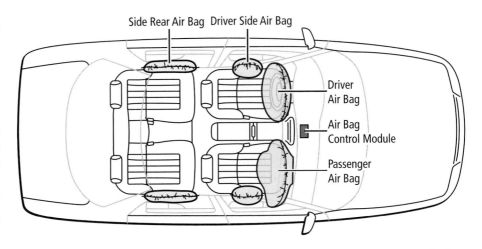

Side Rear Air Bag   Driver Side Air Bag

Driver Air Bag

Air Bag Control Module

Passenger Air Bag

Fig. 6-15 A typical inflatable restraint (air bag) system. *What inflates an air bag on most vehicles?*

Inflator Module The **inflator module** is the module that contains the air bag, ignitor, solid propellant, and cover. The driver side inflator module is located in the center of the steering wheel. See **Fig. 6-16**. The passenger side inflator module is mounted in the right side of the instrument panel. Side inflator modules are located in the door or seat assemblies.

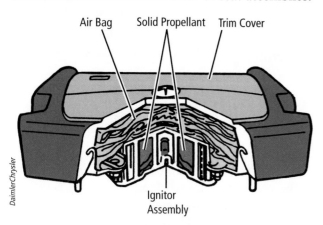

Air Bag   Solid Propellant   Trim Cover

Ignitor Assembly

DaimlerChrysler

Fig. 6-16 A driver-side air bag inflator module. *Where is the passenger side inflator module located?*

Air Bag Control Module The **air bag control module** is the module that monitors system operation, controls the air bag warning light, and stores trouble codes. It is located in the passenger compartment of the vehicle. In some cases a backup power supply and a crash sensor may be located in this module.

Crash Sensors A **crash sensor** is a sensor that closes an electrical circuit when sufficient impact occurs. The crash sensor is also called an impact sensor. There are several of these sensors. They are usually mounted under the hood and in the passenger compartment. The sensor in the passenger compartment may be located inside the air bag control module. The number and location of crash sensors varies among vehicles.

Most air bag systems use two crash sensors. One sensor is on the battery side of the circuit, while the other is on the ground side. The two sensors are calibrated to close at different impact levels. The sensors cannot be interchanged. Both must close at the same time for air bag inflation to occur. The sensors, along with the ignitor, power supply, and wiring make up the "deployment loop." A pair of identical sensors may be connected in parallel. If either one of the sensors closes, that part of the circuit is complete. See **Fig. 6-17**.

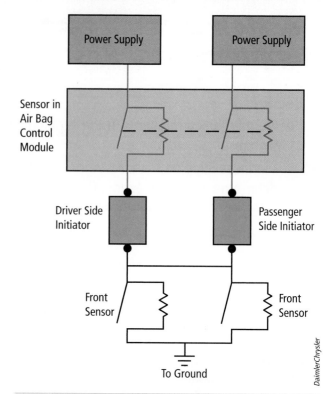

DaimlerChrysler

Fig. 6-17 A typical air bag circuit deployment loop. *What components make up the deployment loop?*

A common type of crash sensor uses a gold-plated steel ball held in place by a magnet. If a crash generates enough force to move the ball away from the magnet, the circuit between the sensor contacts closes. If both sensors in the circuit are closed, the air bag(s) inflate. See **Fig. 6-18**.

Occupant Classification Sensors This system is used to determine whether the front passenger seat is occupied by an infant, a child, or an adult. The occupant module senses (by weight) whether an infant or a small child is in the front seat. Two types of sensors used are the bladder and strain gauge. If it is determined that an infant or a small child is in the front seat, the classification module will send a bus message to the airbag controller to turn off the passenger air bag and illuminate the passenger airbag disable lamp.

Reserve (Backup) Power Supply The reserve power supply stores a voltage high enough to deploy the air bags. This is in case the battery connection is lost in a collision before the crash sensors close. The backup power supply can be a stand-alone unit or located in the control module.

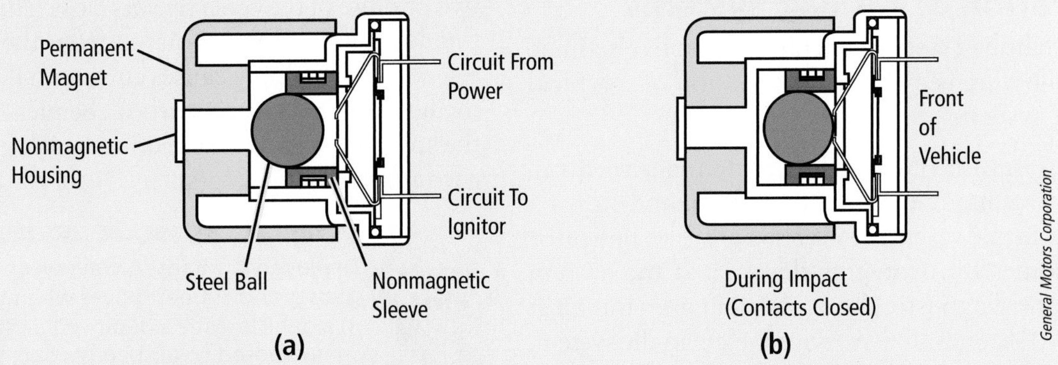

Permanent Magnet

Nonmagnetic Housing

Circuit From Power

Circuit To Ignitor

Steel Ball

Nonmagnetic Sleeve

(a)

Front of Vehicle

During Impact (Contacts Closed)

(b)

General Motors Corporation

Fig. 6-18 The operation of a crash sensor. In the crash sensor shown in **(a)**, a steel ball is held away from the sensor contacts by a magnet. During impact **(b)**, the ball is dislodged and completes the electric circuit to the ignitor. *What causes the ball to move toward the sensor contacts?*

Safety First

Backup Power Supply The backup power supply stays energized for several minutes after the ignition is turned off. When disabling an air bag system, wait at least ten minutes (or the time specified) before beginning work on the air bag system.

Clockspring The clockspring consists of two or more wires coiled inside a plastic housing mounted at the top of the steering column. The clockspring maintains a "hard wired" connection between the steering column wiring and the rotating steering wheel. This ensures good electrical contact between the driver side inflator assembly and the rest of the deployment circuit. Additional wires in the clockspring assembly may be used for the horn, steering wheel controls, or other similar circuits. See **Fig. 6-19**.

Indicator Light Air bag systems use a warning light on the instrument panel to inform the driver about the status of the system.

- The light should be off when the ignition switch is off.
- During the first 10 seconds after the ignition switch is turned on, the light should either stay on or flash on and off.
- The light goes out if the system passes a self-test initiated by the air bag control module.
- If the warning light does not come on, does not stay on or flash as it should, or fails to go out, there is a fault in the system.

Fig. 6-19 The clockspring assembly is mounted at the top of the steering column. *What is the purpose of the clockspring assembly?*

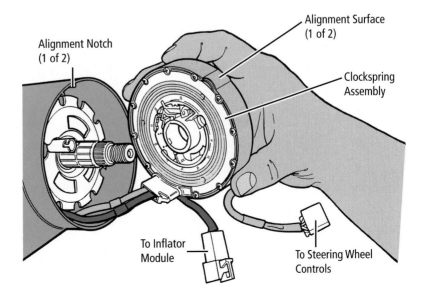

Alignment Notch (1 of 2)

Alignment Surface (1 of 2)

Clockspring Assembly

General Motors Corporation

To Inflator Module

To Steering Wheel Controls

Operation of Air Bag Systems

Most air bag systems operate in a similar manner. The following is a general description of a typical air bag system.

Startup Routine When the ignition is turned on, the control module checks the system and stores a voltage in the reserve power supply. The indicator light comes on or begins flashing. If the system passes the diagnostic check, the light goes out after about 10 seconds. If there is a problem in the system, the light either stays on or begins flashing trouble codes.

The control unit continuously checks the air bag system for possible faults. If none are found, the indicator light remains off. If a fault is detected, the warning light is turned on and a fault code is stored in the module's memory. Fault codes can be read by counting the number of light flashes or by using a scan tool.

Safety First **Air Bag Housing** The metal housing of the air bag module becomes very hot when the bag inflates. To avoid serious injury, do not handle the air bag for at least 20 minutes after deployment occurs.

Air Bag Deployment If the vehicle experiences an impact severe enough to require air bag deployment, two or more of the crash sensors close. This completes the deployment loop. Voltage from the battery or reserve power supply causes current to flow through the ignitor. The ignitor starts a chemical reaction in the solid propellant that produces nitrogen gas. The gas inflates the air bag(s). See **Fig. 6-20**.

Safety First **Deployed Air Bags** Always wear safety glasses and rubber gloves when working in a vehicle with a deployed air bag. If any skin is exposed to air bag residue, wash the affected skin with cool water and soap. Seek medical attention if irritation occurs.

Deployment Chemistry In addition to nitrogen gas, other materials are released during the chemical reaction. Small amounts of sodium azide, sodium hydroxide, and sodium bicarbonate may be found around a deployed air bag. Sodium azide is the primary propellant used in most air bag modules. Only very small amounts are present in a vehicle with a deployed air bag. Sodium hydroxide can irritate the eyes and skin.

Sodium bicarbonate is harmless. The "smoke" and dust released when an air bag deploys is talcum powder or cornstarch. They are used to keep the air bag surfaces from sticking to each other before deployment.

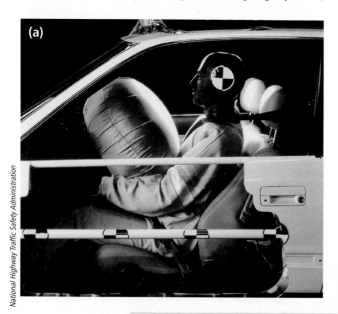
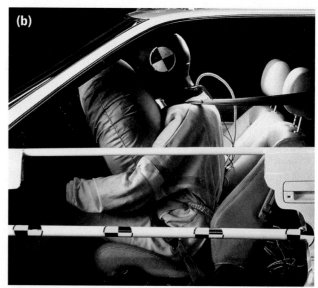

National Highway Traffic Safety Administration

Fig. 6-20 Air bag deployment sequence. Steering wheel at impact point, air bag begins deployment **(a)**. The air bag is fully deployed, protecting the driver from frontal impact **(b)**. *How many crash sensors must sense the impact before the air bag deploys?*

Diagnosis and Repair Special procedures are required when diagnosing and repairing inflatable restraint systems. Failure to follow specific testing and servicing instructions can cause accidental deployment of the air bag(s). In addition, improper servicing and handling of component parts may prevent the system from deploying successfully. Procedures that apply to one system may not apply to another. Always read and follow the vehicle service manual instructions. Pay particular attention to the many safety warnings and precautions.

TECH TIP **Warning Lights.** When diagnosing a problem, always observe the operation of system warning lights. If a light does not come on when it should, begin your diagnosis with the light circuit.

Reading and Erasing Trouble Codes Some inflatable restraint systems use the air bag warning light to display trouble codes. The system is put into diagnostic mode with a jumper wire connection or by cycling a switch. With the ignition on, the technician counts the number of light flashes to determine the trouble code(s) present. In some cases the codes are repeated several times with a slightly longer pause between displays. On other vehicles trouble codes are read with a scan tool connected to the data link connector (DLC) or a separate test connector for the air bag system. On some systems it is possible to read trouble codes using either the flash code or scan tool method.

Erasing trouble codes usually requires the use of a scan tool. With the scan tool connected and the ignition on, follow the instructions on the scan tool display. In some cases the codes will be erased only when the fault is corrected. On some systems, codes can be erased by cycling the driver's door light switch on and off at least five times within seven seconds of turning the ignition on. Always refer to the appropriate service manual for specific information on reading and erasing trouble codes.

Disabling the Air Bag System A variety of complex air bag systems are in use. It is not possible to have a single disabling procedure that is suitable for all applications. Use the procedures specifically recommended for the vehicle you are working on.

The following procedures are often used in various combinations as steps in preventing an air bag from deploying accidentally:
- Turn off the ignition switch.
- Disconnect the battery; isolate the cable from the post.
- Disconnect the clockspring connector at the base of the steering column.
- Connect a shorting clip across the disconnected clockspring connector (if not already in place).
- Wait the recommended time for the reserve power supply to shut down.

Safety First **Disable Air Bags** Disable the air bag(s) before working on the inflatable restraint system or on any components that require you to work near the air bags. This will prevent accidental deployment that could cause serious injuries.

- Remove the air bag fuse.
- Disconnect the reserve power supply.

There is no enabling of the air bag system after disabling. The air bag system automatically enables as long as the system is functional. The air bag warning lamp should illuminate during its bulb check and then extinguish to signal that the system is functioning properly.

Servicing Inflatable Restraint Systems Personal injury and extensive damage to the vehicle may occur if specific repair and replacement procedures are not followed exactly. Read the service manual carefully and perform the necessary steps in the order listed. Read all of the instructions before beginning the procedure. Follow the procedure(s) listed for disabling the system before beginning repairs.

Components of an inflatable restraint system cannot be repaired or adjusted. Defective or damaged parts must be replaced. In addition to the inflator module, some manufacturers require replacement of other deployment loop components if the bag has been deployed. The location and orientation (direction) of sensors are critical. Refer to the vehicle service manual for all service-related information and procedures.

Inflated air bags must be disposed of and documented according to specified regulations.

Excellence in Science

Using a Switching Transistor

Switching transistors are used in everything from supercomputers to sports cars. The electronic switch inside a computer-controlled lighting system is a transistor. Transistors have three connections:
- Collector.
- Base.
- Emitter.

The base electrode acts like a safety valve. A threshold base voltage triggers a large current flow from the collector to the emitter. The transistor switch is closed. All current flow from the collector to the emitter stops if there is no base current. The transistor switch is open. This switching action sends current through a small lamp. For larger lights, it sends current through a relay.

Apply It!

Demonstrating a Transistor's Switching Action

Meets NATEF Science Standards for electrical parameters and semi-conductors.

Materials and Equipment
- 2N3903 general-purpose NPN transistor
- Multimeter
- 330-ohm resistor (R_c)
- Light-emitting diode (LED)
- 1.0 kilo-ohm potentiometer (R_{POT})
- 2.7 kilo-ohm resistor (R_B)
- Breadboard

You can demonstrate a transistor's switching action on a breadboard.

1. Construct the circuit shown here.

2. Adjust the potentiometer to set the base voltage to approximately 0.7 volts or greater. The light-emitting diode will start glowing. The switch is now turned on. The LED emits visible light when it is conducting.

3. Decrease the base voltage to less than 0.6 volts and the LED stops glowing completely. This happens because the transistor has switched off. Current can no longer flow from the voltage supply to ground through the transistor.

4. Explain how the transistor in this experiment is similar to a mechanical switch.

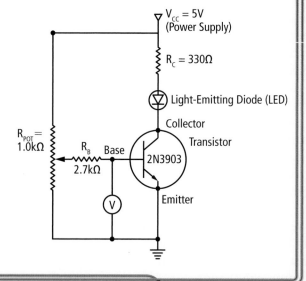

Seat Belts

Seat belts and air bags are designed to be used as a total passenger restraint system. Seat belts should be checked for wear and proper operation.

Seat Belt Retractors and Pretensioners

The seat belt retractor pulls the seat belt into its stored position when the belt is not in use and takes up slack when the belt is being used. See **Fig. 6-21**. To provide additional security during an accident, some seat belt systems use pretensioners. See **Fig. 6-22**.

A pretensioner pulls the seat belt tighter by retracting an extra bit of the seat belt webbing and locking it into place during impact. The pretensioner is deployed by the airbag module, which uses an electrical current to ignite a solid propellant. The pretensioner is not serviceable. After it has deployed, it must be replaced.

Inspecting Seat Belts

Normal use of seat belts may cause wear and deterioration. When inspecting seat belts:

1. Extend the seat belt so its total length can be seen.
2. Check the belts for cuts, wear, and deterioration. After a collision, belt fabric may show damage where the belt passes through the guide plates.

Delphi Safety & Interior Systems

Fig. 6-21 Retracting seat belt.

Delphi Safety & Interior Systems

Fig. 6-22 Seat belt pretensioner. *What is the purpose of the pretensioner?*

3. Attach the two portions of the buckle. Pull sharply on the belt to check buckle operation. Belt should release easily when the buckle release is pressed.
4. Check the belt anchor points for cracking or tearing. Look for sharp or exposed edges that may cut into the seat belt. Be sure the anchor brackets are firmly attached.
5. Check the retractor assemblies for proper operation. When the seat belt is released, it should retract fully, without binding or jamming.

Servicing Seat Belts

A damaged seat belt should be replaced with a new assembly. Refer to the vehicle service manual for the specific removal and installation procedures.

When removing seat belts:

1. Replace any component that is damaged.
2. Wear protective gloves and clothing. The areas where belts are attached may have sharp edges.
3. Remove the anchor brackets and retractor mechanisms. Be careful not to damage the bolt. Apply a solvent to frozen bolts to dissolve any corrosion.
4. Inspect all anchor points for corrosion and damage.

When installing seat belts:

1. Position the belt assembly to ensure the belt is not twisted or kinked.
2. Attach all mounting hardware with the correct hardened bolts.
3. Tighten all mounting bolts to the correct torque specifications.
4. Check the retractor assemblies for proper operation. When the seat belt is released, it should retract fully, without binding or jamming.

SECTION 3 KNOWLEDGE CHECK

1. What is another name for supplemental restraint systems (SRSs)?

2. What type of gas inflates the air bags?

3. What module monitors system operation, controls the air bag warning light, and stores trouble codes?

4. What happens if the battery connection is lost in a collision before the crash sensors deploy the air bags?

5. Why is cornstarch used in air bag systems?

ASE TEST PREP

6. Technician A says that the clockspring is part of the inflator module. Technician B says that the clockspring is located in the air bag control module. Who is correct?

   ⓐ Technician A.

   ⓑ Technician B.

   ⓒ Both Technician A and Technician B.

   ⓓ Neither Technician A nor Technician B.

Section 4
Horn Circuits

Objectives:
- Identify the components in a typical horn circuit.
- **G1** Diagnose incorrect horn operation; perform necessary action.

Vocabulary:
- **horn relay**
- **diaphragm**

Horn Circuit Components

A typical horn circuit consists of either one or two horns, a horn relay, and a horn switch. See **Fig. 6-23.**

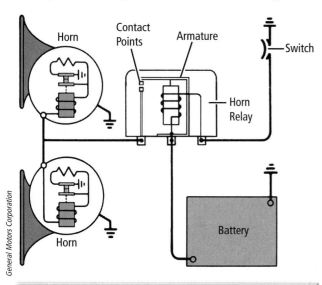

General Motors Corporation

Fig. 6-23 Automotive horn circuits use a relay to supply current to the horns. *Where is the relay winding grounded?*

Horns are usually located near the front of the vehicle under the hood. The **horn relay** is a relay that controls current flow from the battery to the horns. The horn relay may be located under the instrument panel or hood. Most horn switches are located on the steering wheel or on the steering column.

If the horn switch is located on the steering wheel, some provision must be made for continuous electrical contact while the wheel is rotated. Some vehicles use brushes and slip rings to maintain electrical contact in the circuit during wheel rotation. Vehicles with a supplemental restraint (air bag) in the steering wheel may use part of the air bag wiring harness (clockspring) in the steering column for horn switch wiring. See **Fig. 6-24.**

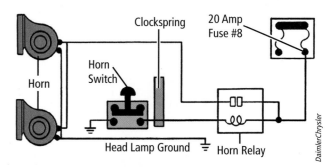

DaimlerChrysler

Fig. 6-24 On vehicles with air bag systems, the clockspring may be part of the horn switch wiring. *If a clockspring is not used, how is the circuit between the steering wheel and column connected?*

Closing the horn switch completes a ground path activating the horn relay. When the relay contacts close, battery voltage is connected to the horns. Current flow through a winding in each horn creates a magnetic field that causes an armature to move a diaphragm. In this case, a **diaphragm** is a thin disk that vibrates in response to electric signals to produce sound waves.

A pair of contact points inside the horn open when the armature movement reaches its limit, opening the circuit. A spring returns the armature and the diaphragm to its original position, closing the contacts. Repeating this cycle many times per second causes the diaphragm to vibrate. Movement of the diaphragm is similar to the cone of a speaker. See **Fig. 6-25.**

Diagnosing Horn Circuit Problems

If the horns do not operate, check the wiring and connections. Check the fuse. If the fuse is good, use a voltmeter or test light to check for voltage at the relay. If voltage is present, have someone operate the horn switch while you check for voltage from the relay. If voltage is present at the relay output, there is an open circuit between this point and the horns.

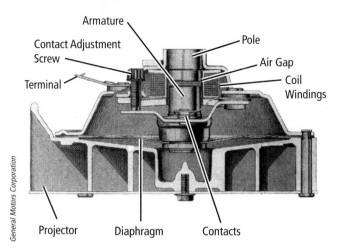

General Motors Corporation

Armature
Contact Adjustment Screw
Pole
Air Gap
Terminal
Coil Windings
Projector
Diaphragm
Contacts

Fig. 6-25 Automotive horns use a vibrating diaphragm to produce sound. *What makes the horn diaphragm vibrate?*

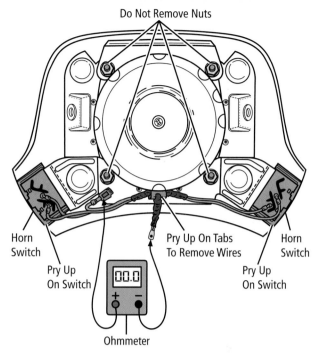

Do Not Remove Nuts
Horn Switch
Pry Up On Tabs To Remove Wires
Horn Switch
Pry Up On Switch
Pry Up On Switch
Ohmmeter

Fig. 6-26 Testing horn switches. Connect one lead of an ohmmeter to the ground wire and the other lead to the positive wire. The meter should read continuity when the horn switch is depressed. Repeat for the other switch. If there is no continuity, replace the switches.

Check the wiring, connections, and ground circuit. If there is no voltage at the relay output, use a jumper wire to ground the horn switch terminal at the relay. Make sure you ground the correct terminal. If the horn sounds, there is an open in the horn switch circuit. If the horn does not sound, the relay is defective.

Test the horn switches. See **Fig. 6-26**. Using an ohmmeter, connect one lead to the ground wire and the other lead to the positive wire. Depress the horn switch, which should have continuity. Repeat for the other switch. If there is no continuity, replace the switches.

Poor sound quality from horns can be caused by high resistance in the circuit, including the ground connection. Some horns can be adjusted using a tone adjustment screw. This screw controls the frequency and current draw of the horn.

SECTION 4 KNOWLEDGE CHECK

1. What makes up a typical horn circuit?

2. What is a horn relay?

3. What may be used to maintain contact between the battery and the horns if the horn switch is located on the steering wheel?

4. What vibrating part is responsible for making horn sounds?

5. What should be checked first if a horn does not operate?

6. What may cause poor sound quality from horns?

ASE TEST PREP

7. Technician A says horns cannot be adjusted. Technician B says that some horns can be adjusted. Who is correct?
   ⓐ Technician A.
   ⓑ Technician B.
   ⓒ Both Technician A and Technician B.
   ⓓ Neither Technician A nor Technician B.

CHAPTER 6 REVIEW

Key Points

Meets the following NATEF Standards for Electrical/Electronic Systems: diagnosing incorrect wiper operation; diagnosing incorrect operation of motor-driven accessory circuits.

- Many small motors have an internal electronic circuit breaker.
- Direct current motors can be reversing or nonreversing.
- Windshield wiper motors have an additional insulated brush to provide two-speed operation.
- Cruise control systems use either a vacuum diaphragm or a stepper motor to control throttle opening.
- Cruise control cannot be engaged below a minimum road speed designed into the system.
- Most inflatable restraint systems use a solid propellant to deploy the air bag(s).
- Inflatable restraint systems have a self-diagnostic capability.
- The inflatable restraint system should be temporarily disabled when working on or near system components.

Review Questions

1. Name a common type of small direct current motor.
2. What is a solid state device that opens a circuit in an over-current condition?
3. What type of motor is used to operate such devices as fuel pumps and windshield wipers?
4. Why remove jewelry before working on electrical circuits?
5. When checking voltage on reversing motors, why should you refer to a wiring diagram?
6. What is the advantage of having the cruise control circuit in the powertrain control module or body control module?
7. What is the lowest speed at which the cruise control may be activated?
8. In an SRS, what part maintains a hard wired connection between the steering column and wiring and the rotating steering wheel?
9. **Critical Thinking** Why is it important to follow manufacturer specifications when servicing air bags?
10. **Critical Thinking** Explain how to inspect seat belts.

Excellence in Communication

Researching Specialty Tools

A specialty tool has a special purpose. It may find use only in a certain area of automotive service or repair.

Some specialty tools may not be frequently used. Because of such infrequent use, you may be tempted to try using a tool you already have instead of a specialty tool. However, there may be consequences if the specified tool is not used. There may also be consequences if the specialty tool is not used correctly.

Damage to a component or a system may result. This may be expensive for you and your employer. It may also delay the repair and the return of the vehicle to the customer.

Apply It!

Meets NATEF Communication Standards for adopting a speaking and writing strategy and supplying information.

1. Using manufacturers' databases, the Internet, and service bulletins, research the specialty tools used in a specific automotive area (e.g., electrical and electronic systems).
2. Identify three specialty tools in that area.
3. For each tool, specify its purpose, the training needed for its use, and how frequently the tool might be used.
4. If possible, identify the consequences of substituting the use of another tool for the use of the specialty tool.
5. Organize your information for a presentation to your team members.

AUTOMOTIVE SERVICE EXCELLENCE
TEST PREP

Answering the following practice questions will help you prepare for the ASE certification tests.

1. Which of the following is an electronic circuit breaker that might be found in a motor?

   ⓐ Rheostat.

   ⓑ Solenoid.

   ⓒ Transistor.

   ⓓ Positive temperature coefficient (PTC) resistor.

2. All of the following are components of a PM motor *except* the:

   ⓐ armature.

   ⓑ commutator.

   ⓒ battery.

   ⓓ brushes.

3. If the direction of current flow through an armature is reversed its:

   ⓐ magnetic polarity is reversed and it rotates in the opposite direction.

   ⓑ magnetic polarity is reversed and it rotates in the same direction.

   ⓒ magnetic polarity is the same and it rotates in the opposite direction.

   ⓓ magnetic polarity is the same and it rotates in the same direction.

4. Technician A says that the park switch shuts off the engine when the car is parked. Technician B says that the park switch supplies power to the windshield wiper motor after the wiper switch is turned off. Who is correct?

   ⓐ Technician A.

   ⓑ Technician B.

   ⓒ Both Technician A and Technician B.

   ⓓ Neither Technician A nor Technician B.

5. Which of the following is not a major component of an electronic/vacuum cruise control system?

   ⓐ Electronic control unit.

   ⓑ Cruise control switch.

   ⓒ Brake (and clutch, if used) switch.

   ⓓ EGR valve.

6. Technician A says that the cruise control must automatically disengage at speeds below 45 mph [72 kph] for safety reasons. Technician B says that the cruise control operates at all vehicle speeds. Who is correct?

   ⓐ Technician A.

   ⓑ Technician B.

   ⓒ Both Technician A and Technician B.

   ⓓ Neither Technician A nor Technician B.

7. What component would a stepper motor be used in place of in a cruise control system?

   ⓐ Vacuum diaphragm.

   ⓑ Solenoid operated clutch.

   ⓒ Clutch arm assembly.

   ⓓ Drum gear and strap assembly.

8. Technician A says that air bags are intended to be used in conjunction with seat belts. Technician B says that some air bag systems inflate on both front and side impact. Who is correct?

   ⓐ Technician A.

   ⓑ Technician B.

   ⓒ Both Technician A and Technician B.

   ⓓ Neither Technician A nor Technician B.

9. A common triggering device for an air bag system is a:

   ⓐ ceramic disc.

   ⓑ gold-plated steel ball.

   ⓒ carbon cylinder.

   ⓓ plastic switch.

10. Technician A says that pretensioners retract some of the seat belt webbing and lock it in place on impact. Technician B says that the pretensioner is integrated into the seat belt assembly and is deployed by the air bag module. Who is correct?

    ⓐ Technician A.

    ⓑ Technician B.

    ⓒ Both Technician A and Technician B.

    ⓓ Neither Technician A nor Technician B.

Engine Performance

Chapter 1
Piston Engine Operation

Chapter 2
Diagnosing Engine Mechanical Problems

Chapter 3
Computerized Engine Controls

Chapter 4
Diagnosing & Repairing Ignition Systems

Chapter 5
Diagnosing & Repairing Air Induction Systems

Chapter 6
Diagnosing & Repairing Fuel Systems

Chapter 7
Using Computer Diagnostics

Chapter 8
Diagnosing & Repairing Emission Control Systems

Piston Engine Operation

Section 1
Internal Combustion Engines

Section 2
Engine Operation

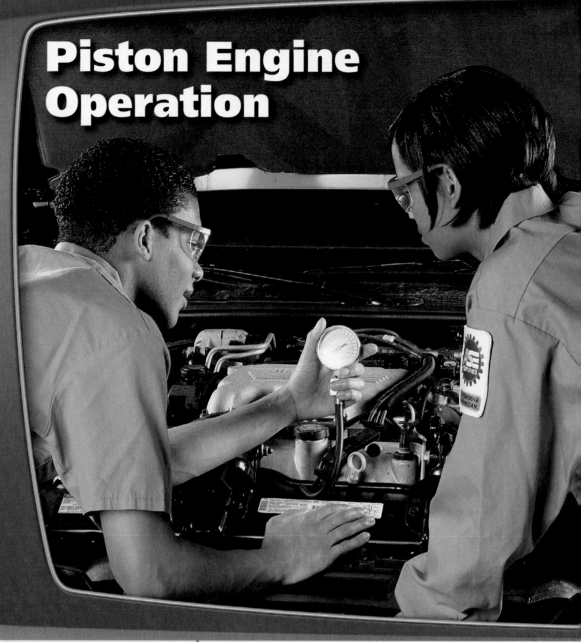

Customer's Concern

Internal combustion engines come in a variety of sizes and power ratings. They supply the mechanical energy needed to put compact, mid-size, and full-size vehicles in motion. Four-cylinder engines power smaller vehicles and provide better fuel economy than larger engines. More powerful six- and eight-cylinder engines are used to power most medium- and full-size vehicles. Ten- and twelve-cylinder engines provide high-performance power for sport models and workhorse power for heavy-duty pickup trucks.

Engine construction may differ by manufacturer, but all piston engines operate on the same principles. A good understanding of these principles will be important in your career as an automotive technician.

Technician's Challenge

As an automotive technician, you need to find answers to these questions:

1. How does an internal combustion engine produce power? How does it convert heat into motion? How is fuel burned inside the engine?

2. What are the basics of engine construction? What parts make up an engine? What is a cylinder, piston, crankshaft, and camshaft?

3. What is the purpose of the air induction, fuel, ignition, lubricating, cooling, and exhaust systems? How do they work together?

Section 1
Internal Combustion Engines

Objectives:
- Describe the function of the pistons.
- Describe the purpose of the connecting rods and crankshaft.
- A7 • Diagnose abnormal exhaust color, odor, and sound; determine necessary action.

Vocabulary:
- engine
- piston
- valve seat

Types of Engines

Automotive engines are internal combustion engines. See **Fig. 1-1**. An **engine** is a machine that turns heat energy into mechanical energy. An internal combustion engine burns fuel internally. The heat produced from burning a fuel creates the power that moves the vehicle.

Most automotive engines are called reciprocating engines because their pistons move up and down inside the cylinders. See **Fig. 1-2**. A **piston** is a cylindrical plug that fits inside the cylinder. It receives and transmits motion as a result of pressure changes applied to it.

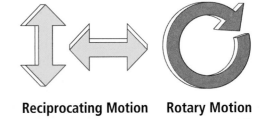

Reciprocating Motion   Rotary Motion

Fig. 1-2 Reciprocating motion is up-and-down or back-and-forth. Rotary motion is motion in a circle.

There are two types of internal combustion piston engines: spark-ignition (gasoline) and compression-ignition (diesel).

Internal combustion piston engines differ in:
- The type of fuel they use.
- The way ignition of the air/fuel mixture occurs.

Spark-Ignition Engine

Most spark-ignition engines run on liquid fuels, such as gasoline, alcohol, or a gasoline/alcohol blend. Some spark-ignition engines run on gaseous fuels, such as propane or natural gas.

Air and fuel enter the engine cylinders to create a combustible mixture. The pistons compress (squeeze) the mixture to about one-eighth of its original volume. The ignition system produces a spark at the spark plug, igniting the compressed mixture. As the mixture burns, temperature and pressure increase in the cylinder. The high pressure forces the piston down in the cylinder. This causes the crankshaft to rotate. Gears and shafts carry this motion to the wheels that drive the vehicle.

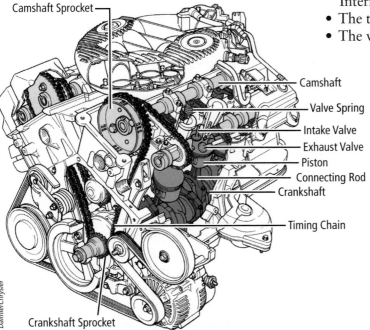

Camshaft Sprocket

Camshaft
Valve Spring
Intake Valve
Exhaust Valve
Piston
Connecting Rod
Crankshaft

Timing Chain

DaimlerChrysler

Crankshaft Sprocket

Fig. 1-1 A V-6 engine with dual overhead camshafts. *A spark ignition engine runs on what fuels?*

Compression-Ignition Engine

A diesel (compression ignition) engine runs on a light fuel oil similar to kerosene. In this type of engine, the piston compresses only air. Compressing air to about one-twentieth of its original volume raises its temperature to 1,000°F [538°C] or higher. The fuel is injected (sprayed) into the cylinder, where it is ignited by the heated air. As the mixture burns, the pressure forces the piston down in the cylinder.

Engine Construction

Spark- and compression-ignition engines are similar in construction. Both have engine blocks and cylinder heads. Both have pistons that move up and down in the cylinders. The cylinders, or cylinder bores, are machined openings through the engine block. A cylinder head covers the top of the cylinders. The bottom of each cylinder is open. The pistons are connected through this opening to the crankshaft.

The two travel limits for a piston are defined as top dead center (TDC) and bottom dead center (BDC). A piston stroke takes place when the piston moves from TDC to BDC or from BDC to TDC. See **Fig. 1-3**.

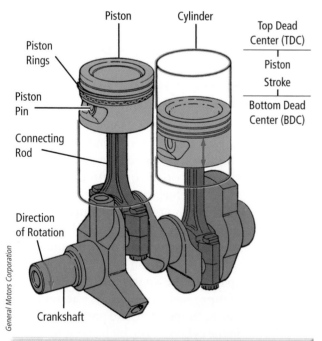

General Motors Corporation

Fig. 1-3 The reciprocating action of pistons in the cylinders. *When does a complete piston stroke take place?*

The Engine Block

The engine block, also called the cylinder block, is a precision metal casting. See **Fig. 1-4**. The block contains the:
- Cylinders, or cylinder bores.
- Pistons and connecting rod assemblies.
- Camshaft, for engines that do not have an overhead camshaft design.
- Crankshaft.

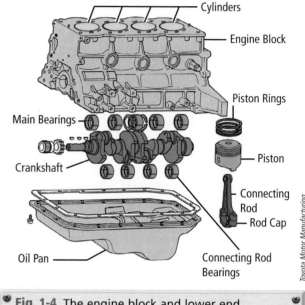

Toyota Motor Manufacturing

Fig. 1-4 The engine block and lower end parts. *Where does the cylinder head attach?*

Figure 1-5 shows the events that take place in the cylinder of a spark-ignition engine. The piston has completed its intake stroke. It is at its lower limit of travel, bottom dead center. See **Fig. 1-5(a)**. The space above the piston contains the air/fuel mixture.

Next, the piston moves up the cylinder toward top dead center. See **Fig. 1-5(b)**. This motion compresses the mixture. As the piston nears top dead center, an electric spark ignites the mixture. The mixture burns rapidly. This creates heat and high pressure that push the piston down in the cylinder. See **Fig. 1-5(c)**.

This downward movement creates power. At the bottom of the power stroke, the piston begins the exhaust stroke and moves up in the cylinder. The exhaust valves open, and the burned gases are pushed from the cylinder. See **Fig. 1-5(d)**.

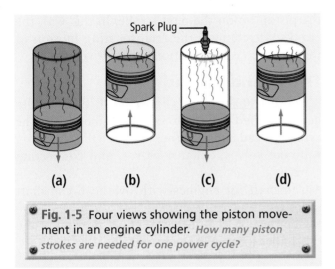

Fig. 1-5 Four views showing the piston movement in an engine cylinder. *How many piston strokes are needed for one power cycle?*

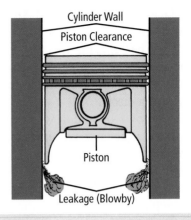

Fig. 1-7 Blowby occurs between the piston and cylinder wall. *What reduces the amount of blowby?*

Pistons and Piston Rings **Figure 1-6** shows a piston and piston rings. Pistons are usually made of an aluminum alloy, which is aluminum mixed with other metals. They are slightly smaller than the cylinders so that they can move up and down freely.

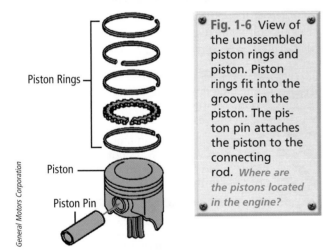

General Motors Corporation

Fig. 1-6 View of the unassembled piston rings and piston. Piston rings fit into the grooves in the piston. The piston pin attaches the piston to the connecting rod. *Where are the pistons located in the engine?*

The small gap between the piston and cylinder wall is known as piston clearance. See **Fig. 1-7**. Piston clearance provides the sliding fit. If not properly sealed, this gap allows some of the compressed air/fuel mixture and combustion gases to leak past the piston. This leakage is called blowby. Blowby reduces power, wastes fuel, and pollutes the air. The piston rings seal

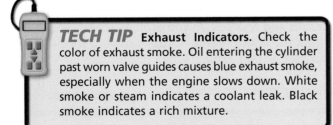

TECH TIP **Exhaust Indicators.** Check the color of exhaust smoke. Oil entering the cylinder past worn valve guides causes blue exhaust smoke, especially when the engine slows down. White smoke or steam indicates a coolant leak. Black smoke indicates a rich mixture.

the gap between the piston and the cylinder wall. Each ring fits into ring grooves cut into the piston. There are two types of piston rings:

- Compression rings form a sliding seal between the piston and the cylinder wall. They reduce or control blowby of combustion gases.
- Oil rings, or oil-control rings, scrape excess oil from the cylinder wall and return it to the crankcase.

Crankshaft The reciprocating motion of the pistons must be changed to rotary motion. Rotary motion is what turns the vehicle's drive wheels. The connecting rods and the crankshaft make this conversion possible. A piston pin connects each piston to the small end of the connecting rod. The connecting rod connects the piston to the crankshaft. See **Fig. 1-8**.

The rod cap and rod bolts attach the connecting rod to the connecting rod journal. The journal holds a split bearing (two halves), or connecting rod

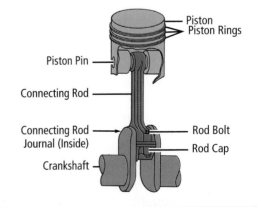

Fig. 1-8 Piston and connecting rod assembly attached to a connecting rod journal on the crankshaft. The piston is shown partly cut away to show how the piston is attached to the connecting rod. *What attaches the piston to the connecting rod?*

bearing, in place in the cap and rod. See **Fig. 1-9**. A slight clearance allows the connecting rod journal to turn inside the bearing. Oil fills this clearance to lubricate the bearing and prevent metal-to-metal contact. As the crankshaft turns, the connecting rod journal moves in a circle.

As the piston moves up and down in the cylinder its connecting rod journal moves in a circle around the centerline of the crankshaft. On the downstroke the connecting rod moves to one side, as its lower end follows the movement of the crankshaft rod journal. As the piston reaches BDC, the connecting rod journal continues to move in a circle. As the journal begins to move up the connecting rod pushes the piston up on the next stroke. In this way, the crankshaft changes the reciprocating motion of the piston to rotary motion at the drivetrain.

The Cylinder Head

Figure 1-10 shows a cylinder head. The cylinder head is bolted to the top of the engine block. The cylinder head contains the:
- Intake valves, exhaust valves, and connecting parts.
- Camshaft for engines with overhead camshaft design.
- Combustion chamber (the upper portion of the cylinder located in the head).

Excellence in Science

Hot Gases Are Really Cool

A diesel engine would have no power without hot air to ignite the fuel within its cylinders. When a diesel engine piston moves up on the compression stroke, it compresses the air above it. This causes the air pressure and temperature to increase within the cylinder. The temperature increases so much that a light spray of fuel ignites as soon as it mixes with the highly compressed air in the top of the cylinder!

Increasing the pressure for a gas (air) trapped in a container increases the temperature. Increasing the temperature increases the pressure. Gas pressure also decreases with decreasing temperature.

Safety First

Personal Protection Use eye protection. Wear gloves and clothing with long sleeves.

Caution Do not heat an empty bottle in the microwave. Always put some water inside the bottle. Never heat the bottle with the top sealed.

Apply It!

Exploring Temperature and Pressure

Meets NATEF Science Standards for understanding the relationship between pressure and temperature and the effect of how adding heat causes vaporization.

Materials and Equipment
- Small plastic bottle with a screw-on top
- Microwave oven and sink or water hose
- 4 tablespoons of water

Here's a simple experiment that you may want to try at home. It's just the reverse of what happens to the air within an engine's cylinder on the compression stroke.

1. Remove the lid from the plastic bottle and rinse it thoroughly.

2. Add 4 tablespoons of water to the bottle. Heat it in a microwave oven for 1 minute.

3. Remove the warm bottle from the oven. Screw on the lid tightly.

4. Run cold water over the bottle for a minute or so. Observe what happens.

Results and Analysis As you probably observed, when the warm plastic bottle is cooled, it collapses. Can you explain why?

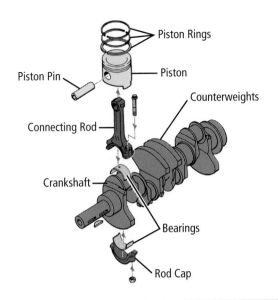

Piston Rings

Piston Pin — Piston

Counterweights

Connecting Rod

Crankshaft

Bearings

Rod Cap

Fig. 1-9 Crankshaft with one piston and connecting rod assembly. This shows how the piston attaches through the connecting rod to the rod journal on the crankshaft. *What is the function of the crankshaft?*

Each cylinder has one or more intake valves and exhaust valves. See **Fig. 1-11.** The intake valve controls the flow of the air/fuel mixture into the cylinder. The exhaust valve controls the flow of exhaust gas from the cylinder. The valves fit in the intake and exhaust ports of the cylinder head.

Most cylinders have two ports, or holes, in the combustion chamber area of the cylinder head. One port is the intake port; the other is the exhaust port. The air/fuel mixture enters the cylinder through the intake port. Burned gases leave the cylinder through the exhaust port. Some engines have multiple intake and exhaust ports and valves.

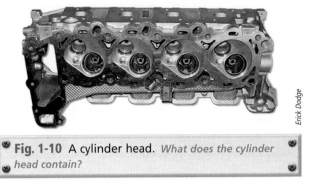

Erick Dodge

Fig. 1-10 A cylinder head. *What does the cylinder head contain?*

When a valve closes, it seals tightly against the valve seat. A **valve seat** is the surface against which the valve face comes in contact to provide a seal against leakage. In the closed position, the valve face and seat should form an air-tight seal. When a valve moves off its seat, the port is open. The air/fuel mixture or exhaust gas can then pass through the port.

The timing of valve opening and closing will vary with engine design. The intake valve opens before the intake stroke begins and closes after it ends. The exhaust valve opens before the exhaust stroke begins and closes after it ends. This valve overlap improves engine "breathing," or the flow of air/fuel mixture and exhaust gases into and out of the cylinders.

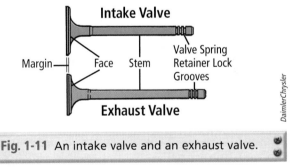

Intake Valve

Margin — | Face   Stem

Valve Spring
Retainer Lock
Grooves

Exhaust Valve

DaimlerChrysler

Fig. 1-11 An intake valve and an exhaust valve.

SECTION 1 KNOWLEDGE CHECK

1. Describe the function of a piston.
2. Which type of engine involves the ignition of fuel by heated air?
3. Describe a piston stroke.
4. What makes up the engine block?
5. What does white exhaust smoke indicate?
6. What is a valve seat?

ASE TEST PREP

7. Technician A says that pistons are usually made of an aluminum alloy. Technician B says that pistons are usually made of stainless steel. Who is correct?
   ⓐ Technician A.
   ⓑ Technician B.
   ⓒ Both Technician A and Technician B.
   ⓓ Neither Technician A nor Technician B.

Section 2
Engine Operation

Objectives:
- Describe how the intake and exhaust valves work.
- Name the four piston strokes of a four-cycle engine.
- Explain the function of each piston stroke.

Vocabulary:
- compression ratio
- valve train
- camshaft
- rocker arm
- flywheel
- intake manifold
- exhaust manifold

Conversion of Energy

An engine converts energy, in the form of a fuel, to motion. The fuel is burned and converted into heat. The heat develops pressure, which applies force to the engine's pistons. The pistons transfer this force, as reciprocating motion, to the engine's crankshaft. The crankshaft converts the reciprocating motion to rotary motion. The rotary motion is transferred through the drive train to provide motion to the vehicle's drive wheels.

Piston Action

The actions of the piston are divided into four strokes. A piston stroke is the movement of the piston from TDC to BDC or from BDC to TDC. The complete power cycle requires four piston strokes. See **Fig. 1-12**.

- Intake.
- Compression.
- Power.
- Exhaust.

This makes the engine a four-stroke, or four-cycle, engine. One complete four-stroke cycle requires two complete revolutions (720°) of the crankshaft.

Intake Stroke During the intake stroke, the piston moves down in the cylinder. The intake valve is open. The downward movement of the piston creates a partial vacuum in the cylinder. Atmospheric pressure forces the air/fuel mixture into the cylinder to fill the vacuum. As the piston moves from TDC to BDC, the crankshaft rotates 180°, or one-half turn.

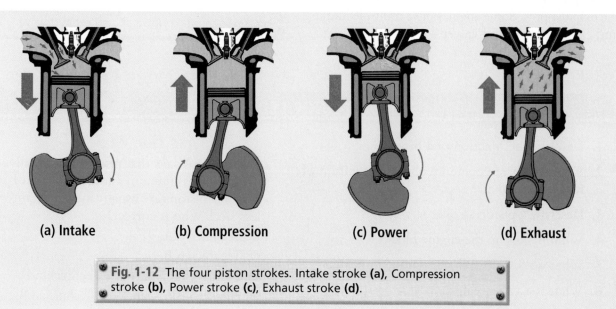

(a) Intake   (b) Compression   (c) Power   (d) Exhaust

Fig. 1-12 The four piston strokes. Intake stroke **(a)**, Compression stroke **(b)**, Power stroke **(c)**, Exhaust stroke **(d)**.

Excellence in Math

Calculating Engine Displacement

Someone may refer to a 350-cubic-inch engine (350 in³) or a 5.7-liter engine. They are using the engine's displacement to describe it. Displacement is the volume swept out when the piston moves from one end of the cylinder to the other.

You can calculate the displacement of an engine if you know the piston stroke length, the cylinder bore diameter, and the number of cylinders.

A Ford Mustang has an eight-cylinder 4.6-liter engine with a cylinder bore diameter of 3.55″ and a piston stroke length of 3.54″. You want to know the engine displacement in cubic inches. You can find this in two ways.

Mathematics Toolbox

$\pi = 3.1416$

Radius of a circle: $r = \dfrac{\text{diameter}}{2} = \dfrac{d}{2}$

Area of a circle: $A = \pi r^2 = \pi \left(\dfrac{d}{2}\right)^2 = \pi \dfrac{d^2}{4}$

Volume of a cylinder: $V = \pi r^2 l$

1 in = 2.54 cm
1 in³ = (2.54 cm)³ = 16.39 cm³
1 liter = 1000 cm³

Method One

You can calculate the volume of each cylinder in cubic inches (in³) and multiply by the number of cylinders.

You first calculate the volume of one cylinder. Remember that:

$$r = \frac{d}{2} = \frac{3.55 \text{ in}}{2} \text{ and } r^2 = \frac{(3.55 \text{ in})^2}{4}$$

$$V = \pi r^2 l = 3.1416 \times \left[\frac{(3.55)^2}{4}\right] \times 3.54$$

$$V = 35.0389323 \text{ in}^3 \cong 35.04 \text{ in}^3$$

Then find the total volume of all eight cylinders:

Total $V = 35.04$ in³ $\times$ 8 $= 280.32$ in³

The manufacturer's specs actually list the engine displacement as 281 in³. Your answer may differ from the manufacturer's value due to rounding off.

Method Two

You can convert 4.6 liters to in³.

The engine displacement is 4.6 liters, which is 4600 cm³.

$$1 \text{ in}^3 = 16.39 \text{ cm}^3, \text{ so } 1 \text{ cm}^3 = \left(\frac{1}{16.39}\right) \text{in}^3.$$

The formula for total volume is:

$$V = 4600 \times \left(\frac{1}{16.39}\right) \text{in}^3 = 280.66 \text{ in}^3$$

This figure is rounded off to 281 in³.

Apply It!

Meets NATEF Mathematics Standards for measuring volume and using both English and metric systems.

A Chevrolet V-8 engine has a cylinder bore diameter of 4″ and a piston stroke length of 3.25″. Calculate the engine displacement in both in³ and liters.

Compression Stroke After the piston moves past BDC on the intake stroke, the compression stroke begins. The intake and exhaust valves are closed. As it moves up, the piston compresses the air/fuel mixture in the space between the top of the piston and the cylinder head. This space is the combustion chamber. The piston compresses the air/fuel mixture to about one-eighth of its original volume.

Compression ratio is the volume in the cylinder with the piston at BDC divided by the volume in the cylinder with the piston at TDC. It is the measure of how much the air/fuel mixture is compressed during the compression stroke. For example, if the mixture is compressed to one-eighth of its original volume, the compression ratio is 8 to 1 (written 8:1). As the piston moves from BDC to TDC, the crankshaft rotates 180°.

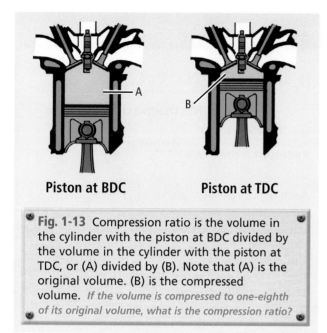

Piston at BDC   Piston at TDC

Fig. 1-13 Compression ratio is the volume in the cylinder with the piston at BDC divided by the volume in the cylinder with the piston at TDC, or (A) divided by (B). Note that (A) is the original volume. (B) is the compressed volume. *If the volume is compressed to one-eighth of its original volume, what is the compression ratio?*

Compression ratios above 9.5:1 may create enough heat to self-ignite the air/fuel mixture without the aid of a spark. In a spark-ignition engine, such detonation can damage the pistons, piston rings, spark plugs, and valves. See **Fig. 1-13**.

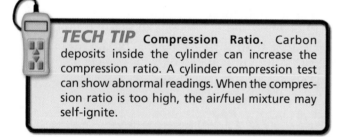

TECH TIP **Compression Ratio.** Carbon deposits inside the cylinder can increase the compression ratio. A cylinder compression test can show abnormal readings. When the compression ratio is too high, the air/fuel mixture may self-ignite.

Power Stroke As the piston nears TDC at the end of the compression stroke, both the intake and exhaust valves are closed. An electric spark jumps the gap at the spark plug. As the mixture burns, high temperatures and pressures are created in the combustion chamber. The force of the expanding combustion gases pushes down on the top of the piston. The connecting rod transmits this force to the crankshaft, which rotates another 180° from TDC to BDC.

Exhaust Stroke As the piston approaches BDC on the power stroke, the exhaust valve opens. After the connecting rod journal passes through BDC, the piston moves up, forcing the burned gases out through the open exhaust port. As the piston moves from BDC to TDC, the crankshaft rotates 180°.

Valve Action

The **valve train** is a series of parts that open and close the valves by transferring cam-lobe movement to the valves. One four-stroke cycle requires two revolutions of the crankshaft. This requires only one revolution of the camshaft. The crankshaft drives the camshaft through gears, sprockets, and a chain or through sprockets and a toothed timing belt. The sprocket driving the camshaft has twice as many teeth as the crankshaft sprocket.

Valve action starts at the camshaft. The **camshaft** is a shaft having a series of cams for operating the valve mechanisms. See **Fig. 1-14**. Each cam is a round collar with a high spot, or lobe. Most camshafts have a cam lobe for each valve in the engine.

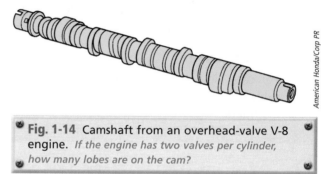

American Honda/Corp PR

Fig. 1-14 Camshaft from an overhead-valve V-8 engine. *If the engine has two valves per cylinder, how many lobes are on the cam?*

In an overhead-camshaft engine, the camshaft mounts in the cylinder head. See **Fig. 1-15**. One end of a rocker arm contacts the tip of each valve stem. A **rocker arm** is a pivoted lever that transfers cam or pushrod motion to the valve stem. The other end of the rocker arm contacts the valve lifter. Valve lifters may be either solid metal or hydraulically operated. In either case, the lifter is used to maintain the desired clearance between the rocker arm and the valve stem. When the rotating camshaft moves a cam lobe in contact with a lifter, the rocker arm pivots to push the valve open. As the camshaft continues to rotate, the lobe moves away from the lifter. Spring tension now closes the valve.

Power Flow

A single-cylinder four-cycle engine has one power stroke for every two rotations of its crankshaft. During the other three strokes, exhaust, intake, and compression, the piston does not deliver power. A single cylinder engine produces power only one-fourth of its running time. The crankshaft increases its rotational speed on the power stroke. It loses speed on the non-power strokes.

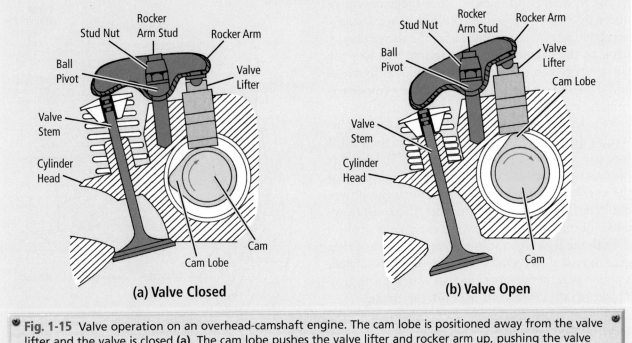

(a) Valve Closed   **(b) Valve Open**

Fig. 1-15 Valve operation on an overhead-camshaft engine. The cam lobe is positioned away from the valve lifter and the valve is closed **(a)**. The cam lobe pushes the valve lifter and rocker arm up, pushing the valve down and opening the port **(b)**. *How many times does the crankshaft turn for one turn of the camshaft?*

In general, an engine with multiple cylinders runs more smoothly. Automotive engines have four or more cylinders to provide a more even and smooth power flow. A complete engine cycle requires two complete rotations of the crankshaft, 720°. In a four-cylinder engine, a power stroke occurs every 180° of crankshaft rotation. A six-cylinder engine provides a power stroke every 120°. An eight-cylinder engine provides a power stroke every 90°. With six or more cylinders, the power strokes follow each other very closely. Before the completion of a power stroke in one cylinder, a power stroke starts in another cylinder. This overlap results in a smoother-running engine.

Even when the power bursts overlap, the flow of power from the pistons to the crankshaft is not completely smooth. The crankshaft tends to speed up on each power stroke and slow down between power strokes. Without a way to store the energy from each power stroke, the engine still runs unevenly.

A **flywheel** is a mechanical device that is used to store energy. When energy sets a flywheel in motion, the weight or mass of the flywheel maintains that motion, storing the energy. A flywheel is mounted on one end of the crankshaft. The device on the other end of the crankshaft is known as the damper. See **Fig. 1-16.**

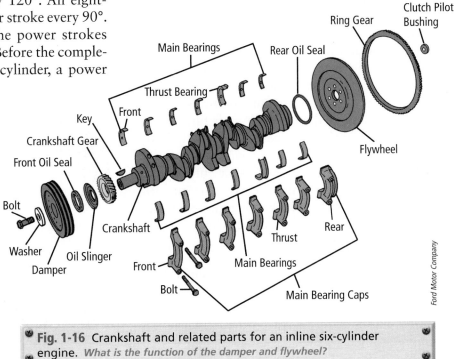

Ford Motor Company

Fig. 1-16 Crankshaft and related parts for an inline six-cylinder engine. *What is the function of the damper and flywheel?*

The flywheel and damper store the energy produced by each power stroke. Between power strokes, the flywheel and damper transfer the stored energy back to the crankshaft. This action balances the energy between the power strokes. The flywheel and damper work together to produce a smoother-running engine.

Vehicles with automatic transmissions use a lightweight drive plate (or flex plate) and a fluid-filled torque converter in place of a flywheel. The weights offset any sudden change in the rotational speed of the crankshaft. They gradually absorb the power burst during the power stroke. They also resist slow-down of the crankshaft between the power strokes.

Both the flywheel and the drive plate have a ring gear mounted to them. When the vehicle is started, a pinion gear on the starter meshes with the ring gear. This turns the crankshaft to crank the engine.

Basic Engine Systems

A spark-ignition, fuel-injected engine requires six basic systems:
- Air induction system.
- Fuel system.
- Ignition system.
- Lubricating system.
- Cooling system.
- Exhaust system.

Air Induction System

The function of the air induction system is to direct clean, filtered air to the intake manifold. The **intake manifold** is a set of tubes, or a casting with several passages. Air or an air/fuel mixture flows through these passages from the throttle valves to the intake ports in the cylinder head. See **Fig. 1-17**. Air entering the engine contains particles of dirt, which can damage the engine. An air filter in the air filter housing cleans the air. A throttle body contains a throttle blade that controls the engine speed by varying the amount of air entering the engine. The intake manifold carries air into the engine's cylinders. The intake manifold is located between the throttle body and the cylinder head.

Fuel System

The fuel system delivers gasoline (or similar fuel) to the engine. See **Fig. 1-18**. Air mixes with fuel to form a combustible air/fuel mixture, which burns quickly. This mixture fills each cylinder, where it is compressed and burned.

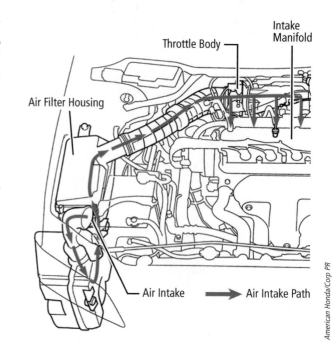

American Honda/Corp PR

Fig. 1-17 Airflow through a remote-mounted air cleaner. The blue arrows show the air intake path. *Which part of an air induction system controls engine speed?*

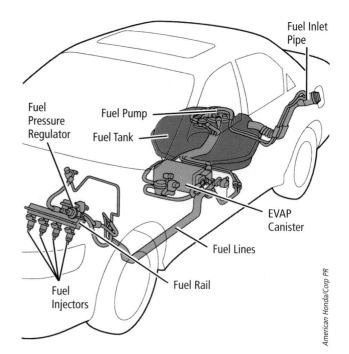

American Honda/Corp PR

Fig. 1-18 The fuel system of a typical fuel-injected car. *Where is the fuel pump located on most fuel-injected vehicles?*

TECHNOLOGY
Hybrid Systems

The hybrid system is a vehicle propulsion system with two power sources: the gasoline engine and the electric motor. The use of power from both the gasoline engine and electrical sources eliminates the need for a battery charging plug and charging station. These are required by vehicles powered only by electricity. The hybrid system produces low emissions and high fuel efficiency by choosing or combining power sources. To reduce fuel consumption and emissions, the engine can be off when stopped or when traveling at low speeds.

The hybrid electrical system uses the most efficient energy source, based on operating conditions and battery voltage. There are two hybrid power source combinations: parallel or series. Each combination uses a gasoline engine, a high voltage battery, and a motor/generator. The motor/generator will operate as an electric motor to start the engine, propel the vehicle, or assist the engine to propel the vehicle. When the hybrid control switches off power to the motor/generator and the vehicle is moving, the motor/generator becomes a generator. It recharges the high voltage battery.

The Parallel System In the parallel system, one power source is the gasoline engine. The other power source is the motor/generator, which receives electrical power from the high voltage battery. In a parallel system, both the gasoline engine and electric motor/generator can propel the vehicle by themselves or in combination.

The Series System The series system uses the gasoline engine to turn the generator to produce electrical current. This generator can charge the high voltage battery or provide electrical power to an electric motor that connects to the transmission. The series system can be modified so that the gasoline engine is connected to the transmission and also turns a motor/generator that recharges the high voltage battery. When the gasoline engine cannot meet the demand, such as under hard acceleration, the motor/generator is turned on to assist the engine. In the series system, the engine must be running to propel the vehicle.

In most hybrid systems the engine is started by a direct-mounted motor and the high voltage battery when the hybrid control system determines that the gasoline engine should be started. The engine will start, depending on conditions such as engine temperature, throttle position, vehicle speed, electrical demand by accessories, and battery condition.

The fuel tank holds a supply of fuel. The fuel pump moves the fuel from the tank to the engine. On most fuel-injected vehicles, the fuel pump is located in the fuel tank.

Safety First

Flammable Materials Gasoline is extremely flammable. Never expose gasoline to a spark or an open flame. The results could be fatal. Rags and other flammable materials exposed to or soaked with gasoline are also hazardous. To avoid the danger of fire or spontaneous combustion, properly dispose of such materials in properly marked containers.

Ignition System

The ignition system (except in diesel engines) uses one or more ignition coils to increase the low voltage of the battery to 20,000 volts or more. This voltage creates the spark that jumps the gap at the spark plug. The spark ignites the compressed air/fuel mixture, causing combustion to begin.

Lubricating System

An engine has many moving metal parts. If metal parts rub against each other, they wear quickly. To prevent this, engines have a lubricating system that coats moving parts with oil. See **Fig. 1-19.** The oil film reduces the friction between the moving parts.

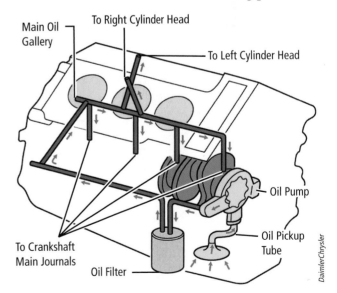

Main Oil Gallery
To Right Cylinder Head
To Left Cylinder Head
Oil Pump
Oil Pickup Tube
To Crankshaft Main Journals
Oil Filter

DaimlerChrysler

Fig. 1-19 Engine lubricating system, showing how the oil flows to the engine parts. *What circulates the oil through the engine?*

The lubricating system has an oil pan (sump) at the bottom of the engine that holds several quarts or liters of oil. An engine-driven oil pump circulates oil from the oil pan, through the engine, and back to the oil pan.

Cooling System

The cooling system keeps the engine at a safe and efficient operating temperature. Where there is combustion, there is heat. Burning the air/fuel mixture raises the temperature inside the engine. Much of the heat leaves the engine through the exhaust gas.

The engine cooling system removes most of the remaining heat. See **Fig. 1-20.** The engine has water jackets, which are open spaces surrounding the cylinders. Engine coolant, a mixture of water and antifreeze, moves through the water jackets. The coolant absorbs the heat and carries it to the radiator. Air passing through the radiator carries away the heat.

Exhaust System

The exhaust system carries exhaust gases away from the engine. See **Fig. 1-21.** The exhaust gases pass from the cylinder, through the exhaust port, and into the exhaust manifold. The **exhaust manifold** is a metal casting with several passages through which exhaust gases leave the engine combustion chambers and enter the exhaust system. The exhaust manifold connects to a header pipe that carries the exhaust gases to a catalytic converter.

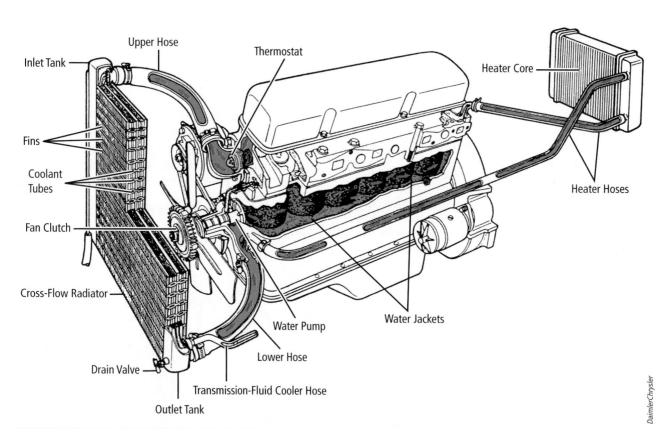

Fig. 1-20 Engine cooling system. Arrows show the flow of coolant through the engine, radiator, and heater hoses to the heater core. *Does hot coolant enter the top or bottom of the radiator?*

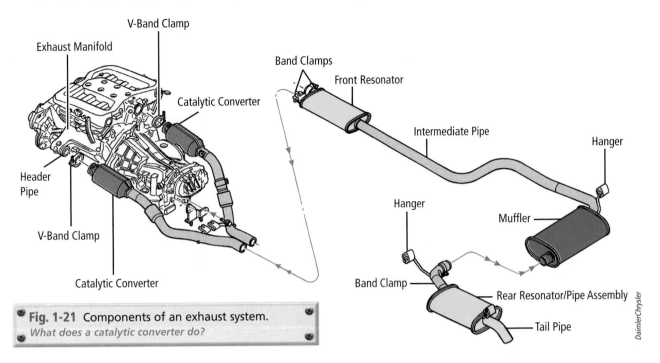

Fig. 1-21 Components of an exhaust system.
What does a catalytic converter do?

The catalytic converter is located between the engine and the muffler. The converter changes harmful exhaust pollutants into harmless gases. The result is that the exhaust gas leaves the catalytic converter with fewer pollutants.

Some vehicles use more than one catalytic converter. The number and location of the converters depends on engine used, the type of vehicle, and whether it has a single or dual exhaust system.

The converter may be equipped with heat shields to prevent unwanted heat from reaching the vehicle's floor pans. The floor pans may also be shielded and insulated from excessive heat.

The exhaust gases then enter the muffler. The muffler reduces the noise created by combustion of the air/fuel mixture. Some exhaust systems use one or more resonators to reduce exhaust noise. The tail pipe safely vents the exhaust gases away from the vehicle.

SECTION 2 KNOWLEDGE CHECK

1. What is the danger of high compression ratios in spark-ignition engines?

2. Explain the crankshaft rotation during the power stroke.

3. Explain how the camshaft interacts with valve lifters.

4. Why aren't single cylinder engines used in cars?

5. What is the purpose of the flywheel and damper?

6. What exhaust system part converts harmful pollutants into harmless gases?

ASE TEST PREP

7. Technician A says that in the hybrid technology series system one power source is the gasoline engine and the other power source is the motor/generator. Technician B says that the system described is the parallel system. Who is correct?

   ⓐ Technician A.

   ⓑ Technician B.

   ⓒ Both Technician A and Technician B.

   ⓓ Neither Technician A nor Technician B.

CHAPTER 1 REVIEW

Key Points

Satisfies the following NATEF Standards for Engine Performance: supporting knowledge for diagnosing engine mechanical problems.

- To be effective, the piston must slide smoothly in the engine cylinder.
- The four piston strokes of a spark-ignition engine take their names from their functions.
- The pistons, connecting rods, and crankshaft work together to convert heat energy to mechanical energy.
- Though similar in design, the intake and exhaust valves have different functions.
- Each piston stroke has a definite function in the power cycle.
- The engine has six basic supporting systems.
- The intake manifold carries air into the engine's cylinders.
- A hybrid vehicle propulsion system uses power sources that produce low emissions and high fuel efficiency.
- The engine cooling system controls engine operating temperature.

Review Questions

1. What part connects the piston to the crankshaft?
2. What part converts the reciprocating motion of the pistons to rotary motion?
3. What part of the engine contains the valve train, intake valves, exhaust valves, and combustion chamber?
4. What is an intake valve?
5. How many complete revolutions does the crankshaft make during a complete four-stroke cycle?
6. What is the measure of how much the air/fuel mixture is compressed during the compression stroke?
7. Describe the valve train.
8. The intake manifold and throttle body are parts of which basic engine system?
9. **Critical Thinking** In what way do the pistons move in a reciprocating engine?
10. **Critical Thinking** What causes some exhaust smoke to be blue?

Excellence in Communication

Explaining Things to Your Customer

The section you just finished reading is titled "Engine Operation." This section uses technical language to provide information on the internal combustion engine.

During your years of servicing vehicles, you may be asked to share your knowledge with customers. A customer may ask, "How does the engine work?" You may wonder why you need to explain this to your customer. The reason is simple. Answering this question is one way to maintain good customer relations.

Because you are an automotive technician, you may think first in terms of technical processes. However, to make clear what you know, you will have to use terms that your customer can understand. Focus on clearly explaining the four piston strokes. This will help you to begin your explanation of how an internal combustion engine works.

Apply It!

Meets NATEF Communications Standards for adapting and using appropriate communication strategies and styles.

1. Fold a sheet of notebook paper in half lengthwise. Head the left half of the sheet "Technical." Head the right half "Customer."

2. In your own words, list on the "Technical" side the steps that occur in each piston stroke.

3. On the "Customer" side, list the important steps that you believe the customer needs to know.

4. Break into teams. Referring to the "Customer" side, explain to your team how the engine works. Ask them whether you have given them enough information. Ask also whether they think you have used words the customer can understand.

AUTOMOTIVE SERVICE EXCELLENCE
TEST PREP

Answering the following practice questions will help you prepare for the ASE certification tests.

1. A term that is used to refer to most automotive engines is:

   ⓐ big block.

   ⓑ reciprocating.

   ⓒ hybrid.

   ⓓ V-8.

2. Technician A says that internal combustion engines can be spark ignition or compression ignition. Technician B says that all internal combustion engines are spark ignition. Who is correct?

   ⓐ Technician A.

   ⓑ Technician B.

   ⓒ Both Technician A and Technician B.

   ⓓ Neither Technician A nor Technician B.

3. The engine block might also be referred to as the:

   ⓐ oil pan.

   ⓑ piston ring.

   ⓒ cylinder block.

   ⓓ camshaft.

4. Technician A says that the small gap between the piston and the cylinder wall is known as the compression ratio. Technician B says that the gap is known as piston clearance. Who is correct?

   ⓐ Technician A.

   ⓑ Technician B.

   ⓒ Both Technician A and Technician B.

   ⓓ Neither Technician A nor Technician B.

5. During the intake stroke, in which direction does the piston move in the cylinder of a V-8 engine?

   ⓐ Up.

   ⓑ Down.

   ⓒ Left.

   ⓓ Right.

6. Technician A says the camshaft is responsible for moving the valves. Technician B says that the camshaft is comprised of a series of collars with raised lobes arranged on a shaft. Who is correct?

   ⓐ Technician A.

   ⓑ Technician B.

   ⓒ Both Technician A and Technician B.

   ⓓ Neither Technician A nor Technician B.

7. How often does an eight-cylinder engine provide a power stroke?

   ⓐ Every 720° of crankshaft rotation.

   ⓑ Every 180° of crankshaft rotation.

   ⓒ Every 120° of crankshaft rotation.

   ⓓ Every 90° of crankshaft rotation.

8. Technician A says that a spark ignition engine system requires an air induction system. Technician B says that a spark ignition system requires a lubricating system. Who is correct?

   ⓐ Technician A.

   ⓑ Technician B.

   ⓒ Both Technician A and Technician B.

   ⓓ Neither Technician A nor Technician B.

9. How many power sources does a hybrid vehicle have?

   ⓐ 1.

   ⓑ 2.

   ⓒ 3.

   ⓓ 4.

10. Technician A says that the ignition system in a diesel engine uses an ignition coil to increase the low voltage of the battery to 20,000 volts or more in order to create a spark across the spark plug gap to ignite the air/fuel mixture. Technician B says that diesel engines do not have spark plugs. Who is correct?

    ⓐ Technician A.

    ⓑ Technician B.

    ⓒ Both Technician A and Technician B.

    ⓓ Neither Technician A nor Technician B.

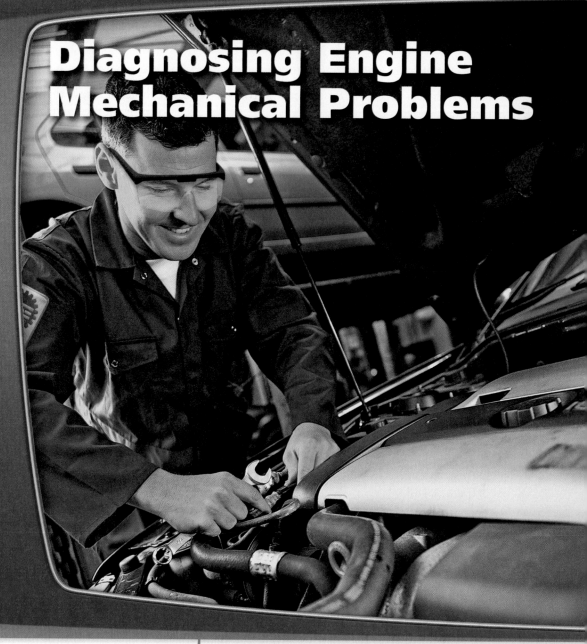

Diagnosing Engine Mechanical Problems

Customer's Concern

Felicia Jones says her car has no power. She used to be able to scale the hills near her home without hesitation. Lately, Felicia has noticed that her car is very sluggish. Even on relatively level roadways, she is not enjoying the responsiveness her car used to provide.

This is Felicia's first visit to your service facility. She rarely returns to the same service center when she needs automotive work. Service center location is the most important thing to Felicia. As a construction laborer, she works at different locations all over the city. Today, Felicia is working near your service center.

Without any service history on Felicia's vehicle, you'll have to gather information about her car by asking questions.

Technician's Challenge

As the service technician, you need to find answers to these questions:

1. Has Felicia noticed any other problems with her car? Has the car undergone any service or repair work lately?

2. What could be causing this problem? Could the problem be a leaking cylinder head gasket or a worn valve seat?

3. What diagnostic tests may help you pinpoint the problem? Could a cylinder-leakage or vacuum test reveal any clues?

4. How can you convince Felicia that it is important to visit the same service center each time she has a problem with her car?

Section 1
General Engine Diagnosis

Objectives:

A2 • Identify and interpret engine performance concern; determine necessary action.

A3 • Research applicable vehicle and service information, such as engine management system operation, vehicle service history, service precautions, and technical service bulletins.

A7 • Diagnose abnormal exhaust color, odor, and sound; determine necessary action.

A8 • Perform engine absolute (vacuum/boost) manifold pressure tests; determine necessary action.

A10 • Perform cylinder cranking compression tests; determine necessary action.

A12 • Perform cylinder leakage test; determine necessary action.

A11 • Perform engine running compression test; determine necessary action.

A13 • Diagnose engine mechanical, electrical, electronic, fuel, and ignition concerns with an oscilloscope and/or engine diagnostic equipment; determine necessary action.

A2 • Identify and interpret engine performance concern; determine necessary action.

A6 • Diagnose abnormal engine noise or vibration concerns; determine necessary action.

Vocabulary:

• service history
• cylinder compression
• cylinder leakage test
• cylinder power balance test
• engine vacuum
• vacuum gauge
• snap-throttle vacuum test
• cranking vacuum test
• automotive stethoscope
• piston slap

Diagnostic Strategy

Diagnosis is the detective work that answers the question, "What is wrong?"

Correctly identifying the cause of a problem is often the hardest part of the job. Make a visual inspection of the engine and its support systems. Check for fuel, oil, and coolant leaks. Check for loose or missing parts. Ask the driver to identify the circumstances in which the problem occurred. See **Fig. 2-1.** If you do not find an obvious cause, form a diagnostic strategy. A diagnostic strategy is a planned, step-by-step procedure you can use to locate a problem.

Gary D. Landsman/The Stock Market

Fig. 2-1 Precise details from the driver can provide valuable diagnostic information.

A diagnostic strategy has five basic rules:

- Get as much information as possible from the driver. This may help direct your diagnostic strategy.
- Know the system. Know how the parts work together and what happens if they fail to work.
- Be aware of the problems that occur often.
- Determine the history of the complaint. Did the problem start suddenly or gradually? Does the problem occur with the engine warm or cold? Does it occur at all speeds?
- Look up the service history of the vehicle. The **service history** is a written service record for the vehicle. It is kept by the service facility. How many miles are on the odometer? Has the vehicle been previously serviced for the same problem?

Safety First **Personal Protection** Keep clothes and hands clear of rotating engine drive belts and pulleys. When using compressed air, always wear safety goggles. Serious injury can result when safety is not observed.

Diagnostic Tests

Worn engine parts cause:

- Engine noise.
- Poor engine performance.
- Increased fuel and oil consumption.
- High exhaust emissions.

Worn engine parts may also cause a loss of compression. Worn or broken pistons and rings, for example, cause increased blow-by and oil consumption. Damaged valves allow leakage between the valves and valve seats. A leaking cylinder head gasket lets compression and combustion gases leak from the cylinder.

Some engine problems can be diagnosed by checking the color and odor of the exhaust. An internal coolant leak into the combustion chamber produces heavy white smoke. Oil entering the combustion chamber past worn valve guides or piston rings produces blue smoke. Rich fuel mixtures may cause black exhaust smoke and a "rotten egg" odor.

Observing and listening will not always lead to a diagnosis. You may need to perform diagnostic tests.

Safety First **Debris** Be sure the areas around exposed spark plug holes and the throttle body air intake are free of dirt, small materials, or loose parts. Small pieces can fall into the engine and cause severe engine damage when the engine cranks.

Cylinder Compression Tests

Cylinder compression is the pressure developed in the cylinder as the engine cranks or runs. The average compression pressure during cranking is about 150 psi [1034 kPa]. Because compression raises the density and temperature of the air/fuel mixture, good compression is vital to proper combustion. When damaged or worn engine parts reduce compression, the engine loses power.

Cylinder compression tests measure compression in each cylinder as the engine cranks. See **Fig. 2-2.** You may have to make two compression tests, a cranking compression test and a running compression test. Wet compression tests are no longer performed due to possible damage to emission control devices such as the catalytic converter and oxygen sensor.

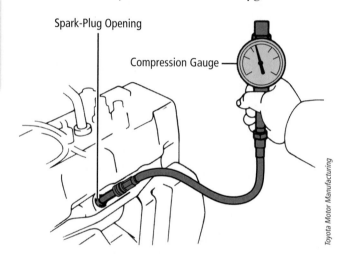
Spark-Plug Opening
Compression Gauge
Toyota Motor Manufacturing

Fig. 2-2 In a compression test, the compression gauge is connected to the spark plug opening.
Why is compression so important to engine performance?

A cranking compression test is made by cranking the engine with a test gauge installed. Depending on results, it may be necessary to make a running compression test. A running compression test is necessary to ensure proper engine volumetric efficiency due to modern engine designs, such as multivalve and dual-cam.

TECH TIP **Compression Readings.** Compression pressure drops about 2 percent for each 1,000' [304.8 m] of altitude. When using the manufacturer's specifications, you must adjust the reading for altitude. Always know the approximate altitude of your service center. This information is available on the Internet.

Cranking Compression Test Perform the cranking compression test first. Perform it without adding oil to the cylinder. To perform this test:

1. Make sure the engine cranks normally and is at normal operating temperature.
2. Disable the ignition or fuel system. Refer to the manufacturer's recommendation for the proper procedures.
3. Loosen the spark plugs about one turn. Use compressed air to blow dirt away from the plug wells.
4. Carefully remove the spark plugs. Be careful not to damage the cylinder head threads.
5. Thread the compression tester into the spark plug hole of the cylinder being tested.
6. Block the throttle plate open for better breathing.
7. Crank the engine at least four compression strokes. Crank the same number of strokes for each cylinder.
8. Record the test results for each cylinder.

Check the vehicle service manual for the specifications for normal compression pressure. Low readings in any cylinder may indicate leaking valves, worn or broken rings, or a defective cylinder head gasket. Low but equal readings in two adjacent cylinders may indicate a blown head gasket.

If the cranking compression is within specs, remove the throttle block, and reinstall the spark plugs and the cables. Restore any circuit that was disabled to prevent starting.

If the cranking compression test results in low readings, pressure is leaking from the cylinder.

Running Compression Test If the compression pressure is normal during the cranking compression test, conduct a running compression test. To perform the running compression test:

1. Remove the spark plug from the desired cylinder.
2. Ground the spark plug wire of the cylinder being tested.
3. Install the compression tester into the cylinder.
4. Start the vehicle and release pressure from the gauge.
5. Allow pressure to build up again.
6. Wait for the gauge to stop moving and release the pressure.
7. Allow pressure to build up again.
8. Wait for gauge to stop moving and record results.
9. Snap the throttle and record results.
10. Repeat for all other cylinders.

Safety First **Grounding Wires** To avoid fire or electric shock, always ensure that the spark plug wire on the cylinder being tested is grounded.

Running compression results will be lower than the results on the cranking compression test. The reason for this is that crankshaft speed is faster. This gives the cylinder less time to fill with air. The typical reading will be 50-60 psi. Manufacturers typically do not provide specifications. You must compare the results for all cylinders. The result for the throttle snap reading should be at least 80% of the cranking compression results.

Low readings on cylinders may indicate:
• Restricted intake.
• Incorrect valve timing.
• Intake valve train problem (carbon/sticking).
High readings on cylinders may indicate:
• Restricted exhaust.
• Exhaust valve train problem (carbon/sticking).

If the running compression test gives a near normal reading, compression is probably leaking past worn piston rings. Other possible causes include worn pistons or scratched cylinder walls.

TECH TIP Loose Carbon. Carbon particles loosened by removing the spark plugs can lodge under a valve and cause a low compression reading. You may need to repeat the test to ensure an accurate reading.

Reinstall the spark plugs and start the engine. Allow the engine to reach normal operating temperature. Repeat the test.

If the compression remains low on the running compression test, there may be leakage past the valves or head gasket. Possible causes of valve leakage include:
• Broken valve springs.
• Carbon deposits on the valve face or seat.
• Incorrect valve adjustment.
• Loose valve seat inserts.
• Burned, sticking, or bent valves.
• Incorrect valve timing.

Improper valve adjustment holds the valves slightly off their seats. Incorrect timing of the camshaft causes the valves to open too early or too late in the combustion cycle. "Engine Repair" in Volume 2 of *Automotive Excellence* discusses camshaft timing.

Common causes of low compression include wear or damage to the rings, pistons, cylinder walls, valves, or head gasket. Remove the cylinder head(s) to repair the problem, except when the cause is an improper valve adjustment or incorrect camshaft timing.

Cylinder Leakage Test

A **cylinder leakage test** is another test that checks a cylinder's ability to hold pressure. Air pressure is applied to the cylinder with the piston at top dead center (TDC) on the compression stroke. In this position, the intake and exhaust valves are closed. See **Fig. 2-3**. If the engine is in good condition, the percent of cylinder leakage will be less than the maximum specified.

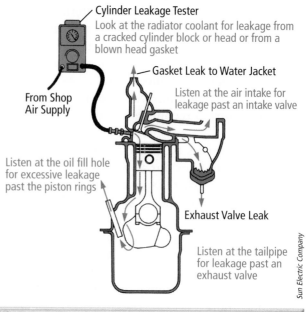

Cylinder Leakage Tester

Look at the radiator coolant for leakage from a cracked cylinder block or head or from a blown head gasket

Gasket Leak to Water Jacket

Listen at the air intake for leakage past an intake valve

From Shop Air Supply

Listen at the oil fill hole for excessive leakage past the piston rings

Exhaust Valve Leak

Listen at the tailpipe for leakage past an exhaust valve

Sun Electric Company

Fig. 2-3 With the piston at TDC, the cylinder leakage test applies pressure to the cylinder through the spark plug hole. *What does a cylinder leakage test indicate that a compression test does not?*

Excellence in Math

Measuring Compression

A customer complains that her vehicle's engine seems to have lost power. You suspect that one or more of the four cylinders may have worn or broken rings or leaking valves. You decide to perform a compression test. You will compare the compression in each cylinder with the manufacturer's specifications in the service manual.

According to the manufacturer, the high-to-low pressure readings in the cylinders should not vary by more than 25 percent of the highest value. This means that the lowest reading must be at least 75 percent of the highest reading.

You perform a dry compression test on the four-cylinder engine. The readings are:

145 psi, 120 psi, 145 psi, and 156 psi

Are these readings within specifications? Note: To convert these readings to metric measurements, remember that 1 psi = 6.895 kPa.

The highest reading is 156 psi; 25 percent of 156 psi is 39 psi.

156 psi − 39 psi = 117 psi

The lowest reading that is within specifications is 117 psi.

Since the lowest reading is 120 psi, and 120 psi is greater than 117 psi, all the readings are within specifications.

You can also find the lowest reading within acceptable range by calculating 75 percent of 156 psi, which would be 117 psi.

Apply It!

Meets NATEF Mathematics Standards for percentages and tolerances.

If the compression readings in the cylinders had been 145 psi, 142 psi, 123 psi, and 105 psi, would the readings have been within specifications? Explain your answer.

To perform a cylinder leakage test:

1. Remove all spark plugs.
2. Remove the air cleaner.
3. Remove the oil-fill cap and dipstick.
4. Remove the radiator cap and fill the radiator to the proper level.
5. Block the throttle wide open.
6. Thread the leakage test adapter with the whistle into the spark plug hole of the number-one cylinder.
7. Crank the engine until the whistle sounds. This means that the number-one piston is moving up on the compression stroke.
8. Continue cranking the engine until the piston is at TDC. Consult the manufacturer's service manual for the proper procedure.
9. Disconnect the whistle from the adapter hose and connect the leak tester.
10. Calibrate the leakage tester as instructed by the manufacturer.
11. Apply the specified air pressure to the cylinder. Record the gauge reading. Observe the percentage of leakage from the cylinder. See **Fig. 2-4**. Specifications vary, but a leakage of more than 20 percent is usually over acceptable limits.
12. Listen at the air intake, tailpipe, and oil-fill openings. Air leaking from the air intake indicates a leaking intake valve. Air leaking from the tailpipe indicates a leaking exhaust valve.

Jack Holtel

Excessive air leaking from the oil-fill opening may indicate worn piston rings. If air escapes from the next spark plug hole, the engine has a blown head gasket between the cylinders. If air bubbles up through the radiator, the engine has a blown head gasket, a cracked cylinder block, or a cracked cylinder head.

13. Check each cylinder in the same way.
14. Remove the throttle block. Reinstall spark plugs and cables. Restore any circuit that was disabled to prevent starting.

Cylinder Power Balance Test

A **cylinder power balance test** checks for weak cylinders by measuring the power being produced by each cylinder. The reading obtained in this test can help to identify problems such as worn pistons or maladjusted fuel injectors.

To perform a cylinder power balance test:

1. Make sure you follow all procedures in the appropriate service manual.
2. Before you perform this test, make sure your instructor has trained you in the use of the engine analyzer.
3. Raise the hood and hook up the engine analyzer.
4. Start the engine and let it idle until the temperature gauge moves into the normal range.
5. Use the engine analyzer to short out the cylinders one at a time. **CAUTION:** Do not short out any cylinder for more than ten seconds. Doing this could damage the catalytic converter.
6. As each cylinder is shorted out, record the vacuum and rpm readings.
7. Turn off the engine and disconnect the engine analyzer.
8. Review your findings. There is a cylinder problem if the vacuum/rpm reading does not drop at least 5 percent when any one cylinder is shorted out or if the difference between the highest reading recorded for a cylinder and the lowest reading recorded for a cylinder is more than 5 percent.
9. A cylinder power balance test will not tell you why the cylinders are producing power at different rates. Some possible reasons inside the engine could be burned valves, worn pistons, or a leaking head gasket.
10. Some possible reasons outside the engine for cylinder power balance problems could be a vacuum leak, a misadjusted carburetor, a faulty fuel injector, an ignition malfunction, or a computer sensor malfunction.

Engine Vacuum

Engine vacuum can be a good indicator of how well an engine is performing. **Engine vacuum** is the low-pressure condition created as the crankshaft turns, pulling the rod and piston down in the cylinder. The **vacuum gauge** is a device that measures intake manifold vacuum in inches of mercury (Hg). See **Fig. 2-5.** There will be some intake manifold vacuum anytime the engine is cranking or running. Note this is not always true if the engine is supercharged or turbocharged.

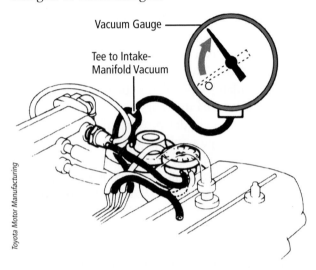

Vacuum Gauge —

Tee to Intake-
Manifold Vacuum

Toyota Motor Manufacturing

> **Fig. 2-5** A vacuum gauge is a common diagnostic tool. *What unit of measure does a vacuum gauge display?*

Engine Vacuum Test Engine speed and load, the position of the throttle plate, and possible engine defects affect engine vacuum. The engine vacuum test (also referred to as the manifold absolute pressure test) checks vacuum readings through a range of engine operating conditions.

To perform an engine vacuum test:
1. Make sure all vacuum hoses are properly connected and not leaking.
2. Connect the vacuum gauge to a source of intake manifold vacuum. Check the manufacturer's service manuals for proper connection points.
3. Start the engine and run it until it reaches normal operating temperature.
4. Record the readings at idle and at several other engine speeds.

The readings on the vacuum gauge provide valuable information. See **Table 2-A.** Keep in mind that engine vacuum decreases about 1″ [25 mm] of mercury per 1,000′ [304.8 m] increase in altitude.

You may need to adjust your readings. The following items describe common gauge readings.
- A high, steady reading at idle between 15″ and 22″ [381 mm and 559 mm] of mercury means normal engine condition.
- A low, steady reading at idle may mean late ignition timing, late valve timing, cylinder leakage, or an air leak at the intake manifold or throttle body.
- A reading that drops back to zero as engine speed steadily increases may mean a restricted catalytic converter, muffler, or exhaust pipe.
- A regular drop and increase in the reading at idle may mean that a single valve is leaking or stuck open.
- An irregular drop and increase in the reading at idle may mean a valve is sticking open part of the time.
- A slow drop and increase in the reading at idle may mean an incorrect air/fuel mixture.

Snap-Throttle Vacuum Test A **snap-throttle vacuum test** is a test that shows the condition of the pistons and piston rings.

To perform a snap throttle vacuum test:
1. Perform steps 1–3 as noted in "Engine Vacuum Test."
2. Increase the engine speed and then quickly release the throttle.
3. Record the reading as the engine speed slows to idle.

A reading of 23″ to 25″ [584 mm to 635 mm] of mercury indicates normal operation.

Cranking Vacuum Test The **cranking vacuum test** is a test that measures engine vacuum while the engine is cranking. To perform a cranking vacuum test:
1. Connect the vacuum gauge to a source of intake manifold vacuum. Check the vehicle service manual for proper connection points.
2. With the engine at normal operating temperature, close the throttle and plug the positive crankcase ventilation (PCV) hose.
3. Disable the ignition or fuel system and crank the engine.

An even vacuum reading, 2″ to 5″ [52 mm to 127 mm] of mercury, at normal cranking speed means the valve timing is correct and the engine is mechanically sound. An uneven reading means

Table 2-A		VACUUM GAUGE READINGS			
Gauge Display	Reading	Diagnosis	Gauge Display	Reading	Diagnosis
	Average and steady at 15"–22".	Everything is normal.		Needle drops to low reading, returns to normal, drops back, and repeats this pattern at a regular interval.	Burned or leaking valve.
	Extremely low reading; needle holds steady.	Air leak at the intake manifold or throttle body; incorrect timing.		Needle drops to zero as engine rpm is increased.	Restricted exhaust system.
	Needle fluctuates between high and low reading.	Blown head gasket between two adjacent cylinders. Check with compression test.		Needle holds steady at 12"–16", drops to 0 and back to about 21" as throttle is opened and released.	Late ignition or valve timing. Leaking piston rings. Check with compression test.
	Needle fluctuates very slowly, ranging 4" or 5".	Incorrect air/fuel mixture.			
	Needle fluctuates rapidly at idle, steadies as rpm is increased.	Worn valve guides.			

Toyota Motor Manufacturing

there is an air leak into one or more cylinders. Burned valves or poor valve seating may cause leakage.

A low or zero reading may indicate that the camshaft timing is incorrect or that the timing belt, gears, or chain has failed.

Exhaust System Backpressure Test The exhaust system backpressure test measures the resistance to the flow of exhaust gases through the exhaust system. To perform an exhaust system backpressure test:

1. Before you perform this test, make sure you have the appropriate service manual for the vehicle you are using.
2. Remove an intake manifold port vacuum line from the intake manifold.
3. Connect a vacuum gauge between the vacuum line and intake manifold port.
4. Connect the tachometer (if necessary).
5. Disconnect the vacuum hose from the EGR valve and plug it.
6. Start the engine and let it idle until it reaches normal operating temperature. Then read and record the vacuum gauge measurement.

7. Gradually increase the engine speed to 2000 rpm. Read and record the vacuum gauge measurement again.
8. If the vacuum gauge does not drop, or it drops less than two inches from the reading made when the engine was idling, the exhaust system is not blocked and you do not need to test further.
9. If the vacuum gauge drops more than two inches from the reading made when the engine was idling, you need to proceed with the backpressure test.
10. If you need to proceed with this test, turn off the engine.
11. If necessary, raise the vehicle on a hoist to gain access to the exhaust manifold connection.
12. Separate the exhaust pipe from the exhaust manifold downstream from the EFE system.
13. Start the engine and gradually increase the speed to 2000 rpm.
14. Observe the operation of the EFE. Make sure your face is at least eighteen inches away from the exhaust manifold.
15. If the arm on it moves freely when the exhaust gases come out, the EFE is working correctly.

16. If the EFE arm does not move when the exhaust gases come out, stop the engine and dismantle and check the EFE system for blockage. If necessary, replace this system before continuing.
17. Read the vacuum gauge. If the gauge reading has still dropped more than two inches from the reading made when the engine was idling, there is an engine problem and engine tests should be made to determine the difficulty.
18. If the gauge reading does not drop or drops less than two inches, there is a blockage in the exhaust system. The exhaust system backpressure test should continue to find out what is causing the blockage.
19. Turn off the engine and reconnect the exhaust manifold to the exhaust pipe.
20. If you are continuing the backpressure test, disconnect the connecting pipe from the catalytic converter downstream from the catalytic converter.
21. Start the engine, gradually increase speed to 2000 rpm, and read the vacuum gauge.
22. If the reading does not drop or drops less than two inches, the blockage is in an exhaust component further downstream, and you need to continue with this procedure. If the reading drops more than two inches, there is a blockage in the catalytic converter, and it should be replaced before continuing.
23. If the reading does not drop more than two inches, reconnect the catalytic converter and disconnect the connecting pipe downstream from the muffler.
24. Start the engine, increase speed to 2000 rpm, and read the vacuum gauge.
25. If the reading does not drop or drops less than two inches, the blockage is in an exhaust component further downstream, and you need to continue with this procedure. (If the reading drops more than two inches, the muffler is blocked, and it should be replaced before continuing.)
26. If the reading does not drop or drops less than two inches, reconnect the muffler and disconnect the connecting pipe downstream from the resonator.
27. Start the engine, increase speed to 2000 rpm, and read the vacuum gauge.
28. If the reading does not drop or drops less than two inches, the blockage is in the tailpipe, and you need to continue with this procedure. (If the reading drops more than two inches, the resonator is blocked, and it should be replaced before continuing.)

29. If the reading did not drop or dropped less than two inches, check the tailpipe for obstruction. If necessary, replace it.
30. If the blockage was not found, repeat this procedure and check your results.

Valve Train Noises

Some engine noises are normal. Others may point to serious problems that require prompt attention. Excessive engine noise should not be overlooked as it could be an indication of a serious engine problem.

Engine noises can travel throughout the engine. They can be hard to isolate and detect. An **automotive stethoscope** is a diagnostic tool that helps isolate and amplify noises in a running engine. See **Fig. 2-6**.

Erick Dodge

Fig. 2-6 To locate noises, technicians use automotive stethoscopes. *What makes the exact location of a noise so hard to detect?*

Valve train noise is a regular clicking noise that occurs at one-half engine speed. When an engine is cold, some valve train noise is normal. Engines with mechanical valve lash adjusters usually produce more noise than do engines with hydraulic lash adjusters.

Too much clearance between the rocker arm (or cam follower) and the valve stem causes excess valve train noise. Other causes of noise include worn valve guides, sticking valves, and sticking or defective hydraulic adjusters. If excess valve train noise occurs when the engine is at normal operating temperature, the engine may need service.

More detailed information on valve train diagnosis and repair is found in Volume 2 of *Automotive Excellence*.

Engine Block Noises

Engine block noises are produced by components within the engine itself. The heavy casting of the block may make some noises difficult to locate or diagnose.

Connecting Rod Noise Connecting rod bearing noise is usually a light knocking or pounding sound. It is most noticeable when engine speed is constant (not speeding up or slowing down). Extreme wear or poor lubrication causes rod bearing noise. This type of wear is also indicated by low oil pressure and high oil consumption.

Piston Pin Noise A loose piston pin creates a noise similar to valve train noise. Piston pin noise has a unique, metallic double knocking sound.

Piston Slap Piston slap produces a muffled, hollow, knocking noise. When the engine is cold, piston slap is usually louder. Although a slight amount of piston slap is normal in many engines, loud, continuous piston slap means that the engine needs service. Overheating, poor lubrication, piston wear, and cylinder wear cause piston slap. Increased oil consumption may also occur.

Crankshaft Knock Worn main bearings cause a rumbling or knocking noise that is loudest when the engine is cold or under heavy load. Worn main bearings may cause low oil pressure and increased oil consumption.

Other Noises Some noises can sound like valve train or engine noises. A leaking exhaust manifold can sound like valve train noise. A loose flywheel can sound like worn main or connecting rod bearings. A loose timing belt or a dented flywheel cover or oil pan that interferes with moving parts can sound like crankshaft noises.

Before disassembling an engine, always verify that the source of the noise is not external. An effective diagnostic strategy can help ensure an accurate diagnosis.

SECTION 1 KNOWLEDGE CHECK

1. What may cause valve leakage?

2. Why are the readings for running compression tests lower than those for cranking compression tests?

3. What may be the problem if a vacuum reading drops back to zero as engine speed increases?

4. What may cause air leakage in a cylinder?

5. What tool may be used to electronically disable individual cylinders?

6. Aside from engine noise, what may also indicate extreme wear or poor lubrication?

7. Explain the sound of piston slap.

8. What causes crankshaft knock?

9. What should you do before disassembling an engine to identify automotive noise sources?

ASE TEST PREP

10. Technician A says that in a running compression test low readings on cylinders may indicate restricted exhaust. Technician B says low readings on cylinders may indicate restricted intake. Who is correct?
    - ⓐ Technician A.
    - ⓑ Technician B.
    - ⓒ Both Technician A and Technician B.
    - ⓓ Neither Technician A nor Technician B.

11. Technician A says that the noise of piston slap is similar to valve train noises. Technician B says that piston pin noise is similar to valve train noise. Who is correct?
    - ⓐ Technician A.
    - ⓑ Technician B.
    - ⓒ Both Technician A and Technician B.
    - ⓓ Neither Technician A nor Technician B.

● Section 2
Diagnosing the Cooling and Lubrication Systems

Objectives:

A5 ● Inspect engine assembly for fuel, oil, coolant, and other leaks; determine necessary action.

A13 ● Diagnose engine mechanical, electrical, electronic, fuel, and ignition concerns with an oscilloscope and/or engine diagnostic equipment; determine necessary action.

A15 ● Verify engine operating temperature; determine necessary action.

A16 ● Perform cooling system pressure tests; check coolant condition; inspect and test radiator, pressure cap, coolant recovery tank, and hoses; perform necessary action.

F3 ● Remove and replace thermostat and gasket.

F6 ● Perform oil and filter changes.

Vocabulary:
● cooling system pressure test
● cooling system thermostat
● pyrometer

Cooling System Tests

Pressurizing a cooling system raises the boiling point of the coolant. The higher boiling point improves the coolant's ability to transfer heat and cool the engine. A high pressure also keeps the coolant from forming vapor bubbles at "hot spots" in the engine. Cooling system pressure usually runs between 14 and 18 psi [97 and 124 kPa].

Frequent need to add coolant indicates a cooling system leak. A compression test or a cylinder leakage test can diagnose internal engine cooling system leaks.

Cooling system tests limit pressure to no more than 18 psi [124 kPa]. Higher pressure can damage the radiator, heater core, and coolant hoses.

Safety First **Radiator Safety** Use extreme caution when removing the radiator cap. The coolant may be under pressure and could cause serious injury.

Cooling System Pressure Test

A **cooling system pressure test** is a test that diagnoses external cooling system leaks. See **Fig. 2-7**.

1. Make sure that the coolant is at the correct level.
2. Attach the pressure tester to the radiator neck, using the proper adapter.

Terry Wild Studio

Fig. 2-7 The cooling system pressure tester checks the cooling system for leaks. *What is the maximum pressure used for this test?*

3. Adjust the pressure to the specified value.
4. Wait a few minutes before looking for leaks around the water pump shaft, coolant hoses, and radiator core.
5. Check inside the passenger compartment for leaks at the heater core.

If you do not see any external leaks, a cylinder leakage test may indicate a coolant leak in the cylinder head, head gasket, or engine block.

By using an adapter that connects the cap to the pressure tester, you can test the radiator pressure cap. The cap must hold the specified system pressure without leaking. If the cap leaks, the coolant can escape through the radiator overflow tube.

The radiator pressure cap has a pressure-relief valve to prevent excessive pressure. When the pressure goes too high, it opens the valve. Excess pressure and coolant then escape into the coolant recovery tank, also called the expansion tank.

To check a coolant hose, squeeze it. It should not collapse easily. Replace any hose that is soft, very hard, damaged, or swollen.

Cooling System Temperature Test

Engine temperature is controlled by engine coolant. The **cooling system thermostat** regulates the flow of coolant through the engine and cooling system. A properly operating thermostat keeps the engine within the correct operating temperature range. There are several different methods for testing thermostats. Refer to the service manual for details. In many cases it may be more practical to replace the thermostat and gasket if its operation is in question.

If the thermostat maintains too low a temperature, efficient combustion cannot occur. Moisture may build up in the engine. If the thermostat maintains too high a temperature, the engine may overheat. Overheating can warp cylinder heads, cause blown head gaskets, score pistons, and cause spark knock (detonation).

A **pyrometer** is an instrument that checks temperature. See **Fig. 2-8.** Pyrometers are either contact or non-contact. Contact types use a probe, which must touch the engine block or thermostat housing to check temperature. Non-contact, or infrared, pyrometers check temperature by measuring heat radiated from the thermostat housing or engine block.

Coolant Condition Check Coolant freezing point can be checked with a float hydrometer or a ball hydrometer.

Place the end of the float hydrometer's rubber tube into the coolant. Draw coolant up into the hydrometer. See **Fig. 2-9.** The position of the float in the coolant is determined by the concentration of antifreeze present. There is a temperature scale on the hydrometer. It shows the temperature at which the coolant will boil. It also shows the temperature at which the coolant will freeze.

A ball hydrometer has four or five balls in a plastic tube. Coolant is drawn into the tube. A stronger antifreeze concentration causes more balls to float.

Erick Dodge

Fig. 2-8 The pyrometer checks engine temperature. *What is another name for a non-contact pyrometer?*

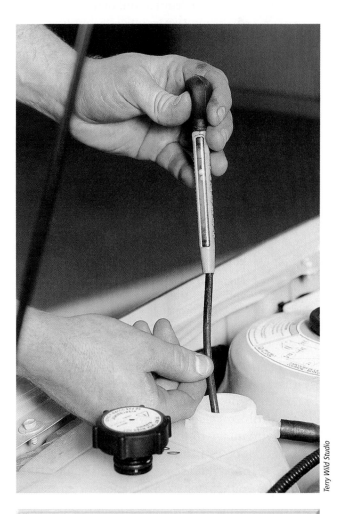

Terry Wild Studio

Fig. 2-9 Antifreeze strength is checked by drawing the coolant into a hydrometer. *What are the two types of hydrometers?*

Excellence in Science

Analyzing Fluids

We use the five senses of smell, taste, touch, sight, and hearing to pick up messages about what is going on around us. For example, our sense of hearing wakes us to our clock radio. Our sense of sight allows us to find our way around the house or to school. Touch may help us estimate temperature when we step out of our house. We use hearing to keep in touch with our friends when we talk with them. Smell may give us a clue as to what is for lunch. Our sense of taste will let us know if lunch was worth the wait.

Automotive technicians also use their senses. In this chapter you learn about diagnostic strategy. When automotive technicians put together a diagnostic strategy they rely on their senses. You learn how observing the color of exhaust can help you diagnose some engine problems. This chapter also explains how listening to engine noise can help a technician detect worn engine parts such as bearings and rocker arms. You are told that some obvious engine problems can be detected by fluid leaks.

Safety First

Poisonous Materials In the past, some technicians detected coolant leaks by taste. Do not taste fluids! The main ingredient in coolant is ethylene glycol, which is poisonous.

Flammable Materials Rags saturated with any flammable fluid must be disposed of properly.

Fluid leaks are often one of the first clues that a technician has in identifying a possible engine problem. Such leaks can occur before the problem becomes serious enough to cause major damage to the engine. With just a little practice you can "fine tune" your senses to help you identify fluid leaks from an engine. This can be your first step in a diagnostic strategy.

You may use a white shop towel to wipe up fluids dripping from the engine or from another location under the vehicle.

Apply It!

Identifying Auto Fluid Leaks

Meets NATEF Science Standards for analyzing fluids, analyzing waste management, and applying safety procedures.

To help train your senses to identify auto fluid leaks, try this.

1. Look around the garage at home, the auto shop at school, or an auto parts store. Pick up samples of the following automotive fluids:
   - Brake fluid.
   - Coolant (antifreeze).
   - Engine oil (new and used).
   - Transmission fluid.
   - Power steering fluid.

2. Get a white paper towel or shop rag. Place a small spot (about the size of a quarter) of each of the fluids you have collected on the towel or rag. Use your senses to learn as much as you can about the properties of each spot. Important clues to look for are:
   - What color is it?
   - Does it have a particular odor?
   - How does it feel? Is it slippery or sticky, for example?

3. Once you have practiced using your senses on these automotive fluids, take one of your white rags out to a parking lot. Look for fluids on the ground. Dip your rag or towel into one of them. See if you can identify it.

4. Determine how to discard the rags and clean up these fluids in an acceptable manner.

Inspecting and Testing a Thermostat Refer to the vehicle service manual for specifications and special procedures. This is a general procedure. To inspect and test the thermostat:

1. On a cool engine, check for pressure and remove the radiator cap.
2. Use a syringe to remove coolant or drain the radiator until it is below the thermostat housing level.
3. Remove the thermostat housing or housing cap.
4. Remove and rinse the thermostat.
5. Visually inspect the thermostat for breaks, corrosion, and improper sealing. Replace the thermostat if any of these are present.
6. Determine the operating (opening) temperature of the thermostat.
7. Replace the thermostat if it does not match the manufacturer's specifications as to type and temperature.
8. Suspend the thermostat, pellet down, in a special thermostat tester or in a cooking pot or heat-proof container of water with a thermometer.
9. Place the pot on a hot plate and gradually raise the temperature of the water, stirring the water as the temperature increases.
10. Make a note of the temperature at which the thermostat begins to open.
11. Apply additional heat to ensure the thermostat will open fully. Make a note of the temperature at which this occurs.
12. Turn off the heat and let the water cool.
13. Note the temperature at which the thermostat closes.
14. Replace the thermostat if it does not meet specifications.
15. Use a putty knife to clean the mating surfaces of the thermostat housing and its mounting surface.
16. Clean out the thermostat pocket and housing.
17. Inspect the housing to ensure it is not warped.
18. Install the appropriate thermostat.
19. Install a new gasket or seal the housing with RTV sealant.
20. Install the thermostat housing or housing cap.
21. Reconnect the radiator hose and refill the radiator with coolant.
22. Make a pressure test.
23. Check for leaks.

TECHNOLOGY

Coolant Heat Storage Tanks

To reduce hydrocarbon emissions, some hybrid vehicles use coolant heat storage tanks. See **Fig. A.** The coolant is kept hot in a tank even when the engine and radiator have gone cold. The hot coolant is used to preheat the engine before starting. Bringing the engine up to operating temperature before starting helps reduce hydrocarbon emissions.

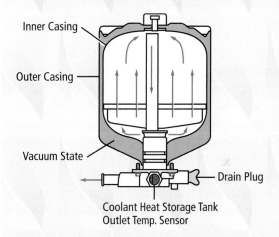

Inner Casing

Outer Casing

Vacuum State

Drain Plug

Coolant Heat Storage Tank Outlet Temp. Sensor

Fig. A Cross section of a coolant heat storage tank.

As a self-check of the tank's insulation and the water pump, the system may turn on the water pump even when the vehicle is off. If this happens while you are changing the coolant, you may be burned by hot coolant. To prevent injury, there are special procedures for changing engine coolant. Always refer to the vehicle's service manual for the proper procedures. The following procedure may not apply to all vehicles.

1. Disable the coolant heat storage water pump by disconnecting it from the power source and control module or by removing the pump altogether.
2. Drain the engine coolant from the coolant heat storage tank.
3. If applicable, drain the coolant from the rest of the system.
4. Reinstall the coolant heat storage water pump and close the system.
5. Refill the coolant system. It may be necessary to operate the coolant heat storage water pump to help recharge the coolant heat storage tank.
6. Operation of the coolant heat storage water pump during this process may set a false DTC in the system and cause the MIL to light. If this happens, be sure to clear the DTC with a scan tool after finishing the service routine.

Inspecting and Testing Mechanical and Electrical Fans Refer to the vehicle service manual for specifications and special procedures. This is a general procedure. To inspect and test the fan components:

1. Using a service manual or other information source, locate a procedure for inspecting and testing a fan, fan clutch, fan shroud/ducting, air dams, and fan control devices. Make sure you follow all procedures in the service manual.
2. Inspect the fan shroud, ducting, and air dams for cracks and missing fasteners. Repair or replace parts as needed.

On mechanical fan applications:

3. Inspect the fan. Check that the blades are not cracked, broken, bent, or loose.
4. Replace cracked, broken, or bent fans. Tighten loose fans.
5. Refer to the service manual for the test to check the fan clutch, if equipped.
6. Replace the fan clutch if it does not meet service manual specifications.
7. On water-pump mounted fans, inspect the water pump for damaged bearings and seals. Replace as necessary.

On electric fan applications:

8. Check that the fan is not loose.
9. Check that the fan motor mountings are not loose. Check for loose or broken wires.
10. Tighten or replace the fan, wires, or mountings as needed.
11. Refer to the service manual for electrical tests to check the fan motor and the fan motor circuit, including the fan switch or relay.
12. If fuses or electrical connections are faulty, repair or replace as needed. Replace the motor and fan switch or relay as needed.

Lubrication System Service

Periodic service of the lubrication system is essential for normal engine operation and service life.

Checking Oil Level

All engines use a metal or plastic rod, called a dipstick, to check the oil level in the engine. The dipstick fits into a tube or other opening that leads to the oil pan. When the dipstick is fully seated, the end should reach into the oil in the pan.

To check the oil level:

1. Make sure the vehicle is level.
2. Shut the engine off and wait a few minutes for the oil to drain back into the pan.

3. Remove the dipstick and wipe it off with a clean shop towel.
4. Reinsert the dipstick so that it is fully seated.
5. Remove the dipstick and note the oil level.

Note the appearance of the oil. Motor oil normally becomes darker with use. Evidence of foam, water, dirt, or the odor of gasoline indicates the need for an oil change. In addition, check the engine for the cause of the contamination.

> **Safety First**
>
> **Hot Engine Oil** Avoid coming in contact with hot oil. If possible, do not tip the filter during removal. Wearing a long-sleeved shirt and a cap will help protect against oil splashes.

Oil and Filter Removal The engine oil and filter should be changed as often as recommended by the manufacturer. Change intervals typically range from 3,000 to 7,500 miles [4,828 to 12,070 kilometers] depending on temperature and type of service. To change the oil and oil filter, position the vehicle so there is access to the oil pan drain plug and the filter. See **Fig. 2-10**. If a lubrication pit is not available, raise and support the vehicle on a lift.

David S. Hwang

Fig. 2-10 Remove the oil filter with an oil filter wrench.

A suggested procedure follows:

1. Start with the engine at normal operating temperature, if possible.
2. Raise and support the vehicle. The vehicle service information provides information on lift points and safety precautions.
3. Place a suitable container under the engine oil drain plug.
4. Remove the drain plug(s). Allow the oil to drain completely.
5. Inspect the drain plug threads and oil pan threads for damage. Replace if required. Reinstall the drain plug(s). Tighten to the recommended torque specification.
6. Move the drain pan under the oil filter.
7. Remove the filter. A special wrench may be required. Pour the oil from the filter into the drain pan.
8. Clean and inspect the filter mounting flange for damage. Replace if required.
9. Dispose of the used oil and filter according to local regulations.

Oil and Filter Replacement Following a standard procedure simplifies the replacement procedure and reduces the chance of error.

The following are general procedures:

1. Check the part number to ensure that the correct filter is being used.
2. Place a thin film of clean engine oil onto the filter gasket. This will ensure proper seating when the filter is tightened.
3. Install the new filter. Tighten it according to the recommended procedure. A typical practice is to turn the filter until the gasket just seats and then turn it another ¾ to 1 full turn.
4. Check to see that the drain plug has been installed and torqued to specifications. Remove the drain pan(s). Lower the vehicle.
5. Remove the fill cap and fill the engine with the recommended amount of the specified oil. Refer to the vehicle service information for oil specifications and engine oil capacity.
6. Start the engine. Quickly check for normal oil pressure and for leaks. Shut the engine off immediately if oil pressure is low or if leaks are found.
7. If oil pressure is satisfactory and no leaks are found, shut the engine off. Let it sit for several minutes. Recheck the oil level. Adjust the level, if needed.

SECTION 2 KNOWLEDGE CHECK

1. Explain how to run a cooling system pressure test.
2. How can you test the radiator pressure cap?
3. Explain how to check a coolant hose.
4. What types of engine problems may be caused by overheating?
5. Explain the difference between a contact and non-contact pyrometer.
6. What can be used to check coolant freezing point?

ASE TEST PREP

7. Technician A says that in oil and filter replacement a thin film of clean engine oil should be placed on the filter gasket to ensure proper seating when the filter is tightened. Technician B says that the filter should be turned until the gasket just seats and then turned another two full turns. Who is correct?
   ⓐ Technician A.
   ⓑ Technician B.
   ⓒ Both Technician A and Technician B.
   ⓓ Neither Technician A nor Technician B.

CHAPTER 2 REVIEW

Key Points

Meets the following NATEF Standards for Engine Performance: diagnosing engine problems and performing engine diagnostic tests.

- A visual check of the engine and its support systems is the first step of the diagnostic process.
- A documented service history can help in planning a diagnostic strategy.
- A diagnostic strategy is a planned, step-by-step procedure.
- The color and odor of exhaust smoke can provide important diagnostic information.
- Compression, cylinder leakage, and engine vacuum tests are used to determine cylinder condition.
- Pressure and temperature tests are used to determine the condition of the cooling system.
- The concentration of antifreeze determines the boiling and freezing point of engine coolant.
- Special procedures must be followed when changing engine coolant in hybrid vehicles.

Review Questions

1. What is a service history?
2. What test can show the condition of the piston and piston rings?
3. What produces a rumbling or knocking noise that is loudest when the engine is cold or under heavy load?
4. What is cylinder compression?
5. Where is the piston when air pressure is applied to the cylinder for a cylinder leakage test?
6. What does a vacuum gauge reading of 18″ indicate?
7. What types of engines will not have some intake manifold vacuum when it is cranking or running?
8. At what coolant temperature do modern engines operate?
9. (Critical Thinking) How does altitude affect compression pressure?
10. (Critical Thinking) What does a ball hydrometer indicate if only one ball is floating?

Excellence in Communication

Using the Scientific Method

The scientific method is a logical approach to problem solving. Use these four simple steps to apply the scientific method.

1. **Observe and Gather Information** Part of this step is talking to the customer. Look and listen for clues to the trouble.

2. **Hypothesize** Use the information you have gathered to make an educated guess about the problem.

3. **Test** Try different methods to see if your hypothesis is correct.

4. **Analyze** Use your test results to determine whether you have found the problem. If you have not, begin again with step one. Having used the method once, you have more information to add to step one. You have eliminated one possibility. Now you can test other possibilities.

Remember, use **OHTA:** Observe, Hypothesize, Test, and Analyze.

Apply It!

Meets NATEF Communications and Science Standards for problem solving using the scientific method.

1. Reread the "Customer's Concern" on the first page of this chapter.

2. Apply **OHTA.**
   - Write down your observations.
   - Write down your hypothesis.
   - Write down the tests you will use to prove your hypothesis.
   - Using the test results, analyze your information to see if your hypothesis is correct.
   - If your hypothesis was not correct, use what you learned to make a new hypothesis to test.

AUTOMOTIVE SERVICE EXCELLENCE
TEST PREP

Answering the following practice questions will help you prepare for the ASE certification tests.

1. A productive diagnostic strategy should include:

   a. getting as much information as possible from the customer.

   b. determining the history of the complaint.

   c. looking up the vehicle's service history.

   d. All of the above.

2. Technician A says that a running compression test is necessary to ensure proper volumetric efficiency. Technician B says that a running compression test is used to determine total system power output. Who is correct?

   a. Technician A.

   b. Technician B.

   c. Both Technician A and Technician B.

   d. Neither Technician A nor Technician B.

3. Which of the following might be the cause of a low reading on a running compression test?

   a. Incorrect valve timing.

   b. Restricted exhaust.

   c. Spark plug misfire.

   d. None of the above.

4. Technician A says that a cylinder leakage test checks a cylinder's ability to hold pressure. Technician B says that a cylinder leakage test is conducted with the piston at top dead center on the compression stroke. Who is correct?

   a. Technician A.

   b. Technician B.

   c. Both Technician A and Technician B.

   d. Neither Technician A nor Technician B.

5. If you suspect a weak cylinder, what type of test should you use to diagnose the problem?

   a. Cylinder leakage test.

   b. Cylinder compression test.

   c. Cylinder power balance test.

   d. None of the above.

6. Technician A says that pressurizing a cooling system raises the boiling point of the coolant. Technician B disagrees and says that raising the pressure of the cooling system decreases the boiling point of the fluid. Who is correct?

   a. Technician A.

   b. Technician B.

   c. Both Technician A and Technician B.

   d. Neither Technician A nor Technician B.

7. What is the usual pressure in psi of a cooling system?

   a. 5–10 psi.

   b. 14–18 psi.

   c. 20–24 psi.

   d. 36–54 psi.

8. Technician A says that the cooling system thermostat serves only to measure engine temperature. Technician B says that the thermostat regulates the flow of coolant through the engine and cooling system. Who is correct?

   a. Technician A.

   b. Technician B.

   c. Both Technician A and Technician B.

   d. Neither Technician A nor Technician B.

9. What device is used to check the coolant freezing point?

   a. A thermometer.

   b. A thermolytic moisture absorption gauge (TMAG).

   c. A float hydrometer.

   d. A digital multimeter.

10. Technician A says that oil and filter changes should be done when the engine is cold. Technician B says that oil and filter changes should be done when the engine is at normal operating temperature. Who is correct?

    a. Technician A.

    b. Technician B.

    c. Both Technician A and Technician B.

    d. Neither Technician A nor Technician B.

Section 1
Sensors

Section 2
Actuators

Section 3
Computerized
Controls

Computerized Engine Controls

Customer's Concern

Last summer, Rosa Santini purchased a new sedan from the dealership where you work. She has returned to the service department every three months or 3,000 miles for routine maintenance. On this cold morning, Rosa has stopped by the dealership to discuss a problem she is having with her sedan. As the weather has cooled, Rosa has noticed her car is more difficult to start and hesitates when she begins her morning commute.

As you discuss the problem with Rosa further, you quickly rule out causes like poor battery connections, low fuel grades, and worn engine parts. It sounds like her engine is not receiving enough fuel. Rosa's car is less than eight months old. How could it be slowed by this type of problem?

Technician's Challenge

As the service technician, you need to find answers to these questions:

1. Aside from when the engine is cold, does Rosa notice the loss of power at any other time? Why would temperature make a difference?

2. Could a faulty actuator or fuel injection problem be responsible for a lack of fuel being delivered to Rosa's engine?

3. How does the PCM relate to this problem? Is a solenoid or relay involved?

4. How can you correct the problem?

● Section 1
Sensors

Objectives:

- Identify commonly used sensors.
- Explain the difference between analog and digital signals.
- **C1** Diagnose ignition system related problems such as no-starting, hard starting, engine misfire, poor driveability, spark knock, power loss, poor mileage, and emissions concerns on vehicles with electronic ignition (distributorless) systems; determine necessary action.
- **C2** Diagnose ignition system related problems such as no-starting, hard starting, engine misfire, poor driveability, spark knock, power loss, poor mileage, and emissions concerns on vehicles with distributor ignition (DI) systems; determine necessary action.
- **B5** Check for module communication LAN/CAN/BUS errors using a scan tool.
- **B7** Obtain and interpret scan tool data.
- **B10** Perform active tests of actuators using scan tool; determine necessary action.
- **B6** Inspect and test computerized engine control system sensors, powertrain control module (PCM), actuators, and circuits using a graphing multimeter (GMM)/digital storage oscilloscope (DSO); perform necessary action.

Vocabulary:

- **sensor**
- **powertrain control module**
- **analog signal**
- **digital signal**
- **data bus**
- **photodiode**
- **thermistor**
- **potentiometer**

Sensors and Electronic Signals

Electronic modules control the operation of many systems on a vehicle. The modules monitor and control engine operation to meet performance, emissions, and fuel economy goals. To do this, several operating conditions must be continuously monitored or measured. A **sensor** is a device that monitors or measures operating conditions. Each sensor generates or modifies an electrical signal based on the condition it monitors. The signals from various sensors are sent to the powertrain control module (PCM). The **powertrain control module** is a sensor that uses information to make decisions about actuator operation. An actuator is an output device controlled by the module. See **Fig. 3-1.**

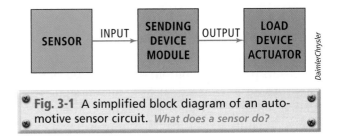

Fig. 3-1 A simplified block diagram of an automotive sensor circuit. *What does a sensor do?*

DaimlerChrysler

Sensors are also needed for automatic climate control, antilock braking, traction control, and other electronically operated systems. While there are many types of sensors, their operating characteristics are similar.

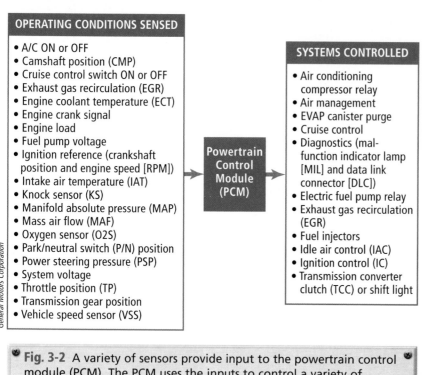

OPERATING CONDITIONS SENSED

- A/C ON or OFF
- Camshaft position (CMP)
- Cruise control switch ON or OFF
- Exhaust gas recirculation (EGR)
- Engine coolant temperature (ECT)
- Engine crank signal
- Engine load
- Fuel pump voltage
- Ignition reference (crankshaft position and engine speed [RPM])
- Intake air temperature (IAT)
- Knock sensor (KS)
- Manifold absolute pressure (MAP)
- Mass air flow (MAF)
- Oxygen sensor (O2S)
- Park/neutral switch (P/N) position
- Power steering pressure (PSP)
- System voltage
- Throttle position (TP)
- Transmission gear position
- Vehicle speed sensor (VSS)

Powertrain Control Module (PCM)

SYSTEMS CONTROLLED

- Air conditioning compressor relay
- Air management
- EVAP canister purge
- Cruise control
- Diagnostics (malfunction indicator lamp [MIL] and data link connector [DLC])
- Electric fuel pump relay
- Exhaust gas recirculation (EGR)
- Fuel injectors
- Idle air control (IAC)
- Ignition control (IC)
- Transmission converter clutch (TCC) or shift light

General Motors Corporation

Fig. 3-2 A variety of sensors provide input to the powertrain control module (PCM). The PCM uses the inputs to control a variety of vehicle systems. *What type of device does the PCM use to control these systems?*

Figure 3-2 lists the operating conditions in a vehicle that are monitored by the powertrain control module (PCM). They include:

- Engine speed.
- Vehicle speed.
- Engine load.
- Engine coolant temperature.
- Intake air temperature.
- Exhaust gas oxygen content.
- Throttle position.
- Crankshaft and camshaft position.
- Engine knock.

Sensors produce an output signal. The output can be either an analog signal or a digital signal. An **analog signal** is a signal that continuously changes. For example, its voltage may change from a minimum (usually 0) to a maximum (usually 5 volts). Any voltage between the minimum and maximum is possible. Many automotive sensors produce analog signals as shown in **Fig. 3-3**.

A **digital signal** is a signal that is either on or off. See **Fig. 3-4**. Digital signals are also known as square wave signals. A digital signal has a rapid rise and fall time (from low to high and from high to low). The signal is either high or low, with no values in between.

Automotive computers and modules use only digital signals. Analog sensor signals must be converted to digital signals before the computer can use them. A solid state device called an analog-to-digital converter produces the signal conversion. Converting analog-to-digital signals may occur in the sensor, the ignition module, or in the computer itself.

Some digital signals transmit information by varying the number of pulses per second. This is known as a changing frequency, or frequency modulation (FM). The frequency of a signal is the number of times it is turned on and off in a specified time, usually one second. Frequency is expressed in hertz (Hz), which are cycles per second. See **Fig. 3-5(a)**. Some mass air flow (MAF) sensors and manifold absolute pressure (MAP) sensors generate a frequency-modulated signal.

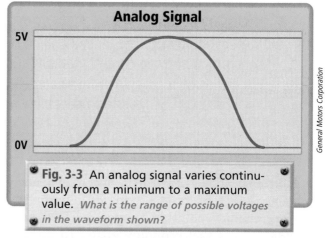

Analog Signal

5V

0V

General Motors Corporation

Fig. 3-3 An analog signal varies continuously from a minimum to a maximum value. *What is the range of possible voltages in the waveform shown?*

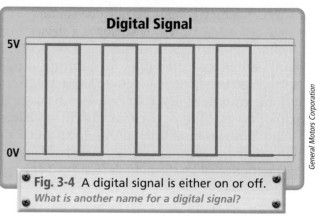

Digital Signal

5V

0V

General Motors Corporation

Fig. 3-4 A digital signal is either on or off. *What is another name for a digital signal?*

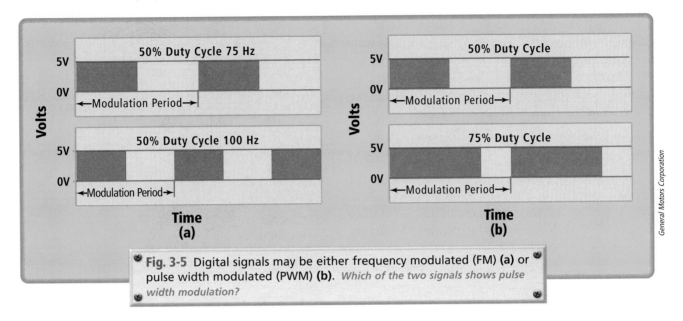

Fig. 3-5 Digital signals may be either frequency modulated (FM) **(a)** or pulse width modulated (PWM) **(b)**. *Which of the two signals shows pulse width modulation?*

Digital signals may also vary in their duty cycle. This is called pulse width modulation (PWM). The signal stays high or low for varying lengths of time. The frequency of a PWM signal does not change. However, the amount of on and off time does change. See **Fig. 3-5(b).** Fuel injectors are examples of actuators that are controlled by a PWM signal.

Reading the Data Stream

The PCM and other electronic components must be able to communicate with each other. This is done through a network of wires called a data bus or data bus network. A **data bus,** also known as CAN/LAN bus, is a wiring harness. It allows components connected to it to share sensor signals and other information needed for normal operation.

A CAN (controller area network) bus is a high-speed network used to support data messaging between multiple ECUs (electronic control modules). The CAN bus uses a twisted pair of wires (to reduce electromagnetic interference) between the ECUs. A LAN is a local area network generally used to connect computers.

The information transmitted on the data bus is known as the data stream. Because a module can share the data stream, each sensor does not need to be connected to each module. This simplifies system wiring and reduces costs and weight.

In addition to connecting modules, sensors, and actuators, the data bus is also connected to the data link connector (DLC). On 1996 and newer vehicles, the DLC is located under the dash near the steering column. On earlier models the DLC may be under the hood or under the dash. Refer to the vehicle service manual for the location.

The DLC allows a technician to read the information on the data stream by using a scan tool. A scan tool, or scanner, is a small, hand-held computer that communicates with the components on the data bus. A scan tool plugs into the DLC. See **Fig. 3-6.** It enables the reading of diagnostic trouble codes (DTCs) and data from the PCM and other related modules and sensors.

On some vehicles the scan tool can be used to give operating commands to components on the data bus. By using the scan tool, a technician can check the operation of most sensors and actuators.

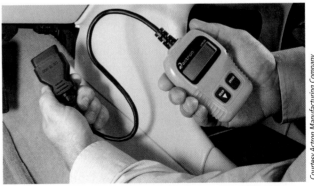

Fig. 3-6 A scan tool is connected to the DLC to read the data stream. *Where is the DLC located on 1996 and newer vehicles?*

Speed and Position Sensors

Speed and position sensors are used to monitor the speed of rotating shafts. These sensors are found on camshafts, crankshafts, and output shafts. In camshafts and crankshafts, the sensor indicates the position of the shaft as well as its speed.

Permanent Magnet Sensors

A permanent magnet (PM) sensor is a small AC-voltage generator. This type of sensor is also called a magnetic pulse generator. It uses a wire coil, a pole piece, a permanent magnet, and a rotating trigger wheel (reluctor wheel) to produce an analog voltage signal. See **Fig. 3-7.**

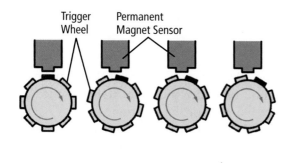

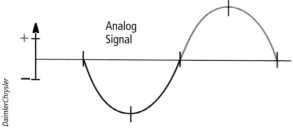

DaimlerChrysler

Fig. 3-7 A permanent magnet sensor produces an analog signal. *What produces the magnetic field in this type of sensor?*

The trigger wheel is mounted on a rotating shaft, such as a crankshaft or distributor shaft. As the trigger wheel rotates, it causes the field from the permanent magnet to move back and forth across the pickup coil. The moving magnetic field induces an analog (AC) voltage in the coil windings. The AC voltage pulses are directly related to the speed of the shaft the trigger wheel is mounted on. Because a PM sensor generates its own voltage, no supply voltage is needed.

There are many variations of the PM sensor. Most often they are used as sensing devices for engine speed, vehicle speed, or wheel speed. The PM sensor has unique notch spacing on the trigger wheel. This allows it to generate a signal that can be used also as a

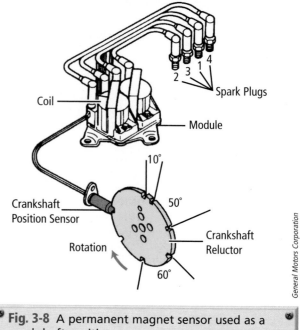

General Motors Corporation

Fig. 3-8 A permanent magnet sensor used as a crankshaft position sensor. *What two items of information can be obtained from a crankshaft position sensor?*

position sensor. In this way, a PM crankshaft sensor can signal engine rpm. It can also signal the position of the piston in cylinder number one. See **Fig. 3-8.**

Testing a Permanent Magnet Sensor Test a permanent magnet sensor as follows:

1. Connect a digital volt-ohm-meter (DVOM) (use AC volt scale) to the two wires leading from the sensor.
2. Crank the engine and observe the voltage. If the output is higher than specified (usually 200–300 mV), the sensor is good.
3. As a second test, check the pickup coil windings with an ohmmeter. If the resistance is higher or lower than normal, replace the sensor.

Hall-Effect Sensors

The Hall-effect sensor acts like an electronic switch. It turns a voltage on or off. In the Hall-effect process, current is continually passed through a semiconductor material or chip in the sensor. When the semiconductor material is exposed to a magnetic field, a small voltage is produced. When no magnetic field is present, the Hall-effect sensor produces no voltage.

A rotating interrupter ring controls the magnetic field. The interrupter ring has alternating metal blades and windows. When used as an ignition-timing sensor in a distributor, there are as many blades and

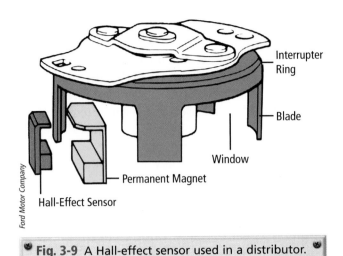

Ford Motor Company

Fig. 3-9 A Hall-effect sensor used in a distributor.
What does a Hall-effect sensor do?

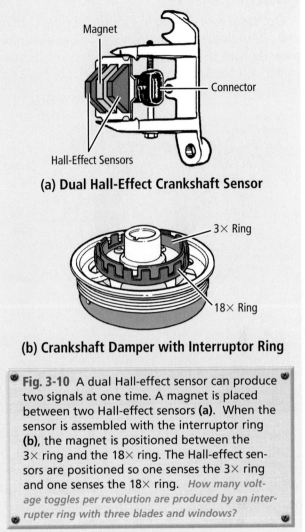

(a) Dual Hall-Effect Crankshaft Sensor

(b) Crankshaft Damper with Interruptor Ring

General Motors Corporation

Fig. 3-10 A dual Hall-effect sensor can produce two signals at one time. A magnet is placed between two Hall-effect sensors **(a)**. When the sensor is assembled with the interruptor ring **(b)**, the magnet is positioned between the 3× ring and the 18× ring. The Hall-effect sensors are positioned so one senses the 3× ring and one senses the 18× ring. *How many voltage toggles per revolution are produced by an interrupter ring with three blades and windows?*

windows as there are cylinders in the engine. The ring either exposes or shields the material from the magnetic field. See **Fig. 3-9.** Because the magnetic field is either exposed or shielded, the Hall-effect sensor does not rely on speed to create a signal. Unlike a PM sensor, no pickup coil or pole piece is used.

When a metal blade is in the space between the magnet and the Hall chip, it blocks the magnetic field. When the magnetic field doesn't strike the semiconductor, the Hall switch is off. No voltage is produced.

As the interrupter ring rotates, a window moves between the magnet and chip. The window allows the magnetic field to strike the chip. This turns on the Hall circuit. A small output voltage is generated. The on-off action of the circuit creates an on-off digital (square wave) signal.

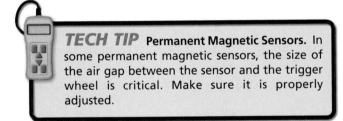

TECH TIP **Permanent Magnetic Sensors.** In some permanent magnetic sensors, the size of the air gap between the sensor and the trigger wheel is critical. Make sure it is properly adjusted.

Hall-effect sensors are used for many of the same applications as PM sensors. They control fuel injection and provide a TACH signal. Some engines use dual Hall-effect crankshaft sensors. In this case a single magnet is used with two Hall-effect sensors and two uniquely shaped interrupter rings. One interrupter ring produces eighteen uniform pulses per revolution. The other ring produces three unevenly spaced pulses. See **Fig. 3-10.**

Testing Hall-Effect Sensors Test a Hall-effect sensor as follows:
1. Use a DVOM to measure voltage on the signal line from the sensor. Refer to a wiring diagram to identify the correct wire.
2. With the ignition switch on, read the voltage.
3. Use the starter to rotate the engine a few degrees. Read the voltage again. If the sensor is good, the voltage will vary when the engine is stopped in various positions. It will vary from high (5–12 volts depending on the system) to low (near 0). It may take several attempts to get the engine to stop so that the interruptor blade is in the correct position for a reading.

Optical Sensors

Optical sensors use light-emitting diodes (LEDs) and photodiodes to produce a sensor signal. A **photodiode** uses the presence or absence of light to switch a reference voltage on and off. See **Fig. 3-11.**

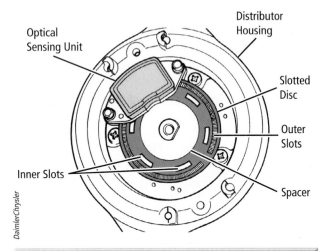

DaimlerChrysler

Fig. 3-11 This is a top view of an optical sensor, which uses light-emitting diodes (LEDs) and photodiodes to toggle a reference voltage. *What is the purpose of the slotted disc?*

Like a Hall-effect sensor, the optical sensor requires a voltage feed for operation. A typical circuit has two LEDs. These are mounted over two photodiodes with a space in between. A slotted metal disc mounted on a shaft rotates between the photodiodes and the LEDs.

Testing Optical Sensors Test an optical sensor in the same manner as a Hall-effect sensor:

1. Use a wiring diagram to identify the signal wire leading from the sensor. Connect a DVOM from this wire to ground.
2. With the ignition on, check the voltage.
3. Crank the engine a few degrees and check the voltage again. As the slotted disc moves between the photodiodes and the LEDs, the reference voltage should toggle to near 0 volts. If voltage is present at the sensor but the output does not toggle, the sensor is defective.

Variable Resistance Sensors

Several types of variable resistors are used as sensors for electronically controlled systems. The resistance in this type of sensor changes as the sensor monitors changing conditions.

Thermistors

A **thermistor** is a solid-state resistor with a resistance that changes with temperature. Two types are used. In a positive temperature coefficient (PTC) sensor, the resistance of the thermistor increases as the temperature increases. In a negative temperature coefficient (NTC) sensor, the resistance decreases as the temperature increases.

Thermistors are commonly used to monitor engine coolant temperature (ECT) and intake air temperature (IAT). In either case, the thermistor is a two-wire sensor. It is connected in series between a reference voltage from the PCM and ground. The reference voltage is usually 5 volts. See **Fig. 3-12.**

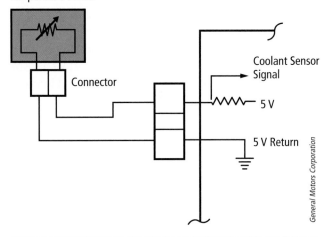

General Motors Corporation

Fig. 3-12 A thermistor is used as an engine coolant temperature (ECT) sensor. *If thermistor resistance is high, will the signal voltage in the PCM be high or low?*

With the ignition on, current flow through the sensor circuit is affected by the thermistor's resistance. If the resistance is high, there is less current flow in the circuit. Less current causes less voltage drop across a resistor in the PCM. The voltage on the sensor side of the PCM resistor is monitored by the PCM as the ECT sensor input.

TECH TIP **Thermistors.** You can quickly check both the ECT and IAT sensors by comparing their temperature or voltage readings on a scan tool. Do this when the engine is cool. Both sensors should read about the same.

The IAT sensor works like the ECT sensor. It is located in the engine air induction system. It provides information on the temperature of the air being drawn into the engine.

Testing Thermistors Test a thermistor as follows:
1. Using a scan tool, check the temperature readout. The temperature should be near normal for the operating conditions involved.
2. Using an ohmmeter, measure the resistance from one sensor terminal to the other. Compare this reading with specifications for the sensor at the test temperature.
3. Replace the sensor if the resistance is out of the specified range.

Potentiometers

A **potentiometer** is a three-wire variable resistor. It is used to monitor movement. The resistance of this sensor changes with the position of the shaft to which it is connected. One use of a potentiometer is the throttle position (TP) sensor on the throttle body assembly. See **Fig. 3-13**.

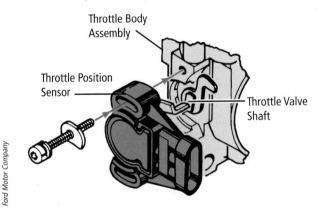

Fig. 3-13 The throttle position (TP) sensor is mounted on the throttle body assembly. *What type of variable resistor is used as a TP sensor?*

The PCM sends a 5-volt reference signal to one terminal of the TP sensor. A second terminal is grounded at the PCM. The voltage on the third TP sensor signal wire will change as the throttle is opened or closed. In most cases, a TP sensor voltage of 0.5 volts indicates a closed throttle. At wide-open throttle (WOT), the voltage will be almost 5 volts. See **Fig. 3-14**.

A potentiometer is also used to indicate the position of the exhaust gas recirculation (EGR) valve and the vane position in a vane-type airflow meter.

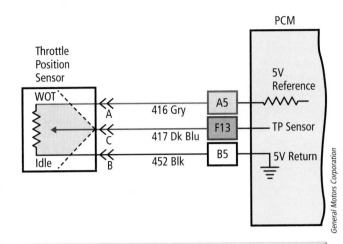

Fig. 3-14 The throttle position (TP) sensor is a potentiometer-type sensor. It receives a 5-volt reference signal from the PCM. *Identify the circuit that carries the TP sensor voltage to the PCM.*

Testing Potentiometer-Type Sensors Test potentiometer-type sensors as follows:
1. Connect a scan tool to the DLC (or use a DVOM) to measure voltage on the sensor signal wire.
2. Turn on the ignition switch. At the closed position the reading should be less than 1 volt. At the open position the reading should be almost 5 volts.
3. If no voltage is present, check to see if there is voltage on the reference wire from the PCM. If the voltage is 0, the reference voltage circuit is open.

Load Sensors

The PCM needs to know the amount of load on the engine. Load sensors provide this information to the PCM. This allows the PCM to calculate the correct spark advance and air/fuel ratios needed for various operating conditions.

On some engines load is calculated by using the inputs from the IAT sensor, TP sensor, and MAP sensor. This is the speed-density method of determining load. Other applications use an airflow sensor to determine the load. Airflow sensors measure the amount of air being used by the engine.

Manifold Absolute Pressure Sensors

The manifold absolute pressure (MAP) sensor is mounted to a source of manifold vacuum. Some MAP sensors are mounted directly on the intake manifold. Others are remotely mounted. They are connected to the manifold by a vacuum hose.

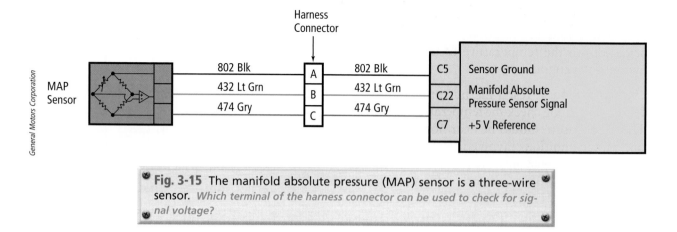

MAP Sensor

Harness Connector

802 Blk
432 Lt Grn
474 Gry

A
B
C

802 Blk
432 Lt Grn
474 Gry

C5 — Sensor Ground
C22 — Manifold Absolute Pressure Sensor Signal
C7 — +5 V Reference

Fig. 3-15 The manifold absolute pressure (MAP) sensor is a three-wire sensor. *Which terminal of the harness connector can be used to check for signal voltage?*

Engine vacuum is the opposite of manifold absolute pressure. When the engine is not running, there is no manifold vacuum. The pressure in the intake manifold is equal to atmospheric pressure. When engine load is low, as during closed throttle operation, vacuum is high and manifold pressure is low.

When there is more load on the engine, the throttle is opened to produce more power. Opening the throttle causes vacuum to decrease and manifold pressure to increase. Manifold vacuum and pressure change with engine load. Because of this, the MAP sensor is important in the speed-density method of calculating load.

Most MAP sensors are similar in appearance. However, several different internal designs are used. In one type of MAP sensor, the PCM monitors the voltage drop across the sensor. In another type, changes in manifold pressure cause the sensor to vary the frequency of the output signal.

On many vehicles the MAP sensor is also used to monitor atmospheric (barometric) pressure. When the key is turned on (engine off), the pressure in the manifold is atmospheric pressure. This value is sent to the PCM. It is used to calculate the amount of fuel needed by the engine. See **Fig. 3-15**.

Checking Manifold Absolute Pressure Sensors

Check the MAP sensor as follows:

1. Connect a scan tool to the DLC. With the key on and engine off, read the scan display. Vacuum should be 0 or voltage should be about 4.5 volts.
2. Start the engine. Manifold vacuum should be in the range of 16–22" [41–56 cm] of mercury. The voltage reading should be about 1–2 volts. If the readings are not as specified, make sure the vacuum line to the MAP sensor is not damaged, plugged, or disconnected.

Airflow Sensors

Several types of airflow sensors are in use. All determine engine load by directly measuring the amount of air entering the engine. Most vehicles that use airflow sensors do not use MAP sensors. However, some vehicles use both.

Mass Air Flow Sensors The mass air flow (MAF) sensor is mounted in the air induction system. This enables air entering the engine to pass through the sensor. See **Fig. 3-16**.

Most MAF sensors measure the amount of electrical energy required to keep a heated element at a specified temperature. Incoming airflow cools the heated element. By measuring the amount of current needed to maintain the specified temperature, the PCM determines the mass of airflow into the engine.

Depending on the application, MAF sensor output may be a varying voltage or a varying frequency.

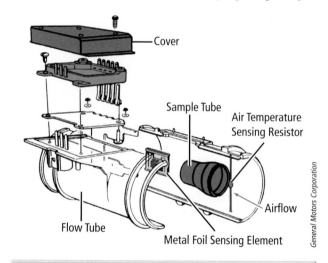

Cover

Sample Tube

Air Temperature Sensing Resistor

Airflow

Metal Foil Sensing Element

Flow Tube

Fig. 3-16 The mass air flow (MAF) sensor directly measures the amount of air entering the engine. *What two types of signals do MAF sensors produce?*

Testing Airflow Sensors There are several types of airflow sensors and signals. As a result, there is no one method to test these sensors. If airflow information is displayed on the data stream, use a scan tool. A scan tool can determine whether the airflow at idle is within specifications. If a vehicle with an identical powertrain is available, compare the airflow data between the two vehicles.

Oxygen Sensors

Oxygen sensors (O2S) detect the presence of oxygen in the exhaust gases. They are similar to spark plugs in appearance. See **Fig. 3-17.**

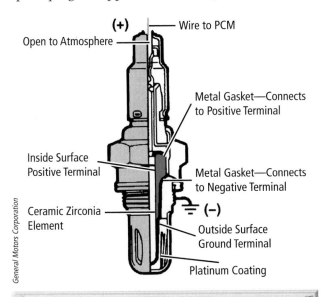

Fig. 3-17 An oxygen sensor. *What does the oxygen sensor do?*

Two types of oxygen sensors are used. Both must reach a specific temperature before they produce a useful signal. In some cases the hot exhaust gases are the only source of heat. These sensors require a warm-up period before they become effective.

Other sensors have a built-in heating element so that they reach normal operating temperature more quickly. They are called heated oxygen sensors (HO2S). Heated sensors also maintain their operating temperature during periods of extended idle when a cool-down might occur.

The number of oxygen sensors used and the number of wires connected to each sensor varies. It depends on the type of sensor and the application.

Several oxygen sensors may be used on the same vehicle. The sensor closest to the engine is primarily responsible for helping the PCM maintain the correct air/fuel ratio. A sensor near the inlet to the catalytic converter is often referred to as the "pre-cat" sensor. The "post-cat" sensor is located at the outlet from the catalytic converter.

Oxygen sensors located before and after the catalytic converter are used only on vehicles with on-board diagnostics-II (OBD-II). These sensors monitor catalytic converter efficiency. See **Fig. 3-18.**

Zirconia Oxygen Sensors

The zirconia oxygen sensor produces a voltage signal. This signal is based on the oxygen content in the exhaust gases.

During normal operation the output from the zirconia O2S varies from 0 to about 1 volt. Low readings (below 300 mV) indicate that the exhaust gas oxygen content is high. This means the air/fuel ratio is lean (excess air). High voltage readings (over 600 mV) mean that the oxygen content of the exhaust is low. This is caused by a rich mixture (excess fuel).

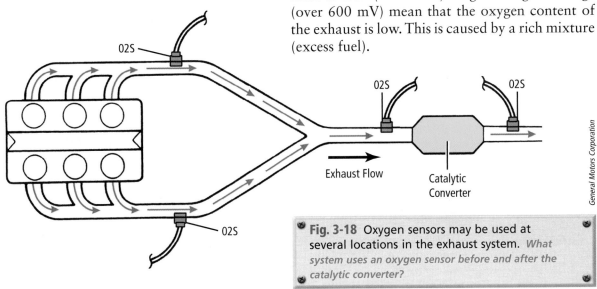

Fig. 3-18 Oxygen sensors may be used at several locations in the exhaust system. *What system uses an oxygen sensor before and after the catalytic converter?*

The O2S reads exhaust gas oxygen content, not the actual air/fuel ratio. Extra oxygen in the exhaust due to a cylinder misfire or exhaust manifold leak will result in a low oxygen sensor voltage reading. This will occur even if the actual air/fuel ratio is normal or slightly rich.

Titania Oxygen Sensors

Titania oxygen sensors are similar in appearance to other O2Ss. This type of sensor changes resistance in response to the amount of oxygen in the exhaust.

In a typical application, a titania sensor is used as the post-cat O2S. The PCM sends a 2-volt signal to the sensor and monitors the resulting return voltage. A voltage near 0 volts indicates a lean exhaust. A voltage near 2 volts indicates a rich exhaust.

Oxygen sensors become less sensitive with age. When this occurs, the time it takes to respond to a change in oxygen content slows. This makes it difficult for the PCM to maintain the desired air/fuel ratio.

Oxygen sensors may become contaminated with carbon and oily deposits. These contaminants may be caused by:

• Rich fuel mixtures.
• Internal coolant leaks.

• Excessive oil consumption.

Correct the condition(s) causing any contamination problems before replacing the sensor.

Checking Oxygen Sensors

In OBD-II, oxygen sensors are designated according to a number scheme. The numbers are 1/1 (upstream bank 1), 1/2 (upstream bank 2), 2/1 (downstream bank 1), and 2/2 (downstream bank 2).

Check oxygen sensors as follows:

1. Use a scan tool or DVOM to observe the output voltage from the O2S. The actual signal will depend on the type of sensor and where it is located. Refer to a service manual for information on the testing of specific O2S.

2. Do not attempt to test a zirconia sensor with an ohmmeter. (It is acceptable to check the heating element for resistance.) **Figure 3-19** shows graphs of typical voltages from an O2S closest to the engine. Voltages from the post-cat sensor will be considerably different.

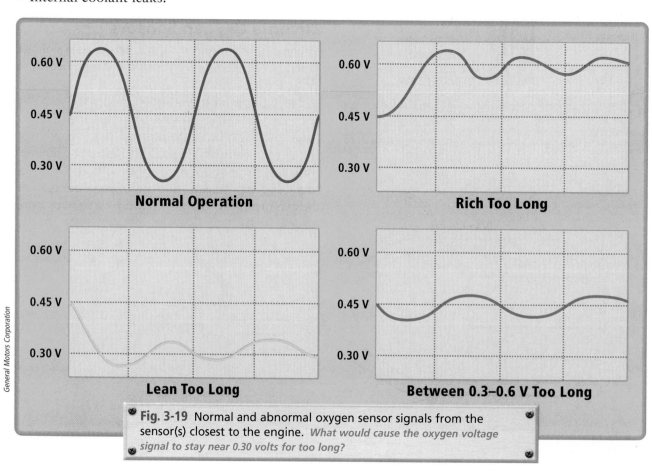

General Motors Corporation

Fig. 3-19 Normal and abnormal oxygen sensor signals from the sensor(s) closest to the engine. *What would cause the oxygen voltage signal to stay near 0.30 volts for too long?*

Excellence **in Science**

Finding Resistance

The Wheatstone bridge is a useful circuit. It can be used to calculate the value of an unknown resistance from known resistances.

A sample circuit is shown here. The input terminals for the bridge are points C and D. The output is across terminals A and B. A voltage source (V_S) is connected across the input terminals (C and D) to energize the bridge.

If R_1 and R_2 have the same ratio as R_3 and R_4, the bridge is balanced and V_{AB}, across the bridge, is zero. Similarly, if R_1 and R_2 are equal, then R_3 and R_4 must be equal to balance the bridge and cause V_{AB} to be zero. In either case, with a balanced bridge, the formula for R_4 is:

$$R_4 = R_3 \times \frac{R_2}{R_1}$$

This equation makes the balanced bridge very useful for measuring any unknown resistance (R_4).

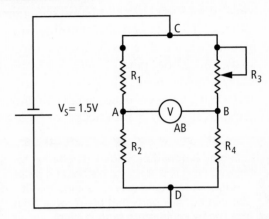

The output voltage of the unbalanced bridge is very sensitive to the difference between the values of R_3 and R_4. The unbalanced output voltage is used to measure many variables. Temperature, pressure, and light level are some measurements made using sensors in place of R_3 and R_4.

Apply It!

Constructing a Wheatstone Bridge

Meets NATEF Science Standards for measuring electrical resistance.

Materials and Equipment
- 1.5-volt power supply (V_S)
- Galvanometer or digital multimeter
- Three 500-ohm resistors (R_1, R_2, R_4)
- 1.0 kilo-ohm potentiometer (R_3)

Let's investigate the balanced and unbalanced Wheatstone bridge.

1. Use the digital multimeter to measure the resistance of each of the fixed resistors (R_1, R_2, and R_4). Record these values.

2. Make sure the power supply is turned off.

3. Construct the circuit shown. Use a length of wire as a circuit between one end of the potentiometer and its center lead. If a galvanometer is not available, use a digital multimeter to measure V_{AB}.

4. Position the potentiometer at its center value. Then adjust its setting several times. Unbalance the bridge so you can observe both positive and negative output voltage (V_{AB}).

5. Adjust the potentiometer to balance the bridge with a zero output voltage for V_{AB}.

6. Disconnect the potentiometer, R_3, from the circuit without changing its setting. Use the multimeter to measure the value of its resistance.

7. Calculate the value of R_4 using the formula:

$$R_4 = R_3 \times \frac{R_2}{R_1}$$

Use your measured values for R_1, R_2, and R_3. Compare your measured value for R_4 to the value you just calculated.

Knock Sensors

A knock sensor (KS) is used on some engines. It allows the PCM to retard ignition timing to control detonation, or spark knock. Ultimately, this reduces nitrogen oxide (NOx) in the exhaust. Detonation occurs when part of the air/fuel mixture self-ignites and "explodes." This uncontrolled burning causes engine parts to vibrate. The resulting sound waves create "spark knock" or "ping." Severe spark knock damages engine components. The KS is mounted on the engine. Here it is exposed to mechanical vibrations, including those caused by spark knock. See **Fig. 3-20.**

Safety First

Engine Detonation Engine detonation can cause serious damage to pistons and piston rings. Never stand over an engine that is detonating. Any parts that break loose from the engine could cause serious injury.

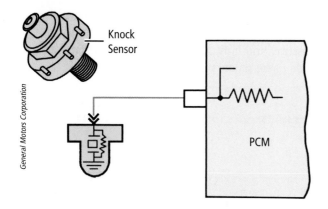

Knock Sensor

PCM

General Motors Corporation

Fig. 3-20 Some engines have a knock sensor (KS) to help control spark knock (detonation). *What does the KS do when spark knock occurs?*

A typical KS contains a piezoelectric crystal. A piezoelectric crystal is a type of crystal that produces a voltage when it is subjected to pressure. Therefore, when vibrations occur, the piezoelectric crystal generates a small AC voltage. This voltage is proportional to the intensity of the knock. This signal is sent to the PCM. The PCM monitors the KS signal. It ignores most vibrations not caused by

detonation. If detonation is occurring, the PCM retards the ignition timing until the knock-related vibrations stop. Normal timing is gradually restored as the conditions causing the spark knock change.

Testing Knock Sensors Test knock sensors as follows:

1. Use a scan tool to observe either ignition timing or the KS signal.
2. With the engine running at about 1,500 rpm, rap lightly with a small hammer on the engine near the sensor. Ignition timing should retard several degrees. Or, you should see a signal from the knock sensor.
3. For specific test procedures, refer to the vehicle service manual.

Knock sensors are electronic devices. Their operation can be affected by heat and mechanical damage. When handling these sensors always use the proper tools. Be careful not to round off the corners of the nut when removing or installing a sensor. If the knock sensor is seized, use a penetrating oil to remove any corrosion before attempting to remove it.

Switches

Sensors normally produce variable input signals. Other input signals are simple on or off signals from mechanically or pressure-operated switches. Switch input to a module is either an on or off voltage. This depends on whether the switch is open or closed. Two types of switch circuits are used.

Power Side Switches

Power side switches are located between a power supply and a module. The voltage source is usually the battery (12 volts). The module provides a ground circuit and monitors the signal. When the power side switch is open, the voltage signal to the module is 0. When the switch is closed, the signal will be the voltage supplied. The switch is also called a "pull-up" switch. When the switch closes, the voltage is "pulled-up" to its highest possible level. See **Fig. 3-21.**

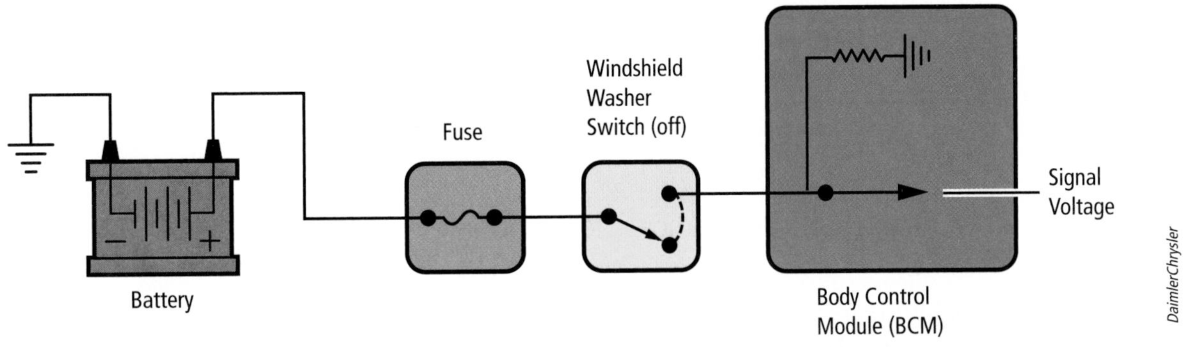

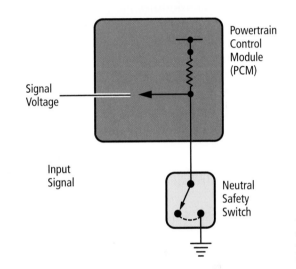

DaimlerChrysler

Fig. 3-21 A power side switch is located between a voltage source (the battery) and a control module. *What are the only two voltage signals that this switch can produce?*

Ground Side Switches

Ground side switches have one terminal connected directly to ground. Power is supplied by the module, which also monitors the circuit. When the switch is open, signal voltage is at its maximum value. When the switch closes, the circuit is connected to ground. The voltage drops to near zero. Because the voltage drops, the switch is often referred to as a "pull-down" switch. See **Fig. 3-22.**

Testing Switches Test switches as follows:

1. Using a DVOM or scan tool, check for voltage on both sides of the switch. When using a DVOM, refer to the vehicle service manual to determine the proper wiring connections for the switch.
2. The voltage should change from low to high or high to low as the switch is operated. The operation of many switches can be monitored on a scan tool. The switch signal should change when the switch is operated.

DaimlerChrysler

Fig. 3-22 A ground side switch is connected directly to ground. *What is another name for a ground side switch?*

SECTION 1 KNOWLEDGE CHECK

1. What kind of output signal changes continuously?
2. What do optical sensors use to produce a sensor signal?
3. What is commonly used to monitor engine coolant temperature and intake air temperature?
4. What is used to indicate the position of the exhaust gas recirculation valve?
5. What does an oxygen sensor do?
6. Where are power-side switches located?

ASE TEST PREP

7. Technician A says that in checking a MAP sensor the vacuum reading should be 4.5 and the voltage should be about 1 volt. Technician B says that the vacuum reading should be 0 and the voltage should be about 4.5 volts. Who is correct?
   - ⓐ Technician A.
   - ⓑ Technician B.
   - ⓒ Both Technician A and Technician B.
   - ⓓ Neither Technician A nor Technician B.

● Section 2
Actuators

Objectives:

- Explain what actuators do and how they perform needed tasks.
- **B10** ● Perform active tests of actuators using scan tool; determine necessary action.

Vocabulary:
- **actuator**
- **solenoid**
- **relay**

Types of Actuators

After electronic modules have evaluated sensor inputs, they operate output devices. These devices, called actuators, cause the desired actions to take place. An **actuator** is an output device that is operated by the PCM or other modules to create motion and perform other tasks. A variety of actuators are used to control automotive circuits and components. Tasks performed by actuators include controlling:

- Air/fuel ratio.
- Idle speed.
- Emission control device operation.

Solenoids

A **solenoid** is an electromechanical device which, when connected to an electrical source such as a battery, produces a mechanical movement.

Solenoids use electromagnetism to produce motion. This motion is used to open and close air or hydraulic passages, apply a magnetic clutch, and lock and unlock doors. Solenoids can be used to control the flow of vacuum to a device. Solenoids may be either normally open (N.O.) or normally closed (N.C.).

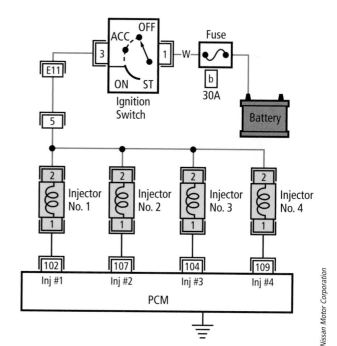

Fig. 3-24 The PCM provides the ground circuit for the fuel injectors. *When a fuel injector circuit is grounded by the PCM, does the fuel injector open or close?*

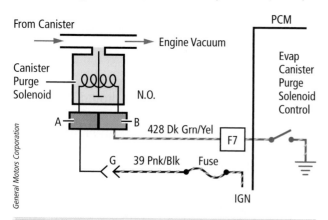

Fig. 3-23 The PCM controls vacuum-operated devices by using solenoids. *Where does this solenoid get its voltage?*

Voltage is applied to most solenoids by the ignition switch. When the solenoid winding is grounded by the PCM, the plunger in the solenoid moves. It either opens or closes a vacuum passage. In this way the PCM controls the operation of vacuum-operated components, such as canister purge valves and exhaust gas recirculation (EGR) valves. See **Fig. 3-23.**

A fuel injector is a special type of solenoid. Battery voltage is supplied to one of the injector terminals. The PCM grounds the other terminal to operate (open) the injector. See **Fig. 3-24.**

By controlling the on and off time (pulse width) of a fuel injector, the PCM controls the amount of fuel injected. See **Fig. 3-25.**

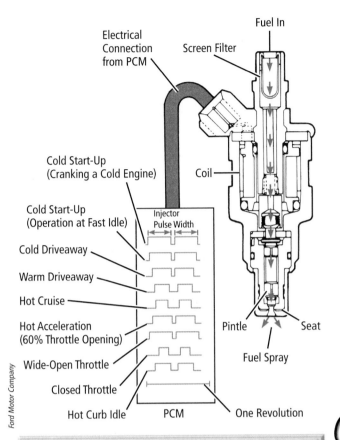

Ford Motor Company

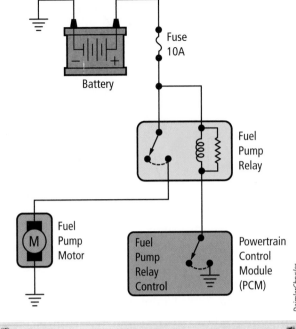

DaimlerChrysler

Fig. 3-26 The electric fuel pump is controlled by a PCM-operated relay. *Where is the fuel pump relay winding grounded?*

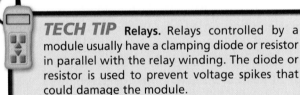

TECH TIP Relays. Relays controlled by a module usually have a clamping diode or resistor in parallel with the relay winding. The diode or resistor is used to prevent voltage spikes that could damage the module.

Relays

A **relay** is a device that is similar to a solenoid except that the motion is used to close a set of electrical contacts. When the relay is not energized, the contacts are open. No current flows in the circuit. When the relay is energized, the contacts close and the circuit is completed. See **Fig. 3-26.**

The PCM energizes the fuel pump relay circuit to operate the electric fuel pump. On many vehicles relays controlled by the PCM are also used to operate the electric engine cooling fan and air conditioning compressor clutch.

Testing Solenoids and Relays Test solenoids and relays as follows:

1. Listen or feel for plunger movement when the coil is energized. If no movement is observed, use a DVOM.
2. Use the DVOM to test for voltage to and from the windings.
3. Use an ohmmeter to check the resistance of the windings.
4. If the electrical checks are acceptable but the relay or solenoid does not work, the relay or solenoid is defective.
5. Special test procedures and equipment may be required to test some fuel injectors. Refer to the vehicle service manual for details.

Relays and solenoids can be tested using a scan tool by following the scan tool's menu to find actuation. While in actuation, relays and solenoids can be turned on and off with the scan tool through a control module for testing.

Stepper Motors

Stepper motors are similar to other small DC motors. However, the movement of the shaft is more precisely controlled. Many fuel-injected engines use a stepper motor as an idle air control (IAC) valve.

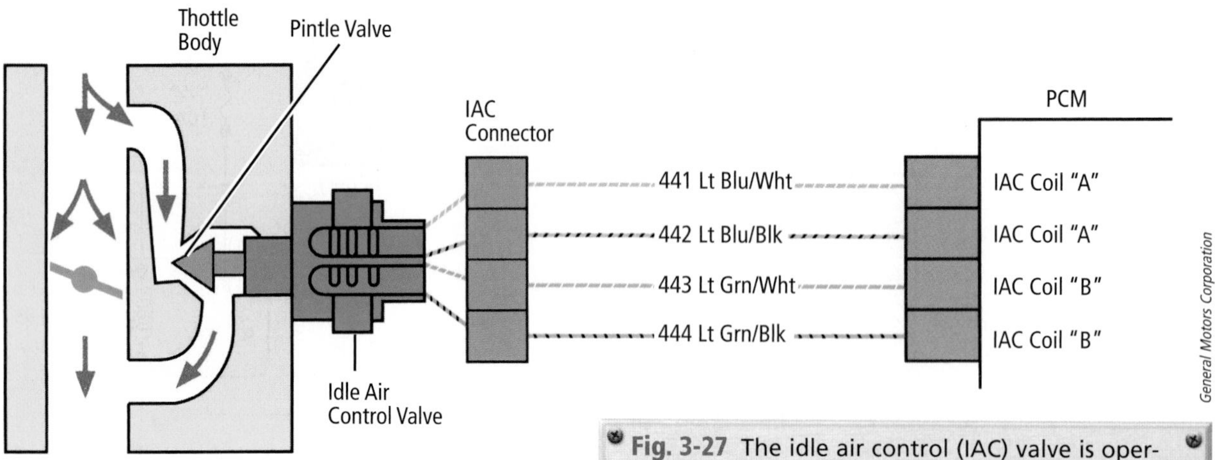

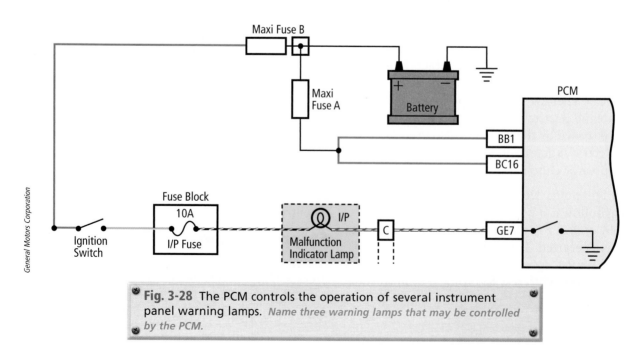

Thottle Body · Pintle Valve · Throttle Body

IAC Connector

441 Lt Blu/Wht — IAC Coil "A"
442 Lt Blu/Blk — IAC Coil "A"
443 Lt Grn/Wht — IAC Coil "B"
444 Lt Grn/Blk — IAC Coil "B"

PCM

Idle Air Control Valve

General Motors Corporation

Fig. 3-27 The idle air control (IAC) valve is operated by a stepper motor. *How does the PCM position the pintle in the exact location needed?*

The IAC valve is a reversible DC motor in the throttle body assembly. A small pintle valve controls airflow to the engine during closed throttle conditions. See **Fig. 3-27**. To control the position of the pintle valve, the PCM sends a pulsing (on and off) voltage through two sets of motor windings. By pulsing voltage to the correct winding, the PCM can position the pintle in the exact location needed for a specified idle speed.

Testing Stepper Motors Test a stepper motor by observing the pintle for normal operation. In some cases a test wiring harness is available to operate the motor using battery voltage. Some stepper motors can be tested using commands given by a scan tool.

Other PCM-Controlled Outputs

The PCM is responsible for turning on some instrument panel warning lamps. The PCM controls the malfunction indicator lamp (MIL), turning it on when certain malfunctions occur. The PCM may also control the coolant over-temperature lamp, charging system warning lamp, and upshift lamp. Warning lamps are turned on when the PCM provides a ground for the lamp circuit. See **Fig. 3-28**.

Testing Warning Lamps Most warning lamps are designed to come on as a "bulb check" when the ignition switch is turned to ON or START. If a warning lamp does not come on when it should, check the fuse and the bulb before checking the PCM circuit.

Maxi Fuse B

Maxi Fuse A

Battery

PCM

BB1

BC16

General Motors Corporation

Fuse Block
10A
I/P Fuse

I/P
Malfunction Indicator Lamp

C

GE7

Ignition Switch

Fig. 3-28 The PCM controls the operation of several instrument panel warning lamps. *Name three warning lamps that may be controlled by the PCM.*

Excellence in Math

Determining Rate of Change

The graph below shows the characteristics of an EFI MAP sensor. The graphed line appears to be a straight line (linear).

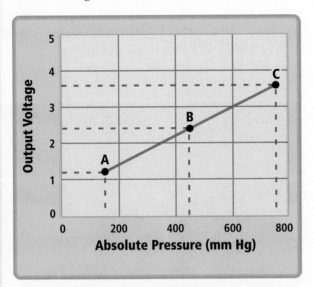

You can find the rate of change of the output voltage per mm Hg from point B to point A using the formula:

$$m = \frac{Y_1 - Y_2}{X_1 - X_2}$$

where point B (450, 2.4) is (X_1, Y_1) and point A (150, 1.2) is (X_2, Y_2).

$$\frac{2.4\ V - 1.2\ V}{450\ mm\ Hg - 150\ mm\ Hg} = 0.004\ V/mm\ Hg$$

You can find the rate of change between points B (450, 2.4) and C (750, 3.6):

$$\frac{3.6\ V - 2.4\ V}{750\ mm\ Hg - 450\ mm\ Hg} = 0.004\ V/mm\ Hg$$

If the change in the vertical quantity divided by the change in the horizontal quantity is constant, then a linear relationship exists between the quantities. The above two calculations show that the rate of change of the output voltage per mm Hg is 0.004.

You can show mathematically that the line is straight. The data shown below were used to plot the line on the graph. If the rate of change between points A and B is the same as the rate of change between points B and C, the line is a straight line.

Look at the data as three sets of numbers in the form (X, Y). They are: A (150, 1.2), B (450, 2.4), and C (750, 3.6). Each pair of numbers identifies a point on the graph.

	Absolute Pressure (in mm Hg)	Output Voltage (in Volts)
A	150	1.2
B	450	2.4
C	750	3.6

Apply It!

Meets NATEF Mathematics Standards for interpreting graphs and solving problems.

1. If the relationship is linear, what should be the rate of change of the output voltage per mm Hg using the sets of numbers for Point A and Point C.

2. Calculate the rate of change of the output voltage per mm Hg between A and C.

Testing an Actuator by Using a Scan Tool

The scan tool is a bi-directional control device. It sends information to and receives information from vehicle control modules. In OBD-II Mode 1, the scan tool requests generic information and receives data from the PCM. Many enhanced scan tools can actuate devices energized by PCMs, body control modules, and other sub-system control modules. These devices include relays, solenoids, stepper motors, and warning devices. The use of the scan tool to energize components can speed the troubleshooting process.

Check the scan tool manufacturer's vehicle-specific instruction manual for its capability to operate a particular actuator or initiate a test sequence. These are listed under headings such as Active Command Mode or Inspection Menu. The list can be quite long. It may include over a thousand different commands for some vehicles. Commands might include those to turn on the fuel pump, operate the door locks, and change the power seat position. Be aware that a factory scan tool may have the capability to perform tests that cannot be performed by aftermarket scan tools. These may include testing the ABS, SRS, and other non-engine related control systems.

Each scan tool has a slightly different method of navigation to its actuation screen. This is a general method. To monitor the operation of an actuator:

1. Connect the scan tool to the vehicle's data link connector.
2. Access the ECU that controls the actuator you want to control.
3. Navigate to the actuation screen.
4. Select the item you would like to turn on.
5. While actuating the component, monitor its operation with the data supplied by the scan tool.

Current Ramping

Current ramping is a unique diagnostic approach used to determine a component's condition. Typical components that can be tested include motors, solenoids, and relays. See **Fig. 3-29**. The tools required include a lab scope and a current multiplier, which is used to amplify the signal. Current waveform "pictures" acquired using the lab scope allow the technician to see more of what the electrons are doing. Defective components will show an erratic low-amperage or high-amperage pattern while the component is working.

Current ramping is fast, non-invasive, and gives a more complete picture of an operation. It also can help find intermittent problems, predict future failure, and verify repairs. Using this diagnostic approach will also help customers understand the need for component repair or replacement.

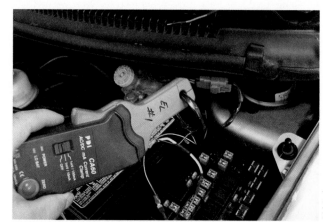

Fig. 3-29 Using a current probe to check a relay.
In what way are defective components revealed?

SECTION 2 KNOWLEDGE CHECK

1. What do solenoids use to produce motion?

2. How does a relay differ from a solenoid?

3. What controls the on and off time of the fuel injector to control the amount of fuel delivered to the engine?

4. What is used to prevent voltage spikes within relays?

5. What is used to check the resistance of solenoid or relay windings?

6. What should be checked if a warning lamp does not come on when it should?

ASE TEST PREP

7. Technician A says that a factory scan tool may have the capability to perform tests that cannot be performed by an aftermarket scan tool. Technician B says that aftermarket scan tools are designed to perform the tests performed by factory scan tools. Who is correct?
   ⓐ Technician A.
   ⓑ Technician B.
   ⓒ Both Technician A and Technician B.
   ⓓ Neither Technician A nor Technician B.

• Section 3
Computerized Controls

Objectives:

B3 • Diagnose the causes of emissions or driveability concerns resulting from malfunctions in the computerized engine control system with stored diagnostic trouble codes.

B6 • Inspect and test computerized engine control system sensors, powertrain control module (PCM), actuators, and circuits using a graphing multimeter (GMM)/digital storage oscilloscope (DSO); perform necessary action.

B1 • Retrieve and record stored OBD I diagnostic trouble codes; clear codes.

A4 • Locate and interpret vehicle and major component identification numbers (VIN, vehicle certification labels, and calibration decals).

B5 • Check for module communication LAN/CAN/BUS errors using a scan tool.

• Explain why sensors and actuators fail.

Vocabulary:

- **on-board diagnostic systems**
- **malfunction indicator lamp (MIL)**
- **random access memory (RAM)**
- **diagnostic trouble code (DTC)**
- **vehicle identification number (VIN)**

On-Board Diagnostic Systems

In the early 1980s, vehicle manufacturers began using on-board diagnostic systems. **On-board diagnostic systems** are computer-controlled test routines that monitor engine control systems. Most on-board diagnostic systems made before 1996 are known as on-board diagnostic I (OBD-I) systems. OBD-I technology was used during the 1980s and early 1990s. The main computer in these systems was known by the following names:

- Engine control module (ECM).
- Electronic engine controller (EEC).
- Single board engine controller (SBEC).

The OBD-I system's diagnostic capabilities had the following limitations:

- It could not identify deterioration of a system.
- It could not monitor all engine-related systems.
- It used nonstandard diagnostic trouble codes, terminology, and diagnostic procedures.

Because of these limitations, OBD-II was developed.

Powertrain Control Module

The engine control module is now referred to as the powertrain control module (PCM). The PCM is sometimes called a processor or microprocessor. It is the heart of the OBD system. Using input from a sensor network, it operates a network of actuators that regulate engine control systems.

The instructions for the PCM are contained in an electronically erasable programmable read-only memory (EEPROM). The EEPROM may also be called a MEMory CALibration (MEMCAL) unit. The EEPROM can be hard-wired into the PCM or it can be removable.

The EEPROM contains engine calibration data in an electronically erasable programmable read-only memory (EEPROM) chip. The calibration data includes operating parameters for functions such as idle speed, air/fuel mixture, and spark advance. Using this data, the PCM controls these engine management functions to provide the best driveability, fuel economy, and lowest emissions.

TECH TIP **Operational MIL.** If ignition timing doesn't respond to changes in engine load, the PCM may be in LOS mode. The MIL is your only visible indicator of a problem. Before diagnosis, be sure that the MIL is operational.

Figure 3-30 shows a typical PCM. The PCM's functions are to:

- Monitor system sensor inputs.
- Control ignition timing and air/fuel mixture.
- Control and monitor emission control systems.
- Perform self-diagnostic checks.

The PCM may also control other systems, such as the transmission.

If certain failures occur, such as an out-of-expected-range signal from the oxygen sensor (O2S), the PCM goes into a limited operating strategy (LOS), or limp-in mode. The driver is alerted to the LOS condition by the malfunction indicator light. The **malfunction indicator lamp (MIL)** is a light that warns the driver of a problem in the systems monitored by the PCM. The MIL is sometimes referred to as the check engine light or service engine soon light.

In LOS mode, factors such as air/fuel mixture and ignition timing are controlled by preset values stored in the PCM. Driveability, fuel economy, and emissions are adversely affected.

Safety First

Jump-Starting A voltage surge during jump-starting could affect the vehicle's electronics, including the PCM. Never attempt to connect to another vehicle while the engine is running and the charging system is in operation. Spikes in voltage can damage electronic modules on either vehicle during jump-starting.

Manufacturers may change the calibration settings of the engine to correct or improve a driveability or emissions control problem. When the calibrations are updated, OBD-I system PCMs with programmable read-only memory (PROM) must be replaced as a unit. PCMs with a removable PROM use a replacement chip. PCMs with an EEPROM may be "flashed," or electronically erased with a scan tool and reprogrammed without removing the module.

Electronic parts such as PROM chips can be seriously damaged by static electricity. High voltage "spikes," known as electrostatic discharge, can ruin sensitive electronic circuits. When handling a PCM, never touch its connector pins or its circuit board. Also, never touch the pins of a replaceable PROM chip.

Safety First

Grounding Disconnect the battery ground cable before servicing the PCM. Wear an approved grounding strap to ground yourself to the vehicle. Grounding places you and the vehicle at the same electrical potential. With everything at the same potential, the danger of electrostatic discharge is minimized.

The PCM also has a random access memory. **Random access memory (RAM)** is a volatile, or erasable, memory that temporarily stores information such as diagnostic trouble codes. A **diagnostic trouble code (DTC)** is a code that identifies a system or component malfunction. In an OBD-I system, the DTC is a two- or three-digit value. In most OBD-I systems, disconnecting the battery or removing the fuse for the PCM erases all codes stored in the RAM. Normally, the technician erases codes with a scan tool.

Diagnostic Trouble Codes

Diagnostic trouble codes (DTCs) are set by the PCM. The codes indicate a monitored sensor circuit that is not providing a return signal within a range of expected values. Driveability and other problems can be diagnosed by reading DTCs. They indicate the circuit or device affected. These codes are explained in the vehicle service manual.

Excellence in Science

Converting Sensor Signals

The PCM depends on sensors to provide the information it needs. Since the PCM is a computer, it needs such information as a voltage or frequency signal. The measured voltage or frequency signal tells the PCM about the engine condition being measured.

Most sensors use a simple circuit called a voltage divider. This circuit converts position, temperature, pressure, and other inputs into a voltage. A simple voltage divider circuit can act as a sensor to convert nonelectrical quantities into a voltage between 0 and 5 volts.

Apply It!

Wiring Voltage Divider Circuits

Meets NATEF Science Standards for electrical measurements.

Materials and Equipment
- 5-volt power source
- DVOM (an analog voltmeter may be used)
- 1000 Ω linear variable resistor or potentiometer
- Strips of sheet metal that can be drilled and bent to make brackets and a lever arm on the resistor shaft
- Insulated hookup wire
- 12″ [30 cm] piece of stiff wire, such as coat hanger wire
- 6″ × 12″ [15 cm × 31 cm] board to use as a base
- Assortment of rubber bands
- Nuts, bolts, and screws

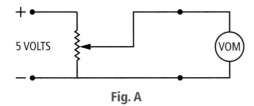

Fig. A

1. Assemble the circuit following the circuit diagram in **Fig. A** and the drawing in **Fig. B**.

2. Test the basic sensor. Rotate the shaft on the resistor while observing the DVOM readings. These readings illustrate the basic sensor behavior that is converting angular position into a voltage.

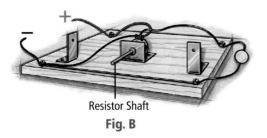

Resistor Shaft

Fig. B

3. Change the sensor circuit so that it converts linear position into a voltage.

   a. Bend a strip of sheet metal around the resistor shaft. Drill and bolt the metal to make a lever arm with a hole level with the holes in the left and right brackets.

   b. Hook one end of the stiff wire through the hole in the lever arm. Put the other end through the hole in the left-hand bracket.

   c. Move the resistor shaft left and right, using the left end of the wire. Observe how the output voltage changes.

4. Convert the position sensor to a force sensor.

   a. Connect a rubber band between the lever arm and the right-hand bracket. Pull on the wire that runs through the left bracket. Observe how a force can be converted into a voltage.

   b. Repeat this step using several strengths of rubber bands.

5. Explain how the strength of the rubber band influences the outcome of the experiment.

Displaying Diagnostic Trouble Codes

Most OBD systems display the DTCs stored in the diagnostic memory of the PCM by displaying the code on a scan tool or scanner.

Most OBD-I systems store two-digit codes that are not standardized by the manufacturer. Refer to the vehicle service manual for a complete listing of all applicable codes. OBD-II systems store five-digit codes that are standardized.

Using a Scanner

The most common method of retrieving DTCs is to connect a scanner (sometimes called a scan tool) to the DLC. Two types of scanners are used—dedicated and generic. See **Fig. 3-31.**

Fig. 3-31 A scanner is used to retrieve DTCs stored in the PCM. *Why would a dedicated scanner provide more information than a generic scanner?*

Dedicated scanners are designed for use on specific vehicles. These scanners normally have more diagnostic capacity and features than do generic scanners. Some of these scanners have a built-in diagnostic database that includes electronic specifications and troubleshooting tips.

Generic scanners are made for use on many different vehicles from different manufacturers. Most of these scanners are programmed with removable cartridges. These cartridges program the scanner for specific applications or system updates.

Scanners display DTCs and other diagnostic data in different ways. Always consult an instruction manual before connecting a scanner.

After the scanner is connected, the scanner menu may request information found in the vehicle identification number (VIN). The **vehicle identification number (VIN)** is a serial number unique to each vehicle that indicates:

- When the vehicle was made.
- The country in which it was made.
- The vehicle make and type.
- The passenger safety system.
- The type of engine.
- The line, series, and body style.
- The assembly plant where the vehicle was produced.

> *TECH TIP* **Entering Scanner Data.** Entering the wrong VIN information or using incorrect scanner software, or a bad DLC connection may cause a NO DATA: message on the scanner. Generic scanners must be individually programmed and configured.

The VIN is inscribed on a plate mounted at the lower corner of the driver's-side windshield. See **Fig. 3-32.** The VIN may also be displayed on a tag mounted on the driver's-side doorjamb. Manufacturer's scan tools read the VIN from the car automatically, eliminating the need to manually enter this information.

Fig. 3-32 The VIN plate is usually located at the base of the windshield on the driver's side. *In what other location is VIN information displayed?*

The scanner may request the tenth character of the VIN, which is the vehicle's model year. The scanner may also request the eighth character in the VIN, which is the engine code. The engine code indicates the type and size of engine installed in the vehicle. Most scanners will also request the third character of the VIN, which indicates the type of vehicle being diagnosed.

The screen on the scanner shows a menu that may include engine, transmission, air bag, or anti-lock brake options. To retrieve engine DTCs, choose the engine menu.

The scanner may also show a diagnostic menu that includes special diagnostic test modes used only by the vehicle's manufacturer. The scanner's instruction manual will describe each diagnostic mode and the type of information it provides. To choose the correct diagnostic mode for the specific vehicle application, follow the instructions included with the scanner.

The diagnostic memory in the PCM may store a "soft" or "hard" DTC. A soft (history) DTC is not currently occurring. It may be an intermittent problem. The soft code illuminates the MIL only when the failure occurs. A hard (current) DTC is present in the system when the MIL is on.

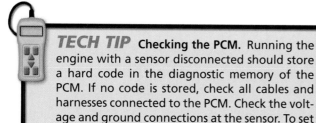

TECH TIP **Checking the PCM.** Running the engine with a sensor disconnected should store a hard code in the diagnostic memory of the PCM. If no code is stored, check all cables and harnesses connected to the PCM. Check the voltage and ground connections at the sensor. To set some codes, the vehicle must be driven.

Snapshot Testing

Most scanners have a snapshot feature that can record serial data at the exact moment a condition occurs. Depending upon vehicle application, the scanner may record up to 100 frames of serial data before and after the fault occurs. Each frame represents a set of serial data that may show which sensor or actuator circuit was not within the expected range. Snapshot tests are useful for diagnosing intermittent failures.

Interpreting Diagnostic Trouble Codes

A DTC may not be directly related to a specific complaint. Always use an effective strategy to diagnose the condition that sets a DTC. An effective strategy might include:

- Listing all displayed DTCs before doing any repair work. Multiple DTCs must be corrected in a specified order.
- Checking the manufacturer's technical service bulletins for factory service information.
- Determining when and how a specific problem occurs.
- Accompanying the customer as he or she drives the car to verify the problem.
- Identifying the problems the customer is most concerned about.
- Inspecting the vehicle's maintenance records. Make sure that all scheduled maintenance is up to date. Find out if other service facilities have tried to repair the problem.
- Inspecting the related sensor and its connections. For example, a cracked vacuum hose to a MAP sensor may cause a DTC in the MAP sensor circuit. A burned-through wire on the oxygen sensor may set a DTC for the oxygen sensor circuit.

Replacing Sensors and Actuators

Before replacing a sensor or actuator, verify that the device is defective by eliminating other possible sources of failure. Check to see if the device is properly positioned and connected. Check for defective wiring, poor connections, and leaking or missing vacuum hoses. Use a DVOM to measure the voltage supply. In some cases you may need to test a circuit at the PCM or other module to see whether a signal is being received or voltage is being supplied.

When troubleshooting an actuator, answer the following:

- Is the PCM trying to activate the device in question?
- Is voltage available?
- Is the actuator capable of producing the desired result?

Verifying the Problem

To operate correctly, a sensor or actuator must have the correct voltage supplied. Most sensors operate at 5 volts. Actuators usually operate at 12 volts. Both sensors and actuators require a good ground circuit, as well.

Blown fuses or open switches can prevent operation. Defective wiring, broken connectors, or deformed or corroded terminals can also cause problems in a circuit.

Use a DVOM to perform voltage drop or resistance tests. This will ensure that the wiring to the module is in good condition. Vehicle service manual wiring diagrams show how components are connected, the color codes for the wires, and the location of splices, connectors, fuses, and switches.

Some actuators, such as motors and solenoids, require a significant amount of current to operate. Make sure the voltage supply to the actuator is present under load. Check the wiring and the connections to the power source. Make sure the device is not shorted or grounded internally.

Data Bus Problems

Sensors and actuators communicate on a data bus that connects most major electronic circuits and components. Poor connections may produce voltage drops that distort the information being transmitted. Loose wires or connections and bent or distorted terminals may result in intermittent connections. Replace damaged wires or terminals. Spray connector blocks and terminals with electronic terminal cleaner.

Mechanical Factors

Sensors and actuators may not work due to mechanical interference. Solenoid plungers may stick or bind. See **Fig. 3-33**. Motor shafts may be too tight or damaged to rotate. Vacuum lines may be plugged or kinked. See **Fig. 3-34**. Make sure the sensor or actuator has the freedom of movement required for correct operation.

Proper sensor operation depends on the correct positioning of the sensor. This is needed to make an accurate measurement. The output of some PCM sensors depends upon the correct air gap. The ECT sensor cannot provide an accurate reading if the coolant level is too low. Solenoid actuators cannot produce the desired range of motion if they are not properly mounted and adjusted.

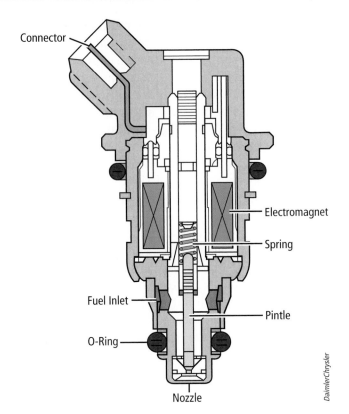

DaimlerChrysler

Fig. 3-33 The fuel injector is a solenoid. The pintle can become clogged with carbon and stick. This can cause the injector to stick open, allowing fuel to leak past the nozzle.

Erick Dodge

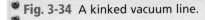

Fig. 3-34 A kinked vacuum line.

Sensor and Actuator Failures

Early failures of sensors and actuators can occur for several reasons:

- Oxygen sensors become less sensitive with age. Replace the sensors if the response or cycling time is too slow.
- Potentiometer sensors may become dirty or damaged. This can cause false or intermittent signals to be sent to the PCM.
- High temperature exhaust gases may damage the exhaust gas recirculation (EGR) valve.
- Carbon deposits may interfere with normal EGR valve operation.
- Accidental voltage spikes and reversed battery polarity can damage the electronic circuits in sensors, actuators, and modules.
- Severe vibration or impact and extreme temperature changes can damage connections inside a sensor or actuator.
- Impact failure is more likely to occur when the vehicle has been in an accident.

Safety First **Oxygen Sensors** Use caution to avoid burns when working with oxygen sensors. You may need a special oxygen sensor wrench. Use it to prevent damage to the sensor during removal and installation.

Precautions

In replacing a sensor or actuator, take the following precautions:

- Read and follow the installation instructions.
- Make sure the ignition is off before removing any connectors.
- Remove the connectors carefully. Connectors are often held in place with plastic retainers.
- Pull only on the connector body, not the wires.
- Some connectors are filled with white silicone grease. Replace this grease as needed.
- Avoid damaging weatherproof seals when removing or installing a connector.
- Apply antiseize compound to oxygen sensor threads before installation.
- Make sure cables and harnesses are routed to prevent heat damage.

Safety First **Exhaust System** The exhaust system stays hot for a period of time after the engine is shut down. Exercise caution to avoid burns.

SECTION 3 KNOWLEDGE CHECK

1. What is an on-board diagnostic system?

2. Explain the purpose of a malfunction indicator lamp (MIL).

3. What is the code that identifies a system or component malfunction?

4. Name the four main functions of the PCM.

5. What does the vehicle identification number (VIN) indicate?

6. What is the difference between a soft DTC and a hard DTC?

ASE TEST PREP

7. Technician A says that the eighth character in the VIN is the vehicle make and type. Technician B says that the eighth character in the VIN is the engine code. Who is correct?

   ⓐ Technician A.

   ⓑ Technician B.

   ⓒ Both Technician A and Technician B.

   ⓓ Neither Technician A nor Technician B.

CHAPTER 3 REVIEW

Key Points

Meets the following NATEF Standards for Engine Performance: inspecting, testing, and replacing sensors and actuators.

- Speed and position sensors are electromagnetic, optical, and Hall-effect.
- Sensors produce either analog or digital signals.
- Actuators control specific engine management systems to provide the best performance with the lowest emissions.
- When sensors or actuators fail, driveability, emissions, and fuel economy are affected.
- Analog signal voltage changes continuously over a range of values.
- Digital signal voltage is either high or low.
- Electronic components communicate on a special wiring harness called a data bus.
- Sensors produce output signals based on the operating condition they are monitoring.
- The output signal of a switch is either on or off.
- Solenoids use electromagnetism to produce motion.
- A relay is used to open and close a set of electrical contacts.

Review Questions

1. What type of device generates or modifies an electrical signal based on the condition it is monitoring?
2. What is another term for digital signal?
3. Name the network of wires that enables the PCM and other electronic components to communicate with each other.
4. What type of sensor is a small AC-voltage generator that produces an analog signal?
5. What type of device controls air/fuel ratio, idle speed, and emission control devices?
6. Where is the VIN located on a vehicle?
7. What do speed and position sensors monitor?
8. What type of sensor has fluctuating resistance as it monitors changing conditions?
9. What type of sensor is mounted to a source of manifold vacuum?
10. **Critical Thinking** Explain how to check manifold absolute pressure sensors.

Excellence in Communication

Decoding Words

There are several methods you can use to learn the meaning of a word you do not know. You may look up a definition in a dictionary or glossary. Another very useful way is to reread the material to see if the word is defined when it is first used.

In the section "Reading the Data Stream," the term data bus is explained in the sentence after the term is mentioned. Another example is in the section titled "Sensors and Electronic Signals." The term sensor is defined in the same sentence where it is first mentioned. These words are usually printed in *italic* or **bold** type.

Note how the definition is organized. It moves from the general to the specific. For example, a sensor is defined as a device that monitors or measures operating conditions. The first part of the definition states that the sensor is a device. The second part states that its purpose is "to monitor or measure operating conditions."

Apply It!

Meets NATEF Communications Standards for writing paragraphs and organizing and comprehending written information.

In reading this chapter, look for definitions as they are presented in the text. (Hint: The words "is" or "is called" are keys to look for.)

1. Look for the definitions of the words listed as "Vocabulary" at the beginning of each section in this chapter. Write the terms and their definitions on a sheet of paper.

2. Find at least five other terms that are defined in this chapter. Add these, with their definitions, to your list.

3. Locate each term on your list in a dictionary. Compare the definitions from this source with your definitions. If there are differences, how do the sources differ?

AUTOMOTIVE SERVICE EXCELLENCE
TEST PREP

Answering the following practice questions will help you prepare for the ASE certification tests.

1. A device that monitors or measures operating conditions is called a:

   ⓐ module.

   ⓑ sensor.

   ⓒ actuator.

   ⓓ None of the above.

2. Technician A says that an analog signal can be read directly by the PCM and other modules. Technician B says that the PCM and other modules can read only digital signals and that analog signals must be converted before they are understood. Who is correct?

   ⓐ Technician A.

   ⓑ Technician B.

   ⓒ Both Technician A and Technician B.

   ⓓ Neither Technician A nor Technician B.

3. A device that allows components connected to it to share sensor signals and other information needed for normal operation is a:

   ⓐ data bus.

   ⓑ digital bus.

   ⓒ scan tool.

   ⓓ None of the above.

4. Technician A says that on 1996 or newer vehicles the data link connector is located under the dash near the steering column. Technician B says that on 1996 or newer vehicles the data link connector is located in the engine compartment. Who is correct?

   ⓐ Technician A.

   ⓑ Technician B.

   ⓒ Both Technician A and Technician B.

   ⓓ Neither Technician A nor Technician B.

5. What tool is used to actively test actuators such as relays and solenoids?

   ⓐ Scan tool.

   ⓑ Ammeter.

   ⓒ Electromagnet.

   ⓓ Digital volt-ohm-meter.

6. Technician A says that stepper motors may be used to control engine components such as the idle air control valve. Technician B says that stepper motors are used where precise movements are required. Who is correct?

   ⓐ Technician A.

   ⓑ Technician B.

   ⓒ Both Technician A and Technician B.

   ⓓ Neither Technician A nor Technician B.

7. When testing a warning lamp that is not functioning properly, before checking the PCM circuit, you should check the:

   ⓐ battery.

   ⓑ generator.

   ⓒ sending unit.

   ⓓ fuse.

8. Technician A says that you should disconnect the battery ground cable before servicing the PCM and wear an approved grounding strap connected to the vehicle. Technician B says this is unnecessary. Who is correct?

   ⓐ Technician A.

   ⓑ Technician B.

   ⓒ Both Technician A and Technician B.

   ⓓ Neither Technician A nor Technician B.

9. The vehicle identification number indicates which of the following?

   ⓐ When the vehicle was made.

   ⓑ Vehicle make and type.

   ⓒ Type of engine.

   ⓓ All of the above.

10. Technician A says that a special wrench may be needed to remove some oxygen sensors without damage. Technician B says that a standard wrench is appropriate. Who is correct?

    ⓐ Technician A.

    ⓑ Technician B.

    ⓒ Both Technician A and Technician B.

    ⓓ Neither Technician A nor Technician B.

Section 1
The Ignition System

Section 2
Spark Distribution Systems

Diagnosing & Repairing Ignition Systems

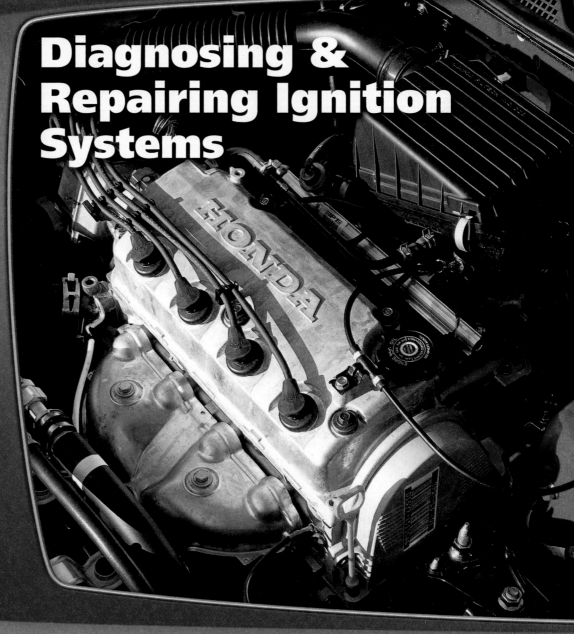

Customer's Concern

Larry Peacock's wife, Sherrie, has been complaining about her car's performance for about a month. Larry simply ignored her complaints. Yesterday, she proved her point. Larry overslept, and by the time he made it to the garage, Sherrie had already left in his car. He had to drive her car to work. Sure enough, Sherrie was having car problems.

When Larry brought the car to your service center, he said it took a long time to get the car started. Once started, he said it was hesitant to accelerate and he noticed a lot of exhaust smoke. Your supervisor says it could be a number of problems, but "the plugs speak volumes about what's happening inside an engine." So, that's where you begin your diagnosis.

Technician's Challenge

As the service technician, you need to find answers to these questions:

1. If the car is a six cylinder, will you expect to see the same problems occurring on all six spark plugs? Why or why not?

2. What spark plug conditions may cause the problems Larry mentioned? Could carbon, oil, or ash deposits be to blame?

3. Will a deposit condition be solved by simply replacing the affected spark plugs? If not, what else may need to be done?

● Section 1
The Ignition System

Objectives:

C1 ● Diagnose ignition system related problems such as no-starting, hard starting engine misfire, poor driveability, spark knock, power loss, poor mileage, and emissions concerns on vehicles with electronic ignition (distributorless) systems; determine necessary action.

C2 ● Diagnose ignition system related problems such as no-starting, hard starting engine misfire, poor driveability, spark knock, power loss, poor mileage, and emissions concerns on vehicles with distributor ignition (DI) systems; determine necessary action.

C3 ● Inspect and test ignition primary circuit wiring and solid state components; perform necessary action.

C5 ● Inspect and test ignition system secondary circuit wiring and components; perform necessary action.

D1 ● Diagnose hot or cold no-starting, hard starting, poor driveability, incorrect idle speed, poor idle, flooding, hesitation, surging, engine misfire, power loss, stalling, poor mileage, dieseling, and emissions problems on vehicles with injection-type fuel systems; determine necessary action.

C6 ● Inspect and test ignition coil(s); perform necessary action.

C8 ● Inspect and test ignition system pick-up sensor or triggering devices; perform necessary action.

A13 ● Diagnose engine mechanical, electrical, electronic, fuel, and ignition concerns with an oscilloscope and/or engine diagnostic equipment; determine necessary action.

B6 ● Inspect and test computerized engine control system sensors, powertrain control module (PCM), actuators, and circuits using a graphing multimeter (GMM)/digital storage oscilloscope (DSO); perform necessary action.

Vocabulary:

● **ignition coil**
● **distributor**
● **indexing mark**
● **dwell angle**
● **duty cycle**

Ignition System Components

The ignition system provides an ignition spark to the proper cylinder at the correct time. Delivering the ignition spark at the correct time produces the maximum power and fuel economy with the lowest exhaust emissions.

All ignition systems share the same operating principles. Ignition systems also share some or all of these basic components. See **Fig. 4-1.**

- Ignition switch.
- Ignition coil.
- Distributor.
- Powertrain control module (PCM).
- Ignition module.
- Ignition wires.
- Spark plugs.

The Ignition Switch

The ignition switch is the master switch for the entire electrical system. When placed in the ON position, the ignition switch connects the ignition system to the battery.

The Ignition Coil

The ignition system consists of two separate but closely related electrical circuits. These circuits are a low-voltage primary circuit and a high-voltage secondary circuit. The **ignition coil** is a device that

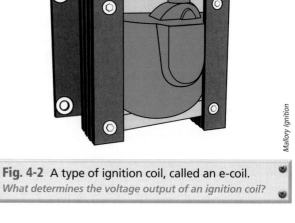

Mallory Ignition

Fig. 4-2 A type of ignition coil, called an e-coil.
What determines the voltage output of an ignition coil?

transforms low voltage from the battery into a high voltage capable of producing an ignition spark. An ignition coil has two windings, a primary winding and a secondary winding. See **Fig. 4-2.**

The ignition coil has two primary winding terminals, B positive (+) and B negative (−). The ignition switch connects the battery to B+. The negative terminal lead is connected to the ignition module.

Depending on the application, ignition coils may have one or two secondary winding terminals. Coils used in distributorless (waste spark) systems have two secondary winding terminals.

The primary coil consists of a few hundred turns of heavy copper wire. The secondary coil consists of several thousand turns of fine copper wire. The ratio between the number of primary and secondary windings determines the voltage output of the coil.

The two coils surround an iron core. The iron core concentrates the magnetic field created when current passes through the primary coil. The ignition module controls current in the primary coil. The current flow produces a magnetic field around the primary coil. When the ignition module stops the current flow, this magnetic field collapses into the secondary coil. This coil produces a voltage as high as 50,000 volts.

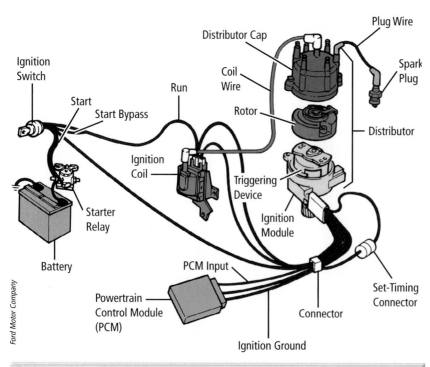

Ford Motor Company

Fig. 4-1 The ignition system components in a distributor ignition.
Where is the ignition module in this system?

This is called available voltage or maximum coil output. On some ignition systems, it can exceed 50,000 volts [50 kilovolts, or 50 kV]. The secondary voltage builds only to the point at which current begins to flow in the secondary circuit. Normally, this is the voltage required to cause a spark to jump across the spark plug gap. This is called the "required" or "firing" voltage.

If the required voltage is 10,000 volts [10 kV], the plug will fire at this voltage. The secondary voltage will not build up higher. Think of the difference between the available and required voltage as ignition reserve voltage.

Firing voltage will be higher than normal when any of the following conditions exist:
• A wider than specified spark plug gap or worn plug electrodes.
• Late ignition timing.
• Higher-than-specified compression ratio.
• Hard acceleration or wide-open throttle operation.
• Lean air/fuel mixtures.
• Large gap in secondary wiring.

Safety First

Sparks An ignition spark can exceed 50,000 volts [50 kV]. Do not hold any ignition wire with your hand while the engine cranks or runs. An ignition spark can give a dangerous electrical shock. Use insulated pliers especially made to hold secondary ignition cables. Sparks from a disconnected coil lead or ignition wire can ignite gasoline or other flammable liquids and gases. Before testing the spark, make sure you clean up any fuel spills and tighten all fuel system connections.

Some of these conditions may occur in only one cylinder at any given time. This is true for wide plug gaps, worn electrodes, or wire problems.

When the spark jumps the gap at a voltage lower than the coil is capable of producing, the coil reserve voltage makes the spark last longer. This is called spark duration. The longer the spark duration, the more likely that all of the air/fuel mixture in the cylinder will ignite. Complete combustion results in better fuel economy and lower exhaust emissions. If the spark plug gap is too wide, the available voltage may not be enough to create a spark. This will result in a cylinder misfire.

Diagnosing the Ignition Coil Check the ignition coil output using a spark tester. See **Fig. 4-3**. This is a modified spark plug that is connected to ground by a clip attached to its shell.
1. Remove a spark plug wire from its plug.
2. Connect the wire to the electrode tip of the spark tester.
3. Connect the ground clip from the spark tester to a proper ground connection, for example the engine block. DO NOT connect the ground clip to a fuel rail or any connection to the fuel system.
4. Crank the engine.

A spark should jump from the spark tester electrode to the shell. If there is a faint spark or no spark, check the distributor cap and rotor (if used) for cracks and burn marks.

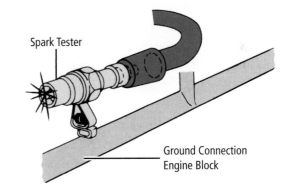

Spark Tester

Ground Connection
Engine Block

Fig. 4-3 A common spark tester. *Why would you not ground the spark tester to the fuel rail?*

The resistance of an ignition coil can be checked with an ohmmeter. See **Fig. 4-4**. Connecting the ohmmeter between the terminals of the primary coil shows the resistance in the primary winding.

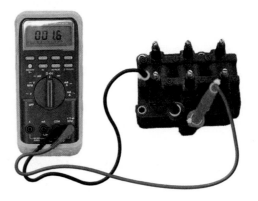

Erick Dodge

Fig. 4-4 Testing the resistance of the primary coil with an ohmmeter. *If a coil were open, what reading would you expect to see?*

On a distributorless ignition system (DIS), attach the ohmmeter to the towers of the coil pack to measure the secondary coil resistance. Removing the spark plug wires allows access to the coil terminals. See **Fig. 4-5**. The vehicle service manual includes the resistance specifications for the type of coil being checked.

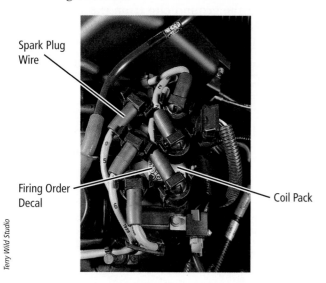

Spark Plug Wire

Firing Order Decal

Coil Pack

Terry Wild Studio

Fig. 4-5 Spark plug wire connections to a six-cylinder DIS (waste spark) coil assembly. *How many plug wires are connected to each individual coil?*

The Distributor

The **distributor** is a device designed to establish base timing and distribute the secondary ignition voltage. It is sometimes referred to as an electronic switch. Depending on the type of distributor ignition system, the distributor design may be a:

- Contact-point type—an obsolete mechanical design used on older vehicles.
- Magnetic-pickup-coil type—a design using a magnetic coil and pickup in the distributor to create the timing signal.
- Hall-effect type—a design using a solid-state magnetic sensing device to create the timing signal.
- Optical-sensor type—a design using a light-emitting diode and photodiode sensor to create the timing signal.

The Powertrain Control Module

The powertrain control module (PCM) is a computer that manages engine and powertrain systems. Within engine management, the PCM is responsible for fuel delivery, ignition timing and some emission control devices.

Ignition timing determines when the spark occurs during the combustion cycle. When the engine is idling, the spark occurs during the compression stroke, a few degrees before the piston reaches top dead center (TDC). As the engine speeds up, the ignition system must make the spark occur earlier (advance the spark). Advanced timing of the spark gives the air/fuel mixture time to burn completely.

The engine needs correct spark advance to deliver maximum power and fuel economy and to control exhaust emissions. If the spark occurs too early, detonation (engine knock) of the air/fuel mixture may occur. Detonation occurs when the air/fuel mixture does not burn evenly. The mixture explodes. This causes a metallic knock or pinging sound. Early ignition causes too much pressure to build in the cylinder before the piston reaches TDC. This causes rough idle, loss of power, and detonation.

If the spark occurs too late, combustion occurs late in the compression stroke. This condition is called retarded timing. With retarded timing, an engine cannot develop maximum power and fuel economy. Late spark timing may cause the engine to overheat.

The PCM calculates and electronically adjusts the spark timing by processing data from electronic sensors. A sensor mounted at the crankshaft or in the distributor senses engine speed. Input from the mass airflow (MAF) sensor, or a combination of inputs from the throttle position sensor (TPS) and manifold absolute pressure (MAP) sensor, indicates engine load. Inputs from the engine coolant temperature (ECT) sensor and intake air temperature (IAT) sensor indicate engine temperature and intake air temperature.

Some engines also use a knock sensor (KS). The knock sensor is mounted on the engine block. The knock sensor detects the vibrations caused by detonation. The PCM uses a signal from this sensor to retard timing to this point where detonation stops.

Before the PCM can calculate ignition timing, it must receive a reference signal indicating when number-one piston is near TDC on the compression stroke. The reference signal is produced by a sensor or triggering device mounted at the crankshaft vibration damper, the crankshaft, the flywheel, or in the distributor.

Ignition triggering devices are sensors that indicate the position of the crankshaft and engine rpm. The crankshaft-position triggering device is called a crankshaft position (CKP) sensor. The function of the CKP is to indicate when the number-one piston nears (TDC) on the compression stroke.

There are three basic designs of ignition triggering devices: magnetic pulse, Hall-effect, and optical (photodiode). These three basic designs are manufactured in many variations. The testing procedure for each variation is specific to each vehicle model. Therefore, it can be described only in general terms.

Magnetic Pulse Sensors Magnetic pulse sensors consist of a pole piece that extends from a permanent magnet and a pickup coil. See **Fig. 4-6**.

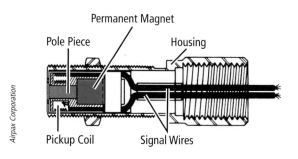

Fig. 4-6 Construction of a typical magnetic pulse sensor. *What type of signal does a magnetic pulse sensor produce?*

A reluctor, or timing disc, mounts on the crankshaft, distributor shaft, or flywheel. See **Fig. 4-7**. The slots or teeth in the reluctor indicate the position of each piston. As the reluctor rotates, a pulse is generated each time a slot or tooth passes the sensor. This signal pulse is sent to the PCM. The PCM signals the ignition module to trigger the ignition sequence.

When checking individual ignition components, test to see that the device does what it is supposed to do. Magnetic pulse sensors are usually tested by checking the circuit resistance. The specification for circuit resistance and the connector terminal location is found in the vehicle service manual. Check the resistance by disconnecting the magnetic sensor. Use a digital volt-ohm-meter (DVOM) to measure the resistance in ohms.

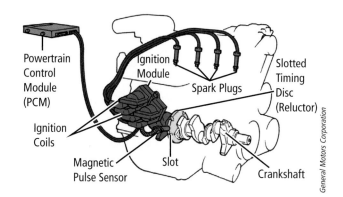

Fig. 4-7 Typical placement of a magnetic pulse sensor. Notice the timing slots cut into the crankshaft. *Why would a magnetic pulse sensor be more accurate when placed on the crankshaft?*

While the engine is cranking, a magnetic pulse trigger circuit should produce a small (about 300 mV) AC, or analog, signal. Therefore, another way to check the sensor is to connect a DVOM set on the AC scale to the two wires leading from the sensor pickup coil. Crank the engine and measure the resulting voltage. If it is equal to or higher than the minimum specified for the vehicle, the sensor is working normally.

The wavelike pulse produced by a magnetic pulse sensor is called an analog signal. This signal is converted to a digital signal by the ignition module or the PCM.

Hall-Effect Sensors Hall-effect sensors use a Hall-effect switch to supply the triggering signal to the ignition module or PCM.

An interrupter ring or shutter is mounted behind the vibration damper, on the camshaft, or on the distributor shaft. Equally spaced windows in the shutter rotate through an air gap between a permanent magnet and the Hall-effect switch. The position and spacing of the shutter windows indicate the TDC position of each piston. See **Fig. 4-8**.

When a shutter window passes through the gap between the magnet and the Hall-effect sensor, the magnetic field reaches the sensor. See **Fig. 4-9**. The sensor produces a small voltage. This action creates the triggering signal sent to the PCM or ignition module.

When the window moves out of the air gap, the magnetic field cannot act on the switch. The sensor produces no voltage. This action drops the triggering signal sent to the PCM or ignition module.

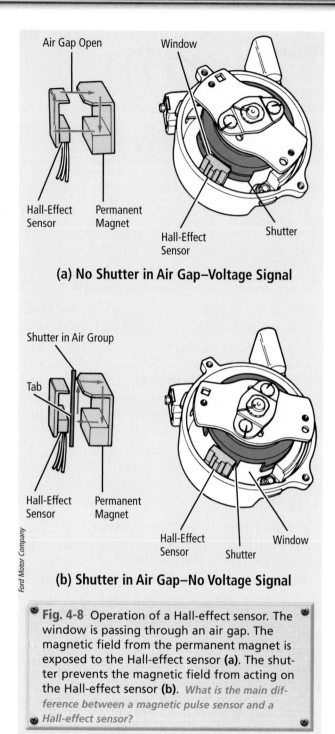

(a) No Shutter in Air Gap–Voltage Signal

(b) Shutter in Air Gap–No Voltage Signal

Ford Motor Company

Fig. 4-8 Operation of a Hall-effect sensor. The window is passing through an air gap. The magnetic field from the permanent magnet is exposed to the Hall-effect sensor **(a)**. The shutter prevents the magnetic field from acting on the Hall-effect sensor **(b)**. *What is the main difference between a magnetic pulse sensor and a Hall-effect sensor?*

This Hall-effect sensor generates a "square-wave" or digital on/off reference signal. The reference signal indicates the position of each piston. The square-wave signal produced by this type of sensor has very sharp turn-on and turn-off times. The signal is extremely accurate.

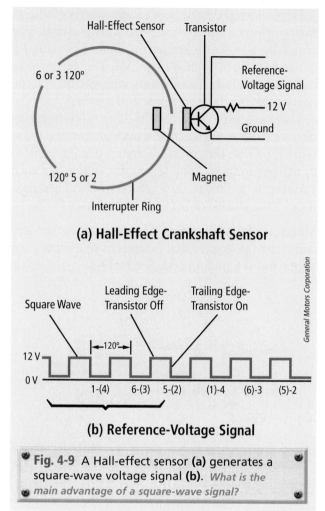

(a) Hall-Effect Crankshaft Sensor

General Motors Corporation

(b) Reference-Voltage Signal

Fig. 4-9 A Hall-effect sensor **(a)** generates a square-wave voltage signal **(b)**. *What is the main advantage of a square-wave signal?*

When checking Hall-effect sensors, first test for the specified voltage at the power terminal. If the voltage is normal, check whether the voltage on the signal wire "toggles" between the signal voltage and near 0 (<300 mV) while cranking the engine. You may also use a light-emitting diode (LED) tester. When connected to the signal wire, the LED should flash as you crank the engine. To determine connector pin connections, refer to the vehicle service manual.

Optical (Photodiode) Sensors A photodiode is an electronic device that uses the presence or absence of light to switch on and off. An LED provides the light source. Photodiode sensors are usually found in distributor ignition (DI) systems.

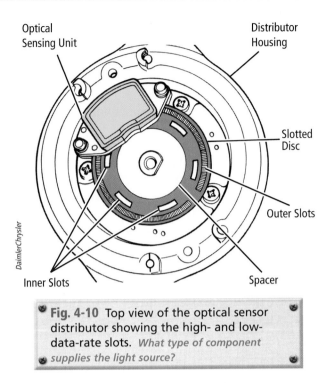

Fig. 4-10 Top view of the optical sensor distributor showing the high- and low-data-rate slots. *What type of component supplies the light source?*

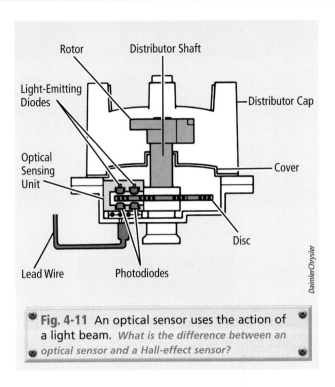

Fig. 4-11 An optical sensor uses the action of a light beam. *What is the difference between an optical sensor and a Hall-effect sensor?*

The timing device is a thin disc with two sets of slots around its outer edge. See **Fig. 4-10**. Each set of slots controls a voltage signal in one of the photodiodes. The outer set, or high-data-rate slots, occur at 2-degree intervals of crankshaft rotation. This timing signal provides input to the PCM for engine crankshaft position and spark advance timing at engine speeds up to 1,200 rpm.

The inner, or low-data-rate, set of slots has the same number of slots as the engine has cylinders. This timing signal shows the TDC position of each piston. This signal triggers fuel injection and times spark advance at engine speeds above 1,200 rpm.

Two light-emitting diodes and two photodiodes are mounted on opposite sides of the slotted disc. See **Fig. 4-11**. The slotted disc rotates between the LEDs and the photodiodes. As the slots move past an LED, the light beam is interrupted and the photodiode turns on and off. This creates an alternating voltage signal. An integrated circuit converts the voltage into digital on-and-off pulses. These pulses provide engine speed and crankshaft position signals directly to the PCM.

This type of sensor may not use a separate ignition module. Instead, the PCM uses the sensor input to control ignition timing.

Photodiode sensors can be tested by connecting a DVOM to the sensor's signal wire. The voltage signal should change from high to low while the engine is cranking. The vehicle service manual should be used to identify the signal wire.

In most trigger circuit designs, one reluctor tooth, shutter window, or timing slot is made larger than the others. This is known as an indexing mark. The **indexing mark** is an indicator that produces a unique signal that tells the PCM when the number-one piston is nearing TDC. This signal is known as a synchronizing pulse, or signature pulse.

The Ignition Module

The ignition module is an electronic switch. It times the ignition spark. When the module switches on, current flows through the primary winding of the ignition coil. When the module switches off, current flow stops. The magnetic field in the primary winding collapses into the secondary winding. The voltage created in the secondary winding creates the spark at the spark plug.

When the engine begins cranking, the ignition module switches the ignition coil on and off. The module also controls the duration of current flow through the primary winding of the ignition coil.

This amount of time is called dwell angle or duty cycle. **Dwell angle** is the number of degrees of distributor or camshaft rotation during which current flows through the primary circuit of the ignition coil. **Duty cycle** is the percentage of time the primary circuit stays switched on.

Dwell is reduced at idle to prevent the coil and module from overheating. Dwell is increased at high speed to produce the highest possible secondary voltage.

Excellence in Math

Calculating MAF Values

A mass air flow (MAF) sensor measures, in grams per second (g/sec), the mass of air that flows through the sensor. When the throttle is opened, more air flows through the sensor. The PCM uses the MAF sensor signal to determine the amount of fuel needed for the airflow. The following data were collected in a lab from a mass air flow (MAF) sensor.

RPM	Airflow (g/sec)
800	10
1000	21
1200	28
1400	36
1600	43
1800	52
2000	59

These data values can be plotted on the graph. Note that airflow increases as rpm increases.

The rate of increase is called the slope. It is usually shown by the letter m. To calculate the slope use the formula:

$$m = \frac{(y_2 - y_1)}{(x_2 - x_1)}$$

To find the rate of increase in the MAF per rpm you need to find the slope of the line between two points, (x_1, y_1) and (x_2, y_2). Let's use 1,000 rpm and 1,400 rpm as the x values of the two points. The points on the graph are $(1,000, 21)$ and $(1,400, 36)$. The slope between these points is:

$$m = \frac{y_2 - y_1}{x_2 - x_1} = \frac{36 - 21}{1,400 - 1,000} = \frac{15}{400}$$
$$= 0.0375$$

On the graph, the slope of the line (m) is 0.04 when rounded to the nearest hundredth.

You can now write a formula to calculate the expected MAF for another rpm value. You can rewrite the slope formula as:

$$(y - y_1) = m (x - x_1)$$

Here (x_1, y_1) is one of the points you already know.

Use the point $(1,000, 21)$ as the point you know to write a formula.

$$y - y_1 = m (x - x_1)$$
$$y - 21 = 0.04 (x - 1,000)$$
$$y - 21 = 0.04x - 40$$
$$y = 0.04x - 19$$

If you know the value of x, you can calculate the value of y using this formula. You can find the expected airflow at 1,100 rpm, $(x = 1,100)$. You solve the equation for y, the expected airflow for 1,100 rpm.

$$y = 0.04 (1,100) - 19 = 44 - 19 = 25 \text{ g/sec}$$

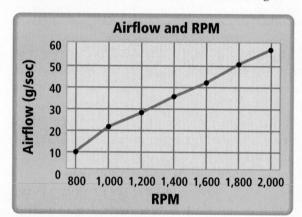

Airflow and RPM

Apply It!

Meets NATEF Mathematics Standards for using tables and graphs, and for determining expected values.

1. Refer to the data point for 1,400 rpm on the graph. What is the x value? What is the y value?

2. Find the rate of increase in airflow per rpm between 1,400 rpm and 1,600 rpm.

3. Was this the same slope as in the example? Why do you think this is so?

4. Write a formula for the line between these two points.

5. Use this formula to calculate the expected airflow at 1,500 rpm.

Diagnosing the Ignition Module Specialized diagnostic equipment is required to test ignition modules. However, a DVOM or a 12-volt test light can be used to see if the ignition module switches the primary ignition circuit on and off. Follow this procedure:

1. Use a wiring diagram to identify the correct terminals.
2. With the ignition ON, check for voltage to the module and the positive terminal of the ignition coil.
3. If voltage is present, connect a test light to the negative (ground) side of the ignition coil.
4. As the engine is cranking, the test light should flicker on and off.
5. If the light does not flicker on and off, check for an open primary coil winding or a defective trigger circuit.
6. If the coil winding and trigger circuit are working, a defective module is indicated.

The Ignition Wires

The ignition wires connect the secondary winding of the ignition coil to the spark plug. The conductive core of the wire is a carbon-impregnated material. See **Fig. 4-12**. An electrical resistance (about 1,000 ohms per inch) is built into the conductive core to reduce electrical interference and radio static. This problem is called electro-magnetic interference (EMI). This interference may cause erratic electrical inputs to the PCM, resulting in driveability complaints.

Diagnosing Ignition Wire Problems The core in an ignition wire may deteriorate or break. This will cause higher than normal resistance or an open circuit. Test this resistance by connecting an ohmmeter to each end of the wire. The resistance should not exceed the manufacturer's specifications. Replace any wire that is open or has higher than normal resistance.

Open ignition wires can also be detected by using an ignition oscilloscope. If the wire is good, the oscilloscope will display a normal waveform pattern. See **Fig. 4-13**. A large break in the ignition wire will cause the waveform to show high firing voltage or other pattern variations.

Ignition wires and spark plug boots may develop cracks that can cause the spark to jump to ground. If you suspect a voltage leak, check wires for damaged insulation.

Fluke Corporation

Fig. 4-13 A good ignition secondary circuit scope pattern (generic).

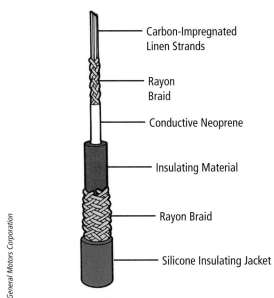

- Carbon-Impregnated Linen Strands
- Rayon Braid
- Conductive Neoprene
- Insulating Material
- Rayon Braid
- Silicone Insulating Jacket

General Motors Corporation

Fig. 4-12 Cutaway view of an ignition wire. *Why do ignition wires use a carbon-impregnated core instead of a metal core?*

The Spark Plugs

The spark plug has a metal shell enclosing a ceramic insulator. See **Fig. 4-14.** The center electrode is in the center of the insulator. The center electrode carries high voltage from the ignition coil to the plug air gap. The spark plug has two or more conductors called electrodes. The electrodes form an air gap between the insulated center electrode and one or more ground electrodes. By jumping the gap between the electrodes, the spark ignites the compressed air/fuel mixture.

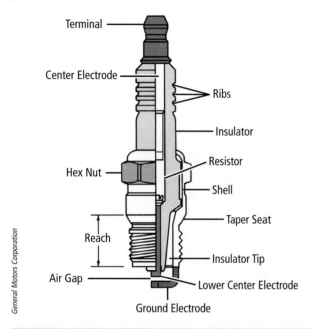

Terminal

Center Electrode

Ribs

Insulator

Resistor

Hex Nut

Shell

Taper Seat

Reach

Insulator Tip

Air Gap

Lower Center Electrode

Ground Electrode

General Motors Corporation

Fig. 4-14 Cutaway view of a resistor-type spark plug. *What are two types of spark plug seats?*

One or more ground electrodes attach to the metal shell. To form an air gap at the center electrode, the ground electrode bends in. Specified gaps may range from 0.035″ [0.90 mm] to 0.080″ [2.03 mm].

Spark plugs are made in different hex sizes. The most common sizes are ⅝″ and ¹³⁄₁₆″. To seal the shell to the cylinder head, some plugs use gaskets. Other plugs use tapered seats on the plugs and in the cylinder head openings. Tapered seat plugs do not use a gasket. Most automotive spark plugs have a resistance built into the center electrode to help suppress EMI. These plugs are called resistor spark plugs.

Spark Plug Threads Spark plugs are made with different thread diameters and thread lengths. The most common thread diameter is 14 mm, but some plugs have diameters of 10 mm or 18 mm. The thread length is also called the thread reach. Thread reach is the distance from the gasket seat (or top of a tapered seat) to the end of the threads.

Safety First

Spark Plugs When installing a spark plug, begin turning it by hand. Do not use a ratchet to start spark plug threads. Doing so could strip the threads and damage the plug.

If the reach is too long, the plug will protrude into the combustion chamber. The piston could strike the plug and cause engine damage. Carbon may also form on the exposed threads. This will make removal difficult. If the reach is too short, the plug may fail to ignite the air/fuel mixture properly. This will cause misfiring. The spark plugs that the engine manufacturer recommends have the correct reach. See **Fig. 4-15.**

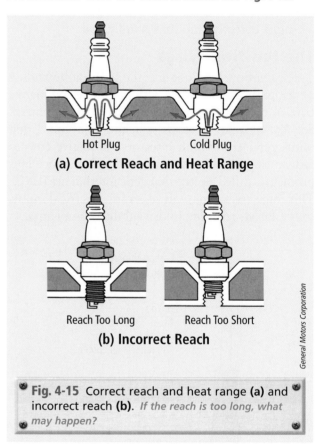

Hot Plug   Cold Plug

(a) Correct Reach and Heat Range

Reach Too Long   Reach Too Short

(b) Incorrect Reach

General Motors Corporation

Fig. 4-15 Correct reach and heat range **(a)** and incorrect reach **(b)**. *If the reach is too long, what may happen?*

Diagnosing Spark Plug Problems Spark plugs usually fail because of electrode wear or fouling deposits. Plugs may also show conditions resulting from overadvanced ignition timing, rich or lean air/fuel mixtures, and excessive oil consumption. See **Fig. 4-16.**

COMMON SPARK PLUG CONDITIONS

NORMAL
Symptoms: Brown to grayish-tan color and slight electrode wear. Correct heat range for engine and operating conditions.
Recommendations: When new spark plugs are installed, replace with plugs of the same heat range.

PRE-IGNITION
Symptoms: Melted electrodes. Insulators are white, but may be dirty due to misfiring or debris in the combustion chamber. Can lead to engine damage.
Recommendations: Check for correct plug heat range, overadvanced ignition timing, lean fuel mixture, insufficient engine cooling, and lack of lubrication.

CARBON DEPOSITS
Symptoms: Dry, sooty deposits indicate a rich mixture or weak ignition. Causes misfiring, hard starting, and hesitation.
Recommendations: Make sure the plug has the correct heat range. Check for a clogged air filter or problem in the fuel system or engine management system. Also check for ignition system problems.

HIGH SPEED GLAZING
Symptoms: Insulator has yellowish, glazed appearance. Indicates that combustion temperatures have risen suddenly during hard acceleration. Normal deposits melt to form a conductive coating.
Recommendations: Install new plugs. Consider using a colder plug if driving habits permit.

ASH DEPOSITS
Symptoms: Light brown deposits on the electrodes caused by oil and/or fuel additives. Excessive deposits may foul the spark, causing misfiring and hesitation during acceleration.
Recommendations: Correct the mechanical condition with necessary repairs. Install new plugs. Also try changing gasoline brands.

DETONATION
Symptoms: Insulators may be cracked or chipped. Can lead to piston damage.
Recommendations: Make sure the fuel anti-knock values meet engine requirements. Use care when setting the gaps on plugs. Avoid lugging the engine.

OIL DEPOSITS
Symptoms: Oily coating caused by poor oil control. Oil is leaking past worn valve guides or piston rings into the combustion chamber. Causes hard starting, misfiring, and hesitation.
Recommendations: Correct the mechanical condition with necessary repairs. Install new plugs.

HEAT SHOCK FAILURE
Symptoms: Broken and cracked insulator tip. Caused by overadvanced timing, low-grade fuel, and severe operating conditions.
Recommendations: Check ignition timing. Use the proper grade of fuel. Check for proper spark plug heat range.

DEPOSIT FOULING
Symptoms: Heavy ash deposits. Ash buildup on portion of plug projecting into combustion chamber, and closest to the intake value. Deposits are result of combustion of fuel and lubricating oil.
Recommendations: Replace plug. Check intake value stem clearances and valve seals. Suspect defective seals if condition is found in only one or two cylinders.

INSUFFICIENT INSTALLATION TORQUE
Symptoms: Overheating of the spark plug and severe damage to spark plug elements. Caused by poor heat transfer between spark plug and engine seat.
Recommendations: Replace plug and torque to manufacturer's specifications.

AC Delco

Fig. 4-16 Causes of common spark plug failures. *What are the two most common causes of spark plug failure?*

Spark Plug Heat Range The heat range is determined by how fast the plug transfers heat from the firing tip to the cylinder head. The length of the lower insulator and the type of metal used in the center electrode determine heat range.

The longer the length of the lower insulator, the higher the operating temperature of the plug. A short insulator transfers heat faster, so the plug has a lower operating temperature. The insulator temperature must be at least 700°F [371°C] to burn off carbon. To prevent preignition, the insulator temperature must not exceed 1,500°F [815°C].

To help conduct heat away from the lower insulator, some spark plugs have copper cores. Many plugs have electrodes made of nickel and chrome alloys that resist corrosion. To extend plug life, some plug electrodes are tipped with precious metals, such as platinum. See **Fig. 4-17**.

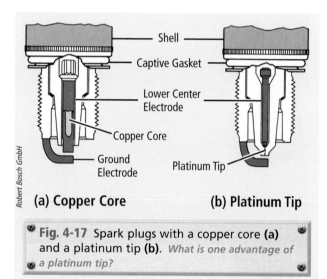

Shell
Captive Gasket
Lower Center Electrode
Copper Core
Ground Electrode
Platinum Tip

Robert Bosch GmbH

(a) Copper Core   **(b) Platinum Tip**

Fig. 4-17 Spark plugs with a copper core **(a)** and a platinum tip **(b)**. *What is one advantage of a platinum tip?*

> **TECH TIP** **Torquing Spark Plugs.** When installing plugs, use the correct torque specification. Overtightening can damage the threads in the cylinder head. Undertightening can cause the spark plugs to overheat. An overheated plug may cause pre-ignition damage to the engine.

Inspecting, Testing, and Replacing an Ignition Control Module This is a general procedure. Refer to the vehicle service manual for specifications and special procedures. To inspect, test, and replace the ignition control module:

1. Make sure you follow all procedures in the appropriate service manual.
2. Ignition control modules turn the ignition coil primary current on and off. Extreme heat can cause module failure.
3. Anytime a vehicle will not start, you need to inspect and test the ignition control module.
4. Consult the vehicle service manual for the location of the ignition control module. These modules may be located on the side of the distributor, in the engine compartment, inside the distributor, or under the dash.
5. If you find a defective ignition control module, replace it by following the directions in the vehicle service manual.

SECTION 1 KNOWLEDGE CHECK

1. Explain the purpose of the ignition coil.
2. What may cause higher than normal firing voltage?
3. What is a spark tester?
4. What tells the PCM when the number-one piston is nearing TDC?
5. What can be used to test for open ignition wires?
6. What are two symptoms of spark plug carbon deposits?

ASE TEST PREP

7. Technician A says that overtightening a spark plug can cause the spark plug to overheat. Technician B says that undertightening a spark plug can damage the threads in the cylinder head. Who is correct?
   - ⓐ Technician A.
   - ⓑ Technician B.
   - ⓒ Both Technician A and Technician B.
   - ⓓ Neither Technician A nor Technician B.

Section 2
Spark Distribution Systems

Objectives:

C5 • Inspect and test ignition system secondary circuit wiring and components; perform necessary action.

D1 • Diagnose hot or cold no-starting, hard starting, poor driveability, incorrect idle speed, poor idle, flooding, hesitation, surging, engine misfire, power loss, stalling, poor mileage, dieseling, and emissions problems on vehicles with injection-type fuel systems; determine necessary action.

C4 • Inspect, test and service distributor.

C7 • Check and adjust ignition system timing and timing advance/retard (where applicable).

A17 • Verify correct camshaft timing.

C2 • Diagnose ignition system related problems such as no-starting, hard starting engine misfire, poor driveability, spark knock, power loss, poor mileage, and emissions concerns on vehicles with distributor ignition (DI) systems; determine necessary action.

C1 • Diagnose ignition system related problems such as no-starting, hard starting engine misfire, poor driveability, spark knock, power loss, poor mileage, and emissions concerns on vehicles with electronic ignition (distributorless) systems; determine necessary action.

Vocabulary:
- **timing light**
- **carbon tracking**
- **distributorless ignition system**

Types of Spark Distribution Systems

The spark distribution system delivers the spark to the correct cylinder in the correct firing order. Spark distribution systems are made in distributor, distributorless (electronic), and direct-ignition types.

Distributor Ignition Systems

The ignition distributor usually performs two tasks. First, most distributors contain a device that triggers the primary circuit on and off. As noted earlier, this device may be a permanent magnet, Hall-effect, or optical-type trigger. The second task performed by the distributor is to conduct the high ignition voltage from the coil wire to the spark plug wires. See **Fig. 4-18.**

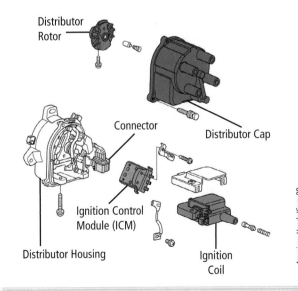

Distributor Rotor

Connector

Distributor Cap

Ignition Control Module (ICM)

Distributor Housing

Ignition Coil

American Honda/Corp PR

Fig. 4-18 Exploded view of a Honda distributor.
What two tasks are performed by a distributor?

Depending on the application, the ignition module may be mounted on the inside or outside of the distributor housing. On other vehicles the module function is built into the PCM.

The distributor assembly includes a cap and rotor. The rotor mounts on the end of the distributor shaft. As the rotor turns, it delivers ignition coil output to the correct ignition wire terminal. The secondary ignition wires are connected to the distributor cap in a specific order.

Distributor ignition systems have provisions for setting the base ignition timing. Follow the manufacturer's procedures when installing a distributor or adjusting base ignition timing.

Base timing is adjusted by using a timing light. The **timing light** is a bright stroboscopic (strobe) light that is usually connected to the number-one spark plug wire. Current flow through the wire causes the timing light to flash. When the light flashes, it shows the position of a timing, or index, mark on the vibration damper in relation to a timing pointer mounted on the front of the engine. See **Fig. 4-19**. Some engines have timing marks located on the flywheel and bell housing.

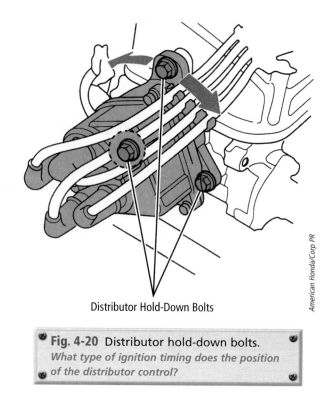

Distributor Hold-Down Bolts

Fig. 4-20 Distributor hold-down bolts. *What type of ignition timing does the position of the distributor control?*

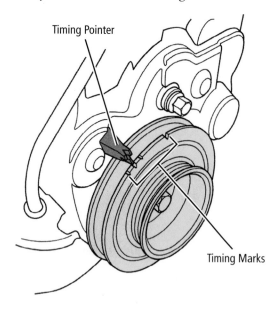

Timing Pointer

Timing Marks

Fig. 4-19 The alignment of the timing pointer and the timing mark. *Where is the base timing index mark?*

With the engine running at the specified rpm, adjust the base timing by loosening the distributor hold-down bolts. See **Fig. 4-20**. Turning the distributor slowly changes the timing. When the timing light shows the timing mark aligned with the timing pointer, you have correctly adjusted the base timing. To prevent the distributor from moving, you must tighten the distributor hold-down bolt(s). Restore the PCM to its normal mode.

Diagnosing the Distributor Ignition System In addition to the previous tests, check the distributor cap for cracks. Check also for carbon tracking. **Carbon tracking** occurs when the spark jumps from a distributor cap terminal to another terminal or to ground. Carbon tracks appear as thin black lines on the inside of the cap. Check distributor rotors for burn-through from the center contact to the distributor shaft. Light-colored pinholes in the rotor material indicate burn-through.

TECH TIP **No-Spark Condition.** An electronic distributor ignition system relies on the distributor to time and distribute the secondary ignition voltage. The camshaft usually drives the distributor. The camshaft is timed to the engine through a series of gears and a timing belt or chain. If the timing belt or chain breaks, ignition timing is affected. If a no-spark condition exists, remove the distributor cap, crank the engine, and look at the rotor or triggering devices. If no motion is seen, the camshaft is not driving the distributor.

Excellence in Science

How Does a Coil Work?

To understand how battery voltage (12 volts) can be increased to as much as 50,000 volts [50 kV] in the secondary coil, you must remember some basic rules of electricity. Electrical current flow through a conductor creates a magnetic field around the conductor. When a magnetic field moves past a conductor, a voltage is induced in the conductor.

An ignition coil consists of two coils of wire. The primary coil is connected to battery voltage and ground. One end of the secondary coil is connected to the output terminal. The type of coil determines where the other end is connected. The primary and secondary coils are close together but not touching.

As current flows through the primary coil, a magnetic field expands outside the wires for a short distance. When current flow stops, the magnetic field moves back into the coil.

When the primary circuit is closed, the moving magnetic field induces a voltage in the secondary coil. This happens when the magnetic field moves out of the primary winding.

When the primary circuit is opened (switched off), a voltage is induced a second time. This happens as the magnetic field again moves across the secondary coil. This process of producing a voltage within a wire or coil is called magnetic induction.

Apply It!

Inducing a Voltage in a Secondary Coil

Meets NATEF Science Standards for ignition coils.

Materials and Equipment
- 2 pieces of plastic pipe. The diameter of the pieces should be about 5 in. The diameters should differ by about ½ in. to ¼ in. You must be able to fit one inside the other.
- 2 pieces of copper wire about 70 ft. of 16–18 gauge wire about 210 ft. of 32–38 gauge wire
- 12-volt power supply
- 2 analog VOMs
- Electrical tape

To see how current flows through a coil, you can build your own coil.

1. Wrap 50 turns of the larger diameter wire around the larger diameter pipe. This is the primary coil. Leave the two ends of each piece of wire near each other to use as terminals.

2. Wrap 150 turns of the smaller diameter wire around the smaller diameter pipe. This is the secondary coil.

3. Use tape to keep the wires from slipping off of the plastic pipe pieces.

4. Place the smaller coil inside the larger coil.

5. Complete a circuit by connecting the larger coil (primary coil) to the power supply.

6. Connect one VOM to this coil. Set it to measure DC volts. Connect the other VOM to the smaller secondary coil to measure DC volts.

7. Close the switch on the power supply. Read the voltage on the primary coil. What is the voltage on the secondary coil?

8. Open the switch. Then close it again while you watch the needle on the VOM that is attached to the secondary coil. What do you see happening to the needle? You must look very carefully.

9. Which voltage is larger, the power supply voltage or the induced voltage?

Distributorless Ignition Systems

A **distributorless ignition system** is an ignition system that does not use a distributor to establish base ignition timing or distribute the secondary ignition voltage. It uses the same type of triggering devices and modules as a distributor-type system. Distributorless ignition uses one ignition coil for every two cylinders. Each coil has its own module circuit.

The cylinders are connected in pairs. When one cylinder is on its compression stroke, the companion cylinder is on its exhaust stroke. When the ignition system is triggered, the spark in the cylinder on compression ignites the mixture. The spark in the companion cylinder is "wasted" because the exhaust gases cannot be ignited. The next time the same pair of cylinders fire, the companion cylinder will be on compression and the other cylinder will be on exhaust. These systems are often referred to as "waste spark" systems. See **Fig. 4-21.**

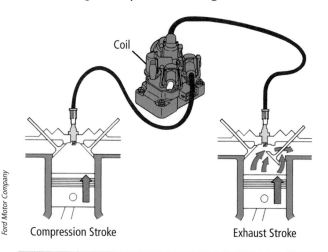

Ford Motor Company

Compression Stroke   Exhaust Stroke

Fig. 4-21 A waste spark system fires two spark plugs on different cylinders at the same time. The pistons are on different strokes. One spark ignites the air/fuel mixture during the compression stroke. The other spark is wasted during the exhaust stroke.

Figure 4-22 shows a crankshaft position (CKP) sensor. The CKP sensor provides the ignition module and PCM with engine speed and crankshaft position information. Some distributorless ignition systems also use a camshaft position (CMP) sensor. The CMP sensor is used to synchronize the firing of the coil packs and to trigger sequential fuel injection. The CMP sensor is usually a Hall-effect sensor. See **Fig. 4-23.**

Crankshaft Position Sensor

Erick Dodge

Fig. 4-22 A crankshaft position sensor on a DaimlerChrysler engine. *What information does the CKP provide?*

Camshaft Position Sensor

Terry Wild Studio

Fig. 4-23 A camshaft position sensor (CMP) mounted on a Ford 3.0L engine. *What information does the CMP provide?*

Diagnosing Distributorless Ignition Systems With no coil distributor cap, rotor, or coil wire, distributorless ignition systems have fewer components to check than distributor type systems. Since one coil fires a pair of spark plugs, a coil or ignition module problem usually affects both cylinders. If one spark plug wire is open or disconnected, the other plug in the pairing may fire at idle. Under load, both cylinders usually fail to fire. To diagnose a problem in distributorless ignition systems:

- Check the trigger circuit, primary circuit, and module in the same way as for other systems.
- Check for a spark from each coil assembly, using the spark tester.
- Test the spark plug wires for continuity, using an ohmmeter.
- Test each coil secondary winding for continuity, using an ohmmeter.
- Refer to the service manual for specific test procedures and specifications.

Direct Ignition Systems

Direct ignition systems use one ignition coil and module circuit for each cylinder. They are also referred to as "coil on plug" (COP) ignition systems. A coil is mounted directly over each spark plug. This eliminates the cap and rotor and all secondary wiring.

One variation of this system mounts an ignition coil near the spark plug and uses a short plug wire to connect the two. In either case, system operation is the same as in other ignition types.

Diagnosing Direct Ignition Systems To diagnose a direct ignition system:

- Check the trigger circuit, primary circuit, and module in the same way as for other systems.
- Check for a spark from each coil assembly, using a spark tester. For COP systems connect the tester to the coil output terminal. It may be necessary to use a secondary (coil or plug) wire to make the required connections.
- Test each coil secondary winding for continuity, using an ohmmeter.
- Refer to the service manual for specific test procedures and specifications.

SECTION 2 KNOWLEDGE CHECK

1. What delivers spark to the correct cylinder in the correct firing order?

2. What two tasks does the ignition distributor perform?

3. Where is the ignition module mounted?

4. Which two parts make up the distributor assembly?

5. What does a flashing timing light indicate?

6. What is another name for a waste spark ignition system?

7. What does the CKP do?

8. Explain how to diagnose problems in distributorless ignition systems.

9. What is another name for a direct ignition system?

ASE TEST PREP

10. Technician A says that the timing light is usually connected to the number-one spark plug wire. Technician B says that the timing light is usually connected to the last spark plug wire. Who is correct?
    - ⓐ Technician A.
    - ⓑ Technician B.
    - ⓒ Both Technician A and Technician B.
    - ⓓ Neither Technician A nor Technician B.

11. In a waste spark system, when one of a pair of cylinders is on the compression stroke, the other cylinder is on the:
    - ⓐ intake stroke.
    - ⓑ power stroke.
    - ⓒ exhaust stroke.
    - ⓓ None of the above.

Key Points

Meets the following NATEF Standards for Engine Performance: inspecting and testing ignition system components.

- An ignition coil has a primary and secondary winding.
- A distributor is a device designed to establish base timing and distribute the ignition spark.
- Ignition triggering devices include magnetic pulse, Hall-effect, and optical types.
- Ignition triggering devices provide crankshaft position and engine rpm information.
- The ignition module switches primary current on and off.
- Spark plug and coil wires have high resistance to control electro-magnetic interference.
- Distributorless (waste spark) ignition systems use one coil for two paired cylinders.
- Direct ignition uses one coil for each cylinder.

Review Questions

1. Name three basic designs of ignition triggering devices.
2. What is an ignition module?
3. What are the most common spark plug hex sizes?
4. What is thread reach?
5. What is the danger of a thread reach that is too long?
6. What should be done for spark plug heat shock failure?
7. What is a symptom of insufficient installation torque?
8. What is a CMP sensor?
9. **Critical Thinking** Why is it important to tighten all fuel connections before testing ignition spark?
10. **Critical Thinking** Why is the word "waste" associated with distributorless ignition systems?

Excellence in Communication

Locating Information

Change is constant in the automotive industry. New models, new systems, new regulations, and modified or new procedures are frequently announced. Each change means new or revised information you will need to use. You also will need to know how to work on older models still in use.

To use this information you will need to find it. Fortunately much of this information has been organized to help you find it quickly. Textbooks, service manuals, and service bulletins usually have tables of contents and indexes. You can refer to these.

This textbook is organized to help you develop your ability to locate material quickly. The table of contents lists the chapters. It gives an overall view of the information in each chapter. Note that each section in every chapter begins with a list of objectives. This list states important skills you should be able to develop as you study the chapter. The index lists subjects, components, and procedures covered in this book. It gives page numbers where you can find the information.

Most service manuals also use a table of contents to organize their information. An overall listing refers you to a specific section. There you will find a detailed listing of the topics covered in the section.

Apply It!

Meets NATEF Communication Standards for using text resources and service manuals to identify information.

1. Refer to the objectives in each section of this chapter.
2. Look through each section and identify the headings that relate to items on the list.
3. Choose one of the objectives.
4. Use a service manual's table of contents to find information about the objective that you selected in Step 3.
5. What similarities and differences do you find between the way these two sources of information are organized?

AUTOMOTIVE SERVICE EXCELLENCE
TEST PREP

Answering the following practice questions will help you prepare for the ASE certification tests.

1. Which of the following conditions could cause higher than normal firing voltage?

   ⓐ Wider than specified spark plug gap or worn plug electrodes.

   ⓑ Low compression ratio.

   ⓒ Abrupt change in the octane rating of the fuel.

   ⓓ None of the above.

2. Technician A says the distributor establishes base timing and distributes the secondary ignition voltage. Technician B says those tasks are the function of the powertrain control module. Who is correct?

   ⓐ Technician A.

   ⓑ Technician B.

   ⓒ Both Technician A and Technician B.

   ⓓ Neither Technician A nor Technician B.

3. Which of the following is the approximate electrical resistance of a spark plug wire that is within specifications?

   ⓐ 1 ohm/in.

   ⓑ 10 ohm/in.

   ⓒ 100 ohm/in.

   ⓓ 1000 ohm/in.

4. Technician A says that you should connect a spark tester to a proper ground such as the engine block. Technician B says that a spark tester may be connected to ground anywhere. Who is correct?

   ⓐ Technician A.

   ⓑ Technician B.

   ⓒ Both Technician A and Technician B.

   ⓓ Neither Technician A nor Technician B.

5. Hall-effect sensors can be checked by first testing:

   ⓐ specified amperage.

   ⓑ specified voltage.

   ⓒ specified resistance.

   ⓓ specified magnetic field strength.

6. A normal spark plug electrode:

   ⓐ should have a yellowish glazing.

   ⓑ can be grayish-tan in color.

   ⓒ contains light brown deposits.

   ⓓ is covered with sooty deposits.

7. What is the minimum temperature required to burn carbon deposits off of a spark plug?

   ⓐ 700°F [371°C].

   ⓑ 800°F [427°C].

   ⓒ 900°F [482°C].

   ⓓ 1000°F [538°C].

8. Technician A says that engine timing in a distributor based ignition system is adjusted by altering the position of the timing chain. Technician B says the timing is adjusted by rotating the distributor until the proper engine timing is reached. Who is correct?

   ⓐ Technician A.

   ⓑ Technician B.

   ⓒ Both Technician A and Technician B.

   ⓓ Neither Technician A nor Technician B.

9. In a distributor ignition system, if a spark jumps from a distributor cap terminal to another terminal or to ground it will be evidenced by:

   ⓐ ash buildup.

   ⓑ large gouges.

   ⓒ carbon tracking.

   ⓓ None of the above.

10. Technician A says that in a waste spark system two plugs fire simultaneously on two different cylinders, one of which is on the compression stroke and the other is on the exhaust stroke. Technician B says that one plug fires on the intake stroke and the other on the exhaust stroke. Who is correct?

    ⓐ Technician A.

    ⓑ Technician B.

    ⓒ Both Technician A and Technician B.

    ⓓ Neither Technician A nor Technician B.

Section 1
Air Induction Systems

Section 2
Sensing Induction Airflow

Diagnosing & Repairing Air Induction Systems

Customer's Concern

Jun Chen is known around town for his beautifully maintained black convertible. He has always trusted its care to your service center. On this cool day, Jun's concern is the car's recent poor performance. The service center manager, Jim, talked to Jun at length and then took the car on a variable-speed test drive. According to Jim, Jun's car operates fine at slower speeds and lower rpm, but when accelerating, the big V-8 does not move the little car quite as quickly as it should.

Jim tells Jun that he suspects the problem is related to the intake manifold. Because you are the facility's top air induction system technician, Jim quickly assigns Jun's car to you. How will you begin your diagnosis?

Technician's Challenge

As the service technician, you need to find answers to these questions:

1. What kind of fuel injection system would you expect to find in Jun's car? Would a multiport or throttle body system be preferable?

2. Is the car equipped with a variable induction system? How could this type of system influence vehicle performance at various speeds and rpm?

3. What could be to blame for poor performance at higher speeds and rpm? Could the secondary or short runners need tuning?

Section 1
Air Induction Systems

Objectives:
- Identify the components of the air induction system that require scheduled service.
- **D8** Check idle speed.
- Check air filter and replace as necessary.

Vocabulary:
- air induction system
- air filter
- powertrain control module (PCM)
- throttle position sensor (TPS)
- idle air control (IAC) valve

Air Induction System Components

The **air induction system** is the system that supplies clean air to the engine and controls the flow of air through the engine. See **Fig. 5-1.** Air enters the air induction system through the air filter. The **air filter** is a ring, cylinder, or panel of filter paper that removes dirt particles and debris from the air. The air may also pass through an electronic device called an airflow sensor. This sensor measures the amount of air entering the engine.

The air then flows around the throttle plate in the throttle body. The throttle plate controls engine speed by varying the amount of air entering the engine. After the air leaves the throttle body, it enters the intake manifold. The air passes through the intake manifold and enters the cylinder head. The air mixes with fuel, passes around the intake valve, and enters the cylinder.

A problem in the air induction system will affect exhaust emissions. An air induction problem can also cause engine performance problems.

The major components of the air induction system include the:
- Air filter and housing.
- Throttle body.
- Intake manifold.

The Air Filter and Housing

The air filter removes dirt, contaminants, and small abrasive particles from the air before it enters the engine. As much as 100,000 cubic feet of air may pass through the air filter every 1,000 miles [1609 km] of driving.

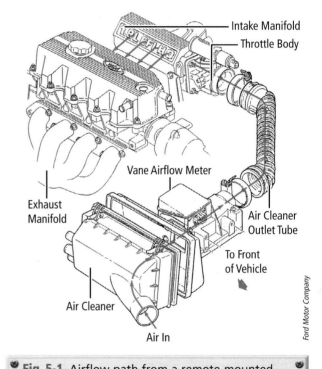

Fig. 5-1 Airflow path from a remote-mounted air cleaner to the intake manifold. *What is the purpose of an airflow sensor?*

Intake Manifold
Throttle Body
Vane Airflow Meter
Exhaust Manifold
Air Cleaner Outlet Tube
To Front of Vehicle
Air Cleaner
Air In
Ford Motor Company

Some air filters are mounted on the throttle body. Others are remotely mounted. For example, some mount on the inner fender and are connected to the throttle body by a tube.

The air filter paper, also called the air filter element or filtering media, must be strong enough to resist tearing. The filter must be flame-resistant in case the engine backfires through the air induction system. To prevent dirt from traveling around the filter, the filter must seal tightly against the air filter housing.

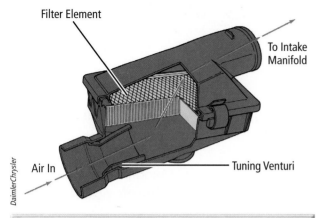

Filter Element

To Intake Manifold

Air In

Tuning Venturi

DaimlerChrysler

Fig. 5-2 The parts of a panel-type air filter assembly. *What is the job of the tuning venturi?*

The air passing from the filter housing, around the throttle plate, and into the engine creates noise. The air filter housing muffles some of this noise. To further reduce noise, some systems have a tuning venturi inside the housing. See **Fig. 5-2**. The shape and size of the tuning venturi compensates for noise created by air turbulence.

Changing the Air Filter Change air filters at specified intervals or sooner if they become dirty. To change an air filter, follow these steps:
1. Carefully remove the air filter housing lid or cover. Make sure nothing falls into the housing. Allowing debris to enter the air inlet or throttle body can damage the engine.

Excellence in Math

Calculating Airflow

Good engine performance requires an adequate supply of clean air. When an engine operates at high rpm a large volume of air is needed. As much as 100,000 cubic feet of air can pass through the air filter every 1,000 miles [1609 km] of driving.

Let's find out how those numbers relate to everyday engine operation. You can calculate the volume of air in cubic feet that flows through an air filter in a minute. This calculation will help you visualize how much air must pass through an air filter every minute the engine is running.

To calculate the volume of air flowing through an air filter you must first know the engine's rpm and displacement. The engine is a four-stroke, 3.0-liter engine running at 2,500 rpm at 100-percent throttle opening.

A four-stroke engine has two crankshaft revolutions for each complete combustion cycle. At an engine speed of 2,500 rpm, each cylinder will fire 1,250 times per minute.

The engine will move its displacement volume of 3.0 liters of air 1,250 times each minute.

3 liters × 1,250 = 3,750 liters each minute

To find the volume in cubic feet, use this conversion formula:

$$1 \text{ liter} = 0.0353 \text{ ft}^3$$

Thus, 3,750 liters/min. = 3,750 × 0.0353 = 132.4 ft³/min.

This volume of air would more than fill a cube 5 feet on a side (125 ft³).

The actual airflow volume will be less than the calculated volume because no filter and intake system is 100% efficient.

Apply It!

Meets NATEF Mathematics Standards for converting measurements between the metric and English systems.

1. Determine the volume of air flowing through an air filter at 2,800 rpm at a 100-percent throttle opening for a 2.8-liter, four-stroke engine. Show your answer in liters/min. and ft³/min.

2. What would happen to the volume of airflow if the engine had twice the displacement volume?

2. Inspect the air filter and housing to make sure that the filter seals correctly against the housing. A poorly fitting filter will show signs of dirty air flowing around its sealing surfaces. Make sure that any seal or gasket used in the air filter housing is intact and in place.

3. Clean the air filter housing with a shop vacuum or a clean shop towel. If required, remove the housing by removing the fastening screws. See **Fig. 5-3**.

4. Make sure that the new air filter fits correctly. Tighten all air inlet connections. Start the engine and make sure it idles correctly.

Terry Wild Studio

Fig. 5-3 The air filter housing must be clean, with the seal firmly attached. *What might happen if dirt and debris are not removed from the air-filter housing?*

The Throttle Body

The throttle body contains the throttle plate, the throttle position sensor, and the idle air control valve. Some throttle bodies also include a coolant passage.

By moving the accelerator pedal, the driver moves the throttle plate, which controls the amount of air entering the engine. The throttle plate is moved mechanically or electronically.

Throttle shaft bushings may wear with use, causing rough idle problems. Varnish can build up around the throttle plate and throttle bore. This may cause a rough idle, sluggish response, or stalling condition.

Vehicle manufacturers apply throttle bore coatings that resist dirt buildup and prevent sticking. Harsh solvents, such as carburetor cleaners, may damage these coatings. Before using any cleaner, follow the vehicle manufacturer's recommendations and procedures.

Most throttle bodies do not require routine adjustment. However, some throttle bodies found on cars may have an idle speed and emissions trim adjustment. When a check of idle speed indicates improper operation, a proper cleaning of throttle plates, bore, and idle air control (IAC) may be necessary. If this has not corrected the problem, trim adjustment should be made according to manufacturer's specifications. To avoid damage to components, consult the vehicle service manual before servicing any throttle body.

Mechanically Operated Throttle On a mechanical throttle, the throttle plate shaft is connected to the accelerator pedal by a cable. Pressing down on the pedal opens the throttle plate. The throttle plate controls the air entering the engine.

Throttle cables may stretch with use, preventing the throttle plate from opening or closing properly. When necessary, adjust throttle cables according to the procedures specified in the vehicle service manual.

Electronically Operated Throttle Instead of a mechanical throttle plate linkage, some vehicles use an electronic throttle control or drive-by-wire system.

A sensor on the accelerator pedal monitors the position of the pedal. The sensor sends a position return signal to the powertrain control module. The **powertrain control module (PCM)** is a computer that monitors and controls ignition timing, emission control devices, and other engine-related systems.

The PCM computes the proper opening for the throttle plate. A small motor mounted on the throttle body opens and closes the throttle plate.

These electronic controls may be part of a traction control system. The system provides input to the PCM. The PCM adjusts the throttle-plate position, the air/fuel mixture, the spark advance, and the shift points of automatic transmissions and transaxles.

Safety First

Electronic Throttle Control Use caution when servicing an electronic throttle control. The throttle is operated by a gear-reduction system strong enough to cause personal injury, should it close on a finger.

Throttle Position Sensor The **throttle position sensor (TPS)** is a variable resistance sensor that sends throttle plate position information to the PCM. See **Fig. 5-4.** As the throttle plate position changes, the return-signal voltage from the TPS changes.

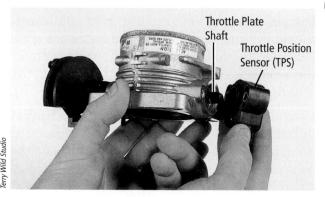

Terry Wild Studio

Fig. 5-4 The TPS attaches to the throttle plate shaft. *What is the purpose of the TPS?*

Check Idle Speed

The idle speed must be checked and adjusted for efficient engine operation.

Idle Air Control Valve The **idle air control (IAC) valve** is a valve that controls engine idle in response to signals from the PCM. As engine load at idle changes, the idle air control valve regulates the amount of air passing by the throttle plate. See **Fig. 5-5.**

An example of engine-idle control is the reaction of the IAC to an increase in engine load from the power steering system. A pressure switch in the power-steering system sends a return signal to the PCM indicating a pressure increase. To maintain a correct idle speed under the increased load, the engine speed must increase.

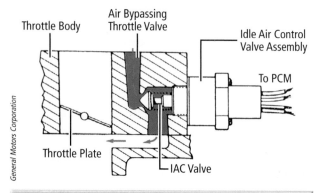

General Motors Corporation

Fig. 5-5 Operation of the IAC valve. A stepper motor changes the position of the conical valve to control idle speed. *When would the IAC valve increase idle speed?*

The PCM moves the IAC valve so it passes more air around the throttle plate. At the same time, the PCM signals the injectors to deliver more fuel to match the added airflow.

TECH TIP **Debris in IAC Valve.** Debris from changing an air filter can collect in the IAC valve. The IAC valve may stick and not respond properly. This will cause a rough or erratic idle and engine stalling. You may need to remove the IAC valve for cleaning.

Checking and Adjusting the Idle Speed and Fuel Mixture Refer to the vehicle service manual for specifications and special procedures. To check and adjust the idle speed and fuel mixture:

1. Make sure you use the appropriate service manual for the type of vehicle you are checking.
2. If the electronic fuel injection system you are checking has self-test abilities, it will produce a code that pinpoints a bad component.
3. If an adjustment is needed, refer to the service manual to interpret the code and find the appropriate adjustment procedure.
4. Let the engine fully warm up before you enter the self-test mode.
5. Vehicles that do not have self-test abilities require special tools to check the operation.

Safety First

Servicing Air Induction System Always make sure the throttle operates correctly after servicing an air induction system. A sticking throttle can "over-rev" the engine, causing major damage to the valve train and pistons. Never try to start an engine by pouring gasoline into an open air intake. An engine backfire can ignite the gasoline and cause serious burns.

The Intake Manifold

The intake manifold connects the throttle body to the intake ports in the cylinder head. The manifold has a set of passages, or runners, through which air or an air/fuel mixture flows.

Fuel must vaporize completely to mix and flow evenly with air. Cold air does not allow for complete vaporization. Unvaporized fuel contains heavy liquid droplets. Inertia prevents these droplets from turning sharp bends and corners as the air/fuel mixture flows through the intake manifold. These droplets tend to travel in a straight line. They collect and puddle at bends in the manifold. Heating or tuning the manifold can eliminate or reduce these problems.

Tuned Intake Manifold Tuning the intake manifold improves the volumetric efficiency of normally aspirated engines. The runners of the intake manifold are designed to specific sizes and lengths. This design helps provide the highest usable pressure to each cylinder. Long runners improve low-speed performance. Short runners improve high-speed performance.

A tuned intake manifold takes advantage of the opening and closing of the intake valves to produce a "ram pressure" effect. See **Fig. 5-6.**

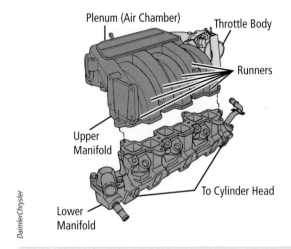

Plenum (Air Chamber)
Throttle Body
Runners
Upper Manifold
To Cylinder Head
Lower Manifold
DaimlerChrysler

Fig. 5-6 An example of a tuned intake manifold. The long runners improve low-speed performance. *What length of runner will improve high-speed performance?*

When an intake valve opens, the air/fuel mixture flows into the cylinder. When the valve closes, this flow stops quickly. The inertia of the moving air/fuel mixture tends to keep it moving. This movement creates pressure as the air/fuel mixture piles up, or "rams," against the closed intake valves. When the valve opens, the pressure forces more air/fuel mixture into the usable volume of the cylinder. This is referred to as increasing the volumetric efficiency.

A tuned intake manifold is most effective at high engine revolutions per minute (rpm). To improve low- and high-rpm performance, some engines have a variable induction system. **Figure 5-7** shows this system on an in-line four-cylinder engine.

The variable induction system has two runners for each cylinder. The long runner, or primary runner, is tuned for low speed. The short runner, or secondary runner, is tuned for high speed.

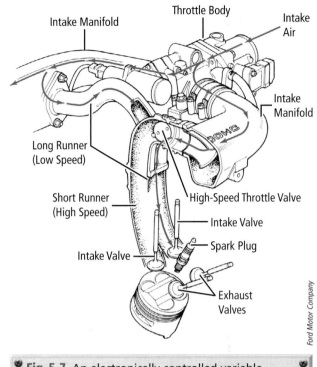

Intake Manifold
Throttle Body
Intake Air
Intake Manifold
Long Runner (Low Speed)
Short Runner (High Speed)
High-Speed Throttle Valve
Intake Valve
Spark Plug
Intake Valve
Exhaust Valves
Ford Motor Company

Fig. 5-7 An electronically controlled variable-induction system has two runners for each cylinder. One runner is for low-speed operation; the other opens for high-speed operation. *What advantage is provided by a variable induction system?*

The primary runners are open. The secondary runners contain a PCM-controlled valve. This valve is closed at low engine rpm. The valve opens at high engine rpm.

At low engine rpm, only the primary runners are open. At high engine rpm, both runners supply cylinders with air or an air/fuel mixture. The tuned induction system improves power and throttle response.

Superchargers and Turbochargers An engine can produce more power when the air/fuel mixture enters the cylinders under pressure. Pressurizing the air/fuel mixture increases its density. A higher density air/fuel mixture creates more power during the power stroke. This is called forced induction. A forced induction engine provides more power than a normally aspirated engine.

Superchargers and turbochargers are two devices that provide forced induction. Both devices increase the pressure in the intake manifold. A supercharger is a mechanically driven air pump. The drive is provided by a belt driven off the crankshaft pulley. A turbocharger is a turbine driven air pump. Exhaust gases routed from the exhaust manifold power the turbine.

Excellence in Science

Measuring Pressure and Vacuum

Pressure and vacuum are important during engine operation. Pressure and vacuum are usually measured in inches or millimeters of mercury. Mercury's density makes it ideal for measuring pressure and vacuum. A mercury barometer or manometer can be made much smaller than a similar device using another liquid such as water.

Pressure and vacuum on a vehicle are usually measured with a mechanical gauge rather than a mercury manometer. These devices include engine compression pressure, fuel pump pressure, tire pressure, and manifold vacuum gauges.

Safety First

Mercury Is Poisonous If a manometer using mercury breaks or spills, do not handle the mercury in any way. Call your instructor and get expert help in cleaning up a mercury spill.

Apply It!

Making a Manometer

Materials and Equipment
- Yardstick
- About 7′ [2.1 m] of clear plastic tubing, with a diameter of about ½″ [13 mm]
- Clear plastic tape
- Small funnel or meat-basting bulb
- Food coloring (any color)

In this activity you will make a simple manometer. A manometer is an instrument used to measure pressure and vacuum.

1. Fold the tubing in half to form a U-shape.

2. Tape the center of the U to the bottom of the yardstick. Tape the tubing to the edges of the yardstick leaving about 6″ of loose tubing on the top of each side.

3. Hang the yardstick so that the loose ends of the tubing are about level with your shoulders.

4. Fill the funnel or meat-basting bulb with colored water to about the 18″ mark.

5. Blow gently into one end of the tubing while watching the water level on both sides. Record the level of fluid on both sides.

6. Find the difference in measurement between the two sides. This number is the amount of pressure you created in inches of water.

7. Gently draw air from one side of the tube to create the same difference in water level as before. This indicates the amount of vacuum you created in inches of water.

SECTION 1 KNOWLEDGE CHECK

1. What is the purpose of the air induction system?

2. What are the three main components of the air induction system?

3. Why is it important to adjust throttle cables?

4. What may happen if debris collects in the idle air control valve?

5. What connects the throttle body to the intake ports in the cylinder head?

6. Why is MFI more efficient than TBI?

ASE TEST PREP

7. Technician A says that the idle air control valve is a valve that controls engine idle in response to signals from the PCM. Technician B says that the idle air control valve controls engine idle in response to signals from the throttle position sensor. Who is correct?

  ⓐ Technician A.

  ⓑ Technician B.

  ⓒ Both Technician A and Technician B.

  ⓓ Neither Technician A nor Technician B.

● Section 2
Sensing Induction Airflow

Objectives:

D6 ● Inspect throttle body, intake manifold and gaskets for vacuum leaks and/or unmetered air.
   ● Diagnose air metering failures.

Vocabulary:
● **manifold absolute pressure (MAP) sensor**
● **mass airflow (MAF) sensor**

Calculating Airflow

A fuel injection system requires an accurate determination of the amount of air flowing into the engine. The PCM uses airflow information to determine the amount of fuel to be injected and the amount of spark advance needed. Airflow can be calculated or measured directly.

Airflow Sensors

On some engines the PCM calculates the airflow using the speed density method. This is a mathematical relationship using the following factors:
• Engine rpm.
• Throttle position.
• Intake air temperature.
• Manifold absolute pressure (MAP).
• Coolant temperature.
• Exhaust gas recirculation.

These variables are measured by a network of sensors that send signals to the PCM. Using this information, the PCM determines the amount of fuel and spark advance needed.

The manifold absolute pressure sensor plays a key role in speed density calculations. The **manifold absolute pressure (MAP) sensor** is a sensor that is mounted on or connected to the intake manifold. See **Fig. 5-8**. With the key on and engine off, the MAP sensor reads barometric pressure. With the engine running, the sensor reads the (low) pressure in the intake manifold caused by piston movement.

Manifold pressure readings are the opposite of manifold vacuum readings. When manifold vacuum is high (at closed throttle, for example), manifold pressure is low. When manifold vacuum is low (at wide-open throttle), the pressure is high. Manifold pressure is an accurate indication of engine load and, indirectly, of airflow. The MAP sensor sends a varying voltage or frequency signal to the PCM as engine load and manifold pressure change.

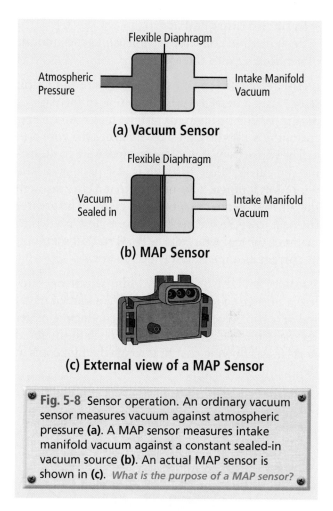

(a) Vacuum Sensor

Flexible Diaphragm — Atmospheric Pressure — Intake Manifold Vacuum

(b) MAP Sensor

Flexible Diaphragm — Vacuum Sealed in — Intake Manifold Vacuum

(c) External view of a MAP Sensor

Fig. 5-8 Sensor operation. An ordinary vacuum sensor measures vacuum against atmospheric pressure **(a)**. A MAP sensor measures intake manifold vacuum against a constant sealed-in vacuum source **(b)**. An actual MAP sensor is shown in **(c)**. *What is the purpose of a MAP sensor?*

Inputs from other sensors are also used in the airflow calculation. The intake air temperature (IAT) sensor measures the temperature of the air. Cool air is more dense than warm air and requires more fuel to maintain the ideal air/fuel ratio, 14.7:1.

The engine coolant temperature (ECT) sensor measures engine temperature by monitoring coolant temperature. A cold engine requires more fuel to maintain the ideal air/fuel ratio. When the engine is at operating temperature, the air is less dense and less fuel is needed.

Measuring Airflow Directly

A **mass airflow (MAF) sensor** measures airflow directly. The MAF is an electronic sensor that measures the amount of air entering the engine. The sensor sends a return signal in the form of voltage to the PCM. The MAF signal is used as a measure of airflow. The five sensors used to measure airflow directly are:

- Vane type.
- Hot-wire induction.
- Heated film.
- Airflow sensor plate.
- Karman-Vortex Path.

Each method continuously measures the amount of air flowing into the engine.

Hot-Wire Induction Sensor A hot-wire induction sensor uses a heated wire. The wire is in the path of the air passing through the airflow meter. An electric current flowing through the wire keeps the wire hot.

The wire is kept at a specific temperature by adjusting the current flow through it. Air passing by the wire cools it down. The more air that passes through the airflow meter, the more heat is lost. The greater the heat loss, the greater the current flow needed to maintain the temperature. The PCM reads the amount of current as a measurement of airflow.

Heated-Film Sensor A heated-film sensor operates like a hot-wire induction sensor. It consists of metal foil or a grid coated with a current conducting material. See **Fig. 5-9.** Current flowing through the material heats it. Air flowing past or through the film cools it.

Like the hot-wire induction sensor, the film is maintained at a specific temperature. The more air that passes through the airflow meter, the more heat is lost. The greater the heat loss, the greater the current flow. The PCM reads the amount of current as a measurement of airflow.

Karman-Vortex Path Sensor The Karman-Vortex Path sensor measures airflow by measuring air turbulence. When air passes over an obstruction, it separates into whirls and eddies. The frequency of the whirls and eddies changes in direct proportion to the amount of air passing over the obstruction. A high level of airflow produces a higher frequency of whirls and eddies than a lower level of airflow. The change in frequency is a measurement of airflow. The higher the frequency, the greater the airflow.

Diagnosing Airflow Sensor Failures

Measuring the airflow into an engine is important. Incorrect airflow measurements will produce incorrect air/fuel mixtures. A defective airflow sensor will send the wrong return signal to the PCM. This will cause the PCM to incorrectly adjust the air/fuel mixture. An incorrect air/fuel mixture can cause starting, fuel economy, drivability, and exhaust emission problems. Several conditions can cause a failure in the airflow sensor system.

Indirect measurement (speed density) systems may have problems with vacuum leaks that occur after the air leaves the throttle body. Air leaking into the intake manifold reduces manifold vacuum. It may also cause the idle speed to increase. Excess air leaking into the intake manifold will also cause a lean air/fuel mixture.

Figure 5-10 shows the network of vacuum hoses that carry vacuum to the actuators. The cause of many vacuum and air leaks is usually a defective vacuum hose or gasket. Rubber and plastic vacuum hoses may develop leaks and cracks due to age or contamination. Manifold and throttle body gaskets may dry out, crack, and deteriorate, allowing air to enter through them.

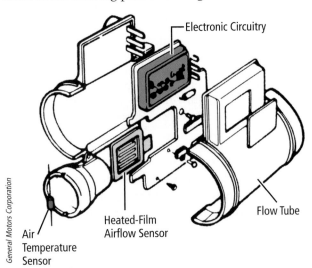

Electronic Circuitry

General Motors Corporation

Air Temperature Sensor

Heated-Film Airflow Sensor

Flow Tube

Fig. 5-9 Mass airflow sensor using a heated film and air-temperature sensor. *What heats the coating?*

Jack Holtel

Arts Automotive, Berkeley, CA

Fig. 5-10 A network of vacuum hoses carries vacuum to actuators. *How can a leak in the vacuum hose network affect engine performance?*

A smoke machine can be used to detect small leaks in hoses that route vacuum or light pressure. The smoke machine emits a harmless smoke, which is sometimes tinted with an ultraviolet dye. Leaks can be identified by the presence of smoke escaping from the system. See **Fig. 5-11**.

Fig. 5-11 A smoke machine can be used to find leaks in vacuum lines.

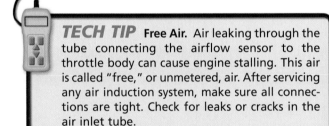

TECH TIP **Free Air.** Air leaking through the tube connecting the airflow sensor to the throttle body can cause engine stalling. This air is called "free," or unmetered, air. After servicing any air induction system, make sure all connections are tight. Check for leaks or cracks in the air inlet tube.

Direct airflow measurement systems may have problems with air entering the engine after the airflow is measured. With this type of leak, the airflow sensor is not measuring all of the air entering the engine. The measurement signal sent to the PCM is not correct. An incorrect airflow measurement will cause the PCM to supply an incorrect air/fuel mixture. It is sensing too little air. It compensates by reducing the amount of fuel the fuel injectors are supplying. The resulting lean mixture will produce engine performance problems.

SECTION 2 KNOWLEDGE CHECK

1. What factors influence speed density?

2. At what throttle position is manifold vacuum low and manifold pressure high?

3. Why is more fuel needed when intake air is cold?

4. What sensor measures airflow directly?

5. What happens if an airflow sensor is defective?

6. How is a smoke machine used to identify air leaks?

ASE TEST PREP

7. Technician A says that the heated film induction sensor operates like a hot-wire induction sensor. Technician B says that the heated film induction sensor operates like a Karman-Vortex path sensor. Who is correct?

   ⓐ Technician A.

   ⓑ Technician B.

   ⓒ Both Technician A and Technician B.

   ⓓ Neither Technician A nor Technician B.

CHAPTER 5 REVIEW

Key Points

Meets the following NATEF Standards for Engine Performance: inspecting the air induction and filtration system and the intake manifold.

- Maximum engine life requires air induction system maintenance.
- Air induction system parts may require periodic cleaning and adjustment.
- A faulty IAC valve in the throttle body will cause idle and stalling problems.
- Airflow sensor operation is critical so the PCM receives correct air metering information.
- A tuned intake manifold provides more power output from the engine.
- Superchargers and turbochargers are two devices that provide forced induction.
- The five types of sensors used to measure airflow directly are: vane type, hot-wire induction, heated film, airflow sensor plate, and Karman-Vortex path.
- Incorrect airflow measurements will produce incorrect air/fuel mixtures.

Review Questions

1. What type of fuel injection system mixes fuel with air as it enters the intake manifold?
2. What is the purpose of the secondary runner in a variable induction system?
3. Name two devices that provide forced induction.
4. Which sensor measures airflow by measuring air turbulence?
5. What controls engine idle in response to engine load?
6. What material makes up the air filter element or filtering media?
7. What contains the idle-air control valve, throttle position sensor, and throttle plate?
8. What controls the amount of air entering the engine?
9. **Critical Thinking** What can be done to eliminate or reduce fuel collecting in the bends of a manifold?
10. **Critical Thinking** What is the purpose of a tuning venturi?

Excellence in Communication

Decoding Acronyms

WYSIWYG, pronounced "wizzy wig" by many computer users, is an acronym for the phrase "What you see is what you get." It is used when talking about displays on a computer screen. In 1941 the term "radio detecting and ranging" was shortened to the acronym RADAR. This acronym is now used as a word. Few people know it is an acronym.

An acronym is a word formed from the first letter or first few letters of the words in a phrase. Every area of work or interest uses acronyms. The automotive industry uses many acronyms for parts, tests, equipment, company names, and products.

As a technician, you need to know what the letters in an acronym stand for. For example, you should recognize TPS as meaning "throttle position sensor." This will save time on the job.

Apply It!

Meets NATEF Communications Standards for interpreting acronyms.

1. Read through this chapter again. As you do this, note the acronyms that are used.
2. List the acronyms. Next to them write the words they stand for.
3. Using a technical dictionary, look up the acronyms you have listed. Does the entry refer you to another entry? What does this tell you about the way acronyms are listed in some dictionaries?

AUTOMOTIVE SERVICE EXCELLENCE
TEST PREP

Answering the following practice questions will help you prepare for the ASE certification tests.

1. Which of the following is a major component of the air induction system?

   ⓐ Air filter and housing.
   ⓑ Throttle body.
   ⓒ Intake manifold.
   ⓓ All of the above.

2. Technician A says that worn throttle shaft bushings may cause rough idle. Technician B says that varnish buildup around the throttle plate and bore may cause rough idle. Who is correct?

   ⓐ Technician A.
   ⓑ Technician B.
   ⓒ Both Technician A and Technician B.
   ⓓ Neither Technician A nor Technician B.

3. Technician A says that the engine should be at a cold relative temperature when the idle speed and fuel mixture are being checked and adjusted. Technician B says that the engine should be at a warm relative temperature when the idle speed and fuel mixture are being checked and adjusted. Who is correct?

   ⓐ Technician A.
   ⓑ Technician B.
   ⓒ Both Technician A and Technician B.
   ⓓ Neither Technician A nor Technician B.

4. Technician A says that the intake manifold connects the throttle body to the intake ports in the cylinder head. Technician B says that the intake manifold connects the throttle body to the tuning venturi and the air filter. Who is correct?

   ⓐ Technician A.
   ⓑ Technician B.
   ⓒ Both Technician A and Technician B.
   ⓓ Neither Technician A nor Technician B.

5. An intake manifold is tuned to:

   ⓐ lengthen service life.
   ⓑ lessen noise.
   ⓒ improve the cyclic rate.
   ⓓ improve volumetric efficiency.

6. Technician A says that airflow can be measured directly. Technician B says that airflow can be calculated. Who is correct?

   ⓐ Technician A.
   ⓑ Technician B.
   ⓒ Both Technician A and Technician B.
   ⓓ Neither Technician A nor Technician B.

7. Which of the following factors is important in speed density calculations?

   ⓐ Engine rpm.
   ⓑ Vehicle speed.
   ⓒ Transmission temperature.
   ⓓ All of the above.

8. Technician A says that a mass airflow sensor continuously measures the amount of air entering into the engine. Technician B says that the measurements are taken at intervals and represent a snapshot of the total amount of air entering the engine. Who is correct?

   ⓐ Technician A.
   ⓑ Technician B.
   ⓒ Both Technician A and Technician B.
   ⓓ Neither Technician A nor Technician B.

9. What device is used to find leaks in hoses that route vacuum or low pressure air?

   ⓐ Digital multimeter.
   ⓑ Smoke machine.
   ⓒ Oscilloscope.
   ⓓ None of the above.

10. Technician A says that an incorrect measurement or calculation of the amount of air entering the engine can cause the air/fuel mixture to become either too rich or too lean. Technician B says lean air/fuel mixtures can cause performance problems. Who is correct?

    ⓐ Technician A.
    ⓑ Technician B.
    ⓒ Both Technician A and Technician B.
    ⓓ Neither Technician A nor Technician B.

6

Diagnosing & Repairing Fuel Systems

Section 1
Automotive Fuels

Section 2
The Combustion Process

Section 3
The Fuel Management System

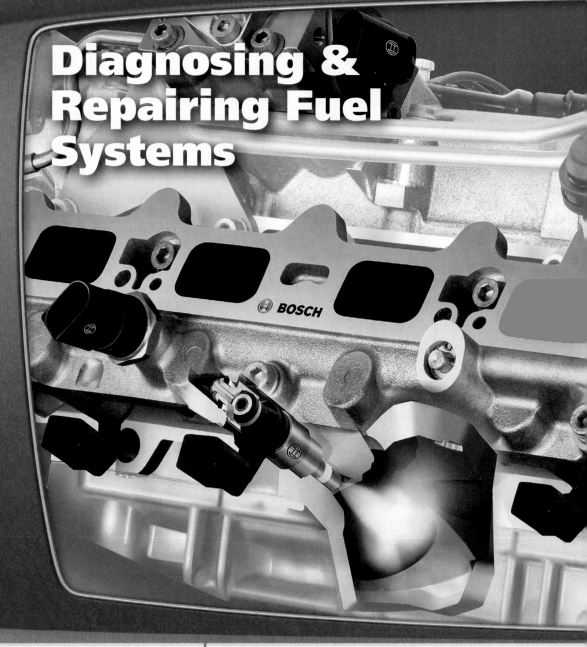

Customer's Concern

Patrick O'Dea owns a uniform service business. He and his employees use a 1998 full-size van, affectionately called Sally, to pick up and deliver uniforms. Much to his employees' disappointment, Patrick says, "We are keeping Sally until she dies."

Today, Patrick is visiting your service center because the van has been stalling at stoplights, and it hesitates at takeoff when lights turn green. It sounds like the air/fuel ratio is out of balance. Service records indicate the van's fuel injectors have never been serviced. Will repair costs outweigh Patrick's will to fix Sally? Is today the day you tell Patrick to consider a new van? Before you can answer these questions, you will need to diagnose the problem.

Technician's Challenge

As the service technician, you need to find answers to these questions:

1. Could the van's problems be caused by a faulty fuel pump, clogged fuel filter, faulty fuel pressure regulator, kinked fuel line, or low-octane fuel?

2. If the above causes are ruled out, the fuel injection system is likely to blame. How will you diagnose a fuel injection problem?

3. Name two solutions to the fuel injection problem. Will you have to ask Patrick's permission before performing these services?

Section 1
Automotive Fuels

Objectives:
- Identify the characteristics of automotive fuels.

Vocabulary:
- antioxidants
- volatility
- octane number
- air/fuel ratio
- stoichiometric ratio

Characteristics of Automotive Fuels

Automotive fuels are hydrocarbon compounds. They contain two basic elements, hydrogen and carbon. The chemical symbol for hydrogen is H. The chemical symbol for carbon is C.

Gasoline

Oil companies refine gasoline from crude oil (petroleum). See **Fig. 6-1.** During the refining process, chemical additives are added to the gasoline. These additives improve the combustion properties of gasoline. They also help protect the engine and fuel system.

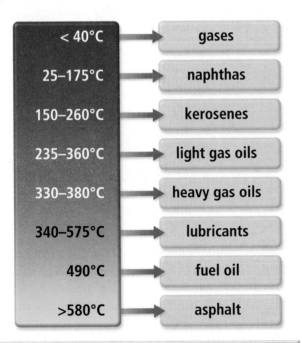

< 40°C	gases
25–175°C	naphthas
150–260°C	kerosenes
235–360°C	light gas oils
330–380°C	heavy gas oils
340–575°C	lubricants
490°C	fuel oil
>580°C	asphalt

Fig. 6-1 An oil refinery "cracking tower" distills the various components of crude oil. *At what temperature range are kerosenes distilled from crude oil?*

> **Safety First**
> **Open Fuel Systems** Gasoline vapor is highly explosive. Never use a trouble light around a disconnected fuel system. Instead, use a low-voltage, battery-powered flashlight. Never use a device like a welder, electric motor, or an appliance with an open-flame pilot light around an open fuel system. When working with an open fuel system, make sure your work area is properly ventilated.

A good-quality gasoline should have:
- Proper volatility, which determines how easily the gasoline vaporizes (turns to vapor).
- The correct octane rating, which minimizes detonation (spark knock).
- **Antioxidants,** which are chemical compounds that prevent formation of varnish in the fuel system.
- Corrosion inhibitors, which prevent rusting of metal parts in the fuel system.
- Anti-icers, added seasonally or by geographical region, that minimize icing in the throttle body and fuel line.
- Detergents, which keep the fuel injectors clean.
- Deposit control agents, which prevent or remove fuel system deposits.

Volatility One measure of how easily a liquid (fuel) vaporizes is known as **volatility.** If volatility is too low, the fuel will not vaporize and mix properly with air. Gasoline that does not vaporize causes incomplete combustion. It leaves the cylinder as unburned hydrocarbons.

If volatility is too high, the fuel may turn to vapor in the fuel system. This condition is vapor lock. Vapor lock prevents normal fuel flow through the fuel system.

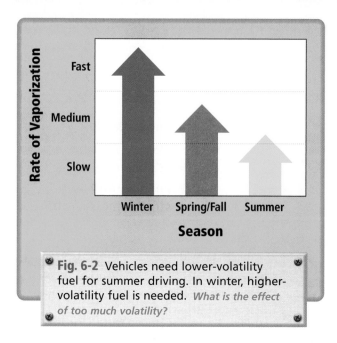

Fig. 6-2 Vehicles need lower-volatility fuel for summer driving. In winter, higher-volatility fuel is needed. *What is the effect of too much volatility?*

Octane Requirements The octane requirements of an engine are determined by combustion chamber design and compression ratio. See **Fig. 6-4**. However, the octane requirement changes with weather, altitude, and driving conditions.

Octane requirements can also be affected by changes in the mechanical condition of the engine. These include:
- Reduced cooling system efficiency.
- Lean air/fuel mixtures.
- Over-advanced ignition timing.
- Increased compression ratio.
- Failure of the exhaust gas recirculation (EGR) valve.

To suit weather conditions and to meet local evaporative emissions standards, refiners adjust volatility. They increase volatility for cold weather and reduce it for hot weather. See **Fig. 6-2**.

Poor-quality gasoline can cause hard starting, hesitation, stalling, and detonation. Changing brands or grades of gasoline may eliminate these problems.

Octane Number The antiknock quality of a gasoline is indicated by its **octane number.** This is also known as the octane rating or octane level. The higher the octane number, the more resistant the gasoline is to detonation (spark knock). A 91-octane gasoline is more knock-resistant than an 87-octane gasoline. A gasoline that detonates easily is a low-octane gasoline.

The octane number is determined by testing gasoline in laboratory engines. Two common laboratory tests determine research (R) and motor (M) octane numbers. The average of these two values $[(R+M)/2]$ is the antiknock index (AKI). This number is posted on the pumps at service stations. See **Fig. 6-3**.

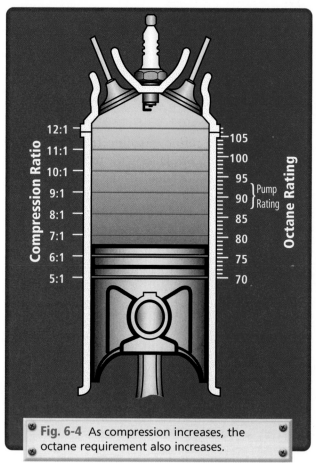

Fig. 6-4 As compression increases, the octane requirement also increases.

Using gasoline with a higher octane rating than is needed wastes money and resources. A high-octane or premium gasoline should be used only when recommended by the manufacturer or when detonation is an ongoing problem.

For example, engines may have a "stack up" of production tolerances as a result of machining or rebuilding. The change in tolerances reduces combustion chamber volume. The compression ratio is increased, causing detonation.

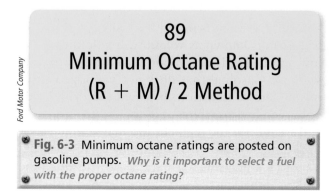

89
Minimum Octane Rating
(R + M) / 2 Method

Ford Motor Company

Fig. 6-3 Minimum octane ratings are posted on gasoline pumps. *Why is it important to select a fuel with the proper octane rating?*

Excellence in Science

Increasing Oxygen in Fuel

Automotive gasoline is a mixture of many different hydrocarbons. When hydrocarbons burn in the combustion chamber of an engine, energy is released. This energy moves the piston to create mechanical energy. To burn a hydrocarbon, oxygen atoms are added to the fuel in the combustion chamber. A spark then ignites the mixture.

In a 100-percent efficient gasoline engine, all hydrocarbons would burn. Only carbon dioxide (CO_2), water (H_2O), and nitrogen (N) would be left to come out the tailpipe. Automotive engines are not 100-percent efficient. Unburned fuel, carbon monoxide (CO), and nitrogen oxides are also produced.

Increasing the amount of oxygen in the combustion chamber will burn more of the fuel. Less CO and unburned fuel will go out the tailpipe. More energy will be released.

Unlike pure hydrocarbons, oxygenated fuels contain hydrogen, carbon, and oxygen atoms.

Blending oxygenated fuels with gasoline will get more oxygen into the chamber.

Ethanol, an alcohol made from corn, is an oxygenated fuel. As ethanol burns, its oxygen atoms are freed to help convert more hydrocarbons. As a result, more fuel burns. Oxygenated fuels lower carbon monoxide levels in the exhaust.

Too much ethanol in a fuel system can harm engine components. Most manufacturers recommend a maximum of 10 percent of ethanol in any fuel.

Gasoline and ethanol will mix. However, gasoline and water will not mix. The gasoline will float on water, forming two layers.

Add water to a gasoline sample that contains ethanol. Now the ethanol will separate from the gasoline and mix with the water. Two layers will again form. The gasoline without the ethanol will float on the mixture of water and ethanol.

Apply It!

Measuring the Ethanol Content of Gasoline

Meets NATEF Science Standards for safety and proper waste disposal.

Materials and Equipment
- 10 ml gasoline
- Eyedropper
- Graduated cylinder with a stopper
- Eye protection

You will use a very small sample (10 ml) of gasoline for this test. Make sure you use gasoline containing ethanol. Before you start, review all of the "Safety First" alerts in this chapter.

Safety First

Personal Safety Use eye protection. Gasoline is very flammable. Keep your sample away from sparks or flames. Be careful not to spill any of your sample.

1. Place the gasoline in the graduated cylinder.

2. Using the eyedropper, add 2 ml of water to the sample.

3. Shake the sample for one minute. Gently remove the stopper several times during this procedure to release pressure.

4. Two layers should now be visible in the cylinder. The bottom layer is ethanol and water, while the upper layer is the gasoline.

5. You added 2 ml of water to the cylinder. Now subtract 2 ml from the measured depth of the bottom layer of water and ethanol. The result is the amount of ethanol. Multiply this number by 10. This is the percentage of ethanol in the original sample.

6. Properly dispose of your sample according to OSHA and EPA guidelines.

Gaseous Fuels

Some engines are designed to run on gaseous fuels, such as liquefied petroleum gas (LPG) or compressed natural gas (CNG). Under pressure, petroleum gas turns into a liquid. Upon release of pressure, the liquid turns back to a gas. CNG is not a liquid. It is natural gas in a compressed state.

An advantage of LPG or CNG is that both have an octane rating over 100. LPG and CNG also burn cleanly. Clean combustion results in reduced exhaust emissions. Gaseous fuels also have disadvantages. They provide less fuel economy. They require a heavy tank capable of holding a high pressure. They also need special injection equipment to meter the fuel into the engine.

TECH TIP Tailpipe Clues. The tailpipe of an engine operating at a stoichiometric ratio will be clean, with only a light gray or tan coloration. Sooty deposits result from rich air/fuel mixtures. Black, oily deposits result from excess oil consumption.

Air/Fuel Ratio

As engine demands and loads change, the fuel system must maintain a proper air/fuel ratio. See **Fig. 6-5.** The **air/fuel ratio** is the proportion of air and fuel, by weight, supplied to the engine's cylinders for combustion. Fifteen pounds of air to one pound of fuel is an example of the ratio of air to fuel by weight. This is written as 15:1.

The ideal air/fuel ratio is the stoichiometric ratio of 14.7:1. The **stoichiometric ratio** provides the most efficient combustion, giving the chemically correct mixture of air to fuel. If the ratio is lower (14:1, for example), there is too much fuel for the available air. If the ratio is higher (16:1, for example), there is excess air (or a shortage of fuel).

Most vehicles manufactured since 1981 use a computer to maintain the stoichiometric ratio. This allows the catalytic converter to be most efficient in lowering exhaust pollutants.

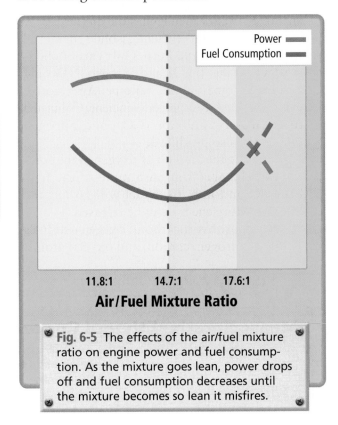

Air/Fuel Mixture Ratio

11.8:1   14.7:1   17.6:1

Fig. 6-5 The effects of the air/fuel mixture ratio on engine power and fuel consumption. As the mixture goes lean, power drops off and fuel consumption decreases until the mixture becomes so lean it misfires.

SECTION 1 KNOWLEDGE CHECK

1. Why should gasoline contain antioxidants?

2. What is volatility?

3. What do R and M represent in relation to octane?

4. What number is posted on the pumps at service stations?

5. What is one advantage of LPG or CNG?

6. If 13.5 pounds of air and 1 pound of fuel are supplied to the engine cylinders, what is the air/fuel ratio?

ASE TEST PREP

7. Technician A says that the stoichiometric ratio provides the most efficient combustion. Technician B says that the stoichiometric ratio gives the chemically correct mixture of air to fuel. Who is correct?

   ⓐ Technician A.

   ⓑ Technician B.

   ⓒ Both Technician A and Technician B.

   ⓓ Neither Technician A nor Technician B.

Section 2
The Combustion Process

Objectives:
- Identify the four factors affecting combustion.
- Identify the characteristics and causes of detonation.

Vocabulary:
- vacuum
- absolute pressure
- detonation

Factors Affecting Combustion

A hydrocarbon fuel and oxygen combine and burn during the combustion process. The burning gases get as hot as several thousand degrees. This high temperature causes the gases in the cylinder to expand very rapidly. This creates a high pressure that forces the piston down in the cylinder.

The combustion of the air/fuel mixture is affected by the following factors:
- Atmospheric air pressure.
- Manifold absolute pressure.
- Humidity.
- Air temperature.

Atmospheric Air Pressure

At sea level and average temperature, a cubic foot of air weighs about 1.25 ounces [35.44 grams]. The total weight of thousands of cubic feet of air pressing down on the earth is about 14.7 psi [101 kPa] at sea level.

Atmospheric pressure is called barometric pressure. Barometric pressure is affected by altitude and weather conditions. As the altitude increases, the barometric pressure decreases. For example, the barometric pressure can be lower in Denver, Colorado, than it is in Los Angeles, California.

High- and low-pressure weather fronts affect barometric pressure. When a low-pressure storm front moves into an area, the barometric pressure usually drops below 29.92″ [101 kPa]. As the low-pressure front moves out, a high-pressure front replaces it. A high-pressure front can increase barometric pressure above 29.92″ [101 kPa].

On any given day, the barometric pressure is constantly changing. The engine's fuel management system must continually adjust to these changing conditions.

The lower the barometric pressure, the lower the air density. Lower air density needs less fuel for complete combustion. Higher air density needs more fuel for complete combustion. Computer-controlled engines have barometric sensors to change the air/fuel mixture as the barometric pressure changes.

Manifold Absolute Pressure

A **vacuum** is a measurement of air pressure that is less than atmospheric pressure. When a piston moves down in a cylinder, the piston creates a partial vacuum, drawing air and fuel into the cylinder. An engine that uses vacuum in this manner is a normally aspirated engine.

The difference between atmospheric pressure and a partial vacuum is **absolute pressure**. Engines measure this difference with a manifold absolute pressure (MAP) sensor.

Throttle opening and engine load affect manifold pressure. A closed-throttle idle may produce a MAP reading as low as 5 psi. A wide-open throttle condition may produce a MAP reading of about 14 psi.

TECH TIP   Barometric Pressure. Barometric pressure also affects the MAP reading. For each 1,000′ [305 m] above sea level, the MAP reading decreases about 1″ [2.54 cm] of mercury.

Humidity

Humidity is measured as a percentage of relative water vapor. Air holding no water vapor has a relative humidity of 0 percent. Air that is completely saturated with water vapor has a relative humidity of 100 percent. A relative humidity reading of 50 percent means the air is holding half as much water as it can hold. An engine running in humid air requires slightly less fuel than an engine running in dry air.

Air Temperature

An increase in air temperature decreases the density of the air. A decrease in air temperature increases the density of the air. The density of the air affects the air/fuel ratio. Dense air requires more fuel.

Abnormal Combustion

During normal combustion, the flame front travels gradually across the combustion chamber. A gasoline with good anti-knock quality produces a smooth pressure rise in the cylinder. See **Fig. 6-6(a)**.

Figure 6-6(b) also shows a form of abnormal combustion known as detonation or spark knock. The flame starts across the combustion chamber. However, before the flame reaches the far side, a portion of the mixture explodes rather than burns. The two flame fronts meet, producing a very rapid pressure rise. The result is a high-pitched metallic pinging noise called **detonation**. A low-octane fuel or a high compression ratio can cause detonation.

The sudden power shocks of detonation can damage an engine. Damaged pistons, rings, and spark plugs are the most frequent result of prolonged (or frequent) detonation.

Safety First

Carbon Monoxide Carbon monoxide is a poisonous gas. It is invisible, it has no odor, and it has no taste.

Avoid working on vehicles in enclosed, unventilated spaces while a vehicle's engine is running. Make sure all engine exhaust is properly and completely vented from the workspace. Attach a length of heat-resistant flexible tubing over the opening of the exhaust pipe(s) of the vehicle. Route the tubing to the outside through a window or suitable opening. Make sure the tubing is attached whenever the engine is operating.

To further reduce the possibility of carbon monoxide poisoning, be sure that your workspace is properly ventilated.

Symptoms of carbon monoxide poisoning include drowsiness, dizziness, headache, and nausea.

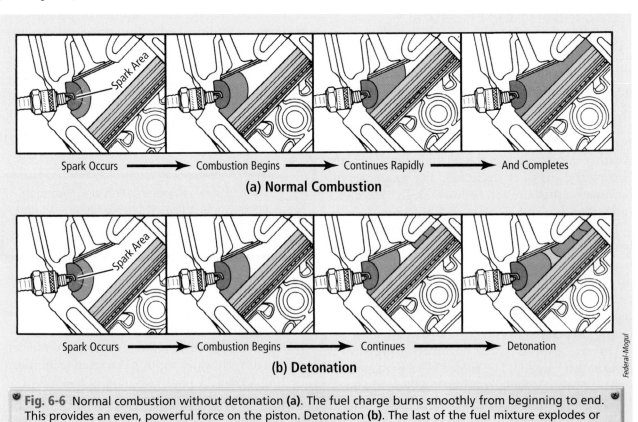

Spark Occurs → Combustion Begins → Continues Rapidly → And Completes

(a) Normal Combustion

Spark Occurs → Combustion Begins → Continues → Detonation

(b) Detonation

Federal-Mogul

Fig. 6-6 Normal combustion without detonation **(a)**. The fuel charge burns smoothly from beginning to end. This provides an even, powerful force on the piston. Detonation **(b)**. The last of the fuel mixture explodes or burns almost instantly to produce detonation (or spark knock). *What can detonation do to an engine?*

Composition of Exhaust Gases

When complete combustion occurs, all the hydrogen and carbon in the fuel combines with oxygen. The resulting exhaust contains only water (H_2O), carbon dioxide (CO_2), and nitrogen (N).

These are basically harmless compounds. But fuel combustion is not always complete, so products of incomplete combustion occur.

Fuel that does not burn completely produces unburned hydrocarbons (HC) and carbon monoxide (CO). In addition, the high temperature of combustion (over 3,000°F [1,650°C]), forms nitrogen oxides (NO_x). See **Fig. 6-7.**

Carbon monoxide is a poisonous gas. Unburned hydrocarbons and nitrogen oxides combine chemically in the presence of sunlight to form smog. Various federal, state, and local agencies regulate the emission of all three of these gases.

There are federal and state emission control requirements. Some state legal emission requirements may be stricter than federal requirements. Emission control problems can be detected in several ways. Constant illumination of the MIL signals an emission system malfunction. Emission control problems are typically checked by an analysis of tailpipe emissions. This is followed by an inspection of emission control components. These components include the MIL, the EGR valve, and the gas cap.

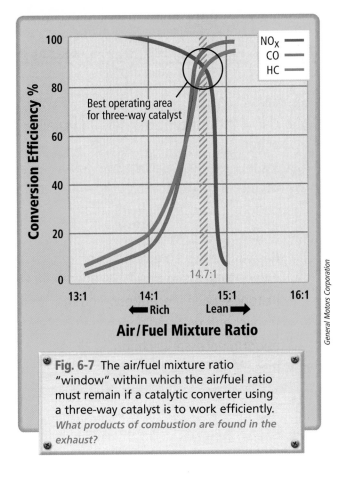

General Motors Corporation

Fig. 6-7 The air/fuel mixture ratio "window" within which the air/fuel ratio must remain if a catalytic converter using a three-way catalyst is to work efficiently. *What products of combustion are found in the exhaust?*

SECTION 2 KNOWLEDGE CHECK

1. What four factors affect combustion?

2. How will an engine's air/fuel mixture adjust to the weather of a stormy day? Why?

3. A car has traveled to the top of a 2,000′ mountain. How will this altitude affect its MAP reading?

4. How will an engine's air/fuel mixture adjust to cooler weather temperatures?

5. What can prolonged or frequent detonation cause?

6. How can you eliminate exhaust fumes in your work environment?

ASE TEST PREP

7. Technician A says that detonation can be caused by a low compression ratio. Technician B says that detonation can be caused by a high compression ratio. Who is correct?
   - **ⓐ** Technician A.
   - **ⓑ** Technician B.
   - **ⓒ** Both Technician A and Technician B.
   - **ⓓ** Neither Technician A nor Technician B.

Section 3
The Fuel Management System

Objectives:

D2 ● Check fuel for contaminants and quality; determine necessary action.

D3 ● Inspect and test mechanical and electrical fuel pumps and pump control systems for pressure, regulation and volume; perform necessary action.

D4 ● Replace fuel filters.

A3 ● Research applicable vehicle and service information, such as engine management system operation, vehicle service history, service precautions, and technical service bulletins.

D5 ● Inspect and test cold enrichment system and components; perform necessary action.

D7 ● Inspect and test fuel injectors.

Vocabulary:
● inertia switch
● fuel pressure regulator
● pulse width
● closed-loop operation

The Fuel Supply System

The fuel management system consists of two subsystems. See **Fig. 6-8.** These are the fuel supply and fuel metering systems. The fuel supply system delivers fuel from the fuel tank to the fuel metering system. The fuel metering system mixes air and fuel and delivers this mixture to the cylinders.

The fuel supply system consists of several basic parts: the fuel tank, fuel pump, fuel filter, fuel pressure regulator, fuel lines, fuel rails, and vapor recovery system.

Fuel Tank

The fuel tank is a dome-shaped tank that holds the fuel. It is made of metal or plastic and contains the fuel pump, the fuel level sensor, and a portion of the vapor recovery system.

The fuel tank cap has a valve that prevents excessive buildup of pressure or vacuum in the fuel tank. Warm temperatures increase fuel vapor pressure. Cool temperatures decrease pressure, creating a vacuum.

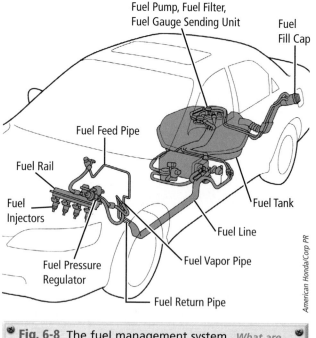

Fuel Pump, Fuel Filter, Fuel Gauge Sending Unit

Fuel Fill Cap

Fuel Feed Pipe

Fuel Rail

Fuel Injectors

Fuel Pressure Regulator

Fuel Tank

Fuel Line

Fuel Vapor Pipe

Fuel Return Pipe

American Honda/Corp PR

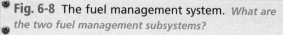

Fig. 6-8 The fuel management system. *What are the two fuel management subsystems?*

Fuel Pump

The fuel pump and fuel sensor are combined as a unit, or module. This module is located inside the fuel tank. The pump in the tank allows it to pressurize the fuel in the fuel lines. See **Fig. 6-9.** The pressurized fuel cannot vaporize in the fuel lines. This reduces the occurrence of vapor lock.

When the ignition switch is turned on, the powertrain control module (PCM) activates the fuel pump relay for a few seconds. The relay supplies power to the fuel pump, which runs briefly to build pressure in the fuel system.

When the engine cranks and starts, the PCM receives an ignition reference, or "tach," signal. This signal tells the PCM that the engine is running. The PCM keeps the fuel pump relay closed and the fuel pump running. On some vehicles, the oil pressure switch serves as a backup to the fuel pump relay. If the relay does not close as it should, the oil pressure switch supplies voltage to the fuel pump when the oil pressure becomes about 2–4 psi [14–28 kPa].

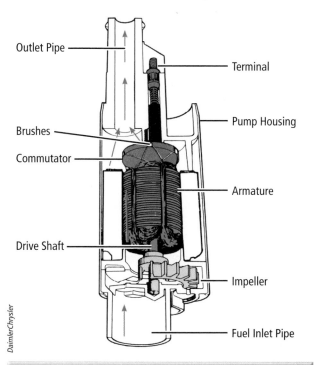

Fig. 6-9 Cutaway of a typical in-tank electric fuel pump. *Why are most fuel pumps located in the fuel tank?*

Some vehicles have an inertia switch in the fuel pump circuit. See **Fig. 6-10.** The **inertia switch** is a switch that disables the fuel pump in the event of an accident. This action prevents fuel from spraying from a broken fuel line.

If accidentally bumped, the inertia switch can disable the fuel pump circuit. The switch must be reset before the fuel pump will operate. The vehicle service manual describes the location and reset procedure for the inertia switch.

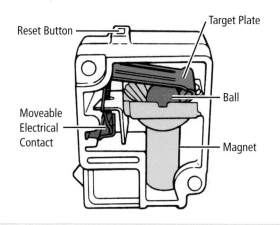

Fig. 6-10 Construction of an inertia switch. During a collision, the ball dislodges from its seat and opens the fuel pump circuit. *Why are inertia switches used?*

Safety First **Fuel Systems** When working on a fuel system, avoid creating any sparks when releasing fuel. A spark can ignite gasoline vapors. An explosion or fire could result in serious injury. After completing repairs, double-check the fuel system for leaks. A small fuel leak can cause a fire or explosion.

Residual Fuel Pressure When a vehicle is shut off, the fuel pump maintains residual pressure in the fuel system. This pressure must be safely released before performing any work on the fuel system. These are the recommended safety practices to follow when removing fuel filters or other fuel system parts.

- Before disconnecting any fuel line, assume that it is pressurized. To prevent personal injury and property damage, follow the manufacturer's recommended procedures.
- Remove the negative battery cable to eliminate the potential for sparks.
- Remove the fuel tank cap to release pressure in the tank. Fuel expansion causes pressure in the fuel tank.

- Some systems are equipped with a Schrader valve. Attach a fuel pressure tester to the Schrader valve, following the manufacturer's procedures. Use the volume release valve on the tester to relieve pressure in the fuel system.
- Many systems do not have a Schrader valve. In these cases, manufacturers recommend removing the fuel tank cap and loosening a fuel line fitting. Cover the fitting with a shop towel to absorb any released fuel.
- You may need special tools to remove fuel filters or fuel lines. Consult the vehicle service manual before attempting any removal or repair.

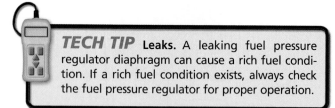

TECH TIP **Leaks.** A leaking fuel pressure regulator diaphragm can cause a rich fuel condition. If a rich fuel condition exists, always check the fuel pressure regulator for proper operation.

Testing the Fuel Pump Fuel pumps must supply fuel at a specified pressure and volume. Follow the manufacturer's procedures when performing fuel pressure and fuel volume tests.

- Pressure and volume can be measured by connecting a fuel pressure gauge to the fuel system. See **Fig. 6-11**.
- System design will determine where the fuel gauge should be connected. If a Schrader valve is present, connect the gauge to it.
- Connecting a pressure gauge to a system without a Schrader valve will require special adapters. It is best to connect the gauge at the inlet on the fuel rail.

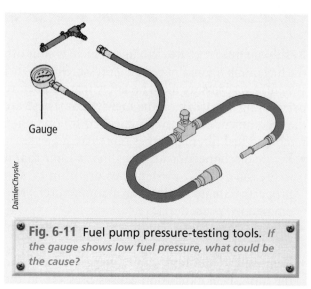

DaimlerChrysler

Gauge

Fig. 6-11 Fuel pump pressure-testing tools. *If the gauge shows low fuel pressure, what could be the cause?*

- Vehicle service manuals provide modulated and unmodulated fuel pressure specifications. Modulated fuel pressure is checked with the fuel pressure regulator enabled. Unmodulated fuel pressure is checked with the fuel pressure regulator disabled. Modulated pressure should be lower than unmodulated pressure. A pinched fuel line, clogged fuel filter, or worn fuel pump can cause low fuel pressure.

It may be possible to use a test valve on the pressure gauge to test fuel volume. Depending upon the system configuration, you may have to connect a jumper wire to the fuel pump lead, or cycle the ignition switch to run the fuel pump. With the fuel pump operating, open the test valve. Discharge the fuel into a graduated container. See **Fig. 6-12**. Remove the fuel pump jumper wire when finished.

Fuel volume is measured by observing the amount of fuel discharged over a specified period of time. The vehicle's service manual will provide procedures and specifications.

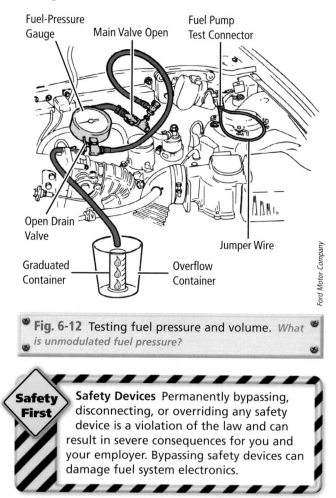

Fuel-Pressure Gauge

Main Valve Open

Fuel Pump Test Connector

Open Drain Valve

Graduated Container

Overflow Container

Jumper Wire

Ford Motor Company

Fig. 6-12 Testing fuel pressure and volume. *What is unmodulated fuel pressure?*

Safety First **Safety Devices** Permanently bypassing, disconnecting, or overriding any safety device is a violation of the law and can result in severe consequences for you and your employer. Bypassing safety devices can damage fuel system electronics.

Fuel Filters

The fuel filters prevent contaminants from entering the fuel system and clogging the fuel injectors. Fuel contamination can cause erratic injector operation, poor engine performance and driveability problems.

The fuel system contains several filters. A paper-type fuel filter, located in the fuel line between the fuel pump and fuel injectors, prevents dirt and other contaminants from entering the fuel system. See **Fig. 6-13**. These filters can become clogged and must be serviced.

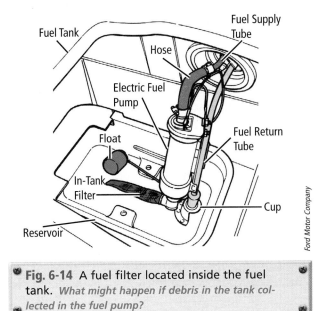

Ford Motor Company

Fig. 6-14 A fuel filter located inside the fuel tank. *What might happen if debris in the tank collected in the fuel pump?*

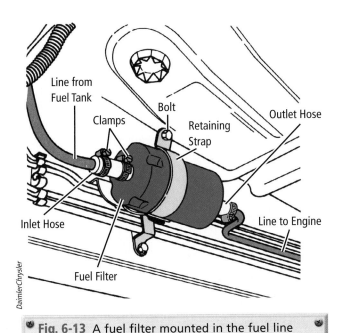

DaimlerChrysler

Fig. 6-13 A fuel filter mounted in the fuel line between the fuel tank and the fuel injectors. *Why do fuel-injected vehicles have several fuel filters?*

Some filters are located in the fuel tank as part of the fuel pump and fuel-level sensor module. See **Fig. 6-14**. These filters protect the fuel pump. They prevent debris, which may collect in the fuel tank, from getting to the pump. These filters seldom require service.

Dirt or debris in the fuel can damage injectors. To diagnose fuel contamination, examine the contents of the fuel filter. Rusty residue indicates the presence of water. Dark, grainy residue shows that the fuel contains dirt. If the filter continues to clog, you may need to clean or replace the fuel tank.

Fuel Pressure Regulator

The **fuel pressure regulator** is a spring-loaded valve built into the fuel pump or the throttle body. It maintains a constant pressure drop across the injectors. Multiport fuel injection (MFI) systems locate the regulator on the fuel rail. See **Fig. 6-15**.

The pressure regulator maintains the correct fuel pressure by allowing unneeded fuel to return to the fuel tank through a fuel return line. The return line must be unrestricted to prevent excess fuel system pressure.

If the pressure regulator is part of the fuel pump assembly, excess fuel returns directly to the fuel tank. Because it has no external fuel return line, this system is called a single-line fuel system.

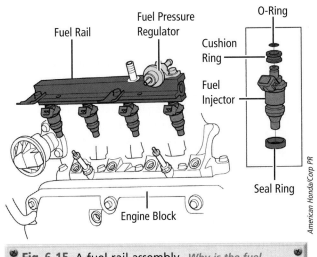

American Honda/Corp PR

Fig. 6-15 A fuel rail assembly. *Why is the fuel pressure regulator on the fuel rail?*

The best fuel economy and lowest exhaust emissions require very accurate regulation of the fuel pressure. See **Fig. 6-16.** Too much fuel pressure makes the air/fuel mixture too rich. An overly rich condition causes loss of power, poor fuel economy, and high exhaust emissions. Too little fuel pressure makes the air/fuel mixture too lean. This will cause hard starting, hesitation, stalling, and loss of power.

Causes of low fuel pressure include a low fuel level in the tank, a clogged fuel filter, a faulty fuel pressure regulator, a restricted fuel line, or a defective fuel pump.

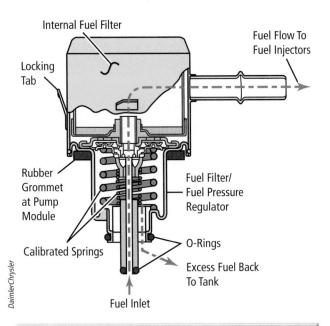

DaimlerChrysler

Fig. 6-16 A typical one-piece fuel filter/regulator. *What problems might result from too much fuel pressure?*

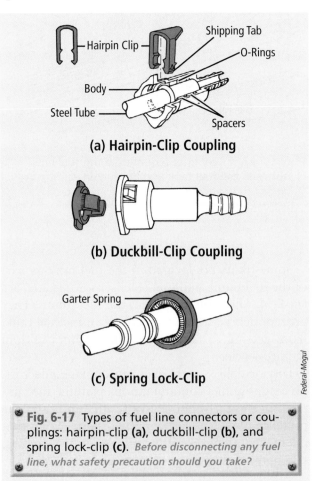

Safety First **Fuel Filter Removal** You will need special tools to remove some fuel filters.

Attempting to remove fuel filters without the correct tools may damage the fuel line connectors, cause a potential fuel leak, and create the risk of fire. When changing a fuel filter, follow the manufacturer's recommended procedures for bleeding pressure from the fuel line. Opening pressurized fuel lines will cause gasoline to spray from the fuel line fitting.

Fuel Lines

The fuel lines transfer fuel from the fuel tank to the throttle body or the fuel rails. Fuel lines are made of plastic, nylon, rubber, or metal. They are also called hoses, tubing, or pipes. A hose is flexible. Tubing may be flexible or rigid. Pipe is usually rigid.

Long fuel lines are usually rigid and made of nylon or steel. The fuel lines must be well supported and must not rub against sharp corners. They should not be kinked or bent unnecessarily. Replace a damaged fuel line. Use a tube bender if you need to shape metal tubing. Nylon fuel lines can be damaged by heat. Protect nylon lines or remove them from the vehicle if grinding, heating, or welding will be done nearby.

Check all fuel hoses for cracks, leaks, and hardness. Hoses deteriorate with time. They should be checked on a regular basis.

Fuel lines have many different types of couplers or connectors. These connectors are found wherever fuel lines are connected, such as in-line fuel filters and fuel rails. See **Fig. 6-17.** Servicing, cutting, shaping, and flaring fuel lines and connectors may require special tools.

Federal-Mogul

Fig. 6-17 Types of fuel line connectors or couplings: hairpin-clip **(a)**, duckbill-clip **(b)**, and spring lock-clip **(c)**. *Before disconnecting any fuel line, what safety precaution should you take?*

Fuel Rails

Fuel rails are found in multiport fuel injection systems. They are an extension of the fuel lines. The fuel rails provide fuel to each injector.

Vapor Recovery System

The vapor recovery system transfers fuel vapors (evaporative emissions) from the fuel tank to an evaporative emissions (EVAP) canister. The EVAP canister stores the vapors until they are burned in the engine. This system is part of a vehicle's emission control system.

Fuel Metering System

The fuel metering system is the second part of the fuel management system. The fuel metering system mixes air and fuel and delivers this mixture to the cylinders. The metering system consists of the powertrain control module (PCM), a network of sensors, and the fuel injectors. See **Fig. 6-18.**

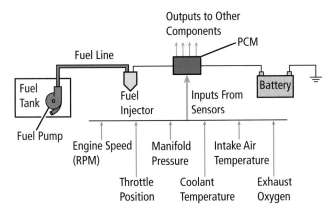

Fig. 6-18 A simplified schematic of an electronic fuel injection system. Sensors (bottom) provide information, or input, to the PCM. The PCM then determines the amount of fuel needed and opens the fuel injector to produce the required air/fuel ratio. *What components are part of the fuel metering system?*

Electronic Fuel Injection

With electronic fuel injection, the PCM controls fuel delivery by controlling injector pulse width. **Pulse width** is the duration in milliseconds that the injector is open. Most vehicles use one of two types of electronic fuel injection (EFI) systems, throttle body or multi-port.

Multiport Fuel Injection The multiport fuel injection system (MFI) has one fuel injector for each cylinder. By injecting fuel directly into the intake port, the MFI system provides a metered amount of fuel to each cylinder.

Multiport systems provide more control of the air/fuel mixture than do throttle body systems. As a result, multiport systems produce lower emissions, while increasing the power output of the engine. Multiport fuel injection systems may be pulsed in banked or sequential order. See **Fig. 6-19.**

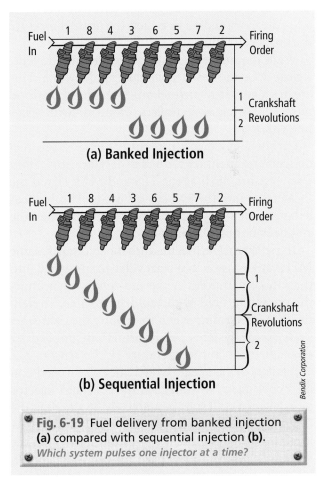

(a) Banked Injection

(b) Sequential Injection

Fig. 6-19 Fuel delivery from banked injection **(a)** compared with sequential injection **(b)**. *Which system pulses one injector at a time?*

Banked Multiport Fuel Injection A banked multiport fuel injection (MFI) system pulses the injectors in separate sets. Banked MFIs injectors on a four-cylinder engine pulse in sets of two. A six-cylinder engine pulses in sets of three. An eight-cylinder engine pulses in sets of four. Banked injection pulses one set of injectors for each revolution of the engine.

With banked injection, each injector delivers only one-half the required amount of fuel per pulse.

Because the injector pulses twice per cycle, it delivers the correct amount of fuel.

Sequential Multiport Fuel Injection In a sequential multiport fuel injection (SFI) system, the fuel injectors are pulsed individually in the firing order of the engine's cylinders. Each injector pulses once every two crankshaft revolutions. All the fuel needed is delivered during that one pulse. Since each injector is individually pulsed, fuel metering is more accurate than with banked injection.

When engine sensors indicate that the throttle is being opened, the PCM may add asynchronous pulses. The asynchronous (not synchronized) pulses do not follow the normal timing sequence. The PCM adds the extra pulses to richen the air/fuel mixture during acceleration.

While the engine is cranking at wide-open throttle, a clear flood mode sharply reduces pulse width. This creates a very lean air/fuel mixture. The clear flood mode clears engine cylinders "flooded" with gasoline vapors.

On some engines, a fuel cut-off mode stops fuel delivery momentarily during deceleration. Data from sensors, such as the TPS and MAP, signal the PCM to go into the fuel cut-off mode. This reduces exhaust emissions and fuel consumption when the engine is not producing power.

To richen the air/fuel mixture for cold starts, some MFI systems use a cold-start valve to spray fuel into the intake manifold. A thermo-time switch limits the operating time of the cold-start valve. To help the PCM determine when to operate the cold-start valve, some systems use information supplied by the engine coolant temperature (ECT) sensor.

A failure of this system would cause a lean condition on a cold start. No voltage at the cold start injector or valve on a cold start would likely be a fault in the necessary inputs or output of the PCM or the PCM itself. If voltage is present at the cold start valve, the valve would have to be tested for proper operation using the manufacturer's recommended procedures.

Powertrain Control Module

The powertrain control module (PCM) controls fuel injector pulse width. The pulses are timed by a triggering signal from the ignition system. The triggering signal occurs so that injection begins at the proper time. Because the fuel sprays through the injector under high pressure, fuel injectors are pulsed for only a few thousandths of a second. One-thousandth of a second is a millisecond. A fuel injector may have a pulse width of only 2 milliseconds at idle. The pulse width at full throttle may be more than 7 milliseconds. See **Fig. 6-20.**

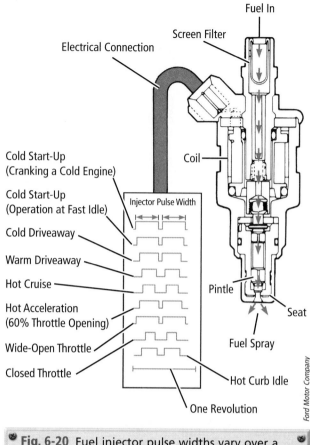

Fig. 6-20 Fuel injector pulse widths vary over a range of engine operation. The longer the pulse width, the greater the amount of fuel injected into the cylinder.

By calculating a specific pulse width for the fuel injector, the PCM controls the air/fuel mixture. If there is a need for more fuel, the PCM increases the pulse width. If the need for fuel is less, the PCM reduces the pulse width.

The injector pulse width can be measured with some professional grade digital volt ohmmeters (DVOM). To measure these values, follow the instructions included with the DVOM. In many cases, you can also read pulse width with a scan tool.

Closed-loop operation is the operation that occurs when the PCM processes electrical inputs from a network of sensors to control fuel delivery and other actuators. The inputs are variable voltage or variable frequency signals.

The signals supply the data needed for the PCM to calculate the air/fuel mixture ratio. The PCM provides ground to control the fuel injectors supplying fuel to the engine.

Excellence in Math

Calculating Miles Per Gallon

Karl brings his vehicle to your service station. He says he doesn't think his vehicle is getting as many miles per gallons (mpg) as it used to. Karl wants to find out if he is right.

Checkpoint 1. Karl has started to keep a log book. In it he lists the odometer reading and number of gallons he buys each time he fills his gas tank. For the first six fill-ups, he calculated the mpg by counting the number of miles between fill-ups.

- Calculate the number of miles driven between his sixth and seventh fill-ups.

49,098 miles − 48,706 miles = 392 miles

- How many mpg did his car get between his sixth and seventh fill-ups?
- Calculate the mpg. He drove 392 miles and used 15.9 gallons of gas.

$$\frac{392 \text{ miles}}{15.9 \text{ gal}} = 24.7 \text{ mpg}$$

Checkpoint 2. Karl wants to know his average mpg for the time he kept his log book. You add the seven mpg figures and divide the total by the number of items you have added (seven) to find the average.

- The sum of the seven numbers is 181.6. The average mpg is:

$$\frac{181.6}{7} = 25.9 \text{ mpg}$$

Note that the average value of a set of numbers is also called the arithmetic mean. The middle value of a set of numbers is called the median.

- Rank the seven mpg values from the largest to the smallest. The median, or middle, value is 26.3 mpg. Karl's vehicle performed better than the median three times. It had lower mileage than the median three times.

You notice that the mpg calculations for the sixth and seventh fill-ups seem low. You ask Karl to keep the log book for two more fill-ups. You will be able see what mileage he gets then.

	Odometer reading	Miles between fill-ups	Gallons purchased	MPG
	46,415			
1	46,830	415	15.6	26.6
2	47,232	402	15.3	26.3
3	47,620	388	15.1	25.7
4	48,043	423	15.9	26.6
5	48,482	439	16.4	26.8
6	48,706	224	9.0	24.9
7	49,098		15.9	

Apply It!

Meets NATEF Mathematics Standards for finding the mean and median and for using addition, subtraction, and division.

Karl returns with figures from his eighth and ninth fill-ups. He bought 15.8 gal. of gas at 49,484 miles and 15.6 gal. of gas at 49,862 miles.

1. How many mpg did the vehicle get for these two fill-ups?

2. Calculate the overall average mpg for the nine fill-ups. Find the average of all nine mpg figures.

3. You can also find the overall average by dividing the total number of miles driven by the total number of gallons of gas used. Try this method. Compare your answers. Your answer should be very close to the first number you calculated. Rounding will account for any difference.

4. Recalculate the median mpg value for the nine fill-ups. You should calculate 25.7 mpg for the median. This value is lower than the median was for the first seven fill-ups. What does this indicate about the performance of Karl's vehicle?

5. Why might calculating the overall mpg the second way cause you to miss a possibly important clue about the vehicle's performance?

The Fuel Injector

The fuel injector is a solenoid-operated valve. It is controlled by the PCM. Because the PCM controls the fuel injector, it is considered an actuator.

The PCM provides a ground connection for the injector circuit. Pulse width is controlled by turning the ground circuit on and off.

When the PCM driver circuit grounds the injector circuit, current flows through the fuel injector coil. A magnetic field pulls the injector armature against the closing spring. As the armature moves, the pintle valve pulls away from the pintle seat. See **Fig. 6-21.** As the injector pintle valve opens, the fuel passes through the nozzle in a fine, cone-shaped spray pattern.

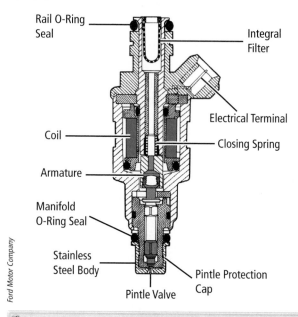

Ford Motor Company

Rail O-Ring Seal
Integral Filter
Coil
Electrical Terminal
Armature
Closing Spring
Manifold O-Ring Seal
Stainless Steel Body
Pintle Protection Cap
Pintle Valve

Fig. 6-21 A cutaway view of an electronic fuel injector. *What part of a fuel injector creates a magnetic field?*

When the injection cycle is completed, the PCM driver opens the ground connection to the circuit. With the ground circuit open, current stops flowing through the injector coil. The pintle valve closes against the pintle seat, and fuel stops flowing through the injector.

The shape of the spray pattern and amount of fuel injected can be affected in many ways. Dirt, carbon, or varnish can clog the nozzle, making the spray pattern uneven. An uneven fuel spray pattern cannot mix properly with the air. An improper mixture causes poor fuel economy, a loss of power, and an increase in exhaust emissions.

TECH TIP **Cleaning Injectors.** Some injectors can be damaged by injector cleaning solvents. Always check the manufacturer's recommendations before attempting this procedure.

Cleaning Fuel Injectors Deposits on the tip of a fuel injector prevent proper fuel delivery and distort the spray pattern. Rough idle, loss of power, and poor fuel economy may result.

Injectors can be cleaned by a flow of injector-cleaning solvent through them. The solvent removes gum, varnish, and other deposits. When cleaning fuel injectors, follow these general guidelines:
1. Make sure the engine is at normal operating temperature.
2. Relieve the fuel pressure and disable the fuel pump.
3. Remove and plug the vacuum hose at the pressure-regulator valve.
4. Follow the instructions for the injector-cleaning equipment you are using. Connect a container of injector cleaner to the fuel rail.
5. Start the engine and let it idle until the container is empty and the engine stalls.
6. Remove the container, restore the connections, and start the engine.

Testing Fuel Injectors Fuel injector types vary from vehicle to vehicle. **Figure 6-22** shows a multiport system. However, these general steps can be used to perform a preliminary diagnosis.
1. Visually inspect for:
   • Broken wires.
   • Fuel leakage.
   • Loose connections.
   • Proper seating of the injector housing into the manifold.
2. With the engine running, use a technician's stethoscope to check for a clicking sound in each injector. A bad injector will not have a pronounced clicking noise.
3. With the engine off, remove the electrical connector from the fuel injector. Attach DVOM leads to each of the fuel injector terminals. Compare the resistance reading to the manufacturer's specifications. Remember that high temperatures increase the resistance reading.
4. Some manufacturers require the use of test procedures that evaluate the injector's ability to deliver a uniform amount of fuel (injector balance test). This requires specialized test equipment. See the service manual for details.

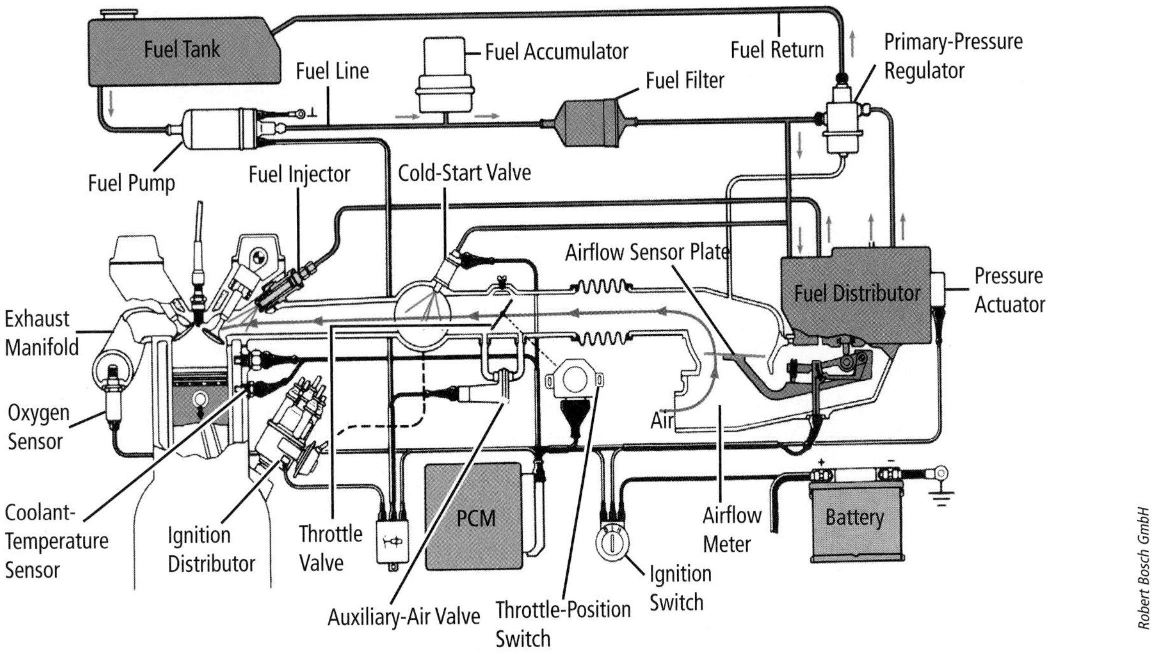

Fuel Tank

Fuel Line

Fuel Accumulator

Fuel Return

Primary-Pressure Regulator

Fuel Filter

Fuel Pump

Fuel Injector

Cold-Start Valve

Airflow Sensor Plate

Fuel Distributor

Pressure Actuator

Exhaust Manifold

Oxygen Sensor

Air

Coolant-Temperature Sensor

Ignition Distributor

Throttle Valve

PCM

Airflow Meter

Battery

Auxiliary-Air Valve

Throttle-Position Switch

Ignition Switch

Robert Bosch GmbH

Fig. 6-22 Schematic layout of the Bosch KE continuous-injection system with an oxygen sensor. *What is the main difference between electronic and mechanical fuel injection systems?*

Replacing Fuel Injectors When replacing a fuel injector, follow procedures provided in the manufacturer's service manual.

Here are general guidelines for replacing a fuel injector.

1. Bleed pressure from the system.
2. Disconnect the negative battery cable.
3. Remove the fuel line and electrical connections to the injector.
4. Remove any hardware holding the injector in place.
5. Carefully remove the injector from the intake manifold.
6. As needed, install new O-rings and washers.
7. Carefully align the new injector in the manifold.
8. Push into position by hand, using thumb pressure to seat the injector.
9. Reconnect the fuel and electrical connections.
10. Replace all attaching hardware.
11. Check for leaks.

Fuel Management Sensors

The PCM uses electronic inputs from a network of sensors on the vehicle to calculate fuel injector pulse width.

Most PCMs supply 5 volts to power the sensor circuits. Technicians refer to this voltage as the reference voltage. The sensors alter the reference voltage and supply it to the PCM as a return-signal. The return-signal is an electrical data stream. The data stream may be in the form of a changing voltage or a changing frequency.

Throttle Position Sensor The throttle position sensor (TPS) sends throttle plate position information to the PCM. See **Fig. 6-23.** As the throttle opens, the return signal voltage from the TPS increases. When the throttle closes, the return-signal voltage decreases.

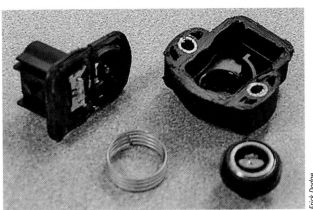

Erick Dodge

Fig. 6-23 A throttle position sensor. *When does the return signal voltage from the TPS increase or decrease?*

The PCM sees the increase in voltage as a need for more fuel. The PCM increases the pulse width signal to the fuel injectors. This provides more fuel.

A decrease in the TPS return signal is seen as a need for less fuel. The PCM decreases the pulse width signal to the fuel injectors. This provides less fuel.

Engine Coolant Temperature Sensor The engine coolant temperature (ECT) sensor is a thermistor type sensor that sends engine coolant temperature information to the PCM. See **Fig. 6-24**. Thermistors change their electrical resistance as the temperature changes. As temperature decreases, the resistance of most thermistors increases. When the thermistor's resistance increases, the return signal voltage decreases, signaling the PCM that the engine is cold.

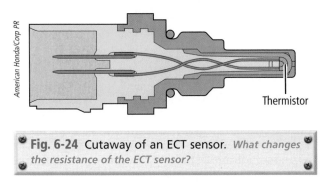

Fig. 6-24 Cutaway of an ECT sensor. *What changes the resistance of the ECT sensor?*

Gasoline does not vaporize well when the engine is cold. A cold engine requires more fuel to start and warm up. When the ECT signals a cold engine, the PCM delivers more fuel by increasing the injector pulse width. As the coolant temperature increases, the PCM reduces injector pulse width, maintaining an appropriate air/fuel ratio.

Intake Air Temperature Sensor The intake air temperature (IAT) is a thermistor type sensor that provides intake air temperature information to the PCM. Cold air is denser and contains more oxygen than warm air. More oxygen requires more fuel to maintain a stoichiometric air/fuel ratio.

As intake air temperature decreases, the PCM increases injector pulse width and supplies more fuel. When air temperature increases, less oxygen is present. The PCM reduces the injector pulse width, decreasing the supply of fuel.

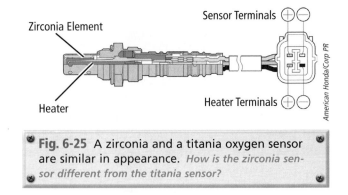

Fig. 6-25 A zirconia and a titania oxygen sensor are similar in appearance. *How is the zirconia sensor different from the titania sensor?*

Oxygen Sensor The oxygen sensor (O2S) provides data showing the amount of oxygen in the exhaust. The PCM uses this data to adjust the air/fuel mixture. Fuel management systems use two types of oxygen sensors. See **Fig. 6-25**.

The zirconia oxygen sensor is the most common design. This design uses a heater to quickly warm it to operating temperature. The zirconia sensor produces its own voltage. At operating temperature, about 600°F (315°C) the sensor produces an output signal of approximately zero to one-volt. A 0.2-volt signal tells the PCM that the exhaust is lean. A 0.8-volt signal tells the PCM that the exhaust is rich.

The titania sensor operates like a resistor. The amount of oxygen in the exhaust changes the sensor's resistance. A high signal from the sensor tells the PCM the exhaust is rich. A low signal from the sensor tells the PCM the exhaust is lean.

Wide-Band Sensor The wide-band air/fuel ratio sensor combines an oxygen-sensing Nernst cell from the narrow-band sensor with an oxygen pump to create a device that gives a wide range response to various air/fuel ratios. The Nernst cell senses exhaust gas oxygen in the same range as a conventional narrow band oxygen sensor. If there is a difference in oxygen levels across the zirconium oxide, or zirconia, sensor element, current flows from one side to the other and produces a voltage.

The wide-band exhaust gas oxygen sensor has many constructional forms. All are basically similar. They consist of two parts: a Nernst reference cell and an oxygen pump cell. They are in a package that contains a reference chamber and heater element. The heater element is used to regulate the temperature of the Nernst cell and the pump. The wide-band sensor operates only in combination with specialized wide-band control circuits that adjust both the pump cell current and the heater.

Manifold Absolute Pressure Sensor The manifold absolute pressure (MAP) sensor provides intake manifold absolute-pressure information. When a vacuum exists in the manifold, absolute pressure is less than atmospheric pressure. Two types of sensors are in use.

The first type produces a voltage signal that changes with the manifold pressure. The high or low signal tells the PCM to decrease or increase the injector pulse width.

The second type produces a frequency signal that changes with manifold pressure. Frequency is measured in cycles per second or hertz. One hertz equals one cycle per second. The signal tells the PCM to decrease or increase the injector pulse width.

Barometric Pressure Sensor The barometric pressure (BARO) sensor measures atmospheric pressure. As atmospheric pressure increases, the oxygen content of the air increases. As oxygen increases, the PCM increases injector pulse width to supply more fuel. When atmospheric pressure decreases, oxygen content decreases. The PCM reduces the injector pulse width to supply less fuel. On some engines barometric pressure is read by the MAP sensor when the ignition switch is first turned ON.

Mass Airflow or Volume Airflow Sensors The mass airflow (MAF) sensor, also called the volume airflow (VAF) sensor, measures the amount of air flowing into the engine. As airflow increases, the PCM increases injector pulse width to supply more fuel. When airflow decreases, the PCM reduces the injector pulse width to supply less fuel.

The MAF sensor measures the volume and density of the air. The VAF sensor measures volume and temperature.

In some closed-loop systems, MAF or VAF sensors replace the MAP sensor. MAF and VAF sensors are direct methods of measuring airflow. MAP systems measure airflow indirectly.

Testing Sensors While you cannot test some sensors directly, a DVOM or Lab Scope can be used to check for normal operation. All sensor circuits can be checked for the presence of a reference voltage. If a reference voltage is not found, follow the procedures that the manufacturer recommends to find the cause. Voltage changes on the return signal wire can be read by using a DVOM or scan tool.

SECTION 3 KNOWLEDGE CHECK

1. What parts of the fuel supply system are found in the fuel tank?

2. What is the function of an inertia switch?

3. Why should the negative battery cable be disconnected before working on the fuel system?

4. What is used to measure fuel pump pressure?

5. How is fuel volume measured?

6. What prevents contaminants from entering the fuel system and clogging fuel injectors?

7. What must be accurately regulated to ensure the best fuel economy and lowest exhaust emissions?

8. On what type of systems would you find a fuel rail?

9. In which type of fuel injection systems are the injectors pulsed individually in the firing order of the engine's cylinders?

ASE TEST PREP

10. Technician A says that the Schrader valve disables the fuel pump in the event of an accident. Technician B says that the fuel pressure regulator disables the fuel pump in the event of an accident. Who is correct?
    ⓐ Technician A.
    ⓑ Technician B.
    ⓒ Both Technician A and Technician B.
    ⓓ Neither Technician A nor Technician B.

11. Technician A says that the engine coolant temperature sensor contains a rheostat. Technician B says that the engine coolant temperature sensor contains a thermistor. Who is correct?
    ⓐ Technician A.
    ⓑ Technician B.
    ⓒ Both Technician A and Technician B.
    ⓓ Neither Technician A nor Technician B.

Engine Performance

CHAPTER 6 REVIEW

Key Points

Meets the following NATEF Standards for Engine Performance: checking fuel for contaminants and quality; fuel filter service.

- Fuel pumps are electrically operated and supply fuel under pressure to the fuel metering system.
- Correct fuel pressure and fuel volume are vital to proper engine operation.
- Fuel contamination can be determined by examining the residue of fuel filters.
- Multiple fuel filters are found on fuel injected vehicles. Some are located in the tank; some are located in the fuel line.
- Fuel injectors can be tested by checking the resistance of the injector coil or by performing an injector balance test.
- A properly operating fuel injector produces a cone-shaped spray pattern.
- An oxygen sensor indicates the amount of oxygen in the exhaust.
- MAF and VAF sensors provide a direct method of measuring airflow.

Review Questions

1. What is the purpose of a filter inside a fuel tank?
2. Name three types of fuel line connectors or couplings.
3. What is an EVAP?
4. What is the purpose of the fuel metering system?
5. What does a cold-start valve do?
6. What is the first step in cleaning fuel injectors?
7. What is the final step in replacing a fuel injector?
8. What is the purpose of the throttle position sensor?
9. What two types of oxygen sensors are used in fuel management systems?
10. **Critical Thinking** What effect may a low fuel level in the tank have on fuel pressure?

Excellence in Communication

Searching a Database

Experience was once the only source of information for mechanics. Vehicle systems were very simple. Anyone with mechanical knowledge could learn to fix a vehicle. Using trial-and-error methods may have wasted some time, but the job was usually done correctly.

With new developments, technical knowledge grew. Previously, one service manual may have been used for a manufacturer's whole line of automobiles. Now there are one or more service manuals per vehicle.

To keep up with the expanding field of automotive technology, computers are now used in dealership service areas. Computer databases provide the same material found in service manuals. Many of these databases can be found in CD-ROM format. Using this electronic service information (ESI) you can quickly and easily locate the information you require.

Many manufacturers also have Web sites that contain much useful information.

Apply It!

Meets NATEF Communications Standards for using databases and manuals to obtain system information.

1. Choose a service manual for a specific vehicle model. Locate the section that deals with how to diagnose fuel supply problems for that vehicle.

2. Use a computer to begin your search in one of the following ways:

   a. Use a manufacturer's CD-ROM database to find the information you need. Locate the section that deals with how to diagnose the fuel system for the vehicle.

   b. Perform an on-line search on the Internet. Select a search engine and look for information using key words or phrases.

3. Compare the information in the service manual with what you located on the manufacturer's database or on the Internet.

AUTOMOTIVE SERVICE EXCELLENCE
TEST PREP

Answering the following practice questions will help you prepare for the ASE certification tests.

1. Which of the following would one expect to find in a quality fuel?

    a Proper volatility.

    b Antioxidants.

    c Detergents.

    d All of the above.

2. Technician A says the higher the octane rating of the gasoline, the less likely it is to detonate. Technician B says the higher the octane rating of the gasoline the more likely it is to detonate. Who is correct?

    a Technician A.

    b Technician B.

    c Both Technician A and Technician B.

    d Neither Technician A nor Technician B.

3. The octane requirements of an engine are dictated by combustion chamber design and by the:

    a number of valves.

    b depth of the spark plug.

    c engine timing.

    d compression ratio.

4. Technician A says that the stoichiometric air/fuel ratio is 16.3:1. Technician B says that the stoichiometric air/fuel ratio is 14.7:1. Who is correct?

    a Technician A.

    b Technician B.

    c Both Technician A and Technician B.

    d Neither Technician A nor Technician B.

5. The difference between atmospheric pressure and a partial vacuum is known as:

    a vacuum.

    b humidity.

    c absolute pressure.

    d barometric pressure.

6. Technician A says that an increase in air temperature decreases the density of air, which requires less fuel. Technician B says that a decrease in air temperature increases the density of air, which requires more fuel. Who is correct?

    a Technician A.

    b Technician B.

    c Both Technician A and Technician B.

    d Neither Technician A nor Technician B.

7. Which of the following is a byproduct of incomplete combustion?

    a H_2O.

    b CO.

    c CO_2.

    d N.

8. Technician A says that when testing pressure in the fuel system, modulated pressure should be lower than unmodulated pressure. Technician B says that modulated pressure should be higher than unmodulated pressure. Who is correct?

    a Technician A.

    b Technician B.

    c Both Technician A and Technician B.

    d Neither Technician A nor Technician B.

9. Serviceable fuel filters may be located:

    a on the fuel rail.

    b in the fuel lines.

    c in the throttle body.

    d all of the above.

10. Technician A says that a visual inspection of fuel injectors should be completed. Technician B says that a digital volt-ohm-meter should be used to test fuel injectors. Who is correct?

    a Technician A.

    b Technician B.

    c Both Technician A and Technician B.

    d Neither Technician A nor Technician B.

Section 1
OBD-II Systems

Section 2
OBD-II Diagnostics

Using Computer Diagnostics

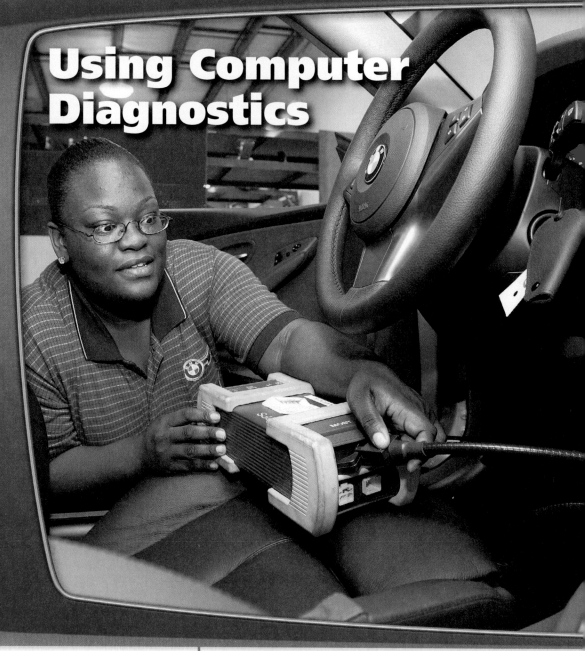

Customer's Concern

Yelena Clarno says her car is jerking and the CHECK ENGINE light will not go out. She says the light came on about a week before the car started jerking. "I sort of ignored the light. I have my car serviced regularly. I figured there should not be anything wrong with it," Yelena reasoned.

As you ask Yelena questions about her car's symptoms, she says the jerking usually occurs when she moves the gearshift to DRIVE. Before she takes her foot off the brake, the car surges or jerks forward. Yelena has also noticed that as she accelerates from a stop to 55 miles per hour, the car jerks three or four more times. "I never thought about it before now, but the jerks seem to coincide with the automatic shifting," Yelena says.

Technician's Challenge

As the service technician, you need to find answers to these questions:

1. When was Yelena's car serviced last? Has the car been serviced by your service center? Are service records available?

2. What could cause the rough shifting and the CHECK ENGINE light to stay on? Can a scan tool assist you with this problem?

3. What kind of OBD-II codes would you expect to see on the scanner screen?

4. How will you proceed with the diagnosis and repair?

Section 1
OBD-II Systems

Objectives:
- Describe the purpose of OBD-II systems.
- Describe the OBD-II system hardware that is used to detect problems.
- Define OBD-II terminology.

Vocabulary:
- diagnostic
- enabling criteria
- warm-up cycle
- drive cycle
- passive test
- active test
- failure record
- trip
- freeze-frame data
- inspection/maintenance (I/M) ready status

Purpose of OBD-II

The abbreviation OBD stands for "on-board diagnostics." OBD-I systems were used on vehicles produced from the early 1980s through the mid-1990s. OBD-I systems were limited in the types of faults they could monitor. They were able to identify only component or system failures. OBD-I could not diagnose emission-related problems resulting from the degradation (slow failure) of components or systems.

OBD-II systems were designed to ensure the accurate monitoring and operation of all emission-related systems and components. OBD-II systems must be able to accurately detect and identify conditions that could increase vehicle emissions by one and one half times the federal standards. OBD-II systems are also able to detect emission-related problems caused by the degradation of systems and components. OBD-II systems monitor the efficiency of catalytic converters. All light-duty gasoline powered vehicles manufactured after 1995 must meet OBD-II requirements. The next generation of this system, OBD-III, is currently under development.

The OBD-II system standardizes the data link connector, basic diagnostic equipment, and diagnostic procedures. Under the Society of Automotive Engineers (SAE) J1930 standards, most diagnostic terms, acronyms, and abbreviations are the same, regardless of the vehicle manufacturer.

Manufacturers may use slightly different components and system designs to control and reduce emissions. These designs may require procedures applicable only to the vehicle being serviced. Always refer to the specific manufacturer's service manuals.

The OBD-II system monitors the following:
- Cylinder misfire.
- Catalytic converter efficiency.
- Fuel trim adjustment.
- Exhaust gas recirculation.
- Evaporative emission control system.
- Secondary air injection.

When a component or system failure occurs with an OBD-I system, a diagnostic trouble code (DTC) is set and the malfunction indicator lamp (MIL) is turned on. OBD-II systems turn on the MIL when a problem causes emission levels to exceed the federal standard limits.

TECH TIP **Performing Interactive Actuator Tests.** Many scanners have a diagnostic mode that allows the technician to manually operate many actuators. Follow manufacturer's directions during such tests.

Excellence in Science

Identifying the Role of a Catalyst

OBD-II systems monitor the efficiency of the catalytic converter. Oxygen sensors measure the oxygen levels going into and out of the converter. Here you will learn about the basic idea of a catalyst.

A catalyst is a chemical material that promotes or encourages a chemical reaction between two other materials. The catalyst itself is not consumed or changed in the reaction.

A vehicle's catalytic converter aids the combining of oxygen with potential pollutants. As a result, fewer polluting chemical compounds are emitted with the other exhaust gases.

The palladium catalyst does not generate oxygen. Palladium is a metallic element. It promotes the further combustion of pollutants with any excess oxygen. The palladium itself is not consumed.

Apply It!

Demonstrating Catalytic Action

Meets NATEF Science Standards for explaining chemical reactions in a catalytic converter.

Materials and Equipment
- Clean, empty, clear plastic beverage bottle
- Large rubber balloon
- Packet of baking yeast
- Hydrogen peroxide, three-percent strength
- Measuring cup
- Measuring spoons
- Funnel
- Masking tape

1. Add approximately ¼ cup of hydrogen peroxide solution of three-percent strength to the empty plastic beverage bottle.

2. Using the funnel, add approximately one teaspoon of yeast to the balloon.

3. Carefully, without spilling any yeast into the bottle, fit the open end of the balloon securely over the open mouth of the bottle.

4. Secure the balloon in place using masking tape.

5. When ready, lift the balloon so that all of the yeast inside the balloon falls into the hydrogen peroxide in the bottle.

6. Swirl the bottle gently to mix the yeast with the hydrogen peroxide.

7. Watch the solution in the bottom of the bottle. The hydrogen peroxide will decompose into water and free oxygen in the presence of a catalyst, called a catalase. Catalase is found in yeast. Although the yeast will become wet from the water, the catalase is still there, unchanged.

8. Record your observations.

9. Watch the balloon. What happens to the balloon as the reaction proceeds?

10. Record your observations.

OBD-II Hardware

OBD-II systems are designed to detect emission-related faults and failures. The diagnostic strategy used for OBD-II is often different from that used for OBD-I. OBD-II adds many new features and technical improvements.

When the engine calibration settings are updated, OBD-I system PCMs with hard-wired programmable read-only memory (PROM) chips must be replaced as a unit. PCMs with a removable PROM need a PROM chip replacement. OBD-II systems use an electrically erasable programmable read-only memory (EEPROM). The EEPROM, also called a flash PROM, is hard-wired into the PCM. The information in the EEPROM can be updated or reprogrammed without replacing the EEPROM.

The data link connector (DLC) for OBD-II is a standardized 16-pin connector. See **Fig. 7-1**. Most of the pin use complies with OBD-II standards. For example, pins 4, 5, 7, and 16 have the same assignments and the same use for all manufacturers.

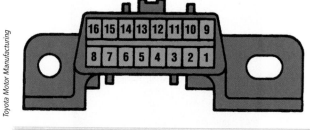

Toyota Motor Manufacturing

Fig. 7-1 The OBD-II DLC is a standardized 16-pin connector. *Where is the DLC located?*

Other pins on the DLC have different uses for specific vehicles or applications. Some pins are used only with original equipment manufacturer's (OEM), or "dedicated," scanners.

On OBD-II vehicles, the location of the DLC is also standardized. The DLC is located under the dash panel near the steering column. Be sure to consult the vehicle service manual for DLC placement. The DLC is indexed to prevent incorrect insertion of the scanner connector. Do not force the scanner connector into the DLC. Look for damage to the DLC, or to its pin connectors. Forcing a connection can result in damage to the DLC or to the scanner connector.

OBD-II Terminology

OBD-II systems use specific standardized terminology. You must learn this terminology before you can understand OBD-II diagnostics. Some of the terms used are:

• **Diagnostic** (also called a monitor)—a procedure used by the PCM to test relevant on-board systems. The MIL will turn on and stay on if the PCM detects a fault occurring on one or two consecutive trips.

• **Enabling criteria**—the sensor inputs supplied during specified driving conditions. They must be received by the PCM before a diagnostic (monitor) can be run. For example, a monitor may require input from the throttle position (TP) sensor, the vehicle speed sensor (VSS), and the mass air flow (MAF) sensor. If any of these sensor inputs are missing, the monitor cannot be run.

• **Warm-up cycle**—the period when the engine coolant temperature rises from ambient temperature to at least 160°F [70°C]. To eliminate false readings from short trips, the temperature must rise at least 40°F [22°C] during a trip.

• **Drive cycle**—a set of driving conditions that "run" all on-board diagnostics. When the monitor is run, the inspection/maintenance (I/M) readiness "flags" will set. The "flag" is an indicator that shows that the monitors have been run. Not all vehicles have I/M flags.

• **Passive test**—a test that checks the performance of a vehicle system or component during normal operation.

• **Active test**—a test that forces a component to operate in a specific way. A scan tool can be used to perform an active test. A valve or solenoid, for example, may intentionally be opened to cause a momentary change in the system. If the PCM doesn't "see" this change occur, it activates the MIL and stores a DTC.

• **Failure record**—may store up to five DTCs in the diagnostic memory. Unlike freeze-frame records, which store only emission-related faults, the failure records store component faults. Multiple DTCs stored in the failure record appear in the order that they occur. These DTCs must be repaired in the order that they occur.

- **Trip**—a key-on, run, key-off cycle in which all of the enabling criteria for a given diagnostic monitor are met. See **Fig. 7-2**.

ALL OBD-II MONITOR STATUS	
FRZ F CAUSED BY DTC	: 00
TASK MANAGER DATA	: 20
1/1 02S MON DATA	: 80
1/2 02S MON DATA	: 80
2/1 02S MON DATA	: 80
2/2 02S MON DATA	: 80
CAT EFFICIENCY DATA BNK1	: 80
CAT EFFICIENCY DATA BNK2	: 80
EGR MONITOR DATA	: 80
LDP MON SWITCH DATA	: 80
LDP MON PINCHED LINE DATA	: 80
LPD MON GROSS LEAK DATA	: 80
LPD MON .040 LEAK DATA	: 80
LPD MON .020 LEAK DATA	: 00
PURGE FLOW MON DATA	: 80
1/1 02 HEATER MON DATA	: 80
2/1 02 HEATER MON DATA	: 80
1/2 02 HEATER MON DATA	: 80
2/1 02 HEATER MON DATA	: 80
1/2 02 HEATER MON DATA	: 80
2/2 02 HEATER MON DATA	: 80
FUEL SYS LEAN BNK1 DATA	: 80
FUEL SYS LEAN BNK2 DATA	: 80
FUEL SYS RICH BNK1 DATA	: 80
FUEL SYS RICH BNK2 DATA	: 80
MIS-FIRE MON DATA	: 80

DaimlerChrysler

Fig. 7-2 This display shows the status of OBD-II monitors for one trip. The information can be used to determine which monitors were running during the trip.

- **Freeze-frame data**—serial data values that are stored the instant an emission-related DTC is set and enters the diagnostic memory. Some manufacturers may refer to this as parameter identification data (PID). Freeze frames provide a snapshot of the conditions present when a DTC is stored. See **Fig. 7-3**.

- **Inspection/Maintenance (I/M) ready status**—shows that a vehicle's on-board diagnostics have been run. These are sometimes called I/M flags.

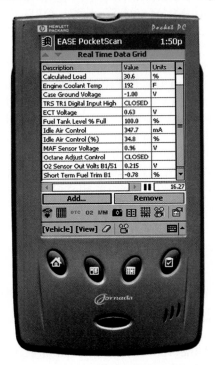

EASE Diagnostics

Fig. 7-3 The freeze-frame data shows what conditions are present.

SECTION 1 KNOWLEDGE CHECK

1. Name the six systems and/or components monitored by the OBD-II system.

2. How does OBD-II indicate that emission levels exceed the federal standard limits?

3. Which pins in the data link connector (DLC) are assigned the same for all manufacturers?

4. Where is the DLC located on OBD-II vehicles?

5. What does the term *trip* mean in relation to OBD-II terminology?

ASE TEST PREP

6. Technician A says that the purpose of OBD-II systems is to ensure accurate monitoring and operation of all emission-related systems and components. Technician B says that the purpose is to diagnose problems in systems and components not related to emission controls. Who is correct?

   ⓐ Technician A.

   ⓑ Technician B.

   ⓒ Both Technician A and Technician B.

   ⓓ Neither Technician A nor Technician B.

● Section 2
OBD-II Diagnostics

Objectives:

- ● Understand the function of a diagnostic monitor.
- B8 ● Access and use service information to perform step-by-step diagnosis.
- B4 ● Diagnose emissions or driveability concerns resulting from malfunctions in the computerized engine control system with no stored diagnostic trouble codes; determine necessary action.
- D1 ● Diagnose hot or cold no-starting, hard starting, poor driveability, incorrect idle speed, poor idle, flooding, hesitation, surging, engine misfire, power loss, stalling, poor mileage, dieseling, and emissions problems on vehicles with injection-type fuel systems; determine necessary action.
- B3 ● Diagnose the causes of emissions or driveability concerns resulting from malfunctions in the computerized engine control system with stored diagnostic trouble codes.
- B6 ● Inspect and test computerized engine control system sensors, powertrain control module (PCM), actuators, and circuits using a graphing multimeter (GMM)/digital storage oscilloscope (DSO); perform necessary action.
- A13 ● Diagnose engine mechanical, electrical, electronic, fuel, and ignition concerns with an oscilloscope and/or engine diagnostic equipment; determine necessary action.
- A3 ● Research applicable vehicle and service information, such as engine management system operation, vehicle service history, service precautions, and technical service bulletins.
- B1 ● Retrieve and record stored OBD I diagnostic trouble codes; clear codes.
- B2 ● Retrieve and record stored OBD II diagnostic trouble codes; clear codes when applicable.

Vocabulary:

- ● **diagnostic executive**
- ● **serial data stream**
- ● **calibration drift**

OBD-II Monitors

Diagnosing OBD-II systems requires a specific knowledge of how DTCs are created, stored, and erased. OBD-II has many classifications of DTCs. These DTCs are stored in specific sequences and by degrees of severity. When diagnosing an OBD-II system, refer to the vehicle service manual.

As mentioned, a monitor is a diagnostic procedure used by the PCM to test relevant on-board systems. A monitor may occur only when enabling criteria (specific sensor inputs) are received by the PCM. Many of these monitors are performed under specific operating conditions. For example, a monitor may occur only when the engine reaches a certain operating temperature, speed, and load, and the transmission is in a certain gear.

OBD-II checks inputs from system sensors including:
- Manifold absolute pressure (MAP) sensor.
- Mass air flow (MAF) sensor.
- Engine coolant temperature (ECT) sensor.
- Crankshaft position (CKP) sensor.
- Camshaft position (CMP) sensor.
- Heated oxygen sensor (HO2S).
- Vehicle speed sensor (VSS).
- Intake air temperature (IAT) sensor.
- Throttle position (TP) sensor.

The **diagnostic executive** is a PCM program that controls the sequencing of tests needed to run the OBD-II monitors. This sequencing procedure organizes and prioritizes the monitor tests. The diagnostic executive includes the following processes:
- Turning the MIL on or off.
- Storing and clearing DTCs.
- Storing freeze-frame data for emissions faults.
- Displaying the status of each diagnostic.

The OBD-II system analyzes data from monitors including:
- Cylinder misfire.
- Catalytic converter efficiency.
- Fuel trim adjustment.
- Exhaust gas recirculation.
- Evaporative emission control.
- Secondary air injection.

OBD-II Diagnostic Trouble Codes

A DTC is displayed as an alphanumeric designator followed by a three-digit number. These codes are displayed on the face of a scanner connected to the DLC. See **Fig. 7-4.**

Code designators fall into four groups:
- Body codes: B0, B1, B2, and B3.
- Chassis codes: C0, C1, C2, and C3.
- Powertrain codes: P0, P1, P2, and P3.
- Network codes: U0, U1, U2, and U3.

Engine performance DTCs are found within the powertrain, or "P," codes. If the first number following P is 0, it indicates a generic, or SAE, code. Generic DTCs are common codes that are uniform throughout the automotive service industry.

If the first number after P is 1, it indicates the DTC is a nonuniform, or manufacturer-specific, code. Manufacturers use these codes in their own diagnostic procedures. Refer to the appropriate service manual to reference these codes. The second number indicates the system that is affected. The following are code numbers of the affected systems:

1—Fuel and air metering (MAP, MAF, IAT, ECT).
2—Fuel injector circuits.
3—Ignition system or misfire (KS, CKP).
4—Auxiliary emission controls (EGR, TWC, EVAP).
5—Vehicle speed control and idle system (VSS, IAC).
6—Computer output circuits (5-volt reference, MIL).
7—Transmission.
8—Transmission.

The last two numbers in an OBD-II DTC refer to the specific fault designation. A DTC of P0137 means that the number-two heated oxygen sensor on cylinder bank number one is producing a low voltage. See **Fig. 7-5.** The number-one cylinder bank contains the number-one cylinder.

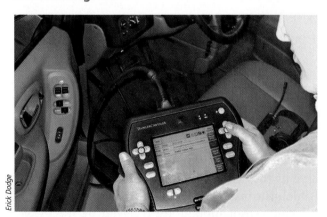

Erick Dodge

Fig. 7-4 Scanners are used to read DTCs. A scanner is connected to the DLC under the dash. *Where are DTCs stored?*

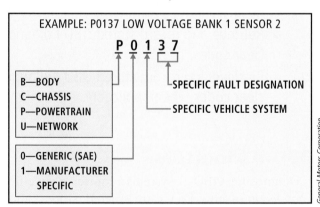

EXAMPLE: P0137 LOW VOLTAGE BANK 1 SENSOR 2

P 0 1 3 7

B—BODY
C—CHASSIS
P—POWERTRAIN
U—NETWORK

SPECIFIC FAULT DESIGNATION

SPECIFIC VEHICLE SYSTEM

0—GENERIC (SAE)
1—MANUFACTURER SPECIFIC

General Motors Corporation

Fig. 7-5 Interpreting an OBD-II DTC. *Where would you look for a list of specific fault designations?*

An OBD-II configuration may have as many as three oxygen sensors per exhaust pipe. The sensor responsible for fuel adjustment is frequently located in the exhaust manifold. It checks the air/fuel mixture. In systems that use three sensors, the second sensor is the pre-catalytic, or pre-cat, sensor. It is located on the input side of the catalytic converter. The final sensor is the post-catalytic, or post-cat, sensor. It is located on the output side of the catalytic converter. A vehicle with a dual exhaust system can have as many as six oxygen sensors.

Setting OBD-II DTCs

The PCM is designed to monitor emission system failures by comparing two or more sensor return signals. To illustrate, the throttle position (TP) sensor, engine rpm (TACH), mass air flow (MAF) sensor, and vehicle speed sensor (VSS) signals are compared. These three sensors should agree that:
- The engine is running.
- The vehicle is in gear.
- The vehicle is moving.

If one of the return signals does not agree with the other three, a DTC is set. The misfire monitor, for example, detects an ignition misfire in a specific cylinder by measuring small changes in crankshaft speed. The return signal from the CKP is the main signal used by the PCM to detect a cylinder misfire. See **Fig. 7-6.**

If the PCM detects a misfire every 200 rpms, it is called a type-A misfire. This type of misfire produces excess hydrocarbons, causing the catalytic converter to overheat. If a type-A failure is detected and a DTC is set, the MIL blinks at a rate of once per second.

A type-B misfire occurs at least once every 1,000 rpms. Type-B misfires result in an emissions failure equal to 1.5 times the Federal Test Procedure (FTP) standards.

If a type-B misfire occurs, the MIL lights up and stays on and a DTC is stored. A DTC for a type-A or type-B misfire is P0300. The DTCs for individual cylinder misfires range from P0301 (number-one cylinder) to P03010 (number-ten cylinder).

Rough road conditions can cause the crankshaft speed to vary. If the varying crankshaft speed is detected, the PCM can incorrectly set a type-B misfire. Many misfire monitors use return signals from the antilock brake system (ABS) to help the PCM determine the roughness of the road surface. The added sensor return signal can prevent a false DTC setting.

TECH TIP Checking Catalytic Converter **Temperatures.** The outlet temperature on a catalytic converter should be at least 100°F [38°C] higher than the inlet temperature. Use an infrared pyrometer to measure the temperature.

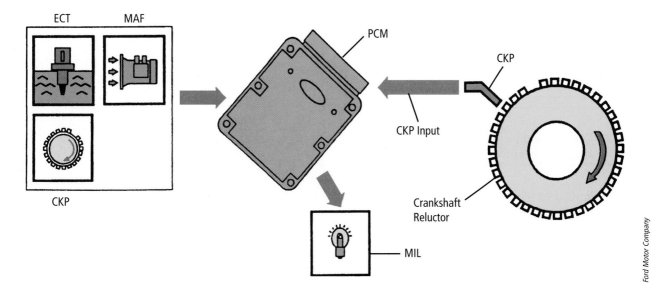

Ford Motor Company

Fig. 7-6 Components of a misfire detection monitor. When the enabling criteria are met for a misfire, a DTC is set in the PCM. *How can driving on a rough road imitate the effect of an engine misfire?*

OBD-II systems monitor emissions by checking the catalytic converter for degradation. If converter efficiency decreases and emissions increase due to component degradation, a DTC is set.

To monitor catalytic converter efficiency, an oxygen sensor is placed at the inlet of the catalytic converter. The pre-cat sensor indicates the amount of oxygen entering the converter. A post-cat oxygen sensor is placed at the converter outlet. The post-cat sensor indicates the amount of oxygen leaving the converter. Under normal operation, all the oxygen in the exhaust leaving the converter is used up.

Diagnostic Flowcharts

A diagnostic flowchart is used to troubleshoot the condition that sets a DTC. See **Fig. 7-7**. Each DTC has a corresponding flowchart in the vehicle service manual. The flowchart provides a step-by-step diagnostic procedure for each DTC. If more than one DTC is stored, the diagnostic flowchart may specify the order in which the DTCs should be corrected.

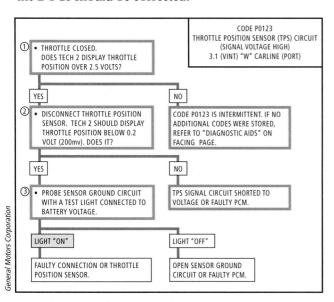

General Motors Corporation

Fig. 7-7 An OBD-II diagnostic flowchart for a TPS circuit. *What conditions could cause a Code P0123?*

A DTC indicates which sensor or actuator circuit is not within expected values. For example, a DTC 21 shows a failure in the throttle position sensor circuit. The problem may be caused by:
- A defective throttle position sensor (TPS).
- An open, shorted, or grounded reference voltage wire.
- High resistance or open TPS ground circuit.
- A defective PCM.

Using a Lab Scope

A lab scope is the commonly used name for a digital storage oscilloscope (DSO). A DSO is used to observe and measure voltage and frequency. The vertical scale displays voltage or amplitude. The horizontal scale displays time or frequency. Both scales are adjustable to provide the best pattern. Changing the scale does not change the actual signal producing the pattern. It changes only the appearance of the pattern. See **Fig. 7-8**.

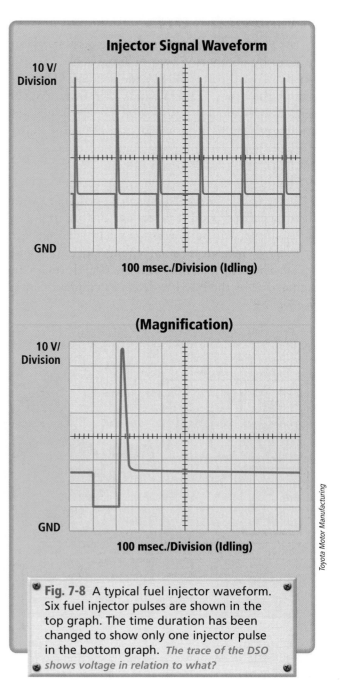

Toyota Motor Manufacturing

Fig. 7-8 A typical fuel injector waveform. Six fuel injector pulses are shown in the top graph. The time duration has been changed to show only one injector pulse in the bottom graph. *The trace of the DSO shows voltage in relation to what?*

The pattern displayed on the screen of the DSO is called a waveform. The waveform is a representation of a signal. It displays circuit activity, showing signal amplitude and frequency. The waveform pattern provides a more accurate view of circuit activity than does a DVOM.

Using a DSO requires training and experience. Many types of waveforms can be displayed. An experienced technician must be able to identify and interpret what is shown.

The DSO can display the two basic types of waveforms produced by sensors and circuits within a vehicle.

- A sine wave is a waveform that alternates between a high and a low value. See **Fig. 7-9(a).** It is also called an analog waveform. The amplitude of the signal alternates smoothly and evenly above and below the base line. Ordinary household alternating current (AC) produces a sine wave when viewed on a DSO. It alternates between 163 volts in the positive direction and 163 volts in the negative direction. The same voltage when measured with a DVOM would show the effective voltage of 110 volts to 120 volts AC.

- A digital signal has very sharp amplitude changes. It is basically an on/off signal. See **Fig. 7-9(b).** The signal changes rapidly from off, or 0 volts, to the applied voltage. The CD player in your home or car produces a digital signal when played. The signal is a series of on/off pulses.

Some sensors in the on-board diagnostics system produce digital signals. The signal changes rapidly from 0 volts to the applied voltage, usually 5 volts. A square wave is a form of digital signal. However, square wave signals may vary in frequency or on/off time (pulse width).

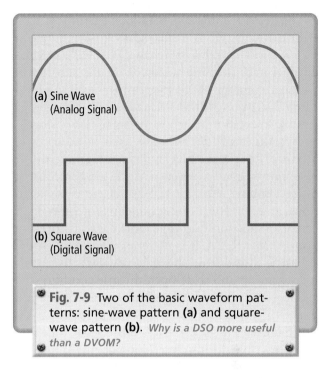

Fig. 7-9 Two of the basic waveform patterns: sine-wave pattern **(a)** and square-wave pattern **(b)**. *Why is a DSO more useful than a DVOM?*

Comparing Sensor Readings

The PCM compares the return signal voltages from the pre-cat and post-cat sensors. As the exhaust leaves the converter, the post-cat oxygen sensor should detect a flat output voltage. If the converter is operating efficiently, the voltage readings will be different. See **Fig. 7-10.** If the converter is not operating efficiently, the sensor readings will be similar. A DTC sets and the MIL activates.

The catalytic converter is most efficient if a stoichiometric fuel ratio is maintained. To maintain efficient operation, the PCM trims the fuel from slightly rich to slightly lean. The return signal voltage from the pre-cat oxygen sensor switches from about 0.8 V (rich) to about 0.2 V (lean). As the mixture becomes lean, a small amount of free oxygen enters the converter. This oxygen helps the converter oxidize the pollutants in the exhaust stream.

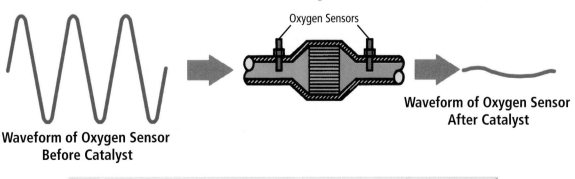

Oxygen Sensors

Waveform of Oxygen Sensor Before Catalyst

Waveform of Oxygen Sensor After Catalyst

Toyota Motor Manufacturing

Fig. 7-10 The pre-cat sensor provides a varying return signal. The post-cat sensor provides a different return signal. *Why are the waveforms different?*

The PCM records short- and long-term fuel trim (FT) readings. FT is displayed as a percentage. A −20% short-term FT means that the PCM is reducing fuel injector pulse width. A +20% short-term FT means that the PCM is increasing the pulse width. The PCM averages the FT readings. If the average reading exceeds a range of values, a DTC is stored.

Two types of fuel trim are used to adjust fuel mixture. Long-term fuel trim changes gradually. It responds to conditions such as the oxygen content of fuel, engine wear, air leaks, fuel pressure variations, and altitude. Long-term trim is a component of basic injection duration. This data is stored in non-volatile RAM. It is not erased, even when the engine is shut down. This information is used during warm-up and wide-open throttle conditions.

Short-term fuel trim is instantaneous correction due to oxygen sensor readings. Under normal conditions, it cycles around the 0% correction value and functions only during closed-loop operation. Short-term trim is part of the corrected injection duration. When short-term trim exceeds ±10% for too long, as with a failing component, the long-term trim begins shifting. It changes the basic injection duration to bring short-term trim within ±10%. Short-term trim can vary as much as ±20%, but this correction method works to keep it within ±10%.

Comparing long- and short-term trim values helps diagnose drivability problems. As long as the system stays within limits, it will make the proper adjustments and keep the engine running as it should. However, when there is a problem in the system, the MIL will light. On most OBD-II vehicles, that limit is when the sum of the long-term and short-term trim exceeds 35%.

Figure 7-11 shows examples of normal and abnormal pre-cat oxygen sensor waveforms. Waveform A shows normal operation. The signal is varying over an expected range of values. Waveform B shows low-level switching activity. The sensor is not responding normally. A contaminated sensor normally causes "B" waveform. Waveform C shows a low voltage bias. The return signal is varying over a voltage range that is too low. Waveform D shows a high voltage bias. The return signal is varying over a voltage range that is too high. A defective oxygen sensor is indicated by waveform "B," "C," or "D."

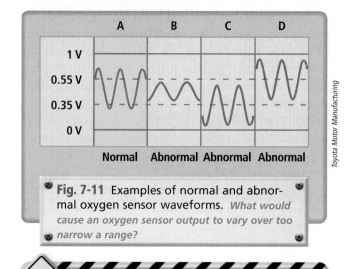

Fig. 7-11 Examples of normal and abnormal oxygen sensor waveforms. *What would cause an oxygen sensor output to vary over too narrow a range?*

Toyota Motor Manufacturing

Safety First

Vapors Leaking EVAP hoses or a defective, loose, or missing fuel tank cap will activate the MIL. These problems allow fuel vapors to escape into the atmosphere, creating a source of pollution.

The evaporative emissions (EVAP) system checks the fuel tank and vapor recovery system for vapor leakage. See **Fig. 7-12**. The EVAP monitor is designed to detect leaks as small as 0.040″ [0.102 cm] in diameter. The EVAP monitor does this by applying either a vacuum or pressure to the purge lines, the canister, and the fuel tank.

Vacuum should be present only when the purge valve allows intake manifold vacuum to enter the purge lines. An EVAP sensor is placed in the purge line to monitor vacuum. A DTC is set if the return signal from the sensor indicates abnormal operation.

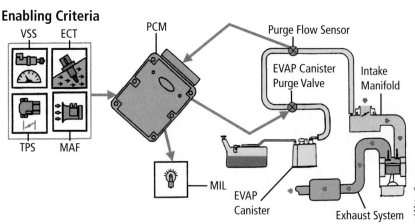

Fig. 7-12 Components of a Ford EVAP monitor. When the EVAP canister purge valve opens, the purge flow sensor tests for vapor flow from the EVAP canister to the intake manifold. *What are the enabling criteria for the EVAP monitor?*

Ford Motor Company

Interpreting Serial Data

Some OBD-I systems provide a serial data stream to indicate how each sensor and actuator is responding to changes in engine operation. The **serial data stream** is information displayed as voltage values or as actual readings such as degrees of temperature, inches of vacuum, or percentage of throttle opening. See **Fig. 7-13.** Connecting a scan tool or similar diagnostic display to the DLC usually retrieves this information.

Serial data is most useful when a condition does not set a DTC. This is called a no-code driveability condition. A no-code condition can occur even if the failure is in a monitored sensor circuit.

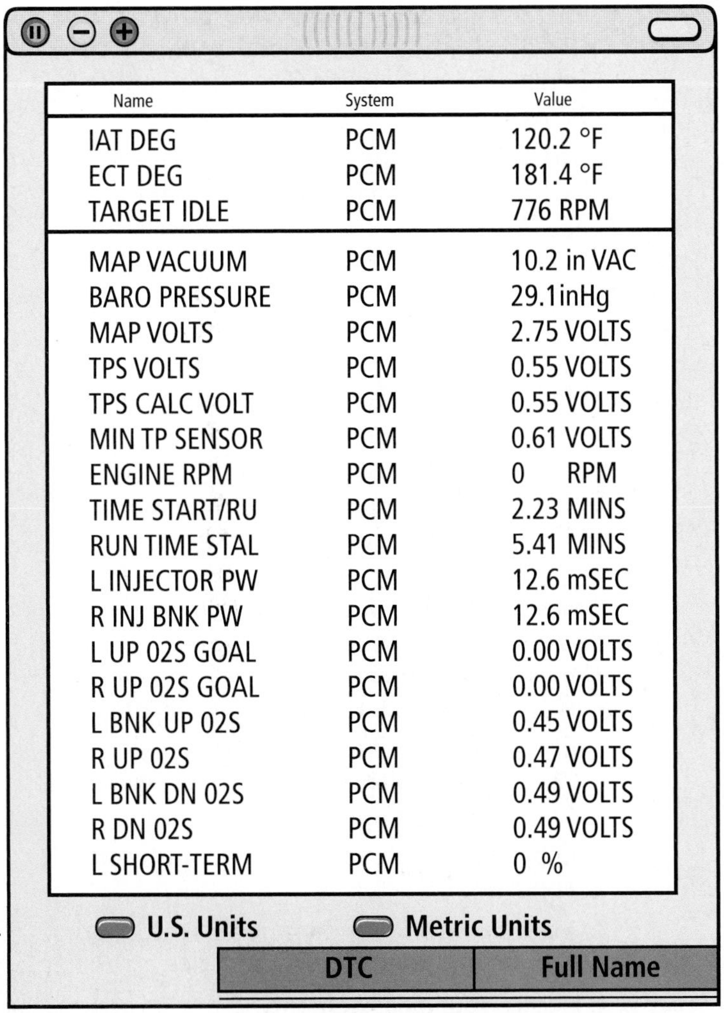

The PCM may need to sense a condition for a predetermined amount of time. If a failure occurs quickly and then returns to within its normal range, the PCM may not record a DTC.

In other cases, age may degrade a sensor's calibration. O2Ss are prone to calibration drift. **Calibration drift** occurs when a component, due to age or contamination, no longer accurately represents the factory setting. The sensor may become contaminated with deposits that reduce its sensitivity. The sensor becomes less responsive to changes in the oxygen content of the exhaust gas. Sensor degradation will not set a DTC if the return signal is within an expected range of values.

You can test most sensors by observing the scanner's serial data stream. Serial data can be compared to specified readings to diagnose no-code conditions. For example, when the engine is cold, the serial data stream from the ECT and IAT can be compared. The two readings, the engine coolant temperature and the intake air temperature, should be within a few degrees of each other.

Serial data may also include return signals from other sensors or systems that affect engine operation. The detonation sensor circuit, for example, is tuned to detect vibrations caused by spark knock. If spark knock occurs, a return signal from the detonation sensor causes the PCM to retard the ignition timing. The detonation sensor should activate very slightly (if at all) under full throttle conditions.

An air leak might occur between the airflow sensor and the throttle body. The leak causes the airflow sensor to indicate that very little air is flowing through the engine at idle. This causes the PCM to reduce the fuel injector pulse width. A lean air/fuel mixture might cause a rough idle or a stall condition.

Systems displaying injector pulse width may offer diagnostic clues. A short pulse width may indicate that the PCM is trying to reduce fuel delivery to the engine because the O2S is sensing a rich exhaust mixture. The actual cause may be a ruptured fuel pressure regulator diaphragm leaking fuel into the intake manifold.

Name	System	Value
IAT DEG	PCM	120.2 °F
ECT DEG	PCM	181.4 °F
TARGET IDLE	PCM	776 RPM
MAP VACUUM	PCM	10.2 in VAC
BARO PRESSURE	PCM	29.1inHg
MAP VOLTS	PCM	2.75 VOLTS
TPS VOLTS	PCM	0.55 VOLTS
TPS CALC VOLT	PCM	0.55 VOLTS
MIN TP SENSOR	PCM	0.61 VOLTS
ENGINE RPM	PCM	0 RPM
TIME START/RU	PCM	2.23 MINS
RUN TIME STAL	PCM	5.41 MINS
L INJECTOR PW	PCM	12.6 mSEC
R INJ BNK PW	PCM	12.6 mSEC
L UP 02S GOAL	PCM	0.00 VOLTS
R UP 02S GOAL	PCM	0.00 VOLTS
L BNK UP 02S	PCM	0.45 VOLTS
R UP 02S	PCM	0.47 VOLTS
L BNK DN 02S	PCM	0.49 VOLTS
R DN 02S	PCM	0.49 VOLTS
L SHORT-TERM	PCM	0 %

☐ U.S. Units   ☐ Metric Units

DTC	Full Name

DaimlerChrysler

Fig. 7-13 Serial data stream. *When is serial data the most useful?*

Excellence in Math

Testing a MAP Sensor

You may use a vacuum gauge and a DVOM to test most MAP sensors indirectly. The table below shows the information needed to test most MAP sensors.

Manifold Vacuum (inches of mercury (Hg))	Voltage (+/−0.04)
5	1.46
8	1.34
9	1.31
10	1.29
11	1.26
12	1.24
13	1.21
14	1.19
15	1.16
16	1.14
17	1.11
18	1.09
19	1.07
20	1.04
21	1.02
22	0.99
23	0.97

Test the MAP sensor at several vacuum values. This should be done on the vehicle. Use a scan tool or DVOM to observe signal voltage.

1. Install a vacuum/pump gauge and slowly apply vacuum.

2. Record readings at the vacuum levels shown in the table.

3. Compare each reading to the value shown in the table.

4. If the output voltages are out of specification, replace the sensor.

5. If output voltages comply with the specifications, consider other possible causes for the complaint.

Output voltage measurements for a possibly defective sensor are:

1.44 V at 5″ of Hg, 1.35 V at 10″ of Hg, 1.22 V at 15″ of Hg, and 1.10 V at 20″ of Hg.

Compare these output voltages with the values in the table. What conclusion do you reach?

- At 5″ of Hg, the specification requirement is between 1.42 V and 1.50 V. This is satisfied.
- At 10″ of Hg, the specification requirement is 1.25 V to 1.33 V. 1.35 V is outside of the requirements.
- At 15″ of Hg, the required interval is 1.12 V to 1.20 V and 1.22 V does not meet that specification.
- At 20″ of Hg, the acceptable measurement must be between 1.00 V and 1.08 V. 1.10 V is out of specification. The sensor needs to be replaced.

Altitude is a factor in obtaining true voltage values at different vacuum levels for your vacuum gauge. Always consider your altitude.

Apply It!

Meets NATEF Mathematics Standards for interpreting specifications and tolerance and standardizing testing equipment.

Also meets NATEF Science Standards for understanding effects of barometric pressure and variances in flow rate in airflow rate sensors.

1. Devise a plan to ensure proper diagnosis of a MAP sensor using your vacuum gauge. As a hint, your plan must include the concept of an "average."

2. Implement your plan after your instructor approves it.

3. Measure several known good sensors on four or five good running vehicles.

4. Record your measurements. Create an accurate table of voltage readings at various vacuum levels.

5. Compare your results with several others of your team. Did every gauge produce the same results?

Retrieving OBD-II DTCs

OBD-II DTCs are accessed by connecting a scanner to the DLC. Unlike some OBD-I systems, "flash code" diagnosis is not possible with OBD-II.

Diagnostic procedures are shown on the scanner's menu. The menu differs with the scanner being used. Dedicated scanners may have more complicated menus.

A single vehicle application has many OBD-II DTCs. For example, OBD-II systems can display over 35 generic oxygen-sensor-related DTCs. A vehicle service manual gives the meaning of each DTC. The repair manual also includes specific procedures needed to diagnose a particular DTC.

A scanner may have several diagnostic modes. The PID mode, used by Ford, supplies serial data information from the PCM. When the PID mode is used, this information is continuously updated. The generic PID data stream includes calculated system values and system status reports. See **Fig. 7-14**.

EASE Diagnostics

Fig. 7-14 A scanner may have several diagnostic modes, including a PID mode useful for diagnosing no-code faults.

TECH TIP **Using Serial Data.** The PID mode is useful for diagnosing no-code faults. The serial data information is continuously updated. The updated information shows what values are being supplied to the PCM.

Clearing OBD-II DTCs

When an OBD-II monitor detects a fault, it stores a DTC and turns on the MIL. Some faults may have to occur for two consecutive drive cycles to activate the MIL. If the MIL is turned on, three consecutive fault-free drive cycles are needed to turn off the MIL. The DTC is cleared after 40 engine warm-up cycles without the fault reoccurring.

DTCs can be manually cleared by a scanner command, although this may not be the accepted practice. OBD-II DTCs should not be cleared until all specified diagnostic and repair operations have been performed. It is best to allow the DTC to clear itself. This practice ensures that the fault, condition, or component causing the DTC has been repaired.

SECTION 2 KNOWLEDGE CHECK

1. What is the diagnostic executive?

2. What do the acronyms MIL, A/C, FLI, ECT, and TP stand for?

3. What four groups do DTCs represent?

4. What does the pre-cat sensor indicate?

5. When does calibration drift occur?

6. What are the two types of fuel trim that are used to adjust fuel mixture?

ASE TEST PREP

7. Technician A says that a DTC is an alphanumeric designator followed by a two-digit number. Technician B says that a DTC is an alphanumeric designator followed by a three-digit number. Who is correct?

   ⓐ Technician A.

   ⓑ Technician B.

   ⓒ Both Technician A and Technician B.

   ⓓ Neither Technician A nor Technician B.

CHAPTER 7 REVIEW

Key Points

Meets the following NATEF Standards for Engine Performance: supporting knowledge for diagnosing OBD-II system problems.

- OBD-II systems standardize the data link connector, basic diagnostic equipment, and diagnostic procedures.
- OBD-II systems detect component degradation and emissions problems.
- A monitor is a diagnostic procedure used by the PCM to test relevant on-board systems.
- A drive cycle "runs" all of the on-board diagnostics on the vehicle.
- A trip is a key-on, run, key-off cycle.
- A diagnostic flowchart is used to troubleshoot the condition that sets a DTC. A DTC indicates which sensor or actuator circuit is not within expected values.
- A digital storage oscilloscope (lab scope) observes both digital and analog waveforms.
- Serial data can be used to diagnose no-code sensor faults.
- DTCs will be cleared automatically if the fault is gone and 40 warm-up cycles have occurred.

Review Questions

1. What is flash PROM?
2. What is the purpose of an inspection/maintenance flag?
3. What type of data provides a snapshot of the conditions present when a DTC is stored?
4. Which system is affected if the second number of a DTC is 7 or 8?
5. What do the last two numbers in an OBD-II DTC represent?
6. What are the last two sensors in a three-sensor OBD-II exhaust configuration?
7. What is another name for a digital storage oscilloscope (DSO)?
8. What do the vertical and horizontal scales of a lab scope show?
9. What system checks the fuel tank and vapor recovery system for vapor leakage?
10. **Critical Thinking** What is the difference between long-term and short-term fuel trim?

Excellence in Communication

Using Communication Strategies

Your customers will vary in their ability to describe a vehicle's problems. They also may vary in their ability to understand what you are telling them. For example, when you talk with a hearing-impaired customer, there are some things you can do to make effective communication easier.

- Allow enough time. Listen carefully to what your customer is telling you.
- Make sure that your customer can see your face and mouth clearly when you speak. Try to have the light fall on your face.
- Speak clearly at your normal speed.
- Avoid speaking over distracting background noises. If possible, move to a quieter area.

You may want to ask your customer, "Do you have any questions?" and, "Would you like me to put my answers in writing?"

You will encounter many other situations in which you need to adapt your communication strategies.

Apply It!

Meets NATEF Communications Standards for adapting listening and speaking strategies to the needs of the customer.

You are standing outside the open doors of your work area. There is heavy traffic on the busy street. Your customer asks you a question about her vehicle.

1. Write a paragraph describing what you should do to make communication clearer.

2. If there were no background traffic noise, would you change your communication strategy? Why or why not?

AUTOMOTIVE SERVICE EXCELLENCE
TEST PREP

Answering the following practice questions will help you prepare for the ASE certification tests.

1. An OBD-II system monitors which of the following?

   ⓐ Cylinder misfire.

   ⓑ Catalytic converter efficiency.

   ⓒ Fuel trim adjustment.

   ⓓ All of the above.

2. Technician A says that OBD-II systems are designed to detect emission-related faults and failures resulting from degradation. Technician B says that OBD-II systems are designed only to detect failures with specific components or systems. Who is correct?

   ⓐ Technician A.

   ⓑ Technician B.

   ⓒ Both Technician A and Technician B.

   ⓓ Neither Technician A nor Technician B.

3. Which of the following is not OBD-II standardized terminology?

   ⓐ Diagnostic.

   ⓑ Trip.

   ⓒ Enabling criteria.

   ⓓ Ground state.

4. Technician A says that a passive test checks the performance of a vehicle system or component during normal operation. Technician B says that an active test forces a component to behave in a specific way. Who is correct?

   ⓐ Technician A.

   ⓑ Technician B.

   ⓒ Both Technician A and Technician B.

   ⓓ Neither Technician A nor Technician B.

5. Serial data values that are stored the instant an emission-related DTC is set and enters the diagnostic memory are referred to as:

   ⓐ failure records.

   ⓑ freeze-frame data.

   ⓒ enabling criteria.

   ⓓ None of the above.

6. Technician A says that diagnostic trouble codes are stored in specific sequences and by degrees of severity. Technician B says that the codes are stored at random. Who is correct?

   ⓐ Technician A.

   ⓑ Technician B.

   ⓒ Both Technician A and Technician B.

   ⓓ Neither Technician A nor Technician B.

7. A diagnostic trouble code with the designator U0 is what type of code?

   ⓐ Body.

   ⓑ Chassis.

   ⓒ Network.

   ⓓ Powertrain.

8. Technician A says that if a type-B misfire occurs the PCM will set a diagnostic trouble code of P0300. Technician B says that if a type-A misfire occurs the PCM will set a diagnostic trouble code of P0300. Who is correct?

   ⓐ Technician A.

   ⓑ Technician B.

   ⓒ Both Technician A and Technician B.

   ⓓ Neither Technician A nor Technician B.

9. What type of data from the scanner can be compared with specified readings to diagnose no-code conditions?

   ⓐ Diagnostic trouble code.

   ⓑ Serial data stream.

   ⓒ Parallel data stream.

   ⓓ None of the above.

10. Technician A says that diagnostic trouble codes can be cleared manually. Technician B says that it is best to let the diagnostic trouble code clear itself. Who is correct?

    ⓐ Technician A.

    ⓑ Technician B.

    ⓒ Both Technician A and Technician B.

    ⓓ Neither Technician A nor Technician B.

Section 1
Automotive
Emissions Controls

Section 2
Emissions Testing

Diagnosing & Repairing Emission Control Systems

Customer's Concern

Shirley Mason was taking her family out for a special dinner when her car stalled at a stoplight. It happened two more times before they got to the restaurant and three times on the way home. Her car has over 90,000 miles on it, but it is in pristine condition. Your service center just completed a 12-point check and a full-service oil change for Shirley last month.

"The car has been idling rough for about two weeks, but the engine dying at stoplights is a new and unwelcome problem," Shirley says. Once you get the car into the service bay and take a look at the engine, you notice sludge around the PCV valve. Could Shirley's visit to your service center last month have contributed to this problem?

Technician's Challenge

As the service technician, you need to find answers to these questions:

1. What is the purpose of the PCV valve? Could the sludge around the PCV valve have anything to do with Shirley's complaints?

2. How will you determine whether the PCV valve needs to be replaced? What can shaking a PCV valve tell you?

3. Should the PCV valve have been replaced prior to these problems? How can you determine the replacement intervals for PCV parts?

● Section 1
Automotive Emissions Controls

Objectives:

E1-1 ● Diagnose oil leaks, emissions, and driveability problems resulting from malfunctions in the positive crankcase ventilation (PCV) system; determine necessary action.

E1-2 ● Inspect, test and service positive crankcase ventilation (PCV) filter/breather cap, valve, tubes, orifices, and hoses; perform necessary action.

E2-1 ● Diagnose emissions and driveability problems caused by malfunctions in the exhaust gas recirculation (EGR) system; determine necessary action.

E2-2 ● Inspect, test, service and replace components of EGR system, including EGR tubing, exhaust passages, vacuum passages, vacuum/pressure controls, filters and hoses; perform necessary action.

E3-1 ● Diagnose emissions and driveability problems resulting from malfunctions in the secondary air injection and catalytic converter systems; determine necessary action.

E3-2 ● Inspect and test mechanical components of secondary air injection systems; perform necessary action.

E3-3 ● Inspect and test electrical/electronically-operated components and circuits of air injection systems; perform necessary action.

E3-4 ● Inspect and test catalytic converter performance.

E4-1 ● Diagnose emissions and driveability problems resulting from malfunctions in evaporative emissions control system; determine necessary action.

E4-2 ● Inspect and test components and hoses of evaporative emissions control system; perform necessary action.

E4-3 ● Interpret evaporative emission related diagnostic trouble codes (DTCs); determine necessary action.

A4 ● Locate and interpret vehicle and major component identification numbers (VIN, vehicle certification labels, and calibration decals).

Vocabulary:

● nitrogen oxide (NO$_x$)
● air injection (AIR) system
● catalyst
● evaporative control (EVAP) system

Gerry Black/Masterfile

Emissions Control Subsystems

Automotive engine emissions come from three sources: crankcase ventilation, fuel vapors, and exhaust system gases. The primary pollutant emissions are unburned hydrocarbons (HC), carbon monoxide (CO), and nitrogen oxides (NO_x). Carbon dioxide (CO_2) and oxygen (O_2) are also emitted from the exhaust. However, they are not considered pollutants. When released into the environment, unburned HC and NO_x form "smog." Smog is a cloudy formation of pollutants.

The primary subsystems of an emissions control system include the:

- Positive crankcase ventilation (PCV) system.
- Exhaust gas recirculation (EGR) system.
- Air injection (AIR) system.
- Three-way catalytic converter (TWC).
- Evaporative control (EVAP) system.

Positive Crankcase Ventilation System

All engines have some blowby. Blowby is mostly unburned gasoline and combustion by-product gases that pass by the pistons into the crankcase.

The positive crankcase ventilation (PCV) system prevents blowby from escaping into the atmosphere by using vacuum to draw filtered air from the air intake into the crankcase. This air mixes with blowby gases in the crankcase. The blowby gases are then drawn through the PCV valve into the intake manifold and burned in the engine's cylinders. See **Fig. 8-1**.

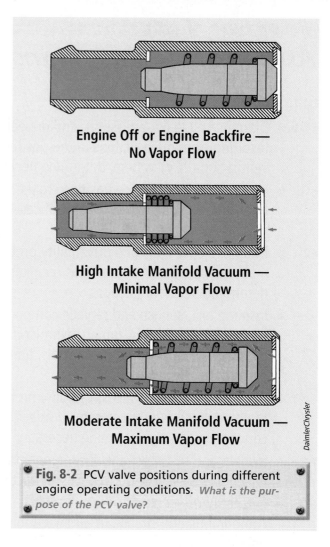

Engine Off or Engine Backfire — No Vapor Flow

High Intake Manifold Vacuum — Minimal Vapor Flow

Moderate Intake Manifold Vacuum — Maximum Vapor Flow

DaimlerChrysler

Fig. 8-2 PCV valve positions during different engine operating conditions. *What is the purpose of the PCV valve?*

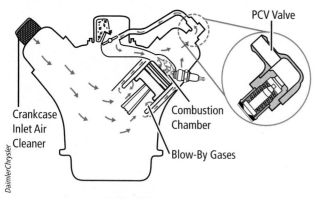

DaimlerChrysler

Fig. 8-1 A PCV system on a V-type engine.

Crankcase Inlet Air Cleaner

PCV Valve

Combustion Chamber

Blow-By Gases

A PCV valve varies the flow of crankcase gases entering the intake manifold. See **Fig. 8-2**. At engine idle, high intake manifold vacuum pulls the valve plunger against the tension spring. This position limits the flow of crankcase gases. Too much flow can cause a rough idle or engine stalling. Under heavier engine load, lower intake vacuum allows the valve plunger to open further. The size of the orifice increases the flow of crankcase gases. At wide-open throttle, a combination of vacuum and spring tension positions the valve plunger to allow maximum flow.

In the event of a backfire, the valve plunger is forced against the valve body. In this position, the backfire cannot ignite crankcase gases.

TECH TIP **Checking the PCV System.** With the engine running, block the oil filler cap open with a square of stiff paper. Vacuum should quickly build up in the crankcase and hold the paper against the inlet. If not, the engine may have a plugged PCV system, high blowby, or a manifold vacuum leak.

With the engine off and no vacuum present, the valve plunger is held against the valve body by spring tension.

Servicing the PCV System Proper operation of the PCV system depends upon the PCV valve being free of sludge deposits. Low-speed driving and high mileage cause deposits to accumulate in PCV passages. This causes poor crankcase ventilation. Auto manufacturers recommend replacing the PCV valve and inlet filter at scheduled intervals. The inlet filter is in the breather cap or in the air intake system. To test the PCV system, check the following:

- If the PCV valve is mounted on the valve cover, remove the PCV valve from its grommet. With the engine running, check for vacuum at the PCV valve. If vacuum isn't present, check the PCV hose and intake manifold port for clogging.
- With the engine off, remove the PCV valve and shake it. A properly operating valve rattles when shaken. If no sound is heard, the valve should be replaced.

If you must repair or replace PCV system components, consult the vehicle service manual.

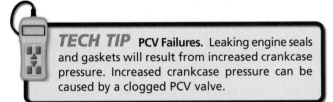

TECH TIP **PCV Failures.** Leaking engine seals and gaskets will result from increased crankcase pressure. Increased crankcase pressure can be caused by a clogged PCV valve.

Exhaust Gas Recirculation System

Nitrogen oxide (NO_x) is a chemical compound that forms when nitrogen (N) and oxygen (O_2) are bonded under high heat. Excess NO_x generally forms when peak combustion temperature exceeds 3,500°F [1,927°C].

Most engines use exhaust gas recirculation (EGR) systems to pass a small amount of exhaust gas into the intake manifold. This reduces NO_x by lowering combustion temperature. Because the exhaust gas is already burned, it is chemically inactive (inert). When the inert exhaust gas is combined with the air/fuel mixture in the cylinder, it reduces the peak combustion temperature.

The exhaust gases flow through a passage connecting the exhaust manifold to the intake manifold. The EGR valve controls the amount of exhaust flowing through this passage. See **Fig. 8-3.**

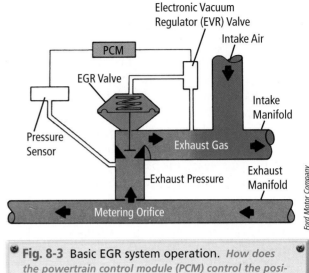

Ford Motor Company

Fig. 8-3 Basic EGR system operation. *How does the powertrain control module (PCM) control the position of the EGR valve?*

Some EGR valves have diaphragms that form a vacuum chamber at the top of the valve. The chamber connects to a vacuum solenoid controlled by the powertrain control module (PCM). The PCM may use return signals from various sensors to operate or "cycle" the vacuum solenoid. These sensors include the engine coolant temperature (ECT), throttle position (TP), manifold absolute pressure (MAP)/mass air flow (MAF), intake air temperature (IAT), and tachometer (TACH).

The PCM may also use a signal from the EGR valve position (EVP) sensor to control the EGR valve. The EVP sensor provides a return signal to the PCM. This signal indicates the position of the EGR valve pintle. See **Fig. 8-4.**

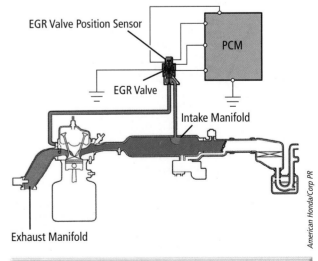

American Honda/Corp PR

Fig. 8-4 A typical EGR configuration. *What information does the EGR valve position sensor provide?*

By changing the duty cycle of the vacuum solenoid, the PCM controls the amount of vacuum that reaches the EGR vacuum chamber. This changes the opening of the EGR pintle valve. This valve controls the exhaust gas flow to the intake manifold.

Some EGR systems use an exhaust backpressure sensor to control exhaust gas circulation. When the engine load is light and backpressure is low, some EGR valve vacuum is vented to the atmosphere. As engine load increases, the backpressure sensor closes the vent. This allows vacuum to open the valve further.

Many current EGR systems use an electronic EGR valve to control the flow of exhaust gas into the intake manifold. A driver circuit in the PCM electronically controls a digital EGR valve. The PCM activates the valve by grounding the valve's solenoid coil. This energizes the solenoid and raises the armature, opening the valve. See **Fig. 8-5**.

OBD-II systems monitor EGR valve operation by opening the valve during deceleration. This increases MAP pressure. The PCM averages a series of EGR tests to determine the amount of EGR flow. If the averaged values do not fall within the expected range, the EGR monitor records a failure. Failure of the EGR system may cause rough idling, detonation (spark knock), and increased emissions.

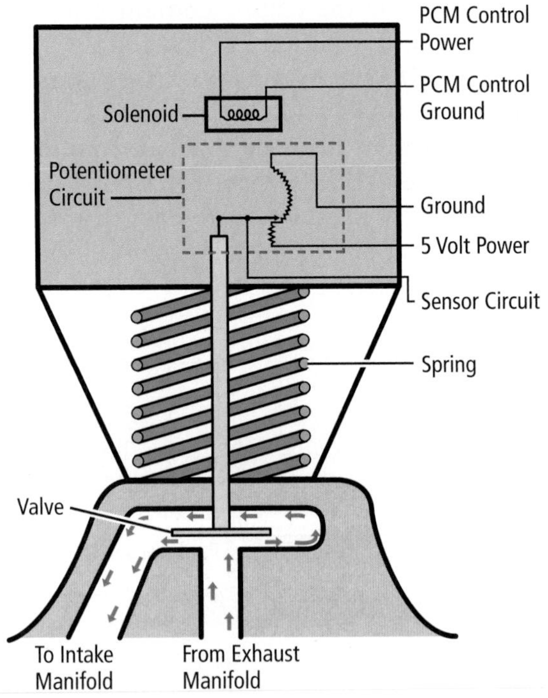

Servicing the EGR System Many different types of EGR valves are used for emissions control. Some may need special diagnostic procedures detailed in service manuals. EGR valves accumulate carbon deposits on the valve pintle and within the valve body. These deposits hold the valve off its seat. This causes rough idle or stalling because exhaust gases leak into the intake manifold.

Carbon may block the exhaust passage leading to the EGR valve. This causes excess NO_x emissions and detonation (spark knock). Detonation can damage pistons and piston rings.

Test most vacuum-operated EGR valves as follows:

- Some EGR valves can be tested by applying vacuum with a hand vacuum pump. See **Fig. 8-6**. If the valve opens, the EGR flow should stall the engine at idle speed. If the valve is cool, open it manually by lifting the vacuum diaphragm.
- If the valve opens and the engine doesn't stall, check the exhaust gas inlet passage for clogging.

Most inoperative EGR valves will set a diagnostic trouble code (DTC) in the PCM's diagnostic memory. OBD-I systems will show an on/off serial data stream for the EGR valve. OBD-II monitors test the EGR valve during each trip, or drive cycle.

DaimlerChrysler

Fig. 8-5 An electronic EGR valve. *What component activates the valve?*

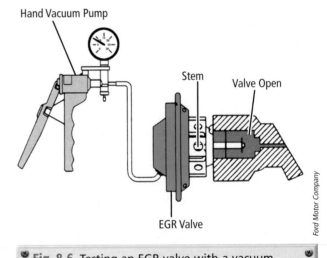

Ford Motor Company

Fig. 8-6 Testing an EGR valve with a vacuum pump. *Can all EGR valves be tested with a vacuum pump?*

A vacuum line that is pinched or that does not allow vacuum to the EGR valve will not allow the valve to open. This will cause engine ping at cruising speed. A new vacuum line will repair this.

A plugged exhaust passage will also cause a no-flow condition with similar symptoms. The passage can be cleaned with a wire brush or metal wire, but replacement may be needed.

The EGR vacuum solenoid uses a small filter to allow air pressure in to help move the diaphragm used to switch from flow to no-flow. If this filter is plugged, it will affect solenoid operation. This will cause no EGR flow. The solenoid should be replaced.

The PCM's serial data stream for electronic EGR valves will show the EGR duty cycle or the percentage of EGR opening. The EGR opening should be zero at idle speed.

If you must repair or replace the EGR system components, consult the vehicle service manual.

Safety First **EGR Valves** EGR valves are very hot, especially if they have been open. If you must touch the EGR valve during testing, wear gloves or use a shop towel to protect your fingers. Handle them carefully. A damaged valve may not operate normally. This may result in component failure of the EGR system.

Inspecting, Testing, Repairing, and Replacing the Valve and Exhaust Passages of an EGR System Refer to the vehicle service manual for specifications and special procedures. This is a general procedure.

To inspect, test, repair, or replace the valve and exhaust passages of the EGR system:

1. Make sure you follow all procedures in the appropriate service manual.
2. Visually inspect the EGR valve and exhaust passages for carbon deposits. These deposits can cause the valve to be stuck open or closed. *Note:* An EGR valve that is stuck open can cause stalling, poor idle, or surging. Detonation, combustion chamber overheating, or high NO_x emissions are possible results of an EGR valve that is stuck closed.

3. If the EGR valve has carbon deposits that are causing clogged passages in the valve, either clean and reuse the valve or replace it. The necessary process depends on the type of valve that is in your vehicle's EGR system. Check your service manual. Clean carbon from all passages in the manifold.
4. If the EGR valve is on a computer-equipped vehicle, be sure to check and clear diagnostic trouble codes.

Inspecting, Testing, Repairing, and Replacing an EGR System's Vacuum/Pressure Controls, Filters, and Hoses Refer to the vehicle service manual for specifications and special procedures. This is a general procedure.

To inspect, test, repair, and replace the vacuum/pressure controls, filters, and hoses of the EGR system:

1. Make sure you follow all procedures in the appropriate service manual. *Note:* If your vehicle has a vacuum-operated EGR system, use a vacuum pump to check for output.
2. Visually inspect the vacuum/pressure controls for looseness or damage.
3. Tighten or replace these controls if they are loose or damaged.
4. Visually inspect the filters for looseness or damage.
5. If the filters are loose or damaged, tighten or replace them.
6. Visually inspect the hoses for looseness or damage.
7. Tighten or replace these hoses if they are loose or damaged. *Note:* The hoses must be properly connected for balanced EGR flow.

Air Injection System

The original **air injection reaction (AIR) system,** currently referred to as the secondary air injection system, is an exhaust emission control system. It reduces HC and CO emissions. It does this by injecting atmospheric air into the exhaust gases. Depending on the vehicle and operating conditions, the air is directed to either the exhaust manifold or the catalytic converter. In either case, the oxygen in the air helps to convert CO and unburned HC into water vapor and CO_2.

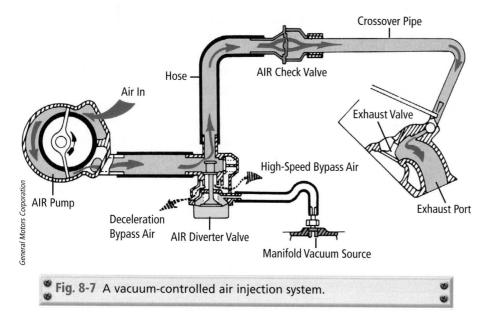

Fig. 8-7 A vacuum-controlled air injection system.

This system is known as a secondary air injection system. The primary components of an air injection system are the air pump, diverter valve, and check valve(s). See **Fig. 8-7.**

Air supplied by the pump travels through the air distribution manifold. The air manifold may be cast into the cylinder head or attached to the exhaust manifold. A belt drives the mechanical air pump from the crankshaft pulley. The pump runs whenever the engine is running.

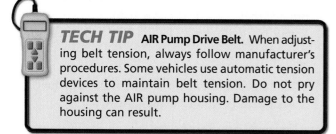

TECH TIP **AIR Pump Drive Belt.** When adjusting belt tension, always follow manufacturer's procedures. Some vehicles use automatic tension devices to maintain belt tension. Do not pry against the AIR pump housing. Damage to the housing can result.

When the engine is cold, air is directed to the exhaust manifold. The air enters the exhaust manifold through tubes or passages provided for this purpose. In the manifold, the air mixes with the hot exhaust gases. The resulting chemical reaction oxidizes the HC and CO into water vapor and CO_2. The heat from this reaction helps both the oxygen sensor and catalytic converter reach normal operating temperature sooner.

If the injected air is allowed to enter the exhaust manifold during deceleration, the mixture in the manifold could ignite and explode. These small explosions can cause annoying popping sounds or damage to the exhaust system.

To prevent this, the diverter valve diverts the air to the atmosphere during the conditions that occur during deceleration. A one-way check valve prevents exhaust gas from backing up into the diverter valve and AIR pump if the pump is not delivering air.

During warmup, the engine is operating in open loop mode. The oxygen sensor signal is not being used. The extra air at the oxygen sensor has no effect on fuel delivery. When the engine goes into closed loop operation, the air must be directed away from the oxygen sensor. To do this, the PCM operates an air management valve that directs the air to the catalytic converter.

The air is injected at a point in the converter where it will help oxidize HC and CO without interfering with the NO_x reduction activity in the converter. On some OBD-II engines the air pump is driven by an electric motor controlled by the PCM. In this case the pump only operates when turned on by the PCM. Most electric air pumps operate only during engine warmup.

Servicing the Air Injection System The air injection system needs little scheduled maintenance. Nevertheless, the system can fail in the following ways:
- Pinched or disconnected air delivery hoses or tubes will prevent normal airflow delivery.
- Defective diverter valves may cause a backfire. To operate correctly, the diverter valve must have a manifold vacuum source.
- Defective check valves allow hot exhaust gases to burn the injection hoses, diverter valve, and AIR pump.
- A leaking check valve or distribution manifold allows oxygen or "false air" to reach the oxygen sensor. This signals a lean condition to the PCM.
- The electrically controlled air pump should be serviced according to manufacturer's specifications.

The diverter valve's operating position may be shown in the PCM's serial data stream.

Excellence **in Science**

Vapor Pressure and Temperature

You stop at the pump to fill your fuel tank. A faint odor of gasoline fills the air. Later, you drive through the automatic car wash. When you leave the car wash, the water on your windshield dries quickly. Both events are related to the concept of evaporation and vapor pressure.

If a dish of water is left on a table for a day, the water level drops noticeably. When a liquid is exposed to air, molecules near the surface escape from it. This process is called evaporation. Condensation occurs when vapor returns to its normal state, such as when water vapor condenses into water droplets on a cold beverage can.

When the number of molecules evaporating equals the number of molecules condensing, an equilibrium has been reached. At a constant temperature, a solid or liquid substance evaporates and reaches an equilibrium pressure with its vapor. This is the vapor pressure for that substance. When the vapor pressure of a liquid equals the external pressure, the liquid boils. When the vapor pressure of water equals the atmospheric pressure at sea level (760 mm Hg), water boils at 100°C [212°F]. At higher altitudes the atmospheric pressure is lower than 760 mm of mercury. At such an altitude, water in an open container will boil at a lower temperature than 100°C [212°F].

Apply It!

Graphing Vapor Pressure

Meets NATEF Science Standards for understanding the relationship of heat and barometric pressure. Also meets NATEF Mathematics Standards for constructing and interpreting graphs.

The vapor pressure of water at various temperatures is shown. You can use this information to show the effects of pressure on the boiling point of water.

1. Use a sheet of standard graph paper. Graph the information in the table. Near the bottom of the page, label the horizontal axis "Temperature." Mark temperatures from −50°C to +120°C in increments of 10°.

2. Near the left edge of the sheet, label the vertical axis "Vapor Pressure." Mark values from 0 to 1,500 mm Hg in increments of 100 mm. Make the graph as tall as possible.

3. Plot the values given in the table as solid dots on the graph.

Results and Analysis

4. Refer to the graph. How does vapor pressure vary with the temperature?

5. Suppose that you are driving high in the mountains. The atmospheric pressure is only about 450 mm Hg. This pressure is much lower than 760 mm Hg, the atmospheric pressure at sea level. At what temperature would water boil on this mountain road?

VAPOR PRESSURE OF WATER			
Temperature [°C]	Vapor Pressure [mm Hg]	Temperature [°C]	Vapor Pressure [mm Hg]
−50	0.030	50	92.5
−10	1.95	60	149
0	4.58	70	234
10	9.21	80	355
20	17.5	90	526
30	31.8	100	760
40	55.3	120	1,489

Catalytic Converter

The catalytic converter changes harmful exhaust pollutants into harmless gases. A **catalyst** is a material that causes a chemical change without being part of the chemical reaction.

The catalytic converter is located between the engine and the muffler. Some engines may have two catalytic converters in each exhaust path. The first converter is located close to the engine so that it will heat up faster. The second is located close to the muffler. It converts the remaining pollutants into harmless gases.

The catalyst body, or substrate, is a bed of pellets or a ceramic honeycomb. The housing of the pellet-type converter is flat. The housing of the honeycomb, or monolith, converter is round or oval-shaped. The housing or shell of the converter is made of stainless steel. This helps prevent burn-through.

The exhaust gas passes over a large surface area coated with a catalyst. Vehicles with catalytic converters must use unleaded gasoline. This is to prevent coating the catalyst with lead and making it ineffective. Excessive oil consumption and coolant leaks into the combustion chamber also reduce converter efficiency.

The catalyst must reach a temperature of about 480°F [249°C] before oxidation begins. When fully operational, the converter temperature ranges between 752°F [400°C] and 1,472°F [800°C]. If excess fuel enters the converter, the operating temperature can exceed 1,800°F [982°C]. At this temperature the substrate will melt and the converter will be destroyed.

The converter is equipped with heat shields to prevent unwanted heat from reaching the vehicle's floor pans.

Two-way converters use platinum or palladium to change or oxidize HC and CO into water vapor (H_2O) and carbon dioxide (CO_2). Three-way converters add rhodium to break up or reduce NO_x to nitrogen (N_2) and oxygen (O_2). See **Fig. 8-8.**

For the catalytic converter to be most effective, the air/fuel mixture must be at the stoichiometric ratio of 14.7:1. The air/fuel mixture must alternate, or "switch," from rich to lean to allow the catalyst to oxidize pollutants more efficiently. Most modern converters contain a base metal known as cerium. Cerium attracts and releases oxygen, which helps oxidize or reduce pollutants.

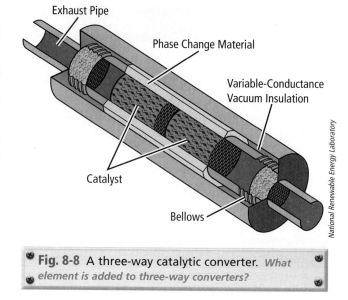

Exhaust Pipe

Phase Change Material

Variable-Conductance Vacuum Insulation

Catalyst

Bellows

National Renewable Energy Laboratory

Fig. 8-8 A three-way catalytic converter. *What element is added to three-way converters?*

Inspecting and Testing the Catalytic Converter

Although catalytic converters are simple devices, they can fail. Perform the following checks:

1. If the substrate is loose in a converter, it will rattle when tapped with a rubber hammer.
2. Test the converter for clogging by using a pressure gauge attached to a special adapter. The adapter can be temporarily installed in place of the oxygen sensor. A special tap can also be temporarily threaded into the exhaust pipe. Either the adapter or tap allows a pressure gauge to be attached. In general, the backpressure shouldn't exceed 1.5 psi [10.3 kPa] at 3,000 no-load rpm.
3. Check the intake manifold vacuum using a vacuum gauge attached to the intake manifold. A 3,000-rpm, no-load condition should show a steady vacuum reading. A progressively decreasing or unusually low vacuum reading may indicate excessive backpressure.
4. Using a noncontact pyrometer, check the converter outlet temperature. When completely warmed up, the converter outlet temperature should exceed the inlet temperature by approximately 100°F [38°C].
5. Thoroughly check the ignition and fuel system for correct operation. An ignition misfire or rich fuel delivery may melt the substrate in a catalytic converter.

Safety First **Catalytic Converters** To prevent severe burns, let hot catalytic converters cool before servicing. Always reinstall heat shields in their original locations. Failing to do so could cause the vehicle's carpet to catch fire.

Replacing the Catalytic Converter A catalytic converter may be attached to the exhaust system, or it may be made as part of the header pipe.

If the catalytic converter is attached to the exhaust system:

1. Remove all clamps and mounting hardware that attach the converter to the exhaust system.
2. Use a hammer or similar tool to loosen the converter.
3. If necessary, use a cutter to loosen the converter from the system.
4. Remove the converter.
5. Install a new converter, using new mounting hardware.
6. Reinstall all heat shields, replacing any that are damaged.

If the catalytic converter is part of the header pipe:

1. Remove the header pipe and converter as a unit. Consult the vehicle service manual for the location of mounting hardware.
2. Install new gaskets as specified by the vehicle service manual.
3. Install a new header pipe and converter.
4. Reinstall all heat shields, replacing any that are damaged.

Legal requirements govern the replacement of catalytic converters. Many converters are covered by original equipment manufacturer (OEM) warranties. A converter should be replaced only by a qualified technician. If the converter is replaced, the repair should be documented. The converter should be disposed of according to applicable regulations.

TECH TIP **Recycling the Converter.** A catalytic converter contains materials and elements that are very rare and expensive. Many of these elements can be recovered through a recycling process. Be sure to check for the proper method of disposing of used converters in your community.

Evaporative Control System

The **evaporative control (EVAP) system** is a system that prevents gasoline vapors in the fuel system from escaping into the atmosphere. The vapors are stored in a charcoal-filled canister. When specific operating conditions are met, a purge valve is opened. Vacuum from the intake manifold draws vapors from the canister. This allows fuel vapors to flow into cylinders to be burned.

OBD-I Evaporative Control System An OBD-I EVAP system consists of the following parts:

- A fuel tank equipped with vapor vent lines leading to a charcoal canister. See **Fig. 8-9.** The canister stores fuel vapors when the engine is shut off.
- A fuel tank cap that prevents fuel vapors from leaking into the atmosphere.
- A vacuum-operated or electrically operated purge valve that controls the flow of fuel vapors into the intake manifold.

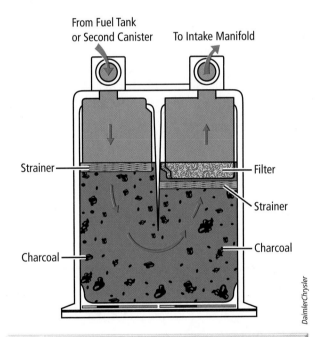

Fig. 8-9 A charcoal canister. *What is the function of this canister?*

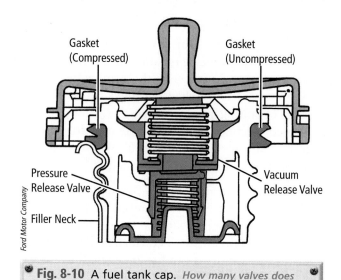

Fig. 8-10 A fuel tank cap. *How many valves does the fuel tank cap have?*

The fuel tank cap on a fuel tank in an EVAP system has a pressure release valve. This valve prevents excess pressure from building in the fuel tank. See **Fig. 8-10.** Tank overfill or pinched vapor purge lines can cause a buildup of pressure. The cap also contains a vacuum release valve to prevent a vacuum from building in the tank caused by gasoline consumption or temperature changes. Most EVAP system malfunctions occur because:

- The fuel tank is overfilled. Fuel station pumps have automatic fuel shut-off nozzles to prevent overfilling.

- The fuel tank cap leaks. If the fuel cap is not fully tightened, or is defective, the MIL light may be turned on in some OBD-II systems.
- The fuel is more volatile than normal. Excess pressure can develop in the fuel tank.
- The purge lines or hoses leak. Many EVAP systems perform vacuum and pressure tests on the entire system. If the tests fail, the MIL light is turned on.
- The purge valve does not open or close when it should. The purge valve must operate properly to remove fuel vapors from the system.

OBD-II Evaporative Control System OBD-II provides diagnostic monitoring of the EVAP system operation. See **Fig. 8-11.** The EVAP monitor checks the operation and condition of EVAP system components. Depending upon the application, OBD-II may add these parts to the EVAP system:
- A canister vent valve.
- A test port with a green cap for testing purposes.
- A leak detection pump (LDP) that pressurizes or introduces a vacuum to the fuel tank for the EVAP system monitor.
- A fuel tank pressure sensor.
- A domed fuel tank equipped with vent valves to prevent overfilling and allow fuel to expand without leaking.
- Rollover valves that prevent fuel from leaking from the tank inlet and outlets if the vehicle tips over.

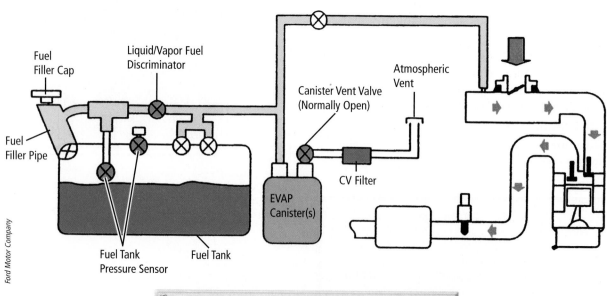

Fig. 8-11 An OBD-II EVAP system. *What is the purpose of an EVAP monitor?*

OBD-II systems test the EVAP system for leaks by admitting a slight amount of vacuum or air pressure into the fuel tank. The operating strategies of these systems may differ. Use the vehicle service manual for diagnosis. In general, an OBD-II system uses a canister vent solenoid to close the system for testing. See **Fig. 8-12.**

For vacuum-operated systems, the PCM monitor begins the test by closing the canister vent valve. The purge valve is opened to allow a small amount of manifold vacuum into the fuel tank. The PCM then closes the purge valve. A fuel tank pressure sensor measures the vacuum in the tank. If the vacuum is lost too quickly, the PCM activates the MIL and sets a DTC in its diagnostic memory.

Some EVAP systems use a leak detection pump (LDP) to pressurize the fuel tank. When the PCM activates the EVAP monitor, the canister vent valve is closed. Then the LDP begins running. If the fuel tank holds pressure, the LDP shuts off. If the LDP does not shut off, the PCM activates the MIL and sets a DTC in the diagnostic memory.

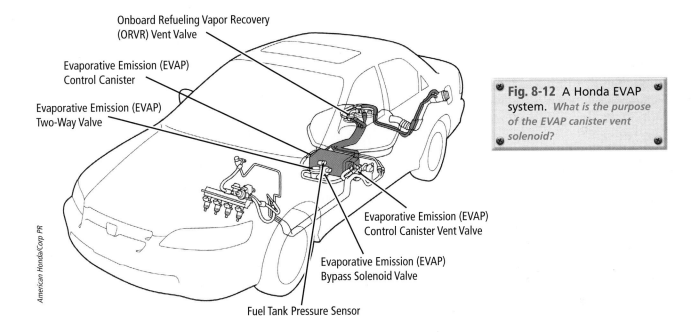

Onboard Refueling Vapor Recovery (ORVR) Vent Valve

Evaporative Emission (EVAP) Control Canister

Evaporative Emission (EVAP) Two-Way Valve

Evaporative Emission (EVAP) Control Canister Vent Valve

Evaporative Emission (EVAP) Bypass Solenoid Valve

Fuel Tank Pressure Sensor

American Honda/Corp PR

Fig. 8-12 A Honda EVAP system. *What is the purpose of the EVAP canister vent solenoid?*

SECTION 1 KNOWLEDGE CHECK

1. Explain how to check the PCV system with a piece of heavy paper.

2. What is the purpose of the EGR?

3. What is the main symptom of a pinched vacuum line or a plugged exhaust passage?

4. Where is the catalytic converter located?

5. What can happen if excess fuel enters the catalytic converter?

6. Where are gasoline vapors stored in the evaporative control (EVAP) system?

ASE TEST PREP

7. Technician A says that the outlet temperature on a completely warmed up catalytic converter should exceed the inlet temperature by approximately 100°F [38°C]. Technician B says that the outlet temperature on a completely warmed up catalytic converter should exceed the inlet temperature by approximately 150°F [66°C]. Who is correct?

   ⓐ Technician A.

   ⓑ Technician B.

   ⓒ Both Technician A and Technician B.

   ⓓ Neither Technician A nor Technician B.

● Section 2
Emissions Testing

Objectives:

- Identify the two types of emissions testing programs.
- A14 ● Prepare 4 or 5 gas analyzer; inspect and prepare vehicle for test, and obtain exhaust readings; interpret readings, and determine necessary action.

Vocabulary:

- no-load test
- load test
- I/M 240 programs
- exhaust gas analyzer

Emissions Testing Programs

Many states have some type of vehicle emissions testing program. These programs vary according to the special needs of a state or locality. All programs require that OEM emissions hardware, including vacuum hoses, be in place and operational. See **Fig. 8-13.** Some programs require using an exhaust gas analyzer to test exhaust emissions. Others rely on the MIL to determine excessive emissions.

Two types of tests are used to check emissions. The **no-load test** is a procedure that checks exhaust emissions at either idle speed only or at idle and 2,500 no-load rpm. This test is most often used on older vehicles that are not required to meet current emissions standards.

A **load test** is a procedure that checks vehicle emissions over a range of operating conditions. The most widely used emissions testing program is the I/M 240 program.

I/M 240 programs are centralized emissions testing programs using test procedures that satisfy federal government standards. Emissions tests performed in dealerships or independent shops are decentralized test programs.

The I/M 240 test uses a chassis dynamometer to simulate specific load and speed conditions encountered in day-to-day driving. The test operator drives the vehicle at speeds up to 55 mph [88 kph] for 240 seconds while the emissions are measured. The emissions specifications depend upon the type of vehicle being tested.

The I/M 240 test may require an EVAP system purge flow test and an EVAP system pressure test. The purge flow test measures the amount of vapor and air flowing through the purge valve. The pressure test pressurizes the fuel tank to 0.5 psi [3 kPa]. The tank must then hold pressure for at least two minutes.

Honda Motor Company

INFORMATION

▷THE FACTORY INSTALLED LONG-LIFE COOLANT MUST BE REPLACED AT 120 MONTHS OR 200,000 KM (120,000 MILES). THEREAFTER, REPLACE COOLANT EVERY 60 MONTHS OR 100,000 KM (60,000 MILES).
▷WHEN ADDING OR REPLACING THE COOLANT, ALWAYS USE Honda RECOMMENDED GENUINE ALL SEASON ANTI-FREEZE/COOLANT TYPE 2. THIS COOLANT IS PRE-MIXED WITH 50% DISTILLED WATER. IT DOES NOT REQUIRE ANY ADDITIONAL MIXING.
▷NEVER DILUTE THE COOLANT, OR THE LIFE OF THE ENGINE MAY BE SERIOUSLY SHORTENED.
▷CHECK OR ADD THE COOLANT AT THE RESERVE TANK, NOT THE RADIATOR.
▷FOR FURTHER INFORMATION ON THE COOLING SYSTEM, READ THE OWNER'S MANUAL OR CHECK WITH YOUR Honda DEALER.

VEHICLE EMISSION CONTROL INFORMATION

THIS VEHICLE CONFORMS TO U.S. EPA TIER 2 BIN 5 AND CFV LEV REGULATIONS APPLICABLE TO 2004 MODEL YEAR NEW PASSENGER CARS AND CALIFORNIA REGULATIONS APPLICABLE TO 2004 MODEL YEAR NEW LEV II LEV PASSENGER CARS. EPA CERTIFICATION TEST FUEL FOR CFV: EPA UNLEADED GASOLINE

CATALYST

TWC, A/F SENSOR, HO2S, EGR, SFI OBDII CERTIFIED

VALVE LASH	IN: 0.23±0.02 mm	4HNXVO2.4JBP	EXHAUST EMISSIONS STANDARDS
(COLD)	EX: 0.30±0.02 mm	4HNXR0140BBA	ARB: LEV II LEV (CERTIFICATION AND IN-USE)
NO OTHER ADJUSTMENTS NEEDED.		2.4L	EPA: TIER 2 BIN 5 (CERTIFICATION AND IN-USE)
			EPA: CFV LEV

TO EVAP CANISTER
PCV VALVE   EVAP CANISTER PURGE VALVE
↓ FRONT

Honda Motor Co.,Ltd.   (U·Y) RAA-A01   KE1AG24G

Fig. 8-13 A typical emission control information decal with vacuum hose routing. *Where is the engine displacement noted?*

Excellence in Math

Calculating Carbon Dioxide

The burning of fossil fuels produces large amounts of carbon dioxide (CO_2) emissions every year. Fossil fuels include coal, natural gas, and petroleum. Gasoline-powered vehicles produce about 20 percent of all CO_2 emissions.

The combustion of gasoline produces about 310 million metric tons of CO_2 every year. How many pounds per year is this?

310 million metric tons
= 310,000,000 metric tons
= 310,000,000,000 kg

Convert kilograms to pounds:

2.2 lb per kg × 310,000,000,000 kg
= 682,000,000,000 lb of CO_2

These numbers are very impressive. However, they are so large that we may not understand their significance.

Let's look at the numbers for one vehicle. One estimate is that burning a gallon of gasoline produces 5 pounds of CO_2. The driver of a 1999 Chevrolet Malibu with a 2.4-liter twin-cam engine could expect to get 23 mpg in city driving. The average driver drives about 12,000 miles each year. How much CO_2 will this car emit in a year?

First find how much gasoline the car will use in a year.

$$\frac{12{,}000 \text{ miles}}{23 \text{ mph}} = 522 \text{ gal}$$

Then determine how much CO_2 is produced by burning 522 gal of gasoline:

522 gal × 5 lb per gal = 2,610 lb of CO_2

Apply It!

Meets NATEF Mathematics Standards for estimating expected outcomes for a normally operating system.

1. Assume that the Grimes family uses its car mainly for city driving. They rarely drive the car on the highway. Most of their trips are relatively short—under 5 miles. Their gas mileage is fairly poor. They average only 14 mpg. They drive 12,000 miles per year. How much CO_2 is emitted by their car in one year?

2. Shirley Patel is a saleswoman who uses her car almost solely for highway driving. She drives 24,000 miles in a year and her car averages 27.5 mpg. How much CO_2 does her car emit in one year?

3. What factors might account for the fact that Shirley Patel's car emits about the same amount of CO_2 as the Grimes' car emits?

4. Bill Jantz commutes back and forth to work on a daily basis. During the daily commute Bill's average fuel economy is 23 mpg. Bill estimates that he drives 18,000 miles each year by going to and from work. Bill also likes to vacation in the mountains. When he drives on the highway from his home to the mountains his car's average fuel economy is 35 mpg. Bill estimates that he drives 6,000 miles each year to vacation in the mountains and return home. How much CO_2 does Bill's car produce each year?

5. Esmeralda Dominguez rides the bus to work each day. The driver estimates that the bus's fuel economy is 15 mpg and that the bus travels 22,000 miles on its route each year. If twenty people ride the bus each day, how much CO_2 is produced per rider per year? How does this amount of CO_2 compare with the amount of CO_2 produced by Bill's car?

Exhaust Gas Analyzers

An **exhaust gas analyzer** is a device used to test the amount of exhaust emissions produced by a vehicle. The analyzer samples the exhaust through a probe placed in the tail pipe. The exhaust sample is drawn into the analyzer, where it is filtered. The filtered exhaust is passed through a detector. The detector measures the content and chemical composition of the exhaust gas. The exhaust gas analyzer can also be used to diagnose ignition and fuel system problems that cause driveability complaints. See **Fig. 8-14**.

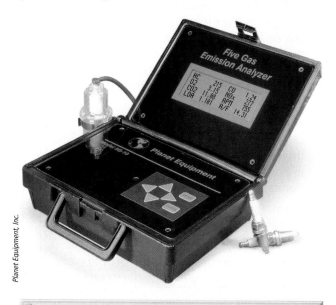

Planet Equipment, Inc.

Fig. 8-14 A portable five-gas emission analyzer. This analyzer records readings for all five gases, plus rpm and the air/fuel ratio. *What five exhaust gases does this instrument analyze?*

Two-Gas Analyzers Two-gas analyzers measure HC and CO. Most of these analyzers are not sensitive enough to measure exhaust emissions on late-model vehicles. Because new vehicles produce very low exhaust emissions, the exhaust gas analyzer must be able to measure very small amounts of polluting gases.

Four- and Five-Gas Analyzers Most exhaust gas analyzers are four- or five-gas analyzers. The four-gas analyzers are the most common. They measure levels of CO_2 and O_2 in addition to HC and CO. Though not harmful emissions, measuring CO_2 and O_2 provides data to evaluate the combustion efficiency of the engine.

The five-gas analyzer measures levels of NO_x, in addition to CO_2, O_2, HC, and CO. NO_x is a toxic pollutant and the primary cause of emission-generated smog. High levels of NO_x are caused by:
- High combustion temperatures resulting from failure of the EGR system.
- High engine temperatures resulting from a defective cooling system or other problems.

Safety First **Carbon Monoxide** Carbon monoxide (CO) is an odorless, invisible gas present in all vehicle exhaust systems. Inhaling CO can cause severe illness or death. Always use exhaust ventilation equipment to remove exhaust gas.

General Testing Procedures Most analyzers require a warm-up period before they will accurately test emissions. The analyzer may also need to be zeroed while sampling clean air. Modern analyzers may use a calibration gas to calibrate the analyzer before it is used to test emissions.

When testing emissions, it is important to check the exhaust system for leaks. A leaking exhaust system affects emissions readings.

Exhaust gas analysis requires special training. In most states, a special license is required to perform federally-mandated emissions testing.

Before testing a vehicle, make sure the engine and exhaust system are warmed to proper operating temperature. An insufficiently warmed vehicle will usually give erroneous readings. Some vehicles may need to be driven before performing an emissions test.

Safety First **Road Test** Before performing a road test, be sure to obtain written permissions from appropriate authorities.

Actual emission values depend on many variables. These include combustion chamber design and emissions control efficiency. Automotive engines tend to produce more emissions as age and mileage increase.

An engine operating at the correct air/fuel ratio will result in the lowest emission levels. The following comments apply to no-load test results.
- HC is measured in parts per million (ppm). Misfires and lean or rich air/fuel mixtures cause excessive HC levels.

- The normal limit for CO should be less than 2 percent. Rich air/fuel mixtures cause excessive CO levels.
- NO_X is a term for various compounds of nitrogen and oxygen. High combustion temperatures cause NO_X. NO_X is not usually measured during no-load testing.
- CO_2 output should peak at 15 percent. Higher CO_2 indicates better combustion.
- O_2 content should be less than 2 percent. Higher levels show a lean air/fuel mixture. Lower levels show incomplete combustion.

TECH TIP **Contaminated Oil.** Engine oil can be contaminated with gasoline. This usually occurs during short-trip driving in cold weather. When the engine is warmed up, the gasoline vaporizes. These vapors cause high HC and CO levels (measured at idle).

Testing Exhaust Emissions with a Four-Gas Analyzer Refer to the vehicle service manual for specifications and special procedures. This is a general procedure. To inspect and test the exhaust emissions of the vehicle:

1. Make sure you follow all procedures in the appropriate service manual.
2. To test exhaust emissions, follow the analyzer operating instructions.
3. When the analyzer is working, the tailpipe probe draws out some of the exhaust gas and carries it through the analyzer. Meters, a display, or a printout show how much of each gas is in the sample of exhaust.
4. Connect the exhaust-gas analyzer to the vehicle, following the analyzer operating instructions.
5. Calibrate the meters on the analyzer, if necessary. The calibration procedure may require a gas sample from a bottle of special calibration gas.
6. Block off or disable the air flow from the air-injection or air-respirator system. Follow the procedure recommended by the vehicle manufacturer. This prevents the additional air from affecting readings.
7. Insert the exhaust-gas pickup or probe into the vehicle tailpipe. Be sure the probe is securely in place. Then connect the shop exhaust system to the tailpipe.
8. Start the engine. With the engine idling at normal operating temperature, take the readings of each gas.
9. Repeat the tests of the exhaust gas with the engine running at 1500 rpm and at 2500 rpm.
10. Compare the readings for each gas with specifications. These may be programmed into the analyzer, or state inspection or other standards may apply.
11. If the vehicle fails the emissions test, determine which gases have bad readings. Review the causes of bad readings. Using this information and the trouble-diagnosis section of the vehicle service manual, make a service recommendation for the vehicle you are testing.

SECTION 2 KNOWLEDGE CHECK

1. What test checks exhaust emissions at either idle speed only or at idle and 2,500 no-load rpm?

2. What are I/M 240 programs?

3. When performing the I/M 240 test, how long should the operator keep the vehicle's speed at 55 mph?

4. Where is an exhaust gas analyzer probe placed during testing?

5. What vehicle conditions cause high levels of NO_X emissions?

6. When is engine oil most likely to become contaminated with gasoline?

ASE TEST PREP

7. Technician A says that the normal limit for CO should be less than 2 percent. Technician B says that the normal limit for CO should be less than 1 percent. Who is correct?
   - ⓐ Technician A.
   - ⓑ Technician B.
   - ⓒ Both Technician A and Technician B.
   - ⓓ Neither Technician A nor Technician B.

Engine Performance

CHAPTER 8 REVIEW

Key Points

Meets the following NATEF Standards for Engine Performance: diagnosing oil leaks and emissions problems; diagnosing emissions and driveability problems.

- Automotive emissions come from three sources: crankcase ventilation, fuel, and exhaust systems.
- Proper operation of PCV system depends on the PCV valve being free of sludge deposits.
- Excess NO_X generally forms when the peak combustion temperature exceeds 3,500°F [1,927°C].
- The air injection (AIR) system reduces HC and CO emissions by injecting fresh air into the exhaust gases.
- The catalytic converter changes harmful exhaust pollutants into harmless gases.
- The EVAP system uses intake manifold vacuum to draw gasoline vapors from the charcoal canister into the intake manifold.
- The I/M 240 test uses a chassis dynamometer to simulate specific load and speed conditions encountered in day-to-day driving.

Review Questions

1. What can shaking a PCV valve tell you?
2. Which exhaust emission control system reduces HC and CO emissions?
3. What is a symptom of defective diverter valves?
4. When inspecting a catalytic converter, what is the first step?
5. What types of emission test programs are carried out at dealerships and independent shops?
6. How long must a fuel tank hold pressure during an EVAP system pressure test?
7. Name three variables that affect emission values.
8. What should O_2 content measure as a percentage?
9. What causes excessive HC emissions?
10. **Critical Thinking** Why must cars with catalytic converters use unleaded gasoline?

Excellence in Communication

Using J1930 Terminology

The Society of Automotive Engineers (SAE) has developed a standardized list of terms and acronyms. It is referred to as Recommended Practice J1930 or J1930, for short. This list was first issued in 1991 and has been updated several times. The U.S. government and the automotive industry accepted the list in 1995 as the industry standard.

J1930 lists terms, definitions, abbreviations, and acronyms. It also provides a method, or rules, to use when naming new items. Using this pattern, new terms will fit in with existing terms on the list. Some older terms have been kept because they are widely used and accepted even though their names don't follow the rules.

Here is an example. Before J1930, the acronym "CPS" could have meant "camshaft position sensor" or "crankshaft position sensor." Now, the term "CMP sensor" identifies the camshaft position sensor. The term CKP sensor refers to the crankshaft position sensor. Now you are less likely to be confused by these acronyms.

The definitions in J1930 are accepted by the automotive industry. This listing can clear up confusion you may have about new terms.

Apply It!

Meets NATEF Communications Standards for using standard definitions and text resources.

1. List the new terms and acronyms in this chapter.
2. Write the definitions for them.
3. Study and learn the items on your list.
4. Form small teams. Everyone on the team should quiz each other until all are familiar with the definitions of the items on the lists.

AUTOMOTIVE SERVICE EXCELLENCE
TEST PREP

Answering the following practice questions will help you prepare for the ASE certification tests.

1. While checking the PCV system you discover that the manifold does not develop vacuum quickly or sufficiently. What is a possible cause?

   ⓐ Engine PCV system is plugged.

   ⓑ Excess blowby.

   ⓒ Manifold vacuum leak.

   ⓓ All of the above.

2. Technician A says that a properly operating PCV valve rattles when shaken. Technician B says that a properly operating PCV valve does not rattle when shaken. Who is correct?

   ⓐ Technician A.

   ⓑ Technician B.

   ⓒ Both Technician A and Technician B.

   ⓓ Neither Technician A nor Technician B.

3. If the EGR valve is opened with the engine at idle, what should occur if the valve is working properly?

   ⓐ Engine should stall.

   ⓑ Engine rpm should increase.

   ⓒ Engine temperature should increase.

   ⓓ All of the above.

4. Technician A says that detonation, combustion chamber overheating, and high NO_X are all possible consequences of an EGR valve that is stuck closed. Technician B says that stalling, poor idle, and surging are all possible consequences of an EGR valve that is stuck open. Who is correct?

   ⓐ Technician A.

   ⓑ Technician B.

   ⓒ Both Technician A and Technician B.

   ⓓ Neither Technician A nor Technician B.

5. If the substrate is loose in a catalytic converter, it will:

   ⓐ rattle when tapped with a rubber hammer.

   ⓑ remain silent when shaken.

   ⓒ have a high resistance when tested with a digital multimeter.

   ⓓ None of the above.

6. Technician A says that the catalytic converter outlet should be about 100°F [38°C] cooler than the converter inlet. Technician B says that the converter outlet should be about 100°F [38°C] warmer than the converter inlet. Who is correct?

   ⓐ Technician A.

   ⓑ Technician B.

   ⓒ Both Technician A and Technician B.

   ⓓ Neither Technician A nor Technician B.

7. Which of the following is not part of an evaporative control system?

   ⓐ A fuel tank with vapor vent lines.

   ⓑ An EGR valve.

   ⓒ A fuel tank cap.

   ⓓ A vacuum or electrically operated purge valve.

8. Technician A says that the fuel tank cap prevents excess pressure from building in the fuel tank. Technician B says that the fuel tank cap is sealed and has no vent valve. Who is correct?

   ⓐ Technician A.

   ⓑ Technician B.

   ⓒ Both Technician A and Technician B.

   ⓓ Neither Technician A nor Technician B.

9. What pollutant does a five-gas analyzer test for that two- and four-gas analyzers do not?

   ⓐ CO_2.

   ⓑ O_2.

   ⓒ CO.

   ⓓ NO_X.

10. Technician A says that an exhaust gas analyzer works by reading the vehicle's serial data stream. Technician B says that an exhaust gas analyzer draws exhaust from the tailpipe into the analyzer for assessment. Who is correct?

    ⓐ Technician A.

    ⓑ Technician B.

    ⓒ Both Technician A and Technician B.

    ⓓ Neither Technician A nor Technician B.

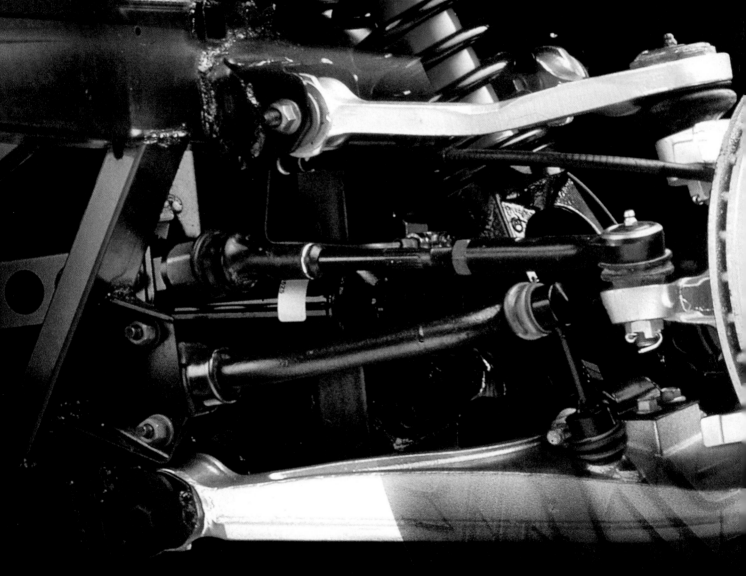

Suspension & Steering

Chapter 1
Diagnosing & Repairing Tires and Wheels

Chapter 2
Diagnosing & Repairing Steering Systems

Chapter 3
Diagnosing & Repairing Suspension Systems

Chapter 4
Diagnosing, Adjusting, & Repairing Wheel Alignment

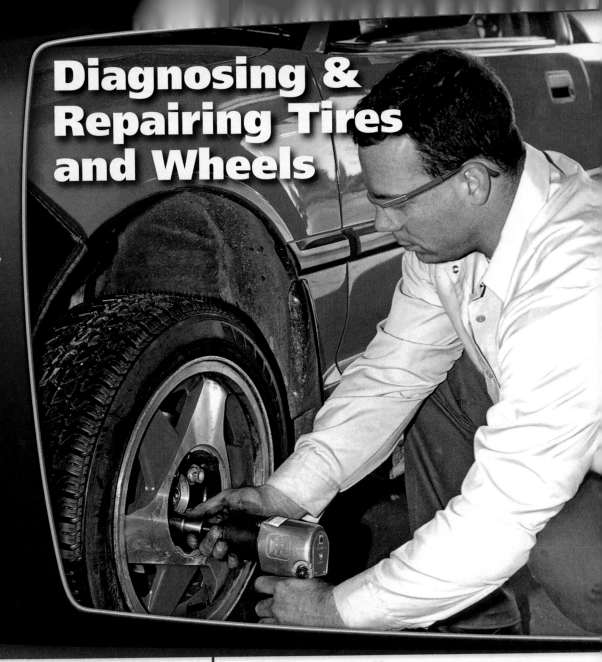

Diagnosing & Repairing Tires and Wheels

Section 1
Tires

Section 2
Wheels

Section 3
Tire Dismounting, Mounting, and Balancing

Customer's Concern

Ryan Maguire recently accepted a job transfer from Orlando to Detroit. Ryan has never traveled north of Georgia. The climate change has been a real adjustment for him this winter. Last night, Detroit received six inches of snow. When Ryan pulled out of his driveway this morning, he said his car didn't respond to his steering efforts. In fact, he ended up on the curb across from his house. He thinks that his tires are either frozen or there is something wrong with his steering system.

As you politely explain how to maneuver a vehicle on snow and ice, you think to yourself that there is probably nothing wrong with Ryan's car. However, to ease his fears, you assure him that you'll take a look at it.

Technician's Challenge

As the service technician, you need to find answers to these questions:

1. What is the first thing you will examine on Ryan's car? Could an overinflated tire increase control problems on snow?

2. How might tire tread design affect the handling of Ryan's car? What kind of tire tread design would you recommend?

3. The wear indicators on the front tires of Ryan's front-wheel-drive car are flush with the tread. Will tire rotation solve the handling problems?

Objectives:
- Identify different types of tire construction.
- Identify and determine tire dimensions.
- Identify and read tire sidewall markings.
- **A4** Locate and interpret vehicle and major component identification numbers (VIN, vehicle certification labels, calibration decals).
- Identify and determine wheel dimensions.
- **E13** Inspect, diagnose, and calibrate tire pressure monitoring system.
- **E2** Inspect tires; check and adjust air pressure.
- **E1** Diagnose tire wear patterns; determine necessary action.
- **E6** Diagnose tire pull (lead) problem; determine necessary action.
- **E4** Rotate tires according to manufacturer's recommendations.

Vocabulary:
- ply
- aspect ratio
- inflation pressure

Tire Construction

Tires provide the only connection between the vehicle and the road surface. For that reason, they are obviously very important. You may not plan to become a tire and wheel specialist. However, you need to understand basic tire design, tire diagnosis, and the handling of tires.

Tires serve several functions:
- Tires provide the traction required to negotiate the terrain. Tires are specially designed for use on different surfaces. These surfaces may be dry paved roads, wet roads, gravel roads, and roads covered with snow or ice.
- Tires act as part of the suspension. The air-cushioned support is part of the shock-absorbing action needed to reduce shock and vibration from the body and frame.
- The tire's construction, size, inflation pressure, and tread design enable proper handling during straight-line driving and proper operation during turns and braking.

First, let us look at the difference between tube and tubeless tires. Tube tires have an inner tube inside the tire. This separate component holds the inflation air that supports the vehicle. Today, only some trucks and some motorcycles use tube tires. The vast majority of tires today are tubeless. See **Fig. 1-1.**

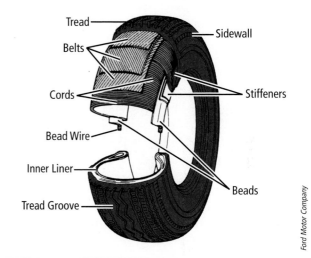

Tread — Sidewall
Belts — Stiffeners
Cords —
Bead Wire —
Inner Liner — Beads
Tread Groove —

Ford Motor Company

Fig. 1-1 Cutaway view showing construction of a typical tubeless radial tire. *What is the purpose of a tire inner tube?*

Tubeless tires contain air without the need for an inner tube. A leakproof seal is created where the tire bead seals against the wheel's flange. The tubeless tire must be nonporous. The wheel must be leak-free at all welds and seams. High-quality manufacturing standards for tires and wheels have eliminated the need for inner tubes, reducing the cost of tires. This has also reduced friction, heat buildup, and weight.

Bias-Ply, Bias-Belted, and Radial

Ply refers to a layer of cord, fiberglass, steel, or other construction materials used to create a tire carcass. The carcass is the tire "body" beneath the tread and sidewalls. Tire makers can apply tire plies either diagonally or radially, as shown in **Fig. 1-2**. Bias plies, also called diagonal plies, run at a bias, or diagonal, angle across the tire from bead to bead. Because the plies intersect, they rub against each other, creating heat as the tire runs. Also, such tires tend to "squirm" when the vehicle is driven. Bias-belted tires include stabilizer belts placed under the tread area.

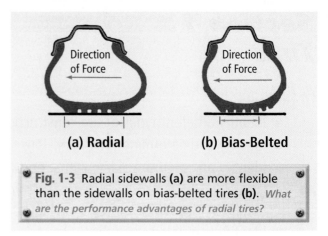

(a) Radial   **(b) Bias-Belted**

Fig. 1-3 Radial sidewalls **(a)** are more flexible than the sidewalls on bias-belted tires **(b)**. *What are the performance advantages of radial tires?*

Radial tires feature plies that run bead-to-bead, parallel to each other, with stabilizer belts under the tread. These plies reduce heat. The tires tend to run more smoothly and quietly. A radial-ply construction is also more flexible, creating a softer sidewall. During turns more tread stays in contact with the road. See **Fig. 1-3**. This results in better handling and improves high-speed stability. Radial tires also create a lower "rolling resistance." Radial tires, therefore, need less energy to roll forward. This increases fuel economy. All late-model vehicles have radial tires.

Run-Flat Tires

Tire makers design some tires to operate with little or no inflation pressure. These tires are called run-flat or zero-pressure tires. See **Fig. 1-4**. They feature a reinforced sidewall and bead design intended to support the vehicle if a cut or puncture causes loss of inflation pressure. Typically, tire makers design these tires to operate at around 50 mph [80 kph] for 50–100 miles [80–161 km] with no internal pressure before the sidewalls are damaged. This provides enough time for the driver to reach a service facility or dealership.

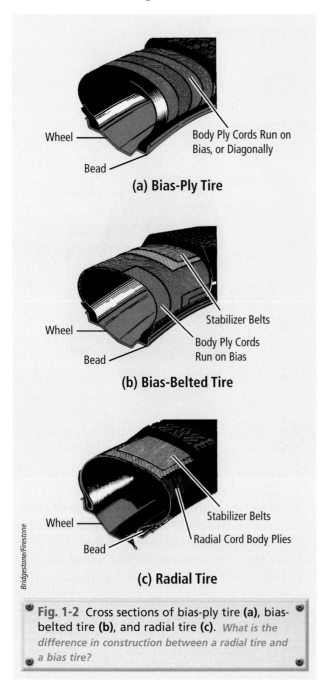

Wheel —

Bead —

Body Ply Cords Run on Bias, or Diagonally

(a) Bias-Ply Tire

Wheel —

Bead —

Stabilizer Belts

Body Ply Cords Run on Bias

(b) Bias-Belted Tire

Wheel —

Bead —

Stabilizer Belts

Radial Cord Body Plies

(c) Radial Tire

Bridgestone/Firestone

Fig. 1-2 Cross sections of bias-ply tire **(a)**, bias-belted tire **(b)**, and radial tire **(c)**. *What is the difference in construction between a radial tire and a bias tire?*

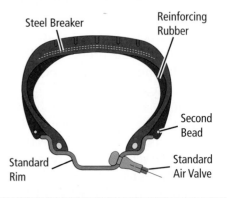

Steel Breaker

Reinforcing Rubber

Second Bead

Standard Rim

Standard Air Valve

Fig. 1-4 A typical run-flat tire. *What is the advantage of a run-flat tire?*

Tire Dimensions

It is important to understand the dimensions used in tire construction and design. See **Fig. 1-5**. The most important dimensions are:

- **Overall diameter.** This is also called the tire diameter. This is the measurement from the top of the tire tread on one side of the tire to the top of the tire tread on the side of the tire directly opposite. This measurement runs through the center of the tire as viewed from the side.
- **Section width.** This refers to the tire's width measured at the tire's widest point (not the tread). Essentially, this is the width of the tire at the sidewall area.
- **Tread width.** This is the measurement from the outside edge of the tread to the inside edge of the tread.
- **Section height.** This is the height of the tire from the bead seat to the tread surface when the tire is mounted and inflated.
- **Wheel size.** This is the diameter of the bead area (where the tire meets the wheel).

The size of the tires on most of today's passenger vehicles is identified using both standard and metric dimensions. For example, a 245/60R15 tire has a section width of 245 mm. The second number (in this case, 60) refers to the tire's aspect ratio, explained below. The R means that the tire is of radial construction. The last number refers to the wheel diameter required for that tire. In this case, 15 refers to a 15-inch rim.

Aspect Ratio

A tire's **aspect ratio** is the relationship between the tire's section height and section width. This ratio of section height to section width may also be referred to as the profile ratio. The section height is a percentage of the section width. For example, a 60-series tire has a section height that is 60 percent as big as the tire's section width. The lower the number of the aspect ratio, the shorter the tire, compared to its section width. See **Fig. 1-6**. For example, a 235/50R15 tire is shorter than a 235/60R15 tire. The number 235 means that the section width is 235 mm. If this tire has an aspect ratio of 60, it means that the section height is 60 percent of the section width. If it is a 50-series tire, the section height is 50 percent of the section width.

A "lower profile" tire has a shorter section height. Because of its lower section height, it provides less sidewall height. The shorter the sidewall, the less the sidewall can flex. Lower section height results in a more responsive tire that reacts faster during turns.

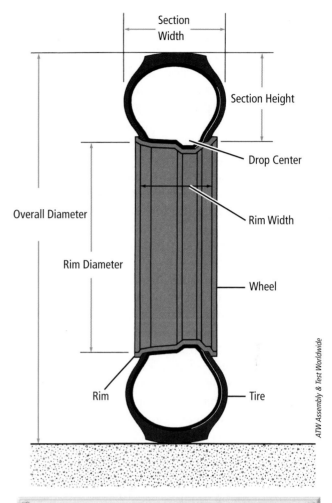

Fig. 1-5 Tire and wheel dimensions. Note tire overall diameter, section width, rim width, and section height. Rim diameter and rim width are wheel dimensions discussed later in this chapter. *Explain tire section width. What does this dimension represent?*

In some cases, the tradeoff is that a shorter sidewall may mean that the tires give a stiffer ride. However, tire manufacturers can design short sidewall tires that provide a comfortable ride. Thus, this is not a hard and fast rule.

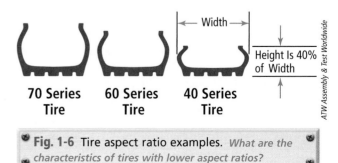

Fig. 1-6 Tire aspect ratio examples. *What are the characteristics of tires with lower aspect ratios?*

Tire Tread

The part of the tire that contacts the road is called the tire tread. The tread serves several functions, including providing traction. Tire makers design treads to provide traction and stability in specific conditions. Although tread designs vary, in general a tread pattern with more grooves and wider tread grooves provides better traction in wet or less-than-ideal traction conditions, such as in rain, snow, gravel, and dirt.

Tire makers design most passenger vehicle tire treads to perform on both dry and wet roads. When tire makers design a tire for use on loose ground, such as snow or dirt, the tread pattern has wider tread blocks and deeper tread grooves. This gives a more aggressive grip.

In appearance and performance, tread patterns may be symmetric or asymmetric. A symmetric tread pattern has the same pattern on each side of the tread (as compared to the center of the tread). An asymmetric tread pattern may have a different style or shape of tread on the left side of the tire's tread area as compared to the right side of the tread area.

Tires may also have directional tread. This means that the tire has been designed to rotate in only one direction. This is often the case with tires with asymmetric treads. The tire maker may have designed the tire for best performance if one side of the tread faces outside, or outboard, and the other side faces inside, or inboard. While you may move symmetric, nondirectional tread tires to any other position on the vehicle, and they may rotate in either direction, you may use a directional tread tire with only one direction of forward rotation.

An asymmetric tire moved to the other side of a vehicle will still have the outboard tread in the outboard position. Only the direction of rotation will have changed. A symmetric tire can be directional, but you can mount either sidewall outboard, depending on which side of the vehicle it is located. See **Fig. 1-7**. To rotate the tires on a vehicle, you may move directional tires from front to rear or rear to front. However each tire must remain on the same side of the vehicle.

If you want to move a directional tire to the other side of the vehicle, you must dismount it from the wheel and remount it to reverse the position of the tire. Always pay attention to sidewall positioning marks. If the tire is directional, a sidewall marking such as an arrow will indicate the forward direction in which the tire must rotate. Also, some asymmetrical tread tires require mounting with a particular sidewall facing outboard. If you mount a tire incorrectly, the vehicle may not handle as well. The tire may not provide directional stability.

The areas of the tread that contact the road are the tread blocks. The larger grooves that separate the tread blocks are the tread grooves. The very narrow slits that further separate the tread blocks are the tread sipes.

Tire makers design tread grooves in tires to allow water to pass through the tread on wet roads. These grooves also separate tread blocks to allow additional tread cooling. Tire makers design the smaller, narrow tread sipes to provide additional grip on wet roads. Sipes open as the tread hits the ground. They close when the tread leaves the ground.

(a)   (b)   (c)   (d)

Fig. 1-7 Examples of tire tread designs. Mud and snow (M&S) tread **(a)**. Notice the great number of narrow slits (sipes). These aid traction in rain and snow. A typical mud and snow tire for light truck use **(b)**. The tread blocks help to grab and throw out snow and mud for increased traction. A typical symmetric tread design **(c)**. A nonsymmetric, or asymmetric, tread **(d)**. *What is the advantage of a varying tread design on a tire?*

Tire Sidewall Markings

The sidewall of a tire provides a great deal of information. See **Fig. 1-8**. The marks may look confusing. However, they are actually easy to interpret.

Information typically provided on a sidewall includes:

- Aspect ratio.
- Brand name.
- Construction components.
- Construction type.
- Date of manufacture.
- Load index.
- Manufacturer and plant code number.
- Maximum inflation pressure.
- Maximum load marking.
- Model name.
- Serial number.
- Speed rating.
- Tire size code number.
- Tire-size designation.
- Treadwear indication number.
- Tube requirement.
- Uniform Tire Quality Grading (UTQG) marking.
- US Department of Transportation (DOT) safety standard code.

Aspect ratio, tire size code number, and tire size designation. Tire sidewalls indicate size in either metric or alphanumeric form. A tire-size designation

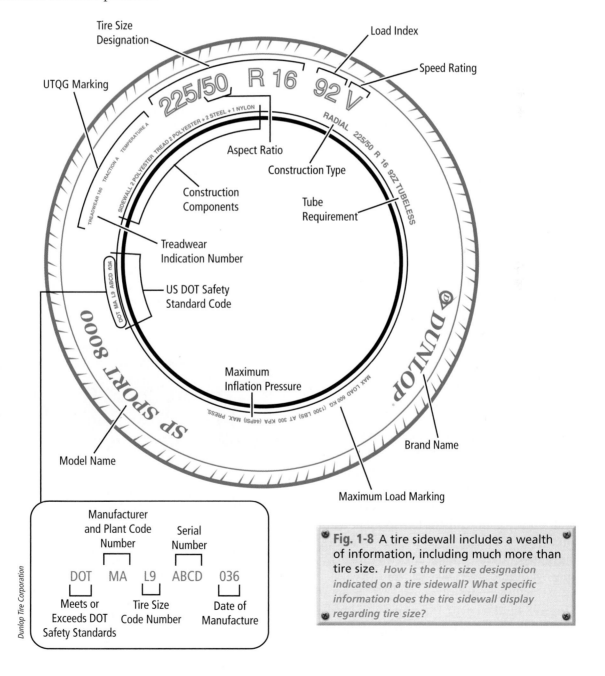

Fig. 1-8 A tire sidewall includes a wealth of information, including much more than tire size. *How is the tire size designation indicated on a tire sidewall? What specific information does the tire sidewall display regarding tire size?*

will show section width, aspect ratio, and rim diameter. For example, a designation of 215/65R14 means that the tire section width is 215 mm, the aspect ratio is 65, and the tire requires mounting on a 14-inch diameter rim. The R means that the tire is of radial construction.

Brand name and model name. The tire sidewall includes the brand (maker's) name and the tire model. For example, a Pirelli P600 tire is the P600 model of a tire that Pirelli makes.

Construction components and construction type. There are two tire sidewall markings related to the tire's construction. The construction components marking indicates the number of plies and the materials used to make the plies for the sidewall, the radial belts, and the backup plies under the belts. The construction type marking indicates whether or not the tire is a radial tire.

Load index. Load index, or load range, numbers give the maximum allowable load for that tire. For instance, a tire may have markings showing a maximum load of 2,200 lbs [999 kg]. This means that one corner of the vehicle can weigh no more than 2,200 lbs [999 kg], because that tire is capable of safely supporting only that amount of weight. In selecting any tire for any vehicle, always consider load ranges.

Maximum inflation pressure. The maximum inflation pressure marking indicates the maximum pressure that the tire can handle. This is not necessarily the pressure that the tire needs to operate on a specific vehicle. The vehicle owner's manual will give the recommended inflation pressure.

Maximum load marking. The maximum load marking indicates the maximum amount of weight the tire can carry when the tire is inflated to its maximum pressure. Any weight above the specified maximum results in unsafe operation.

Speed rating. The sidewall may include a speed rating. For example, in the designation 255/50ZR16, the speed symbol Z indicates the speed rating. This speed rating refers to the maximum allowable operating speed of the tire.

The speed rating indicates the tire's certified top speed. It does not indicate the top speed potential of the tire. Only DOT-approved tires are speed-rated.

The speed rating system is determined by the Rubber Manufacturers Association (RMA). This uses a letter designation from A to Z, from a low of 3 mph [5 kph] to over 168 mph [270 kph]. Passenger vehicle speed ratings are concentrated in the 100 to over-168 mph [161 to over-270 kph] range.

Safety First

Inflation Pressure The maximum inflation pressure marking indicates the maximum allowable inflation pressure for that tire. If, for example, the maximum inflation pressure marking states 65 psi [448 kPa], do not inflate the tire to 65 psi [448 kPa]. Instead, refer to the owner's manual for the correct inflation pressure. Excess inflation will degrade vehicle handling, ride, and braking performance, as well as cause premature wear at the tire center. Excess inflation may also result in failure of the tire.

Table 1-A lists currently used speed ratings related to passenger vehicle tires, and their meaning.

Note that a higher-letter does not necessarily indicate a higher speed rating. For instance, an H-rated tire carries a higher speed rating than does an S-rated tire.

Tire makers use the speed rating as an industry reference number. The speed rating does not mean that you should drive at those speeds. The speed rating is simply an indication of the tire's certified top sustainable speed.

UTQG marking. The Uniform Tire Quality Grading (UTQG) marking indicates subjective tire performance ratings regarding tread wear, wet braking traction, and resistance to temperature. This information is useful only in comparing different models of tires within the same manufacturer's line.

Treadwear indication number. The treadwear indication number included in the UTQG gives a rough indication of how fast the tread will wear.

Table 1-A	Speed Rating Passenger Vehicle Tires	
Speed Rating	**Speed**	
	mph	kph
S	112	180
T	118	190
U	124	200
H	129	208
V	149	240
W	168	270
V*	over 130	over 210
Z	over 149	over 240
Z*	over 168	over 270

(*Unlimited rating)

The lower the number, the faster the tread will wear. A tire with a treadwear rating of 140 will probably wear faster than one with a treadwear rating of 300.

Tube requirement marking. The tube requirement marking on a sidewall will indicate whether the tire needs a tube. The marking usually states either TUBE or TUBELESS.

DOT safety standard code. The US Department of Transportation (DOT) safety standard code indicates that the tire meets accepted tire safety standards and that the US DOT has approved the tire for use on roads in the United States. If the tire is not DOT-approved, the maker does not intend it for use on public roads. For example, typical race tires are not DOT-approved. They may not offer the tread or sidewall protection needed for street use.

A tire marked M&S is designed as a "mud and snow" tire. The marking might be M&S, M+S, or M/S. They all mean the same thing. Tire makers design mud and snow tires to provide better grip and handling in less-than-ideal conditions while also providing proper performance on dry and rainy roads. You can use M&S tires year-round. They are not snow-only tires.

Checking Tire Pressure

Inflation pressure is the measurement of the compressed air in a tire, expressed in pounds per square inch (psi) or kilopascals (kPa). Check tire inflation pressure when the tire is "cold." A tire is cold when its temperature is the same as the ambient temperature. The ambient temperature is the temperature of the surrounding air. Do not check inflation pressure when the tire is hot, after the car has been driven for a long period. Tires generate heat when the vehicle is driven. This raises inflation pressure. After a vehicle is parked, the tire begins to cool. This reduces inflation pressure. The inflation pressure listed in vehicle owner's manuals are "cold" pressures. This information is also on the door decal. See **Fig. 1-9**.

Some late-model vehicles use an electronic low-tire-pressure warning system. A low-tire-pressure warning system features a special tire-pressure sensor mounted inside the wheel rim. If tire pressure falls below a pre-set level, this tire-pressure sensor sends a radio signal to a receiver module in the vehicle. See **Fig. 1-10**. A warning light then glows on the dash to indicate low tire pressure. The light gives the driver an early warning of an underinflation problem. This allows the driver to avoid excessive tire wear and handling problems.

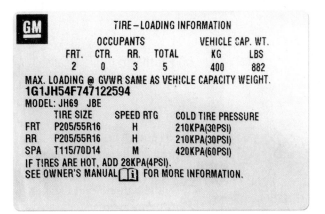

GM	TIRE—LOADING INFORMATION					
	OCCUPANTS				VEHICLE CAP. WT.	
	FRT.	CTR.	RR.	TOTAL	KG	LBS
	2	0	3	5	400	882

MAX. LOADING @ GVWR SAME AS VEHICLE CAPACITY WEIGHT.
1G1JH54F747122594
MODEL: JH69 JBE

	TIRE SIZE	SPEED RTG	COLD TIRE PRESSURE
FRT	P205/55R16	H	210KPA(30PSI)
RR	P205/55R16	H	210KPA(30PSI)
SPA	T115/70D14	M	420KPA(60PSI)

IF TIRES ARE HOT, ADD 28KPA(4PSI).
SEE OWNER'S MANUAL [i] FOR MORE INFORMATION.

Fig. 1-9 Information about proper tire pressure can be found on the door decal. *Where else is this information found?*

SmarTire Systems, Inc.

Fig. 1-10 Tire-pressure sensor mounted on inside of wheel rim. *How does a tire-pressure sensor work?*

Tire Inspection

Inspect a tire periodically for wear and damage. Check the tire tread for signs of uneven wear. Look for indications of worn suspension parts and improper inflation pressures. Look for problems that might result from poor wheel alignment or wheel balance.

A thorough tire inspection involves checking tire noises. Some tire noises are caused by improper mounting, wheel defects, vibrations, or tire

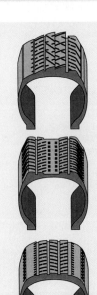
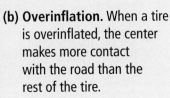

(a) **Feathering.** This is caused by incorrect toe.

(d) **One-side wear.** This can be caused by excessive camber.

(b) **Overinflation.** When a tire is overinflated, the center makes more contact with the road than the rest of the tire.

(e) **Cupping.** This can be caused by improperly balanced wheels, worn shock absorbers, and/or worn ball joints.

(c) **Underinflation.** When a tire is underinflated, the outer portion of the tire makes more road contact than the center of the tire.

Fig. 1-11 Tire wear patterns. *What should you look for when checking the wear pattern of each tire?*

imbalance. To determine whether there are problems, drive the vehicle on a smooth road at a variety of speeds. Listen for noise changes during acceleration and deceleration. The tire noise should remain constant, even while the engine, driveline, and exhaust noises vary.

Check for patterns of tire wear as shown in **Fig. 1-11.** Check the tire for sidewall damage such as cuts, bulges, and scuffs. Bulges may indicate that the plies have separated or broken. Any tire with sidewall damage that appears more serious than simple cosmetic abrasions may no longer be safe. Replace such a tire as soon as possible.

Tires feature wear indicator bars, also called treadwear indicators (TWI), on the tread areas.

Safety First

Proper Inflation Proper inflation is critical to tire performance and safety. Underinflated tires will react slower during turns and maneuvers, will create more heat within the tire, and will promote outer tread wear. Overinflated tires will ride more harshly, and will promote center tread wear. Check tire inflation at least once per month, and always before any long trip. There should be a quality tire inflation gauge in the vehicle at all times. Remember, whenever inflating or deflating a tire, wear safety goggles.

Treadwear indicators are raised ribs molded into the tread. Their location is indicated by a small triangular symbol with the letters TWI on the tire sidewall. The height of the treadwear indicators is such that, when they are flush with the tread surface, the tread has worn enough to require replacement of the tire. See **Fig. 1-12.**

Treadwear Indicator

Fig. 1-12 Treadwear indicators. When tread wears down to a predetermined level, these wear indicator bars become flush with the tread surface and easily visible. This indicates the need to replace the tires. *Why is it important to inspect a tire's treadwear indicator bars?*

You should also check for radial and lateral runout (even roundness). Testing for runout is discussed later in this chapter.

Tire Rotation

Rotating tires, or tire rotation, is the relocating of each tire and wheel assembly from one wheel position to another. Tire rotation prolongs the life of the tire. Typically, a front-wheel drive vehicle's front tires will wear faster than the rear tires, because the front tires also steer the vehicle. By rotating the tires, the additional wear can be spread over all the vehicle's tires. Tires should usually be rotated every 5,000–10,000 miles [8,000–16,000 km]. The recommended rotation mileage for a specific vehicle can be found in the vehicle owner's manual.

Rotation patterns may vary, depending on the vehicle. See **Fig. 1-13.** Typically, on a rear-wheel drive vehicle, you bring the rear tires forward. Move the left-rear tire to the left-front location and the right-rear tire to the right-front location. You also move the front tires to the rear in a crisscross pattern. Move the left-front tire to the right-rear and the right-front tire to the left-rear.

On a front-wheel drive vehicle, move the front tires straight rearwards and move the rear tires forward in a crisscross pattern. Remember to cross the nondrive wheels.

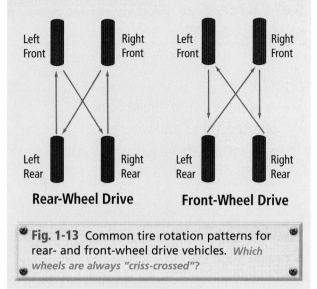

Rear-Wheel Drive   Front-Wheel Drive

General Motors Corporation

Fig. 1-13 Common tire rotation patterns for rear- and front-wheel drive vehicles. *Which wheels are always "criss-crossed"?*

With directional tires, the direction of each tire's forward rotation must remain constant. When moving directional tires, heed the directional arrow and any sidewall marking that indicates outboard side or inboard side. In some cases, tires may be location-specific. For example, a tire may be directional and intended for only right-front use. You cannot move this type of tire to a different location. To make sure you install the tires in the proper positions, read the sidewall information. When in doubt, refer to the vehicle service manual.

SECTION 1 KNOWLEDGE CHECK

1. What is the layer of cord, fiberglass, steel, or other construction materials that create the tire carcass?

2. Explain the concept of a zero-pressure tire.

3. What is section width?

4. Explain the difference between directional and nondirectional tread tires.

5. What is the section width of a 245/60R15 tire?

6. What causes a tire's center ribs to wear faster than the outer ribs?

ASE TEST PREP

7. Technician A says that a static balancer is also called a bubble balancer. Technician B says that a static balancer is also called a dynamic balancer. Who is correct?

   ⓐ Technician A.

   ⓑ Technician B.

   ⓒ Both Technician A and Technician B.

   ⓓ Neither Technician A nor Technician B.

Section 2
Wheels

Objectives:
- Identify wheel dimensions.
- Inspect tires and wheels.
- **E10** Reinstall wheel; torque lug nuts.

Vocabulary:
- rim diameter
- rim width
- wheel offset
- wheel backspacing
- bolt circle
- torque

Wheel Construction

Wheels are made of steel or an alloy (typically an aluminum alloy). Wheel makers construct wheels in a number of ways. A one-piece wheel is usually an alloy wheel cast or machined as a one-piece part. A two-piece wheel features a rim and a center section. These two separate pieces are joined by either a series of welds or by a rivet or bolt-together connection.

A three-piece wheel involves two rim sections (inboard rim and outboard rim) and a center section. These are secured together with small bolts and nuts. Technicians often refer to three-piece wheels as "modular" wheels. This is because they allow different rim width and offset setups by using rim sections of different sizes.

Wheel makers either cast or forge alloy wheels. Forged alloy wheels are stronger. They are normally used for higher-stress applications, such as on trucks and performance vehicles.

Wheel Dimensions

Wheel dimensions include rim diameter, rim width, wheel offset, wheel backspacing, and bolt circle.

The **rim diameter** is the measurement from a point on the inside bead seat to the point on the inside bead seat directly across the diameter of the wheel. The rim diameter refers to the bead seat diameter, not the total outside diameter. For example, a 15-inch wheel features a 15-inch bead seat diameter. However, the total outside diameter may measure 17 inches.

Rim width is the measurement from the inside bead seat wall to the opposite bead seat wall. A 7-inch wheel will measure 7 inches between the bead seat walls. However, the total outside width could be several inches more.

Wheel offset is the location of the wheel's centerline as viewed from the front, relative to the location of the mounting face of the wheel hub. See **Fig. 1-14.** The mounting face is the rear of the hub face that contacts the hub. If the mounting face is at exactly the midpoint of the rim width, the wheel has a zero offset. If the center of the rim width is outboard relative to the mounting face, the wheel has a

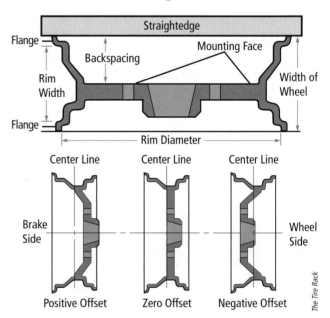

Fig. 1-14 Wheel dimensions. Rim width, backspacing, and offset are shown here. Remember that rim diameter is measured from bead seat to bead seat, not from outer rim flanges. Using a straightedge provides a line of reference that allows easy and accurate measurement of backspacing. The straightedge is laid on top of the rim surface on the brake side of the wheel.
What is wheel backspacing?

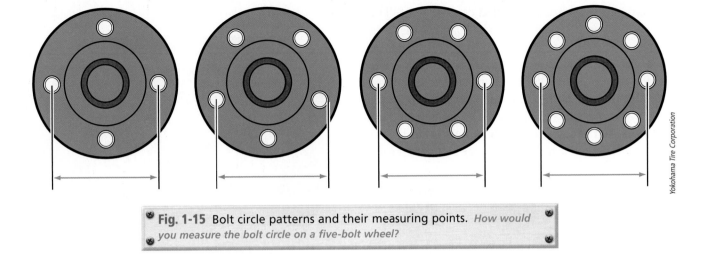

Fig. 1-15 Bolt circle patterns and their measuring points. *How would you measure the bolt circle on a five-bolt wheel?*

negative offset. If the center of the rim width is inboard relative to the mounting face, the wheel has a positive offset.

The wheel offset affects track. Track is the distance between the center of the right tire's tread and the center of the left tire's tread. Negative offset creates a wider track, while positive offset creates a narrower track. The offset dimension is critical for clearance and handling.

Wheel backspacing is the distance from the wheel's mounting surface to the rear edge of the wheel rim. Backspacing is important only when considering inboard clearance between the wheel/tire and the wheelwell and suspension or frame.

Bolt circle refers to the bolt hole pattern in the wheel's center section. This is where the wheel bolts to the hub. Determine the bolt circle by drawing a circle passing through the center of each of the wheel's bolt holes. The bolt circle can refer also to the position of the bolt holes in the wheel's center section.

Depending on the vehicle, the number of bolt holes may vary from four to eight. The number of bolt holes affects the measurement of the bolt circle. See **Fig. 1-15.** If the wheel has four, six, or eight bolt holes, measure from the center of one hole to the center of the opposite hole. If the wheel has five bolt holes, measure from the center of one hole to the outer edge of the bolt hole that is farthest away.

Wheel Fasteners

Wheel fasteners are extremely important. Never take them for granted. Using the wrong style or size of fastener or improperly tightening a fastener can damage the wheel or brake rotor or cause the wheel to fail.

Technicians often refer to a wheel fastener as a "lug nut," although this term is not always correct. The word "lug" is a slang term for a threaded stud used in a wheel application. When a technician refers to "lugs," this is a reference to the threaded studs to which the wheel attaches. "Lug nuts" refer to the nuts used to fasten the wheel to the studs. Some wheels use nuts, or lug nuts, while other wheels use bolts, or lug bolts. Most commonly, vehicles will feature stationary threaded studs installed onto the hub or brake rotor hub. The separate fasteners used to secure the wheels on these vehicles are nuts. However, some vehicles feature threaded bolt holes in the hubs and use separate bolts to secure the wheel.

The size and style of a wheel fastener are important. Naturally, the thread diameter and pitch of the nut or bolt must match the stud or hole at the hub. Older vehicles use standard threads on lug studs, while newer vehicles use metric threads. These threads are not interchangeable.

The "seat style" is extremely important. There are three accepted styles of fastener seats: tapered (or conical), ball (or acorn), and mag. Because seat engagement is critical to a safely secured wheel, you must never mix these styles.

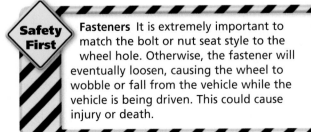

Safety First

Fasteners It is extremely important to match the bolt or nut seat style to the wheel hole. Otherwise, the fastener will eventually loosen, causing the wheel to wobble or fall from the vehicle while the vehicle is being driven. This could cause injury or death.

Tapered seats are also called conical seats. They have a tapered hole in the wheel and a matching tapered shoulder under the nut or bolt head. Ball seats are also called acorn or radiused seats. They have a rounded, ball-shaped pocket at the wheel hole and a matching rounded contact area under the nut or bolt head. Mag-style holes have a countersunk, flat recess around the wheel hole. The nut or bolt for such a hole has a large flat washer that fits in a recess. See **Fig. 1-16**.

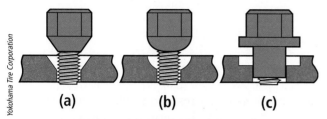

Yokohama Tire Corporation

(a)   **(b)**   **(c)**

Fig. 1-16 Examples of three fastener seat styles: tapered (conical) **(a)**, ball (acorn) **(b)**, and mag **(c)**. Never mix styles of fasteners. You must match the fastener seat style with that of the wheel hole. *Why is it important to match the seat style of the fastener to the seat style in the wheel's mounting holes?*

Wheel Inspection

Inspect the wheel for damage. Inspect the wheel bolt holes for distortion or being out-of-round. Inspect the flange of the wheel for bends or curb damage. Inspect the entire wheel for cracks or defects that may cause air to leak. Steel rims may be repaired, depending on the type of damage. However, damaged mag-type wheels typically need to be replaced.

Tire and Wheel Assembly

Follow the proper procedure when removing or installing a tire and wheel assembly. See **Fig. 1-17**. Improper removal or installation can result in damage to the assembly or cause it to fail.

Removing a Tire and Wheel Assembly

To remove a tire and wheel assembly from a vehicle:
1. Set the parking brake.
2. Position a floor jack under the lift point for the wheel to be removed.
3. Use wheel blocks or chocks to block the wheel diagonally opposite the wheel being removed.
4. Holding the wheel to be removed, loosen the lug nuts one-half turn.

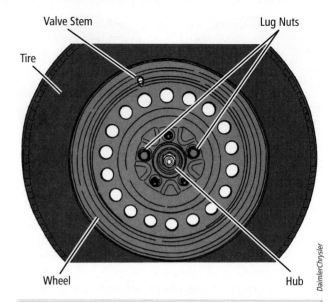

Valve Stem   Lug Nuts

Tire

Wheel   Hub

DaimlerChrysler

Fig. 1-17 Common wheel, tire, lug nut, and hub configuration. *Why is it important to follow the proper procedure when removing or installing a tire and wheel assembly?*

5. Using the floor jack, raise the vehicle until the tire is 2 inches [51 mm] above the floor.
6. Position a safety stand under the vehicle frame or lift point.
7. For vehicles using position-specific wheels, mark the wheel position before removal.
8. Remove the lug nuts and the wheel from the stationary threaded studs on the hub or brake rotor hub.

Installing a Tire and Wheel Assembly

To install a tire and wheel assembly on a vehicle:
1. Position the wheel on the stationary threaded studs of the hub or brake rotor hub.
2. Hand-tighten the lug nuts on the hub studs to align the tire and wheel on the hub.
3. Remove the safety stand.
4. Lower the vehicle and remove the floor jack.
5. Tighten the lug nuts using a torque wrench in the tightening sequence specified. Torque is a force that gives a twisting or rotating motion. (Torque patterns are discussed in more detail in the next section.)
6. Remove the wheel chocks or blocks.
7. Release the parking brake.

Measuring Torque

Torque is a twisting or turning force. It can cause a twisting or rotating motion. In an engine, torque is applied to the crankshaft. This happens when the piston is driven down by the combustion stroke. This force is transferred to the wheels by the transmission, transaxle, or differential. Torque is also applied to fasteners such as bolts or nuts when they are tightened by a wrench.

Nearly every bolt or nut on a vehicle has a torque specification set by the manufacturer. Undertightening may cause the fastener to loosen and create a mechanical or safety problem. Overtightening can also cause problems. Fasteners that are overtightened may deform the part they are holding in place. Torque specifications should always be followed in tightening wheel lug nuts. Overtightening lug nuts on aluminum wheels can deform the wheel shape.

Torque is measured in pound-feet (lb-ft) or inch-pounds (in-lbs). In the metric system, the units are newton-meters (n-m). Most torque wrenches use these units.

Torque is applied by pulling the handle of the torque wrench. Some torque wrenches are made to click or beep when the torque pre-set on them is reached. Others have a dial which measures the torque when force is applied to the handle.

Apply It!

Relating Handle Length to Torque

Meets NATEF Science Standards for measuring tightening force and relating torque to force.

Materials and Equipment
- Torque wrench with a dial that measures torque produced
- Hollow metal rod to be attached to the wrench handle
- ½-in hex head bolt
- Vise
- Empty 1-gallon paint can with handle
- Sand for weight
- Scale
- Yardstick

1. Add sand to the 1-gallon paint can to produce a 2-lb [0.9-kg] weight.

2. Attach the bolt securely in a vise so that it will not turn.

3. Attach the wrench to the bolt. Make sure that the handle is tilted up enough that the weight will not slip off when it is attached.

4. Attach the metal rod to lengthen the wrench handle.

5. Add the weight to the handle 6″ [15 cm] from the socket. Record the torque reading on the dial.

6. Repeat the procedure with the weight 1′ [30 cm] from the socket. Record the weight.

7. Repeat this procedure moving the weight out 6″ [15 cm] each time.

Results and Analysis

8. Did the torque change each time you moved the weight?

9. Did the amount of force placed on the bolt change?

10. You may have seen someone attach a longer handle to a wrench to make it easier to tighten a nut. Is this helpful?

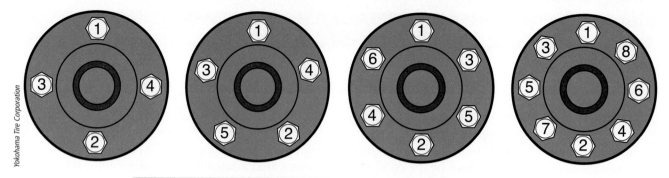

Yokohama Tire Corporation

Fig. 1-18 Torque wrench tightening patterns for 4-, 5-, 6-, and 8-bolt wheels. *What problems can occur if you tighten wheel fasteners excessively or unequally?*

Applying Torque

Torque is a turning or twisting force producing torsion and rotation around an axis. Torque is measured in pound-feet or newton-meters. The tightening torque used to install a wheel on the vehicle is important. You must consider both the amount of torque and the tightening pattern.

The level of tightness must be proper, and it must be identical for all fastener locations. An undertightened fastener may eventually loosen and fail. An overtightened fastener may cause thread damage. The stud or bolt shank may be stretched too far and break, or the nut or threads in the hub may be damaged. Overtightening may also cause the hub or brake rotor to warp which will adversely affect braking action.

You must tighten the fasteners on any wheel in the proper pattern. See **Fig. 1-18**. Spread the torque load as evenly as possible across the face of the wheel's center section. Uneven tightening can distort the wheel or brake rotor. This will cause vibration when driving or brake-pedal pulsation during braking.

You can use a pneumatic wrench to remove a wheel. However, never use one to install a wheel. Without exception, to tighten any wheel fastener, use only a quality torque wrench.

Remember, when installing a wheel, always follow the torque values in the vehicle service manual. Tighten only in the recommended patterns.

Safety First

Tightening Patterns It is important to tighten fasteners in the specified pattern. Not following this pattern can damage brake system components. This damage can result in loss of braking performance and increased risk of brake system failure and personal injury.

SECTION 2 KNOWLEDGE CHECK

1. What is the advantage of a forged alloy wheel?

2. What measurement is important when considering inboard clearance between the wheel/tire and the wheelwell and suspension or frame?

3. What is another name for an acorn seat?

4. How far off the ground should you raise a tire that needs to be changed?

5. What can happen if a wheel fastener is overtightened?

6. Using a clock face as a descriptive guide, explain the sequence for tightening the lug nuts of a six-bolt wheel.

ASE TEST PREP

7. Technician A says that a three-piece wheel involves two rim sections and a center section. Technician B says that a three-piece wheel is also referred to as a "modular" wheel because it allows different rim width and offset setups by using rim sections of different sizes. Who is correct?

    ⓐ Technician A.

    ⓑ Technician B.

    ⓒ Both Technician A and Technician B.

    ⓓ Neither Technician A nor Technician B.

Tire Dismounting, Mounting, and Balancing

Objectives:

E8 ● Dismount, inspect, repair, and remount tire on wheel.

E9 ● Dismount, inspect, and remount tire on wheel equipped with tire pressure sensor.

E11 ● Inspect and repair tire.

E12 ● Repair tire using internal patch.

E3 ● Diagnose wheel/tire vibration, shimmy, and noise; determine necessary action.

E5 ● Measure wheel, tire, axle, and hub runout; determine necessary action.

E7 ● Balance wheel and tire assembly (static and dynamic).

Vocabulary:

● index mark
● dynamic balancing

Dismounting

Repairing wheels and tires requires knowledge of tire dismounting and mounting, valve stem installation, and balancing techniques.

Mount or dismount a tire with the wheel and tire off the vehicle. To remove a tire from a wheel or to install a tire on a wheel, use a tire-changing machine.

Before you begin to dismount a tire, determine whether you want to remount the tire on the same wheel. If you do, place an index mark on the tire and the wheel, using a piece of chalk. An **index mark** will provide a reference so that you can remount the tire on the wheel in the same position. Sometimes, altering the mounting position of the tire on the wheel can create a vibration or a pull. This is due to the variables of wheel and tire runout and balance.

Remove any balancing weights from the wheel, using wheel weight pliers. This tool grips and removes clip-on style wheel weights from the wheel rim. It makes weight removal easy and reduces the chances of damaging the wheel. With the balancing weights removed, place the tire and wheel assembly on a tire changer.

A tire changer, or tire mounting machine, is a machine designed to mount or dismount a tire. See **Fig. 1-19.** Some machines operate manually. However, most are pneumatic (air powered). The machine should feature a method of separating the tire bead's grip at the wheel rims and slipping the tire beads over the rim edges during tire removal or installation. Various styles of changers are available. Make sure you receive proper training in the operation of the changer you plan to use.

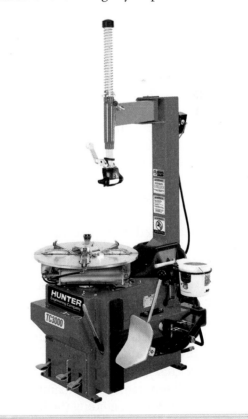

Courtesy Hunter Engineering Company

Fig. 1-19 A tire changer. *What should you do before you dismount a tire?*

The first step is to remove the air from the tire. To relieve all of the internal air pressure from the tire, unthread and remove the valve core from the valve stem. To unthread a valve core, use only a quality valve-core removal tool. Unthread the core slowly, allowing the pressurized air to escape before you fully remove the core.

With the pressurized air released from the tire, you can release the tire bead from the wheel rim. Technicians refer to this procedure as "breaking the bead." A powerful bead breaker arm is used to push the tire bead free from the rim, immediately adjacent to the rim edge.

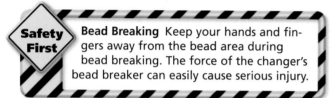

Safety First

Bead Breaking Keep your hands and fingers away from the bead area during bead breaking. The force of the changer's bead breaker can easily cause serious injury.

Once the bead breaks loose from the rim in one spot, rotate the tire and wheel assembly to a different position to continue breaking the rest of the bead loose. You must break the bead on both the front and the rear sides of the tire.

Once you have unseated the bead from the rim, use the proper procedure to remove the tire from the wheel. Do this as follows:

1. Lubricate the tire bead and wheel rim flange with soapy water. A bead lubricant is available for this purpose.
2. Use a bead separator tool to lift the bead from the rim. **Warning:** Some wheels are equipped with tire pressure sensors. The sensors send signals to electronic dash panels to warn the driver of low tire pressure. The sensors may be clamped to the center of the wheel with a large strap clamp, or they may be located in the tire valve stem area. Check before inserting the bead separator tool. If a sensor is present, take care not to contact or damage it with the tool. Many vehicles today have the low pressure dash display but use no pressure sensors at the wheel. These vehicles use information from the ABS wheel speed sensor to recognize a low tire pressure condition.

On some tire changers, such as a rim-clamp type changer, the bead separator tool remains stationary as the wheel and tire turn, guiding the bead up and off the wheel rim. Very wide wheels and delicate custom wheels should be handled using these changers. On other types of changers, the tool may install onto the changer's center shaft or the tool may be

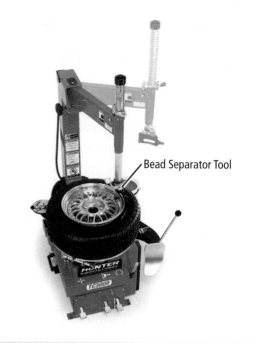

Bead Separator Tool

Courtesy Hunter Engineering Company

Fig. 1-20 On some types of tire changers, the bead separator tool remains stationary as the wheel and tire turn.

part of an overhead boom and rotate around the stationary wheel. Regardless of the type used, all tire changers accomplish the same task. See **Fig. 1-20.**

Once you have removed the top of the tire from the rim, lift the tire so that the rear tire bead contacts the upper wheel rim. Then remove the rear tire bead, using the same process.

TECH TIP **Valve Stems.** Before mounting any tire, install a new valve stem. Installing a new valve stem ensures that you will not have a valve stem leakage problem.

Mounting

Before mounting a tire, check the wheel and tire for damage and runout, make any needed tire and wheel repairs, and install a valve stem. Once these items are completed, the tire-mounting procedure can begin.

Tire and Wheel Repair

Replace all damaged wheels. Bent or cracked rims and cracked center sections present dangerous failure possibilities. To assist in your detection of damage, perform lateral and radial runout checks of the wheel, hub, and axle. Depending on the damage, repair of some aluminum wheels may be possible. However, you must leave wheel repairs to shops that specialize in that type of work. Never attempt any wheel repair on your own.

It is possible for you to perform some minor tire repairs. You can usually repair a small puncture in the tread area (such as what a nail might cause). Various types of plugs and patches are available to allow quick and easy repairs of small punctures. Be aware that training in the use of any plug or patch is necessary.

Insert a tire plug into the puncture to seal the air leak. It is important to follow the steps recommended for specific plug kits. Improperly installed plugs can come out or can cause a tire separation.

Internal Patch A type of tire patch kit is shown in **Fig. 1-21.** Most technicians prefer an internal patch because it is a permanent repair. To apply an internal patch:

1. Locate the puncture and, using a rasp, file the hole to remove burrs from the steel belts.
2. Using a tire buffer, buff the puncture area from the inside of the tire just enough to rough up the area.
3. Apply tire vulcanizing glue to the puncture area and to the tire patch.
4. Allow the glue to get tacky. Then install the patch, using a patch roller to push the patch securely into the tire.

Note that tire repair can be performed only when the puncture occurs in the tread area. Repair specialists may handle more extensive damage. If the repair involves more than a small puncture in the tread, it is best to replace the tire.

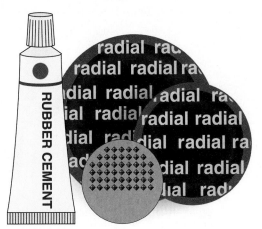

Fig. 1-21 A tire patch kit. *Why should tires be patched instead of plugged?*

Jack Holtel

Fig. 1-22 Pull-through rubber air valve stem. The rubber body creates a seal at the stem hole in the rim. *How often should you replace a pull-through air valve stem? Why?*

Valve Stems

Inspect the valve stem. The air valve stem mounts in a hole located in the wheel rim. This allows inflation and deflation. There are two basic styles of stems: the one-piece "pull-through" style and the "modular" style. The pull-through style relies on an interference fit in the rim hole. See **Fig. 1-22.** The valve stems that you will usually see will be the rubber pull-through type. You will most often find modular valve stems on custom wheels and some racing wheels.

To install a pull-through valve stem:

1. Lubricate the valve stem body.
2. Pull the valve stem through the rim hole and seat it. The rubber outer body of the stem creates an airtight seal at the rim hole.

To install a modular-style valve stem:

1. Insert the valve stem into the hole. The threaded stud portion of the stem protrudes through the outer rim surface.
2. Thread a nut over the stud and secure the valve stem in place. A rubber washer on both sides of the rim provides the airtight seal.

Because of stress during installation and removal, pull-through valve stems tend to split and deteriorate. Whenever servicing a wheel and tire assembly, install a new pull-through stem instead of reusing an old stem.

Safety First

Valve Core Use caution when working with a valve core. Never stand in the path of the core. Make sure the core aims away from your body. Make sure also that no one is standing in the path of the core. The valve core can become a dangerous projectile, causing personal injury.

Mounting Procedure

The procedure for mounting a tire is as follows:

1. Remove the old valve stem. Clean the valve mounting hole in the rim.
2. Lubricate the new valve stem's outer body.
3. Remove the valve core. Pull the new stem into position using a tire valve stem installation tool. Leave the core out for now.
4. Clean and lubricate the tire beads thoroughly. Position the rear tire bead over the wheel's outer rim flange.
5. Using the changer's installation tool, hold one section of the bead down over the wheel rim.
6. As the wheel rotates on the changer, use the tool to guide the tire bead past the rim flange.
7. Drop the tire down until the outer bead contacts the outer wheel rim flange. Repeat the process until the tire is fully engaged within the rim area. See **Figs. 1-23** and **1-24**.
8. Some tires and wheels have small colored dots. If so, orient the tire and wheel so that the dots align. This is "match-mounting." The dots indicate runout areas. On the tire the dot indicates the "high" runout peak. On the wheel the dot indicates the "low" runout peak. By matching these marks, you place the high and low runout areas together. With this orientation the high and low runout areas tend to cancel each other out. This lessens the chance of creating a severe runout problem. If there is no mark on the wheel, align the paint mark on the tire with the valve stem.

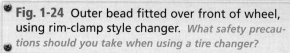

Fig. 1-24 Outer bead fitted over front of wheel, using rim-clamp style changer. *What safety precautions should you take when using a tire changer?*

9. Install an air chuck onto the valve stem. See **Fig. 1-25**. While standing away from the changer, initially inflate the tire using 40 psi [275 kPa] to seat the tire beads. Never use more than 40 psi [275 kPa] to inflate any passenger vehicle tire initially.
10. When the beads seat fully against the rim bead seats, you will hear a distinct "pop" noise. Check to see that the beads seat fully and uniformly at both the rear and front bead areas.
11. Carefully remove the air chuck from the valve stem, allowing the internal pressure to escape.
12. Install the valve core. Inflate the tire to its recommended inflation pressure.

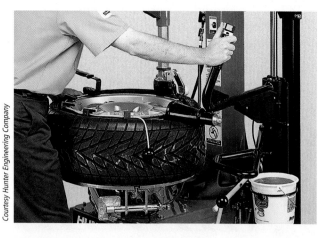

Fig. 1-23 Install the rear bead over the front of the rim first. Here the technician uses a rim-clamp style changer (also called an overhead changer). The bead tool remains stationary while the tire and wheel turn, feeding the bead over the rim. *What type of wheels should be handled with a rim-clamp style changer?*

Fig. 1-25 When inflating the tire to seat the beads, use a clip-on air chuck. This allows you to move away from the changer during initial inflation. This helps you avoid injury. *Why is it important to follow safety precautions when inflating a tire during the mounting process?*

13. Examine the bead edges for air bubbles. Air escaping at the bead areas will show in the excess lubrication as bubbles. If you see air bubbles, deflate the tire and break the beads loose. Examine the bead and rim for dirt or obstructions that may be causing the leak.

14. Balance and mount the tire and wheel on the vehicle. Check lateral and radial runout on both the tire and wheel. A dial indicator can be used to measure runout. The dial indicator must be mounted to a rigid stand or bracket. The dial indicator's plunger is pressed against the tire or wheel surface to be measured. As the tire and wheel assembly rotates, runout is shown on the dial indicator's gauge. See **Fig. 1-26.**

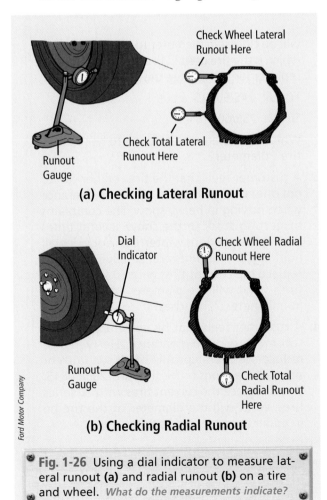

Check Wheel Lateral Runout Here

Check Total Lateral Runout Here

Runout Gauge

(a) Checking Lateral Runout

Dial Indicator

Check Wheel Radial Runout Here

Runout Gauge

Check Total Radial Runout Here

(b) Checking Radial Runout

Ford Motor Company

Fig. 1-26 Using a dial indicator to measure lateral runout **(a)** and radial runout **(b)** on a tire and wheel. *What do the measurements indicate?*

Balancing

To avoid vibration or shimmy during operation, check any tire and wheel assembly for balance. Wheel balancers are machines designed to locate and eliminate imbalance from an assembled tire and wheel. There are two types of balancing methods: static and dynamic.

Static Balancing

Static balancing involves placing the tire and wheel assembly on a machine called a static balancer (also called a bubble balancer). The static balancer features a pedestal with a bubble level. The assembly mounts onto the pedestal in a horizontal position. The front of the wheel faces upward.

A bubble level at the center of the balancer post indicates heavy and light areas of the assembly as the bubble moves off center. To center the bubble level, add balancing wheel weights to the light areas. The balancing wheel weights can be either clip-on or adhesive style.

Most technicians consider static balancing to be inaccurate and outdated. This method does not take into account the dynamic motion of the assembly as it rotates during operation.

Dynamic Balancing

Dynamic balancing, also called spin balancing, is much more accurate. See **Fig. 1-27.** In **dynamic balancing** a dynamic balancer spins the tire and wheel assembly in an upright position. This allows dynamic balancing in more than one plane. The balancer's digital readout indicates how much weight is required and at what location you need to place weights.

Courtesy Hunter Engineering Company

Fig. 1-27 Dynamic spin balancer. Today's computerized balancers make it easy to balance any tire and wheel assembly. Readouts show the weights you need and where to place them. *Why is the use of a dynamic balancer preferred over the use of a static "bubble" balancer?*

Determining Tire Diameter

You can use the markings on a tire's sidewall to determine the tire's overall diameter. The sidewall information gives you the section width, the aspect ratio, and the rim diameter. For a tire with the markings 225/70R15, the rim diameter is 15″. The section width is 225 mm. The section height is 70 percent of 225 mm:

$$0.70 \times 225 \text{ mm} = 157.5 \text{ mm.}$$

You need both these dimensions to calculate the diameter of the tire. Refer to **Fig. 1-5**. The overall diameter is twice the section height plus the rim diameter. One of these numbers is given in the metric system and the other in the English (customary) system. You must decide which system you want to use.

To use the metric system, first convert 15 inches to millimeters. Remember that 1″ = 25.40 mm. So, $15 \times 25.40 = 381$ mm.

The tire diameter, in millimeters, is:

$$(2 \times 157.5 \text{ mm}) + 381 \text{ mm} = 696 \text{ mm}$$

To use the English system, convert 157.5 mm to inches. Use the conversion factor 1 mm = 0.039″. So, 157.5 mm × 0.039 = 6.14 in.

The tire diameter, in inches, is:

$$(2 \times 6.14 \text{ in}) + 15 \text{ in} = 27.28 \text{ in}$$

Apply It!

Meets NATEF Mathematics Standards for using and converting English (customary) and metric units.

Tire diameter is an important consideration when changing tires. On a car with an antilock brake/traction control system, tire diameter can affect system performance. It is preferable to replace old tires with new tires of the same diameter if at all possible.

Measuring a tire's diameter directly is not always possible. In the case of badly worn or damaged tires, calculating a tire's diameter is a more accurate way of determining the original specification of the tire.

Properly calculating a tire's diameter takes practice. With experience, you should be able to quickly calculate a tire's diameter based on the information provided on the sidewall of the tire.

1. Look at the two tire diameter calculations in the example above. Does 27.28″ equal 696 mm?

2. A customer tells you she is considering two possible replacement tires. She asks you which will be closest in diameter to her current tire, which is the tire used in the example. The two replacement tires have these markings:

Tire A: 245/60R15

Tire B: 255/60R15

Which tire's diameter is closest to her current tire's diameter?

3. A customer feels that the tires on her car do not offer enough traction or ground clearance when driving in heavy snow. She complains of getting stuck in the snow several times during the previous winter. Current sidewall markings on her tires are: 225/30R16. If you replace the current tires with 60 series snow tires, what will the diameter of the tire be in millimeters? In inches?

4. A customer feels that his current tires have too much ground clearance. He wants to reduce the overall profile of his car. Current sidewall markings on his tires are: 200/60R15. If you replace the current tires with 20 series tires, what will the diameter of the tire be in millimeters? In inches?

Some electronic wheel balancers may also be capable of measuring the road force variation of a tire. A tire can be within runout specifications and in perfect balance yet have excessive road force variation. This can cause vehicle vibration.

Think of a tire as being a cushion around a wheel. It should flex the same and have the same tension equally around its circumference. Any excessive variation in tire flexibility or tension, while not visible, will cause vibration. When a wheel has some runout the tire can sometimes be relocated to another position on the wheel to bring road force variation within specifications. This is called match-mounting the tire to the wheel. If this is not possible, the only correction is to replace the tire.

Many new tires will not meet road force variation specifications. The only way to determine this is to test them on a wheel balancer with this capability. The wheel balancer forces a large roller on to the tire tread surface under high pressure and takes a dynamic runout measurement. This type of wheel balancer is becoming more popular today.

On-the-Vehicle Balancing

Other balancers, called on-the-vehicle balancers, are motorized units with rollers that contact the tire tread while the tire and wheel assembly is on the vehicle. The rollers spin the entire rotating assembly on the vehicle. This system uses a strobe light technology that quickly provides accurate balancing of wheels on the vehicle. The strobe indicator flashes to indicate the exact placement of wheel weights. No special wheel adaptors or attachments are required. This assembly includes the tire, wheel, brake rotor, and hub. These wheel balancers are not common today. However, they are still sometimes used for vehicle vibration diagnosis.

Balancing Safety

Make sure you receive proper training for the specific balancer that you plan to use. Also, make sure you use any available safety features properly. A dynamic balancer may feature a protective hood that lowers over the tire and wheel assembly during spinning. Never remove this hood. It provides protection from flying debris, such as stones or dislodged wheel weights.

SECTION 3 KNOWLEDGE CHECK

1. Why is it important to remount a tire in the same position on a wheel?

2. What tool should be used to grip and remove a clip-on wheel weight from the wheel rim?

3. What common mixture may be used as a bead lubricant?

4. What problems are caused by improperly installed tire repair plugs?

5. What part mounts in a hole located in the wheel rim to allow inflation and deflation?

6. What machines are designed to locate and eliminate imbalance from an assembled tire and wheel?

ASE TEST PREP

7. Technician A says that a pull-through valve stem is installed in the same way as a modular valve stem. Technician B says that a modular valve stem is another term for a pull-through valve stem. Who is correct?

   ⓐ Technician A.

   ⓑ Technician B.

   ⓒ Both Technician A and Technician B.

   ⓓ Neither Technician A nor Technician B.

CHAPTER 1 REVIEW

Key Points

Meets the following NATEF Standards for Suspension & Steering: diagnosing and repairing wheels and tires; mounting tires; balancing wheels and tires; checking tire and wheel runout.

- Tire functions include providing traction, acting as part of the suspension system, and enabling proper handling and operation.
- Aspect ratio refers to the relationship between the tire's section height and section width.
- A tire tread may be symmetric or asymmetric as well as directional or nondirectional.
- Tire inflation pressure should be checked when the tire's temperature is the same as the ambient temperature.
- Tires should be rotated at recommended mileage intervals.
- The fastener torque must be considered when installing a wheel on a vehicle.
- Most technicians prefer an internal patch because it is a permanent repair.
- A low-tire-pressure warning system features a sensor mounted inside the wheel rim.
- Special care must be taken in removing a tire from a wheel equipped with a tire pressure sensor.

Review Questions

1. What type of tires have plies that run bead-to-bead parallel to each other, with stabilizer belts under the tread?
2. What is the term for the measurement from the top of a tread on one side of a tire to the top of the tread on the opposite side of the tire?
3. What term refers to the relationship between a tire's section height and section width?
4. Name five items of information that you can gather from a tire's sidewall.
5. What does a speed rating of "T" indicate?
6. What is the measurement of the compressed air in a tire?
7. What may cause cracked treads?
8. How often should tires be rotated?
9. **Critical Thinking** Explain how to rotate the tires on a front-wheel drive vehicle.
10. **Critical Thinking** Consider the effects of tire underinflation. Underinflated tires will promote tread wear in what part of the tire?

Excellence in Communication

Interpreting Information

The vehicle identification number (VIN) has become an important source of data regarding the vehicle. Insurance companies and police departments consider it to be like a "fingerprint" that identifies the automobile. The 17-character VIN provides background data and production information for the vehicle. If you know how to interpret the letters and numbers, you can tell where the car was assembled. You can even tell the color of the original paint. Vehicle service manuals have charts that allow you to decode VIN information.

Another code system is used on tires. The information on the sidewalls also gives a wide range of information. Size, manufacturer, and various ratings can be found in the letters and numbers on the sidewalls. Information given in both letters and numbers is alphanumeric information. Some alphanumeric information also

includes other symbols such as punctuation marks and mathematical symbols. As the technician, you need to know the meanings of these letters and numbers. This will allow you to provide your customers with a safe, comfortable ride.

Apply It!

Meets NATEF Communications Standards for identifying and using information written as alphanumeric codes.

Refer to **Fig. 1-8.**

1. List the various types of information that can be found on the tire sidewall.
2. Examine a tire. Write down the information presented by the letters and numbers on the tire.

TEST PREP

Answering the following practice questions will help you prepare for the ASE certification tests.

1. Tires provide:
   - ⓐ the only connection between the vehicle and road surface.
   - ⓑ the motive force of the vehicle.
   - ⓒ a variable wheel base.
   - ⓓ the stopping force of the vehicle.

2. Technician A says that the vast majority of cars on the road today use tube tires. Technician B says that tubeless tires contain a tube, but it is in a different location than on tube tires. Who is correct?
   - ⓐ Technician A.
   - ⓑ Technician B.
   - ⓒ Both Technician A and Technician B.
   - ⓓ Neither Technician A nor Technician B.

3. Which of the following materials is not used to craft a tire ply?
   - ⓐ Cord.
   - ⓑ Fiberglass.
   - ⓒ Steel.
   - ⓓ Silicon.

4. Technician A says that on vehicles equipped with a tire pressure sensor, a lamp glows on the dash to indicate low tire pressure. Technician B says that the glowing lamp indicates that the tire has exceeded its maximum rpm rating. Who is correct?
   - ⓐ Technician A.
   - ⓑ Technician B.
   - ⓒ Both Technician A and Technician B.
   - ⓓ Neither Technician A nor Technician B.

5. Wheels are usually made from which type of material?
   - ⓐ Iron or alloy.
   - ⓑ Tungsten or alloy.
   - ⓒ Steel or alloy.
   - ⓓ Manganese or alloy.

6. Technician A says that wheel offset is the distance between a wheel's mounting surface and the edge of its rim. Technician B says that offset is the location of the wheel's centerline relative to the mounting face of the wheel hub. Who is correct?
   - ⓐ Technician A.
   - ⓑ Technician B.
   - ⓒ Both Technician A and Technician B.
   - ⓓ Neither Technician A nor Technician B.

7. Which of the following is not a type of wheel fastener seat style?
   - ⓐ Tapered.
   - ⓑ Ball.
   - ⓒ Offset.
   - ⓓ Mag.

8. Technician A says that you should check for the location of a tire pressure sensor before inserting a bead breaker. Technician B says that tire pressure sensors are not necessarily in the wheels. Who is correct?
   - ⓐ Technician A.
   - ⓑ Technician B.
   - ⓒ Both Technician A and Technician B.
   - ⓓ Neither Technician A nor Technician B.

9. Tire beads and rim should be lubricated with:
   - ⓐ motor oil.
   - ⓑ soapy water.
   - ⓒ heavy grease.
   - ⓓ graphite.

10. Technician A says that you should check the wheel and tire for damage and runout before mounting the tire. Technician B says that you should make needed repairs and install a valve stem before mounting a tire. Who is correct?
    - ⓐ Technician A.
    - ⓑ Technician B.
    - ⓒ Both Technician A and Technician B.
    - ⓓ Neither Technician A nor Technician B.

CH A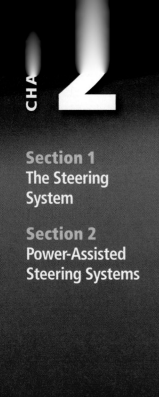

Section 1
The Steering
System

Section 2
Power-Assisted
Steering Systems

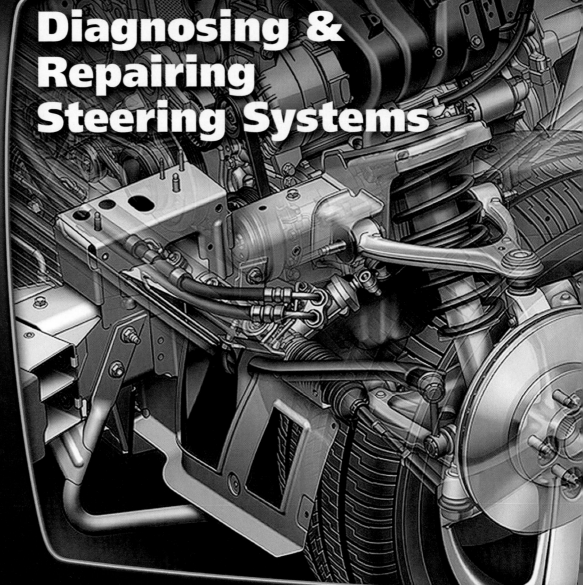

Diagnosing & Repairing Steering Systems

Customer's Concern

Charla Banks has always appreciated the responsiveness of her sports car's steering. She especially enjoys driving at highway speeds along the smooth pavement and gentle curves of the two-lane road she travels on during her daily commute to work. Until lately, Charla's car also handled well at the slower pace of city traffic. However, in the past week or so, she has heard whining noises as she turns the steering wheel when traveling at lower speeds. Charla's also noticed that it's become difficult to turn the steering wheel at lower speeds and stops.

Charla's car has always been cared for by your service center. When she brings her car to you after a week of noise and steering trouble, she's desperate for your help.

Technician's Challenge

As the service technician, you need to find answers to these questions:

1. Why is it important to listen to Charla's observations about this steering problem? How can her descriptions help you?

2. What do you need to know in order to diagnose the problem? What questions should you ask Charla about the problem?

3. After listening to Charla, taking notes on her observations, and getting answers to your questions, how will you isolate the problem? What checks will you make?

Objectives:

- Identify the major components of the steering system.
- **A2** • Identify and interpret suspension and steering concern; determine necessary action.
- **B1** • Disable and enable supplemental restraint system (SRS).
- **B2** • Remove and replace steering wheel; center/time supplemental restraint system (SRS) coil (clock spring).
- **B3** • Diagnose steering column noises, looseness, and binding concerns (including tilt mechanisms); determine necessary action.
- **B6** • Inspect steering shaft universal-joint(s), flexible coupling(s), collapsible column, lock cylinder mechanism, and steering wheel; perform necessary action.
- Identify the two main types of steering gear systems.

Vocabulary:

- power-assisted steering
- recirculating-ball steering gear
- tie rod
- rack-and-pinion steering gear
- steering ratio

Steering System Components

The steering system may be either manual or power-assisted. A manual steering system relies solely on the driver to provide the steering force. **Power-assisted steering** is a system that uses hydraulic or electric power to help the driver apply steering force.

For both manual and power-assisted steering, the basic components are the same. As the driver turns the steering wheel, the steering shaft rotates within the steering column. The steering shaft connects to a steering gear (either a separate gearbox or the pinion gear of a rack-and-pinion unit). The movement of this gear causes the steering linkage to move left or right. The linkage connects the steering gear to the steering arms which are attached to the wheels.

A steering system has these major components:

- The steering wheel, steering column, and steering shaft are parts of the driver input portion.
- The steering gear changes the rotary input motion of the steering column into linear output motion.
- The steering linkage connects the linear output of the steering gear to the steering arms. The road wheels turn whenever the steering arms move.
- The ball sockets allow suspension action without binding the steering linkage.

Steering Wheel

The steering wheel attaches to the steering shaft by one or more threaded fasteners. In most vehicles the steering wheel secures with a single nut.

Steering wheels have a slight interference fit on the shaft. You remove the steering wheel by removing the center mounting nut. Then pull the wheel off using a steering wheel puller as shown in **Fig. 2-1.** Never use a hammer to force the steering wheel off. Use only the proper puller.

Steering Wheel Puller

Steering Wheel

DaimlerChrysler

Fig. 2-1 Steering wheel puller mounted to steering wheel. *Why do you need a special puller to remove a steering wheel?*

When a steering wheel is equipped with a supplemental restraint system (air bag), this system must be disarmed according to the manufacturer's instructions before the air bag can be removed. Remove the steering wheel with the steering locked in a straight-ahead position. Maintain this position until the steering is reattached in a centered position. This maintains proper index between the steering and the SRS clock spring.

Disarming the Supplemental Restraint System and Removing the Steering Wheel Be sure to wear appropriate personal protective equipment and follow all appropriate safety procedures. This is a general procedure. Refer to the vehicle service manual for specifications and special procedures.

1. Be sure to follow all procedures in the appropriate service manual.
2. Disconnect the negative battery cable, and wait the appropriate length of time for the SRS system to be totally disarmed.
3. Turn the ignition key to the "run" position to unlock steering.
4. Steer the front wheels to the straight-ahead position and lock the steering column with the steering wheel centered. Remove the ignition key.
5. Remove the necessary trim and fasteners to loosen the SRS air bag assembly from the steering wheel.
6. Tilt the SRS air bag assembly up and disconnect all wiring connectors. Remove the air bag assembly and store it in a safe place with the trim side (air bag side) facing up.
7. Remove the steering shaft nut. Use an awl to scribe an index mark on the shaft and steering wheel hub.
8. Install the proper steering wheel puller, and remove the steering wheel from the steering shaft.
9. Do not unlock the steering while the steering wheel is removed. This ensures that when the steering wheel is replaced with the scribed marks aligned, the steering wheel will still be indexed properly with the SRS clock spring.
10. If a new SRS clock spring is to be replaced while the steering wheel is removed, check to see that the new clock spring is locked in the neutral or centered position by a factory-installed plastic pin or tape. If the pin or tape is not in place, do not use this clock spring.
11. Do not remove the index pin or tape until after the new clock spring has been installed.

12. The steering wheel can now be reinstalled. Align the scribe marks. Torque the nut to specifications.
13. Reattach all wire connectors to the SRS air bag assembly. Replace all fasteners and removed trim.
14. Reconnect the battery cable.

Steering Column

The steering column is the housing that contains and supports the steering shaft. Many vehicles have a tilt mechanism to adjust the steering wheel or the steering column up or down. The design of some steering columns allows them to telescope in or out in addition to tilting. See **Fig. 2-2.**

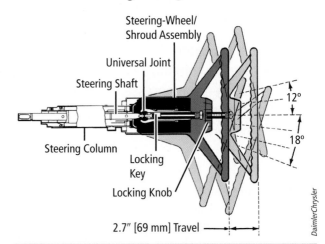

Steering-Wheel/ Shroud Assembly

Universal Joint

Steering Shaft

Steering Column

Locking Key

Locking Knob

12°

18°

2.7" [69 mm] Travel

DaimlerChrysler

Fig. 2-2 Tilt and telescopic steering. Some systems allow the steering wheel to pivot. Others allow the entire column to raise or lower. *What are the advantages of a steering wheel with tilt and telescopic adjustments?*

The steering column also houses the ignition switch and lock. The column-mounted lock allows you to lock the ignition and steering operations to inhibit theft of the vehicle. If the ignition switch or lock is damaged for any reason, replace according to manufacturer procedures.

To protect the driver, some steering columns are designed to collapse in a front-end collision. The steering column collapses as the steering wheel is forced into contact with the driver.

These steering columns are slightly precollapsed, expanded, or constructed of multiple parts bonded together by plastic. This allows the column to easily compress or collapse during an accident. Likewise, the steering shaft also compresses. The steering shaft may be a two-piece shaft, with one shaft splined into the other and fastened with a plastic rivet.

If the column is collapsed, the plastic rivet will be sheared and the shaft will also collapse. Be careful when working on these steering columns. Never hammer on the steering shaft. Doing so will damage the plastic parts or collapse the column.

Steering Column Couplers Steering column couplers allow the steering shaft connections to pivot at various angles during steering operation. These flexible couplers serve as pivot points between the upper and lower shafts and at the steering gear connection.

Depending on the vehicle, the type of coupler will vary. However, these couplers are either universal joints, flexible couplers, intermediate couplers, or a combination of these couplers. The purpose of a coupler is to connect the upper and lower steering shafts together in the steering shaft assembly. See **Fig. 2-3**.

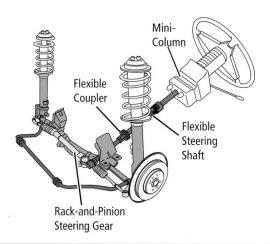

Fig. 2-3 Steering column assembly. Note steering column coupler at lower end of column. *Why do steering assemblies need a coupler?*

Loose or worn couplers can result in unresponsive steering. A seized coupler can cause stiff or uneven operation of the steering wheel. A failed coupler can cause a complete loss of steering. You should always inspect couplers whenever the vehicle has suffered a front-end collision. Replace the damaged couplers according to manufacturer specifications.

Steering Column Diagnosis In the event of a front-end collision, or air bag deployment, inspect the steering column and steering wheel. Then inspect the coupler for any damage and replace if needed. Refer to the manufacturer's manual for these procedures.

If you hear a chirp, squeak, or rubbing sound, inspect the shroud, intermediate shaft, steering column, and steering wheel.

If the steering catches, binds, or sticks, check the shaft and couplers, including the tilt mechanisms, for bind. If excess play exists in the steering wheel, check the steering-shaft couplers for wear or damage and determine any needed repairs. Refer to the manufacturer's manual.

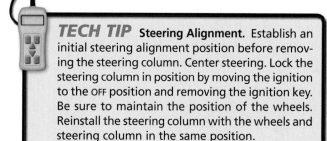

TECH TIP **Steering Alignment.** Establish an initial steering alignment position before removing the steering column. Center steering. Lock the steering column in position by moving the ignition to the OFF position and removing the ignition key. Be sure to maintain the position of the wheels. Reinstall the steering column with the wheels and steering column in the same position.

Steering Gear Systems

Two main types of steering gear systems are in common use. They are recirculating-ball systems and rack-and-pinion systems. A third type in limited use is the worm-and-roller steering gearbox.

Recirculating-Ball System This type of steering is used primarily on trucks, vans, some larger vehicles, and most passenger vehicles made prior to the 1980s. The **recirculating-ball steering gear** is an assembly that uses a series of recirculating balls on a worm gear to transfer steering-wheel movement to road wheel movement. See **Fig. 2-4**.

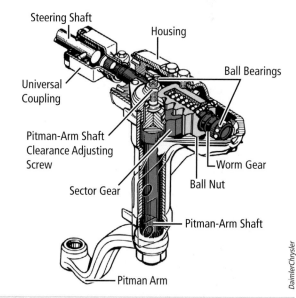

Fig. 2-4 A recirculating-ball system. Input-shaft rotation causes the output shaft to rotate at a 90° angle to the input shaft within the steering gear. *How is rotary motion of the steering wheel changed to linear movement of the tie rod?*

The steel balls within the gear housing constantly recirculate within the guide paths. They move from one end of the ball nut through return guides to reenter the ball nut at the opposite end. The balls provide low-friction contact points between the worm gear and the internal grooves of the ball nut.

The steering-linkage system used with the recirculating-ball system is a parallelogram linkage. A number of separate parts connect the steering gear output to the road wheels. See **Fig. 2-5.**

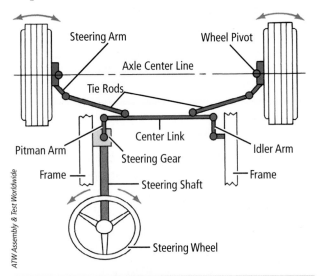

Fig. 2-5 Recirculating-ball system using a parallelogram linkage. *What steering system component provides the driver input?*

The steering gearbox uses an output device called a pitman arm. The pitman arm connects to a center link (also called a drag link or a relay rod). The center link runs horizontally, from left to right. The opposite end of the center link attaches to an idler arm. The pitman arm and the idler arm act as the center link's anchor points. The two ends of the center link pivot at their anchor points.

Two tie rods connect to the center link. A **tie rod** is an adjustable-length rod that, as the steering wheel turns, transfers the steering force and direction from the rack or linkage to the steering arm. One tie rod connects the center link to the left steering arm. The other connects to the right steering arm. To allow free motion as the road wheels turn and as the suspension compresses and rebounds, each attachment point of the tie rods uses a separate lubricated ball socket. See **Fig. 2-6.**

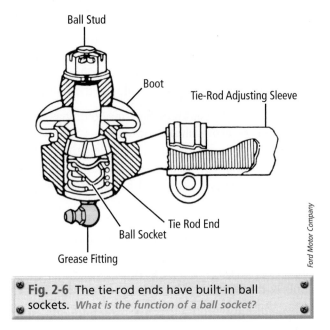

Fig. 2-6 The tie-rod ends have built-in ball sockets. *What is the function of a ball socket?*

Rack-and-Pinion System Most passenger vehicles have rack-and-pinion steering. This steering system uses a **rack-and-pinion steering gear** in which a pinion on the end of the steering shaft meshes with a rack of gear teeth on the major cross-member of the steering linkage. Because a rack-and-pinion system uses fewer parts, it provides space-saving and weight-saving features. See **Fig. 2-7.** Because smaller cars have limited space, a rack-and-pinion design is practical for these vehicles.

The steering shaft connects to an input shaft on the rack-and-pinion unit. When the steering wheel turns, the steering shaft rotates, which rotates a pinion gear on the input shaft.

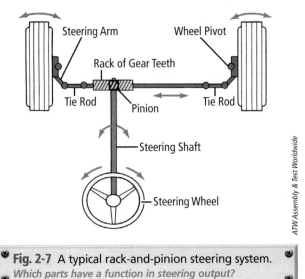

Fig. 2-7 A typical rack-and-pinion steering system. *Which parts have a function in steering output?*

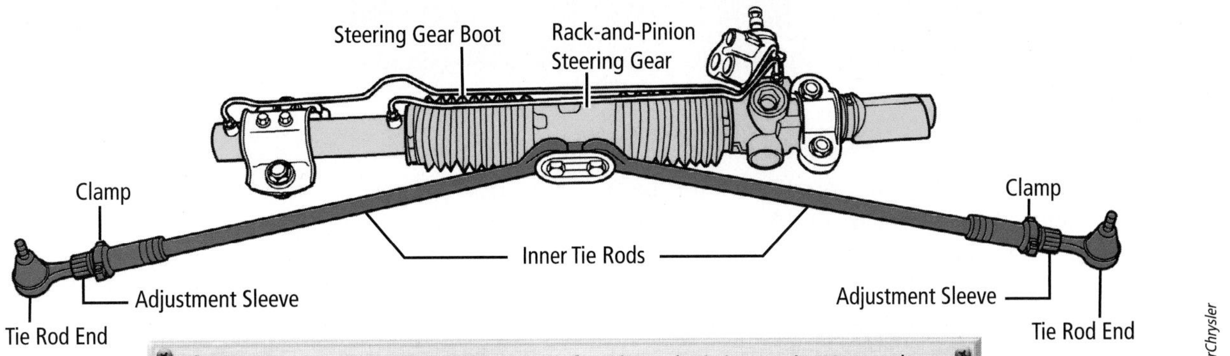

Steering Gear Boot   Rack-and-Pinion
Steering Gear

Clamp   Clamp

Inner Tie Rods

Adjustment Sleeve   Adjustment Sleeve

Tie Rod End   Tie Rod End

DaimlerChrysler

Fig. 2-8 A typical center-link type of rack-and-pinion unit. Note where the tie rods connect to the rack. *Why do some vehicles use center-link rack-and-pinion units?*

The pinion gear mates to a horizontal toothed rack inside the rack-and-pinion housing. As the pinion gear rotates, it forces the toothed rack to slide to the right or left inside the housing. Each end of the rack attaches to an inner and outer tie rod assembly. The tie rods are attached to the steering arms.

A rack-and-pinion system:
- Has fewer parts to inspect, maintain, and service.
- Uses fewer parts than a recirculating-ball steering system.
- Needs less space than a recirculating-ball steering system.

Another style of rack-and-pinion steering is the center-link type. Its basic function is the same as other rack-and-pinion units. However, as the name indicates, the tie rods attach at the center of the rack housing. See **Fig. 2-8.** Because a center-link design is more compact, it is used in smaller vehicles with limited space in the chassis.

Rear-wheel steering systems, although not widely used, have been around since as early as 1980. Before that, some manufacturers used compliant bushings that allowed rear suspensions to steer when acted on by cornering forces. However, compliant bushing systems did not use a steering gear or mechanism to change wheel position.

Newer systems used on high-end performance vehicles and large SUVs use electric rack-and-pinion steering gears or steering motors attached to the rear wheels to vary steering angles. These systems improve handling stability and ease of parking in confined areas. A computer is used to control the rear wheel angles. Using vehicle speed data and data provided by angle sensors from the front steering, these systems are capable of optimally adjusting the rear wheels in response to conditions.

- At low speeds, the wheels steer in opposite directions, reducing the turning radius for ease of parking.
- At high speeds, wheels steer in the same direction to improve maneuverability.
- In a sharp turn, the rear wheels turn in the opposite direction of the front wheels.

In the event of a system failure, these systems are equipped with centering springs that drive the rear wheels into the nonsteering position.

When performing an alignment on these vehicles, be sure to follow the manufacturer's service procedures. Special tools and procedures may be required.

Special Tools

A number of tools are available that will help you disassemble several steering system components. Some components are difficult to take apart because of either a press-fit or an interference-fit. These tools help make sure that none of the parts are damaged during disassembly.
- Pitman arm puller—Disconnects the pitman arm from the steering gear output shaft.
- Drag link socket wrench—Connects and disconnects the drag link from the pitman arm or idler arm.
- Ball joint press—Presses the ball joint tapered stud out of the steering arm (or knuckle) mounting hole.

Other special tools used with steering systems include the inner tie-rod end tool and the tie rod puller. These tools are described later in this chapter.

TECH TIP **Hand Grease Gun.** This is not a special tool, but it is an important one! You must remember to use the hand grease gun to lubricate the grease fittings found on any ball joint or tie-rod end after your service work is completed.

Altering Force with Levers

Power steering systems are complex mechanical systems. They use gears and levers in combination. The gears and levers themselves are called simple machines. Simple machines are devices used to increase force. The inclined plane, wheel and axle, the wedge, and the cam are also simple machines. Simple machines may change the direction, speed, or distance another part moves.

There are three types of levers:

• First-class.

• Second-class.

• Third-class.

Every lever has three parts:

• The effort point.

• The fulcrum, or pivot.

• The resistance point.

Force applied to the effort part of a lever causes the lever to pivot at its fulcrum. This transfers the force to the resistance part of the lever. The drawing below shows the differences in levers. Notice that in the first-class lever the effort and resistance move in opposite directions. In the second- and third-class levers, effort and resistance move in the same direction.

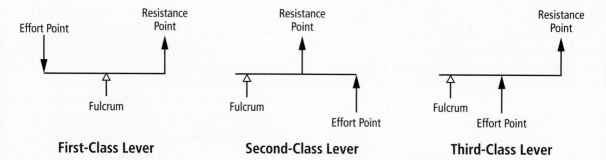

First-Class Lever   **Second-Class Lever**   **Third-Class Lever**

Apply It!

Identifying Levers

Meets NATEF Science Standards for using levers to alter force.

Look carefully at these drawings of mechanical parts. **Figs. A, B, C**. Find the effort point, fulcrum, and resistance point on each lever. Then decide which of the three types of levers each part uses.

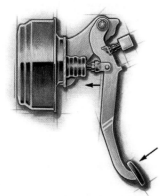

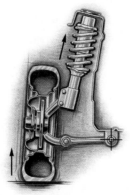

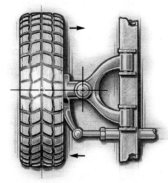

Fig. A Brake Pedal Assembly   **Fig. B MacPherson-Strut Suspension Assembly**   **Fig. C Independent Front Suspension Assembly**

Steering Ratio

Steering ratio is the number of degrees that the steering wheel must turn to turn the road wheels 1°. See **Fig. 2-9.** In this figure the steering wheel turns 17.5° to turn the road wheels 1°. The steering ratio is 17.5:1.

A steering ratio can provide a mechanical advantage. It can change a small input force into a larger output force. As the driver applies a relatively small input force to the steering wheel, a much greater force is output to the road wheels. For example, a 10-pound force moves the steering wheel 17.5°. With a 17.5:1 steering ratio, a much greater force is applied to move the road wheels 1°.

Some steering gear systems provide variable-ratio steering. The steering ratio changes as the steering wheel turns from its straight-ahead position.

A typical change might be from a ratio of 16:1 to 13:1. The steering ratio remains constant at 16:1 for the first 40° of steering wheel movement, left or right of center. This high ratio offers better steering control for highway driving. As the steering wheel turns beyond 40°, the steering ratio decreases to 13:1. The steering wheel does not have to turn as far to turn the road wheels. This lower ratio helps the driver when cornering or parking. See **Fig. 2-10.**

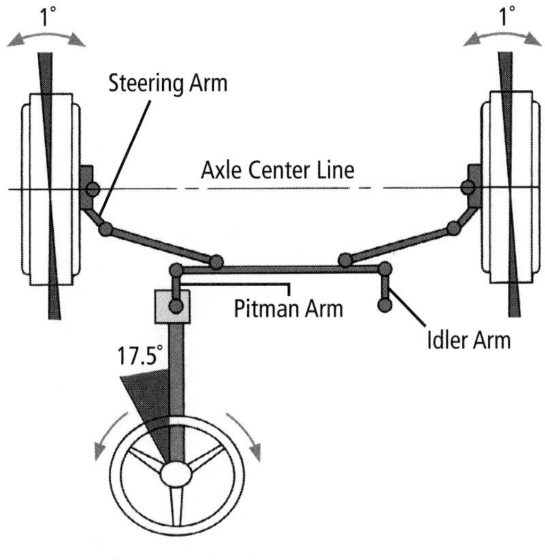

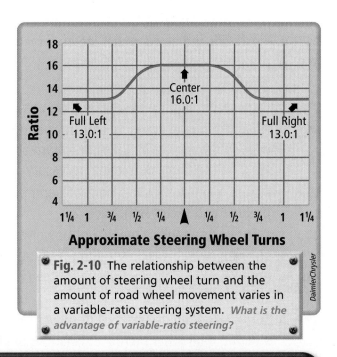

ATW Assembly & Test Worldwide

Fig. 2-9 In this example the steering ratio is 17.5:1. When the steering wheel turns 17.5°, the road wheels turn 1°. *Will a higher ratio, for example 25:1, make the road wheels easier or harder to control?*

DaimlerChrysler

Fig. 2-10 The relationship between the amount of steering wheel turn and the amount of road wheel movement varies in a variable-ratio steering system. *What is the advantage of variable-ratio steering?*

SECTION 1 KNOWLEDGE CHECK

1. What type of power helps the driver apply steering force in a vehicle equipped with power-assisted steering?

2. What tool is used to remove a steering wheel?

3. What is the purpose of a steering column coupler?

4. What is a tie rod?

5. Explain what a steering ratio of 15:1 means.

6. What is the advantage of a lower steering ratio?

ASE TEST PREP

7. Technician A says that the drag link socket wrench is designed to disconnect the pitman arm from the steering gear output shaft. Technician B says that the drag link socket wrench is designed to connect and disconnect the drag link from the pitman arm or idler arm. Who is correct?

   ⓐ Technician A.

   ⓑ Technician B.

   ⓒ Both Technician A and Technician B.

   ⓓ Neither Technician A nor Technician B.

Objectives:

A2 • Identify and interpret suspension and steering concern; determine necessary action.

B13 • Remove, inspect, replace, and adjust power steering pump belt.

B14 • Remove and reinstall power steering pump.

B15 • Remove and reinstall power steering pump pulley; check pulley and belt alignment.

B10 • Determine proper power steering fluid type; inspect fluid levels and condition.

B11 • Flush, fill, and bleed power steering system.

B12 • Diagnose power steering fluid leakage; determine necessary action.

B16 • Inspect and replace power steering hoses and fittings.

B5 • Diagnose power steering gear (rack and pinion) binding, uneven turning effort, looseness, hard steering, and fluid leakage concerns; determine necessary action.

B7 • Adjust manual or power non-rack and pinion worm bearing preload and sector lash.

B8 • Remove and replace manual or power rack and pinion steering gear; inspect mounting bushings and brackets.

B18 • Inspect, replace, and adjust tie rod ends (sockets), tie rod sleeves, and clamps.

B9 • Inspect and replace manual or power rack and pinion steering gear inner tie rod ends (sockets) and bellows boots.

B4 • Diagnose power steering gear (non-rack and pinion) binding, uneven turning effort, looseness, hard steering, and fluid leakage concerns; determine necessary action.

B20 • Inspect and test non-hydraulic electric-power assist steering.

B19 • Test and diagnose components of electronically controlled steering systems using scan tool; determine necessary action.

B21 • Identify hybrid vehicle power steering system electrical circuits, service and safety precautions.

• Observe proper safety precautions when working with steering-wheel mounted air bags.

A3 • Research applicable vehicle and service information, such as suspension and steering system operation, vehicle service history, service precautions, and technical service bulletins.

Vocabulary:

• power steering pump
• variable-assist power steering

Bill Bachman/Photo Researchers

Power-Assisted Steering System Components

A power-assisted steering system uses devices to assist the driver's input force. See **Fig. 2-11**. The components in a hydraulic power-assisted system include:

- A power steering pump.
- A power steering fluid reservoir.
- A drive belt that drives the power steering pump.
- Power steering fluid.
- Hoses and tubes that connect the pump to the steering gear.
- A power-assisted steering gear assembly.

All hydraulic power-assisted steering systems work in the same way. A hydraulic pump, the **power steering pump,** pressurizes the hydraulic fluid. Hydraulic hoses and tubes attached to the pump provide fluid to the steering gear. Pressure from the fluid is applied to a piston inside the gear housing. When the steering wheel turns, a control valve opens and closes fluid passages inside the gear housing. Pressurized fluid moves the piston. The piston applies force to the steering gears.

The power steering pump may have a built-in fluid reservoir, or the reservoir may mount in a remote location. A remote-mounted reservoir connects to the system with two hoses. One hose connects the reservoir to the power steering pump. This hose provides the pump with fluid. The other hose connects the reservoir to the steering gear, which allows fluid to circulate back to the reservoir.

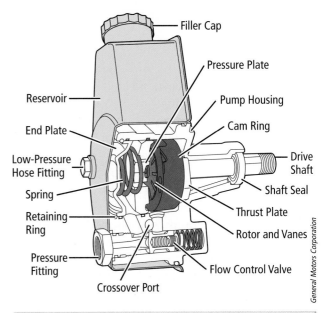

Fig. 2-12 Typical rotary-vane type power steering pump. *How does the pump pressurize fluid?*

Power Steering Pump

A power steering pump is a hydraulic pump that provides an assist to the steering system. It produces very high fluid pressures, which reduces the steering effort needed by the driver. Pressure may reach 2,000 psi [13,790 kPa]. To pressurize the fluid, the pump may use a rotary-vane design or a gear-and-roller design.

The rotary-vane type, which is very common, uses a rotor that rotates inside a cam ring. The rotor applies pressure to the fluid as the area between the rotor, the vane, and the cam ring becomes smaller. See **Fig. 2-12**.

In most cases a belt connected to the engine's crankshaft pulley drives the power steering pump. The pump usually mounts at the front of the engine where there is belt access. Some pumps, however, mount in remote locations and an electric motor drives them.

Checking the Power Steering Pump Belt Visually check the pump drive belt for excess wear. Look for cracks and missing pieces of belt material. If you find any defects, you must replace the belt.

Check that the belt fits properly on the drive pulley. Older vehicles may use a V-belt that fits into a V-groove on the pulleys. Other vehicles may use a ribbed belt that mates to ribs in a drive pulley.

Check belt tension, using a belt-tension gauge. Tension will vary with the vehicle. Newer vehicles may have an automatic belt-tensioning system.

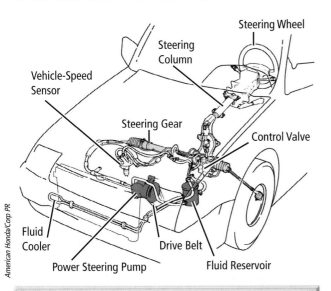

Fig. 2-11 A typical hydraulic power-assisted system using a remote-mounted fluid reservoir. *What is the purpose of the two hoses connecting the fluid reservoir?*

Removing and Installing the Power Steering Pump

1. Before servicing, allow the engine to cool.
2. Remove the power steering pump drive belt. Inspect and replace if needed. Refer to the manufacturer's manual for the vehicle.
3. Disconnect the pump suction hose. Be careful not to spill power steering fluid. Place a plastic bag over the end of the hose to prevent spillage. Secure the bag with a rubber band.
4. Remove the oil-pressure switch from the pump, if so equipped.
5. Disconnect the pump's pressure feed tube. A union bolt or banjo-type bolt will likely secure this tube. A sealing washer may be under the bolt head. Be careful not to lose this part.
6. Remove the pump from the engine. Inspect the pump, pump pulley, and pump seals and gaskets. Replace if needed, following procedures noted in the vehicle's service manual.
7. When replacing a power steering pump with a new unit, it is usually necessary to transfer the pulley. Some pulleys are retained by a nut. Other pulleys are pressed on. These require special pullers for removal and reinstallation. Note the position of the pulley on the shaft before removal. To retain belt alignment, be sure to duplicate this position on installation of the pulley. Follow vehicle service manual procedures.

Install a pump in the reverse order of the removal process.

Power Steering Fluid

Power steering systems can create very high pressures and temperatures. These systems, therefore, require a specific type of hydraulic fluid.

Many manufacturers recommend a particular power steering fluid, and some manufacturers recommend a particular automatic transmission fluid. It is important to use the proper, recommended fluid. Information stating the proper fluid for a particular system may be found on the power steering reservoir cap or in the owner's manual or vehicle service manual. Some manufacturers now recommend flushing the power steering system and changing the fluid at various mileage or time intervals. This is also required when replacing a defective steering gear or pump.

The condition of the power steering fluid should be routinely checked to determine needed service. Dirty fluid should be changed. Metal particles in the fluid indicate a failing pump or steering gear.

Foaming of the fluid indicates the presence of air. This can be caused by a low fluid level or a possible leak that allows air to enter the suction side of the system.

Checking Power Steering Fluid

1. Park the vehicle on a level surface.
2. With the engine off, check the level and condition of the fluid in the reservoir. See **Fig. 2-13.**
3. If the system is hot, check that the fluid level is within the HOT level range.
4. If the system is cold, check that the fluid is within the COLD level range.
5. Start the engine and allow it to idle.
6. Turn the steering wheel lock to lock several times to boost fluid temperature.
7. Check the fluid for signs of foaming. If foaming is evident, you must bleed the power steering system of air.

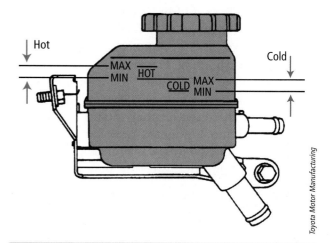

Toyota Motor Manufacturing

Fig. 2-13 Fluid level in reservoir will vary depending on fluid temperature. *Why is it important to park the vehicle on a level surface when checking fluid level?*

Bleeding the Power Steering System

1. Raise the front wheels off the ground. With the engine off, slowly turn the steering wheel from lock to lock several times. Look for foaming in the fluid reservoir.
2. Lower the vehicle onto the ground.
3. Start the engine and allow it to idle for several minutes.
4. With the engine running, turn the steering wheel to full lock, either right or left, and keep it there for 2–3 seconds.
5. Turn the steering wheel to the opposite full-lock position and keep it there for 2–3 seconds.
6. Repeat this process several times.

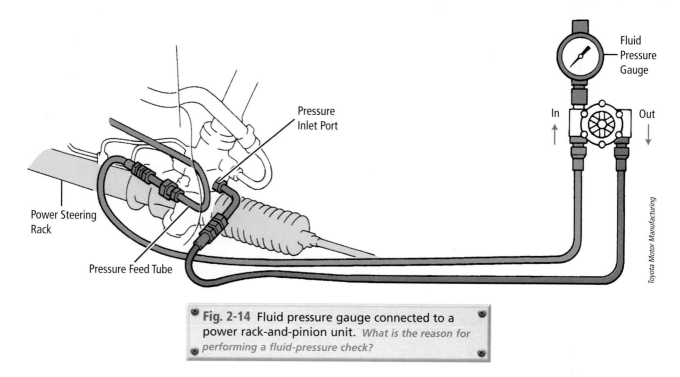

Power Steering Rack

Pressure Inlet Port

Pressure Feed Tube

Fluid Pressure Gauge

In

Out

Toyota Motor Manufacturing

Fig. 2-14 Fluid pressure gauge connected to a power rack-and-pinion unit. *What is the reason for performing a fluid-pressure check?*

7. Stop the engine and check the fluid in the reservoir for foaming. If foaming continues check the entire power steering system for fluid leaks. Diagnose and determine any needed repairs. Refer to the vehicle's service manual. Flush and fill power steering system and repeat the preceding steps.

8. Once you no longer see foaming, measure the fluid level in the reservoir while the engine is idling.

9. Stop the engine, wait a few minutes, and remeasure the fluid level.

Pressure-Testing the Power Steering System
Before performing a pressure test, inspect all hoses, tubes, and fittings. If any hose is soft, brittle, cracked, or shows signs of wear, it must be replaced. Any tube that is rusted, dented, cracked, or otherwise damaged must be replaced.

To determine whether the pump, hoses, tubes, and steering gear are operating under proper pressures, perform a fluid pressure test.

1. With the engine off, install a fluid-pressure gauge on the high-pressure (feed) tube at the steering gear. Using a power rack-and-pinion system as the example, disconnect the pressure feed tube from the rack-and-pinion steering gear housing. Attach the feed tube that runs from the pump to the gear to the IN position of the gauge. See **Fig. 2-14.**

2. Connect the pressure inlet port of the steering gear to the OUT position of the gauge.

3. With the engine idling and the gauge valve open, turn the steering wheel from full left to full right several times.

4. Close the valve on the gauge and note the gauge reading. You should see a pressure reading of about 925 psi [6,378 kPa], though this may vary depending on the system. Always check the manufacturer's service manual. Do not keep the pressure-gauge valve closed for more than 10 seconds. Do not allow the temperature to become too high during this test.

5. Open the valve fully.

6. Measure the fluid pressure at engine speeds of 1,000 rpm and 3,000 rpm. The difference in fluid pressure should be about 71 psi [490 kPa] or less.

7. With the valve fully open, turn the steering wheel to a full-lock position. Fluid pressure should be at least 925 psi [6,378 kPa]. Specific pressure specifications will vary.

8. Turn the engine off. Allow the system to cool before disconnecting the gauge. Determine any needed repairs. Refer to the vehicle's service manual.

9. Once you have reconnected the tubes to the steering gear, bleed the system and check the fluid level.

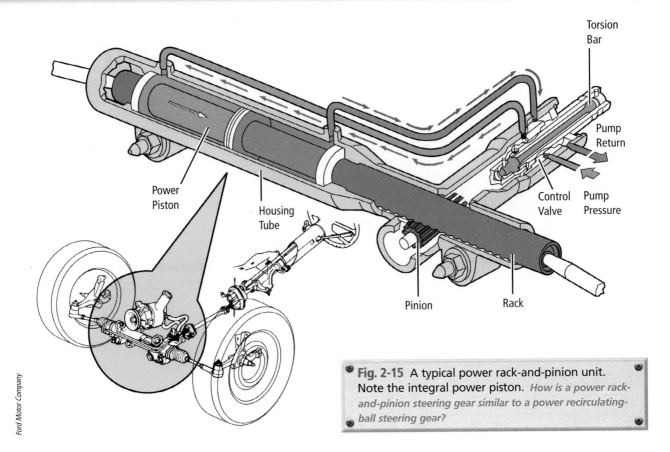

Power
Piston

Housing
Tube

Pinion

Rack

Torsion
Bar

Pump
Return

Control
Valve

Pump
Pressure

Ford Motor Company

Power Rack-and-Pinion Steering Gearbox

A power rack-and-pinion steering gearbox contains an integral (built-in) power piston and cylinder. See **Fig. 2-15.** It is similar in construction to a power recirculating-ball steering system, which has a power piston and cylinder built into the steering gear.

Diagnosing Problems Common power-assisted steering complaints include:
• Vibration.
• Looseness.
• Hard steering problems.
 Possible causes include:
• Underinflated tires.
• Dry or worn ball joints.
• Defective or worn steering column components.
• Bad power steering pressure switch.
• Leaking steering gear assembly.
• Low power steering fluid.
• Low power steering pump pressure.
• Bent or chipped toothed rack.

Servicing a Power Rack-and-Pinion Gearbox Power rack-and-pinion gearboxes with internal problems or external leaks are typically not serviced. They

are replaced as a whole unit. If the bellows boot is torn or damaged, it can be replaced. Remove the clamps and the outer tie rod end and slide a new bellows boot and clamps into place. See **Fig. 2-16.** The inner and outer tie rod ends can also be serviced. This type of service can typically be performed with the unit still installed in the vehicle.

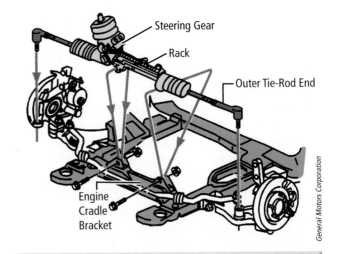

Steering Gear

Rack

Outer Tie-Rod End

Engine
Cradle
Bracket

General Motors Corporation

Reading a Variable-Ratio Steering Graph

In a variable-ratio steering gear, the steering ratio varies as the steering wheel moves away from the straight-ahead position. Look at the graph. What does the graph indicate at Points A, B, and C in terms of variable-ratio steering?

Point A is the straight-ahead position. The steering wheel is not turned. The ratio is 16:1, which means the steering wheel must be turned 16° to pivot the front wheels 1°. At Point B, a full left turn, and at Point C, a full right turn, the ratio is 13:1, which means the steering wheel must be turned 13° to pivot the front wheels 1°. The ratio for a full right turn is equal to the ratio for a full left turn. The direction is the only difference.

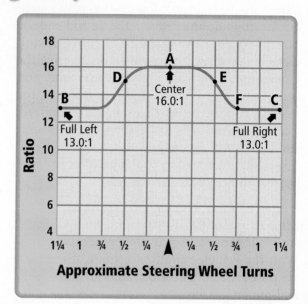

Apply It!

Meets NATEF Mathematics Standards for interpreting graphs.

1. What is the ratio at Point F?

2. What is the ratio at Points D and E? What do these points have in common? What is the difference?

3. Write a brief paragraph explaining why a lower steering ratio helps in city driving during cornering or parking. Identify other situations where a low steering ratio would help.

4. A manufacturer's specification on the steering gear ratio is 15.0:1 at center and 12.0:1 at greater than ½ turn of the steering wheel. After measuring the turn ratio on a vehicle, you discover that the steering gear ratio is 26.0:2.2 at center and 24.3:2.2 at greater than ½ turn. Is this vehicle operating within the manufacturer's specifications?

5. If a steering gear ratio is 36.8° of steering wheel rotation to 1.8° of wheel rotation, how far, in degrees, must the steering wheel be turned to move the front wheels 1°?

6. If a steering gear ratio is 22° of steering wheel rotation to 2° of wheel rotation, how far, in degrees, must the steering wheel be turned to move the front wheels 1°?

7. A manufacturer's specification on the steering gear ratio is 13.5:1 at center and 10.5:1 at greater than ½ turn of the steering wheel. After measuring the turn ratio on a vehicle, you discover that the steering gear ratio is 27.0:2 at center and 21.0:1.4 at greater than ½ turn. Is this vehicle operating within the manufacturer's specifications?

8. If a vehicle has a steering gear ratio of 10.0:1, how far, in degrees would the steering wheel have to be moved to move the wheels 36°?

Inspecting and Servicing Power Rack-and-Pinion Gearbox Inner and Outer Tie Rod Ends

1. Raise the vehicle on a hoist.
2. Inspect the bellows boot for cracks or damage.
3. Inspect the inner and outer tie rod ends for play or looseness.
4. If the outer tie rod end is loose or has play, loosen the locking nut and remove the tie rod end. Be careful to note the number of turns. Install the new tie rod end, threading it on by using the same number of turns. Tighten the locking nut.
5. If the inner tie rod end is loose or has play, the outer tie rod and bellows boot must be removed. The inner tie rod is removed using a special socket and is replaced as a whole unit.
6. The vehicle will need to be aligned after any type of steering service is performed.

Removing a Power Rack-and-Pinion Gearbox Specific procedures will vary depending on the vehicle, but the following steps provide a general outline:

1. With the vehicle raised on a hoist, disconnect the power steering hose connections at the rack-and-pinion gearbox.
2. Allow the power steering fluid to drain into a container.
3. Disconnect the steering sensor from the rack housing, if so equipped.
4. Disconnect the outer tie-rod ends from the steering arms using a tie-rod puller. This tool allows the separation of the tie-rod end from the steering arm, without damaging either component.
5. Disconnect the steering coupler from the pinion shaft.
6. Remove the bolts that attach the rack-and-pinion housing to the frame.
7. Remove the rack unit from the vehicle. On some vehicles it may be necessary to first raise the engine and transmission or to lower the engine cradle bracket.
8. Inspect the mounting bushings and mounting brackets. If cracked, oil-soaked, or otherwise damaged, replace them with new bushings and brackets.
9. Inspect tie-rod ends for faulty movement or damage to the ball-joint boot. Replace if needed. Boot installation is shown in **Fig. 2-17**.

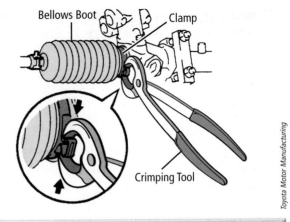

Bellows Boot   Clamp

Crimping Tool

Toyota Motor Manufacturing

Fig. 2-17 The boot clamp is tightened with a special crimping tool.

10. Before you install the rack and pinion assembly, center the rack and install the tie rods and tie-rod ends. Adjust the tie rods to the previous length using the inner tie rod end tool. This tool allows the technician to rotate the tie rod to thread or unthread thereby adjusting the tie rods. Pre-adjusting the tie rods will provide a starting point for the toe-in adjustment. Front wheel alignment is necessary after any front-end steering component replacement.

Power Steering Pressure Switch

Most vehicles equipped with power steering have a pressure switch installed on the high-pressure side of the system. The switch monitors system pressure and supplies information to the engine powertrain control module (PCM). When the switch senses a high pressure load, the PCM may slightly raise engine speed to increase pump pressure.

Electronic Controls

Electronic controls are used in variable-assist power steering. They are also used in electronic rack-and-pinion power steering.

Variable-Assist Power Steering Many vehicles have speed-sensitive power steering. This is a variable-assist system. **Variable-assist power steering** is power steering that uses electronic controls to determine how much power assist the steering needs. See **Fig. 2-18**. Note the electronic power steering controller, the solenoid valve at the rack-and-pinion, and the steering-angle sensor at the steering column. Some vehicles may have the solenoid built into the power steering pump. Electronic variable-assist power works with either rack-and-pinion steering or recirculating-ball steering.

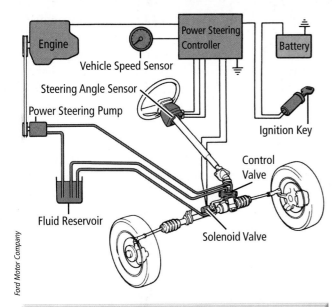

Ford Motor Company

Fig. 2-18 An example of a variable-assist power steering system in a vehicle equipped with rack-and-pinion steering. *What component provides the variable rate of power assist and how?*

Electric Motor-Assisted Power Steering

Hybrids have electric motor-assisted power steering (EMPS). A torque sensor mounted on the steering gear receives information from wheel speed sensors. The electronic control unit (ECU) uses this information to determine the force of the power assist. The ECU actuates a DC motor to provide a power assist to the steering effort. The EMPS system does not depend on the engine for its power source. Thus, it can provide a power assist even when the engine is stopped. Because it receives its power from a DC motor, this system improves fuel economy. The DC motor consumes energy only when the motor is stopped. This system also differs from the conventional hydraulic power steering system in that it does not require hydraulic steering fluid.

When the vehicle is moving at less than 20 mph [32 kph], the solenoid valve keeps the pressure orifices open, providing full power assist for low-speed and parking maneuvers. When vehicle speed increases, the solenoid valve begins to restrict fluid flow to the steering gear. The result is a slight increase in steering effort and improved road feel.

Whenever there is a need for sudden or severe steering action, the solenoid valve opens the orifices, providing full power assist.

Vehicles equipped with a variable-assist power steering system have a separate diagnostic connector. The connector allows the technician to retrieve diagnostic codes from this system using a scan tool.

Electronic Rack-and-Pinion Power Steering Electronic rack-and-pinion power steering uses an electric motor to provide the power assist. It does not use a hydraulic system. Instead of using a flat rack with straight teeth as in a standard rack, this type of steering gear uses a helical-gear rack driven by a fast-acting electric motor. See **Fig. 2-19**.

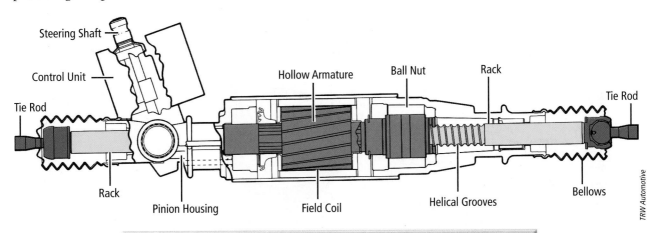

TRW Automotive

Fig. 2-19 A typical electronic rack-and-pinion power steering gear. The electric motor consists of the hollow armature and the field coil. *What provides the input signal to the PCM?*

Electronic rack-and-pinion steering is not yet very common but will probably find greater use in the future. Some vehicles with four-wheel steering use hydraulically assisted rack-and-pinion steering on the front wheels and computer-controlled electronic rack-and-pinion steering on the rear wheels.

A torque sensor mounted on the pinion shaft measures input steering torque. As torque is applied, a signal is sent to the PCM. The PCM sends a signal to the electric motor, providing the power assist. Electronically controlled steering systems can be tested and diagnosed using a scan tool.

Steering-Wheel Air Bags

Many vehicles produced since the late 1980s have a steering-wheel air bag. The air bag is mounted in the center of the steering wheel. See **Fig. 2-20.** If the vehicle hits an object with enough force, a fabric quickly inflates, using a built-in gas-charged canister. This inflated fabric protects the driver from injury caused by contact with the steering wheel, dash, or windshield.

Front impact sensors detect the force and direction of any impact. The sensors connect to an air-bag control module. This module is calibrated for a specific range of impact force. If the impact is strong enough, the control module triggers the air bag.

Accidental discharge of an air bag can cause injury to anyone close to the air bag. The noise a deploying air bag creates can damage hearing.

Never place an undeployed air bag face down on a solid surface, such as a worktable. If accidentally deployed, the air bag expands with great force. Never carry or handle an air bag carelessly. Always carry an air bag with the face (the interior trim side) pointing away from the body.

When cleaning a vehicle after an air-bag deployment, always wear safety glasses, rubber gloves, a dust mask, and long-sleeved clothing. Sodium hydroxide powder is a residue of air-bag deployment. The powder can irritate skin. Flush any exposed areas with cool water. If you experience nasal or throat soreness, get some fresh air. If the soreness continues, get medical attention.

Always store air bags in a cool, dry location, away from excessive heat and static electrical activity. Store the bags facing up. Air bags are not reusable. You must dispose of them properly.

Safety First

Air Bags Always follow the procedures in the vehicle service manual for air bag removal and installation. To prevent accidental discharge of the air bag, the battery and specific fuse may require disconnection. Always take special precautions when handling or storing an air bag assembly. Never attempt to remove a steering wheel until you understand and are prepared to follow the service manual's safety instructions.

Steering Column

Clock Spring

Air Bag

Federal Mogul

Fig 2-20 Placement of the air-bag module within the steering wheel. *Why are air bags mounted in the steering wheel?*

Steering Angle Sensor

Many newer vehicles are equipped with a steering angle sensor, which is located in the steering column. This sensor will allow various control modules such as the variable-assist power steering and some stability control systems to know the exact direction in which the driver wants to steer the vehicle. See **Fig. 2-21**. It does this by sending a signal to the control module when the driver turns the wheel. This sensor uses LEDs (light emitting diodes) and photodiodes (light sensing diodes) to track the steering wheel position. The LEDs shine on the photodiodes through windows cut in a flange. These windows allow light to pass through. When the wheel is turned, the light is alternately interrupted to produce a digital signal that is sent to the control module. The sensor can be accessed by using a scan tool connected to the appropriate control module.

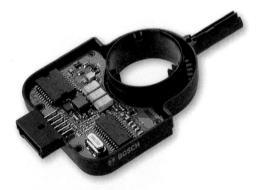

Fig. 2-21 A steering angle sensor may be located in the steering column of a newer car.

Clock Spring

Most vehicles today use a clock spring located in the steering column to serve as the electrical connection. The clock spring connects the air bag, the horn, and the other electrical controls located in the steering wheel. The clock spring allows a positive electrical connection to be maintained when the driver turns the wheel. Many clock springs use a ribbon that contains copper wire encased in flexible plastic and wound in a circle. When the steering wheel is turned, the ribbon can wind or unwind to maintain an electrical path for current to flow without interruption.

TECH TIP **Clock Springs.** Caution should be taken to lock the steering wheel in place when servicing the steering system. If the steering wheel is turned with the steering system disconnected, the clock spring might be turned past its limit. This will cause irreparable damage to the clock spring. Also, the clock spring must be positioned correctly when it is reinstalled. Otherwise, damage to the clock spring will result when the steering wheel is turned completely in either direction.

SECTION 2 KNOWLEDGE CHECK

1. What is the purpose of the two hoses of a remote-mounted power steering pump?

2. Explain how to check the power steering fluid if the system is hot.

3. Name the three common power-assisted steering complaints.

4. What happens within a variable-assist power steering system as speed increases?

5. Why is it necessary to wear safety gear when cleaning a vehicle after an air-bag deployment?

ASE TEST PREP

6. Technician A says that some manufacturers recommend flushing the power steering system and changing the fluid at various mileage or time intervals. Technician B says that flushing the power steering system is required when replacing a defective steering gear or pump. Who is correct?
   - ⓐ Technician A.
   - ⓑ Technician B.
   - ⓒ Both Technician A and Technician B.
   - ⓓ Neither Technician A nor Technician B.

Key Points

Meets the following NATEF Standards for Suspension & Steering: steering systems diagnosis and repair.

- Power-assisted steering systems may be hydraulic or electronic.
- Many vehicles have steering columns with tilt and telescopic mechanisms. Some steering columns are designed to collapse in a collision.
- Recirculating-ball steering gear designs use a series of linkage parts. These include the pitman arm, center link, idler arm, tie rods, tie-rod ends, and steering arms.
- There are two types of rack-and-pinion link designs.
- The steering ratio is the number of degrees that the steering wheel needs to turn so that the road wheels turn 1°.
- Power steering systems require a specific type of hydraulic fluid.
- The power steering pressure switch monitors system pressure and supplies information to the engine electronic control module.
- Hybrid electric motor-assisted power steering units do not depend on the engine for their power source.

Review Questions

1. What is the purpose of the steering column?
2. What is a symptom of loose or worn steering column couplers?
3. Name the steering assembly that uses a series of recirculating balls on a worm gear to transfer steering-wheel movement to road-wheel movement.
4. What is the purpose of a ball joint press?
5. What kind of rack-and-pinion system features tie rods that are attached at the center of the rack housing?
6. What should be used to check belt tension?
7. In what way does variable-assist power steering differ from regular power steering?
8. What is the purpose of a power steering pressure switch?
9. **Critical Thinking** What does foaming in the power steering fluid reservoir indicate?
10. **Critical Thinking** Where should air bags be stored?

Excellence in Communication

Learning About New Systems

Today's highly trained technician cannot make mistakes when servicing vehicles. A technician must not guess or use outdated information to service any system, especially a new or unfamiliar system.

Air bags are now an important part of vehicle safety. When air bags became a service item, even experienced technicians had to read and study to learn how to service them. They had learned that all new systems need careful study through reading. Successful technicians know they cannot rely on guesswork.

Your textbook has pointed out precautions you need to take when servicing air bags. However, manufacturer's service manuals will give you the specific information that you will need to take care of their air bag systems properly. Besides the basic precautions, you will learn how to install and service air bags so they will function correctly.

Apply It!

Meets NATEF Communications Standards for study habits and methods to use information provided by manufacturers.

1. Locate service manuals from two different manufacturers. Choose a vehicle with an air bag system from each manual.
2. Read the section about air bags in each manual.
3. Take notes on specific information for each manufacturer's system.
4. Compare the information you found.

AUTOMOTIVE SERVICE EXCELLENCE
TEST PREP

Answering the following practice questions will help you prepare for the ASE certification tests.

1. How many fasteners is the steering wheel usually secured with?

   ⓐ 4.

   ⓑ 3.

   ⓒ 2.

   ⓓ 1.

2. Technician A says that a steering wheel puller should always be used when removing a steering wheel. Technician B says that a hammer should be used. Who is correct?

   ⓐ Technician A.

   ⓑ Technician B.

   ⓒ Both Technician A and Technician B.

   ⓓ Neither Technician A nor Technician B.

3. To protect the driver, some steering columns are designed to:

   ⓐ warn the driver of understeer.

   ⓑ warn the driver of oversteer.

   ⓒ collapse in a front-end collision.

   ⓓ lock movement of the wheel when braking.

4. Technician A says that steering column couplers allow the steering shaft to pivot at various angles during steering operation. Technician B says that steering column couplers are used to connect the steering column to the drive shaft. Who is correct?

   ⓐ Technician A.

   ⓑ Technician B.

   ⓒ Both Technician A and Technician B.

   ⓓ Neither Technician A nor Technician B.

5. The power rack-and-pinion system:

   ⓐ has more parts to inspect than the recirculating ball system.

   ⓑ has more parts to service than a recirculating ball system.

   ⓒ provides space-saving and weight-saving features.

   ⓓ is impractical for small cars.

6. Technician A says that in a hybrid car a torque sensor mounted on the steering gear receives information from wheel speed sensors. Technician B says that an electronic control unit (ECU) actuates a DC motor to provide power assist to the steering effort. Who is correct?

   ⓐ Technician A.

   ⓑ Technician B.

   ⓒ Both Technician A and Technician B.

   ⓓ Neither Technician A nor Technician B.

7. What type of gear teeth are found on electronic rack-and-pinion power steering systems?

   ⓐ Helical.

   ⓑ Straight.

   ⓒ Elliptical.

   ⓓ Chamfered.

8. Technician A says that front impact sensors detect the force of an impact. Technician B says that front impact sensors detect direction of an impact. Who is correct?

   ⓐ Technician A.

   ⓑ Technician B.

   ⓒ Both Technician A and Technician B.

   ⓓ Neither Technician A nor Technician B.

9. How should an undeployed air bag always be stored?

   ⓐ Face down.

   ⓑ Face up.

   ⓒ On a side.

   ⓓ None of the above.

10. Technician A says that an improperly installed clock spring can be damaged if the steering wheel is turned too far. Technician B says that the steering wheel should be locked when servicing the system. Who is correct?

    ⓐ Technician A.

    ⓑ Technician B.

    ⓒ Both Technician A and Technician B.

    ⓓ Neither Technician A nor Technician B.

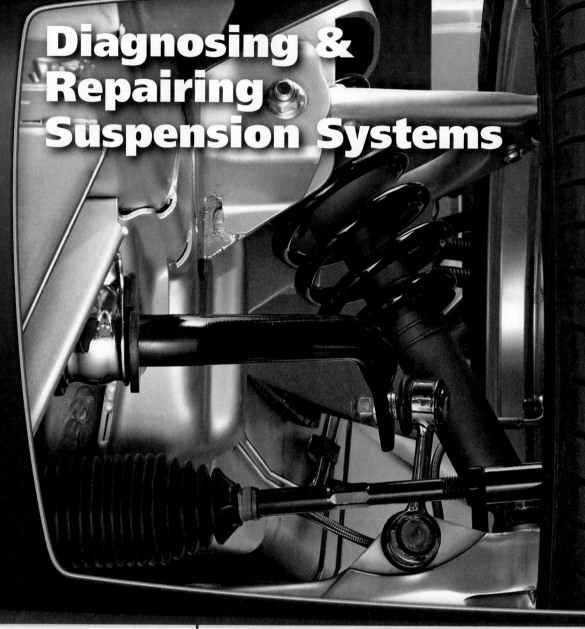

CHAPTER 3

Section 1
The Suspension System

Section 2
Front Suspension Systems

Section 3
Rear Suspension Systems

Diagnosing & Repairing Suspension Systems

Customer's Concern

Miguel Lopez and three of his colleagues traveled in his minivan to a convention in Chicago last weekend. While out on the highway, Miguel says his van handled fine. Once they got into the city, however, he says the van seemed to be bouncing a lot. Chicago driving involves a lot of stops and starts, and Miguel says the bouncing nearly made him and his co-workers carsick. The front of the van would lurch toward the pavement when he applied the brakes and then bounce fitfully back and forth when he stopped. Cornering was not fun either. The van rocked from side to side in sharp turns.

Miguel is embarrassed about the way his van bounced around Chicago. He needs to get it fixed before he takes the same colleagues to Cincinnati next Tuesday.

Technician's Challenge

As the service technician, you need to find answers to these questions:

1. Did Miguel notice any "bouncing" before his trip? Did the problem just become apparent with frequent stopping? Could the added weight of extra occupants and luggage have contributed to the problem?

2. What could be causing the problem? Could it be worn or broken leaf springs, coil springs, shocks, struts, or bushings?

3. How will you diagnose and repair the suspension problem? What safety precautions will you take before servicing the suspension system?

Section 1
The Suspension System

Objectives:

C2-1 • Remove, inspect, and install coil springs and spring insulators.

C3-1 • Inspect, remove, and replace shock absorbers.

C1-9 • Remove, inspect, and install stabilizer bar bushings, brackets, and links.

C1-7 • Remove, inspect, and install short and long arm suspension system coil springs and spring insulators.

C1-1 • Diagnose short and long arm suspension system noises, body sway, and uneven riding height concerns; determine necessary action.

C1-5 • Remove, inspect, and install upper and/or lower ball joints.

C1-11 • Lubricate suspension and steering systems.

C3-2 • Remove, inspect, and service or replace front and rear wheel bearings.

C3-3 • Test and diagnose components of electronically controlled suspension sytems using a scan tool; determine necessary action.

      • Remove and reinstall sealed wheel bearing assembly.

Vocabulary:
- sprung weight
- unsprung weight
- coil spring
- leaf spring
- torsion bar
- air spring
- anti-sway bar
- control arm
- ball joint
- live axle

Suspension System Components

The suspension system is located between the axles and the body or frame of a vehicle. The job of the suspension system is to:
- Support the vehicle.
- Provide a cushion effect between the body and the road.
- Allow the tires to maintain solid contact with the road.
- Maintain wheel alignment.

The suspension system provides for improved vehicle handling and for cushioning road shock. The suspension system controls the stability of a vehicle during lane changes, straight-line driving, turning, and braking.

Compression or jounce occurs when the suspension system moves closer to the body. During braking, the front of the vehicle noses down toward the

Safety First

Suspension Systems When servicing any suspension system, always be aware of the pressures and forces that exist in a compressed spring. Never attempt to remove any suspension component without taking the required steps given in the vehicle's service manual. Failure to do so could cause serious injury.

road. When turning, the side of the body opposite the direction of a turn changes height. The result is that both sides of the body are not at the same height from the ground.

Rebound occurs as the suspension moves away from the body. After completing a stop and nosing down or after completing a turn, the body returns to a normal level position.

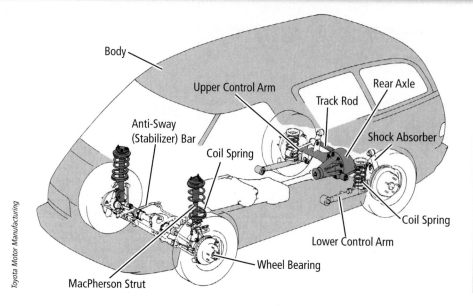

Body
Upper Control Arm
Rear Axle
Track Rod
Anti-Sway
(Stabilizer) Bar
Shock Absorber
Coil Spring
Coil Spring
Lower Control Arm
Wheel Bearing
MacPherson Strut

Toyota Motor Manufacturing

Fig. 3-1 Main parts of a vehicle suspension system. Suspension systems vary depending on the vehicle. This system has MacPherson struts in front and coil springs in the rear. *What are the functions of the suspension system?*

The basic parts of a suspension system are springs, shock absorbers, anti-sway bars, control arms, ball joints, axles, and wheel bearings. Other suspension system parts will vary, depending on the vehicle. See **Fig. 3-1**. The functions of the basic parts are as follows:

• Springs support the body.
• Shock absorbers control spring action by damping the springs. This helps to control how fast the springs compress and rebound. Damping also helps to prevent the springs from "oscillating" or vibrating.
• Anti-sway bars are a type of torsion bar that connects the lower suspension to both sides of the frame or body. These bars prevent the body from "leaning" too far during turns.
• Control arms position the wheels on the frame or body and maintain the wheel alignment to the frame or body.
• Ball joints enable suspension parts to pivot and rotate.
• Axles provide a positioning point for the wheels. They serve as the center point for wheel position and rotation.
• Wheel bearings enable the tires and wheels at the end of the axle to rotate smoothly, freely, and safely at high speed.

Springs

Automotive suspension systems commonly use four types of springs:
• Coil springs.
• Leaf springs.
• Torsion bars.
• Air springs.

Springs are used to support **sprung weight**. This includes the weight of the vehicle body and/or frame, engine, transmission, cargo, and passengers. **Unsprung weight** refers to the weight that the springs do not support. This includes wheels, tires, brakes, lower control arms, and drive axles.

Vehicle makers try to make unsprung weight as light as possible. This is one reason why many vehicles come equipped with lighter aluminum wheels. As unsprung weight increases, so does the roughness of the ride.

Coil Springs A length of spring-steel rod wound into a coil is known as a **coil spring**. The rod can be the same diameter from end to end, giving the spring a constant spring rate. The rod may be tapered or wound with unevenly-spaced coils, giving the spring a variable spring rate. See **Fig. 3-2**.

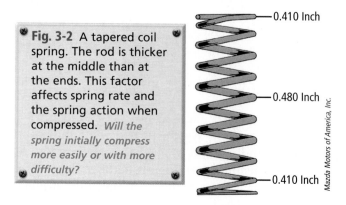

Fig. 3-2 A tapered coil spring. The rod is thicker at the middle than at the ends. This factor affects spring rate and the spring action when compressed. *Will the spring initially compress more easily or with more difficulty?*

0.410 Inch

0.480 Inch

0.410 Inch

Mazda Motors of America, Inc.

Spring rate and action are determined by the spring rod thickness, the number of coils, and the spacing between the coils. A variable-rate coil may compress easily initially. But, as it compresses, it becomes more difficult to squeeze together.

Leaf Springs A spring that consists of single- or multiple-spring steel bands is called a **leaf spring**. See **Fig. 3-3.** Some springs use a high-strength composite material. Leaf springs are formed in an arc shape. The thickness of the band(s) and the length of the spring dictate the spring rate.

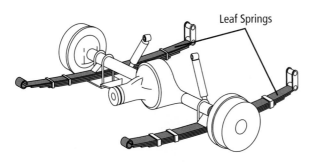

Leaf Springs

Fig. 3-3 Longitudinally mounted leaf springs.

A monoleaf spring has one leaf. A multi-leaf spring has two or more bands stacked together. A leaf spring mounts to the body at each end and attaches to the axle at the center of the leaf. As vehicle weight bears down on the spring, the weight acts against the arc of the leaf. At least one end of a leaf spring must be mounted with a shackle to the vehicle. The shackle acts as a hinge and allows the arc of the spring to change as spring loading changes.

A longitudinally mounted leaf spring positions front-to-rear. A transverse mounted leaf spring positions side-to-side parallel to the axle. If a vehicle uses longitudinal leaves, it requires one spring per side (one left and one right). If a vehicle uses a transverse leaf spring, it needs only one.

Torsion Bar Once used only on early domestic and import vehicles, torsion bar suspension is commonly used on a variety of vehicles. A **torsion bar** is a steel rod that twists to provide spring action. See **Fig. 3-4.** One end of the bar attaches to the vehicle frame, while the opposite end attaches to the lower control arm.

Torsion bars are positioned either longitudinally or transversely. Longitudinal positioning attaches the front end of the bar to the lower control arm and the rear of the bar to the frame. Transverse positioning connects the frame to the lower control arms.

Air Springs An **air spring** consists a cylindrical bag filled with compressed air. See **Fig. 3-5.** Air springs are used primarily in automatic level control suspension systems.

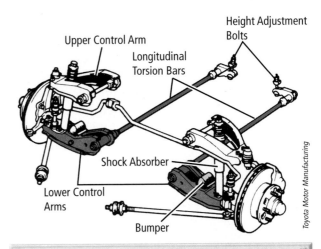

Upper Control Arm
Height Adjustment Bolts
Longitudinal Torsion Bars
Shock Absorber
Lower Control Arms
Bumper

Toyota Motor Manufacturing

Fig. 3-4 A front suspension system using torsion bar springs. Torsion bars mount transversely (side-to-side) or, as shown here, longitudinally (front-to-rear). *How does a torsion bar provide spring action?*

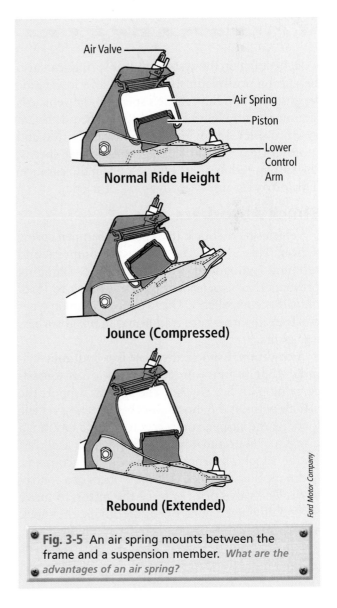

Air Valve
Air Spring
Piston
Lower Control Arm

Normal Ride Height

Jounce (Compressed)

Rebound (Extended)

Ford Motor Company

Fig. 3-5 An air spring mounts between the frame and a suspension member. *What are the advantages of an air spring?*

Sensors in an automatic level-control suspension system detect changes in the vehicle's ride height, or ground clearance. As a vehicle takes on weight, a height sensor detects the change in ride height. An air compressor is activated to provide additional air to the air springs. The added air raises the vehicle back to normal ride height. Upon removal of the weight, the system allows the springs to bleed-off enough air to return the vehicle to its original ride height.

Depending on the system, the air springs can also be automatically adjusted to raise and lower ride height based on the vehicle's speed. If the vehicle is stationary or traveling at slow speeds, the ride height is set to a level providing a comfortable ride and more normal ground clearance. At higher speeds, the system reduces the vehicle's ground clearance. This provides more aerodynamic efficiency.

Shock Absorbers

Vehicles have shock absorbers to dampen spring action. This allows the spring to compress and rebound (unload) at a controlled rate. Damping prevents the suspension from continuing to load/unload uncontrollably. The two most common types of shock absorbers are traditional shock absorbers and struts.

A traditional shock absorber is a hydraulic cylinder that mounts independently of any load-carrying part. See **Fig. 3-6**. The springs support the vehicle without the shock absorber affecting vehicle load. As the suspension reacts to vehicle motion, a piston moves up and down inside the shock absorber. As the shock absorber compresses and rebounds, hydraulic fluid is forced through orifices of a control valve. The valve orifices force the piston to move up and down at a controlled rate, giving the shock absorber its damping characteristics.

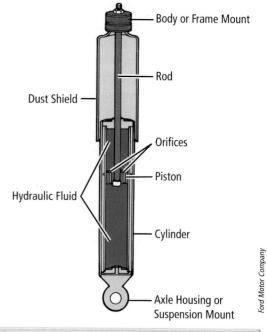

Ford Motor Company

Fig. 3-6 A traditional shock absorber. Internal valving allows the shock absorber to absorb and control spring action. *How do shock absorbers dampen spring action?*

Some shock absorbers also use compressed nitrogen gas. As the shock absorber cycles, the gas reduces foaming or aeration of the hydraulic fluid. Gas-charged shock absorbers have become very common.

Shock absorbers mount with the top attached to the frame or upper control arm and the lower end attached to the lower control arm or axle housing.

A strut serves as a key part of the suspension. It is located between the lower control arm and the body. Struts are also shock absorbers. A traditional shock absorber and a strut both provide damping control for the springs.

Several special types of shock absorbers are used. They include spring-assisted shock absorbers, adjustable shock absorbers, and air-assisted shock absorbers.

Spring-Assisted Shock Absorbers Spring-assisted shock absorbers use a coil spring installed over the shock absorber body. See **Fig. 3-7(a)**. For applications where added cargo load is present, the assist spring provides additional load-carrying assistance. The shock absorber serves as a hydraulic damper for the spring action. The assist spring on the shock absorber also provides additional support for the body and frame.

Adjustable Shock Absorbers Adjustable shock absorbers provide a way to tailor the handling of a vehicle. An adjustable shock absorber has a variable setting for the internal valving. See **Fig. 3-7(b)**. The shock absorber can be set for soft to firm damping. These shock absorbers allow adjustment for damping only and have no effect on load carrying.

Some adjustable shock absorbers have an external dial or adjustment screw. Others must be disconnected to set the adjustment. Once disconnected, they must be fully compressed and rotated in relation to the internal piston.

Air-Assisted Shock Absorbers Air-assisted shock absorbers are traditional shock absorbers with an air chamber between the inner and outer shock absorber tubes. See **Fig. 3-7(c)**. The chamber can be inflated with compressed air to provide additional load-carrying ability. This is helpful when the rear cargo area is heavily loaded. The compressed air acts as an assist to the normal operation of the shock absorber.

Inspecting Shock Absorbers When checking the operation and condition of shock absorbers, do the following:

- Perform a bounce test. Push down on the front end of the vehicle firmly and release. The front end of the vehicle should rise once and immediately settle. If the front end bounces more than once, the shock absorber is worn and should be replaced.
- Visually inspect the shock absorber for leakage. A light film of oil near the top seal is normal. If excessive leakage is seen, replace the shock absorber.
- Look for damage, such as dings and dents. If evident, replace the shock absorber.
- Inspect the shock absorber piston rod for scratches, gouges, corrosion, and bending. If there is damage, replace the shock absorber.

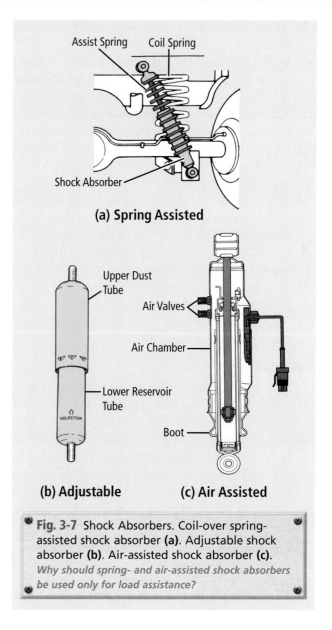

(a) Spring Assisted

(b) Adjustable   (c) Air Assisted

Fig. 3-7 Shock Absorbers. Coil-over spring-assisted shock absorber **(a)**. Adjustable shock absorber **(b)**. Air-assisted shock absorber **(c)**. *Why should spring- and air-assisted shock absorbers be used only for load assistance?*

Servicing Shock Absorbers If the shock absorber appears faulty when you check for operation and condition, replace it. Use the procedures indicated in the specific vehicle's service manual.

Following is a general procedure for removing and servicing the basic shock absorber:

1. While the weight of the vehicle is on the suspension, remove the upper mount nut. This is where the top of the shock absorber attaches to a mount on the frame or body. To remove the nut, use a special hex tool to hold the shock absorber piston rod.
2. Disconnect any special air hose connectors, if applicable.

3. Raise the vehicle and support it on jack stands.
4. Remove the two bottom bolts (front) or bottom nut (rear) and washers where the shock absorber attaches to the lower control arm or axle.
5. Remove the shock absorber from the vehicle.
6. Position the new shock absorber on the vehicle.
7. Install the two bottom bolts (front) or bottom nut (rear) and washers where the shock absorber attaches to the lower control arm or axle.
8. Align the shock absorber piston rod with the upper mount. If equipped, cut the restraining wire to allow the rod to expand to the full length.
9. Install the rod in the upper mount by lowering the vehicle. Using a special hex tool to hold the rod, install the nut where the top of the shock absorber attaches to the upper mount.
10. Tighten the nuts and bolts as specified in the vehicle's service manual.

Anti-Sway Bars

The anti-sway bar is also called a stabilizer bar, sway bar, or anti-roll bar. An **anti-sway bar** is a device that helps reduce body sway. On a front suspension, the ends of an anti-sway bar connect to the two lower control arms. The center portion of the bar mounts to both sides of the vehicle frame. See **Fig. 3-8.** When one front wheel moves up, the bar twists in an attempt to pick up the opposite wheel. This action helps to balance the force between the two sides of the vehicle, reducing body "roll."

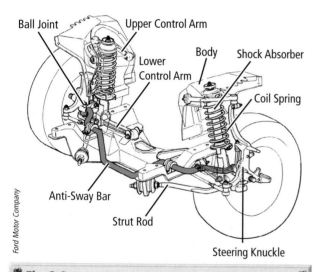

Ford Motor Company

Ball Joint Upper Control Arm
Body Shock Absorber
Lower Control Arm
Coil Spring
Anti-Sway Bar
Strut Rod
Steering Knuckle

Fig. 3-8 An anti-sway bar mounts laterally and connects the suspension to the frame. *How does an anti-sway bar improve handling?*

The anti-sway bar mounts to the frame with rubber or urethane isolator bushings and retainers. See **Fig. 3-9.** These allow the bar to pivot, while reducing the transfer of road noise or vibration to the body. If handling problems occur, always check these bushings. Also check the end link bushings for wear and damage.

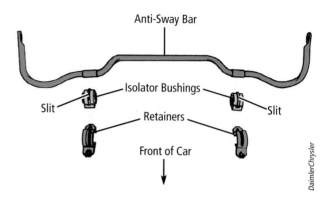

Anti-Sway Bar
Isolator Bushings
Slit Slit
Retainers
Front of Car

DaimlerChrysler

Fig. 3-9 An anti-sway bar is mounted with isolator bushings. *What function do the isolator bushings perform?*

Servicing Anti-Sway Bars An anti-sway bar does not support vehicle weight. Initially, the bar may be installed with the vehicle on jack stands and the wheels hanging. Do not fully tighten the bushing mounts or end links with the suspension extended. Tighten the bushing mounts or end links only when the weight of the vehicle is on the suspension. This will prevent binding of the bar bushings. Refer to the vehicle's service manual for specific details and procedures.

Inspect the anti-sway bars as follows:
- Inspect the bushings that mount the bar to the frame. If these bushings appear loose, worn, damaged, or oil-soaked, they should be replaced.
- Inspect the end links and the end-link bushings. Look for signs of wear, disintegration, and missing bushings. Inspect the end link for heavy corrosion and bending. Replace any part showing signs of wear or damage.

Control Arms

A **control arm** is a device that provides the connection points of the suspension for up/down pivoting movement. Because they look like the letter A when viewed from above, they are called A-type control arms. Technicians also refer to A-type control arms as wishbones.

Excellence in Science

How Stress Affects Springs

Applying a force to a spring creates a stress. There are three types of stress: tension, compression, and shear.

- Tension occurs when two forces act on opposite ends of an object and are directed away from each other. This stretches the object.

- Compression occurs when two forces act on opposite ends of an object but are directed toward each other. This squeezes the object.

- Shear occurs when parallel forces act in opposite directions on opposite sides of an object. This twists the object.

When a coil spring in the suspension system reacts to the vehicle going over a "speed bump," the coil is compressed as the wheels move over the bump (compression stress). As the wheels move down the bump, the wheels and the frame begin to move in opposite directions (tension stress). If these two stresses are controlled, the ride is smooth.

When tension stress is applied to a spring, the spring stretches. When the force is removed, the spring returns to its original shape. This property is called elasticity. As more force is applied to the spring, the spring becomes still longer.

The scientist Robert Hooke observed that the amount of stretch depended on three properties:
- The amount of force applied to the object.
- The type of material used to make the object. Metals differ in their elasticity and stretch at different rates.
- The dimensions of the object. The longer a spring is, the more it stretches. The thicker the coil is, the less it stretches.

Applying more force to any object will eventually stretch it to the point where it cannot return to its original shape.

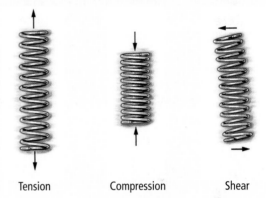

Tension   Compression   Shear

Apply It!

Testing Hooke's Idea

Meets NATEF Science Standards for explaining stress forces and the elasticity of springs.

Materials and Equipment
- Small return spring
- Spring scale
- Ruler
- Set of weights (Flat washers can be used.)

1. Place the spring on the end of the spring scale.

2. Measure the length of the spring.

3. Add weight to the spring. Measure the length of the spring again.

4. Subtract the new length of the spring from its starting length. The result is the stretch.

5. Divide the weight on the spring by the amount of stretch. The result is the spring constant.

6. Repeat the procedure two more times with different weights. Determine and record the spring constant. Do not exceed the elastic limit of your spring.

7. Did the spring stretch more as you increased the amount of weight?

8. Did the measured spring constant also increase? Explain.

The inboard end of the control arm is wider, with two pivoting connections (one at the front and one at the rear). Here the control arm attaches to the vehicle frame. The outer end tapers to a point where the control arm attaches to the steering knuckle with a ball joint.

The wider inboard end of the control arm prevents the suspension from deflecting in or out during braking and hard cornering. The A-shape of the control arm acts as a brace. This prevents wheel alignment changes during braking or cornering.

Control arms may be of different lengths, where the lower arm is longer than the upper arm. This is a short-arm/long-arm (SLA) system. The top of the coil spring rests in a fixed spring seat at the vehicle body or frame. The bottom of the spring rests on the lower control arm.

Some vehicles use a lower control arm that looks like a straight beam, instead of having a shape like an A. See **Fig. 3-10**. This single-beam style provides only one bushing attachment point at the frame.

The single-beam type control arm still allows the suspension travel to take place when the wheel wants to move up or down. However, this type of control arm would deflect under braking and hard cornering.

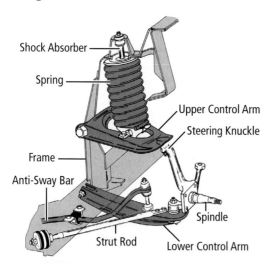

When a single-beam-type lower control arm is used, an additional strut rod is added. Without proper bracing of the control arms, the wheels would move slightly forward and rearwards. This rod is sometimes used for a caster adjustment.

Ball Joints

Ball joints are also called ball-and-socket joints. A **ball joint** is a lubricated attachment that connects two suspension parts to allow pivoting movement. An automotive suspension uses ball joints at the connection points between the control arms and the steering knuckle assemblies. The tapered stud provides a secure press fit at the steering knuckle mounting point. See **Fig. 3-11**. Some ball joints have a straight stud and are attached by a pinch bolt.

Ball joints allow the suspension to move up and down. They also allow the steering knuckle to pivot when the wheels turn left or right.

Fig. 3-10 This is an SLA design. The lower control arm is a single-beam type. It is longer than the upper control arm. Normally, the coil spring mounts between the lower control arm and the frame. When the coil spring mounts between the upper control arm and the frame as shown, technicians refer to this as an SLA-2 design. *Why do some front suspensions require the use of a strut rod?*

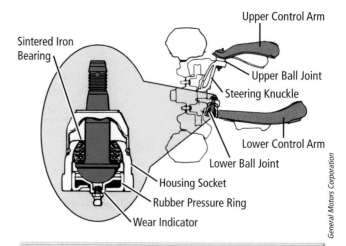

General Motors Corporation

Fig. 3-11 A ball joint provides the connection between the steering knuckle and the control arm. *Why is the ball joint in the form of a ball?*

Ball joints must be checked for looseness and wear. Some ball joints have a built-in wear indicator. The indicator shows when the ball and internal ball socket have worn beyond the point of useable life.

Some ball joints are designed to be used where spring tension forces the ball more tightly into the socket. These are called compression ball joints. Other ball joints are designed to be used where spring tension will try to pull the ball from the socket. These are called tension ball joints. Each type must be designed to appropriately handle this particular spring tension safely during its normal lifetime.

Ball joints have been used on short-arm/long-arm (SLA) and strut systems for the last half-century. Today most automobiles use struts, but many light trucks and SUVs continue to use SLA systems. It is very important to know the proper way to inspect and replace ball joints. Improper inspection of ball joints may return many unsafe vehicles to the highways. In addition, improper replacement procedures can be very dangerous to the service technician.

In either the original SLA system or the SLA-2 system, there is one control arm that contains the loaded ball joint (the one that has spring tension applied). The other control arm contains the follower ball joint (the one that has no spring tension applied). It just holds the steering knuckle to the control arm and goes along for the ride, with very little stress. It is usually the loaded ball joints that fail because of the stress of the spring tension.

When the vehicle is in a configuration that has spring tension applied to the loaded ball joint, it is impossible to test the ball joints and measure for excessive wear. All ball joints in this configuration would seem to be good because none would show any play.

To test the ball joints, spring tension must be removed from the loaded joint and both joints must be checked for excessive play. See **Fig. 3-12**. Ball joints must be checked for vertical (up-and-down) play, called axial play, and for lateral (side-to-side) play, called radial play. Neither the upper nor the lower joint should exceed the manufacturer's maximum limits for axial and radial play. The maximum axial and radial play limits for loaded ball joints may range from 0.050″ to 0.250″, depending on manufacture design. What would be acceptable for one manufacturer's design could be very dangerous for another. In general, most follower joints should not have any perceptible axial or radial play.

To test ball joints, you must sufficiently unload the spring tension, following a correct and safe procedure. The original SLA system has the spring

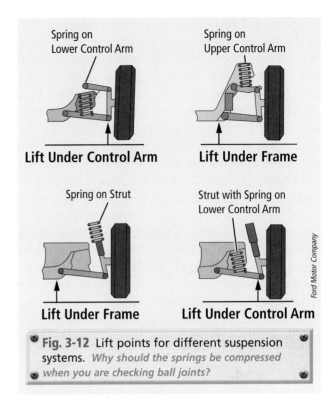

Spring on Lower Control Arm

Spring on Upper Control Arm

Lift Under Control Arm

Lift Under Frame

Spring on Strut

Strut with Spring on Lower Control Arm

Lift Under Frame

Lift Under Control Arm

Ford Motor Company

Fig. 3-12 Lift points for different suspension systems. *Why should the springs be compressed when you are checking ball joints?*

tension applied to the lower control arm. The spring is located between the frame and the lower control arm. Therefore, the lower ball joint is the loaded joint, and the upper ball joint is the follower joint.

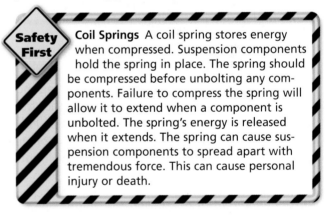

Safety First

Coil Springs A coil spring stores energy when compressed. Suspension components hold the spring in place. The spring should be compressed before unbolting any components. Failure to compress the spring will allow it to extend when a component is unbolted. The spring's energy is released when it extends. The spring can cause suspension components to spread apart with tremendous force. This can cause personal injury or death.

Jack up or place this type of vehicle on vehicle jack stands under the lower control arms as close to the lower ball joints as possible. The weight of the vehicle should compress the spring, allowing the steering knuckle and upper control arm freedom to move up and down. Now the ball joints can be tested without spring tension applied. Place a pry bar under the wheel, and lift up and down. A dial indicator or appropriate measuring device can measure the ball joint movement or play between the ball sockets and ball studs. Check for both axial and radial play, and compare them with the manufacturer's specifications.

The SLA-2 design has the spring tension applied to the upper control arm. The spring is allocated between the car body or frame and upper control arm. Therefore, the upper ball joint is the loaded joint, and the lower joint is the follower joint. Jack up this type of vehicle under the vehicle frame or lift it on a vehicle frame contact lift, allowing the lower control arm to extend to its limit and forcing the upper control arm against the rubber bumper on the vehicle frame. This should unload the tension on the steering knuckle and lower control arm. If this does not occur, you must lower the vehicle and place a special wedge between the frame and the upper control arm to compress spring tension when the vehicle is lifted again. A block of wood can be used if a special wedge is not available. With the steering knuckle and lower control arm hanging free unloaded, a pry bar can be used under the wheel to check the play in the ball joints against the manufacturer's specifications.

TECH TIP **Using a Pry Bar.** Always use a pry bar to lift the wheel steering knuckle and control arm. These items together can be quite heavy; if you try to lift the wheel with just your hand you may mistakenly decide that this heavy weight is a ball joint with no perceptible play.

If you feel excessive play in the suspension system during this test, do not assume that it is all in the ball joint. Have someone lift the pry bar indicating the play, and look behind the wheel to see whether the play is coming from the ball joint socket and ball stud. Measure this play, using a dial indicator or other appropriate measuring tool. This is the clearance you are trying to verify. Excessive play from such sources as a loose wheel bearing, a loose steering linkage, or a worn inner control arm bushing can cause you to mistakenly blame the ball joints. If excessive play exists in these other items, corrections should be made there also.

To check ball joints on the typical strut system you can usually jack up the vehicle under the frame or lift on a frame contact lift, allowing the struts to fully extend. Place a pry bar somewhere near the ball joint between the lower control arm and strut, and check for play by prying in a manner that will show movement between the ball joint socket mounted to the control arm and the ball joint ball stud connected to the strut. Measure this clearance,

and compare it with the manufacturer's specifications. Be careful not to puncture the ball joint rubber boot.

Replacing Ball Joints Consult the vehicle manufacturer's instructions for proper replacement of ball joints. The general procedure is as follows:
1. Relieve the spring tension by setting up the vehicle in the same configuration as that used in testing the ball joints.
2. Remove the wheel.
3. A spring compress may be attached to the spring for safety and to keep the spring compressed during service.
4. Properly disconnect the ball joint stud from the steering knuckle, using a ball joint fork or press for tapered studs. Some straight studs are held in place simply by using a pinch bolt.
5. Remove the old ball joint from the control arm, and replace it with a new ball joint. Some ball joints are pressed in. Some are screwed in with a special socket and others are held in place with rivets or bolts and nuts.
6. Torque all fasteners, and install cotter pins as necessary.
7. If the new ball joint has a grease fitting, it should be properly lubricated. Use caution not to over-lubricate and rupture the rubber boot.
8. Replace the wheel, and torque to specifications.
9. Check the vehicle's wheel alignment.

Axles

An axle is a support suspension member on which the wheels are mounted. A **live axle** supports part of the vehicle weight and drives the wheels connected to the axle shafts. If the wheels on the live axle pivot for steering, the axle is a steerable live axle.

A dead axle is a non-drive axle. It carries a portion of the vehicle weight and the non-driven wheels. Since a dead axle is a non-drive axle, the rear axle of a front-wheel drive vehicle is a dead axle. The rear axle is a support member to which the rear wheels are attached. It is connected to the vehicle body or frame by springs and shock absorbers.

Wheel Bearings

The wheel bearing consists of three parts: a friction element, an outer race, and an inner race. The friction element can be either ball or roller bearings. The outer race provides the outside contact area for the ball or rollers. It is pressed in the hub of the front axles and rear axles of a front wheel drive vehicle. It rotates with the wheel of a dead axle or is stationary in the hub of a live axle. The inner race provides the inner contact surface for the ball or rollers. The inner race action is equivalent to the action of either a live or dead axle. At no time should both races be in motion.

There are four basic categories of wheel bearings: load carrying (radial), load and thrust carrying, low friction, and high friction. Radial load-carrying bearings are cylindrical roller or ball bearings. Radial and thrust load-carrying bearings are tapered roller or ball bearings. This type of bearing can handle the thrust load of the wheel rotation when cornering without the risk of bearing deterioration.

Low friction bearings are ball bearings because of the spherically shaped friction element. The contact point of ball to race is minimal and provides a lower coefficient of friction. With a smaller contact area, it can handle smaller weight loads.

Wheel bearings are classified as adjustable or non-adjustable. Each wheel hub has an inner bearing and an outer bearing. The bearings work together to support the wheel evenly during operation of the vehicle. They also allow the wheels and axles to rotate smoothly with minimal friction, while supporting a partial or full vehicle load. See **Fig. 3-13.**

Adjustable wheel bearings require periodic lubrication according to the vehicle service manual specifications. The drive wheels on front-wheel drive vehicles usually have permanently lubricated, non-adjustable bearings. Non-adjustable, permanently lubricated wheel bearings are becoming more common on all types of vehicles.

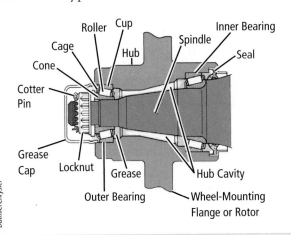

DaimlerChrysler

Fig. 3-13 A cutaway view of an adjustable wheel bearing in a wheel mounting flange or rotor. *Why do the drive wheels on a front-wheel drive vehicle not require lubrication servicing?*

Servicing Adjustable Wheel Bearings The specific procedures to remove and service wheel bearings vary, depending on the vehicle make and model. Some general guidelines are as follows:

1. Raise the vehicle and support the frame on jack (axle) stands.
2. Check the wheel bearings for end play by grasping the tire at the bottom and top. Rock the tire in and out. Proper wheel bearing preload will usually give only 0″–0.003″ of play. Any perceptible play usually indicates a need for adjustment or service.
3. Remove the wheel and tire assembly.
4. Remove the grease cap.
5. Remove the brake calipers, if required. Carefully suspend the calipers with safety wire. This avoids straining the flexible brake hose.
6. Remove the cotter pin, locknut, and washer.
7. Remove the outer bearing, hub, inner bearing, and wheel seal from the spindle.
8. Clean all parts and inspect for signs of excessive wear. Also look for scored or rough surfaces on the race or bearing.
9. Pack the bearings in wheel bearing grease.
10. Install the inner wheel bearing and seal in the hub.
11. Install the hub, outer wheel bearing, washer, and locknut on the spindle. Tighten the locknut to the specified torque value and adjust proper preload according to specifications. Install new cotter pin.
12. Install the grease cap.
13. Install the brake calipers, if removed earlier.
14. Install the wheel and tire assembly. Tighten lug nuts to the specified torque.
15. Remove the jack stands and lower the vehicle.

Servicing Nonadjustable Wheel Bearings Nonadjustable wheel bearings are usually factory-lubricated and sealed. They require no routine service. They are replaced when they fail or when they become worn or noisy. In some cases the wheel hub can be removed from the vehicle, the old bearing pressed out, and a new bearing pressed in. Many manufacturers service the wheel hub and bearing in a single assembly. The old part is simply unbolted, and a new part is bolted on.

Active Suspension Systems

Various manufacturers have designed electronically controlled suspension systems. Many of these systems can be diagnosed by using an appropriate scan tool. Follow manufacturer's instructions to obtain diagnostic trouble codes (DTCs) from the body control module (BCM) or suspension control module.

The purpose of an active suspension system is to maintain full suspension control during all suspension activity, including acceleration, braking, and cornering. See **Fig. 3-14.**

An on-board computer receives signals from a host of sensors. These include a steering sensor, accelerometer, and gyroscope. The sensors detect up and down movement of the wheels and angle changes of the body (forward pitch during braking, rear pitch during acceleration, or sideways pitch during cornering). The sensors send the motion information to the computer.

Instead of conventional shock absorbers and springs, an active system uses electronically controlled hydraulic actuators. The computer controls valves in the hydraulic actuators in response to sensor information. The effect of the system is to maintain a proper level of ride comfort and handling.

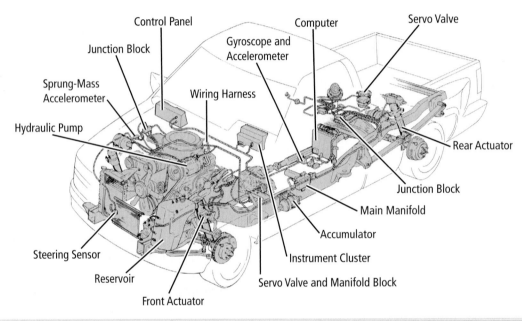

General Motors Corporation

Fig. 3-14 An active suspension system uses sensors and an electronic management system. In the example shown here, hydraulic actuators change their valving and pressures according to commands sent by the on-board computer. *What components replace springs and shock absorbers in an active suspension system?*

SECTION 1 KNOWLEDGE CHECK

1. What causes compression or jounce?

2. What is the purpose of ball joints in a suspension system?

3. What are the four types of springs commonly used in automotive suspension systems?

4. Explain how to perform a bounce test when inspecting shock absorbers.

5. What is a control arm?

6. Which type of wheel bearings need periodic lubrication?

ASE TEST PREP

7. Technician A says that a ruptured gasket in a ball joint can allow lubricant to escape. Technician B says that many ball joints are sealed and cannot be lubricated. Who is correct?

   ⓐ Technician A.

   ⓑ Technician B.

   ⓒ Both Technician A and Technician B.

   ⓓ Neither Technician A nor Technician B.

Section 2
Front Suspension Systems

Objectives:

- Identify the different front suspension designs.
- **A2** Identify and interpret suspension and steering concern; determine necessary action.
- **C1-6** Remove, inspect, and install steering knuckle assemblies.
- **C1-7** Remove, inspect, and install short and long arm suspension system coil springs and spring insulators.
- **C1-2** Diagnose strut suspension system noises, body sway, and uneven riding height concerns; determine necessary action.
- **C1-10** Remove, inspect, and install strut cartridge or assembly, strut coil spring, insulators (silencers), and upper strut bearing mount.
- **C1-8** Remove, inspect, install, and adjust suspension system torsion bars; inspect mounts.

Vocabulary:

- **double A-arm suspension**
- **MacPherson strut**

Preliminary Suspension Checks

The front suspension system is responsible for:
- Supporting the weight of the vehicle front end.
- Providing wheel alignment.
- Providing steering control.
- Providing adequate handling during straight-line driving, lane changes, and turns.

When a front suspension system problem exists, before performing extensive diagnosis or beginning disassembly, do the following preliminary checks:
- Inflate the tires to the correct pressure. Make sure that all tires are the same size.
- Inspect vehicle ride height. A low ride height indicates a broken or weak spring, shock, or strut. The dimensions and points where the measurements should be made are contained in the vehicle service manual.
- Inspect the springs for collapsed or broken coils or broken leaves. Look for shiny spots where coils or leaves may have rubbed together. This is a sign that the springs are weak or were overloaded. It could also mean that the shock absorbers are worn out. Worn shocks may allow excess spring movement.

When diagnosing the cause of a front suspension system problem, relate the function of each subsystem or component to the system as a whole and determine its influence on the vehicle. Refer to the vehicle service manual for details.

If needed, replace the shock absorbers. Then move on to the more difficult replacements as required. Replace worn bushings or ball joints if they do not meet the standards in the vehicle service manual. Replace major suspension parts. Then perform a wheel alignment as specified in the vehicle service manual.

Coil-Spring Front Suspension

There are a variety of coil-spring front suspension designs. Some front suspensions have a double A-arm design. A **double A-arm suspension** uses two control arms, one upper and one lower, and a coil spring. The shock absorber mounts between the body/frame and the lower control arm.

As the spring compresses and rebounds during suspension travel, the control arms pivot up and down. The control arms carry the steering knuckle/spindle assembly along in an up or down direction.

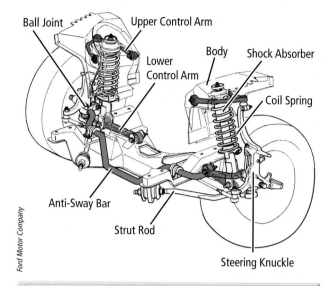

Ball Joint
Upper Control Arm
Lower Control Arm
Body
Shock Absorber
Coil Spring
Anti-Sway Bar
Strut Rod
Steering Knuckle

Ford Motor Company

Fig. 3-15 Suspension designs vary considerably. This front suspension uses a lower control arm and an upper control arm.

The control arms attach to the frame/body with bushings. These bushings allow the control arms to pivot at this connection. Control arm bushings are generally made of rubber or a urethane material. These bushings must be checked for looseness and wear. See **Fig. 3-15**.

The outer ends of the control arms attach to the steering knuckle with lubricated ball joints. The ball joints should be checked for looseness, wear, and binding. A failed ball joint can cause the control arm to lose its connection to the steering knuckle. This results in suspension failure.

Some front suspensions use a single lower control arm. In this type, the top of the coil spring is positioned in a fixed spring seat on the frame. The bottom of the spring rests on the lower control arm.

Steering Knuckle Service

Steering knuckles are used in all types of front suspension/steering systems. The steering knuckle is the part that the front axle or wheel attaches to. The knuckle is attached to ball joints, a MacPherson strut, or a king pin. The steering knuckle is steered by the tie rod. The steering knuckle often includes the steering arm and spindle cast as one part. This is usually referred to as a steering knuckle assembly.

Steering knuckles rarely require service. The parts that attach to the steering knuckle, however, may require service. When steering knuckles are damaged by wheel bearing failure or a collision, they are generally replaced. This is done by following the proper replacement procedure and safety precautions, especially as they relate to the replacement of related parts such as ball joints and MacPherson struts. Steering knuckles should be inspected for cracks, bent steering arms, or damage caused by wheel bearing failure.

Servicing Coil-Spring Front Suspensions

The specific procedures to remove a coil spring vary, depending on the vehicle make and model. However, the following are some general guidelines when removing and servicing a coil spring.

1. While the weight of the vehicle is on the suspension, install a pair of spring compressors on the coil spring.
2. Raise the vehicle and support the frame on jack stands.
3. Remove the wheel and tire assembly.
4. Remove the shock or brake components as required. Some vehicles require the removal of the brake rotor and calipers to gain access to the retaining bolts. Carefully suspend the calipers with safety wire to avoid straining the flexible brake hose.
5. Compress the coil spring using the spring compressors installed earlier. Once the coil spring is compressed enough to remove tension from the spring seats, remove the spring retainer, the spring, and insulators from the vehicle.
6. Slowly release the spring compressors and remove from the old spring.
7. Install the spring compressors on the new spring.
8. Position the new spring and insulators in the vehicle.
9. Carefully release the spring tension, making sure the ends of the coil spring properly position in both the upper and lower spring seats.
10. Install the spring retainer, if required.
11. Install the shock or brake components as required.
12. Install the wheel and tire assembly.
13. Remove the jack stands and lower the vehicle.

Strut-Type Front Suspension

A strut-type front suspension includes a shock absorber and a steering knuckle extension in a single unit. The bottom of the strut body attaches to the steering knuckle and serves as an extension of the "upright" of the knuckle.

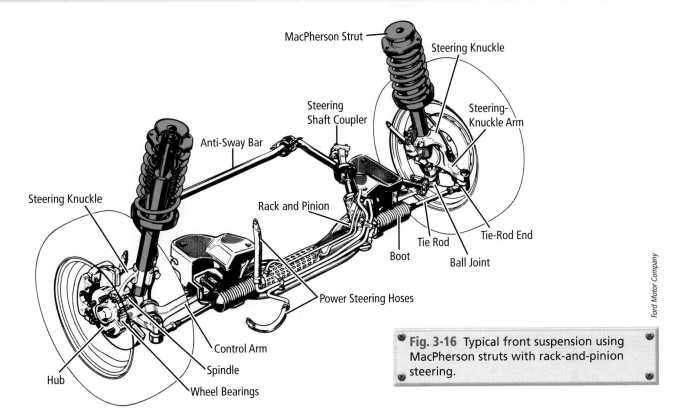

MacPherson Strut

Steering Knuckle

Steering Shaft Coupler

Steering-Knuckle Arm

Anti-Sway Bar

Steering Knuckle

Rack and Pinion

Tie Rod

Tie-Rod End

Boot

Ball Joint

Power Steering Hoses

Control Arm

Spindle

Hub

Wheel Bearings

Ford Motor Company

Fig. 3-16 Typical front suspension using MacPherson struts with rack-and-pinion steering.

The most common type of strut is the MacPherson strut. This combines the shock absorber and coil spring in a single unit. See **Fig. 3-16**. A true **MacPherson strut** incorporates the strut body, coil spring, and shock absorber as an assembled unit.

The coil spring rests on a fixed lower spring seat that is part of the strut body. An upper spring seat holds the top of the coil spring captive on the strut. This allows installation or removal of the spring and shock absorber assembly as a unit.

The upper spring seat attaches to the vehicle frame/body. A bearing under the upper spring seat allows the strut assembly to pivot when the wheels turn. Because the top of the strut/spring attaches directly to the frame/body, there is no need for an upper control arm.

A vehicle with torsion bar springs and strut suspension may use a modified strut. A "modified MacPherson strut" uses a shock absorber mounted inside a strut tube but without a captive coil spring.

Some vehicles may also use a modified strut with a separately-mounted coil spring. The coil spring seats between the lower control arm and the frame.

Inspecting Strut-Type Front Suspensions

When checking struts, do the following:
- Perform a "bounce" test. Push down on the front end of the vehicle firmly and release. The front end of the vehicle should rise once and immediately settle. If the front end bounces more than once, the strut is worn, and should be replaced.
- Visually inspect the strut for leakage. A light film of oil near the top seal is normal. If excessive leakage is seen, replace the strut.
- Look for damage such as strut body dings and dents. If any are evident, replace the strut.
- Inspect the strut-rod for scratches, gouges, corrosion, and bending. If damaged, replace the strut.
- Refer to the vehicle service manual for any specific checks that should be performed.

Servicing Strut-Type Front Suspensions

The shock absorbers used in strut-type suspensions may be serviceable. In some struts, the shock absorber attaches to the strut tube with a removable nut so that the shock absorber can be replaced. Some struts, however, use shock absorbers that are not removable.

For these struts, replace the entire strut housing and shock absorber as a unit. All struts allow removal of the coil spring and upper spring seat.

The strut-type front suspension has the advantage of saving weight and space. The strut requires no upper control arm and no upper ball joint. The control arms are not needed, because the strut attaches to the vehicle body at a recessed area called the strut tower. The strut also combines the coil spring and shock absorber into one compact unit. See **Fig. 3-17**.

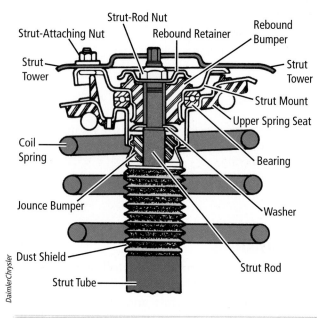

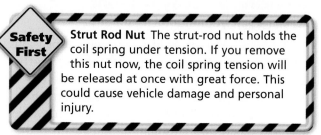

Fig. 3-17 A cutaway view of a MacPherson strut, showing the attachment to the strut tower. *Why is no upper control arm required?*

Depending on the vehicle make and model, specific procedures for removing and servicing a front MacPherson strut assembly vary. Rear MacPherson struts are generally serviced using these same procedures. The following are some general guidelines:

1. While the weight of the vehicle is on the suspension, loosen the strut-rod nut. Loosen the nut only slightly to relieve the majority of tightening torque. Do not remove the nut at this time!

Safety First **Strut Rod Nut** The strut-rod nut holds the coil spring under tension. If you remove this nut now, the coil spring tension will be released at once with great force. This could cause vehicle damage and personal injury.

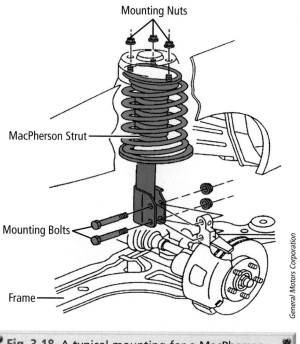

Fig. 3-18 A typical mounting for a MacPherson strut. There are three upper mounting nuts and two lower mounting bolts. *On a MacPherson strut front suspension, what allows the top of the strut to turn and pivot during steering?*

2. Raise the vehicle and support the frame on jack stands.
3. Remove the wheel and tire assembly.
4. Remove the two bottom mounting bolts, where the bottom of the strut attaches to the spindle unit. See **Fig. 3-18**.
5. A brake hose or line may attach to the strut for support. If so, disconnect the hose or line from the strut. Do not disconnect the brake line from the caliper. In some cases the brake rotor and caliper may need to be removed to gain access to the strut bolts. Carefully suspend the caliper with safety wire to avoid straining the flexible brake hose.
6. Remove the upper strut tower nuts where the top of the strut attaches to a mount on the body. Carefully remove the strut assembly from the vehicle. Do not remove the top strut-rod nut at this time.
7. To disassemble the strut unit, place the strut in an approved strut compressor tool. See **Fig. 3-19**. Some of these compressor tools are hand-held units. Some are wall or bench mounted. Always follow the specific disassembly procedure outlined in the vehicle service manual.

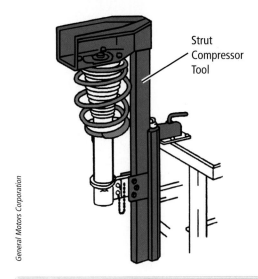

General Motors Corporation

Fig. 3-19 A strut compressor tool specified for use on Pontiac vehicles. A variety of strut compressors are available. Use only a compressor approved for the type of vehicle being serviced. In addition to being able to compress the coil spring, safety is the primary consideration. *When compressing a coil spring, what precautions must be taken?*

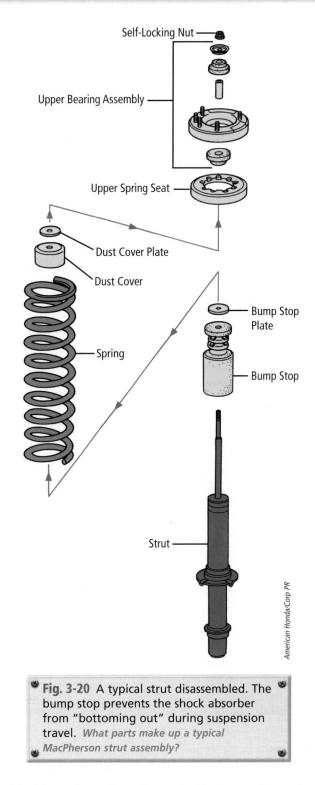

American Honda/Corp PR

Fig. 3-20 A typical strut disassembled. The bump stop prevents the shock absorber from "bottoming out" during suspension travel. *What parts make up a typical MacPherson strut assembly?*

8. Once the coil spring is compressed enough to remove tension from the spring seats, remove the strut-rod nut.
9. Remove the upper bearing assembly, upper spring seat assembly, and dust shield (if used). Remove the coil spring from the strut. Then remove the bump stop and plate (if used). See **Fig. 3-20**.
10. Store the strut spring safely. Follow the guidelines in the service manual. Inspect the strut. Some strut designs use a removable shock absorber. If this is the case, the shock absorber is attached inside the strut tube with a threaded collar nut.
11. Using a special spanner wrench, remove the collar nut and pull the shock absorber out of the strut tube. Remove the shock absorber insert. Make sure the tube is clean inside and install a new insert. Old strut designs used "wet" shock absorber inserts. These have a supply of cooling oil inside the strut tube. More current designs do not use this separate oil bath. The unit is self-contained.
12. Place the new shock absorber properly in the strut tube. Add the correct amount of cooling oil, if required. Install a new threaded collar nut. Torque the nut to factory specifications. Install the bump stop and plate (if used).

13. Place the coil spring onto the strut. Properly position the bottom of the coil spring into the lower spring seat of the strut.
14. With the spring in a compressed state, install the dust shield (if used), followed by the upper spring seat and the upper bearing assembly.
15. Install a new strut-rod nut and torque the nut to specification.

Suspension Springs When servicing suspension springs, always follow proper procedures. To avoid personal injury:
- Always use a quality spring compressor. Follow the recommendations of the vehicle maker for its use.
- Always wear safety glasses or goggles.
- Do not store the spring in its compressed state.
- Never place any part of your body directly over a compressed spring. If a compressed spring slips from the compressor, the energy of the spring can cause serious or fatal injury.

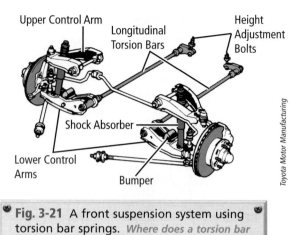

Fig. 3-21 A front suspension system using torsion bar springs. *Where does a torsion bar mount to provide spring action?*

16. Carefully release spring tension, making sure the ends of the coil spring properly position in both the upper and lower spring seats.
17. Reinstall the strut assembly in the vehicle.
18. Check the wheel alignment, as the strut position affects camber, caster, and toe angle.

TECH TIP **Strut Reassembly.** When reassembling a strut, never use an impact wrench to tighten the shock absorber piston rod nut. This will cause the piston rod to spin inside the shock absorber, possibly damaging the seals.

Torsion Bar Front Suspension

Torsion bar suspension supports the weight of the vehicle by using a twisting spring action. There are a variety of torsion bar front suspension designs. Some use a double-A arm design. This design uses two control arms, one upper and one lower, and a torsion bar. See **Fig. 3-21**. The shock absorber mounts between the body/frame and the lower control arm.

One end of the torsion bar is positioned in a fixed seat in the lower control arm. The other end of the torsion bar is fastened in an adjustable anchor in the frame. A screw assembly provides adjustment on the torsion bar by twisting a lever on the anchor end.

As the torsion bar twists during suspension travel, the control arms pivot up and down. The control arms carry the steering knuckle/spindle assembly along in an up or down direction.

Servicing Torsion Bar Front Suspensions The specific procedures to remove a torsion bar vary, depending on the vehicle make and model. Following are some general guidelines for removing and servicing a torsion bar.

1. Inspect the torsion bar and suspension for damaged or worn parts. Look for shiny spots where parts may have shifted and rubbed together. This is a sign that the torsion bars are weak or were overloaded or that the shock absorbers are worn out. Worn shock absorbers may allow excess torsion bar movement.
2. Raise the vehicle and support the frame on jack stands.
3. Remove the wheel and tire assembly.
4. Remove the shock or brake components, as required.
5. Carefully suspend the caliper with safety wire to avoid straining the flexible brake hose.
6. Loosen the torsion bar locking nut on the height adjustment bolts.
7. Mark the position of the height adjustment bolts.
8. Loosen the height adjustment bolts until all tension is relieved from the control arm.
9. Remove the torsion bar, bushings, and control arm, using the procedures specified in the vehicle service manual.
10. Inspect the torsion bar, bushings, and control arm for wear or damage.
11. Install the torsion bar, bushings, and control arm, using the procedures specified in the vehicle service manual.

12. Tighten the height adjustment bolts until the bolts are positioned at the point marked during removal.
13. Tighten the torsion bar locking nut on the height adjustment bolts.
14. Install the shock or brake components, as required.
15. Install the wheel and tire assembly.
16. Raise the vehicle and remove the jack stand support under the frame.
17. Lower the vehicle.
18. Inspect the vehicle for height and level.
19. If the vehicle is not at the correct height and level, repeat the procedures as required.
20. Perform a wheel alignment after replacing front suspension components if specified in the vehicle service manual.

TECH TIP **Ride Height.** Vehicle ride height is critical for proper wheel alignment, handling, and control during braking. While performing any suspension work, always check ride height. A ride height lower than manufacturer's specification may indicate worn or broken springs or damaged suspension components.

Twin I-Beam Front Suspension

Some trucks use a twin I-beam independent front suspension. See **Fig. 3-22**. The I-beams provide the function of lower control arms. Each wheel spindle attaches to the outer end of a separate forged I-beam axle. The opposite end of each I-beam attaches to the frame with a flexible bushing joint. For each I-beam axle, a coil spring is located between the I-beam and an upper spring seat on the frame.

Each I-beam is braced with a radius rod. The rod attaches the I-beam to the frame, rearward of the axles. The radius rods locate the I-beam axles. They prevent the I-beams from moving forward or rearward during vehicle movement and suspension travel.

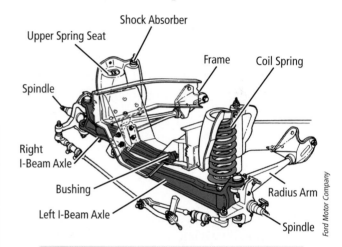

Fig. 3-22 A typical twin I-beam front suspension. The beams pivot on large rubber bushings, where they attach to the truck frame. *Why are the I-beams braced with a radius rod?*

SECTION 2 KNOWLEDGE CHECK

1. Name the three preliminary checks you can make on a front suspension system.
2. What type of front suspension includes a shock absorber and a steering knuckle extension in a single unit?
3. What is the purpose of a strut compressor tool?
4. How can a torsion bar be adjusted?
5. Which way do the control arms of a torsion bar front suspension pivot?
6. Why is it important to mark the position of the height adjustment bolts before removal?

ASE TEST PREP

7. Technician A says that the strut-type front suspension has the advantage of saving space and weight. Technician B says that in this type of front suspension the strut requires an upper control arm and an upper ball joint. Who is correct?
   a Technician A.
   b Technician B.
   c Both Technician A and Technician B.
   d Neither Technician A nor Technician B.

Section 3
Rear Suspension Systems

Objectives:

- Describe the three types of rear suspension designs.
- **A2** Identify and interpret suspension and steering concern; determine necessary action.
- **C2-2** Remove, inspect, and install transverse links, control arms, bushings, and mounts.
- **C2-3** Remove, inspect, and install leaf springs, leaf spring insulators (silencers), shackles, brackets, bushings, and mounts.
- **C2-1** Remove, inspect, and install coil springs and spring insulators.
- **C2-4** Remove, inspect, and install strut cartridge or assembly, strut coil spring, and insulators (silencers).
- Identify and service the parts of a MacPherson strut.

Vocabulary:

- **trailing arms**
- **track bar**

Preliminary Suspension Checks

The rear suspension system is responsible for:
- Supporting the weight of the rear of the vehicle.
- Providing wheel alignment.
- Providing adequate handling during straight-line driving, lane changes, and turns.

Before performing extensive diagnosis or beginning disassembly of any parts of the vehicle, perform the following preliminary checks:
- Inflate the tires to the correct pressure.
- Make sure that all tires are the same size.
- Inspect vehicle ride height. A low ride height indicates a broken or weak spring, shock, or strut. The dimensions and points where the measurements should be made are contained in the vehicle service manual.
- Inspect the springs for broken or collapsed coils or broken leaves. Look for shiny spots where coils or leaves may have rubbed together. This is a sign that the springs are weak or were overloaded. It could also mean that the shock absorbers or shock absorber inserts are worn out. Worn shocks may allow excess spring movement.

If needed, replace the shock absorbers or shock absorber inserts. Then move on to the more difficult replacements as required. Replace worn bushings or ball joints if they do not meet the standards in the vehicle service manual. Replace major suspension parts. Then perform a wheel alignment as specified in the vehicle service manual.

Leaf-Spring Rear Suspension

Many vans, trucks, and older passenger vehicles use leaf-spring rear suspensions. Leaf springs can be designed and built to support very heavy loads.

A leaf spring attaches to the frame at both ends with hangers and a shackle. Large U-bolts attach the spring to the rear axle. See **Fig. 3-23.** As the spring bends during suspension travel, the shackle pivots to allow the spring to lengthen and shorten. This helps soften the ride and prevent shock and vibration from reaching the body and frame. A rubber bumper on the frame cushions the axle if the suspension should "bottom out."

On a multi-leaf spring, the individual leaf plates tend to slide on one another as the spring assembly flexes. To prevent noise, plastic or nylon insulators are placed between the individual leaf plates.

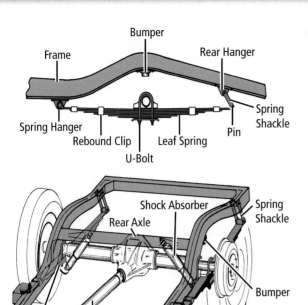

Bumper
Frame
Rear Hanger
Spring Shackle
Spring Hanger
Rebound Clip
Leaf Spring
Pin
U-Bolt

Shock Absorber
Spring Shackle
Rear Axle
Bumper
Leaf Spring
Driveshaft
Spring Eye

Fig. 3-23 A leaf-spring rear suspension using two longitudinal springs. *How is a multi-leaf spring pack held in alignment?*

Rebound clips or clamps wrap around the multi-leaf spring packs to keep the individual leaf plates in alignment with one another and to help keep the insulators in place. A single center bolt holds the individual leaf plates together at the spring midpoint or center. It also acts as a dowel to locate the axle housing to the spring assembly. Bonded rubber and metal bushings are used at each end of the main leaf and the shackle.

This type of leaf spring design requires no normal service or lubrication. Leaf springs should be routinely inspected for damage. If springs become noisy, the bushings and insulators should be inspected for wear. Insulators can be replaced by removing the rebound clips and prying the leaves apart. To replace bushings, remove the spring assembly. Press out the old bushings, and press in the new ones.

Some manufacturers have reduced the number of parts and the need for insulators and rebound clips by using a mono-leaf spring. This design uses only one leaf in the spring assembly. Some of these springs are made of a nonmetallic fiberglass material.

Leaf springs attach to the vehicle frame in front of and behind the axle, running parallel with the length of the frame. They cannot bend sideways. Therefore, the use of rear leaf springs helps locate the rear axle and prevent unwanted sideways movement of the axle.

Servicing Leaf-Spring Rear Suspensions

The specific procedures to remove a leaf spring vary, depending on the vehicle make and model. However, here are some general guidelines to follow when removing and servicing a leaf spring.

1. Raise the vehicle and support the frame on jack stands.
2. Remove the wheel and tire assembly.
3. Remove the shock or brake components as required. Carefully suspend the caliper with safety wire to avoid straining the flexible brake hose.
4. Support the axle with jack stands.
5. Remove the U-bolts and lower shock mount from the axle and leaf spring.
6. While supporting the rear of the leaf spring, remove the pins and rear shackle from the rear hanger and spring eye.
7. While supporting the front of the leaf spring, remove the pin and front spring eye from the spring hanger. Lower the spring from the axle.
8. Replace the shock absorbers or leaf springs as required. Replace worn bushings if they do not meet the standards given in the vehicle service manual.
9. While supporting the front of the leaf spring, install the pin and front spring eye in the spring hanger.
10. While supporting the rear of the leaf spring and the axle, install the pins and rear shackle in the rear hanger and spring eye.
11. Install the lower shock mount and U-bolts on the axle and leaf spring. Tighten the U-bolts as specified in the vehicle service manual.
12. Remove the jack stand support from under the axle.
13. Install the shock or brake components as required.
14. Install the wheel and tire assembly.
15. Raise the vehicle and remove the jack stand support under the frame. Lower the vehicle.
16. Perform a rear wheel alignment after replacing rear suspension components if specified in the vehicle service manual.

Calculating Spring Loads

A constant-rate spring, or linear-rate spring, requires a load of 600 pounds to compress the spring 1 inch. The same spring requires 1,200 pounds to compress it 2 inches. What load will be required to compress the spring 4 inches?

One way to calculate the answer is by using proportions. As a proportion:

$$\frac{1''}{600\ \text{lb}} = \frac{2''}{1,200\ \text{lb}}$$

$$\frac{1''}{600\ \text{lb}} = \frac{4''}{c}$$

where c is the load needed to compress the spring 4 inches. Solving for c, this load is 2,400 pounds.

An alternative way to find the necessary load is to find the rate of increase. Use the formula:

$$m = \frac{(y - y_1)}{(x - x_1)} \text{ or } m = \frac{(1,200 - 600)}{(2 - 1)} = 600\ \text{lb/in.}$$

Remember, the rate of increase is called the slope and is identified by the letter m. This formula shows you that for every change of 1 inch in the spring compression, a 600-pound load will be needed.

Rewrite the formula as:

$$y - y_1 = m(x - x_1)$$

Substitute for y_1, m, and x_1 in the formula and solve for y as follows:

$$y - 600 = 600(x - 1)$$
$$y = 600x - 600 + 600 = 600x$$

For an x value of 4 inches:

$$y = 600(4) = 2,400 \text{ or } 2,400 \text{ pounds.}$$

Apply It!

Meets NATEF Mathematics Standards for proportions, calculating, and evaluating algebraic expressions.

1. What load will be required to compress the spring 2.5 inches? Arrive at a value using both methods.

2. Consider another spring where $m = 660$ lb/in. Which of these springs would be more suitable for a heavily loaded vehicle? Explain your answer.

Coil-Spring Rear Suspension

To prevent the rear axle from moving forward, rearward, or sideways, coil springs on the rear suspension require additional "locating" devices. A system of lower, or upper and lower, control arms prevents the axle from moving. The control arms attach to the frame/body with bushings. Technicians refer to these arms as **trailing arms.**

Control arm bushings allow the control arms to pivot at the frame/body. These bushings are generally made of rubber or a urethane material. They must be checked for looseness and wear.

As an added measure to prevent rear axle movement, some systems use a track bar or panhard rod. See **Fig. 3-24.** A **track bar** is a straight bar positioned parallel to the rear axle. One end of the bar attaches to the axle. The other end of the bar attaches to the frame or body. The bar mounts on bushings. This

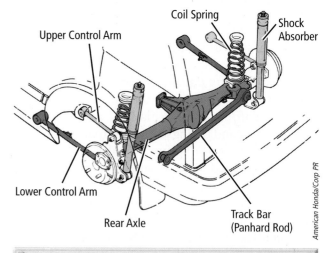

Coil Spring
Shock Absorber
Upper Control Arm
Lower Control Arm
Rear Axle
Track Bar (Panhard Rod)

American Honda/Corp PR

Fig. 3-24 The track bar (also called a panhard rod) attaches to both the frame and the rear axle housing. *What is the purpose and advantage of using a track bar?*

allows the bar to pivot when the axle moves up and down during suspension travel. The bar provides better vehicle control and handling during turns.

Servicing Coil-Spring Rear Suspensions

The specific procedures to remove a coil spring vary, depending on the vehicle make and model. Use the procedure provided in the service manual for the vehicle you are servicing.

Strut-Type Rear Suspension

An independent rear suspension, where the rear wheels can move up and down independently of each other, is a strut-type suspension. In a rear suspension, a strut is a structural unit that locates and connects the wheel spindle to the frame. The strut also incorporates the shock absorber.

The struts may be MacPherson struts, where the shock absorber and the coil spring mount are assembled as a unit. They may instead be modified

> **Safety First**
>
> **Springs** In most cases, a coil spring must be compressed to remove it. Depending on suspension design, spring service will vary. Always follow the instructions of the vehicle manufacturer. If using a spring compressor, use only the type of spring compressor recommended by the vehicle manufacturer. When removing or installing coil springs, take extreme caution to avoid injury. Compressed coil springs store a great deal of energy.

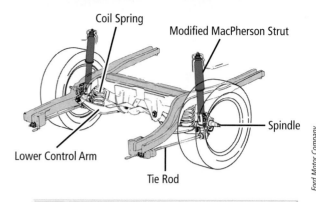

Ford Motor Company

Fig. 3-25 Rear strut suspension featuring modified MacPherson struts. *In what ways is a modified MacPherson strut different from a MacPherson strut?*

MacPherson struts. With modified MacPherson struts, the strut and coil springs are an unassembled unit, with the coil spring mounting independently between a lower control arm and the frame. See **Fig. 3-25.**

Servicing Strut-Type Rear Suspensions

Specific procedures vary, depending on the vehicle make and model. The shock absorbers used in strut-type suspensions may be serviceable. If the shock absorber attaches to the strut tube with a removable nut, the shock absorber can be removed. Some struts, however, use shock absorbers that are not removable. For these struts, replace the entire strut housing and shock absorber as a unit. All struts allow removal of the coil spring and upper spring seat.

SECTION 3 KNOWLEDGE CHECK

1. What might low ride height indicate in relation to the rear suspension system?

2. What cushions the axle if the suspension "bottoms out"?

3. What are trailing arms?

4. What part attaches the axle to the frame and provides better vehicle control during turns?

5. What rear suspension part locates and connects the wheel spindle to the frame?

6. Why is it important to use the spring compressor recommended by the vehicle manufacturer?

ASE TEST PREP

7. Technician A says that rear-suspension leaf springs can bend sideways. Technician B says that rear-suspension leaf springs cannot bend sideways. Who is correct?
   ⓐ Technician A.
   ⓑ Technician B.
   ⓒ Both Technician A and Technician B.
   ⓓ Neither Technician A nor Technician B.

Suspension & Steering

CHAPTER 3 REVIEW

Key Points

Meets the following NATEF Standards for Suspension & Steering: diagnosing and repairing leaf, coil, torsion bar, and strut suspension systems.

- The basic parts of a suspension system are springs, shock absorbers, anti-sway bars, control arms, ball joints, axles, and wheel bearings.
- Compression occurs when the suspension moves closer to the body. Rebound occurs when the suspension moves away from the body.
- Suspensions can use a variety of spring types.
- The two most common shock absorbers are "traditional" and strut. Shock absorbers can also be spring-assisted, adjustable, and air-assisted.
- The most common type of strut is the MacPherson strut.
- An active suspension system uses an on-board computer and sensors to maintain full control of the suspension.
- There are a variety of front suspension designs including leaf, coil, torsion bar, and strut.
- There are a variety of rear suspension designs including leaf, coil, and strut.

Review Questions

1. What is the term for springs that consist of single- or multiple-spring steel bands formed in an arc shape?
2. What type of shock absorber features a chamber of air between the inner and outer shock absorber tubes?
3. How many times can a vehicle bounce and still pass the bounce test?
4. What should you do with a shock absorber that is dinged or dented?
5. What type of wheel bearings are found on the drive wheels of front-wheel drive vehicles?
6. What is the purpose of an active suspension system?
7. What is the purpose of a rear suspension system?
8. Name the independent rear suspension system that allows the rear wheels to move up and down independently of each other.
9. **Critical Thinking** What does the term *live axle* suggest about the function of the axle?
10. **Critical Thinking** What is unsprung weight?

Excellence in Communication

Using a Dictionary

You will often read technical material that is new to you. As you read, you will find words that you do not know. Many of these unfamiliar words will not be explained in either the text or the glossary.

In your trade, you deal with flammable materials as well as parts that ensure the safety of your customer. Your skills and understanding are critical. Therefore, you need to find the meaning of an unfamiliar word. You also need to check words that have meanings you are not sure of.

When you look up a word in a dictionary, you may find a definition directly related to automobiles. "Shock" is one example. Among the definitions, you will find one related to vehicles. For example "shock absorber" is defined. If there is

no auto-related definition, as with "preliminary," you will find one you can adapt for your use. "Coming before" is a definition that can be applied to the word "preliminary" in the section, "Preliminary Suspension Checks."

Apply It!

Meets NATEF Communications Standards for using a dictionary.

1. Reread section 2 of this chapter.
2. List words you cannot define.
3. Look up these words in the dictionary. Write out their definitions. Save this list to help you as you study this chapter.

AUTOMOTIVE SERVICE EXCELLENCE
TEST PREP

Answering the following practice questions will help you prepare for the ASE certification tests.

1. Which of the following is not a function of the suspension system?

   ⓐ To support the vehicle.

   ⓑ To provide a cushion effect between the body and the road.

   ⓒ To generate power for the vehicle.

   ⓓ To maintain wheel alignment.

2. Technician A says that unsprung weight includes the weight of the vehicle body/frame, engine, transmission, cargo and passengers. Technician B says that sprung weight includes wheels, tires, brakes, lower control arms, and drive axles. Who is correct?

   ⓐ Technician A.

   ⓑ Technician B.

   ⓒ Both Technician A and Technician B.

   ⓓ Neither Technician A nor Technician B.

3. Spring rate and action are determined in part by:

   ⓐ weight.

   ⓑ spring rod thickness.

   ⓒ volume.

   ⓓ resistance.

4. Technician A says that a torsion bar is a steel rod that twists to provide spring action. Technician B says that torsion bars will be positioned either longitudinally or transversely. Who is correct?

   ⓐ Technician A.

   ⓑ Technician B.

   ⓒ Both Technician A and Technician B.

   ⓓ Neither Technician A nor Technician B.

5. When diagnosing a front suspension system problem, which of the following preliminary checks should be conducted?

   ⓐ Inflate tires to correct pressure.

   ⓑ Inspect vehicle ride height.

   ⓒ Inspect the springs for collapsed or broken coils or broken leaves.

   ⓓ All of the above.

6. Technician A says that the steering knuckle attaches the steering column to the axle. Technician B says that the steering knuckle is the part that the front axle or wheel attaches to. Who is correct?

   ⓐ Technician A.

   ⓑ Technician B.

   ⓒ Both Technician A and Technician B.

   ⓓ Neither Technician A nor Technician B.

7. Wheel bearings are classified as:

   ⓐ cylindrical or roller bearings.

   ⓑ tapered roller or ball bearings.

   ⓒ adjustable or non-adjustable bearings.

   ⓓ low-friction or high-friction bearings.

8. Technician A says that leaf springs can be designed to support very heavy loads. Technician B disagrees and says that the physical limitations of the leaf spring prevent it from supporting heavy loads. Who is correct?

   ⓐ Technician A.

   ⓑ Technician B.

   ⓒ Both Technician A and Technician B.

   ⓓ Neither Technician A nor Technician B.

9. Which of the following devices is used to help stabilize strut-type rear suspensions?

   ⓐ Trailing arms.

   ⓑ Track bar.

   ⓒ Panhard rod.

   ⓓ None of the above.

10. Technician A says that wheels in a strut-type rear suspension operate as one unit. Technician B says that the wheels in a strut-type rear suspension operate independently. Who is correct?

   ⓐ Technician A.

   ⓑ Technician B.

   ⓒ Both Technician A and Technician B.

   ⓓ Neither Technician A nor Technician B.

Section 1
Alignment and
Driveability

Section 2
Wheel Alignment
Procedures

Diagnosing, Adjusting, & Repairing Wheel Alignment

Customer's Concern

"This crazy car has a mind of its own," Lucy Chen says laughingly. "I struggle to steer it one way, and it fights me to go the other way." After a good-natured chuckle, you assure Lucy that you will set the sedan straight and persuade it to follow her lead again soon.

In fact, setting the car straight may literally be the answer. In talking with Lucy further, you realize she's describing hard steering and steering kickback. You tell her these are symptoms of some wheel alignment problems. The cause shouldn't take very long to identify. Lucy gives you permission to start your diagnosis and repair procedures as she heads to the waiting room for a fresh cup of coffee.

Technician's Challenge

As the service technician, you need to find answers to these questions:

1. How many different causes may lead to hard steering and steering kickback? Which cause will you investigate first?

2. Once an alignment pre-check rules out the easier causes for Lucy's problem, what is the next step? Is alignment equipment necessary?

3. If the sedan's caster is the problem, what factors will help you determine how to adjust it? Are shims needed or is there another way to adjust caster?

Alignment and Driveability

Objectives:

D4 ● Check and adjust front and rear wheel camber; perform necessary action.

D5 ● Check and adjust caster; perform necessary action.

D6 ● Check and adjust front wheel toe and center steering wheel.

D9 ● Check and adjust rear wheel toe.

D8 ● Check SAI (steering axis inclination) and included angle; determine necessary action.

D7 ● Check toe-out-on-turns (turning radius); determine necessary action.

D11 ● Check for front wheel setback; determine necessary action.

D12 ● Check front cradle (subframe) alignment; determine necessary action.

Vocabulary:

● camber angle
● caster angle
● toe
● steering axis inclination
● scrub radius
● included angle
● turning radius
● setback
● thrust line
● thrust angle

Driveability

Wheel alignment angles have an effect on vehicle driveability. Incorrect wheel alignment causes:
• Vehicle wander.
• Vehicle drift and instability.
• Vehicle pulling to the left or right.
• Hard steering effort.
• Torque steering on front-wheel-drive vehicles.
• Slow or abnormal steering return.
• Uneven tire wear.
  The wheel alignment angles are:
• Camber angle.
• Caster angle.
• Toe.
• Steering axis inclination.
• Scrub radius.
• Included angle.
• Turning radius.
• Setback.
• Thrust angle.

Wheel Alignment Angles

Wheel alignment angles relate to the inward or outward tilt of the wheels.

Camber Angle

The angle of inward or outward tilt of a wheel is known as the **camber angle.** The camber angle is sometimes simply called camber. This angle is compared to true vertical when viewed from the front or rear of the vehicle. When the top of the wheel tilts in, the wheel has a negative camber angle. When the top of the wheel tilts out, the wheel has a positive camber angle. When camber is true vertical, there is "zero" camber. See **Fig. 4-1.**

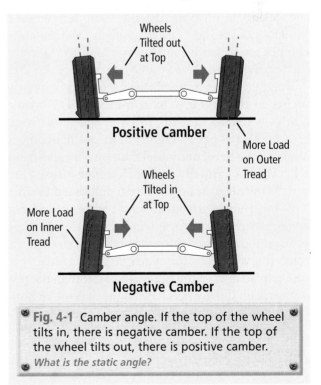

Fig. 4-1 Camber angle. If the top of the wheel tilts in, there is negative camber. If the top of the wheel tilts out, there is positive camber.
What is the static angle?

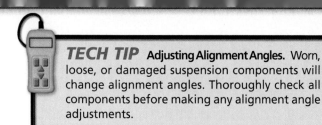

Camber is measured in degrees. The initial setting for camber is called the static angle. The intent of the static angle is to anticipate wheel travel. The static angle may initially be set positive. When the suspension compresses during normal driving, the movement pulls the wheel into a true vertical position. The camber adjustment determines what portion of the tire tread contacts the road surface.

As a vehicle's suspension goes through its loaded and unloaded movement, its wheels travel through an arc. As the suspension compresses and rebounds, camber angle changes. Vehicle manufacturers adjust camber to compensate for suspension action. They do this so that the entire tire tread is in contact with the road during normal driving.

Camber affects directional pull. A vehicle will always pull in the direction of the wheel that has the most positive camber. If camber is positive on the left-front wheel and negative on the right-front wheel, the vehicle will pull to the left. If the right-front wheel has more positive camber, the vehicle will pull to the right.

Ideally, a vehicle in motion should have the same camber angle on both the right and left wheels. However, if the right and left wheels have the same camber angle, the vehicle would pull to the right on a crowned road.

Road crown is present when the road is slightly higher in the center than at the sides. The crown allows water to run off. To compensate for road crown, vehicles have a slightly more positive camber angle on the left-front wheel than on the right-front wheel. This camber angle difference allows the vehicle to travel straight with no pull to either side.

Camber angle affects tire wear. Since the camber angle tilts the top of the wheel in or out, camber changes the angle at which the tire tread contacts the road. If a wheel has too much negative camber, the inside tread area of the tire wears faster than the rest of the tread. If the wheel has too much positive camber, the outside of the tread area will wear faster.

Caster Angle

The angle between true vertical and an imaginary line drawn through the upper and lower ball joints is known as the **caster angle**. Caster angle is sometimes referred to simply as caster. Caster is viewed from the side of the vehicle.

Caster is measured in degrees. When the upper ball joint is behind the lower ball joint, the wheel has positive caster. See **Fig. 4-2**. When the upper ball joint is forward of the lower ball joint, the wheel has negative caster. When the upper ball joint is directly over the lower ball joint, the wheel has zero caster. The caster angle affects directional control of the vehicle and steering wheel return.

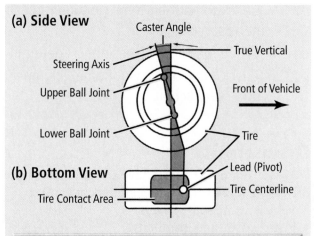

Fig. 4-2 Caster angle. Side view **(a)**. Draw a line through the upper and lower ball joints. Compare this line, called the steering axis, to true vertical. Bottom view **(b)**. The angle between these two lines is the caster angle. Positive caster causes the steering axis to pass through the road surface ahead of the center of the tire contact area. This allows the steering axis to lead the tire along the road surface for better control and stability. *What driveability conditions does caster affect?*

The caster angle on a vehicle equipped with MacPherson struts is measured differently. It is the difference between true vertical and a line drawn from the upper strut mount to the lower ball joint. Since the strut mount is a part of the vehicle body, caster is not always adjustable. See **Fig. 4-3**.

A slight amount of positive caster is desirable. Positive caster helps to keep the front wheels pointed straight ahead. This prevents vehicle wander. However, excessive positive caster requires more steering effort, creates low-speed shimmy, and causes excessive steering wheel return, or "snap-back."

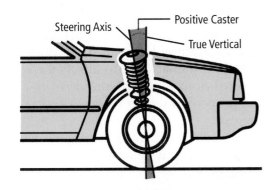

Steering Axis — Positive Caster — True Vertical

Fig. 4-3 The caster angle on a vehicle equipped with MacPherson struts is created by the difference between the true vertical line at the wheel center and the steering axis, a line drawn from the upper strut mount to the lower ball joint. *How is caster measured on a vehicle with MacPherson struts?*

Rear chassis height affects the front wheel caster angle. As the load on the rear increases, the rear chassis height decreases and the front chassis height increases. The caster angle becomes more positive as the front unloads. As rear chassis height increases, front chassis height decreases. The caster angle becomes more negative as the load on the front increases. See **Fig. 4-4.**

A zero or negative caster adversely affects driveability. It causes the vehicle to wander, instead of tracking in a straight line. It increases steering effort by reducing steering return. The steering wheel must be manually returned to a straight-ahead position following a turn.

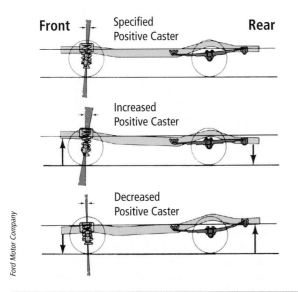

Front — Specified Positive Caster — **Rear**

Increased Positive Caster

Decreased Positive Caster

Fig. 4-4 Rear chassis height affects the front wheel caster angle. *As rear suspension loading increases, what happens to the front caster angle?*

Caster has a great impact on vehicle directional stability. Caster angle should be equal side to side. If the right-front wheel has less positive caster than the left, the vehicle will pull to the right. If the left-front wheel has less positive caster than the right, the vehicle will pull to the left.

Technicians do not generally consider caster a factor in tire wear. Caster, however, does affect tire wear during turns.

Toe

Toe is the measurement by which the front of a wheel points inward or outward, compared to a true straight-ahead position. Toe is viewed from the top of the vehicle. Toe is measured in inches, millimeters, or degrees.

When the wheels are pointed in, the wheels have toe-in. The wheels are closer together at the front than they are at the rear of the wheels. When the wheels are pointed out, the wheels have toe-out. The wheels are further apart at the front than they are at the rear of the wheels. When the right and left wheels aim straight ahead and parallel, the wheels have zero toe. See **Fig. 4-5.**

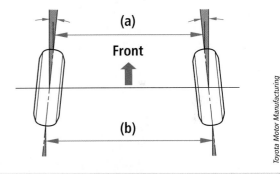

(a) **Front** **(b)**

Fig. 4-5 Toe is the amount by which the front of the wheel points inward or outward compared to a true straight-ahead position. For wheels with toe-in, the distance between the wheels at the front **(a)** is less than the distance between the wheels at the rear **(b)**. *How does the toe angle affect tire wear?*

The goal is to have zero toe. The wheel with the greatest amount of toe-out will pull the vehicle in the direction of that wheel. However, the initial toe setting may be in or out to compensate for vehicle type and vehicle motion.

Typically, a slight toe-in is set on rear-wheel-drive vehicles. This setting compensates for vehicle motion and play in the steering and chassis parts. As the vehicle moves forward, the front wheels will pull out.

A slight toe-out is set on vehicles with front-wheel-drive. The torque action of front-wheel-drive pulls the wheels inboard when power is applied to move the vehicle forward. When a toe-out angle is set, the wheels will achieve a zero toe as the vehicle moves forward.

Improper toe is a major factor in tire wear. When a wheel has too much toe-out, the tread wears faster towards the inside of the tire. The wear may create a "feathered" edge pattern on the tread. When a wheel has too much toe-in, the tread wears faster towards the outside of the tire. Toe usually does not affect directional pull.

Steering Axis Inclination

The difference between a true vertical line drawn through the center of the wheel and an imaginary line drawn through the upper and lower ball joints is known as **steering axis inclination** or SAI. On a strut-equipped vehicle, consider the upper strut mount as the location of the upper ball joint. Steering axis inclination is viewed from the front of the vehicle. See **Fig. 4-6.**

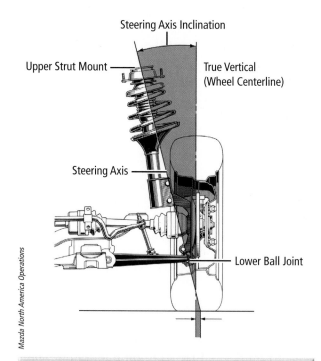

Steering Axis Inclination

Upper Strut Mount

True Vertical (Wheel Centerline)

Steering Axis

Lower Ball Joint

Mazda North America Operations

Fig. 4-6 Steering axis inclination, or SAI, is a fixed, non-adjustable angle. SAI is the angle created between a true vertical line drawn through the wheel center and the steering axis, a line drawn through the upper ball joint or upper strut mount and the lower ball joint. *What might an incorrect SAI indicate?*

SAI is a negative camber angle of the steering axis. The upper ball joint is further inboard as compared to the lower ball joint. The setting of SAI affects steering stability. It also affects the wheel's ability to return to a straight-ahead position after a turn. A proper SAI setting reduces steering effort and tire wear.

SAI is not adjustable. It is a fixed angle designed into the suspension system by the manufacturer. Even though SAI is not adjustable, this angle should be checked during a wheel alignment. An incorrect SAI can be a signal of frame or suspension system damage.

Incorrect SAI could result from:
- A bent control arm.
- A bent spindle.
- Badly worn ball joints.
- Damage to vehicle frame or unibody structure.

Scrub Radius

Scrub radius, also called steering offset, is the distance between the steering axis and the centerline of the tire tread contact area. If the steering axis meets the road surface at a point outside the tire centerline, the scrub radius is negative. If the steering axis meets the road surface at a point inside the tire centerline, scrub radius is positive. See **Fig. 4-7.** If the steering axis and the tire centerline intersect at the road surface, the scrub radius is zero. Scrub radius affects steering effort, steering return, and stability.

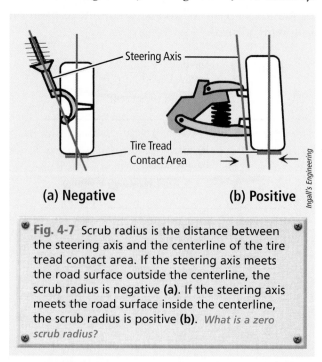

Steering Axis

Tire Tread Contact Area

(a) Negative

(b) Positive

Ingall's Engineering

Fig. 4-7 Scrub radius is the distance between the steering axis and the centerline of the tire tread contact area. If the steering axis meets the road surface outside the centerline, the scrub radius is negative **(a)**. If the steering axis meets the road surface inside the centerline, the scrub radius is positive **(b)**. *What is a zero scrub radius?*

Rear-wheel-drive vehicles with unequal-length control arms have a positive scrub radius setting. Front-wheel-drive vehicles with a MacPherson strut front suspension have a negative scrub radius setting. Scrub radius, like SAI, is not adjustable.

Even though scrub radius is not adjustable, it should be checked during a wheel alignment. If incorrect, it can be a signal of suspension system or structure damage.

Included Angle

The camber angle plus the SAI angle is known as the **included angle**. Incorrect included angle may indicate a suspension or vehicle structure problem. The included angle is another reference that can be checked when diagnosing wheel alignment problems. See **Fig. 4-8.**

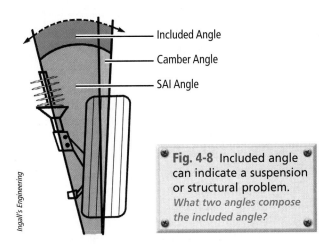

Fig. 4-8 Included angle can indicate a suspension or structural problem. *What two angles compose the included angle?*

Turning Radius

The **turning radius,** also called toe-out on turns, is the difference in the angles of the front wheels in a turn. During a turn, the two front wheels travel in concentric circles that have a common center. The outer wheel must travel a greater distance and make a wider turn than the inner wheel. Since the inner wheel travels a shorter distance, it must turn at a greater angle and follow a smaller radius than the outer wheel.

For example, when the inner wheel turns at an angle of 20°, the outer wheel may turn at an angle of 18°. The inner wheel toes out more in the turn. See **Fig. 4-9.** This difference in toe should not vary by more than about 1.5° from the manufacturer's specifications. An incorrect turning radius angle may indicate a suspension or vehicle structure problem.

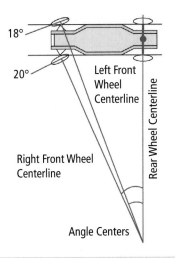

Fig. 4-9 Turning radius (toe-out on turns). To avoid scrubbing, the inner wheel must turn a tighter radius. The two front wheels should turn at different angles. *Why does the inner wheel turn in a smaller radius than the outer wheel?*

Setback

Wheel **setback** is the difference between the wheelbase on one side of the vehicle and the wheelbase on the other side. Wheelbase is the distance between the center of the front wheel and the center of the rear wheel on the same side of the vehicle. Setback, therefore, is a condition in which the distance between the left-front and left-rear wheels is different from the distance between the right-front and right-rear wheels. See **Fig. 4-10.**

On front-wheel-drive vehicles, improper location of the engine cradle or subframe will create a setback condition. If the wheelbase is shorter on one side of the vehicle, the vehicle will pull in the direction of the shorter wheelbase. If a customer complains of a pull and if the steering wheel is off-center, check setback.

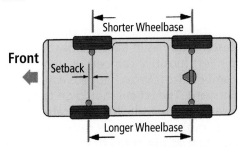

Fig. 4-10 Setback is the difference between the wheelbase on one side of the vehicle and the wheelbase on the other side. The vehicle will pull in the direction of the shorter wheelbase. *How is wheelbase measured?*

Angles in Wheel Alignment

Caster, camber, steering axis inclination, directional pull, and toe angle are discussed throughout this chapter. Definitions and diagrams explaining them appear in different places. You can better understand these terms if you can see how they are related to each other.

In this activity, you will make your own simple model of a vehicle "front end." Then you will be able to see how factors such as caster, camber, directional pull, and toe angle affect steering and tire wear.

Apply It!

Demonstrating Caster, Camber, and Toe

Meets NATEF Science Standards for understanding the relationship between circular motion, linear motion, and friction.

Materials and Equipment
- 1.5″ diameter furniture caster wheel unit, with pivot pin and plastic bearing insert.
- Masking tape, as wide as the wheel
- A flat non-slip surface (to simulate the road)

1. Put two layers of masking tape around the wheel. The taped wheel simulates the tire. It also reduces slipping on the "road" surface.

2. Hold the wheel unit by the plastic bearing insert so that the pivot pin is vertical. The wheel should be ahead of the pivot pin. Push the wheel unit across the surface. Notice how the wheel swings around so that its axle is behind the vertical pivot pin. The wheel has self-aligned. It now trails behind the pivot pin.

3. Hold the unit with the wheel in front of the pivot pin. Tilt the pivot pin toward you and push. Increase the tilt angle until the wheel unit no longer rotates to put the axle behind. You have included enough positive caster to make the wheel self-aligning by moving the pivot point ahead of the steering axis.

4. Tilt the pivot pin toward you at the same caster angle as in Step 3. Now tilt the pivot pin left (positive camber) or right (negative camber). Note what happens when you push forward. The wheel should go to the opposite side of the tilt. This illustrates how camber angle can change caster angle. Also, notice that the "tape tire" contacts the surface on only one side, leading to tire wear.

5. Hold the pivot pin tilted toward you at the same caster angle as in Step 3. Now push the unit with the axle turned from the direction of push. You will see the wheel straighten out. This is directional pull.

6. Hold the wheel unit by its frame instead of the pivot pin. Twist the frame slightly left or right of the direction of your push. As you push the unit, you should see and feel the "tape tire" sliding on the surface. This is what happens when the toe angle is incorrect and is why toe is a factor in tire wear.

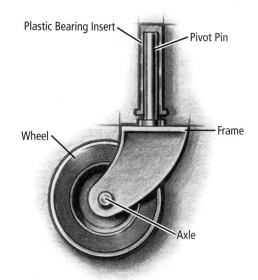

Plastic Bearing Insert — Pivot Pin — Wheel — Frame — Axle

Thrust Angle

The geometric centerline is a line drawn from the midpoint of the rear of the vehicle to the midpoint of the front of the vehicle. The **thrust line** is a line drawn perpendicular to the rear axle. It bisects the total toe of the rear wheels. It points toward the front of the vehicle in the same direction as the rear wheels.

If the thrust line and the geometric centerline are not parallel, a **thrust angle** exists. See **Fig. 4-11**. The thrust angle is positive if it is to the right of the geometric centerline. It is negative if it is to the left of the geometric centerline. A thrust angle means that the rear wheels aim in a direction offset to the center of the front of the vehicle.

A thrust angle causes the vehicle to steer or wander in the direction opposite to the thrust line. If the rear axle aims to the left, the vehicle will pull to the right, and vice-versa. A thrust angle can cause excessive tire wear that resembles toe wear.

If the vehicle has rear toe adjustments, the thrust angle can be set to zero degrees. This permits a total four-wheel alignment. If the vehicle does not have rear-wheel toe adjustments, the front-wheel toe is set to correspond with the rear-wheel toe. The wheels will then track properly with a centered steering wheel. This is called a thrust line alignment.

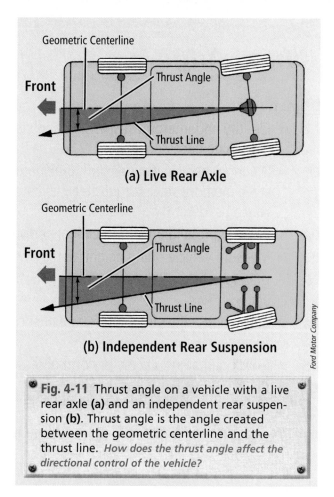

(a) Live Rear Axle

(b) Independent Rear Suspension

Ford Motor Company

Fig. 4-11 Thrust angle on a vehicle with a live rear axle **(a)** and an independent rear suspension **(b)**. Thrust angle is the angle created between the geometric centerline and the thrust line. *How does the thrust angle affect the directional control of the vehicle?*

SECTION 1 KNOWLEDGE CHECK

1. Explain negative camber.

2. What is the initial setting for camber?

3. Why is positive caster desirable?

4. Define toe.

5. Define scrub radius.

6. Define turning radius.

ASE TEST PREP

7. Technician A says that as the load on the rear increases, the rear chassis height decreases and the front chassis height increases. Technician A says that the caster angle becomes more positive as the front unloads. Technician B says that the caster angle becomes more negative as the front unloads. Who is correct?

   ⓐ Technician A.

   ⓑ Technician B.

   ⓒ Both Technician A and Technician B.

   ⓓ Neither Technician A nor Technician B.

Wheel Alignment Procedures

Objectives:

A2 ● Identify and interpret suspension and steering concern; determine necessary action.

D1 ● Diagnose vehicle wander, drift, pull, hard steering, bump steer, memory steer, torque steer, and steering return concerns; determine necessary action.

D2 ● Perform pre-alignment inspection; perform necessary action.

D3 ● Measure vehicle riding height; determine necessary action.

E6 ● Diagnose tire pull (lead) problem; determine necessary action.

D4 ● Check and adjust front and rear wheel camber; perform necessary action.

D5 ● Check and adjust caster; perform necessary action.

D6 ● Check and adjust front wheel toe and center steering wheel.

D9 ● Check and adjust rear wheel toe.

D10 ● Check rear wheel thrust angle; determine necessary action.

Vocabulary:
● **inner tie-rod end tool**
● **tie-rod puller**
● **steering wheel holder**

Complaints

Wheel alignment requires several different checks and adjustments. Wheel alignment involves:
- Checking camber, caster, and toe.
- Diagnosing possible problems.
- Adjusting caster, camber, and toe to the specifications in the vehicle's service manual.
- Centering the steering wheel when adjustments are complete.
- Road-testing the vehicle.

Many driveability conditions may appear to be wheel alignment problems. However, broken, worn, or loose steering system or suspension components may be at fault.

Table 4-A lists those complaints, causes, and corrections relating specifically to wheel alignment.

Pre-alignment Inspection

Many service facilities use a checklist to help with the pre-alignment inspection. The list may begin with a road test so that the technician can see how well the vehicle handles. Driving the vehicle will answer such questions as "does it pull?" or "does it steer hard?" Other items in the checklist may include measuring and recording tire pressure, checking steering linkage, ball joints, power steering belt and fluid, and general tire and brake condition. The checklist should also include such items as measuring camber, toe, and caster.

Before performing any wheel alignment, always check tire pressure. Tire pressure affects vehicle pull. If the front tire is significantly underinflated, the vehicle will pull in the direction of the underinflated tire. Tire pressure also affects wandering, ride quality, tire wear, and driveability.

Check that tires on the same axle are the same size. Tires of different sizes cause pull and directional problems. Look for bent wheels and damaged hubs.

Always measure chassis height and compare measurements to the specifications in the vehicle's service manual. Incorrect height has a direct effect on camber, caster, and toe settings.

Inspect the suspension and steering system for damaged, missing, and worn parts. Check the steering gear, steering linkage, ball joints, wheel bearings, springs, shocks, stabilizer bar links and bushings, control arms, and control arm bushings. Replace any damaged or worn parts. Many service facilities require a pre-alignment checklist.

Table 4-A

WHEEL ALIGNMENT DIAGNOSIS

Complaint	Possible Cause	Check or Correction
1. Hard steering	a. Low or uneven tire pressure b. Too much caster c. SAI incorrect	a. Inflate to correct pressure b. Check and adjust caster c. Check for damaged suspension or frame components
2. Wander or drift	a. Excessive toe-out b. Too little caster c. Thrust angle incorrect d. Excessive play in steering (bump steer can occur when wheels hit a bump in the road)	a. Check and adjust toe-out b. Check and adjust caster c. Check and adjust thrust angle d. Check and adjust or replace necessary parts
3. Pulls to one side	a. Uneven caster b. Uneven camber c. Incorrect setback d. Thrust angle incorrect e. Defective tire f. Power steering gear control valve out of adjustment g. Memory steer h. Torque steer on hard acceleration (FWD vehicle)	a. Check and adjust caster b. Check and adjust camber c. Check and adjust setback d. Check and adjust thrust angle e. Cross-switch front tires to prove tire defective; replace defective tire f. Adjust or repair power steering gear control valve g. Loosen and re-torque rubber bushings in steering linkage with wheels in straight-ahead direction; these bushings are found in idler arms and MacPherson struts h. Inspect FWD axles; explain to customer this is common on some high-power vehicles
4. Shimmy	a. Wheels out of balance b. Too much caster c. Incorrect or unequal camber	a. Check runout. Check and rebalance wheels b. Check and adjust caster c. Check and adjust camber
5. Steering kickback	a. Tire pressure low or uneven b. Excessive positive caster	a. Inflate to correct pressure b. Check and adjust caster
6. Poor steering return	a. Excessive negative caster b. SAI incorrect	a. Check and adjust caster b. Check for damaged suspension or frame components
7. Improper tire wear	a. Wear at tread sides from under inflation b. Wear at tread center from over inflation c. Wear at one side of tread due to camber d. Feathered tread wear due to toe e. Uneven or scalloped wear f. Thrust angle incorrect	a. Inflate to correct pressure b. Adjust tire pressure c. Check and adjust camber d. Check and adjust toe e. Rotate tires, balance tires and align wheels f. Check and adjust thrust angle
8. Excessive sway in turns	a. Caster incorrect b. Damaged stabilizer/sway bar or related components c. Weak springs	a. Check and adjust caster b. Inspect, repair, or replace stabilizer/sway bar or related components c. Inspect springs; replace as necessary
9. Vehicle unstable	a. Low or uneven tire pressure b. SAI incorrect	a. Inflate to correct pressure b. Check for damaged suspension or frame components
10. Steering wheel off-center	a. Setback incorrect b. Bent steering linkage c. Toe not properly set with steering wheel centered d. Thrust angle incorrect	a. Align engine cradle or subframe b. Inspect and replace damaged steering linkage c. Properly adjust toe with steering wheel centered d. Adjust thrust angle or do thrust line alignment

Correct wheel alignment has several benefits. These include:

- Improved tire wear. Improper alignment is a major cause of premature tire wear.
- Improved fuel efficiency. Fuel efficiency will increase as rolling resistance decreases. Rolling resistance is the resistance of the tires on the road. Correct alignment will set all four wheels parallel. If the tires carry the correct inflation pressure, this will minimize rolling resistance.
- Improved handling. Correct alignment will eliminate pulling and vibrations.
- Smoother ride. The correct alignment of system components will reduce road shock.

Safety First

Road Test Before performing a road test, be sure to obtain written permissions from appropriate authorities.

Alignment Equipment

Accurate wheel alignment requires the skillful use of specialized equipment. Specialized wheel alignment equipment provides easy-to-read diagrams and illustrations. In some instances, the equipment shows exactly how much adjustment is needed at each wheel. The display monitor shows the camber, caster, toe, thrust angle, toe-out on turns, SAI, and included angle of each wheel. The system contains alignment specifications for various vehicle makes and models. It will store information related to an individual alignment job as well as other pertinent vehicle and customer information. Equipment manufacturers provide training or documentation on the use of their equipment. See **Fig. 4-12**.

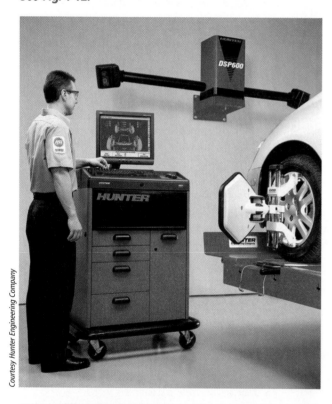

Fig. 4-12 The computer in this alignment system uses special software to simplify the alignment process.

Regardless of the equipment used, the goal is to measure wheel alignment angles and to monitor changes to those angles. A skilled wheel alignment technician understands why angles change and how to achieve the required adjustments. It is critical that you understand the theory of wheel alignment, rather than simply depending on the alignment equipment.

Types of Wheel Alignment

There are three basic types of wheel alignment. A front-wheel alignment on the vehicle's geometric centerline, a thrust line alignment, and a total four-wheel alignment.

Four-Wheel Alignment

The total four-wheel alignment should always be done when there are means of adjustment on all four wheels. If the rear wheels are not adjustable, then the thrust line alignment should be done. This allows the front-wheel toe to correspond to the rear-wheel toe and provides proper tracking of all four wheels. With up-to-date alignment equipment there is no need to do a front-wheel alignment using the geometric centerline of the vehicle. This will not ensure proper wheel tracking and involves the same amount of labor as the thrust line alignment. See **Fig. 4-13**.

Fig. 4-13 A four-wheel alignment system in use. The alignment heads attach to the wheels and transmit wheel position information to the system's computer. *What is the advantage of using a computer-aided alignment machine?*

The location of the rear axle can dramatically affect the directional control of a vehicle. The rear wheels dictate the "thrust angle" of the vehicle. This, in turn, affects the geometry of the front wheels.

Rear-Wheel Alignment

Rear-wheel-drive vehicles (those with a fixed-rear-axle housing assembly) offer no rear toe or camber adjustment. If the rear thrust angle is incorrect, it may be due to an improperly mounted axle housing or a damaged frame. If frame damage exists, it must be repaired before performing an alignment.

Some vehicles have independent suspension systems. An example of such a system is shown in **Fig. 4-14**.

Independent rear suspensions on front- and rear-wheel-drive vehicles may provide adjustment of camber and toe. Adjustment is made by rotating the cam adjuster bolts where the rear control arms mount to the frame.

Depending on the design, cam adjusters may provide adjustment only for the toe. If the vehicle has rear MacPherson struts, rear camber adjustment is at the lower strut mounting point. Loosen the two mounting bolts that secure the strut to the knuckle or install adjuster bolts at these locations. For specific procedures, refer to the vehicle's service manual.

For camber adjustment, some rear hubs (on front-wheel-drive vehicles) may allow the use of shims to change the angle of the rear spindles.

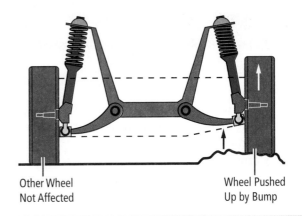

Other Wheel Not Affected

Wheel Pushed Up by Bump

Fig. 4-14 With Independent suspension each wheel can move independently. *What is the advantage of this type of suspension system?*

Many four-wheel-drive trucks and sport utility vehicles may require the use of tapered shims to alter the spindle angle as well. Because there are so many different suspension designs, many alignment methods are available. A number of specialty tools are in common use for this purpose. See **Fig. 4-15**. Always refer to the service manual.

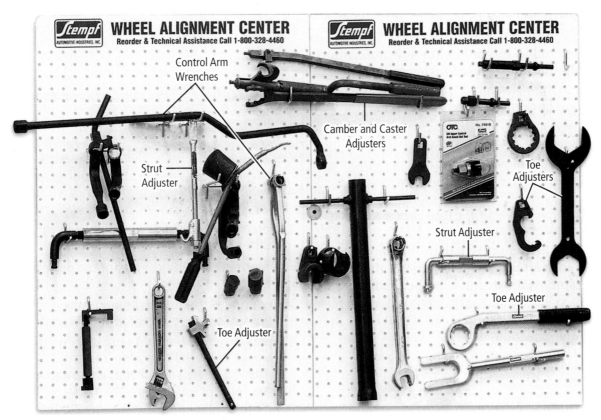

Fig. 4-15 Different suspension designs require the use of different specialty tools.

Measuring Camber

Manufacturer's specs give the information needed to make decisions about camber adjustment.

Camber angle tolerance is given as a range of acceptable values. This range can be written as an inequality. A mathematical inequality is a statement that uses the symbols $<, \leq, >, \geq$.

For example, if the camber angle tolerance is given as $1° \pm 0.5°$, the inequality is $0.5° \leq c \leq 1.5°$. This statement is read as camber angle, c, is greater than or equal to $0.5°$ and less than or equal to $1.5°$.

For a certain customer's vehicle, the camber angle tolerance in degrees is $0.75° \pm 0.5°$. You measure the right rear wheel camber of your customer's vehicle. It measures $1.4°$.

For this car, you will:

1. Determine the tolerance interval graph and indicate the optimal value.

2. Determine the adjustment for the optimal or preferred setting.

3. Determine the minimum and maximum adjustment for an acceptable measure.

4. Write a mathematical inequality for the camber, c, and tolerance interval you have determined.

The range, $0.75° \pm 0.5°$, means that the optimal, or desired, setting is $0.75°$.

The lower level of the tolerance interval is:
$$0.75° - 0.5° = 0.25°$$
The upper level of the tolerance interval is:
$$0.75° + 0.5° = 1.25°$$

Since $1.4°$ is greater than the upper level tolerance, you must adjust the camber. The necessary adjustment must be made in the negative direction. For the optimal setting, the adjustment must be $1.4° - 0.75° = 0.65°$ in the negative direction.

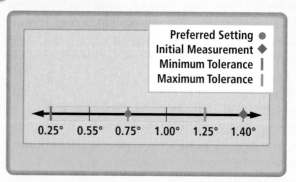

The minimum adjustment would be:
$1.4° - 1.25° = 0.15°$ in the negative direction.
The maximum acceptable adjustment would be:
$1.4° - 0.25° = 1.15°$ in the negative direction.

The graph indicates the preferred setting and the initial measurement. The graph also indicates the minimum and maximum tolerance values of camber angle.

In this situation, the mathematical inequality for an acceptable camber measurement, c, is:
$$0.25° \leq c \leq 1.25°.$$

Apply It!

Meets NATEF Mathematics Standards for using angle measurements and tolerance intervals.

Assume that the camber of a front wheel of a vehicle is $-0.29°$ and the tolerance is $0.31° \pm 0.50°$.

1. Determine the tolerance interval graph and indicate the optimal value.

2. Determine the adjustment for the optimal or preferred setting.

3. Determine the minimum and maximum adjustment for an acceptable measure.

4. Write a mathematical inequality for the camber, c, for the tolerance interval.

In the workplace you will probably compare the measured camber with the specs. With practice, you will learn to do this mentally without writing down all the steps you have taken.

Alignment Adjustments

The general methods of making alignment adjustments are covered here. Always refer to the vehicle service manuals for the specific make and model of vehicle when making alignment adjustments. If alignment adjustments are available on the rear wheels, these adjustments must be made before adjusting the front wheels.

Camber

Depending on the vehicle design, there are several methods for adjusting camber. Some adjustment methods use spacer shims. Other methods use rotating eccentric control arm shafts or eccentric cam bolts. On some strut-equipped vehicles, camber is adjusted by moving the upper or lower mounting points.

If a vehicle uses multiple control arms, such as in a short-arm/long-arm (SLA) system, camber is adjusted by adding or removing shims. The shims are located where the upper control arm connects to the frame. In some designs, these shims are inboard of the upper control arm. In other designs, the shims are outboard of the upper control arm.

Adding or removing shims of equal thickness at the front and rear location affects camber angle. Adding or removing shims of unequal thickness at the front and rear locations affects camber and caster. See **Fig. 4-16.**

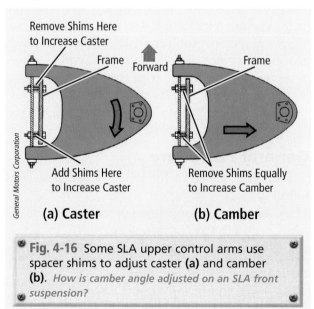

Remove Shims Here
to Increase Caster

Frame Forward Frame

Add Shims Here
to Increase Caster

Remove Shims Equally
to Increase Camber

(a) Caster **(b) Camber**

General Motors Corporation

Fig. 4-16 Some SLA upper control arms use spacer shims to adjust caster **(a)** and camber **(b)**. *How is camber angle adjusted on an SLA front suspension?*

When the upper control arm moves inward, the camber angle becomes more negative. When the upper control arm moves outward, the camber becomes more positive. See **Fig. 4-17.**

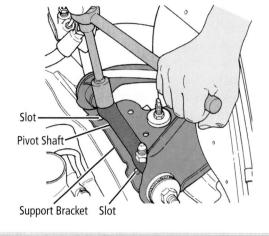

Slot

Pivot Shaft

Support Bracket   Slot

DaimlerChrysler

Fig. 4-17 Adjusting both caster and camber using slots (elongated holes) in the frame. *How is camber affected when the control arm is moved inward?*

Some vehicles have an offset upper control arm. Camber adjustment is made by rotating the control arm. The rotation moves the upper control arm inward or outward.

On other vehicles, camber is adjusted at the lower control arm. The lower control arm pivot bolt may be eccentric, or it may have eccentric washers. Camber is adjusted by rotating the eccentric adjusters. When the lower control arm moves inward, the camber angle becomes more positive. When the lower control arm moves outward, the camber angle becomes more negative.

On some vehicles with MacPherson struts, camber is adjusted at the bottom of the strut at the steering knuckle. Loosening the two lower strut-mounting bolts creates enough movement to allow some camber adjustment. If there is not enough movement, replace the upper or lower strut mounting bolt with an adjuster bolt that uses an eccentric washer. See **Fig. 4-18.**

Fig. 4-18 Camber adjustment on a MacPherson strut front suspension. *Where is the camber adjustment?*

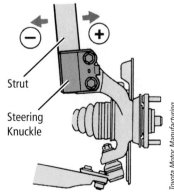

Strut

Steering
Knuckle

Toyota Motor Manufacturing

Some vehicles equipped with MacPherson struts may provide a small amount of camber adjustment at the top of the strut mounts. The mounts have elongated mounting holes. These holes allow inward and outward movement of the strut. However, new vehicle designs do not commonly employ this method. Installing aftermarket specialty adjuster kits serves the same purpose.

Some vehicles may allow camber and caster adjustment by sliding the upper control arm inward or outward. This type of upper control arm is attached with bolts through slotted holes in the frame. When movement at both the front and rear elongated holes is equal, only camber angle changes. If movement is unequal at these holes, both the camber angle and the caster angle change.

Caster

Depending on the vehicle design, caster angle is set by a number of methods. If the suspension is a short-arm/long-arm (SLA) system, caster adjustment is similar to camber adjustment. Spacer shims are located at the upper control arm. When an unequal thickness of shims is added or removed from the front and rear shim locations, caster angle is affected.

If the vehicle has a lower strut rod, the strut rod may have a threaded adjustment. The threaded adjustment lengthens or shortens the strut rod. If you shorten the strut rod, the caster angle becomes more negative. If you lengthen the strut rod, the caster angle becomes more positive.

If the upper or lower control arm has adjuster bolts, both camber and caster can be adjusted. If both front and rear bolts are adjusted an equal amount, only camber is affected. If the adjustment is unequal, the control arm will pivot slightly. Forward or rearward pivot of the control arm changes the caster angle.

If the upper control arm fastens to the frame through slotted holes, the control arm can be moved inward or outward. If the movement is unequal, the caster angle will change.

On some vehicles equipped with MacPherson struts, there may not be an adjustment for caster angle. If caster angle is incorrect, replace the control arm or strut or install aftermarket cam bolts in the lower control arm.

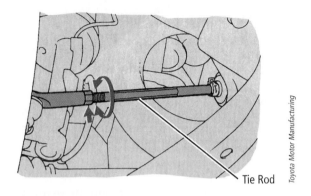

Tie Rod

Toyota Motor Manufacturing

Fig. 4-19 The toe is adjusted at the tie rods. *How do you adjust toe?*

Toe

Toe is adjusted at the tie rods. Rotating the tie rods effectively lengthens or shortens the rods. See **Fig. 4-19.**

On some vehicles, the tie rod connects to the tie rod end using a separate "adjuster sleeve." This sleeve is simply an internally threaded tube. When rotated, the sleeve changes the length of the tie rod.

When adjusting toe, any adjustment must be applied equally to both tie-rod ends. The right and left tie rods should be as equal in length as possible. Never perform the total toe adjustment on only one tie rod.

After adjusting toe, always be sure to tighten the lock nuts/jam nuts fully to factory torque values.

Several specialty tools can assist in the adjustment process. An **inner tie-rod end tool** resembles pliers or a crescent wrench. It grips the tie rod, allowing you to rotate the tie rod at its adjustment connection. A **tie-rod puller** allows you to separate the tie rod end's tapered stud from the steering arm.

General Procedure

The order of tasks for wheel alignment is as follows:

1. Check tire pressure and correct as needed.
2. Check tire size for mismatch.
3. Check tires for unusual or uneven wear.
4. Measure chassis height and correct as needed. Check for unusual loads in the passenger and cargo areas.
5. Check for loose, binding, worn, or damaged parts (wheel bearings, steering linkage, steering gears, suspension pivots, ball joints, and shocks).

6. Position the vehicle on the alignment rack and connect alignment equipment.

7. Using the alignment equipment, check existing angles (camber, caster, toe, included angle, SAI, thrust angle, toe-out on turns, setback). Determine which angles require adjustment.

8. Adjust rear camber where possible.

9. Adjust/address thrust angle. Correct rear toe, if possible.

10. Adjust front caster.

11. Adjust front camber.

12. Center steering wheel.

13. Adjust front toe.

14. Road test the vehicle, checking for steering control, directional stability, drifting, and wandering. Check for pull, both while cruising and during braking.

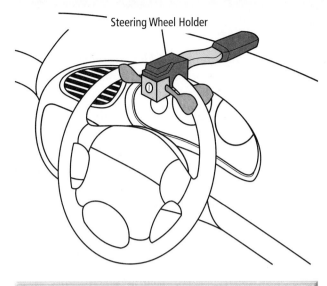

Steering Wheel Holder

Fig. 4-20 A steering wheel holder.

Safety First **Road Test** Before performing a road test, be sure to obtain written permissions from appropriate authorities.

Safety First **Steering Wheels** Always follow the procedures in the vehicle service manual for steering wheel removal or installation. This is especially important when working with a steering wheel assembly that has an air bag. To prevent accidental discharge of the air bag, the battery and specific fuse may require disconnection. You must always take special precautions when handling or storing any air bag assembly! Until you understand and are prepared to follow the service manual's safety instructions, never attempt to remove a steering wheel.

Current alignment equipment usually requires the steering to be locked in the straight-ahead position before adjusting front toe. A special tool called a **steering wheel holder** or lock can be used to hold the steering wheel in a straight-ahead position while toe adjustment is being accomplished. See **Fig. 4-20.** Tie rods on each front wheel are usually adjusted independently to adjust the individual toe of each front wheel. This ensures proper total toe and a centered steering wheel.

SECTION 2 KNOWLEDGE CHECK

1. What may cause steering kickback?

2. Why would you perform a thrust line alignment?

3. When are shims used to adjust camber?

4. Where is toe adjusted?

5. What is a tie-rod puller?

6. What should you check for when road testing a vehicle after wheel alignment?

ASE TEST PREP

7. Technician A says that on some vehicles camber can be adjusted by using spacer shims. Technician B says that on some vehicles camber can be adjusted by using eccentric cam bolts. Who is correct?

   ⓐ Technician A.

   ⓑ Technician B.

   ⓒ Both Technician A and Technician B.

   ⓓ Neither Technician A nor Technician B.

CHAPTER 4 REVIEW

Key Points

Meets the following NATEF Standards for Suspension & Steering: wheel alignment diagnosis; wheel alignment adjustment.

- Incorrect wheel alignment causes driveability problems and uneven tire wear.
- Wheel alignment angles are camber angle, caster angle, toe angle, scrub radius, included angle turning radius, setback, steering axis inclination, and thrust angle.
- Wheel camber angle adjustment determines what portion of the tire tread contacts the road.
- The wheel caster angle affects directional control of the vehicle and steering wheel return.
- The ideal toe angle setting is zero. Toe-in or toe-out causes uneven tread wear.
- The steering axis inclination is a reference angle and cannot be adjusted.
- Before doing a wheel alignment, check such items as condition of suspension and steering parts.
- Wheel alignments should always be a total four-wheel alignment.

Review Questions

1. What is the caster angle when the upper ball joint is behind the lower ball joint?
2. What side of the tire wears faster when a wheel has too much toe-out?
3. What may cause incorrect steering axis inclination?
4. What is the camber angle plus the SAI angle?
5. What is wheel setback?
6. What wheel alignment problem may cause excessive sway in turns?
7. What is the first step in wheel alignment?
8. What is the purpose of a steering wheel holder?
9. **Critical Thinking** What is the geometric centerline?
10. **Critical Thinking** Describe thrust angle.

Excellence in Communication

Reading Service Manuals

Twenty-five years ago, a mechanic would rarely have consulted a service manual. Today, however, vehicles are too complicated for any one technician to know everything about them. Today's technicians must consult service manuals and databases to be sure they are following the manufacturers' procedures.

Today's technician must read carefully. No longer can the tightening of nuts and bolts be left to guesswork. Specific torque values are now required to tighten fasteners correctly. Torque is a twisting or turning force. You must

be able to read, understand, and follow directions for a specific procedure. You must also know what special tools you will need.

Most service manuals include torque specifications. They also include pictures and part numbers for special tools.

Apply It!

Meets NATEF Communications Standards for using service manuals and comprehending and applying written information.

1. Select a service manual in your lab or school media center.

2. Look up the procedure for wheel alignment, which requires the tightening of fasteners to a specific torque. Look up another procedure that has specific torque requirements.

3. Look for the special tools identified by the manufacturer for the proper alignment of wheels. Look up another procedure that requires the use of special tools.

Safety First **Special Tools** If you fail to read about special tools and specifications, you may perform incorrect repairs or maintenance. Such errors can affect the vehicle's performance, as well as your safety and the safety of your customer.

Answering the following practice questions will help you prepare for the ASE certification tests.

1. A symptom of incorrect wheel alignment is:
   - ⓐ the same camber on right and left wheels.
   - ⓑ road crown.
   - ⓒ slow steering return.
   - ⓓ torque steering on rear-wheel-drive vehicles.

2. Technician A says that camber angle is the angle of inward or outward tilt of a wheel. Technician B says that camber angle is compared with true vertical when viewed from the front or rear of the vehicle. Who is correct?
   - ⓐ Technician A.
   - ⓑ Technician B.
   - ⓒ Both Technician A and Technician B.
   - ⓓ Neither Technician A nor Technician B.

3. Why is a little positive caster desirable?
   - ⓐ It prevents vehicle wander.
   - ⓑ It provides added lift.
   - ⓒ It lowers wind resistance.
   - ⓓ It increases tire contact with the road.

4. Technician A says that toe is how much the front of a wheel points inward or outward, compared to a true straight-ahead position. Technician B says that toe is viewed from the top of the vehicle and is measured in inches, millimeters, and degrees. Who is correct?
   - ⓐ Technician A.
   - ⓑ Technician B.
   - ⓒ Both Technician A and Technician B.
   - ⓓ Neither Technician A nor Technician B.

5. What is the thrust line of a vehicle?
   - ⓐ An in-dash gauge that measures the force driving the vehicle.
   - ⓑ The axis on which lateral g-force is applied.
   - ⓒ A line drawn perpendicular to the rear axle, pointing to the front wheels, that bisects the total toe of the rear wheels.
   - ⓓ The direction in which torque is applied to the wheels.

6. Technician A says that tires of different sizes can cause pull and directional problems. Technician B says that you should measure chassis height and compare measurements to the manufacturer's specification during a pre-alignment check. Who is correct?
   - ⓐ Technician A.
   - ⓑ Technician B.
   - ⓒ Both Technician A and Technician B.
   - ⓓ Neither Technician A nor Technician B.

7. Which of the following is not a cause of excessive sway in turns?
   - ⓐ Incorrect caster.
   - ⓑ Damaged stabilizer/sway bar or related components.
   - ⓒ Weak springs.
   - ⓓ Oversized struts.

8. Technician A says that a vehicle may be unstable because of low or uneven tire pressure. Technician B says that instability may be the result of incorrect steering axis inclination (SAI). Who is correct?
   - ⓐ Technician A.
   - ⓑ Technician B.
   - ⓒ Both Technician A and Technician B.
   - ⓓ Neither Technician A nor Technician B.

9. How many different types of wheel alignment are there?
   - ⓐ One.
   - ⓑ Two.
   - ⓒ Three.
   - ⓓ Four.

10. Technician A says that camber is adjusted using shims. Technician B says that camber can be adjusted by rotating eccentric control arm shafts. Who is correct?
    - ⓐ Technician A.
    - ⓑ Technician B.
    - ⓒ Both Technician A and Technician B.
    - ⓓ Neither Technician A nor Technician B.

A

ABS channel A hydraulic line from the ABS actuator to the wheel.

ABS diagnostic connector The diagnostic connector that allows technicians to access the control module using a scan tool designed for the vehicle being serviced.

absolute pressure The difference between atmospheric pressure and a partial vacuum.

accumulator In an antilock brake system, a device that stores fluid under pressure. Fluid is stored to provide pressure for one or two brake applications.

active listening The skill of paying attention and interacting with the speaker.

active test A test that forces a component to operate in a specific way.

actuator An output device that is operated by the PCM or other modules to create motion and perform other tasks.

air bag A balloon-type passenger safety device that inflates automatically on vehicle impact.

air bag control module The module that monitors system operation, controls the air bag warning light, and stores diagnostic trouble codes.

air filter Any device such as porous paper or a wire mesh filter that prevents airborne particles from entering machinery.

air induction system The system that supplies clean air to the engine and controls the flow of air through the engine.

air injection (AIR) system An exhaust emission control system that reduces hydrocarbon and carbon monoxide emissions.

air spring A spring that consists of a cylindrical bag filled with compressed air.

air/fuel ratio The proportion of air and fuel, by weight, supplied to the engine cylinders for combustion.

alternating current Electrical current that changes its direction of flow in a regular and predictable way.

analog signal A signal that continuously changes from positive to negative.

antilock brake system A system on motor vehicles that prevents the wheels from locking while braking. This system improves the driver's ability to control the vehicle while braking in panic stops and other emergencies.

antilock warning light Yellow or amber light on the instrument panel that indicates a problem in the antilock brake system.

antioxidants A chemical compound that prevents formation of varnish in the fuel system.

antiseize compound A lubricant that prevents bolt threads from locking, or seizing.

anti-sway bar A type of torsion bar that connects the lower suspension to both sides of the frame or body. This helps reduce body sway. Also called an anti-roll bar.

armature The part of the starter that rotates. It contains many individual windings or coils through which electric current flows, producing magnetic fields.

aspect ratio The relationship between the tire's section height and section width. Also called profile ratio.

Automotive Service Excellence (ASE) A nonprofit national institute dedicated to improving the quality of motor vehicle service and repair. ASE promotes testing and certification for service and repair professionals.

automotive stethoscope A diagnostic tool that helps isolate and amplify noises.

automotive system A system made up of two or more parts that work together to perform a specific task.

auxiliary parking brake A parking brake that uses a separate set of brake linings.

B

backing plate The metal plate on which many of the drum brake components are mounted.

ball joint A lubricated attachment that connects two suspension parts to allow pivoting movement.

battery An electrochemical device that stores electric current in chemical form so that it can be released as electricity for cranking the engine and powering the electrical load.

battery jumper box A portable power pack used for jump starting vehicles.

bench test A test of a component that has been removed from the vehicle.

bolt circle The bolt hole pattern in the wheel's center section. This is where the wheel bolts to the hub.

brake bleeding The process of flushing air or contaminated fluid from the braking system.

brake drum micrometer A micrometer specially adapted to the measurement of brake drums.

brake fluid A chemically inert hydraulic fluid used in hydraulic brake systems to transmit force and motion through a closed system of tubing or brake lines.

brake grabbing A condition in which the brakes apply more quickly than expected when compared with the pedal effort applied.

brake hardware Assorted small parts that attach to the brake shoes.

brake lines The tubes and hoses connecting the master cylinder to the wheel cylinders or calipers in a hydraulic brake system.

brake master cylinder A component that provides pressurized fluid to the remote cylinders.

brake pads The parts of disc brake systems that apply friction to the brake rotor.

brake pedal fade A temporary reduction of brake effectiveness.

brake pedal free play The amount of pedal movement before the pushrod touches the piston inside the master cylinder.

brake shoe A carrier to which the brake lining is attached that is used to force the lining in contact with the brake drum.

brake spoon A tool used to adjust drum brakes.

brush In an electric motor, a block of conducting substance, such as carbon.

C

calibration drift A condition in which a component, due to age or contamination, no longer accurately represents the factory setting.

caliper In a disc brake system, the housing that contains the pistons and the brake pads.

caliper mounting brackets Devices that hold the calipers in place.

camber angle The angle of inward or outward tilt of a wheel, measured in degrees. Often called camber.

camshaft A shaft having a series of cams for operating the valve mechanisms.

carbon tracking A condition that occurs when the spark jumps from a distributor cap terminal to another terminal or to ground. Carbon tracks appear as thin black lines on the inside of the cap.

caster angle The angle between true vertical and an imaginary line drawn through the upper and lower ball joints, measured in degrees. Often called caster.

catalyst A material that causes a chemical change without being part of the chemical reaction.

Celsius The unit by which temperature is measured in degrees.

charging current test A test that measures the maximum current output of the generator at a specified voltage.

charging voltage test A test that determines whether a generator's output is within the normal range.

circuit boards Electronic circuits printed on a plastic board.

circuit breaker A resettable protective device that opens an electric circuit to prevent damage when the circuit is overheated by excess current flow.

clamping diode A diode that provides a path to use up unwanted voltage. Used when high voltage could damage the module that controls the circuit.

closed-loop operation The operation that occurs when the powertrain control module (PCM) processes electrical inputs from sensors and provides output controls to actuators.

coil spring A length of spring-steel rod wound into a coil.

cold-cranking amps (CCA) The amount of current a fully charged battery can supply at 0°F [-18°C] for 30 seconds.

commutator A device consisting of a series of copper segments placed side by side to form a ring around the armature shaft.

compression ratio The volume in the cylinder with the piston at bottom dead center (BDC) divided by the volume in the cylinder with the piston at top dead center (TDC).

conductor A material that contains free electrons that allow electrical current to flow easily.

control arm The device that provides the connection points of the suspension system for up/down pivoting movement.

control valve A valve that regulates the flow of atmospheric pressure and vacuum to the two separate chambers in the vacuum power booster.

cooling system pressure test A test that diagnoses external cooling system leaks.

cooling system thermostat A device that regulates the flow of coolant through the engine and cooling system, keeping the engine within the correct operating temperature range.

cranking vacuum test A test that measures engine vacuum while the engine is cranking.

cranking voltage/current draw test A test that measures battery voltage and current during engine cranking.

crash (impact) sensors The sensors in an air bag system that close an electrical circuit to activate the system when sufficient impact occurs.

cruise control vacuum servo A device that uses a vacuum-operated diaphragm to hold the throttle linkage open.

current flow The movement of electrical energy through a conductor.

cylinder compression The pressure developed in the cylinder as the engine cranks.

cylinder leakage test A test that checks a cylinder's ability to hold pressure.

cylinder power balance test A test that checks for weak cylinders by measuring the power being produced by each cylinder.

 D

data bus A wiring harness that allows components connected to it to share sensor signals and other information.

deceleration sensor A sensor that tells the control module whether the vehicle is moving or stopped.

detonation Commonly referred to as spark knock or ping. In the combustion chamber of a spark-ignition engine, an uncontrolled second explosion (after the spark occurs at the spark plug), with spontaneous combustion of the remaining compressed air/fuel mixture, resulting in a pinging sound.

diagnostic A procedure used by the powertrain control module (PCM) to test relevant on-board systems.

diagnostic executive A powertrain control module (PCM) program that controls the sequencing of tests needed to run the OBD-II monitors.

diagnostic trouble code (DTC) A code that identifies a system or component malfunction.

diaphragm A thin disk that vibrates in response to electric signals to produce sound waves.

digital signal A signal that is either on or off. The voltage is either high or low, with no values in between. Also called a square wave signal.

diode A solid-state electronic device that allows the passage of an electric current in one direction only.

direct current Electrical current that flows in a single direction.

disc brake wear indicator A device that alerts the driver to the need for brake service.

disc brakes A brake in which brake pads, in a vise-like caliper, grip a revolving disc to stop it.

discard diameter The maximum allowable diameter of the brake drum. The number is cast into the drum.

distributor A device designed to establish base timing and distribute the ignition spark.

distributorless ignition system An electronic ignition system without a separate ignition distributor. Sensors signal the position of the crankshaft to the powertrain control module (PCM), which then electronically times and triggers the system and controls the distribution of the secondary voltages.

diversity A mix of different people.

double A-arm suspension A suspension system that uses two control arms, one upper and one lower, and a coil spring.

drive cycle A set of driving conditions that "run" all on-board diagnostics.

drum brake self-adjuster A device on drum brakes that compensates for lining wear by automatically adjusting the shoe-to-drum clearance.

drum brakes A brake in which curved brake shoes press against the inner circumference of a metal drum to produce the braking action.

dual-braking system A type of braking system that has a dual-piston master cylinder, two fluid reservoirs, and two separate hydraulic systems. One hydraulic system controls the brakes of two wheels. The other hydraulic system controls the remaining two wheels.

duo-servo drum brakes Brakes in which the action of one shoe reinforces the action of the other shoe.

duty cycle The percentage of time the primary circuit stays switched on.

dwell angle The number of degrees of distributor or camshaft rotation during which current flows through the primary circuit of the ignition coil.

dynamic balancing A balancer that spins the tire and wheel assembly in an upright position. This allows balancing in more than one plane. Digital readouts show where to place weights.

E

electric brake pad wear indicator An indicator that depends on a sensor wire in the pad lining. When the wire contacts the brake rotor at a predetermined depth, a circuit is completed that illuminates the brake wear indicator light on the instrument panel.

electrolyte A compound that conducts an electrical current in a water solution.

electromagnetic display A gauge that uses electromagnetism to move an indicating needle.

electromagnetic field The space around an electromagnet that is filled with invisible lines of force. The strength of the field depends on the level of current flow and the number of wires in the coil.

electronic circuit tester A device that is used to safely test electronic circuits. It uses light-emitting diodes (LEDs) to display test results. Also called a logic probe.

enabling criteria The sensor inputs supplied during specific driving conditions.

engine A machine that turns heat energy into mechanical energy. A device that burns fuel to produce mechanical power.

engine vacuum The low-pressure condition created as the crankshaft turns, pulling the piston down in the cylinder.

Environmental Protection Agency (EPA) A government agency. It requires facilities to keep track of, handle, an dispose of hazardous materials properly.

ergonomics The study of workplace design. It studies the tools used, the lighting, and the type of movements required by the employee on the job.

evaporative control (EVAP) system A system that prevents gasoline vapors in the fuel system from escaping into the atmosphere.

exhaust gas analyzer A device used to test the amount of exhaust emissions produced by a vehicle.

exhaust manifold A metal casting with several passages through which exhaust gases leave the engine combustion chambers and enter the exhaust system.

F

failure record A record of up to five diagnostic trouble codes (DTCs) in the diagnostic memory relating to component faults.

field-serviceable part A part that can be repaired.

fire emergency plan A plan that includes the location of fire exits, where employees should meet outside, and what is expected of each person.

fixed caliper disc brakes Disc brakes that use a caliper that is fixed in position and cannot move.

floating caliper disc brakes Disc brakes that use a caliper that is free to move sideways on bushings and guide pins.

flywheel A mechanical device used to store energy that helps smooth out the engine power surges from the power strokes.

freeze-frame data Serial data values that are stored the instant an emission-related diagnostic trouble code (DTC) is set and enters the diagnostic memory.

friction The resistance to motion between two objects or surfaces that touch.

fuel pressure regulator A spring-loaded valve built into the fuel pump or the throttle body. It maintains a constant pressure drop across the injectors.

fuse A safety device that contains an element that is calibrated to melt when the current level in the circuit exceeds the rating of the fuse.

fusible link A short length of insulated wire connected in the circuit. Typically it is four gauge sizes smaller than the wires it is protecting. Like a fuse, it is designed to melt when current flow exceeds the rating for the circuit.

G

gear ratio The number of rotations a pinion gear must make to rotate a driven gear one time.

general workplace equipment Equipment that is shared by many technicians and used for a variety of tasks.

generator A device that converts mechanical energy into electrical energy.

H

halogen lamp A bulb filled with halogen gas. Halogen is a chemically inactive gas that protects the filament from burnout and allows it to operate at a higher temperature.

hand tool A tool that does not use a motor and obtains its energy from the person using it.

hazardous materials Materials and wastes that pose a danger to human health and the environment.

high-intensity discharge (HID) lamp A lamp in which light is produced when high voltage creates an arc between two electrodes. Mercury vapor or xenon gas is used in HID lamps.

honing To restore or resize or bore a cylinder by using rotating cutting stones.

horn relay A relay that controls current flow from the battery to the horns.

hydraulic pressure The pressure applied to a liquid to create the force.

hydraulics The process by which pressure is applied to a liquid to transfer force or motion.

hydrometer An instrument that determines the density of a liquid.

I

I/M 240 programs Centralized emissions testing programs using test procedures that satisfy federal government standards.

idle air control (IAC) valve A valve that controls engine idle in response to signals from the PCM.

ignition coil A device that transforms low voltage from the battery into a high voltage capable of producing an ignition spark.

incandescent bulb A bulb that uses tungsten filament placed in a vacuum inside a glass bulb. Used for side marker, license plate, and interior lights.

included angle The camber angle plus the steering-axis inclination (SAI) angle.

index mark A mark that will provide a reference so that you can remount the tire on the wheel in the same position.

indexing mark An indicator that produces a unique signal that tells the powertrain control module (PCM) when the number-one piston is nearing top dead center (TDC).

inertia switch A switch that disables the fuel pump in the event of an accident. This action prevents pressurized fuel from spraying from a broken fuel line.

inflation pressure The measurement of compressed air in a tire, expressed in pounds per square inch (psi) or kilopascals (kPa).

inflator module The module that contains the air bag, igniter, solid propellant, and cover.

inner tie-rod end tool A tool that resembles pliers or a crescent wrench. It grips the tie rod, allowing rotation of the tie rod at its adjustment connection.

inspection/maintenance ready status A record that shows a vehicle's on-board diagnostics have been run.

insulator A material that is a poor conductor of electricity.

intake manifold A set of tubes, or a casting with several passages, through which air or air/fuel mixture flows from the throttle valves to the intake ports in the cylinder head.

integral braking system A system in which the brake booster, master cylinder, pump, accumulator, and pressure modulator are combined as a single unit.

integral parking brake A parking brake that uses the same brake shoes or pads as the service brakes.

interference nut A self-locking nut that will not loosen.

J

jam nut A second nut that is tightened against the adjusting nut to keep it from moving.

jump starting The process of starting the engine in one vehicle by connecting it to the battery in another vehicle.

jumper wire A short piece of wire used as a temporary connection between two points on a circuit.

K

key-off load A device that draws current even when all switches are turned off. Examples are computer and radio memory circuits. Also called parasitic drain.

kinetic friction The resistance between objects that are in contact and in relative motion.

L

lateral acceleration sensor In antilock brake systems (ABS), a device that senses hard cornering during braking.

leading-trailing drum brakes Brakes in which the action of one shoe does not affect the action of the other shoe.

leaf spring A spring that consists of single or multiple-spring steel bands (leaves).

lift point A place on a vehicle frame where a lift, floor jack, or safety stand can be placed. Lift points are designated by the manufacturer.

liquid crystal display (LCD) A display panel that is placed in front of an incandescent or halogen light bulb.

live axle The shaft through which power travels from drive axle gears to driving wheels.

load test A test that measures terminal voltage while the battery is supplying a large current for 15 seconds. Also called a high rate discharge test.

low brake fluid level sensor A switch that illuminates the brake warning light to indicate low fluid level.

M

MacPherson strut A strut that combines a coil spring and a shock absorber into a single assembly using only a beam-type lower control arm.

malfunction indicator lamp (MIL) A light that warns the driver of a problem in the systems monitored by the powertrain control module (PCM). Also referred to as check engine light or the service engine soon light.

manifold absolute pressure (MAP) sensor A sensor that is mounted on or connected to the intake manifold.

mass airflow (MAF) sensor A sensor that measures the amount of air entering an engine.

master technician An automotive technician who is ASE-certified in all eight automobile/light truck areas.

material safety data sheet (MSDS) An information sheet that identifies chemicals and their components. It also lists the possible health and safety problems and describes safe use of the chemical.

memory holder A memory protection device that prevents temporary failure of electronic components.

metering valve A valve that controls, or delays, the flow of brake fluid to the front brakes.

multimeter A tester that measures voltage, current, and resistance. Also called volt-ohm-meter (VOM).

N

National Automotive Technicians Education Foundation (NATEF) An organization that certifies automotive training programs.

National Institute for Occupational Safety and Health (NIOSH) An organization that tests and certifies safety equipment.

nitrogen oxide A chemical compound formed when nitrogen and oxygen bond under high heat.

no-load test A test that checks exhaust emissions at either idle speed only or at idle and 2,500 no-load rpm.

nondirectional finish A finish that does not have machining grooves.

nonintegral braking system A system that uses traditional brake system components, such as the master cylinder and brake booster.

O

Occupational Safety and Health Administration (OSHA) The organization created to enforce safe and healthful working conditions.

octane number An indicator of the antiknock quality of a gasoline. The higher the octane number, the more resistant the gasoline is to detonation.

Ohm's law A law that applies the mathematical relationship between voltage, resistance, and current in an electrical circuit.

on-board diagnostic systems Computer-controlled test routines that monitor and control vehicle systems.

on-car brake lathe A device used to perform brake rotor machining on the vehicle.

open circuit The condition that occurs when the electrical path is broken within the circuit.

open-circuit voltage test A test that checks the state of charge of a battery.

operator's manual A document that specifies procedures for the proper use and maintenance of tools and equipment.

oscilloscope A test device that displays voltage changes within a certain time period.

overrunning clutch A device that prevents the engine from driving the starter. This roller or sprag clutch transmits torque in only one direction.

oversteer A condition that results when the rear tires lose adhesion during cornering.

P

parallel circuit The electric circuit formed when two or more electric devices have their terminals connected together, positive to positive and negative to negative, so that each may operate independently.

park switch A switch that supplies power to the wiper motor after the windshield wiper switch is turned off.

parking brake equalizer A device that balances the braking forces so both rear brakes are applied evenly.

parking brakes The brakes used to keep a parked vehicle from moving. They are usually on the rear wheels and are mechanically operated.

Pascal's law A law that states that when there is an increase in pressure at any point in a confined liquid, there is an equal increase in pressure at every other point in the container.

passive test A test that checks the performance of a vehicle system or component during normal operation.

pawl A ratchet tooth that is used to lock a device.

pedal pulsation A throbbing or vibration of the pedal.

personal protective equipment (PPE) Equipment worn by workers to protect against hazards in the environment.

photocell A device that uses light energy to create current flow.

photodiode A device that uses the presence or absence of light to switch a reference voltage on and off.

piston A cylindrical plug that fits inside a cylinder. It receives and transmits motion as a result of pressure changes applied to it.

piston slap A muffled, hollow, knocking noise.

pitch The length from a point on a fastener thread to a corresponding point on the next thread. It is calculated by dividing one inch by the number of threads per inch.

ply A layer of cord, fiberglass, steel, or other material used to create a tire carcass.

pneumatic motor A motor powered by compressed air.

pneumatic tool A tool powered by compressed air.

polarity The quality of an electronic component or circuit that determines the direction of current flow.

positive temperature coefficient (PTC) resistor A solid-state device used as a circuit breaker that opens a circuit when an over-current condition occurs.

potentiometer A three-wire variable resistor used to monitor movement. The resistance of the sensor changes with the position of the shaft to which it is connected.

power piston In a power brake booster, the interface between the front and rear pushrods. It is attached to or suspended from the diaphragm.

power steering pump A hydraulic pump that provides an assist to the steering system.

power-assisted steering A system that uses hydraulic or electric power to help the driver apply steering force. Also called power steering.

powertrain control module (PCM) An electronic module or computer that receives input from various engine and powertrain sensors and responds by sending output signals to various actuators.

pressure differential valve The valve that senses the pressure in each branch of a hydraulic circuit.

proportioning valve A valve that reduces the amount of braking force at the rear wheels on front disc and rear drum brake systems.

pulse-width In fuel injection systems, the duration during which a fuel injector supplies fuel.

pyrometer An instrument that checks temperature. A contact pyrometer must touch the heat source to check temperature. A non-contact, or infrared, pyrometer measures the heat radiated from the heat source.

R

rack-and-pinion steering gear Steering gear in which a pinion on the end of the steering shaft meshes with a rack of gear teeth on the major cross-member of the steering linkage.

random access memory (RAM) A volatile, or erasable, memory that temporarily stores information such as diagnostic trouble codes.

recirculating-ball steering gear An assembly that uses a series of recirculating balls on a worm gear to transfer steering wheel movement to road wheel movement.

rectification The process by which AC voltage is changed to DC by diodes.

relay An electrical device that opens or closes a circuit in response to a voltage signal.

repair order A document that organizes the information the service technician needs to know about the vehicle in order to service it properly.

reserve capacity The measure of how many minutes a battery can supply a load of 25 amps at 80°F [27°C].

residual pressure check valve A valve that maintains a residual pressure of about 6–18 psi [41–124 kPa] in the brake lines.

resistance The opposition to a flow of current through a circuit or electrical device; measured in ohms.

rheostat A variable resistor.

rim diameter The measurement from a point on the inside bead seat to the point on the inside bead seat directly across the diameter of the wheel.

rim width The measurement from the inside bead seat wall to the opposite bead seat wall.

rocker arm A pivoted lever that transfers cam or pushrod motion to the valve stem.

rotor (brake) A disc-shaped device made from cast iron or sintered iron. It has a flat friction surface machined onto both sides against which the brake pads are pressed. It is attached to the spindle or hub and rotates on the wheel bearings.

rotor (generator) The part of the generator that rotates inside the generator housing. It creates the rotating magnetic field of the generator.

rotor runout The wobble of the brake rotor.

S

scan tool An electronic device used to read a vehicle's data stream and trouble codes. Also called a scanner.

scores Grooves or deep scratches on a smooth surface. Scoring is caused by debris or metal-to-metal contact.

screw thread A fastener that has a spiral ridge, or screw thread, on its surface.

scrub radius The distance between the steering axis and the centerline of the tire tread contact area. Also called steering offset.

sensor A device that monitors or measures operating conditions. It generates or modifies an electrical signal based on the condition it is monitoring.

serial data stream Information displayed as voltage values or as actual readings, such as degrees of temperature.

series circuit An electrical circuit in which the devices are connected end to end, positive terminal to negative terminal. The same current flows through all the devices in the circuit.

service history A written service record for a vehicle.

Service Technicians Society (STS) An association for automotive and transportation professionals that provides a forum for the exchange of technical information and industry trends.

setback The difference in length between the wheelbase on one side of the vehicle and the wheelbase on the other side.

setscrew A fastener used to secure a collar or gear on a shaft.

short circuit A condition occurring when two or more electrical conductors are in contact where no connection is intended.

sliding caliper disc brakes Disc brakes that use a caliper that is held in place by a retainer, a spring, and a bolt.

slip rings Devices that allow current to flow through the field coil while it rotates.

snap-throttle vacuum test A test that shows the condition of the pistons and the piston rings as the engine speed decreases to idle.

solenoid An electromechanical device that produces a mechanical movement when connected to an electrical source such as a battery.

specialized tool A tool designed for a certain use. A specialized tool may be a hand tool or a power tool.

specific gravity The weight per unit volume of a substance as compared with the weight per unit volume of water.

spontaneous combustion Fire caused by chemical reactions with no spark.

spool valve A valve that shuttles back and forth to open and close ports for the pressurized power steering fluid. It resembles a spool that carries sewing thread.

sprung weight Vehicle weight, including the engine, body and frame, transmission, and cargo, that is supported by the springs.

star wheel An adjusting nut with indexing arms for positive and accurate rotation, as on a brake or clutch.

starter A high torque electric motor that cranks the engine.

starter relay An electrical device that opens or closes the high-voltage circuit to the starter.

starter solenoid An electromechanical device that moves the pinion gear into mesh with the ring gear on the engine flywheel or drive plate.

static friction Resistance between objects that are in contact but at rest.

stator windings The stationary coils or windings in a generator.

steering axis inclination The difference between a true vertical line drawn through the center of the wheel and an imaginary line drawn through the upper and lower ball joints.

steering ratio The number of degrees that the steering wheel must turn to turn the road wheels 1°.

steering wheel holder A device used to hold the steering wheel in a straight-ahead position while toe adjustment is being accomplished.

stepper motor A small DC motor used to position a component very precisely.

stoichiometric ratio The ratio (14.7:1) that provides the most efficient combustion, giving the chemically correct mixture of air to fuel.

System of International Units (SI) A system of measurement that uses meters, liters, and grams. Also called the metric system.

T

terminal voltage The voltage measured across a battery under specified conditions.

thermistor A solid-state resistor in which resistance changes with temperature.

thread-locking compound A compound used to prevent threaded fasteners from loosening.

throttle position sensor (TPS) A variable resistance sensor that sends throttle plate position information to the powertrain control module (PCM).

thrust angle The relationship between the position of the rear axle and the centerline of the vehicle.

thrust line A line drawn perpendicular to the rear axle. It bisects the total toe out of the rear wheels.

tie rod An adjustable-length rod that, as the steering wheel turns, transfers steering force and direction from the steering gear or linkage to the steering arm.

tie-rod puller A tool that allows you to separate the tie rod end's tapered stud from the steering arm.

timing light A bright stroboscopic light used to set ignition timing. It is usually connected to the number-one spark plug wire. Current flow causes the timing light to flash and show the position of the timing mark on the vibration damper in relation to a timing pointer mounted on the front of the engine.

toe The measurement by which the front wheel points inward or outward, compared to a true straight-ahead position.

tone wheel In an antilock brake system (ABS), a toothed ring that rotates with the wheel. The teeth pass through the wheel speed sensor's magnetic field, causing a voltage signal that is sent to the ABS system.

torque A turning or twisting force producing torsion and rotation around an axis. Torque is measured in pound-feet or Newton-meters.

torsion bar A steel rod that twists to provide spring action.

track bar A straight bar positioned parallel to the rear axle.

trailing arms Suspension linkage supporting wheel assembly aft of a transverse pivot axis.

transfer cable(s) A cable in the parking brake system that runs between the rear wheels or from the equalizer to each rear wheel.

transmission jack A jack that is used to support the transmission when it is serviced or replaced.

trip A key-on, run, key-off cycle in which all of the enabling criteria for a given diagnostic monitor are met.

turning radius The difference in the angles of the front wheels in a turn. Also called toe-out on turns.

U

understeer A condition that results when the front tires lose adhesion during cornering.

unsprung weight Vehicle weight, including the wheels, tires, brakes, drive axles, and lower control arms, that is not supported by the springs.

V

vacuum A measurement of air pressure that is less than atmospheric pressure.

vacuum booster A device that uses vacuum to supply additional energy to boost brake application pressures.

vacuum gauge A device that measures vacuum in inches of mercury (Hg).

vacuum storage system A device that stores engine vacuum in the booster.

valve seat The surface against which a valve comes to rest to provide a seal against cylinder leakage.

valve train A series of parts that open and close the valves by transferring cam-lobe movement to the valves.

variable-assist power steering Power steering that uses electronic controls to determine how much power assist the steering needs.

vehicle identification number (VIN) A serial number unique to each vehicle. The number indicates the year, assembly plant, and country in which the vehicle was made; the vehicle make and type; the passenger safety system; the engine type; and the line, series, and body style.

vehicle speed sensor A small AC-signal generator driven by a shaft in the transmission that generates a voltage pulse proportional to vehicle speed.

volatility A measure of how easily a liquid (fuel) vaporizes.

voltage A measurement of the pressure that causes electrical energy (current) to flow.

voltage drop test A test that checks for high resistance across a cable, component, or connection.

voltage regulator A device used to control the generator output voltage.

voltage regulator test A test that checks that the voltage regulator can keep the charging system at a predetermined voltage.

W

warm-up cycle The period when the engine coolant temperature rises from ambient temperature to at least 160°F [71°C].

wheel backspacing The distance from the wheel's mounting surface to the rear edge of the wheel rim.

wheel cylinder A cylinder that converts the hydraulic pressure from the master cylinder into mechanical movement.

wheel lockup A condition that occurs when braking causes tires to lose traction, resulting in skidding.

wheel offset The location of the wheel's centerline as viewed from the front, relative to the location of the mounting face of the wheel hub.

wheel speed sensor Inputs wheel speed to the ABS control module.

wiring diagram A drawing that shows the wires, connectors, and load devices in an electrical circuit.

Z

Zener diode A diode that can conduct current flow in a reverse direction without being damaged.

A

ABS. *See* antilock brake system
absolute pressure, EP453
accessory motors, EL331–336
accident prevention. *See* Safety
accumulators, BR185, BR214
acronyms, EP446
ACTE. *See* Association for Career and Technical Education
active listening, HB46
active tests, EP473
actuators, EP389, EP402–406
    fuel injectors as, EP464–465
    hydraulic, BR209, BR213, BR214–215
    replacing, EP411–413
    testing, EP405
adjustable shock absorbers, SS555
adjusting screws, BR143
adjusters, one-shot drum brake, BR143
air
    atmospheric air (barometric) pressure, EP453
    leaks of, EP445
    temperature of, EP454
air bag systems. *See* supplemental restraint systems
air chisel sets, HB73
air compressors, HB73
air filters and housings, EP364, EP437–439
airflows, EP443
    calculating, EP438, EP443
    diagnosing failures of sensors of, EP444–445
    direct measurement of, EP444
airflow sensors, EP395–397
air/fuel ratio, EP452
air induction systems, EP364, EP437–445
    air filter and housing, EP437–439
    intake manifold, EP440–441
    sensing induction airflows in, EP443–445
    throttle body, EP439–440
air injection (AIR) systems, EP491–493
air pressure regulators, HB73
AIR pump drive belts, EP492
alignment, steering, SS533
alignment, wheel. *See* wheel alignment
Allen wrenches, HB53
alternating current (AC), EL231
    rectifying AC voltage, EL293
alternators, EL289
American Vocational Association. *See* Association for Career and Technical Education (ACTE)
analog signals, EP390, EP421
analyzer, four-gas, EP501
angle of incline, BR203
antifreeze. *See* coolants
antiknock index (AKI), EP450
antilock brake systems (ABS), BR206–225
    channels in, BR210–212
    components of, BR213–217
    diagnosing and repairing, BR217–220
    diagnostic connectors, BR217–218
    graphs, BR210

    integral, BR207
    nonintegral, BR207
    pedal pulsations in, BR166
    slip ratio in, BR210
    speed sensors in, BR128
    stability control in, BR223
    traction control in, BR221
    warning lights, BR214, BR216–217, EL325
antilock brake system-traction control modules (ABS-TCSs), BR221
antioxidants, in gasoline, EP449
antiseize compounds, HB83
antisqueal compound, BR168, BR170
anti-sway bars, SS556
appearance, personal, HB45
armatures, EL274
asbestos, HB95, BR116, BR140
    in brake pads, BR154
ASE. *See* Automotive Service Excellence
aspect ratio, SS509
Association for Career and Technical Education (ACTE), HB37
atmospheric air (barometric) pressure, EP453
A-type control arms (wishbones), SS556, SS558
attitude, positive, HB45
auditory alerts, HB93
automatic transmissions, EP364
automotive emissions, EP488
    control systems for, EP137–140
    testing for, EP498–501
automotive industry, HB33–41
    career opportunities, HB38–41
    work environment, HB40–41
automotive parts stores, HB41
automotive salespersons, HB41
Automotive Service Excellence (ASE) Certification, HB35–37, HB42
automotive systems, HB33–35. *See also* individual systems
axles, SS560
axle stands. *See* safety stands

B

backing plates, in drum brakes, BR140
back injuries, preventing, HB96
backup lights, EL316
balancing tires, SS525, SS527
ball (ball-and-socket) joints, SS558–560
barometric pressure, EP453
barometric pressure (BARO) sensors, EP467
barrier creams, HB95
batteries, EL234–235, EL252–271
    absorbed glass mat (AGM), EL255
    charging, EL265
    in charging systems, EL289
    construction of, EL253–255
    damage to, EL267
    high-voltage, on hybrids, HB104, EL268
    hybrid vehicle, EL255, EL268
    inspection and testing of, EL258–263

operation of, EL255–277
overcharged, EL303
replacement of, EL265–266
servicing of, EL264–269
in starter systems, EL273–274
testing and warranties, EL261
undercharged and overcharged, EL302–303
battery carriers, EL266
battery chargers, HB67
battery jumper boxes, EL269
battery load tests, EL260
battery management systems, EL255
battery plates, EL253–255
battery post cleaners, HB61
battery ratings, EL256
battery terminal pliers, HB61
battery terminal puller, HB61
battery testers, EL261
bead breaker arms, on tire changers, SS522
bead separator tools, SS522
bearing packers, HB67
belts, EL298–300
belt-tension gauges, HB67, EL300, SS539
bench bleeds, BR128–129
bench grinders, HB67
bench test, EL304
bias-belted tires, SS508
bleeding automotive systems
ABS systems, BR219–220
hydraulic braking systems, BR133–135
power steering system, SS540–541
bleeding emergencies, HB97
blowby, EP357, EP488
blowguns, HB61, HB99–100
body language, HB47
bolt circles, SS517
bolts, HB79–81
broken, removing, HB82
standards for, HB80
boosters, hydraulic brake, BR184–186. *See also* power
brake boosters
brake bleeding, BR133. *See* bleeding automotive systems
brake boosters, BR185, BR189
brake cleaner, aqueous, BR116–117
brake drag, BR128
brake drums, BR151–153. *See also* drum brakes
cleaning, BR150
out-of-round, BR149
brake dust, HB95, BR116–117, BR145, BR169
brake fluid, BR114–117, BR125–126, BR186
contamination of, BR115
leaking from calipers, BR167
loss of, BR150
metering valves, BR131
safety concern for, BR148
brake fluid level sensors, EL326–327
brake fluid reservoirs. *See* master cylinder fluid
reservoirs
brake grabbing, BR147
brake hardware, BR141
brake lathes, standard, BR176

brake light circuits, EL315
brake light switches, EL326–327
brake lines (hoses), BR109, BR112, BR129
brake linings, BR142
burnishing, BR171
brake master cylinders, BR109, BR112, BR122
diagnosing, BR127–129
in dual-braking systems, BR113, BR130
leaks in, BR127
low fluid level in, BR147–148, BR167
operation of, BR125–126
pistons in, BR122
plugged air vents in, BR148
quick-takeup, BR126–127
brake pads, BR159–160
inspecting, BR169–170
replacing, BR170–171
brake pad wear indicator, electric, EL327
brake pedal fade, BR114
brake pedals
adjustment of height, BR128
in cruise control systems, EL337–338
driver adjustable, BR128
free play in, BR147
for parking brakes, BR199
pulsations of, BR148–149, BR216
ratios, BR183
soft or spongy, BR147–148
in vacuum booster systems, BR181–182
vibrations in, BR149
brake shoe adjusting gauges, BR154–155
brake shoes
adjusting, BR154–155
for auxiliary parking brakes, BR202
in drum brakes, BR140, BR153
in duo-servo drum brakes, BR142–143
installing, BR154
in leading-trailing drum brakes, BR142
linings for, BR142
brake spoons, BR151
brake systems, BR109–111
antilock (ABS), BR207–223
brake fluid in, BR114–117
brake master cylinders in, BR124–130
diagnosing, BR145–150, BR164–168
disc brakes, BR158–179
drum brakes, BR138–157
dual-braking, BR113
friction and, BR110–111
hydraulic, bleeding, BR133–135
hydraulic boosters for, BR184–186
hydraulic circuits in, BR130
hydraulics in, BR121–123
noise in, BR150
parking brakes, BR192–205
power boosters for, BR180–191
safety procedures for servicing, BR116–117
service brakes, BR109, BR112–113
servicing rotors in, BR173–177
types of brakes in, BR109–110
vacuum boosters for, BR181–184

valves in, BR131–133
See also antilock brake systems (ABS)
brake warning lights, BR193, EL325–326
    in ABS systems BR216–217
    brake wear indicator lights, EL327
    circuits for, EL315
    to indicate parking brakes on, BR193
    as indicator of problems, BR150, BR168
    switches and sensors for, EL325–327
brake wear indicator lights, EL327
braking, regenerative, BR220
brushes, in generators, EL291
bulbs
    diagnosing, EL316–318
    types of, EL309–311
    in warning lights, EL322

C

cables
    connections between, EL275
    jumper cables, HB66, EL267–269
    for parking brakes, BR199–202
calibration drift, EP481
caliper mounting brackets, BR159
calipers
    for disc brakes, BR159–163
    fluid leaking from, BR167
    low drag calipers, BR162–163
    removing and replacing, BR170–171
    repairing, BR171–173
calipers, vernier, HB78
camber angle, SS577–578
    adjusting, SS589–590
    demonstrating, SS582
    measuring, SS588
camshaft position (CMP) sensors, EP432
CAN bus, EP391
camshafts, BR184, EP362–363
carbon dioxide, EP499, EP500–501
carbon monoxide, HB90, EP454–455, EP500–501
carbon scrapers, HB61
carbon tracking, EP430
careers, automotive, HB38–41
    employers in, HB38–40
    preparation for, HB42–47
    work environment in, HB40–41
caster angle, SS578–579, SS582, SS590
catalysts, EP494
catalytic action, EP472
catalytic converters, EP366–367, EP397, EP472,
    EP477–478, EP494–495
Celsius temperature scale, HB74, BR116
**center high-mounted stop (brake) lights
    (CHMSLs),** EL315
central processing unit (CPU), EL321
charcoal canisters, EP495
charging current tests, EL301
charging systems, EL288–307
    components of, EL289–292
    diagnosis of, EL302–303

generators in, EL303–305
    instrument panel charge indicators, EL296–297
    operation of, EL292–296
    testing, EL298–302
charging voltage test, EL300–301
chemical generators, EL234
chemicals *See* hazardous materials and wastes
chisels, HB59
    air chisel sets, HB73
circuit breakers, EL238
    for accessory motors, EL335
    in headlight switches, EL313
    in permanent magnet motors, EL331
circuits, electrical. *See* electrical circuits
circuit testers (logic probes), EL241–242
clocksprings, EL343, SS547
closed-loop operation, EP462
coil on plug (COP) ignition systems, EP433
coil springs, SS552
coil-spring front suspensions, SS563–564
coil-spring rear suspensions, SS572–573
cold-cranking amps (CCA), EL256
combination valves, BR133
combustion, EP453–455
commitment, HB45
communication, HB45–47
    nonverbal, HB47
communications applications
    acronyms, decoding, EP446
    clear explanations, EP368
    communication strategies, BR136, EP484
    databases, searching, EP468
    dictionary, using, SS574
    electrical symbols, EL250
    exploded view diagrams, BR156
    finding information, EP434
    J1930 standards, EP502
    memos, writing, EL270
    new systems, SS548
    obtaining information from customers, EL286
    reading customer actions, BR136
    reading diagrams, BR178
    recording information, BR190
    researching specialty tools, EL350
    responsibilities in, EL328
    safety information, BR204
    schematic wiring diagrams, EL306
    scientific method, EP386
    service manuals, reading, SS592
    taking notes, BR118
    using technical illustrations, BR224
    VIN information, SS528
    words, decoding, SS574, EP414
commutators, EL274
composite headlights, EL313
composite master cylinders, BR125
compressed air, tools powered by, HB73
    safety in using, HB99–100
compressed natural gas (CNG), EP452
compression, cylinder, EP372
compression, measuring, EP372–374

compression ratios, EP361–662, EP540

compression rings, EP357

compression stroke of piston, EP360–362

compression testers, HB77

computers
  for active suspension systems, SS562
  in dealership service departments, HB39
  personal, HB65
  See also on-board diagnostic systems;
    powertrain control modules

computer scan tools. *See* scan tools

conductors, EL230, EL235–236

connecting rods, EP357–358, EP379

connectors (electrical), EL236
  repair of, EL236–237

controller area network (CAN) bus *See* CAN bus

control arms, SS556, SS558, SS564

control modules
  in ABS systems, BR213–214, BR217, BR221
  air bag, EL342
  body (BCM), EL315, EL331, EL337
  ignition, EP428
  See also powertrain control modules

control valves, BR183

conversions
  analog and digital signals, EP390
  fractions and decimal, HB74–76
  metric and customary, HB74–76
  temperature scales, BR116

coolants, EP380–384

cooling system pressure tests, EP380–381
  tools for, HB65

cooling system temperature tests, EP381–384

cooling systems, EP366
  diagnosing, EP380–384

cooling-combustion gas detectors, HB65

courtesy lights, EL314

CPR (cardiopulmonary resuscitation), HB97

crankcases, EP488–489

cranking vacuum tests, EP376–377

cranking voltage/current draw tests, EL280–282

crankshaft position (CKP) sensors, EP421–432

crankshafts, EL273–274, EP357–358, EP362–364
  noises from, EP379

crash sensors, EL342–343, SS546

creeper (tool), HB68

crowfoot wrench sets, HB54

cruise control systems
  diagnosing and repairing, EL339–340
  electronic systems, EL339
  electronic/vacuum systems, EL337–338

cruise control vacuum servos, EL337

current, EL230–231, 301

current flow, EL230–231, EL244
  in ignition coils, EP431
  in nonreversing motors, EL332
  in reversing motors, EL332

current ramping, EP406

customer
  questioning, EL286
  reading clues, BR136

cylinder blocks. *See* engine blocks

cylinder heads, EP358–359

cylinder leakage test, EP374

cylinder leakage testers, HB65

cylinder power balance test, EP375

cylinders, in engines, EP362–364
  compression tests on, EP372–374
  leakage tests on, EP374–375
  noises in, EP379

D

dampers, EP363–364

data bus, EP391, EP412

data link connectors (DLCs), EL345, EP391
  in OBD-II systems, EP473, EP476, EP483

data streams, EP391, EP465
  freeze-frame data in, EP474
  serial, EP481, EP483

databases, searching, EP468

daytime running lights (DRLs), EL309, EL315, EL327

dealerships, new car, HB38–39

decal, emission control information, EP498

deceleration, graphing, BR174

deceleration sensors (G-sensors), BR216

decimal numbers, conversions for, HB75

depth gauges, HB77

detonation, engine, EP400, EP454

diagnostic, EP473

DGMM. *See* multimeter, digital graphing (DGMM)

diagnostic executives, EP476

diagnostic flowcharts, EP478

diagnostic tools, HB65

diagnostic trouble codes (DTCs), EP408–411,
    EP473–478, EP480–483
  from air bag systems, EL345
  from ABS control modules, BR214
  from cruise control systems, EL337
  displays of, EP410–411
  indicator lights for, EL296–297
  interpreting codes, EP411
  interpreting serial data, EP481
  lab scopes for, EP478–479
  in OBD-II systems, EP408–411, EP475–483
  scan tools to read, BR218, EL242, EL339

diagnostics. *See* on-board diagnostic systems

diagonally split braking systems, BR113, BR130

diagrams
  diagnostic flowcharts, EP478
  electrical schematic diagrams, EL306
  exploded view, BR156
  reading, BR178
  technical illustrations, BR224
  wiring, EL29–240

dial indicators, HB77, SS525

diaphragm, EL348

dictionaries, EP468

diesel engines, EP356, EP358

digital displays, EL321, EL324

digital multimeters (DVOMs), HB68, EL241, EL317

digital ratio adapter controllers (DRAC), BR216

digital signals, EP390–391

digital storage oscilloscopes (lab scopes; DSOs), EP478–479

dimmer switches, EL313

diodes, EL247–248
in charging systems, EL292
clamping, EL247
light-emitting diodes (LEDs), EL248, EL311

direct current (DC), EL230
accessory motor circuits using, EL31, EL334
rectifying AC voltage to, EL293

direct ignition systems, EP433

discard diameter, BR152

disc brakes, BR109, BR112–113
brake master cylinder pistons in, BR122
brake pads and calipers on, BR169–173
construction of, BR159–161
diagnosing problems with, BR164–168
installing brake fluid for, BR115
operation of, BR161–163
power boosters for, BR181
quick-takeup master cylinders for, BR126–127
servicing rotors in, BR173–177

disc brake wear indicators, BR163

dismounting tires, SS521–522

displacement, engine, EP361

distributor ignition systems, EP429–430

distributorless ignition systems (DIS), EP420, EP432–433

distributors (in ignition system), EP420, EP429–430

diversity, workplace, HB45

door panel, removing and reinstalling, EL336

DOT. *See* Transportation, U.S. Department of (DOT)

drain pans, HB68

drills, electric, HB66

drill sets, HB66

drive belts and pulleys, safety around, HB100

drive cycles, EP473

drop lights, HB102

drum brakes, BR109, BR112–113
diagnosing problems with, BR145–150
duo-servo, BR142–143
leading-trailing, BR142
operation of, BR139–144
as parking brakes, BR139, BR193
removing, BR152
residual pressure check valves used with, BR133
servicing, BR151–155
types of, BR142

dual-braking systems, BR113, BR130–131

duo-servo drum brakes, BR142–143

duty cycles, EP423

dwell angles, EP423

dynamic (spin) balancing of tires, SS525, SS527

E

ears, protective equipment for, HB96

EGR valves, EP489–491

electrical and electronic systems
accessory motor circuits in, EL331–336
actuators, EP402–406
batteries in, EL253–257
brake warning lights, EL325–326
charge system indicator lights, EL296–297
charging systems in, EL289–296
cruise control systems, EL337–340
electrical components of, EL234–238
electronic components of, EL247–249
electronic lighting controls, EL314–315
electronic signals in, EP389–391
generators in, EL234, EL290–292
horns, EL348–349
instrument panel displays, EL320–324
lighting systems, EL309–319
relays, EP403
sensors, EP389–401
starting systems in, EL273–285
switches, EP400–401
wiring diagrams and symbols used for, EL239–240

electrical circuits, EL231, EL233
for accessory motors, EL331–336
diagrams of, EL239–240
grounded, EL245, EL323, EL335
for lighting systems, EL311–314
measurement of resistance in, EL244
schematic diagrams of, EL306
troubleshooting, EL243–246
voltage divider circuits, EP409
Wheatstone bridges, EP399

electrical safety, HB98–99, HB102, EL333
with hybrid vehicles, HB104
lockout/tagout for, HB93
with power tools, HB98–99, HB102
spikes, EP408

electrical schematic diagrams, EL306

electrical test equipment, EL240–243

electricity, EL229–233
calculating wattage, EL310
electromagnetism and, EL275, EL277
static electricity, HB92

electric locks, diagnosing, EL336

electric power tools, HB66. *See also* tools
safety, HB98–99, HB102

electrohydraulic brake systems, BR186

electrolytes, EL254–255, EL262

electromagnetic (analog) displays, EL320–321

electromagnetic fields, EL275

electromagnetic induction, EL290

electromagnetism, EL275, EL277

electronics, automotive. *See* electrical and electronic systems

electrostatic discharges (spikes; ESDs), EL249, EP408

emergencies, responding to, HB97

emergency brakes. *See* parking brakes

emission control systems, EP487–497
air injection system in, EP491–492
catalytic converters in, EP494–495
evaporative control system in, EP495–497
exhaust gas recirculation system in, EP489–491

positive crankcase ventilation system in, EP488–489
emissions testing, EP498–501
employability skills, HB45
employers, automotive, HB38–40
   material safety data sheets kept by, HB93
   "Right to Know" law and, HB90
electric motor-assisted power steering (EMPS), SS543
enabling criteria, EP473
engine, internal combustion, EP355
energy, alternative source, HB48
engine blocks, EP356–358, EP379
engine coolant recovery equipment, HB68
engine coolant temperature (ECT) sensors, EP394–395, EP420, EP443, EP466
engine displacement, calculating, EP361
engine performance
   calculating airflow for, EP438
   emission control systems in, EP487–497
   increasing oxygen in fuel for, EP451
   OBD-II systems for, EP471–474
   on-board diagnostic systems for, EP407–408, EP475–483
engine vacuum, EP376
   tests for, EP376–378
engines, compression-ignition, EP356
engines, internal combustion, EP355–359
   air induction systems for, EP437–442
   components of, EP356–359
   diagnosing noises in, EP378–379
   diagnosing problems in, EP371–378
   generators powered by, EL289
   jump starting, EL267–269
   octane requirements of, EP450
   operation of, EP360–364
   sensors in, EP389–413
   starting systems for, EL273
   systems in, EP364–367
engines, spark-ignition, EP355
Environmental Protection Agency (EPA), HB90
equipment, general workplace, HB64–73
ergonomics, HB96
ethanol, EP451
evacuation routes, HB93
evaporative control (EVAP) systems, EP480, EP495–497
evaporative emissions (EVAP) canisters, EP461
   analyzing, EP501
exhaust evacuation system, HB90
exhaust gas analyzers, EP500–501
exhaust gases, EP455
exhaust gas recirculation (EGR) systems, EP395, EP489–491
exhaust manifolds, EP366–367
exhaust smoke, EP357
exhaust stroke of piston, EP360, EP362
exhaust system backpressure test, EP377–378
exhaust systems, EP366–367, EP413
   oxygen sensors in, EP397–398, EP466
exhaust valves, EP359
exit doors and aisles, HB89, HB92–93

exploded view diagrams, BR156, BR224
extension cords, HB66
eyes, protective equipment for, HB63, HB94
   safety glasses, HB62

F

face shields, HB68, HB94
Fahrenheit temperature scale, BR116
failure records, EP473
fans, inspecting and testing, EP384
fasteners, HB79–84
feeler gauge, HB77
feet, protective equipment for, HB94–95
fender covers, HB68
field coil starters, EL274
field serviceable part, BR187
files (tools), HB62
finish, nondirectional, BR175
fire emergency plan, HB92
fire extinguishers, HB91
fire safety, HB91–93
first aid kits, HB97
fixed caliper disc brakes, BR161, BR170
flare-nut (tubing) wrenches, HB54
flasher units, EL316
flashlight, HB62
flat rates, HB42
fleet facilities, HB40
floating caliper disc brakes, BR161, BR170–171
floor jack, HB69, HB100–101
   safe use of, HB100–101
fluid-pressure gauges, SS541
fluids, analyzing, EP382
flywheels, EP363–364
four-channel ABS, BR212
four-stroke engines, EP360
four-wheel alignments, SS586
four-wheel-drive vehicles, BR217
fractions, conversions for, HB75
free air, EP445
freeze-frame data, EP474, EP483
frequency modulation (FM), EP390–391
friction, BR110–111
   and inertia, BR144
   kinetic, BR111
   in stopping, BR110
   wheel lockup and, BR207
front suspension systems, SS563–569
   coil-spring, SS563–564
   leaf-spring, SS570–571
   strut-type, SS564–568
   torsion bar, SS568–569
   twin I-beam, SS569
front-rear split braking systems, BR113, BR130
front-wheel-drive (FWD) vehicles, BR130
fuel cells, HB48
fuel filters, EP459
fuel injection systems
   electronic, EP461–462

multiport fuel injection, EP461–462
sensing induction airflows for, EP443–445
fuel injectors, EP464–465
fuel lines, EP460–461
fuel management sensors, EP465–467
fuel management system, EP456–467
    fuel metering system, EP461–462
    fuel supply system, EP456–461
    powertrain control modules in, EP462–467
    sensors in, EP465–467
fuel metering system, EP461–462
fuel mixture, checking, EP440
fuel pressure gauges, EP458
fuel pressure regulators, EP458–460
fuel pumps, EP457–458
fuel rails, EP459, EP461
fuel supply system, EP456–461
fuel systems, EP364–365
    combustion in, EP453–455
    fuel management system, EP456–457
    fuel metering system, EP461–462
    fuel supply system, EP456–461
    powertrain control modules in, EP462–467
    See also fuel injection systems
fuel tank caps, EP456, EP495–496
fuel tanks, EP456
fuel trim, EP480
fuel vapors, EP480, EP495–497
fuels
    air/fuel ratio, EP452
    calculating miles per gallon, EP463
    combustion of, EP453–455
    gaseous, EP452
    gasoline, EP449–451
    increasing oxygen in, EP451
fuse pullers, HB62
fuses, EL237, EL313
fusible links, EL237–238

G

gases, EP358
gasket scrapers, HB62
gaskets, HB84–85
gasoline, EP364–365, EP449–451
    calculating miles per gallon, EP463
    contamination of, EP459
    ethanol in, EP451
    fire prevention and, HB91–92
    increasing oxygen in, EP451
    vapors from, EP480, EP495–497
gas pressure, EP358
gauges, HB77–78
    belt-tension, HB67, EL300, SS539
    brake shoe adjusting, BR154–155
    diagnosing and servicing, EL324
    in electromagnetic displays, EL320–321
    fluid-pressure, SS541
    fuel pressure, EP458
    thermoelectric, EL322
    thickness, HB77

    thread-pitch, HB81
    vacuum, EP376–378
gear ratio, EL279
gearboxes, SS542–544
general workplace equipment, HB65–73
generator housings, EL292
generators, EL234, EL290–292
    action of, EL290
    servicing, EL303–304
    voltage regulators for, EL295–296
geometric centerline, SS583
grease guns, hand, SS535
grinding wheels, HB67
    machine guards for, HB98–100
    safe use of, HB98–100
guide pins, BR161

H

hacksaws, HB62
Hall-effect sensors, EP392–393, EP421–422
halogen lamps, EL310, EL317
hammers, HB60
hand levers, for parking brakes, BR193, BR199
hand tools, HB52–63
    proper use of, HB51–53, HB98
    safe use of, HB51–52, HB98
    storing and maintaining, HB51–53
    types of, HB53–63
    See also Tools
hands and arms
    ergonomics and, HB96
    protective equipment for, HB95
hazardous materials and wastes, HB90–91
    asbestos, HB95, BR116, BR140, BR154
    brake dust, BR116–117, BR145, BR169
    mercury, EP442
hazard warning lights, EL316
head gaskets, HB84–85
headlights
    aiming, EL318–319
    automatic controls for, EL314–315
    electrical circuits for, EL312–313
    replacing, EL317–318
    switches for, EL312–313
head, protective equipment for, HB96
heated glass, diagnosing, EL333
heated-film sensors, EP397
high-efficiency particulate air (HEPA) filter vacuum systems, HB95
high-intensity discharge (HID) lamps, EL311
hoists, HB69, HB102, BR116
honesty, HB45
honing, BR172
Hooke, Robert, SS557
horn relays, EL348–349
horns, EL348–349
horn switches, EL348–349
hoses, brake lines, BR109, BR112, BR129
hot-wire induction sensors, EP444
humidity, EP453

hybrid technology
    alternative energy sources, HB 48
    braking, regenerative, BR220
    coolant heat storage tanks, EP383
    electric-motor assisted power steering, SS543
    high voltage in hybrids, EL268
    hybrid power systems, EP365
    hybrid vehicle auxiliary battery, EL255
    hybrid warning lights, EL326
    safety precautions for hybrids, HB104
    tools for hybrids, HB86
hydraulic actuators, BR209, BR213–215
hydraulic boosters, BR184–186
hydraulic brake fluid. *See* brake fluid
hydraulic brake systems
    bleeding, BR133–135
    electrohydraulic, BR186
hydraulic circuits, BR130
hydraulic lifts, BR134
hydraulic power-assisted steering systems, SS539
hydraulic presses, HB69
hydraulic pressure, BR121–123
hydraulic pressure storage systems, BR189
hydraulic systems, BR121–137, BR217
hydraulics, BR121–123
hydrogen, as fuel, HB48
hydrometers, EL258–259, EP381

idle air control (IAC) valves, EP403–404, EP440
idle speed, checking, EP440
ignition coils, EP418–420
ignition control modules, EP428
ignition modules, EP423, EP425
ignition oscilloscopes, EP425
ignition switches, EL273, EP418, SS532
ignition systems, EP355–356, EP365, EP418–433
    accessory motors controlled by, EL335
    ignition coils in, EP418–420
    ignition modules in, EP423, EP425
    ignition switches in, EP418
    ignition wires in, EP425
    powertrain control modules in, EP420–423
    spark distribution system in EP429–433
    spark plugs in, EP426–428
ignition wires, EP425
ignition wrench sets, HB54
I/M 240 programs, EP498
impact sensors. *See* crash sensors
impact sockets, HB73
impact wrenches, HB73
incandescent bulbs, EL309–310
included angle, SS581
incremental adjusters, on drum brakes, BR143
independent service facilities, HB39
indexing marks, EP423
index mark, SS521
indicator lights, EL296–297
    for air bag systems, EL343
Industry Planning Council (IPC), HB37
initiative, HB45

inertia, and friction, BR144
inertia switches, EP457
inflation pressure, of tires, SS512–513
inflator modules, EL342
information, recording, BR190
inspection/maintenance (I/M) ready status, EP474
inspection mirrors, HB62
instrument panels
    brake warning lights on, EL325
    charge indicators on, EL296–297
    diagnosing and servicing, EL324
    displays on, EL320–324
    lighting of, EL314
insulators, EL230
intake air temperature (IAT) sensors, EP394–395,
    EP420, EP443, EP466
intake manifolds, EP364, EP440–441
    for vacuum boosters for brakes, BR181–182
intake stroke of piston, EP360
intake valves, EP359
integral braking systems, BR209–210
integral master cylinders, BR124
integral parking brakes, BR193
    rear disc, BR195–196
    rear drum, BR194
interior lighting, EL314
internal combustion engines. *See* engine, internal
    combustion
International Standards Organization (ISO) flare,
    BR129
internal threads, repairing, HB83–84
IPC (Industry Planning Council), HB37

J1930 standards for diagnostics, EP471, EP502
jacks, HB69, HB100–101
jump starting, EL267–269
jumper cables, HB66, EL267–269
jumper wires, EL243
jumper wire set, HB62

K

Karman-Vortex path sensors, EP444
key-off loads (parasitic drains), EL253, EL261, EL263
kinetic energy, converting, BR222
kinetic friction, BR111
knock sensors (KS), EP400, EP420

L

lab scopes (digital storage oscilloscopes; DSOs),
    EP478–479
ladder safety, HB89
lateral acceleration sensors, BR216
lathe, on-car, BR175–176
leading-trailing drum brakes, BR142
leaf springs, SS553
leaf-spring front suspensions, SS570–571
levers, BR188, BR197, SS536
license lights, EL313

lift point, HB100
lifts, HB100–101, BR134
light-emitting diodes (LEDs), EL248, EL311
    in instrument panel displays, EL321
    in optical sensors, EP394, EP422–423
lighting systems, EL308–329
    automatic controls, EL314–315
    brake warning lights, EL325–326
    diagnosing problems in, EL316–318
    electrical circuits for, EL311–314
    electronic controls for, EL314–315
    high-intensity discharge head-lamps, EL311
    instrument panel displays, EL320–324
    light sources, EL309–311
    warning lights, EL315–316
lights
    automatic controls for, EL314
    drop, HB102
    flashlights, HB62
    headlights, EL312–313
    headlights, aiming, EL318–319
    light-emitting diodes (LEDs) for, EL248
    replacing, EL317–318
    test lights, HB63, EL241
    timing lights, EP430
    trouble/work lights, HB62
    See also warning lights
liquid crystal displays (LCDs), EL321–322
liquified petroleum gas (LPG), EP452
listening skills, HB46
live axle, SS560
load devices, EL238
load index (load range), SS512
load-leveling sensors, SS554
load-sensing proportioning valves, BR132
load sensors, EP395–397
load tests, EL260, EP498
lock washers, HB81
lockout/tagout, HB93
logic probes (electronic circuit testers), EL241–242
low drag calipers, BR162–163
lubricants, BR176
    for ball joints, SS558
    bead lubricants, SS522
    for threads, HB83–84
lubrication systems, EP365–366, EP384–385
lug nuts (wheel fasteners), SS517–518
lungs, protection for, HB95

M

machine guards, HB99
MacPherson struts
    camber adjustments on, SS589
    caster angle on vehicles with, SS578, SS590
    front, SS565–566
    rear, SS573
MAF values, calculating, EP424
magnetic fields, EL292–293
magnetic pulse generators, EP392
magnetic pulse sensors, EP421

magnetism, EL277
malfunction indicator lamp (MIL), EL297
    activated by fuel vapors, EP480
    controlled by powertrain control modules,
        EP404
    in OBD-II systems, EP477, EP483
    in on-board diagnostic systems, EP407–408,
        EP471
mallets, HB60
manifold absolute pressure (MAP), EP453
manifold absolute pressure (MAP) sensors,
        EP395–369, EP467
    in calculating airflow, EP443
    in combustion process, EP453
    in ignition system, EP420
    testing, EP482
manometers, EP442
manual bleeding of hydraulic braking systems,
        BR133–135
mass airflow (MAF) sensors, EP396, EP444, EP467
    in ignition system, EP420
    MAF values calculated by, EP424
master cylinder fluid reservoirs
    diagnosing problems with, BR127
    installing brake fluid in, BR115
master cylinders. See brake master cylinders
master puller sets, HB69
master technician, HB35
material safety data sheet (MSDS), HB93, HB97
math applications
    ABS slip ratio, BR210
    airflow, calculating, EP438
    angle of incline, BR203
    brake pedal ratio, BR183
    calculating resistance, EL282
    camber angle, measuring, SS588
    carbon dioxide, calculating, EP499
    compression, measuring, EP374
    engine displacement, calculating, EP361
    hydraulic pressure, calculating, BR123
    MAF values, calculating, EP424
    MAP sensor, testing, EP482
    metric system, EL334
    miles per gallon, calculating, EP463
    Ohm's law, EL232, EL257
    out-of-round brake drums, BR149
    rate of change, determining, EP405
    rotor thickness, measuring, BR177
    sine waves, EL294
    spring loads, calculating, SS572
    temperatures, converting, BR116
    tire diameter, determining SS526
    variable-ratio steering graphs, reading, SS543
    watts, calculating, EL310
math skills, HB43
measurement tools, HB76–77
measuring systems, HB74–75
mechanical generators, EL234
memory holders, EL265
memos, writing, EL270
mercury (element), EP442

metering valves, BR131, BR135
metric system, HB74–75
  conversions, HB74–75
  prefixes, EL334
micrometer, HB77
  brake drum, BR152
MIL. *See* malfunction indicator lamp
miles per gallon, calculating, EP473
monitors, EP473
motors
  accessory, EL331–336
  diagnosing problems with, EL334–336
  in electronic rack-and-pinion power steering
    systems, SS545
  nonreversing, EL332
  permanent magnet, EL331
  pneumatic, HB52
  reversing, EL332
  stepper, EL339, EP403–404
mounting tires, SS522–525
MSDS. *See* material safety data sheet
mufflers, EP367
multimeters, EL 240–241
  digital, EL241, EL317
  digital graphing (DGMM), EL242
multiport fuel injection (MFI) systems, EP461–462
  fuel pressure regulators in, EP459–460
  replacing fuel injectors in, EP465

N

**National Automotive Technicians Education Foundation
  (NATEF),** HB37, HB42
**National Institute for Automotive Service Excellence
  (ASE),** HB35
  Automotive Service Excellence (ASE) certification
    exams, HB37, HB42
**National Institute for Occupational Safety and Health
  (NIOSH),** HB95
negative temperature coefficient (NTC) sensors, EP394
neon lights, EL311
**NIOSH. National Institute for Occupational Safety and
  Health,** HB95
nitrogen oxide, EP489
noises
  in brakes, BR150
  charging system noise, EL303
  from disc brakes, BR167–168
  in engines, diagnosing, EP378–379
  protection for ears against, HB96
  from tires, SS513–514
no-load test, EP498
nonintegral braking systems, BR209–210
nonreversing motors, EL332
nonvented rotors, BR160
note taking, BR118
nuts,
  interference, BR201
  jam, BR201
  wheel, tightening, BR155

O

OBD-II monitors, EP475–476
OBD-II systems, EP471–474
  components of, EP473
  diagnostic trouble codes in, EP476–483
  evaporative control system in, EP496–497
  exhaust gas recirculation systems and, EP490
  monitors for, EP475–476
  terminology of, EP473–474
  See also on-board diagnostic systems
**Occupational Safety and Health Administration
  (OSHA),** HB89
  footwear standards of, HB94
  lockout/tagout required by, HB93
  safety notices required by, HB92–93
octane number, EP450
odometers, EL321–322
Ohm's law, EL232–233
  applied to series circuits, EL257
  to calculate resistance, EL232, EL282
  to calculate wattage, EL310
  resistance measurement in, EL244
ohmmeters, EP419–420
oil
  contaminated, EP501
  used, disposal of, HB91
  waste-oil receptacles for, HB72
oil cans, HB69
oil filter, EP384
oil filter wrench, HB70
oil pumps, EP365–366
oil rings, EP357
on-board diagnostic systems, EP407, EP471–474
  diagnostic trouble codes for, EP408–411,
    EP475–483
  evaporative control system in, EP495–497
  J1930 standards for, EP471, EP502
  OBD-II systems, EP471–474
  OBD-II terminology for, EP473–474
  powertrain control modules in, EP407–408
  See also OBD-II systems
on-car brake lathes, BR175–176
one-channel ABS, BR211–212
open circuits, EL243, EL335
open-circuit voltage (OCV) test, EL258–259
operator's manual, HB64
optical (photodiode) sensors, EP394, EP422–423
oscilloscopes, EL242
  ignition oscilloscopes, EP425
  lab scopes (digital storage oscilloscopes),
    EP478–479
OSHA. *See* Occupational Safety and Health
  Administration (OSHA)
output terminal tests, EL304
outside micrometers, HB77
overrunning clutches, EL278–279
oversteer, BR223
oxy-acetylene torches, HB70
oxygen, in fuel, EP451
oxygen sensors, EP397–398, EP413, EP466

P

palladium, EP472

panhard rods (track bars), SS572–573

parallel circuits, EL231, EL233

parasitic drains (key-off loads), EL253, EL261, EL263

park switches, EL333

parking brake equalizers, BR199–200

parking brake switches, EL326

parking brakes, BR109, BR143, BR192–205

    auxiliary, BR193, BR198, BR202

    ball-ramp, BR196

    cam-rod, BR196

    controls for, BR199–200

    diagnosis and repair of, BR168, BR200–202

    drum brakes as, BR139, BR193

    equalizer for, BR199–200

    integral, BR193

parking lights, EL313

parts catalog, electronic, HB39

parts cleaning tanks, HB70

parts manager, HB41

Pascal, Blaise, BR134

Pascal's law, BR121

passive tests, EP473

pathogens, bloodborne, HB97

pawl, BR199

PCV valves, EP488–489

pedestal grinders, HB67

permanent magnet (PM) sensors, EP392–393

permanent magnet motors, EL331

permanent magnet starters, EL274

personal protective equipment (PPE), HB94–96

photocell, EL234

photodiode sensors. *See* optical sensors

photodiodes, EP394

photoelectric generators, EL234

pickup tools, HB61–62

piezoelectric generators, EL234

pinion gears, EL278–279

piston rings, EP357

pistons

    in composite master cylinders, BR125

    for disc brakes, BR162–163

    for drum brakes, BR141

    hydraulic pressure in, BR121–122

    in internal combustion engines, EP355–358

    noises from, EP379

    power pistons, BR182–183

    in quick-takeup master cylinders, BR126–127

    strokes of, EP360–362

piston slap, EP379

pitch, of fasteners, HB80–81

planetary gears, EL279, EL285

pliers, HB57

    battery terminal, HB61

    snap-ring, HB70

    wheel weight, SS521

ply, SS508

pneumatic motors, HB52

pneumatic tools, HB52, HB73

    safe use of, HB89–90

polarity, EL241

pollutants, EP488

positive crankcase ventilation (PCV) systems, EP488–489

positive temperature coefficient (PTC) sensors, EP394

potentiometers, EP395

power (electrical), EL244

power brake boosters, BR109

    diagnosing problems with, BR187–189

    hydraulic boosters, BR184–186

    push rod adjustment, BR128

    vacuum boosters, BR181–184

power flows, EP362–364

power mirrors, EL334

power pistons, BR182–183

power rack-and-pinion steering gearboxes, SS542–SS544

power seats, EL334

power side switches, EP400–401

power steering. *See* steering systems, power-assisted

power steering fluid, BR186, SS540–541

power steering pressure switches, SS544

power steering pump belts, BR189, SS539

power steering pumps, SS539–540

power stroke of piston, EP360, EP362–364

power tools. *See* electric power tools

power windows, EL335

power-assisted steering systems, SS531, SS538–547

    electronic rack-and-pinion power steering, SS545–546

    power rack-and-pinion steering gearbox for, SS542–544

    power steering fluid for, SS540–541

    power steering pumps for, SS539–540

    variable-assist power steering, SS544–545

powertrain control modules (PCMs), EL321, EL337, EP407–408, EP462–467

    airflow calculated by, EP438

    diagnostic trouble codes read by, EP408–411

    in electronic rack-and-pinion power steering systems, SS545–546

    electronically operated throttle and, EP439

    in evaporative control systems, EP497

    in exhaust gas recirculation systems, EP489–490

    fuel management sensors and, EP465–467

    in fuel metering system, EP461–462

    fuel pump relay controlled by, EP457

    in ignition system, EP420–423

    incorrect sensor readings sent to, EP444–445

    inputs from sensors to, EP389–391

    load sensors for, EP395–397

    OBD-II diagnostic trouble codes set by, EP477–478

    OBD-II monitors performed by, EP475–476

    in OBD-II systems, EP473, EP479–480

    in on-board diagnostic systems, EP407–409

outputs controlled by, EP404
relays and, EP403
sensor signals converted by, EP409
in sequential multiport fuel injection systems, EP461–462
solenoids and, EP402
POZIDRIV® screwdrivers, HB58
PPE. *See* personal protective equipment (PPE)
pressure
absolute, EP453
barometric, EP453
engine, measuring, EP442
hydraulic, BR121–122
measuring, EP442
temperature and, EP358
vapor pressure, EP493
pressure bleeders, BR135
pressure bleeding of hydraulic braking systems, BR135
pressure differential valves, BR131
printed circuits, EL236
PROM (programmable read-only memory) chips, EP408
for OBD-II systems, EP473
proportioning valves, BR132, BR208
prying tools, HB60
pullers
battery terminal, HB61
fuse, HB62
master puller sets, HB69
spark plug boot, HB70
steering wheel pullers, SS531–532
tie-rod, SS590
pulleys, HB100
pulse width, EP461–462
pulse width modulation (PWM), EP391
pumps
in ABS systems, BR214
in air injection system, EP492
fuel pumps, EP457–458
leak detection, EP496
power steering pumps, SS539–540
punches, HB59
pyrometers, EP381

Q

questioning customers, EL286
quick-takeup master cylinders, BR126–127

R

rack-and-pinion steering gear system, SS531, SS534–535
electronic, SS545–546
power gearboxes for, SS542–544
radial tires, SS508
radiator pressure caps, EP380
random access memory (RAM) chips, EP408
ratchets, air, HB73

rate of change, determining, EP405
ratio, air/fuel, EP452
reading skills, HB43
rear antilock brake systems (RABS), BR211–212
rear disc integral parking brakes, BR195–196
rear drum integral parking brakes, BR194
rear suspension systems, SS570–573
coil-spring, SS572–573
leaf-spring, SS570–571
strut-type, SS573
rear wheel alignment, SS587
rear-wheel antilock systems (RWAL), BR211–212
hydraulic actuators in, BR214–215
wheel speed sensors in, BR216
rear-wheel-drive (RWD) vehicles, BR130
recirculating-ball steering gear system, SS533–534
rectification, of AC voltage, EL293
recycling, HB91
reinitialization, EL266
relay and solenoid starters, EL276, EL284
relays, EP403
testing, EP403
remote starter switches, HB66
repair orders, completing, HB44
reserve (backup) power supplies, EL342–343
reserve capacity, EL256
residual pressure check valves, BR133, BR148
resistance (electrical), EL231
calculating, EL282
excessive, EL245
finding, EP399
measurement of, EL244
and Wheatstone bridges, EP399
resistors
positive temperature coefficient (PTC), EL331
potentiometers, EP395
thermistors, EP394–395
resistor spark plugs, EP426
respirators, HB95
respect for others, HB45
responsibility, HB45
retail facilities, HB39
reversing motors, EL332
rheostats, EL312
"Right to Know" law, HB90
rim diameter, SS516
rim width, SS516
rivets, HB92
road crown, SS578
road tests, SS585
rocker arm, EP362
rotating tires, SS515
rotor, generator, EL291
rotor assemblies, generator, EL291
rotor runout, BR164
rotors, brake, BR159–160
measuring thickness, BR177
servicing, BR173–177
run-flat tires, SS508

S

SAE markings (on bolts), HB79
safety, HB88–105, BR204
  ABS pedal pulsations, BR216
  accident prevention, HB89–93
  air bags, EL344–345, SS546
  antilock brake systems (ABS), BR208
  asbestos, HB95, BR116, BR140, BR154
  automotive waste disposal, HB92
  batteries, EL235, EL254–255, EL258–259,
    EL265, EL266–267
  batteries, charging, EL255
  batteries, disconnecting, EL265
  batteries, hot, EL267
  battery acid, EL266–267
  bleeding ABS systems, BR219
  brake dust, BR117, BR145, BR153, BR169,
    BR189
  brake fluid, BR114–115, BR125, BR128
  brakes, BR167
  brake repairs, BR172
  brake shoe linings, BR140
  brake warning lights, EL325
  cable connections, EL275
  carbon monoxide, HB90, EP454, EP500
  catalytic converters, EP495
  charging systems, EL303
  clothing, EP372
  coil springs, SS573
  compressed gases, HB103
  compressed springs, SS551
  coolant, EP380
  detonation, engine, EP400
  DOT tire safety standard codes, SS513
  EGR valves, EP491
  electrical, HB31
  electrical circuits, EL333
  electronic modules, EL335
  emergency response, HB97
  engines, running, EL301
  ergonomics and, HB96
  evacuation routes, HB93
  exhaust evacuation system, HB90
  exhaust systems, EP413
  exposed areas, EP372
  fire safety, HB91–93
  first-aid, HB97
  floor jack, HB100–101
  fluids, EP382
  fuel filters, EP460
  fuel system leaks, EP457–458
  fuses, EL237
  gasoline, EP365, EP451
  gasoline vapors, EP449, EP480
  gauges, thermoelectric, EL322
  gloves, insulated, HB104
  grinding wheel, HB98–100
  grounding wires, EP373
  halogen lamps, EL311
  hand tools, use of, HB51–52
  hazardous materials and wastes, HB90–92
  headlight aimers, EL318
  HID lamps, EL311
  hot engine oil, EP384
  with hybrid vehicles, HB104
  hydraulic boosters, BR185
  hydraulic system, BR217
  hydrogen peroxide, EP472
  ignition sparks, EP419
  jumper cables, EL269
  jumper wires, EL243
  jump starting, EL267, EP408
  ladders, HB89
  load-leveling sensors, SS554
  load tests, EL260
  lock-out/tag-out, HB93
  manufacturer recommended procedures, HB89
  mercury, EP442
  Occupational Safety and Health Administration,
    HB89
  overriding safety devices, EP458
  oxygen sensors, EP413
  parking brakes, BR143, BR193, BR201
  PCM servicing, EP408
  personal protective equipment, HB94–97
  power steering fluid, BR186
  precautions, HB89–90
  probes, use of, EL242
  proper tire inflation, SS512, SS514
  regulations, HB89
  reserve power supply, EL343
  responsibilities for, EL328
  in road tests, BR155, BR170–171, BR220,
    EP500, SS585, SS591
  safety glasses, BR219
  safety notices, HB92–93
  in servicing brake systems, BR115, BR117
  servicing suspension springs, SS568
  servo solenoid valves, EL340
  soldering, EL246
  solid-state components, EL249
  spark plugs, EP426
  springs, SS559
  steering wheels, installing and removing, SS591
  for strut suspensions, SS566
  sulfuric acid, EL262
  temperature and pressure, EP358
  for terminals, EL236
  test lights, EL241
  testing air bag systems, EL341
  throttles, EP439, EP440
  tightening fasteners, SS520
  tire changers (mounting machines), SS522,
    SS525
  tire patch, internal, SS523
  tools, insulated, HB104
  tools, specialized hybrid, HB104
  tools, use of, HB98–100
  valve cores, SS523
  visual clues, BR204
  voltage, EL302

welding, HB85, HB103
wheel fasteners, SS517
wheel lockups, BR211
windows, power, EL335
workplace equipment, use of, HB100–103
safety glasses, HB62, BR219
safety notices, HB92–93
safety stands (axle stands), HB67, HB101
scan tools (scanners), HB65, EL242
   to test on actuator, EP405
   connected to data link connector, EP391
   to diagnose air bag system, EL345
   diagnostic modes for, EP483
   diagnostic trouble codes read by, EL339,
      EP410–41, EP476
   interactive diagnostic mode in, EP471
   snapshot testing by, EP411
schematic diagrams, EL306
Schrader valves, EP458
science applications
   catalytic action, EP472
   deceleration, graphing, BR174
   electrolytes, EL262
   electromagnetism, EL277
   fluids, analyzing, EP382
   friction, BR110
   gas pressure, EP358
   generator action, EL290
   grounded circuits, EL323
   hydraulics, BR134
   ignition coils, EP431
   increasing oxygen in fuel, EP451
   inertia and friction, BR144
   kinetic energy, converting, BR222
   levers, BR188, BR197, SS536
   magnetism, EL277
   pressure and vacuum, measuring, EP442
   resistance, finding, EP399
   resistance, measuring, EL244
   sensor signals, EP409
   spring elasticity, SS557
   switching transistors, EL346
   torque, measuring, SS519
   vapor pressure, EP493
   Wheatstone bridges, EP399
   wheel alignment angles, SS582
science skills, HB43
scientific method, EP386
scores (on rotors), BR169
screw extractor sets, HB70
screw threads, HB79–80
screwdrivers, HB58
screws, HB79, HB82
scrub radius (steering offset), SS580–581
sealants
   anaerobic, HB84–85
   aerobic, HB85
sealed-beam headlights, EL313
seat belt pretensioners, EL346
seat belt retractors, EL346
seat belts, EL341, EL346–347

seat covers, HB70
secondary cells (batteries), EL255
self-adjusters, on drum brakes, BR143, BR151,
   BR154–155
self-tapping screws, HB82
semiconductors, EL247
sensors, EP389–413
   in active suspension systems, SS562
   airflow, diagnosing failures of, EP444–445
   in antilock brake systems, BR208–209
   barometric pressure (BARO), EP467
   brake fluid level, EL326–327
   calibration drift in, EP481
   camshaft position (CMP), EP432
   crankshaft position (CKP), EP421–422
   crash, EL242–243, SS546
   deceleration, BR216
   in distributorless ignition systems, EP432–433
   engine coolant temperature (ECT),
      EP394–395, EP420, EP443, EP466
   of engine speed and position, EP392–394
   in exhaust gas recirculation systems, EP395,
      EP489
   fuel management, EP465–467
   Hall-effect, EP392–393, EP421–422
   heated-film, EP444
   heated oxygen, EP397
   hot-wire induction, EP444
   in ignition system, EP420–421
   intake air temperature (IAT), EP394–395,
      EP420, EP443, EP466
   Karman-Vortex path, EP444
   knock (KS), EP400
   lateral acceleration, BR216
   load, EP395–397
   load-leveling, SS554
   low brake fluid level, EL326
   magnetic pulse, EP421
   manifold absolute pressure (MAP), EP395–396,
      EP443, EP453, EP467, EP482
   mass airflow, EP396, EP424, EP444, EP467
   negative temperature coefficient (NIC), EP394
   in OBD-II systems, EP480
   occupant classification, EL342
   optical (photodiode), EP394, EP422–423
   oxygen, EP397–398, EP466
   permanent magnet (PM), EP392–393
   positive temperature coefficient (PTC), EP394
   replacing, EP411–413
   signal frequencies generated by, EP389–391
   signals of, connecting, EP409
   signals produced by, EP389–391
   signals, nonverbal, HB47
   steering angle, SS547
   thermistors as, EL248, EP394–395
   throttle position, EP395, EP420, EP440,
      EP465–466
   tire-pressure, SS513, SS522
   titania oxygen, EP398, EP466
   vane-type, EP444
   variable resistance, EP394–395

vehicle speed (VSS), EL321
voltage generating, EP397–400
volume airflow (VAF), EP467
wheel speed, BR216
wide-band, EP466
zirconia oxygen, EP397–398, EP466
sensor signals, connecting, EP409
serial data streams, EP474, EP481, EP483
series circuits, EL231
    Ohm's law applied to, EL257
serpentine belts, EL298–299
service brake systems, BR109, BR112–113
service departments, dealership, HB39
service dispatchers, HB40
service history, HB44, EP372
service managers, HB41
service manuals, SS548, SS592
service plug, on hybrids, HB104
Service Technicians Society (STS), HB37
service consultant, HB40
servo solenoid valves, EL340
setback (angle), SS581
setscrews, HB82
shock absorbers, SS554–556
supervisors, HB40
short circuits, EL245
short-arm/long-arm (SLA) system, SS558, SS589–590
SI (System of International Units). *See* metric system
side marker lights, EL313
sidewall markings on tires, SS511–513
signal frequencies, EP389–391
signals, electronic, EP389–391
sine waves, EL294
single-diaphragm vacuum boosters, BR182–184
skids, BR207
skin, injuries to, HB95
sliding caliper disc brakes, BR162, BR170–171
slip rings, EL291
smoke machine, EP445
snap rings, HB81
snapshot testing, EP411
snap-throttle vacuum tests, EP376
Society of Automotive Engineers (SAE), HB37, BR114
    J1930 standards of, EP471, EP502
socket sets, HB55
sockets, impact, HB73
soldering, EL246
soldering guns, HB66
soldering irons, HB66
solenoid starters, EL275–277
    testing, EL284, EP403
solenoids, EP402
    starter, EL273–274, EL284
solid-state components, EL247–248
solid-state digital displays, EL321
solvents, BR173
spark distribution system, EP429–433
spark plug boot pullers, HB70
spark plug gap gauge, HB78

spark plugs, EP355, EP426–428
    carbon particles near, EP373
    spark duration and, EP419
spark plug sockets, HB56
spark testers, EP419
speaking skills, HB46
specialized tools
    ball joint presses, SS535
    bead separator tools, SS522
    defined, HB51
    drag link socket wrench, SS535
    exhaust gas analyzers, EP500–501
    inner tie rod end tools, SS590
    to make ISO flares, BR129
    pitman arm pullers, SS535
    for power-assisted steering systems, SS535
    for pressure bleeding, BR135
    researching, EL350
    steering wheel puller tools, SS531
    tie rod pullers, SS590
    for wheel alignment, SS586
    See also tools
specialty centers, HB39
specific gravity, EL258–259
speed
    cruise control systems for, EL337–340
    deceleration sensors for, BR216
    stopping distances and, BR174
    tire speed ratings, SS512
speed sensors. *See* wheel speed sensors
speedometers, EL321
spikes (electrostatic discharges), EL249, EP408
spills, HB90
split point, BR132
spontaneous combustion, HB92
spool valves, BR185
spring-assisted shock absorbers, SS554–555
springs, SS552–554
    air, SS553–554
    calculating loads on, SS572
    stressing, SS557
sprung weight, SS552
stability control, in ABS systems, BR223
stabilizer (anti-sway) bars, SS556
starter drive assemblies, EL278–279
starter no-load bench tests, EL283–284
starter relays, EL273–274
starter solenoids, EL273–274
    testing, EL284
starters, EL273–274
starting systems, EL273–274
    components of, EL274
    diagnosing, EL280–284
    operation of, EL275–279
    servicing, EL285
star wheel, BR151
static angle, SS578
static balancing of tires, SS525
static electricity, EL249
static friction, BR111

stator assemblies, EL291
stator windings, EL291
steering, BR223
steering angle sensor, SS547
steering axis inclination (SAI), SS580
steering column couplers, SS533
steering columns, SS532–533
steering gear systems, SS533–535
steering knuckle, SS564
steering offset (scrub radius), SS580–581
steering ratio, SS537
   variable-ratio steering graphs of, SS543
steering systems
   components of, SS531–535
   electronic rack-and-pinion power, SS545–546
   hydraulic power-assisted, SS539
   power-assisted, SS531, SS538–547
   rear wheel, SS535
   special tools for, SS535
   steering ratios, SS537
   variable-assist power steering, SS544–545
   See also electric motor-assisted power steering (EMPS)
steering wheel puller tool, SS531
steering wheels, SS531–532, SS546, SS591
   air bags attached to, SS546
   removing, SS532
   in steering ratio, SS537
step-bore cylinders, BR126
stepper motors, EL339, EP403–404
stethoscopes, automotive, HB65, EP378
stoichiometric ratio, EP452
stopping distances, BR174
strobe light, SS527
strut compressor tools, SS566–567
strut-type front suspensions, SS564–568
STS (Service Technicians Society), HB37
superchargers, EP441
supplemental restraint systems (air bags; SRS),
    EL341–347, SS546
   components of, EL341–343
   disarming, SS532
   operation of, EL344–345
   seat belts, EL346–347
   service manuals for, SS548
suspension systems
   active, SS562
   alignment angles affected by, SS578
   anti-sway bars in, SS556
   automatic level control, SS554
   axles in, SS560
   ball joints in, SS558–560
   components of, SS551–552
   control arms in, SS556, SS558
   double A-arm, SS563
   front, SS563–569
   leaf spring, SS570–571
   rear, SS570–573
   shock absorbers in, SS554–556
   springs in, SS552–554
   strut-type rear, SS573
   wheel bearings in, SS560–561

switches, EL238, EP400–401
   brake light, EL326–327
   dimmer, EL313
   ground side, EP401
   headlight, EL312–314
   horn, EL348–349
   ignition, EL273, EP418, SS532
   ignition modules as, EP423
   inertia, EP457
   multifunction, EL313
   park, EL333
   parking brake, EL326
   power side, EP400–401
   power steering pressure switches, SS544
   remote starter, HB66
   switching transistors, EL346
symbols, electrical, EL240, EL250
System of International Units (SI; metric system),
    HB74–75

T

tachometer, HB77
tail lights, EL313
tail pipes, EP367, EP452
tandem (dual) diaphragm vacuum boosters, BR184
tap and die sets, HB71
tape measures, HB77
teamwork, HB45
technical illustrations, using, BR224
technicians, automotive, HB35–47
   employers of, HB38–40
   hand tools owned by, HB51–63
   master technician, HB35
   safety responsibilities of, EL328
   skills needed by, HB43–47
   work environment of, HB40–41
telephone skills, HB46
temperature
   of air, EP454
   battery performance and, EL256, EL259–260
   converting between scales, BR116
   pressure and, EP358
   pyrometers to measure, EP381
   thermistors to sense, EL248
   voltage regulation and, EL295
terminal voltage, EL257
terminals (electrical), EL236
test lights, HB63, EL241
thermistors, EL248, EP394–395
thermoelectric gauges, EL322
thermostat, EP381, EP383
thickness gauges, HB77
thread dressings, HB83
thread inserts, HB81
thread-locking compounds, HB84
thread-pitch gauges, HB81
thread repair kits, HB71
three-channel ABS, BR212
throttle, electronically generated, EP439
throttle bodies, EP339–440, EP364

throttle position sensors (TPS), EP395, EP420, EP440, EP465–466

thrust angle, SS583

thrust line, SS583

tie rods, SS534, SS591

timing lights, EP430

tire changers (mounting machines), SS521–522

tire inflator chucks, HB77

tire pressure, SS513, SS584

tire pressure gauges, HB78

tire-pressure sensors, SS513, SS522

tires
    in alignment pre-check, SS584
    balancing, SS525, SS527
    construction of, SS507–510
    diameter, determining, SS526
    dismounting, SS521–522
    inflation pressure of, SS513
    patching of, internal SS523
    inspecting, SS513–515
    mounting, SS522–525
    rotating, SS515
    sidewall markings on, SS511–513
    tire and wheel assemblies, SS518
    See also wheels

tire treads, SS510

titania oxygen sensors, EP398, EP466

toe, SS579–580, SS590–591

tone wheel, BR209

tools
    air chisel sets, HB73
    air compressors, HB73
    air pressure regulators, HB73
    air ratchets, HB73
    Allen wrench sets, HB53
    axle stands, HB67, HB101
    battery carriers, EL266
    battery chargers, HB67
    battery post cleaners, HB61
    battery terminal pliers, HB61
    battery terminal pullers, HB61
    bearing packer, HB67
    belt-tension gauges, HB67, EL300, SS539
    bench (pedestal) grinders, HB67
    brake lathes, standard, BR176
    carbon scrapers, HB67
    chisel holders, HB59
    chisels, HB59
    compressed-air blowguns, HB61
    compression testers, HB77
    constant velocity universal joint service tools, HB67
    creeper, HB68
    depth gauges, HB77
    diagnostic tools, HB65
    dial indicators, HB77, SS525
    digital multimeters, HB68, EL241, EL317
    drain pans, HB68
    drills, HB66
    ear protection, HB96
    electrical test equipment, EL240–243

electronic battery testers, EL261
engine coolant recovery equipment, HB68
ergonomics and, HB96
extension cords, HB66
face shields, HB68, HB94
feeler gauge sets, HB77
fender covers, HB68
files, HB62
flashlight, HB62
floor jack, HB69, HB100–101
fluid-pressure gauges, SS541
fuse pullers, HB62
gasket scrapers, HB62
hacksaws, HB62
hammers, HB60
hand grease guns, SS535
hoists, HB69, HB102
hydraulic presses, HB69
hydrometers, EL258–259, EP381
ignition oscilloscopes, EP425
impact sockets, HB73
impact wrenches, HB73
inner tie-rod end, SS590
inspection mirrors, HB62
jumper cables, HB66
jumper-wire sets, HB62
lab scopes (digital storage oscilloscopes), EP478–479
manometers, EP442
master puller sets, HB69
measurement, HB76–77
memory holders, EL265
ohmmeters, EP419–420
oil cans, HB69
oil filter wrenches, HB70
on-car brake lathes, BR175–176
outside micrometers, HB77
oxy-acetylene torches, HB70
parts cleaning tanks, HB70
pickup tools, HB61–62
pliers, HB57, HB61, HB70
for power-assisted steering systems, SS535
proper use of, HB51–53
prying tools, HB60
punches, HB59
pyrometers, EP381
remote starter switches, HB66
for removing batteries, EL265–266
safe use of, HB98–103
safety glasses, HB62
safety stands, HB67, HB101
scan tools, HB65, EL242, EL339, EL345, EP391, EP410–411, EP471, EP483
screw extractor sets, HB70
screwdrivers, HB58
seat covers, HB70
snap-ring pliers, HB70
socket sets, HB55
soldering guns, HB66
soldering irons, HB66
spark plug boot pullers, HB70

spark testers, EP419
steering wheel holder, SS591
steering wheel pullers, SS531
stethoscopes, automotive, HB65, EP378
storing and maintaining, HB53
strut compressor tools, SS566–567
tachometer, HB77
tap and die sets, HB71
tape measures, HB77
test lights, HB63, EL241
thickness gauges, HB77
thread repair kits, HB71
thread-pitch gauges, HB81
tie rod puller, SS590
timing lights, EP430
tire inflator chucks, HB71
tire pressure gauges, HB78
torque, SS520
torque wrenches, HB54, SS519–520
trouble/work lights, HB54
tube quick-disconnect tool sets, HB71
tubing benders, HB71
tubing cutter/flaring sets, HB71
twist-drill sets, HB66
vacuum gauges, HB78, EP376–378
valve-core removing tools, HB72
V-blocks, HB72
vernier calipers, HB78
vises, HB72
volts-ampere testers, EL301–302
waste-oil receptacles, HB72
wheel chocks, HB72
wheel weight pliers, SS521
wire brushes, HB63
workbenches, HB72
wrenches, HB54
See also special tools
torque, HB83–84, EL279, SS519–520, SS546
torque wrenches, HB54, SS519–520
torsion bar front suspensions, SS568–569
torsion bars, SS553, SS568–569
Torx head screwdrivers, HB58
track bars (panhard rods), SS572–573
traction control systems (TCSs), BR221
trailing arms, SS572
transfer cables, BR202
transistors, EL247–248
switching, EL346
transmission jacks, HB102
transportation, U.S. Department of (DOT)
brake fluid standards of, BR114
dual-braking systems required by, BR130
tire safety standard code of, SS513
treadwear indicators (wear indicator bars), SS512, SS514
trip (diagnostic), EP474
tube quick-disconnect tool sets, HB71
tube tires, SS507
tubeless tires, SS507
tubing benders, HB71
tubing cutter/flaring sets, HB71

tuning venturi, EP438
turbochargers, EP441
turning radius, SS581
turn signal lights, EL315–316
twin I-beam front suspensions, SS569
twist-drill sets, HB66

understeer, BR223
Uniform Tire Quality Grading (UTQG), SS512
United States Customary (USC) system, HB76
conversions for, HB74–76
unsprung weight, SS552

vacuum, EP376, EP442, EP453
vacuum bleeding of hydraulic braking systems, BR135
vacuum boosters, BR181–184
vacuum gauges, HB78, EP376–378
vacuum pumps, HB65, BR181
vacuum storage system, BR187
valve-core removing tools, HB72
valves
combination, BR133
control, BR183
EGR, EP489–491
fuel injectors, EP462–465
in fuel tank caps, EP496
idle air control, EP403–404, EP440
intake and exhaust, EP359
in internal-combustion engines, EP362
metering, BR131, BR135
PCV, EP488–489
pressure differential, BR131
proportioning, BR132, BR208
residual pressure check, BR133, BR148
Schrader, EP458
servo solenoid, EL340
spool, BR185
valve seat, EP359
valve stems, on tires, SS522, SS523
valve train, EP362
vane-type sensors, EP444
vapor lock, EP449
vapor pressure, EP493
vapor recovery system, EP461
variable resistance sensors, EP394–395
variable-assist power steering, SS544–545
variable-ratio steering graphs, SS543
V-blocks, HB72
vehicle identification number (VIN), HB44, EP410–411, SS528
vehicle lifts. *See* lifts
vehicle speed sensor (VSS), EL321
vehicle stability control, BR223
vented rotors, BR160
ventilation, need for good, HB90
vernier calipers, HB78
VIN. *See* vehicle identification number